Semantic Web:

Ontology and Knowledge Base Enabled Tools, Services, and Applications

Amit P. Sheth
Kno.e.sis Center, Wright State University, USA

Managing Director:	Lindsay Johnston
Editorial Director:	Joel Gamon
Book Production Manager:	Jennifer Yoder
Publishing Systems Analyst:	Adrienne Freeland
Assistant Acquisitions Editor:	Kayla Wolfe
Typesetter:	Christina Henning
Cover Design:	Jason Mull

Published in the United States of America by
Information Science Reference (an imprint of IGI Global)
701 E. Chocolate Avenue
Hershey PA 17033
Tel: 717-533-8845
Fax: 717-533-8661
E-mail: cust@igi-global.com
Web site: http://www.igi-global.com

Library of Congress Cataloging-in-Publication Data

Semantic web : ontology and knowledge base enabled tools, services, and applications / Amit Sheth, editor.
    pages cm
 Includes bibliographical references and index.
  ISBN 978-1-4666-3610-1 (hardcover) -- ISBN 978-1-4666-3611-8 (ebook) -- ISBN 978-1-4666-3612-5 (print & perpetual access) 1. Semantic Web. I. Sheth, A. (Amit), 1959- editor of compilation.
  TK5105.88815.S42745 2013
  025.042'7--dc23
                                    2012046681

British Cataloguing in Publication Data
A Cataloguing in Publication record for this book is available from the British Library.

The views expressed in this book are those of the authors, but not necessarily of the publisher.

Table of Contents

Section 3
Web of Data and Applications

Detailed Table of Contents

Section 1
Ontology Engineering and Knowledge

Chapter 1

Lijuan Zhu, Washington State University, USA
Uma Jayaram, Washington State University, USA
Okjoon Kim, Washington State University, USA

This paper formulates an approach to use the semantic web for knowledge management in the product design domain to provide enhanced capabilities of authoring/updating, querying/reasoning, searching, and visualization of information. Engineering has unique challenges, due to the pervasive use of CAD models and underlying interoperability and integration issues. The authors propose a distributed model composed of a host hybrid-data repository, external public linked data sources, a semantic data management engine, and a web-based user interface layer. The hybrid-data repository consists of ontologies to preserve knowledge for the product design domain and a conventional product data base to utilize legacy design data. Near full integration with a web based environment is achieved. The importance of accessing product related CAD data that has been instantiated in ontology models, querying them, and then displaying the data on a web interface in real time with other legacy data, such as hand sketches and notes that have been scanned and relevant information from conventional rational databases public linked data sites, is a useful and transformational capability. The system clearly facilitates design and information management beyond traditional CAD capabilities and creates a foundation for important capability improvements in the domain.

Chapter 2

Edward Heath Robinson, The University of South Florida, USA

The agentivity of social entities has posed problems for ontologies of social phenomena, especially in the Descriptive Ontology for Linguistic and Cognitive Engineering (DOLCE) designed for use in the semantic web. This article elucidates a theory by which physical and social objects can take action, but that also recognizes the different ways in which they act. It introduces the "carry" relationship, through which social actions can occur when a physical action is taken in the correct circumstances. For example, the physical action of a wave of a hand may carry the social action of saying hello when entering a room. This article shows how a system can simultaneously and in a noncontradictory manner handle statements and queries in which both nonphysical social agents and physical agents take action by the carry relationship and the use of representatives. A revision of DOLCE's taxonomic structure of perdurants is also proposed. This revision divides perdurants into physical and nonphysical varieties at the same ontological level at which endurants are so divided.

Chapter 3

Onto-Relational Learning is an extension of Relational Learning aimed at accounting for ontologies in a clear, well-founded and elegant manner. The system QuIn supports a variant of the frequent pattern discovery task by following the Onto-Relational Learning approach. It takes taxonomic ontologies into account during the discovery process and produces descriptions of a given relational database at multiple granularity levels. The functionalities of the system are illustrated by means of examples taken from a Semantic Web Mining case study concerning the analysis of relational data extracted from the on-line CIA World Fact Book.

Section 2
Reasoning and Ontology Development

This paper presents a novel semi-automatic approach to construct conceptual ontologies over structured data by exploiting both the schema and content of the input dataset. It effectively combines two well-founded database and data mining techniques, i.e., functional dependency discovery and association rule mining, to support domain experts in the construction of meaningful ontologies, tailored to the analyzed data, by using Description Logic (DL). To this aim, functional dependencies are first discovered to highlight valuable conceptual relationships among attributes of the data schema (i.e., among concepts). The set of discovered correlations effectively support analysts in the assertion of the Tbox ontological statements (i.e., the statements involving shared data conceptualizations and their relationships). Then, the analyst-validated dependencies are exploited to drive the association rule mining process. Association rules represent relevant and hidden correlations among data content and they are used to provide valuable knowledge at the instance level. The pushing of functional dependency constraints into the rule mining process allows analysts to look into and exploit only the most significant data item recurrences in the assertion of the Abox ontological statements (i.e., the statements involving concept instances and their relationships).

Chapter 5

This paper presents an approach to ontology construction pursued through the induction of concept descriptions expressed in Description Logics. The author surveys the theoretical foundations of the standard representations for formal ontologies in the Semantic Web. After stating the learning problem in this peculiar context, a FOIL-like algorithm is presented that can be applied to learn DL concept descriptions. The algorithm performs a search through a space of candidate concept definitions by means of refinement operators. This process is guided by heuristics that are based on the available examples. The author discusses related theoretical aspects of learning with the inherent incompleteness underlying the semantics of this representation. The experimental evaluation of the system DL-Foil, which implements the learning algorithm, was carried out in two series of sessions on real ontologies from standard repositories for different domains expressed in diverse description logics.

Chapter 6

This paper presents novel algorithms for learning semantic relations from an existing ontology or concept hierarchy. The authors suggest recommendation of semantic relations for supporting continuous ontology development, i.e., the development of ontologies during their use in social semantic bookmarking, semantic wiki, or other Web 2.0 style semantic applications. This paper assists users in placing a newly added concept in a concept hierarchy. The proposed algorithms are evaluated using datasets from Wikipedia category hierarchy and provide recommendations.

Chapter 7

Defeasible logic is a non-monotonic formalism that deals with incomplete and conflicting information, whereas modal logic deals with the concepts of necessity and possibility. These types of logics play a significant role in the emerging Semantic Web, which enriches the available Web information with meaning, leading to better cooperation between end-users and applications. Defeasible and modal logics, in general, and, particularly, deontic logic provide means for modeling agent communities, where each agent is characterized by its cognitive profile and normative system, as well as policies, which define privacy requirements, access permissions, and individual rights. Toward this direction, this article discusses the extension of DR-DEVICE, a Semantic Web-aware defeasible reasoner, with a mechanism for expressing modal logic operators, while testing the implementation via deontic logic operators, concerned with obligations, permissions, and related concepts. The motivation behind this work is to develop a practical defeasible reasoner for the Semantic Web that takes advantage of the expressive power offered by modal logics, accompanied by the flexibility to define diverse agent behaviours. A further incentive is to study the various motivational notions of deontic logic and discuss the cognitive state of agents, as well as the interactions among them.

Section 3
Web of Data and Applications

Chapter 8

Alfio Ferraram, Università degli Studi di Milano, Italy

Andriy Nikolov, The Open University, UK

François Scharffe, University of Montpellier, France

By specifying that published datasets must link to other existing datasets, the 4th linked data principle ensures a Web of data and not just a set of unconnected data islands. The authors propose in this paper the term data linking to name the problem of finding equivalent resources on the Web of linked data. In order to perform data linking, many techniques were developed, finding their roots in statistics, database, natural language processing and graph theory. The authors begin this paper by providing background information and terminological clarifications related to data linking. Then a comprehensive survey over the various techniques available for data linking is provided. These techniques are classified along the three criteria of granularity, type of evidence, and source of the evidence. Finally, the authors survey eleven recent tools performing data linking and we classify them according to the surveyed techniques.

Chapter 9

Fergal Monaghan, SAP Research, UK

Siegfried Handschuh, National University of Ireland, Galway, Ireland

David O'Sullivan, National University of Ireland, Galway, Ireland

With the advent of online social networks and User-Generated Content (UGC), the social Web is experiencing an explosion of audio-visual data. However, the usefulness of the collected data is in doubt, given that the means of retrieval are limited by the semantic gap between them and people's perceived understanding of the memories they represent. Whereas machines interpret UGC media as series of binary audio-visual data, humans perceive the context under which the content is captured and the people, places, and events represented. The Annotation CReatiON for Your Media (ACRONYM) framework addresses the semantic gap by supporting the creation of a layer of explicit machine-interpretable meaning describing UGC context. This paper presents an overview of a use case of ACRONYM for semantic annotation of personal photographs. The authors define a set of recommendation algorithms employed by ACRONYM to support the annotation of generic UGC multimedia. This paper introduces the context metrics and combination methods that form the recommendation algorithms used by ACRONYM to determine the people represented in multimedia resources. For the photograph annotation use case, these result in an increase in recommendation accuracy. Context-based algorithms provide a cheap and robust means of UGC media annotation that is compatible with and complimentary to content-recognition techniques.

Chapter 10

Iván Cantador, Universidad Autónoma de Madrid, Spain

Pablo Castells, Universidad Autónoma de Madrid, Spain

Alejandro Bellogín, Universidad Autónoma de Madrid, Spain

Recommender systems have achieved success in a variety of domains, as a means to help users in information overload scenarios by proactively finding items or services on their behalf, taking into account or predicting their tastes, priorities, or goals. Challenging issues in their research agenda include the sparsity of user preference data and the lack of flexibility to incorporate contextual factors in the recommendation methods. To a significant extent, these issues can be related to a limited description and exploitation of the semantics underlying both user and item representations. The authors propose a three-fold knowledge representation, in which an explicit, semantic-rich domain knowledge space is incorporated between user and item spaces. The enhanced semantics support the development of contextualisation capabilities and enable performance improvements in recommendation methods. As a proof of concept and evaluation testbed, the approach is evaluated through its implementation in a news recommender system, in which it is tested with real users. In such scenario, semantic knowledge bases and item annotations are automatically produced from public sources.

Chapter 11

Steven O'Hara, University of Texas at San Antonio, USA

Tom Bylander, University of Texas at San Antonio, USA

Query answering usually assumes that the asker is looking for a single correct answer to the question. When retrieving a textual answer this is often the case, but when searching for numeric answers, there are additional considerations. In particular, numbers often have units associated with them, and the asker may not care whether the raw answer is in feet or meters. Also, numbers usually denote a precision. In a few cases, the precision may be explicit, but normally, there is an implied precision associated with every number. Finally, an association between different reliability levels to different sources can be made. In this paper, the authors experimentally show that, in the context of conflicting answers from multiple sources, numeric query accuracy can be improved by taking advantage of units, precision, and the reliability of sources.

Chapter 12

Jakub Šimko, Slovak University of Technology, Slovak Republic

Michal Tvarožek, Slovak University of Technology, Slovak Republic

Mária Bieliková, Slovak University of Technology, Slovak Republic

The effective acquisition of (semantic) metadata is crucial for many present day applications. Games with a purpose address this issue by transforming computational problems into computer games. The authors present a novel approach to metadata acquisition via Little Search Game (LSG) – a competitive web search game, whose purpose is the creation of a term relationship network. From a player perspective, the goal is to reduce the number of search results returned for a given search term by adding negative search terms to a query. The authors describe specific aspects of the game's design, including player motivation and anti-cheating issues. The authors have performed a series of experiments with Little Search Game, acquired real-world player input, gathered qualitative feedback from the players, constructed and evaluated term relationship network from the game logs and examined the types of created relationships.

Preface

This book is a compilation of the International Journal on Semantic Web and Information Systems (IJSWIS) Volume 7. It is composed of high quality manuscripts pertaining to various aspects of Semantic Web that are relevant to computer science and information systems communities. In addition to being a premier outlet of high quality archival research in Semantic Web, IJSWIS also had high impact factor of 2.3 in the year of the publications covered here and belongs among the top journals in World Wide Web with over 7 citations per publication on average (Microsoft Academic Search, http://bit.ly/www-j1).

The chapters in this book are divided in three parts. The first part on *Ontology Engineering and Knowledge* management has three chapters that deal with ontology engineering, relational learning and knowledge extraction. The second part on *Reasoning and Ontology Development* has four chapters that focus on reasoning. Three of them use induction form of reasoning for various uses in formal ontology development. The final and the third section of the book on *Web of Data and Applications* consist of five chapters that cover Web of Data and variety of applications involving semantic processing of data. After presenting the overview of twelve chapters in this book, I briefly provide my take on some of the exciting new progress and exciting things to come in near future in Semantic Web.

SECTION 1: ONTOLOGY ENGINEERING AND KNOWLEDGE MANAGEMENT

The first chapter "Online Semantic Knowledge Management for Product Design Based on Product Engineering Ontologies," by Lijuan Zhu, Uma Jayaram, and Okjoon Kim, formulates an approach to use the semantic web for knowledge management in the product design domain to provide enhanced capabilities of authoring/updating, querying/reasoning, searching, and visualization of information. Engineering has unique challenges, due to the pervasive use of CAD models and underlying interoperability and integration issues. The authors propose a distributed model composed of a host hybrid-data repository, external public linked data sources, a semantic data management engine, and a web-based user interface layer. The hybrid-data repository consists of ontologies to preserve knowledge for the product design domain and a conventional product data base to utilize legacy design data. Near full integration with a web based environment is achieved. The importance of accessing product related CAD data that has been instantiated in ontology models, query them, and then display the data on a web interface in real time with other legacy data, such as hand sketches and notes that have been scanned and relevant information from public linked data sites, is a useful and transformational capability. The system clearly facilitates design and information management beyond traditional CAD capabilities and creates a foundation for important capability improvements in the domain.

The agentivity of social entities has posed problems for ontologies of social phenomena, especially in the Descriptive Ontology for Linguistic and Cognitive Engineering (DOLCE) designed for use in the semantic web. The second chapter, "A Theory of Social Agentivity and its Integration into the Descriptive Ontology for Linguistic and Cognitive Engineering," Edward Heath Robinson elucidates a theory by which physical and social objects can take action, but that also recognizes the different ways in which they act. It introduces the "carry" relationship, by which it allows social actions to occur when a physical action is taken in the correct circumstances. For example, the physical action of a wave of a hand may carry the social action of saying hello when entering a room. This article shows how a system can simultaneously and in a noncontradictory manner handle statements and queries in which both nonphysical social agents and physical agents take action by the carry relationship and the use of representatives. A revision of DOLCE's taxonomic structure of perdurants is also proposed. This revision divides perdurants into physical and nonphysical varieties at the same ontological level at which endurants are so divided.

The third chapter "AL-QuIn: An Onto-Relational Learning System for Semantic Web Mining" is by Francesca A. Lisi. Onto-Relational Learning is an extension of Relational Learning aimed at accounting for ontologies in a clear, well-founded and elegant manner. The system $\mathcal{AL}$ - QuIn supports a variant of the frequent pattern discovery task by following the Onto-Relational Learning approach. It takes taxonomic ontologies into account during the discovery process and produces descriptions of a given relational database at multiple granularity levels. The functionalities of the system are illustrated by means of examples taken from a Semantic Web Mining case study concerning the analysis of relational data extracted from the on-line CIA World Fact Book.

SECTION 2: REASONING AND ONTOLOGY DEVELOPMENT

Chapter 4 titled "Semi-Automatic Ontology Construction by Exploiting Functional Dependencies and Association Rules" by Luca Cagliero, Tania Cerquitelli, and Paolo Garza presents a novel semi-automatic approach to construct conceptual ontologies over structured data by exploiting both the schema and content of the input dataset. It effectively combines two well-founded database and data mining techniques, i.e., functional dependency discovery and association rule mining, to support domain experts in the construction of meaningful ontologies, tailored to the analyzed data, by using Description Logic (DL). To this aim, functional dependencies are first discovered to highlight valuable conceptual relationships among attributes of the data schema (i.e., among concepts). The set of discovered correlations effectively support analysts in the assertion of the Tbox ontological statements (i.e., the statements involving shared data conceptualizations and their relationships). Then, the analyst-validated dependencies are exploited to drive the association rule mining process. Association rules represent relevant and hidden correlations among data content and they are used to provide valuable knowledge at the instance level. The pushing of functional dependency constraints into the rule mining process allows analysts to look into and exploit only the most significant data item recurrences in the assertion of the Abox ontological statements (i.e., the statements involving concept instances and their relationships).

The next chapter, "Concept Induction in Description Logics Using Information-Theoretic Heuristics," by Nicola Fanizzi presents an approach to ontology construction pursued through the induction of concept descriptions expressed in Description Logics. The author surveys the theoretical foundations of the standard representations for formal ontologies in the Semantic Web. After stating the learning problem in this peculiar context, a FOIL-like algorithm is presented that can be applied to learn DL concept descriptions. The algorithm performs a search through a space of candidate concept definitions by means of refinement operators. This process is guided by heuristics that are based on the available examples. The author discusses related theoretical aspects of learning with the inherent incompleteness underlying the semantics of this representation. The experimental evaluation of the system DL-Foil, which implements the learning algorithm, was carried out in two series of sessions on real ontologies from standard repositories for different domains expressed in diverse description logics.

Chapter 6 titled "Using Similarity-Based Approaches for Continuous Ontology Development" by Maryam Ramezani presents novel algorithms for learning semantic relations from an existing ontology or concept hierarchy. The author suggest recommendation of semantic relations for supporting continuous ontology development, i.e., the development of ontologies during their use in social semantic bookmarking, semantic wiki, or other Web 2.0 style semantic applications. This chapter assists users in placing a newly added concept in a concept hierarchy. The proposed algorithms are evaluated using datasets from Wikipedia category hierarchy and provide recommendations.

The motivation behind the seventh chapter, titled "A Modal Defeasible Reasoner of Deontic Logic for the Semantic Web," by Efstratios Kontopoulos, Nick Bassiliades, Guido Governatori, and Grigoris Antoniou, is to develop a practical defeasible reasoner for the Semantic Web that takes advantage of the expressive power offered by modal logics, accompanied by the flexibility to define diverse agent behaviours. Defeasible logic is a non-monotonic formalism that deals with incomplete and conflicting information, whereas modal logic deals with the concepts of necessity and possibility. These types of logics play a significant role in the emerging Semantic Web, which enriches the available Web information with meaning, leading to better cooperation between end-users and applications. Defeasible and modal logics, in general, and, particularly, deontic logic provide means for modeling agent communities, where each agent is characterized by its cognitive profile and normative system, as well as policies, which define privacy requirements, access permissions, and individual rights. Toward this direction, this article discusses the extension of DR-DEVICE, a Semantic Web-aware defeasible reasoner, with a mechanism for expressing modal logic operators, while testing the implementation via deontic logic operators, concerned with obligations, permissions, and related concepts. A further incentive is to study the various motivational notions of deontic logic and discuss the cognitive state of agents, as well as the interactions among them.

SECTION 3: WEB OF DATA AND APPLICATIONS

By specifying that published datasets must link to other existing datasets, the 4th linked data principle ensures a Web of data and not just a set of unconnected data islands. In Chapter 8 titled "Data Linking for the Semantic Web," Alfio Ferrara, Andriy Nikolov, and François Scharffe propose the term data linking to name the problem of finding equivalent resources on the Web of linked data. In order to perform data linking, many techniques were developed, finding their roots in statistics, database, natural language processing and graph theory. The authors begin this paper by providing background information and terminological clarifications related to data linking. Then a comprehensive survey over the various techniques available for data linking is provided. These techniques are classified along the three criteria of granularity, type of evidence, and source of the evidence. Finally, the authors survey eleven recent tools performing data linking and we classify them according to the surveyed techniques.

The next chapter is "ACRONYM: Context Metrics for Linking People to User-Generated Media Content" by Fergal Monaghan, Siegfried Handschuh, and David O'Sullivan. With the advent of online social networks and User-Generated Content (UGC), the social Web is experiencing an explosion of audio-visual data. But the usefulness of the collected data is in doubt, given that the means of retrieval are limited by the semantic gap between them and people's perceived understanding of the memories they represent. Whereas machines interpret UGC media as series of binary audio-visual data, humans perceive the context under which the content is captured and the people, places, and events represented. The Annotation CReatiON for Your Media (ACRONYM) framework addresses the semantic gap by supporting the creation of a layer of explicit machine-interpretable meaning describing UGC context. This paper presents an overview of a use case of ACRONYM for semantic annotation of personal photographs. The authors define a set of recommendation algorithms employed by ACRONYM to support the annotation of generic UGC multimedia. This paper introduces the context metrics and combination methods that form the recommendation algorithms used by ACRONYM to determine the people represented in multimedia resources. For the photograph annotation use case, these result in an increase in recommendation accuracy. Context-based algorithms provide a cheap and robust means of UGC media annotation that is compatible with and complimentary to content-recognition techniques.

The tenth chapter "An Enhanced Semantic Layer for Hybrid Recommender Systems: Application to News Recommendation" written by Iván Cantador, Pablo Castells, and Alejandro Bellogín. Recommender systems have achieved success in a variety of domains, as a means to help users in information overload scenarios by proactively finding items or services on their behalf, taking into account or predicting their tastes, priorities, or goals. Challenging issues in their research agenda include the sparsity of user preference data and the lack of flexibility to incorporate contextual factors in the recommendation methods. To a significant extent, these issues can be related to a limited description and exploitation of the semantics underlying both user and item representations. The authors propose a three-fold knowledge representation, in which an explicit, semantic-rich domain knowledge space is incorporated between user and item spaces. The enhanced semantics support the development of contextualisation capabilities and enable performance improvements in recommendation methods. As a proof of concept and evaluation testbed, the approach is evaluated through its implementation in a news recommender system, in which it is tested with real users. In such scenario, semantic knowledge bases and item annotations are automatically produced from public sources.

The next chapter is "Numeric Query Answering on the Web," by Steven O'Hara and Tom Bylander. Query answering usually assumes that the asker is looking for a single correct answer to the question. When retrieving a textual answer this is often the case, but when searching for numeric answers, there are additional considerations. In particular, numbers often have units associated with them, and the asker may not care whether the raw answer is in feet or meters. Also, numbers usually denote a precision. In a few cases, the precision may be explicit, but normally, there is an implied precision associated with every number. Finally, an association between different reliability levels to different sources can be made. In this paper, the authors experimentally show that, in the context of conflicting answers from multiple sources, numeric query accuracy can be improved by taking advantage of units, precision, and the reliability of sources.

The effective acquisition of (semantic) metadata is crucial for many present day applications. Games with a purpose address this issue by transforming computational problems into computer games. In the final and the twelfth chapter 12 "Semantics Discovery via Human Computation Games," Jakub Šimko, Michal Tvarožek, and Mária Bieliková present a novel approach to metadata acquisition via Little Search

Game (LSG) – a competitive web search game, whose purpose is the creation of a term relationship network. From a player perspective, the goal is to reduce the number of search results returned for a given search term by adding negative search terms to a query. The authors describe specific aspects of the game's design, including player motivation and anti-cheating issues. The authors have performed a series of experiments with Little Search Game, acquired real-world player input, gathered qualitative feedback from the players, constructed and evaluated term relationship network from the game logs and examined the types of created relationships.

RECENT PROGRESS AND UPCOMING CHALLENGES

Against the backdrop of the research presented in the above twelve chapters, let me now review my views on some of the most exciting progresses, current challenges and the times to come in the Semantic Web arena in near future.

Growing Role of Background Knowledge: Semantic Web researchers and early entrepreneurs knew (as exemplified by the first patent on developing and using Semantic Web technologies awarded in 2001 that with moderate effort, it is possible to create background knowledge and populated ontologies by aggregating and disambiguating high quality information and facts from multiple sources. It has also been long known that by using such knowledge bases, we can substantially improve information extraction and develop a variety of semantic tools and applications including semantic search, browsing, personalization, advertisement, etc. Over the past 3-5 years, several efforts to create such knowledge bases took place, of which Freebase is a showcase. What has drawn everyone's attention to this aspect of semantic approach is Google's acquisition of the company that created Freebase and significantly extending techniques largely known, but scaling it to the next level, to create Google Knowledge Base (GKB). Further on, applying GKB to enhance search (and I am sure other applications in future), has forever changed the importance of creating and using background or domain models for semantic applications. I believe this form of semantic application building will see the fastest growth in the near future. I have discussed related thoughts in my article titled "Semantics Scales Up".

Growing Pains for Linked Open Data (LOD): Publication of over 300 large data sets with 30+ billion triples certainly draws the attention of many. Data holders will continue to find LOD an attractive vehicle to publish and share their data, so it will continue to grow at a rapid pace. Some of the data sets, more than others, will find additional usage as data reference, interlinking, and transformation. But in the near term, broader or aggregate usage of LOD will be a slog because we are running into some of the harder technical challenges: questionable quality of data and provenance, unconstrained and uneven use of semantics (e.g. same-as used inconsistently) and limited use of richer relationship types (part-of relationship, causality), and poor interlinking (lack of high quality alignment). We will need to have better handle of these issues along with a better ability to identify the most relevant and high quality data sets (a semantic search for LOD) and better alignment tools (not limited to just same-as), before we can start realizing the true promise of LOD. So, I would give it another five years to fully develop.

Democratization of Semantics: So far, we have paid the majority of our attention to knowledge representation, languages, and reasoning. Furthermore, a majority of the work focuses on documents in enterprises and on the Web, or uses structured data transformed into triples. But, what is even more exciting, is how semantics and Semantic Web technology (primarily through annotating data with respect to background knowledge or ontologies) is being used for improving interoperability and analysis of different types of textual and non-textual data, esp. social data and data generated by sensors, devices, or Internet of Things. These types of data have long overtaken traditional document-centric data and structured databases in terms of volume, velocity, and variety. The type of semantics one needs to deal with for such (relatively) nontraditional data is of amazing variety. For example, in the Twitris system (http://twitris.knoesis.org), besides semantic annotation for spatial, temporal, and thematic elements associated with the tweets, semantics (aka meaning) also includes understanding people (about the poster and receiver), network (about interactions and flow of message), sentiment, emotion, and intent. For more in-depth treatment, see our just published book on semantics empowered Web 3.0. This is probably the most important development in my view and is likely to garner a much larger share of attention related to the application of semantics and semantic web technologies.

Amit Sheth
Kno.e.sis Center, Wright State University, USA

REFERENCES

Sheth, A. (2011, November). Semantics scales up: Beyond search in Web 3.0. *IEEE Internet Computing*, *15*(6), 3–6. doi:10.1109/MIC.2011.157.

Sheth, A. P., & Thirunarayan, K. (2012). *Semantics empowered Web 3.0: Managing enterprise, social, sensor, and cloud-based data and services for advanced applications. Synthesis Lectures on Data Management*. Morgan and Claypool Publishers.

Section 1
Ontology Engineering and Knowledge

Chapter 1
Online Semantic Knowledge Management for Product Design Based on Product Engineering Ontologies

Lijuan Zhu
Washington State University, USA

Uma Jayaram
Washington State University, USA

Okjoon Kim
Washington State University, USA

ABSTRACT

This paper formulates an approach to use the semantic web for knowledge management in the product design domain to provide enhanced capabilities of authoring/updating, querying/reasoning, searching, and visualization of information. Engineering has unique challenges, due to the pervasive use of CAD models and underlying interoperability and integration issues. The authors propose a distributed model composed of a host hybrid-data repository, external public linked data sources, a semantic data management engine, and a web-based user interface layer. The hybrid-data repository consists of ontologies to preserve knowledge for the product design domain and a conventional product data base to utilize legacy design data. Near full integration with a web based environment is achieved. The importance of accessing product related CAD data that has been instantiated in ontology models, querying them, and then displaying the data on a web interface in real time with other legacy data, such as hand sketches and notes that have been scanned and relevant information from conventional rational databases public linked data sites, is a useful and transformational capability. The system clearly facilitates design and information management beyond traditional CAD capabilities and creates a foundation for important capability improvements in the domain.

DOI: 10.4018/978-1-4666-3610-1.ch001

INTRODUCTION

The assumption that a single user works with a single computer system and a single application characterized by a centralized local knowledge base is out of date and rapidly getting revised (Gil, 2011), especially in engineering. There is a tremendous volume and diversity of product design data that engineers now create through the use of multiple design and analysis tools. There are issues unique to engineering that are related to compatibility of data across the applications, interoperability, and the widespread use of the CAD model as the master model. The issue is compounded because the engineers are often distributed globally. The CAD models are local-based and sharing of that data in near real time over the internet is a big challenge. Although engineers are now working with these multiple systems and multiple applications in a distributed manner, there needs to be progress in parallel in terms of using new approaches and technologies to support the management and sharing of this engineering data.

Traditionally, the process to build applications to share data has depended on hand-tuned and ad hoc techniques to integrate information (Seagram, 2009). Recently, ontology-based approaches have been used for managing product data. An ontology is a data model that represents a domain and is used to reason about the objects in that domain and relations between them. Using description languages, such as Resource Description Framework (RDF) and Web Ontology Language (OWL), data can be made explicit with semantic relationships, and thus there are powerful possibilities for mitigating miscommunication between engineers because everyone will interpret an ontology the same way. Using these approaches, ontology modeling allows engineers in a specific domain to represent design knowledge in a relatively flexible manner along with a formal and machine manipulatable standard

in a context-dependent way. Machines can now be used to solve relatively complex problems that require application of domain knowledge. However, in order to realize the full potential of ontologies and create knowledge-contextual design environments, we need to extend the scope of sharing and reusing product design knowledge that has been captured in existing ontology models.

The Semantic Web provides a common framework that allows data to be shared and reused across applications, enterprises, and community boundaries (Herman, 2009). Currently Semantic Web applications are used for personal information management, travel planning, and exchange of data in telecommunication and legal domains (Sheth, 2010). A few Semantic Web applications have been developed for product design in the engineering domain, but more powerful and germane applications would serve to streamline knowledge sharing, and ultimately enhance individual and group contributions to the field of engineering.

The monolithic and "silo" nature of CAD data in each CAD system and the great difficulty in viewing this data in any way other than in a CAD system or as a "dumb" model is definitely a major concern in many small and large design companies. If the Semantic Web can help alleviate this problem and allow real time querying and display of this data, it essentially creates a "lightweight" version of the CAD system and this information is now on the web, can be shared, can be dynamically collated, and does not need the CAD system after the initial instantiation process.

This research aims to explore a product design semantic knowledge management system (PD-SKMS) and realize a knowledge-contextual design environment for product engineers by integrating design knowledge with Semantic Web technologies. This paper makes four significant contributions that differentiate it from other research groups in this domain:

1. It constructs a knowledge-contextual design environment based on concepts of semantic knowledge management.
2. It provides applications with the capability to query/reason and author/update on a host hybrid-data repository.
3. It develops a novel approach to present rich, dynamic visualizations of product data semantics through the Web.
4. It provides for the extension of knowledge sources by linking to external public linked data sources in a seamless manner.

Through these contributions this work seeks to provide a completed and implemented framework and solution to publish product data semantics on the Web. Relevant technologies/tools related to the semantic web are identified, integrated, and implemented for the product engineering domain. This work is significant because these capabilities allow in one integrated system the deployment of heterogeneous data sources, implementation of semantic querying and reasoning on product data semantics, and visualization of semantic data in a dynamic and interactive way are very novel and significant for the product data domain. Very few existing Semantic Web applications, especially for product design in engineering domain, have been developed as completely as PD-SKMS. The development work is also expected to provide the foundation for important capability improvements.

The paper is organized as follows: the next section introduces background of this research and prior work. The Semantic Web technologies adopted in this paper are then briefly described. The following section discusses the motivation and underlying architecture of PD-SKMS. The details of the components deployed in PD-SKMS are explained and PD-SKMS with test scenarios is demonstrated. Following these six sections, a conclusion and further work are presented.

BACKGROUND

Semantic Web

The Semantic Web is an evolution of the World Wide Web and enables machines to interpret and analyze the requests of end-users, facilitates communication between users, and perform much of the tedious work engineers often undertake such as finding, sharing, and combining information on the Web (Wikipedia, 2011a).

A key aspect of the Semantic Web is using generic metadata for sharing information. Applications allowing users to make connections and understand relationships that were previously hidden are very powerful and compelling. Using description languages, such as Resource Description Framework (RDF) and Web Ontology Language (OWL), which are standardly used in the Semantic Web, data can be made explicit with semantic relationships, and thus computer systems are capable of exchanging data based on its meaning. Exchanging data based on its meaning is key to the usefulness of the Semantic Web as it makes possible the Semantic Web's ability to integrate data from different sources that use different schemas.

Linked Data

Linked Data refers to a set of best practices for publishing and connecting structured data on the Web (Wikipedia, 2011b). In this framework numerous individuals and groups can publish Linked Data and contribute to the building of a Web of Data, which thereby lowers the barrier previously preventing practices that allowed reusing, integrating, and applying data from multiple, distributed and heterogeneous sources (Watson, 2010). There are already some useful public Linked Data sources including, but not limited to DBpedia, Freebase, and FOAF. In order to address the potential usefulness of these data sources, an approach for a seamless integration of these linked data sets based on an upper level ontology is addressed (Jain, Hitzler, Yeh, Verma, & Sheth, 2009).

Traditional Knowledge Management Systems for the Engineering Domain

A knowledge-based system can support creative design in various ways, such as by providing better user interfaces, bigger knowledge bases, better knowledge representations, and a computational model with a flexible search mechanism (Gero & Maher, 1993). A common approach to capturing and storing product data from design tools is employing database technologies. For example, systems permitting database queries over data extracted from a CAD system have been developed and used in the field (Koparanova & Risch, 2002). However, the external query system outside the CAD system must be transferred to standardized data exchange formats for interoperability with the CAD system. Therefore, traditional database systems are not applicable for data management involving heterogeneous but interrelated data, because not all the data can be conveniently fit into a structured database system (Frankin, Halevy, & Maier, 2005). Traditional database systems are also incapable of providing an environment for semi-automatically created relationships between data, or improving and maintaining existing relationships between data, which our research intends to provide for.

Another option for supporting knowledge capturing and reasoning for engineering analysis and design tasks is a context based modeling approach (CML) (Nicklas, Ranganathan, & Riboni, 2010), which have been used to capture and store data. This approach does not provide support for interoperability as it emphasizes the development of context models for particular applications or application domains instead. In recent years, neutral definitions based on STEP and ISO EXPRESS

(Murshed, Dixon, & Shah, 2009) have been used to capture product data in the engineering domain. However, the EXPRESS schema language has a major shortcoming because it lacks extensibility. Traditional rule-based expert systems put greater emphasis on implementing technologies than on the knowledge itself (Welty, 1999). Moreover, the old expert systems are monolithic, and computer-centric. Modern ontology-driven expert systems will make raw knowledge programmable and enable the domain expert to be a good "communicator" that can share knowledge/expertise (Morris, 2008).

Ontology-Based Approaches for the Engineering Design

In the product engineering domain, a large amount of product information is described through design documents for user requirements, customer dialogs, survey reports, and other similar texts. Often the concepts of customer preferences are implicit within these documents. Work has been done in using ontologies to address this issue (Li, Raskin, & Ramani, 2008; Li, Yang, & Ramani, 2009). Eliciting and extracting information specific to these preferences are essential to achieving success in product development (Cao, Ramani, Li, Raskin, Liu, & Li, 2010). In order to accomplish this, an approach has been introduced to identify influential relationships using ontology alignment and semantic relatedness techniques in order to improve knowledge management in product development processes (Witherell, Krishnamurty, Grosse, & Wileden, 2009). However, it is agreed that further development is needed in this area. This is specifically true regarding the needs for retrieval of previous designs as well as the need to capture knowledge and information from current designs to support future engineering tasks (Heisig, Caldwell, Grebici, & Clarkson, 2010). An approach for CAD interoperability by using a shared CAD ontology to represent features has been proposed (Tessier & Wang, 2011). The feature data structure stores both the data for features and the boundary representation (B-Rep) data. However, as of now, their current research goes from Pro/E up to the ontology model and does not as yet go past to a different CAD system. Requirements for the development of an industry-ready application of semantic knowledge management systems have been presented (Briendel et al., 2011) and include incorporation of legacy information, robustness of the software to support multiple file types, and ability to share information across platforms. It is believed that ontologies will be broadly adopted and integrated into knowledge/information management systems for the engineering domains by the engineering community due to its high degree of usefulness.

Online Semantic Tools for the Engineering Domain

Past approaches for knowledge representation and retrieval are outdated and ineffective in today's climate of widespread computer-based social networking and computational literacy. Large communities on the Web, such as Facebook, Flickr, LinkedIn, and Twitter, demonstrate that individuals are increasingly collaborating over the Internet, and in large numbers. Given this general collaboration, creating a web-based system that links engineers in a professional setting that enables them to share non-proprietary models and information while providing an opportunity to trouble-shoot problems collaboratively, will be significant to helping professionals make advancements in the field.

There are numerous efforts in the product engineering domain to move toward using Internet technology for data sharing. For example, domain ontologies have been built for products and services in order to use Semantic Web technologies for the automation of E-Business tasks. This research yielded a fully-fledged ontology for the product and services domain, reflecting more than 25,000 product types in 75,000 ontology classes (Hepp,

2006). The author further proposed an ontology named GoodRelations that satisfies representational needs in e-commerce scenarios (Hepp, 2008; Hepp & Radinger, 2010). However, GoodRelations places more attention on the business domain, e.g., product price and company data, instead of the product design domain, which would benefit the work of engineers. A design repository was created to enable storage and retrieval of design artifact knowledge via a web interface (Szykman, Sriram, Bochenek, Racz, & Senfaute, 2000). This was a very important stage toward utilizing the capabilities of the Web, but the primary focus of the work was not on using semantic technologies. The STEP module, using XML, can be rendered dynamically in a Web browser environment in response to user input, and can be independent of an HTTP server (NIST, 2002). In other work, Semantic Wikis have been used to form a central knowledge base for semantic a search engine which performs computational Fluid Dynamics Simulations and assists airfoil design (Fowler, Crowder, Guan, Shadbolt, & Wills, 2010). Similarly, the semantic tools provided by the EU-funded WIDE project supports innovative product design in the automotive field (Sevilmis & Stork, 2005).

In summary, though strides have been made towards utilization of Web technology, there are currently few online semantic tools that have been developed and published for use in the engineering domains. More effort needs to be expended in this area and research work is needed to bring Semantic Web technologies into the product development process in a more concrete form. Our research endeavors to provide such a system.

Our Previous Work

In our previous work, we designed and implemented rich ontology models for the product design domain (Zhan, Jayaram, Kim, & Zhu, 2010; Zhu, Jayaram, & Kim, 2009; Kim, Jayaram, & Zhu, 2009, 2010). Using these models and integration approaches we have built a product semantic repository that is now used in the work presented in this paper as an underlying data source of PD-SKMS.

Further, we exploited and extended the semantic representation with reasoning mechanisms (Zhu, Jayaram, & Kim, 2010, 2012), which makes two important tasks possible. The first is querying and retrieving existing product data information, while the second, through rule definitions, derives new product data information that is not explicitly expressed in given information models. Although local-based, this sets up a foundation to deploy and implement querying and reasoning capabilities in PD-SKMS. However, it should be noted that in PD-SKMS, different technologies will be adopted to implement querying and reasoning capabilities given that PD-SKMS is a web based framework and the results will be published online.

This previous work serves as a good launching point to now investigate the applicability of the Semantic Web technologies to product design in the engineering domain.

SEMANTIC WEB TECHNOLOGIES

The Semantic Web is a group of methods and technologies that allow machines to understand and process data based on the meaning of the data. It is comprised of standards such as XML, RDF, RDF Schema, and OWL, all of which are organized in the Semantic Web Stack (Wikipedia, 2010), as shown in Figure 1.

RDF is a simple language for expressing data models, which represent objects ("resources") and their relationships. RDF Schema extends RDF. OWL adds vocabulary for describing properties and classes.

SPARQL (Prud'hommeaux & Seaborne, 2007) makes queries on Semantic Web data sources and it is considered a key Semantic Web technology. SPARQL can be utilized to identify data quality problems in the Semantic Web (Fürber & Hepp,

Figure 1. Semantic WebStack (Wikipedia, 2010)

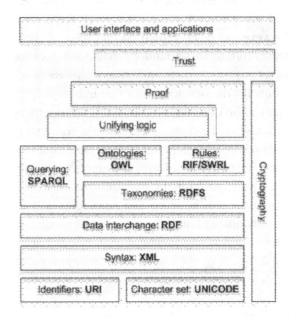

2010). Table 1 shows a simple SPARQL SELECT query example for the product design domain. This query finds all assemblies containing sub components which have a volume greater than 1000 cm^3 in a product design domain ontology (PRO-AO).

Since SPARQL is widely adopted by the Semantic Web community, the work in this paper adopts SPARQL as the query language for product semantic data.

OBJECTIVE AND SOLUTION

Objective

The fundamental objective of this paper is to propose a model that enables semantic knowledge management, including authoring, querying/reasoning, visualization, and publishing product data semantics for the product design domain (Figure 2). The functional requirements of this model include:

Table 1. SPARQL example for product design domain

SPARQL SELECT Query Example: SPARQL0
PREFIX PRO-AO: <http://www.wsu.edu/vrcim-onto/PRO-AO.owl#>
SELECT ?assembly ?subcomponent ?volume
WHERE {
?assembly PRO-AD: has_component ?subcomponent .
?subcomponent PRO-AD: has_volume ?volume .
        FILTER (? volume > 1000) .
} ORDER BY ?assembly ?volume

- Being able to access and integrate heterogeneous data across host semantic repositories, host rational databases, and external public linked data;
- Being able to provide querying/reasoning as well as authoring/updating services on the hybrid-data repository for engineers on the Web according to authentications assigned to them;
- Being able to visualize and manifest semantic data with multiple views. These displayed data will come from disparate data sources.

Solution

A distributed and completed model is proposed as shown in Figure 3. The components of this architecture are:

1. Host Hybrid-Data Repository (HDR)
2. External Public Linked Data (EPLD)
3. Semantic Data Management Engine (SDME)
4. Web-Based User Interfaces

HDR and SDME reside on a host server, while EPLD is composed of public data sources residing on external servers. Engineers on the Web can access the Web-based user interfaces with Web browsers on any client machine.

HDR consists of Product Semantic Repositories (PSR) capturing design knowledge for the product design domain, and a conventional Product Database (PDB) storing legacy design data. SDME supplies querying/reasoning and authoring/updating services on PSRs, searching and updating services on PDB, as well as querying service on external publicly-linked data. Through Web-based user interfaces, engineers can inquire/contribute design information/knowledge from/to PSRs and PDB, and also query relevant information from external public linked data sources. The querying results from all these disparate data

Figure 2. Functionality desired and data sources in PD-SKMS

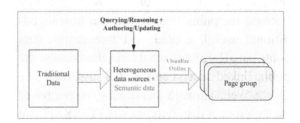

Figure 3. Underlying architecture of PD-SKMS

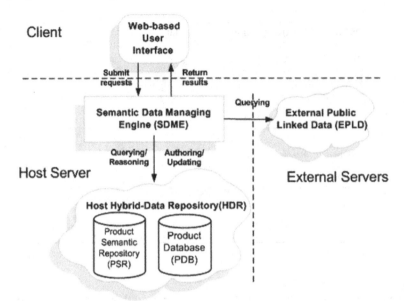

sources will be combined and displayed in Web-based user interfaces.

Key Steps

The key steps to create the PD-SKMS are shown in Figure 4. To start with, the product data semantics will be built for product data in the engineering domain. This work has been completed as part of our prior work as discussed before. Also, legacy design data, such as design parameters, sketches of product, expert notes, and materials information will be stored in a conventional database.

In addition, the solution calls for extending the data sources to external publicly linked data which has been introduced in the background section. It is believed that this extension will greatly improve the quality of the outcomes and the querying capability of PD-SKMS not only because the public linked data can provide additional useful, related, and free design data contributed by professionals, but also because the public linked data is composed of structured data on the Web. Through this linking, output based on the product data semantics in PD-SKMS can

be combined with relevant data from the external data source seamlessly.

Next, a uniform data management engine will be designed to provide querying/reasoning as well as authoring/updating services on these heterogeneous data sources discussed above.

Last, and perhaps most important, our solution will support a novel approach to visualize the structured data in PD-SKMS and publish it online. This is a significant step because the powerful capabilities of the Semantic Web will be applied in the product design domain for rich, fast, and dynamic information presentation; something that has been not been addressed adequately in this domain.

An Engineering Design Process Mapped to the PD-SKMS

Designing is question intensive and usually promotes the asking of additional and deeper questions (Eris, 2002). Particularly, design information establishes the need for answering questions about the product design being created, and verifying or refuting conjectures about that design (Kuffner &

Figure 4. Key steps for the PD-SKMS

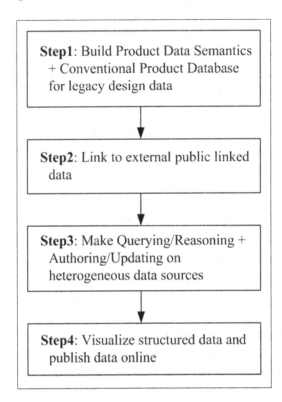

Figure 5. Design process yields requirements for PD-SKMS

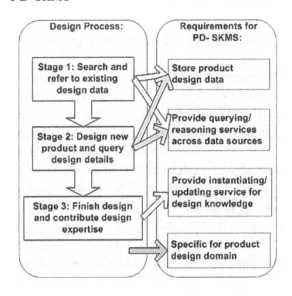

Ullman, 1990). However, as discussed in previous sections, product development teams currently face challenges in sharing and reusing especially large amounts of existing product data. Thus, PD-SKMS seeks to manage and share product design data during designing processes through the use of Semantic Web technologies.

Figure 5 shows a simplified outline of a design process yielding requirements for PD-SKMS. Consider the situation of an engineer performing a design task for a product. The design activities can be divided into roughly three stages. In the initial stage, the engineer would most probably search and refer to the existing design data corresponding to similar products, using it as a model for the current project. In the second stage, the engineer will need to determine if it is appropriate to reuse portions of the product data obtained from the first stage to design the new product. Frequently this

engineer will search and make queries/reasoning on this system to clarify/identify some design details, such as parameters, analysis, materials and so on. Finally, after this engineer finishes the design successfully, he/she may contribute the design expertise to the repository in order to help other engineers when dealing with the similar product design.

The online PD-SKMS is designed for the product design domain to enable practicing engineers to search and refer to existing designs, present queries and requests for design tasks, and input their opinions/expertise for design problems, thus allowing them to actively collaborate with colleagues.

The key components of the PD-SKMS are now described in detail.

DESCRIPTION OF HOST HYBRID-DATA REPOSITORY COMPONENT

The HDR consists of a semantic repository and a relational database.

Management of Product Data Semantics

Product Semantic Repository (PSR)

The semantic repository is designed as storage for the ontology models. In previous work, we created a 3-layered ontology structure: (1) General Domain Ontology (GDO); (2) Domain Specific Ontology (DSO); (3) Application Specific Ontology (ASO). ASO is built on DSO and GDO while DSO is built on GDO. We also built ASOs for some design tools/applications, e.g., PRO-AO for a ProEngineer CAD application, CAT-AO for a CATIA CAD application, and others. Moreover, product data semantics are instantiated by an ontology instantiation process. For example, we use CAD APIs to extract information from the CAD models, e.g., models for the Hubble Space Telescope or a wind turbine and instantiate the concepts to create owl files, e.g., PRO-AO-HubbleTelescope.owl.

There are two methods for storing and managing these ontologies. The first is to store them in a local file system on a server. The second is to use an independent database to store the ontologies. The second method may be preferable given the fact that an independent database has the capability of managing numerous ontology models efficiently while supplying uniform APIs to other applications for searching and accessing the data contained within it. We use this approach.

Sesame (http://www.openrdf.org/) is an open source Java framework for storing, querying, and reasoning with RDF(S), and it provides the necessary tools to parse, interpret, and query RDF(S). As a plug-in, OWLIM (http://www.ontotext.com/owlim/) is a high-performance Storage and Inference Layer (SAIL) for Sesame, and it partially supports OWL. OWLIM is based on a native RDF rule-entailment engine. The supported semantics can be configured through the definition of custom rule-sets. Currently, OWLIM is the fastest OWL-supported repository available.

Sesame supports both local and remote access through HTTP connection. Several query languages, including SPARQL, are applicable to Sesame. In our framework, administrator engineers on the Web are allowed to add, delete, and manage semantic data stored in Sesame remotely through a Web-based interface. A local-based tool is also developed to help the administrator manage the PSR locally. Figure 6 illustrates the interior organization of PSR.

Management of Legacy Design Data: Product Database (PDB)

There are two reasons to integrate a conventional database into HDR. Firstly, as a conventional approach to capturing and storing product data from design tools, relational databases still store much legacy design data, e.g., information related to CAD models and design rules, as well as their interdependencies on material, production unit, manufacturer capabilities, and others. Failing to utilize all this information would represent a significant loss to the field.

Secondly, the relational database organizes and stores queries, comments, design materials, such as videos, documents, CAD models, and other similar texts, which may be provided by engineers through the Web.

Table 2 lists some schemas and tables we include in PDB currently.

Figure 6. Organization of product semantic repository

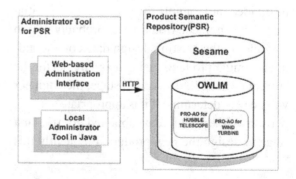

Table 2. Structure of PDB

Schema	Table	Column
hubbledb	Basic-parameter	Id, pname, length, weight, maxdiameter, speed, accuracy, power, startdate
	Imglib	Id, imgname, sourcefile, type, description
	Doclib	Id, docname, sourcefile, type, description
Wind turbinedb	Videolib	Id, vedioname, sourcefile, type, description
	Comments	Id, author, content, topic, postdate
	Queries	Id, author, content, topic, postdate

Integration of Product Data Semantics and Legacy Design Data (PSR and PDB)

In PD-SKMS, the semantic repository storing ontology models are combined with a conventional database.

This is because we believe the semantic repository cannot replace the relational database at this time. Firstly, although some approaches exist to convert typical relational data into RDF, the conversion is still a challenging job and is not adopted so commonly currently. Secondly, the usage of semantic representation is still restricted in some ways. Although it is flexible enough to define new properties between concepts and then use these properties to make statements on existing resources, not every user on the Web is willing to reorganize his/her thinking with concepts and properties in a semantic way. Most engineers are accustomed to natural language, which is informal and unstructured.

The combined approach is also very powerful because it allows for a phased transition from raw data to semantic data as new data is made available, without holding up anything in the interim waiting for processing and translation. A database can be used to store all inputs from engineers. Some of the inputs, about design expertise, rules, and other descriptors are stored in PDB first, then are processed and translated to knowledge representation, e.g., ontologies in OWL, and finally captured into PSR. This aspect of processing and translation is not a focus of this paper.

DESCRIPTION OF EXTERNAL PUBLIC LINKED DATA (EPLD) COMPONENT

Linking data resources in RDF can extend the usefulness of the Web so that both human and software agents can utilize these data resources. We have designed an external public linked data component called EPLD. By querying EPLD deployed in PD-SKMS, engineers using this system may provide in-depth linked design information through these public resources.

Currently, two public linked data sources are selected for EPLD. These are DBpedia, (http://dbpedia.org/) which contains the RDF information that points to and categorizes data contained in Wikipedia, and Freebase (http://wiki.freebase.com/wiki/Main_Page), a community-driven web portal that allows people to enter facts as structured data. Currently, PD-SKMS connects with DBpedia and Freebase through the EPLD by calling the Web services of keyword searching supported by these two data sources.

EPLD is expected to extend the querying capability of PD-SKMS and supply more related product information for product engineers. We plan to publish semantic data of PD-SKMS on the Web in the near future and provide linking services to the Semantic Web applications on the Web.

DESCRIPTION OF SEMANTIC DATA MANAGEMENT ENGINE (SDME) COMPONENT

The next key component is the semantic data management engine. Information is only valuable if it can be managed such that it can be accessed readily and for the desired and appropriate purpose.

Figure 7 shows the workflow of SDME. As discussed, two kinds of back ends are supported by SDME: PSR and PDB. Through querying and reasoning on PSR, the engineers are able to access product data semantics/design knowledge captured in product design domain ontologies; through querying on PDB, users can retrieve design information/materials from the product relational database. The SPARQL query language is used to access semantic data in PSR while SQL is used to access data in PDB.

An engineer might need the following information which is typical for an assembly product:

1. Components of this assembly.
2. Details of the components, including name, volume, materials.
3. Constraint information for every component.
4. Details of a constraint, including assembly reference, component reference.
5. Internal relationship between components.
6. Geometry attributes of constraint reference.

Querying

The existing product data semantics can be retrieved by direct querying on PSR. For example, information a), b), c) and d) are explicitly captured in the ontologies, so they can be retrieved out by SPARQL1 and SPARQL2 (Table 3) from PSR. These two SPARQL queries are given as examples in this section. These can be easily extended to retrieve other product data semantics.

SPARQL1: Retrieve product data for a), b) and c)

There are two types of components defined in the ontology: *Part* and *SubAssembly*. *SubAssembly* is different from *Part* because it is composed of more parts and subassemblies. *Part* and *SubAs-*

Figure 7. Workflow of SDME

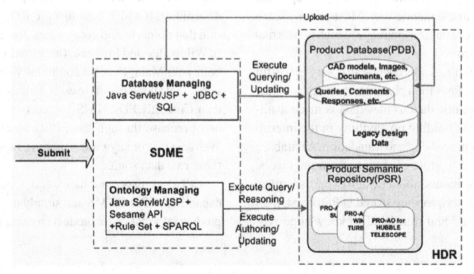

Table 3. Query examples in the repository using SPQRL

```
SPARQL SELECT Query on PSR: SPQRQL1 for a), b) and c)
SELECT *
WHERE {
        { ?component rdf:type ?class .
          ?class rdfs:subClassOf PRO-AO:Component .
          ?component PRO-AO:has_name ?name .
          ?component PRO-AO:has_volume ?volume .
          OPTIONAL {?component PRO-AO:has_constraint ?constraint
                          ?constraint PRO-AO:has_assemblyreference
                          ?assembleto .}
        } UNION
        {?component rdf:type ?class .
          ?class rdfs:subClassOf PRO-AO:Component .
          ?component PRO-AO:has_name ?name .
          ?component PRO-AO:has_component ?subcomponent .
          OPTIONAL {?component PRO-AO:has_constraint ?constraint .
                          ?constraint PRO-AO:has_assemblyreference
                          ?assembleto .}
        }
        } ORDER BY ?component
```

```
SPARQL SELECT Query on PSR: SPQRQL2 for d)
SELECT *
WHERE {
?labelconstraint PRO-AO:has_assemblyreference ?assemblyreference .
?labelconstraint PRO-AO:has_assemblyref_item  ?arefitem .
?labelconstraint PRO-AO:has_componentreference ?componentreference.
?labelconstraint PRO-AO:has_componentref_item ?crefitem . }
```

sembly have some common properties, such as *has_*name, *has_constraint*, but property *has_component* is appropriate for *SubAssembly*, not for *Part* while property *has_volume* is appropriate for *Part*, not for *SubAssembly* (This is because the volume was captured for *Part*, but not for *SubAssembly*). Hence, SPARQL1 queries *Part* and *SubAssembly*, respectively, and returns the union of the two result sets. Here OPTIONAL means to retrieve the constraint information for a component if this component has constraints. In this way, the base component of an assembly will also be included in the final result set.

SPARQL2: Retrieve product data for d)

This query returns assembly reference, assembly reference model item, component reference, and component model item for one constraint.

Reasoning

Product data semantics not explicitly represented in ontologies can be inferred by reasoning on existing product data semantics through rule definitions. Ontology is different from databases, programming languages, or other modeling tools because it is built on a logic base, which enables the explicit, formal declaration of information models, and hence supports inferences by logical rules. We have published papers (Zhu, Jayaram, & Kim, 2010, 2012) that discuss ontology reasoning with SWRL/SQWRL for product design ontologies.

Since PSR in PD-SKMS is built on OWLIM, which is based on a native RDF rule-entailment engine, some custom rule-sets have been defined for OWLIM to realize inferences.

For example, information e) and f) cannot be retrieved directly from the ontologies since they are not explicitly represented. However, with the following rules, they can be inferred from the existing product data semantics.

RuleSet1: This rule set infers the internal relationship between two components (Table 4).

It is believed that the more closely two components are related, the more probable it is that their design parameters are interrelated. Two components are regarded closely related if:

Rule1: They are assembled directly with some constraints.

Rule2: They are connected by an intermediate component.

For large-scale assemblies this rule set will make it much easier to figure out the internal relationships between components. SPARQL3 takes advantage of inferences by RuleSet1 and returns the components closely related (assembleon and assembledwith) to one component.

RuleSet2: In the CAD ontologies, the exact type of model item referenced by a constraint is not captured during ontology instantiation. For example, the model items referenced by the constraint Mate are captured as instances of Surface, but whether these surfaces are

planar or cylindrical is not known. RuleSet2 (Table 5) can help infer the exact type of these surfaces. As illustrated, two rules for Mate are given, which infer the surfaces referenced by Mate are planar. Other rules for Insert and Align are also defined in this rule set but not shown.

More rules can be defined in SDME and help to derive new product data semantics.

Authoring/Updating on PSR

Apart from the ontologies and instantiation described above, currently, SDME implements the instantiation and update for PSR by RDF manipulations. That means information can be input in a pattern like: Subject-Predicate-Object.

For example, an engineer inputs: a) Mirror-Truss as *Subject*; b) has_material as *Predicate*; c) Aluminum as *Object* in a given user interface. The statement: MirrorTruss (Subject) has_material (Predicate) Aluminum (Object) will be created and added/removed to/from the semantic repository by the following code in Table 6.

Table 4. Reasoning for information e) internal relationship between components

```
Ruleset1 for d)
Id: rule1
    x <PRO-AO:has_constraint> y
    y <PRO-AO:has_assemblyreference> z
    -------------------------------
    x <PRO-AO:assembleon> z

Id: rule2
    x <PRO-AO:assembleon> y
    y <PRO-AO:assembleon> z
    -------------------------------
    x <PRO-AO: assembledwith > z
```

```
SPARQL SELECT Query on PSR: SPQRQL3
SELECT *
WHERE {
{?x  PRO-AO:assembleon ?y .} UNION
{?x  PRO-AO:assembledwith ?z . }}
```

Table 5. Reasoning for information f) geometry attributes of constraint reference

```
Ruleset2 for e)
Id: myrule3
   x <rdf:type> <PRO-AO:Mate>
   y <rdf:type> <PRO-AO:Surface>
   x <PRO-AO:has_assemblyref_item> y
   -------------------------------
   y <rdf:type> <PRO-AO:Plane>

Id: myrule4
   x <rdf:type> <PRO-AO:Mate>
   y <rdf:type> <PRO-AO:Surface>
   x <PRO-AO:has_componentref_item> y
   -----------------------------
     y <rdf:type> <PRO-AO:Plane>
...
```

However, as discussed in precious sections, human users are used to expressing thoughts in natural languages, which are informal and unstructured. It is not easy to translate this information into design knowledge in a formal and structured manner. The processing and translating aspect is not the focus of our work and there are many research groups working on this issue (Davies, Grobelnik, & Mladenic, 2008). We will be informed by the work of others in this area.

Searching and Updating on PDB

The technologies for searching and updating conventional databases are much more mature. Through PDB in PD-SKMS, an engineer gets legacy design data and related design materials such as videos, images, documents, etc. Moreover, he/she will be allowed to upload these materials. Queries, comments from engineers are also stored in PDB and are available to visit later. For example, one could connect to the database, select a document from a Doclib table and insert a comment to a Comments table, which are listed in Table 2.

DESCRIPTION OF WEB-BASED INTERFACE FOR VISUALIZATION OF SEMANTIC DATA

There is much potential in using product data semantics and the Semantic Web to create new

Table 6. Authoring/Updating on PSR

```
Code 3 for RDF manipulation
Graph myGraph = myRepository.getGraph();
ValueFactory myFactory = myGraph.getValueFactory();
String namespace = " http://www.wsu.edu/vrcim-onto/PRO-AO.owl#";
URI Subject = myFactory.createURI(namespace, "MirrorTruss");
URI myPredicate = myFactory.createURI(namespace, "has_material");
Literal myObject = myFactory.createLiteral("Aluminum ");
myGraph.add(mySubject, myPredicate, myObject);

...

myRepository.addGraph(myGraph);
myRepository.removeGraph(myGraph);
```

approaches to present and visualize product data and the relationships between them. A clear and efficient knowledge presentation will result in better user experience, improve knowledge understanding for users, and make tacit knowledge more explicit. Efficient presentation can be facilitated by the Web, and one contribution of this paper is providing a novel approach to presenting product data semantics through this medium.

From the existing frameworks for publishing structured data, PD-SKMS chooses Exhibit as the visualizing tool for product semantic data. Exhibit (Huynh, Karger, & Miller, 2007) is a lightweight framework for publishing structured data on standard web servers. It allows creators to publish richly interactive pages and exploit the structure of data for better browsing and visualization. Figure 8 shows the visualization process for query results from SDME.

Each time after executing SPARQL for querying or reasoning tasks, SDME will return a list of tuples. Here a JSON (JavaScript Object Notation) Translator has been developed in PD-SKMS to translate these tuples into JSON, which is the native format for Exhibit.

Since the querying results from public linked data are structured data (XML from DBpedia and JSON from Freebase) in PD-SKMS, Exhibit is also used to visualize these results from EPLD.

Figure 9 gives a complete visualization process for semantic structured data obtained by SDME.

To further illustrate this, the first segment in Table 7 is the JSON data converted from querying results of SPARQL1 (which can be seen in Table 4) by using JSON Translator. The second segment shows how to integrate Exhibit with JSON data into a Web-based user interface. Most Exhibit applications published on Web present the static data which is created before presenting and cannot be changed during presenting. Different from these applications, PD-SKMS presents dynamic semantic data according to the different query/reasoning tasks.

In the next section, the web-based user interfaces containing rich, dynamic visualizations of product data semantics using Exhibit will be shown as part of a case study.

CASE STUDY USING THE PD-SKMS FOR A DESIGN TASK

As a test case, PD-SKMS has been set up as a design environment for a *Hubble Space Telescope* related design exercise. The Hubble Space Telescope (Figure 10, I) has been used since 1990, and some components needed to be repaired or redesigned in order to improve the quality of images sent back to earth. Our simplified assembly model in PRO/E (Figure 10, II) includes 47 parts and 4 sub-assemblies. Specifically, (Figure 10, III) shows the optical system of the Hubble Space Telescope, which consists of two mirrors,

Figure 8. Visualizing semantic data with Exhibit technology

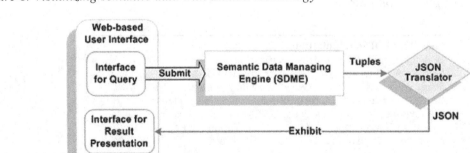

Figure 9. Visualization for retrievals of structured data from SDME

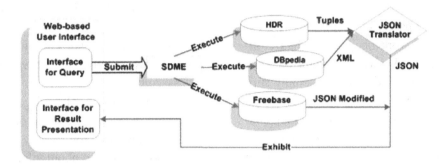

Table 7. JSON data inlined in Exhibit technology

Segment of JSON data for querying results of SPQRQL1:
```
{
component:"HUBBLE_BOTTOMCIRCULARHANDLE168_HUBBLE_ASSEM
BLY",
label:"HUBBLE_BOTTOMCIRCULARHANDLE168_HUBBLE_ASSEMBLY",
name:"HUBBLE_BOTTOMCIRCULARHANDLE",
type:"Component",
subtype:"Part",
constraint:"Align_Offset11",
assembleto:"HUBBLE_BASE18_HUBBLE_ASSEMBLY",
volume:"283.23",
domain:"http://www.wsu.edu/vrcim-onto/PRO-
AO.owl#HubbleTelescope",
author:"VRCIM Lab@WSU" },
...
```

Segment of HTML for presenting query results with Exhibit
```
<link type="inline" rel="exhibit/data" />
<script src="http://static.simile.mit.edu/exhibit/api-2.0/exhibit-
api.js?bundle=false" type="text/javascript"></script>
...
```

Figure 10. Example assembly: Hubble Space Telescope

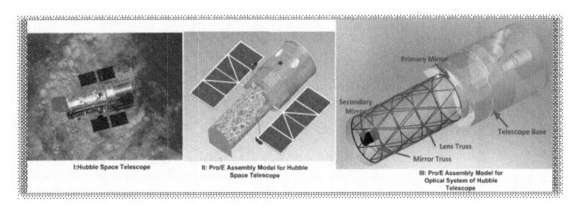

supporting trusses, and the apertures (openings) of the instruments.

The Hubble Space Telescope was a good candidate for our work because we had completed the modeling/knowledge capturing work for the Hubble Space Telescope assembly supported by a REU NSF Grant, and some design data had also been stored in a conventional database. Secondly, there is much interest in the engineering community related to the design of telescopes, and it is a worthwhile project to continue adding knowledge to so professionals may use this information. However, the resources that have been published for *Hubble Space Telescope* on the Web, especially information about design parameters, e.g., dimensions of every component, are currently limited.

The PD-SKMS intends to provide a knowledge-contextual design environment for engineers who are looking for design information/knowledge of a space-based telescope. Specifically, this system will tie together different kinds of data to show that semantic data management makes the design task much easier by exploiting product data semantics with extensible and sophisticated queries. The capabilities include:

1. Performing inquiries about product data semantics of the Hubble Space Telescope assembly.
2. Performing reasoning on product data semantics of the Hubble Space Telescope assembly.
3. Making inquiries about legacy design data of the Hubble Space Telescope assembly by searching on PDB.
4. Making inquiries about information related to the Hubble Space Telescope by querying EPLD.
5. Visualizing and manifesting semantic data in multiple views for the user.

The schematic of the main Web-based user interface for PD-SKMS is given in Figure 11. This user interface provides entries to PSR, PDB, and EPLD for engineers. The site administrator can also access and manage PSR through the Web-based tool supported by Sesame

Toolkits

Table 8 lists the toolkits adopted in the development of PD-SKMS and some key toolkits have been introduced in previous sections.

Figure 11. Schematic of main web-based user interface for PD-SKMS

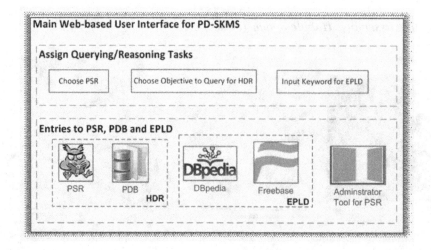

Table 8. Toolkits adopted by PD-SKMS

Component in PD-SKMS	Toolkit
PSR	Sesame, OWLIM, Tomcat
PDB	MySQL
SDME	Sesame API+SPARQL, SQL+JDBC, Java Servelt
Web-base User Interface	JSP, Javascript, Exhibit

Scenario 1: Query on PSR and PDB and Exhibit Product Data Semantics (Capabilities 1), 3), and 5)

In this scenario, SDME executes SPQRQL1 and SPQRQL2. The query results including: a) components of *Hubble Space Telescope* assembly; b) details of these components, including name, volume, materials, and other similar aspects; c) constraint information for every component; d) details of constraints, including assembly reference, component reference, and others will be retrieved without accessing CAD systems once the product data has been captured into the ontologies. The retrieved semantic data are presented using Exhibit technology which provides several ways to display the structured data.

In Pane 1 of Figure 12, the semantic data are classified according to their types (which is called *Facet in Exhibit*). For example, all instances of *Component* are listed in the facet of *Component*. Pane2 of Figure 12 can show all components (51 in total, including *Part* and *SubAssembly*) of the Hubble Space Telescope assembly with a thumbnail view. These components are sorted by their volumes in this view.

As compared to the thumbnail view, Figure 13 presents a table view of the same retrieved product data shown in Figure 12. As shown in this figure, the relationships between data are easily identified in a tabular view. We can read the name, type, volume, subcomponent, constraint, and other factors for every component. Different colors are used to categorize the type of components. For example, *SubAssembly* is colored in orange while *Part* is colored in yellow.

Figure 12. Product data semantics presented on the web for Hubble Space Telescope assembly-I: thumbnail

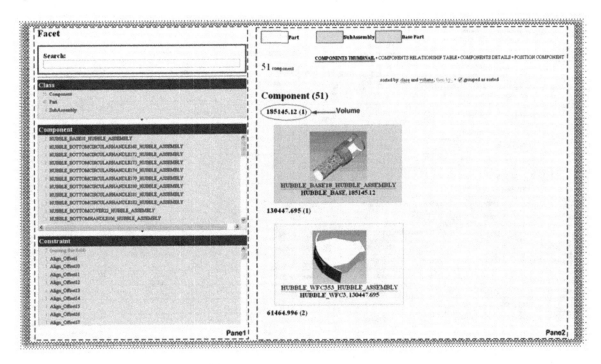

In addition, the semantic data can be displayed dynamically and extensively. For example, by clicking any constraint, e.g., *Insert1*, a mini window will pop up to display the details of this constraint. This dynamic character provides much convenience for browsing the interrelated information.

By connecting to PDB, legacy design information can be retrieved as well. Figure 14 shows the drawing draft and a PRO/E model with some design parameters for *Base* part of *Hubble Space Telescope* created in our previous work.

It is worthwhile to compare the ease and speed of bringing up this kind of data for large models, the ease of assimilating this data in this form for an engineer, and also the accessibility of this on the web with the much more cumbersome approach of starting up a CAD system and viewing individual parts and assemblies, one by one, on a local machine.

Scenario 2: Reasoning on PSR – (for Capability 2) and 5))

Consider an engineer wanting the design information of an optical system of the *Hubble Space Telescope* (Figure 10), by just inputting "truss" in the "Search" facet (Figure 15). The lens truss (the first item in results of Figure 15) and top mirror truss (the 2nd item in results), as well as all related components: top mirror (the 3rd item in results) and truss assembly (the 4th item in results), are filtered out from all components of the *Hubble Space Telescope* assembly.

Further, this engineer may want to know more about the design context of every component, such as how one component affects the design parameters of the other components if some changes are made. The RuleSet1 in the previous section can infer the closely related components based on constraint information, and it enables the inference of design context of components. Figure 15 also displays the inference results by

Figure 13. Product data semantics presented on the web for Hubble Space Telescope assembly-II: tabular view

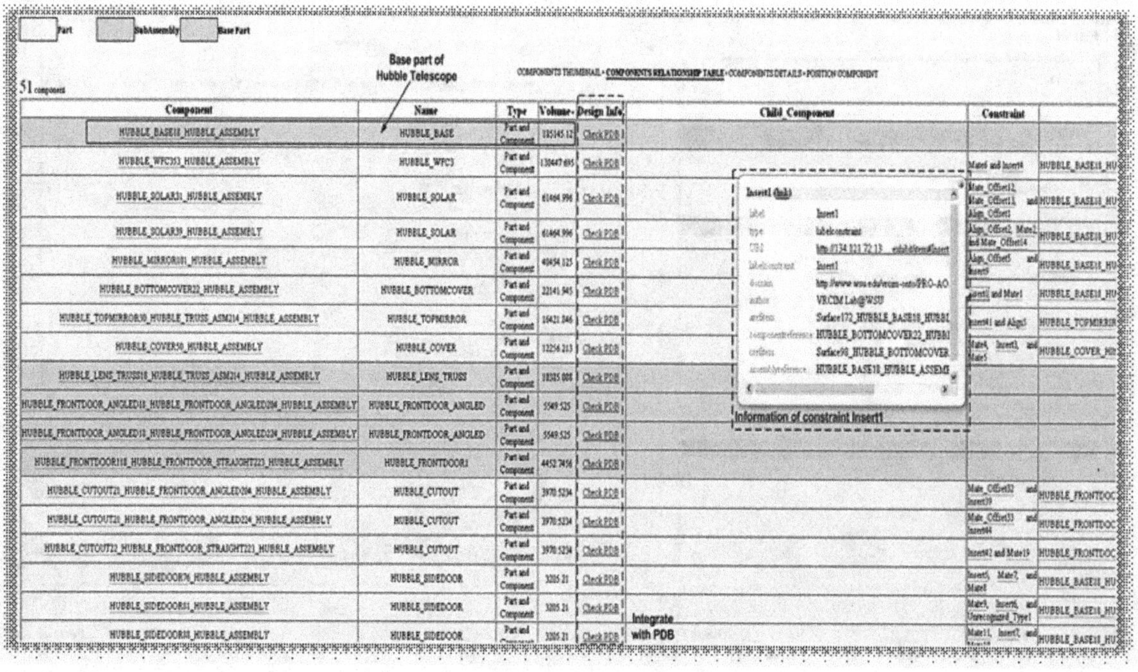

Figure 14. Design information in PDB for base part of Hubble Space Telescope

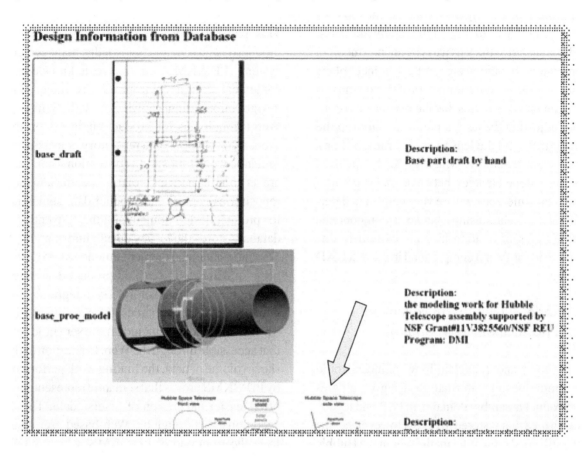

Figure 15. Product data related to truss of Hubble Space Telescope

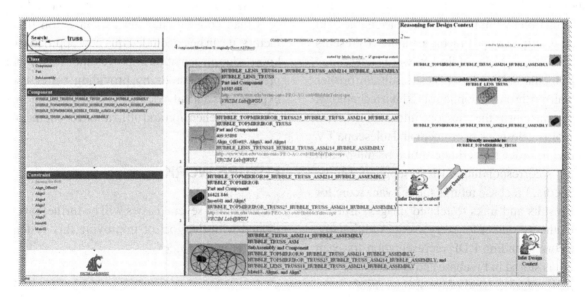

RuleSet1 for the top mirror (the 3rd item in results of Figure 15). This figure shows that the top mirror is assembled directly on the top mirror truss, and connected to the lens truss by an intermediate component. In other words, if this engineer plans to modify the design parameters of the top mirror, e.g., the mirror's radius, he/she may need to consider adjusting the design parameters for top the mirror truss and the lens truss accordingly. For a large-scale assembly, which typically involves complex dependencies between many components, this inference will be very helpful in determining the relationships between components. These kinds of relationships are extremely difficult to identify and comprehend in current CAD systems.

Scenario 3: Link to Public Linked Data (for Capability 4) and 5))

Scenarios 1 and 2, explain how engineers could determine design information using ontologies for product assembly domains in PSR and legacy design data that is stored in PDB. However, he/she may still need more information about the Hubble Space Telescope, such as background, history, the information irrelevant to design, or information about telescopes general. EPLD offers this kind of information by linking to publicly available data such as DBpedia and Freebase. Figure 16 presents the resulting queries of the key word "telescope" in DBpedia and Freebase. These results are further visualized through adoption of Exhibit technology. DBpedia returns the telescope information in two domains: telescope instrument and telescope TV show. In order to facilitate future reading, each result's corresponding URL is supplied. Unlike DBpedia, Freebase returns the relevant score for the results and links to related images, articles, and other resources for every result. Additionally, the corresponding RDF representation for each result is stored in Freebase and is accessible with a GUID number as id of the special result.

CONCLUSION

This paper has proposed and implemented a product design semantic knowledge management system (PD-SKMS) to realize a knowledge-contextual design environment by integrating design information/knowledge with Semantic Web technologies for product engineers on the Web. A host hybrid-data repository consisting of semantic repositories and a conventional database are set up as the back ends of this system. Semantic repositories capture the product data semantics for product design domain and the conventional database stores the legacy design information. A Semantic data management engine (SDME) has been implemented to exploit product data in the host hybrid-data repository. By integrating the publicly linked data sources, the capacity of PD-SKMS is extended to include more semantic data that accessible through the Web. In addition to the sheer volume of data, the linking work performed by PD-SKMS proves that semantic representation offers easier integration of diverse data. This is accomplished through the Web-based user interface, the front end of PD-SKMS, which allows engineers to assign querying/reasoning tasks. It also presents the data retrievals in rich, dynamic visualizations that are easier to interpret and access than conventional modes. Based on these factors, it can be concluded this new approach for knowledge presentation improves upon traditional presentation methods by providing better user experiences and advancing the process of knowledge comprehension and utilization for engineers.

FUTURE WORK

Additionally, several issues will be further investigated with the goal of improving this system. These issues include:

Figure 16. Linking results from DBpedia and freebase

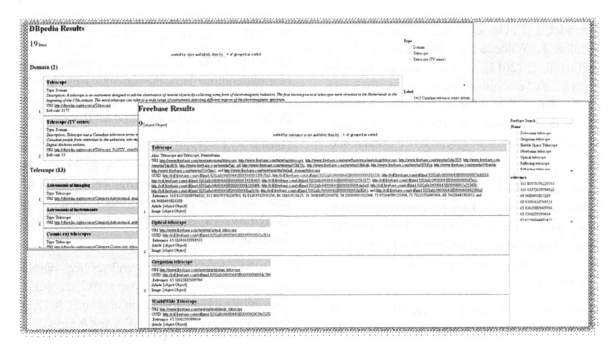

- Extending the host hybrid-data repository.

More design information/knowledge in the product design domain for various products are needed to extend the current repository and evaluate PD-SKMS further. We expect to collaborate with other research groups to incorporate the Semantic Web elements.

- Enhance the capabilities of the Semantic Data Management Engine.

One important component of this work is allowing the engineer authoring/updating privileges in the product semantic repository. Also, more SPARQL queries and rule sets will be defined to extend the querying/reasoning capability of SDME and exploit the enhanced product data semantics.

- Become involved in the world of publicly linked data.

In this paper two publicly linked data sources are linked to PD-SKMS. These data repositories can supply additional information for engineers. However, the contribution of EPLD is limited for now. In the coming future, PD-SKMS will explore more publicly linked data sources, one of which is productontology.org (Hepp, 2011). At the same time we will publish the semantic data for the product design domain on the Web and thus use this work to contribute to the Semantic Web community.

ACKNOWLEDGMENT

This work was partially supported by National Science Foundation (NSF) Grant No. DMI 0523052; Hubble Space Telescope assembly is supplied by NSF Grant#11V3825560/ NSF REU Program: DMI. We also acknowledge contributions by Matthew Poppe in modeling the Hubble Space Telescope and populating the ontologies.

REFERENCES

Briendel, J. T., Grosee, I. R., Krishnamurty, S., Altidor, J., Wildeden, J., Trachtenberg, S., & Witherell, P. (2011). Towards industrial implementation of emerging semantic technologies. In *Proceedings of the ASME International Design Engineering Technical Conferences & Computers and Information in Engineering Conference*.

Cao, D. X., Ramani, K., Li, Z., Raskin, V., Liu, Y., & Li, Z. (2010). Developing customer preferences for concept generation by using engineering ontologies. In *Proceedings of the ASME International Design Engineering Technical Conferences & Computers and Information in Engineering Conference*.

Davies, J. F., Grobelnik, M., & Mladenic, D. (2008). *Semantic knowledge management: Integrating ontology management, knowledge discovery, and human language technologies*. New York, NY: Springer.

Eris, O. (2002). *Perceiving, comprehending, and measuring design activity through the questions asked while designing* (Unpublished doctoral dissertation). Stanford University, Stanford, CA.

Fowler, D., Crowder, R. M., Guan, T., Shadbolt, N., & Wills, G. (2010). Requirements for semantic Web applications in engineering. In *Proceedings of the ASME International Design Engineering Technical Conferences & Computers and Information in Engineering Conference*.

Franklin, M. J., Halevy, A. Y., & Maier, D. (2005). From databases to dataspaces: A new abstraction for information management. *SIGMOD Record*, *34*(4), 27–33. doi:10.1145/1107499.1107502.

Fürber, C., & Hepp, M. (2010). Using SPARQL and SPIN for data quality management on the semantic web. *Business Information Systems*, *47*(2), 35–46. doi:10.1007/978-3-642-12814-1_4.

Gero, J. S., & Maher, M. L. (1993). *Modeling creativity and knowledge-based creative design*. Mahwah, NJ: Lawrence Erlbaum.

Gil, Y. (2011). Interactive knowledge capture in the new millennium: How the semantic web changed everything. *The Knowledge Engineering Review*, *26*, 45–51. doi:10.1017/S0269888910000408.

Heisig, P., Caldwell, N. H. M., Grebici, K., & Clarkson, P. J. (2010). Exploring knowledge and information needs in engineering from the past and for the future – results from a survey. *Design Studies*, *31*(5), 499–532. doi:10.1016/j.destud.2010.05.001.

Hepp, M. (2006). Products and services ontologies: A methodology for deriving OWL ontologies from industrial categorization standards. *International Journal on Semantic Web and Information*, *2*(1), 72–99. doi:10.4018/jswis.2006010103.

Hepp, M. (2008). GoodRelations: An ontology for describing products and services offers on the Web. In A. Gangemi & J. Euzenat (Eds.), *Proceedings of the 16th International Conference on Knowledge Engineer: Practice and Patterns* (LNCS 5268, pp. 329-346).

Hepp, M. (2011). *The product types ontology: Good identifiers for product types based on Wikipedia*. Retrieved April 20, 2011, from http://www.productontology.org/

Hepp, M., & Radinger, A. (2010). *eClassOWL- The Web ontology for products and services*. Retrieved April 18, 2011, from http://www.heppnetz.de/projects/eclassowl/

Herman, I. (2009). *W3C Semantic Web Frequently Asked Questions*. Retrieved February 20, 2011, from http://www.w3.org/RDF/FAQ

Huynh, D. F., Karger, D. R., & Miller, R. C. (2007). Exhibit: Lightweight structured data publishing. In *Proceedings of the 16th International World Wide Web Conference*.

Jain, P., Hitzler, P., Yeh, P. Z., Verma, K., & Sheth, A. P. (2009). Linked data is merely more data. In *Proceedings of the AAAI International Conference on Linked Data Meets Artificial Intelligence* (pp. 82-86). Retrieved April 18, 2011, from http://www.aaai.org/ocs/index.php/SSS/SSS10/paper/download/1130/1454

Kim, O., Jayaram, U., Jayaram, S., & Zhu, L. J. (2009). An ontology mapping application using shared ontology approach and a bridge ontology. In *Proceedings of the ASME International Design Engineering Technical Conferences & Computers and Information in Engineering Conference.*

Kim, O., Jayaram, U., Jayaram, S., & Zhu, L. J. (2010). ITrain: Ontology-based integration of information and methods in computer-based training (CBT) and immersive training (IMT) for assembly simulation. In *Proceedings of the ASME International Design Engineering Technical Conferences & Computers and Information in Engineering Conference.*

Koparanova, M. G., & Risch, T. (2002). Completing CAD data queries for visualization. In *Proceedings of the International Database Engineering and Applications Symposium* (p. 130).

Kuffner, T. A., & Ullman, D. G. (1990). The information requests of mechanical design engineers. *Design Studies, 12*(1), 42–50. doi:10.1016/0142-694X(91)90007-J.

Li, Z., Raskin, V., & Ramani, K. (2008). Developing engineering ontology for information retrieval. *Journal of Computing and Information Science in Engineering, 8*(1), 011003. doi:10.1115/1.2830851.

Li, Z., Yang, M. C., & Ramani, K. (2009). A methodology for engineering ontology acquisition and validation. *Artificial Intelligence for Engineering Design, Analysis and Manufacturing, 23*(1), 37. doi:10.1017/S0890060409000092.

Morris, J. (2008). *The role of ontology in modern expert systems development.* Retrieved March 20, 2011, from http://www.slideshare.net/jcmorris/the-role-of-ontology-in-modern-expert-systems-dallas-2008-presentation

Murshed, S. M. M., Dixon, A., & Shah, J. J. (2009). Neutral definition and recognition of assembly features for legacy system reverse engineering. In *Proceedings of the ASME International Design Engineering Technical Conferences & Computers and Information in Engineering Conference.*

Nicklas, D., Ranganathan, A., & Riboni, D. (2010). A survey of context modeling and reasoning techniques. *Pervasive and Mobile Computing, 6*(2), 161–180. doi:10.1016/j.pmcj.2009.06.002.

NIST. (2002). *STEP/EXPRESS and XML.* Retrieved February 25, 2011, from http://xml.coverpages.org/stepExpressXML.html#step-part28

Prud'hommeaux, E., & Seaborne, A. (2007). *W3C: SPARQL query language for RDF.* Retrieved February 25, 2011, from http://www.w3.org/TR/rdf-sparql-query/

Segaran, T., Evans, C., & Taylor, J. (2009). *Programming the semantic Web.* Sebastopol, CA: O'Reilly Media.

Sevilmis, N., Stork, A., Smithers, T., Posada, J., Pianciamore, M., Castro, R., et al. (2005). Knowledge sharing by information retrieval in the semantic Web. In A. Gómez-Pérez & J. Euzenat (Eds.), *Proceedings of the Second European Semantic Web Conference: Research and Applications* (LNCS 3532, pp. 251-287).

Sheth, A. (2010). Computing for human experience: Semantics-empowered sensors, services, and social computing on the ubiquitous Web. *IEEE Internet Computing, 14*(1), 88–91. doi:10.1109/MIC.2010.4.

Szykman, S., Sriram, R. D., Bochenek, C., Racz, J. W., & Senfaute, J. (2000). Design repositories: Engineering design's new knowledge base. *IEEE Intelligent Systems*, *15*(3), 48–55. doi:10.1109/5254.846285.

Tessier, S., & Wang, Y. (2011). Ontology-based representation and verification to enable feature interoperability between CAD systems. In *Proceedings of the ASME International Design Engineering Technical Conferences & Computers and Information in Engineering Conference*.

Watson, M. (2010). *Practical semantic Web and linked data application*. Retrieved February 20, 2011, from http://www.markwatson.com/

Welty, C. (1999). Ontologies: Expert systems all over again? In *Proceedings of the American Association for Artificial Intelligence National Conference*.

Wikipedia. (2010). *Semantic web stack*. Retrieved March 25, 2011, from http://en.wikipedia.org/wiki/Semantic_Web_Stack

Wikipedia. (2011a). *Linked data*. Retrieved March 25, 2011, from http://en.wikipedia.org/wiki/Linked_Data

Wikipedia. (2011b). *Semantic web*. Retrieved March 25, 2011, from http://en.wikipedia.org/wiki/Semantic_Web

Witherell, P., Krishnamurty, S., Grosse, I., & Wileden, J. (2009). Semantic relatedness measures for identifying relationships in product development processes. In *Proceedings of the ASME International Design Engineering Technical Conferences & Computers and Information in Engineering Conference*.

Zhan, P., Jayaram, U., Kim, O., & Zhu, L. J. (2010). Knowledge representation and ontology mapping methods for product data in engineering applications. *Journal of Computing and Information Science in Engineering*, *10*(2). doi:10.1115/1.3330432.

Zhu, L. J., Jayaram, U., & Kim, O. (2012). Semantic applications enabling reasoning in product assembly ontologies: Moving past modeling. *Journal of Computing and Information Science in Engineering*, *12*(1). doi:10.1115/1.3647878.

Zhu, L.J., Jayaram, U., Jayaram, S. & Kim, O. (2010). Querying and Reasoning with Product Engineering Ontologies-Moving Past Modeling. Proceeding of 2010 ASME IDETC/CIE Conference.

Zhu, L.J., Jayaram,U., Jayaram, S. & Kim, O. (2009). Ontology-Driven Integration of CAD/CAE Applications: Strategies and Comparisons. Proceeding of 2009 ASME IDETC/CIE Conference

This work was previously published in the International Journal on Semantic Web and Information Systems, Volume 7, Issue 4, edited by Amit P. Sheth,, pp. 36-61, copyright 2011 by IGI Publishing (an imprint of IGI Global).

Chapter 2
A Theory of Social Agentivity and its Integration into the Descriptive Ontology for Linguistic and Cognitive Engineering

Edward Heath Robinson
The University of South Florida, USA

ABSTRACT

The agentivity of social entities has posed problems for ontologies of social phenomena, especially in the Descriptive Ontology for Linguistic and Cognitive Engineering (DOLCE) designed for use in the semantic web. This article elucidates a theory by which physical and social objects can take action, but that also recognizes the different ways in which they act. It introduces the "carry" relationship, through which social actions can occur when a physical action is taken in the correct circumstances. For example, the physical action of a wave of a hand may carry the social action of saying hello when entering a room. This article shows how a system can simultaneously and in a noncontradictory manner handle statements and queries in which both nonphysical social agents and physical agents take action by the carry relationship and the use of representatives. A revision of DOLCE's taxonomic structure of perdurants is also proposed. This revision divides perdurants into physical and nonphysical varieties at the same ontological level at which endurants are so divided.

INTRODUCTION

The Descriptive Ontology for Linguistic and Cognitive Engineering (DOLCE) is an ontology for "comparing and elucidating the relationships with other future modules in the [WonderWeb ontology] library, and also for clarifying the hidden assumptions underlying existing ontologies or linguistic resources such as WordNet" (Masolo, Borgo, Gangemi, Guarino & Oltramari, 2003, p. 13). It was developed as part of an effort to create basic infrastructure for the semantic web, and has

DOI: 10.4018/978-1-4666-3610-1.ch002

been used as a foundational ontology for creating domain-level ontologies, such as Bottazzi and Ferrario's (2009) preliminary ontology of organizations. When DOLCE is extended and used to examine domains in more detail (as with Bottazzi and Ferrario, 2009, and the considerations of the geopolitical domain in Robinson, 2010), some issues arise that were not immediately apparent when the foundational ontology was examined in isolation.

The purpose of this article is to resolve issues uncovered in Bottazzi and Ferrario (2009) and Robinson (2010) regarding the agentivity of social objects. "Since ontologies are seen as the semantic web's 'basic infrastructure', it is becoming increasingly important to ensure that ontologies can reflect the social reality that we live in" (Wood & Galton, 2009, p. 268). Thus, the goal of this article is to expand DOLCE with the ability to far more accurately describe social agentivity. How can an ontology simultaneously and in a noncontradictory manner explain the agentivity of both physical and social objects, especially since many nonphysical social objects depend upon the actions of physical agents to perform actions? In order to address this, a theory of social agentivity is proposed that is consistent with DOLCE's basic assumptions. It is then shown how this theory can be encoded into DOLCE with some revision of its basic taxonomic structure of perdurants. The goal of this effort is to capture the natural language notion that some physical and social objects have the capacity to be agentive while recognizing the commonsense notion that they act in different ways. For example, both human beings and corporations can be agents, but corporations, being nonphysical entities, can only act indirectly though human beings authorized to act on their behalf. DOLCE has been chosen as the foundational ontology for this research because it already includes an agentive/non-agentive distinction. This in contrast with other ontologies, such as OCHRE, the Object-Centered High-level Reference Ontology, which "does not distinguish

agentive vs. non-agentive entities" (Masolo et al., 2003, p. 79) and BFO, Basic Formal Ontology, which notes that its category *substantial entity* is taken to include "organizations and other agents" (p. 58) but does not further elaborate on agentivity.

This effort is undertaken with the assumption of social realism: that is, that "social reality exists, that entities such as claims, prices, financial transactions, elections, trials, and weddings are not mere fictions and that our talk of such entities is not a mere collection of roundabout ways of talking about other things" (Smith, 2008, p. 42). Taking a philosophically informed approach to information systems can lead to better information systems research (Lee, 2004). This is especially true in the area of ontology design for the semantic web, because, even though the technical aspects of ontology design may be derived from earlier research on databases, ontology design includes "methods similar to those employed in philosophy, including the methods used by logicians when developing formal semantic theories" (Smith, 2003, p. 161).

The structure of this article is as follows: (1) the meaning of the term "social" as it is used in this article is discussed, (2) a summary of the current problems in DOLCE that this research proposes to solve is provided, (3) the theory of social agentivity is elucidated and informally introduced into DOLCE, and finally (4) some preliminary formal axioms are supplied.

THE MEANING OF "SOCIAL" AND THE EXISTENCE OF SOCIAL OBJECTS

"Social action occurs when thought processes intervene between a stimulus, an actor, and their subsequent response. In other words, it is a process whereby an individual attaches a subjective meaning to his or her action" (Ryan, 2005, p. 714). Trypuz (2008), with reference to Kemke (2001), writes that social actions are actions undertaken by an agent "which have an effect on another agent and are caused and determined by certain social rules and behaviors (shaking hands or kissing someone)" (p. 216, parenthetical in original). Masolo, Vieu, Bottazzi, and Ferrario (2004) distinguish between two senses of sociality: a weak sense and a strong sense. An object is social in the weak sense if it is immaterial and the product of a community. Objects are social in the strong sense if, in addition to the above criteria, "its very conventional constitution involves a network of relations among social agents" interpreted in terms of collective intentionality, actions, and deontic constraints (p. 267).

Weber (1978) writes,

Not every type of contact of human beings has a social character; this is rather confined to cases where the actor's behavior is meaningfully oriented to that of others. For example, a mere collision of two cyclists may be compared to a natural event. On the other hand, their attempt to avoid hitting each other, or whatever insults, blows, or friendly discussion might follow the collision, would constitute "social action. (p. 23)

In this article, the physical motions the cyclists make to avoid hitting one another would not be considered social actions, and neither would any blows exchanged between the two following the collision. Those are regarded as physical actions[1]. The term "social" does not necessarily refer to nonphysical entities created by two or more individuals, but rather the subjective meaning given to a physical action by one or more intentional minds. Therefore, it is possible for a human being to perform a social action completely alone. A lone individual might be physically shifting cards from one stack to another, but these physical actions may carry the social action of playing solitaire. Likewise, a hermit can develop certain physical motions that to him or her constitute the performance of a religious ceremony, a social action.

In some research, social actions are actions taken by a group, whether the entire group acts in unison, or the groups are represented in some way. Ware (1988) writes on the subject of "secondary actions of collectives" where a group is attributed action through "the action of a representative or leader" which constitutes action on behalf of the whole (p. 53). Here, a social action can take place even if the action is not ascribed to a group, but to a single socially constructed individual. The existence of these singular social entities is similar to the distinction explained in Stoutland (2008) between "plural" and "collective" social agents. This distinction is based on whether or not the social entity in question is referred to in the plural (such as using the word "they" with a group of people), or in the singular (such as using the word "it" with a corporation). If a corporation takes an action, it is not considered that the action was taken by the entire group of people affiliated with the corporation, but rather by the single corporate entity itself.

The existence of such social entities is, however, debated. Karl Popper (1945) argued that explanations of the activities of social entities should be given only in terms of individual actions. Even theories that do recognize social entities may not regard them as "genuine" objects in the world (Ware, 1988), and further debate can be held regarding whether such social entities are "nonentities, useful fictions, hypothetical, theoretical, or reduced" (p. 49). In contrast, scholars such as Stoutland (2008) claim that "there are irreducible social agents that intentionally perform social action" (p. 533). Johansson (2004) discusses leveled ontologies in which higher level entities (such as social entities) depend on the levels below them (such as biological entities) but higher level entities cannot be reduced to lower level entities.

John Searle is well known for his work on the ontological construction of social reality. His formulation "X counts as Y in context C," such that a physical act (X) "counts as" a social act (Y) in context C, might be thought to provide a starting point for codifying social action. Unfortunately, Searle's account can only provide limited assistance in answering the questions set forth in this article. This is because, despite being centrally concerned with "how there can be a social and institutional reality in a world consisting of physical particles" (Searle, 2008, p. 20), he is emphatically "not interested in the category of social objects" (Smith & Searle, 2003, p. 305).

Searle writes that "Social objects are always … constituted by social acts; and, in a sense, the object is just the continuous possibility of the activity. A twenty dollar bill, for example, is a standing possibility of paying for something" (Searle, 1995, p. 36, original emphasis), and that "What we think of as social objects, such as governments, money, and universities, are in fact just placeholders for patterns of activities" (p. 57, original emphasis). Smith points out that this "seems to come threateningly close to a skeptical theory of social objects, according to which there are not social objects (like California drivers licenses) after all, but only (somewhat vaguely) 'patterns of activities'" (Smith & Searle, 2003, p. 288, original emphasis).

Searle also writes, "The notion of a social object seems to me at best misleading, because it suggests that there is a class of social objects as distinct from a class of non-social objects" (p. 302). DOLCE operates with exactly that assumption. Searle claims that this situation gives rise to contradictions such as there being one object that is both a physical piece of paper and a social dollar bill. His position is that, "when I am alone in my room, that room contains at least the following 'social objects.' A citizen of the United States, an employee of the state of California, a licensed driver, and a tax payer. So how many objects are in the room? There is exactly one: me" (p. 302). Differently, DOLCE employs the notion of qua-individual, hinted at in the WonderWeb Deliverable D18 (henceforth D18), which describes and provides the founda-

tional axiomatization of DOLCE, and described in Masolo et al. (2004) and Masolo, Guizzardi, Vieu, Bottazzi, and Ferrario (2005). When a role classifies a particular endurant, a third entity emerges, called a qua-individual.

A semiskeptical approach to social objects would be difficult to reconcile or integrate with DOLCE, given that it includes the category *Social Object*. Eliminating social objects by integrating a Searleian approach into DOLCE would likely require so much disruption to DOLCE's taxonomic structure (and possibly its basic philosophical approach) that it might become unrecognizable. This DOLCE-based theory of social agents and actions is not based on Searle's formulation. Instead, a theory of social action is presented that begins with the acceptance of the existence of social objects. This is not because DOLCE's assumptions and structures should be accepted for their own sake (they should be reviewed and revised as necessary), but rather to investigate the topic from within the framework of social realism and thus the acceptance of social objects. This effort could be compared and contrasted with a theory of social agentivity based on a Searle's approach in future research.

PROBLEMS WITH AGENTIVITY IN DOLCE

"Depending upon how we define agency it may be possible to argue that anything can have agency" (Wight, 2004, p. 271). A brick may be said to be the agent that caused the window to break, but according to a narrower understanding of agency, "an action (or event) is caused by an exertion of power by some agent endowed with will and understanding" (Rowe, 1999, p. 15, parenthetical in original). In this sense, agents are capable of what Kemke (2001) calls "real" actions. "Real actions" are "generally volitional, intentional and thus done consciously and under our control,"[2] and "the effect associated with the action corresponds to the motive or intention of the actor as reason for performing the action" (p. 8). Similarly, for Boella and van der Torre (2004), agents are those entities that are able to make autonomous decisions based on their own beliefs, desires, and goals. DOLCE takes this narrow view of agentivity and recognizes two different categories of agents: *Agentive Physical Object and Agentive Social Object. Agentive Physical Objects* are ascribed intentions, beliefs, and desires. D18 provides "human person" as an example of an *Agentive Physical Object*. This is specifically contrasted with "legal person," which is provided as an example of an *Agentive Social Object* (and, more specifically, a *Social Agent*).[3] DOLCE does not have a category for agents that are neither physical nor social.

Bottazzi and Ferrario (2009) and Robinson (2010) leave issues surrounding the agentivity of social entities unresolved. With regard to organizations, Bottazzi and Ferrario (2009) write that in legal and moral philosophy, "organisations are considered as having a personality and identity of their own and thus as being agentive entities" (p. 228), but they challenge this position based on the "peculiar" way in which organizations act, "namely through the actions of some agents who, in virtue of the roles they play, are delegated to act on their behalf" (p. 228), and thus "it is not very obvious that they can really be classified as agentive entities" (p. 228). They do not take an ultimate stand on the agentivity of organizations in that article, but they do tentatively place *Organization* under the category of Non-agentive *Social Object* because of the manner in which organizations act.

This approach can be difficult to reconcile with the existing DOLCE structure as described in D18. Robinson (2010) encountered such difficulty when he argued that states (in the geopolitical sense of the term) were not organizations, but rather legal persons. This places states in the category *Social Agent* and would make them agentive. This sets up the odd situation that if organizations are denied agentivity on the basis of the peculiar way in which they act (that is, through certain institutionalized actions of physical agents playing certain roles), then it would seem strange to grant agentivity to legal persons, as they are even more "abstract" entities than organizations and seem no more capable of taking direct action than are organizations. Perhaps the agentivity of the organization should not be denied when it is granted to the legal person.

The following theory should not be taken as an attempt to make a conclusive metaphysical argument concerning the agentivity of social entities, but rather to elucidate a solution to the problem of social agents in the context of DOLCE. DOLCE is a descriptive ontology, and thus "aims at capturing the ontological stands that shape natural language and human cognition. It is based on the assumption that the surface structure of natural language and the so-called commonsense have ontological relevance" (Masolo et al., 2003 p. 7, original emphasis).[4] Thus, it would seem that regardless of whether or not organizations and legal persons are agents in an ultimate philosophical or metaphysical sense, these entities should, by virtue of the surface structure of natural language, be granted agentivity for the purposes of DOLCE. Nevertheless, it does seem intuitive that social entities (such as Fiat, Apple, and the Bank of Italy) are agentive in a different way than are physical entities, such as human beings, cats, or rhinoceroses. Further, as noted in Trypuz (2008), DOLCE contains no concept of action itself.

A THEORY OF SOCIAL ACTIONS AND SOCIAL AGENTIVITY

In everyday conversation, people often attribute agentivity to nonphysical social entities. The United States may declare war, IBM may sell ten thousand computers, General Motors may bring a lawsuit against another company, New York City may enact regulations about smoking in public places, NATO may hold military exercises, or the 9/11 Commission may investigate what happened on certain days. In these cases, natural language suggests that there is an entity (nonphysical and social though it is) that takes action in the world. However, even after cursory consideration, it seems that these actions are of a different character than physical actions taken by physical entities, such as a human being stabbing another with a sword, pushing a table or throwing a rock, a cat bumping its food bowl, or a bear striking another with its paw. In all of the social cases given above, some physical agent performs some action on behalf of the social entity. Thus, one might conclude that social objects are not agentive after all. In some ontologies, it might be possible or desirable to reduce the agentivity of social agents to the agentivity of physical agents, but this seems undesirable and incorrect within the framework of a descriptive ontology where the surface structure of language is intended to have ontological relevance. In order to explain how the agentivity of social entities can exist in harmony with physical agents in an ontology, this section will present a theory of how physical objects can take social actions. Then it will extend that theory into how social objects can take social actions.

Physical Agents and Social Actions

To account for how a physical agent (such as a human being) can perform social actions, the notion of a physical action carrying a social action is introduced. When a physical agent performs a physical action, that action may carry a social action. As a simple example, a human being can raise his or her hand. Sometimes raising the hand has no social meaning, but in certain situations, the raising of the hand carries the social action of expressing a greeting to another human being. Here, the physical action is the raising of the hand and the social action is an expression of greeting. If a woman raises her hand in greeting, then both the statements "The woman raised her hand" (a statement concerning the physical action) and

"The woman expressed greeting" (a statement concerning the social action) are true. This is similar to the way in which Smith (2008) notes that moving an arm can mean different things in different contexts. Sometimes it may express greeting, but it might also signal an infantry unit to halt, or indicate the refusal of an offer. In still other contexts, raising the arm may be an expression of farewell.

As a more complex example, in the Colosseum of ancient Rome, a victorious gladiator looks to his emperor to decide whether or not the life of his defeated foe should be spared. The emperor will perform one of two social actions: either condemn the defeated gladiator to death or spare his life. Either social action the emperor decides to perform will be carried by a physical action. In order to condemn the man, the emperor will make the "thumbs down" sign. To spare his life, the emperor will make the "thumbs up" sign. The spectators may give either sign in order to cheer for their preferred choice, but merely performing the physical action of pointing the thumb up or down does not condemn or spare the defeated gladiator. Only the thumbs up or thumbs down sign from the human being playing the role of the emperor of Rome carries the social action of sparing or condemning the man. The emperor is not feeling generous, and points his thumb downward, condemning the gladiator. Note that, here again, the statements "The emperor gave a thumbs down" (concerning the physical action) and "The emperor condemned the gladiator" (concerning the social action) are both true. One might argue that signaling thumbs up or thumbs down merely communicated the decision to the victorious gladiator, but this can be rejected. Even if the emperor decided and intended to spare the gladiator's life, but in a moment of confusion gave the thumbs down sign instead, the emperor would have actually condemned the gladiator by the physical act of pointing his thumb downward, which carried the social act of condemnation.

Performing a social action may or may not depend upon the intention of the person who makes the action.[5] For example, a tourist may make a physical hand gesture that carries no offensive social action in his or her own culture, but happens to carry a highly offensive social action in the culture he or she is currently visiting. The tourist was totally ignorant of this fact when the gesture was made. Did the physical hand gesture carry the offensive social action? In the context where the gesture was made, it would appear that it does, although ignorance of what the tourist was doing might absolve him or her of the responsibility for the action to some people. Alternatively, consider a hermit who developed the physical actions that carry a religious ceremony, but never communicated that information to anyone. Completely accidentally, another person performs the exact physical motions the hermit specified as carrying the religious ceremony. Has the second person performed the religious ceremony? Probably not, since part of the required context for performing the religious ceremony may be intending to perform it. In another instance, one might perform the physical actions, but only intend to practice them for later performance. In this case, the ceremony would not have been performed during the practice.

Certain situations may prevent the social act from being carried. For example, making certain markings on a sheet of paper with certain other markings already on it may ordinarily carry the social action of agreeing to a contract, but being under duress may cause the social action not to be carried. Also, a single physical act may carry different social actions in different situations. Making certain marks with a pen on a sheet of paper is a physical act that can carry different social actions depending on the situation. Besides agreeing to a contract, making certain marks on a sheet of paper might carry the social action of signing an autograph or granting permission for other actions to happen. The physical act of homicide may carry the social act of murder in some situations; in others it may be the social act of manslaughter, the severe social act of treason, or (in self-defense or another situation of justifiable homicide) not carry a crime at all.

It is possible to assign new social actions to existing physical actions. For instance, a club could have a particular physical action performed by two people that carried the social action of the club's secret handshake. If a third party compromised the secret handshake, the club might adjust its norms so that a new physical action carried the social action of performing the secret handshake. In addition to physical actions being able to carry different social actions in different contexts, a single physical action may carry multiple social actions. For instance, perhaps the secret club finds itself on the wrong side of the government and its secret handshake is outlawed. Now, whenever the members performed the specific physical action, those actions would carry not only the social action of the secret handshake, but also the commission of a crime.

In this example, it is important to consider whether the government bans the physical action or the social action. If the government bans the social action, then even if the secret club reassigned the secret handshake to a new physical action, performing that new physical action would still carry the secret handshake, and thus, the social act of the commission of a crime. If the government bans the physical action, then the club could be free to reassign the secret handshake to a new physical action, but the original physical actions would still carry the commission of a crime. Banning the physical act might occur when the physical action and the social action it carried became intertwined in the mind of the public and significant emotional weight was attached to the action.[6] Of course, it is certainly possible that the government might ban both.

Not only can a single physical action carry multiple social actions, but also the same social action can be carried by different physical actions. Consider the social action of expressing greeting.

It might be carried by raising the hand, by shaking hands, or by making certain utterances. This can especially be seen cross-culturally when different cultures have the same social actions (such as getting married, getting divorced, adopting a child, or crowning a monarch) but very different physical actions that carry those social actions. A speech act is also a physical action that can carry social actions. Speech acts of certain kinds and under the right circumstances can carry social actions or bring about certain social conditions. Searle (1995) wrote on the subject of "declarations" in which "the state of affairs represented by the propositional content of the speech act is brought into existence by the successful performance of that very speech act" (p. 34).

In order for one social act to be performed, another social action might be required to precede it, and another social action required to precede that one, and so on and so forth. The requirements for each of these social acts can leave the physical acts necessary to carry them unspecified. For example, perhaps before some other social action can happen, the social action of a greeting is required, but the physical action that carries the greeting is not specified. It could be a handshake, raising the arm, or even a head nod. Figure 1 provides a diagrammatic overview of the various ways in which physical and social actions can carry social actions as they have been described in this section.

When do Certain Actions Carry Other Actions?

It is important to be able to determine when one action carries another. As mentioned above, there may be certain situations (such as being under duress) that might prevent the carry relation from holding between two actions. But more generally, it is important to understand that this relation may hold between two actions only in certain circumstances or when certain conditions are met.

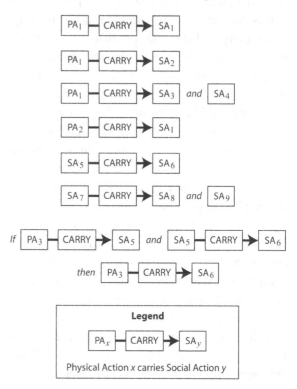

Figure 1. Diagram of different methods by which physical and social actions can carry other actions

An appropriate context for the carry relation to hold may be created by multiple criteria, none of which may alone be sufficient for the physical action to carry the social action. Both temporal and spatial location may be important parameters for defining an appropriate context, but may neither be sufficient nor necessary alone.

For example, certain social actions may only be carried at certain times, such as only during the fourteenth century, or only during the hour before sunset. Others may only be carried when performed in the correct spatial location, such as in Europe, or the territory of Venezuela. *Temporal Location* and *Spatial Location* are neither *Endurants* nor *Perdurants* in DOLCE, but rather members of the class *Quality*. Thus, temporal and spatial parameters might be reduced to saying the entity performing the action must have the correct qualities. Other parameters might include the relations of belonging to a certain group or being classified by a certain role. It might be required that an individual be in the presence of other certain individuals, or the event be happening before, after, or during the occurrence of another event. For example, the spatiotemporal qualities of a hand wave alone are insufficient to determine what social action (if any) has been carried. If the hand wave is preceded by one's arrival, then "hello" may be carried; if the hand wave is followed by the individual departing, then "goodbye" may be carried.

Combinations are certainly possible and even likely. Certain social actions may only be carried in certain spatial locations at certain times, such as within the bounds of Venezuela in the hour before sunset, or only in Europe during the fourteenth century. But, beyond physical and temporal location, other factors may come into play to define a context. For instance, a social action may only be carried if someone of a particular social class performs the action, or by someone playing a certain role. These can be combined with spatial or temporal location parameters. Perhaps a certain social action is only carried if a certain physical action is performed by a member of the landed gentry in fourteenth century Europe, or by a person playing the role of priest in the hour before sundown within the territory of Venezuela.

The conditions necessary for one action to carry another must be given in a description (a *Non-agentive Social Object*). Following Bottazzi and Ferrario (2009), descriptions "are always encoded in at least one physical support" (p. 227). For example, the description could be written in a book or memorized in the brain of a human being. The physical actions that occurred and the circumstances in which they occurred can be compared with the criteria enumerated in the description in order to determine whether or not a social action was carried.

Social Agents and Action Through Representation

How social objects come into being is not at issue in this article. Their existence is presupposed. The explanation for how social agents take action is partially based on the comments in Bottazzi and Ferrario (2009) on organizations, but is broadened to incorporate the action of any agentive social object. Here, however, rather than *denying* certain social objects agentivity because of the indirect way they act in the world, it is put forward that such entities should be *granted* agentivity *because* of it.

In this article, representation is the key to the ability of nonphysical social objects being able to take action. Bottazzi and Ferrario (2009) describe two relations, delegation and its specification, the representation relation. They write,

Generally speaking, the representation relation is a delegation relation that holds between agents that are classified by two roles: the representative and the represented role. Differently from the delegation relation, if the representation relation holds, the delegator cannot perform him/herself the action that (s)he wants or needs the delegate to do. Sometimes it is the case that there is a contingent impediment, other times the delegator is intrinsically unable to perform what (s)he is delegating. The case of organisations is clearly one of these. Organisations, as immaterial entities, cannot act without a physical agent who acts for them. (p. 234)

Agentive Social Object is a broader class than *Organization*, so the above can be generalized. The representation relation can hold between an *Agentive Social Object* and an *Agentive Physical Object* that are classified by the appropriate roles. *Agentive Social Objects* cannot act unless there are physical agents that act for them. The representation relation can form a transitive chain in which one *Agentive Social Object* is represented by other *Agentive Social Objects*. At the end of this chain is either a physical agentive object or a qua-individual. For instance, the transitive chain of representation might terminate with an entity such as "the Duke of Edinburgh," regardless of what physical agent may be playing that role at the time.

If an *Agentive Physical Object* represents an *Agentive Social Object* (either directly or through a chain of other *Agentive Social Objects*) and that *Agentive Physical Object* performs a physical action on behalf of the *Agentive Social Object* that carries a particular social action, then the *Agentive Social Object* has performed the social action. An *Agentive Social Object* need not be represented by the same *Agentive Physical Object* for all purposes. Further, there may be only a very limited set of actions that an individual is authorized to take on behalf of the *Agentive Social Object*. For example, Bottazzi and Ferrario (2009) write that the action that an agent may perform on behalf of an organization must be institutionalized within the organization. Specifically, "The president does not hit a piece of wood with a stick on behalf of the organization he is president of (unless this is a symbolic gesture with some further meaning), but he can very easily sign a contract on behalf of it" (p. 228, parentheses in original).

A single *Agentive Social Object* may be represented by several other entities, with each entity representing it for different purposes. For example, the government of Latvia (an *Organization*, and an *Agentive Social Object*) may represent the state of Latvia (another *Agentive Social Object*). A particular suborganization within the Latvian government, the Latvian Ministry of Foreign Affairs, may represent the state of Latvia for the purposes of its foreign relations. For the purposes of its relations with the state of Estonia, the state of Latvia may specifically be represented by an *Agentive Social Object* (and qua-individual), the "Latvian Ambassador to Estonia" (created when an *Agentive Physical Object* plays a certain role).

When the *Agentive Physical Object* playing the role of Latvian Ambassador to Estonia performs the physical action of making some markings on a sheet of paper, and those markings are of a certain type, and other markings on the paper are of a certain type, this may carry the social action of agreeing to a treaty with Estonia. Thus, Latvia has agreed to a treaty with Estonia. See Figure 2 for a diagrammatic overview of a social agent performing a social action by way of representation, and Figure 3 for an overview of a social agent performing a social action by way of a representation chain.

Bottazzi and Ferrario (2009) write, "it seems fair to say that every organisation not only has at least an affiliate, but also at least a representative, i.e., someone who can act on its behalf" (p. 235). This may or may not be the case for organizations, but even if it is, it is not something that can be generalized to *Agentive Social Objects* as a whole. For example, ordinarily, a state's government represents the state, but in the case where the government is destroyed, disbanded, or overthrown, there may well be no representative of the state. Destruction of a government is not identical with destruction of a state, and the state may continue despite having no government to represent it. A human being in a coma serves as another example. The legal person, the *Social Agentive Object*, still exists, but the *Physical Agentive Object*, the human being, is unable to act on the legal person's behalf. Many times, a spouse or other family member is authorized to represent the legal person in the coma. But, if the person has no family, spouse, or other human being to act on his or her behalf, there may be no way for that legal person to act.

It was explained above that an agent can be restricted to representing an entity for only certain purposes (although there is nothing preventing one agent from representing a *Social Agentive Object* for all purposes). Therefore, it is possible that a *Social Agentive Object* might lose its representative for a particular purpose. For instance, the

Figure 2. Diagram of a social agent performing a social action by way of representation

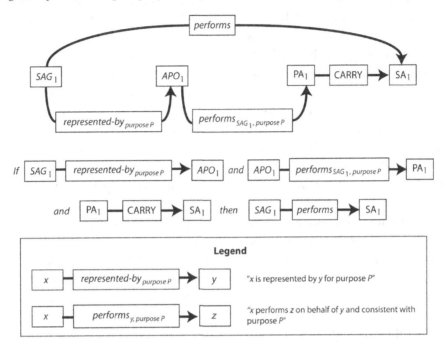

Figure 3. Diagram of a social agent performing a social action by way of a representation chain. Note that in this case SAG$_2$ does not perform SA$_1$. Consider a law firm representing a client by filing a lawsuit. The represented client files suit by way of representation through the law firm.

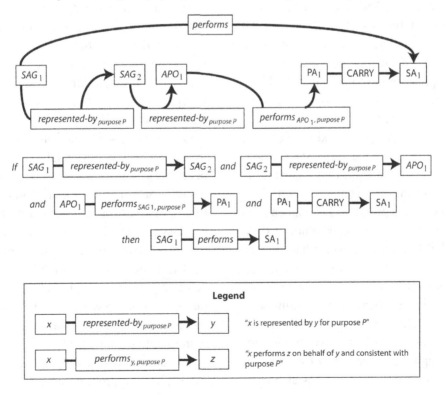

representative might be assassinated. Until a new representative is reappointed, the *Social Agentive Object* may be unable to take action with regard to that purpose. This might be especially significant if that representative cannot be replaced. Perhaps the representative of a *Social Agentive Object* for purpose *p* might be required to be a male of a particular familial line, but if the person assassinated happened to be the last male of that line, then the *Social Agentive Object* might no longer be able to perform actions with regard to purpose *p*.

In other situations, there may be no procedure for replacing a representative for purpose *p*. This might be especially relevant in the cases of terrorist or insurgent organizations. An opposing force may go out of its way not to kill enemy leadership so that there will be someone to negotiate with. If its leadership is dead, an insurgent force may have no one to represent it for the purposes of political negotiations, and they might have no process to reappoint a representative for that purpose. Such a conflict might drag on, rather than being concluded by those authorized to represent the force for that purpose. The insurgent force may still have representatives for other purposes, such as violence[7] (conducting ambushes or planting explosive devices) or religious proclamations. This could have implications as to what responsibility for the actions of certain individuals might or might not fall upon the organization as a whole.

Thought must be given to the kind of entity a purpose is, in order to place it within the DOLCE hierarchy. One could suppose that a purpose is something that inheres in an entity, and thus be a *Quality*. However, according to D18, an entity's qualities must exist as long as the entity exists. DOLCE explicitly does not consider that a quality might only intermittently inhere in an entity. This means that an entity could not have no purpose, acquired one later, and then at further future time lose its purpose again. Perhaps the existence of intermittently inhering qualities should be reevaluated, even though the larger issue of whether an entity's purpose inheres in it at all is also open

debate (i.e., does the purpose of a person's life inhere in the life or in the person, either permanently or intermittently?).

At least for the reason of the prohibition on the intermittent inherence of a quality in an entity, this article will understand a purpose as a *Non-agentive Social Object*. Purposes has no direct spatial qualities (and thus is a *Non-physical Object*), and also are *Social Objects*, at least in the sense that they depend on intentional minds (and thus contrast with the merely private experiences which fall under the category *Mental Object*).

Consideration also needs to be given to whether or not any social object can be represented. The answer appears to be no, since it seems *Agentive Social Objects* can be distinguished from *Non-agentive Social Objects* because they can be represented. Just as the purpose of this article is not to analyze how *Social Agentive Objects* come into being, it is not its purpose to investigate the ontological distinctions between agentive and non-agentive social objects.[8] For present purposes it is enough to understand that some social objects are of such a character that they can be represented and others are not. How that determination can be made could be the subject of deeper investigation. It is not the case that a non-agentive social object can become agentive simply by someone claiming to represent it (i.e., an economic system, a *Non-agentive Social Object*, cannot become agentive simply because someone claims to represent it). In spite of both being socially created, there appears to be something intrinsic to the nature of *Agentive Social Objects* that allows them to have representatives (or in other words, to be able to be classified by the represented role) that *Non-agentive Social Objects* do not share.

The status of an *Agentive Social Object* that has no representatives should be contrasted with that of a *Non-agentive Social Object*. While it seems that an *Agentive Social Object* without a representative is not agentive, it is still potentially agentive (and will be fully agentive again when it reacquires a representative). Whatever intrinsic characteristic of the *Agentive Social Object* that allows it to have representatives is still present even at the times where there are no representatives, and this characteristic seems to be enough to distinguish agentive from non-agentive social objects. At this time, DOLCE does not recognize a category of "potentially agentive objects," social or otherwise.

Introduction of Physical and Nonphysical Perdurants into DOLCE

According to DOLCE's taxonomic structure endurants are "wholly present (i.e., all their proper parts are present) at any time they are present" (Masolo et al., 2003, p. 15, parentheses in original). It also recognizes a distinction between the physical and the nonphysical, and hence the social. This distinction is based on whether or not the entity has direct spatial qualities, such as spatial location. Physical endurants have direct spatial qualities, nonphysical entities cannot. DOLCE's taxonomy of perdurants, entities that "extend in time by accumulating different temporal parts, so that, at any time they are present, they are only partially present, in the sense that some of their proper temporal parts (e.g., their previous or future phases) may be not present" (p. 15, parentheses in original), does not include such a distinction. For reference, see Figure 4 for a diagram of the original DOLCE structure for endurants and perdurants. An ontological distinction between physical and nonphysical endurants is proposed at the same level at which the distinction between physical and nonphysical perdurants is recognized. The taxonomy proposed is diagrammed in Figure 5, and examples of physical and social states, processes, achievements, and accomplishments are provided in Table 1.

Figure 4. Original DOLCE taxonomic structure for endurants and perdurants as described in D18. The categories amount of matter, feature, and arbitrary sum are not shown due to space limitations.

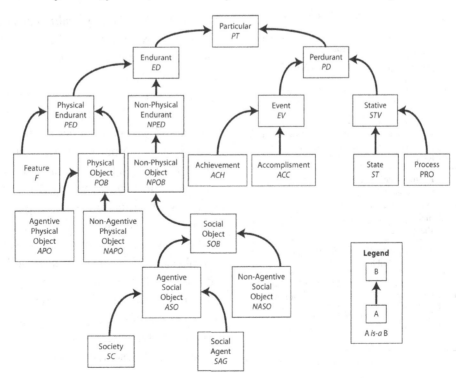

Figure 5. Proposed DOLCE taxonomic structure for endurants and perdurants. Also shown are the categories concept, description, role, and norm from Bottazzi and Ferrario (2009). The categories amount of matter, feature, and arbitrary sum are not shown due to space limitations.

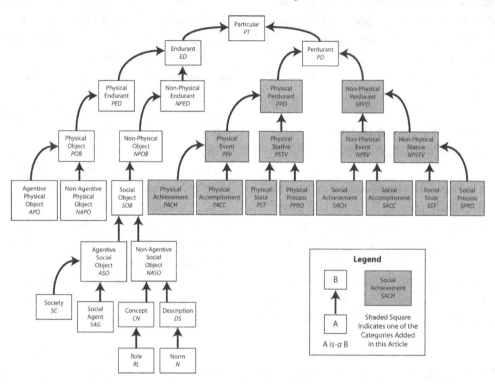

Table 1. Examples of proposed new categories

Category	Examples
Physical Achievemen	Reaching the summit of K2, a departure, a death
Physical Accomplishment	An ascent, the demolition of a building, attacking an individual
Physical State	Being solid, being red, being sitting, being pregnant, being hungry, being translucent, being cold, being liquid
Physical Process	Photosynthesis, combustion, bioluminescence, coagulation, evaporation, sublimation, freezing, melting, running, making marks on a sheet of paper
Social Achievement	The moment a boxing match is won, the moment a bill becomes law
Social Accomplishment	A theatrical performance, a conference, a war, a family get-together, a cocktail party
Social State	Being excommunicated, being at war, being at peace, being under judicial review
Social Process	Educating, declaring war, making peace, writing

The nature of the physical/nonphysical distinction in the taxonomy of perdurants is still open to question. As mentioned above, only physical endurants are allowed to have direct spatial qualities. Perdurants are only allowed direct temporal qualities. "The temporal regions of endurants and the spatial regions of perdurants are inherited by means of the participation relation" (p. 74). Since all perdurants are only allowed to have spatial qualities indirectly (by virtue of the spatial qualities of endurants that are participating in them), using the direct/indirect spatial qualities distinction to divide perdurants into physical and nonphysical categories is not possible.[9] More to the point of this article is the distinction between the physical and the social. The critical distinction between the physical and social perdurants put forward in this article is that social processes are dependent upon society (or at least a single intentional mind) that is able to provide subjective meaning to physical actions. Photosynthesis and combustion are physical processes that are not dependent upon intentional minds. Agreeing to a contract or receiving a university degree are dependent upon intentional minds.

Following the distinction between the physical and nonphysical, the distinctions that DOLCE makes between kinds of perdurants are maintained. These include *Event* and *Stative* being distinguished based on cumulativity, the distinction between *Achievement* and *Accomplishment* being atomicity, and *State* and *Process* being distinguished by homeomericity. But, as shown in Figure 5, the perdurant side of the taxonomy switches from distinguishing "physical" and "nonphysical" to distinguishing "physical" and "social" at the same ontological level at which the endurants are so divided. This immediately prompts the question of whether there are nonphysical nonsocial perdurants. Insofar as DOLCE recognizes nonphysical, nonsocial endurants (Mental Object) and the perdurant side of the ontology potentially mirrors the endurant side, their possible existence should be considered.

Mental Process might be the obvious perdurant complement to *Mental Object*. The existence of mental objects and processes can be argued for or against, depending upon the theory of mind to which one subscribes. For instance, it is possible that mental objects and processes are only the physical objects and processes of the brain. Insofar as DOLCE subscribes to no particular theory of mind, the question is left open here, although the inclusion of Mental Object would seem to suggest the inclusion of *Mental Process* as well.

Other potential candidates for nonsocial nonphysical statives might be emotional or spiritual statives. Changes in emotional state (such as being happy or becoming sad) may also be actual physical changes in the brain and thus physical perdurants. Medication for chronic depression creates a chemical (physical) change in the brain, and thus going from depression to happiness may

be a physical process. With regard to spiritual statives, a great deal will depend on the realism to which the ontology subscribes. If "being saved" is an actual state of a nonphysical soul, then it might be a candidate for a nonsocial, nonphysical stative. Nonsocial, nonphysical perdurants have not been included in the proposed ontology in this article, but it remains open to their inclusion in future revisions if warranted.

Participation vs. Performance

Participation is a relation of central importance in DOLCE. According to Masolo et al. (2003),

In DOLCE, the main relation between endurants and perdurants is that of participation: an endurant "lives" in time by participating in some perdurant(s). For example, a person, which is an endurant, may participate in a discussion, which is a perdurant. A person's life is also a perdurant, in which a person participates throughout its all [sic] duration. (p. 16)

To explain action, one needs a stronger relation than mere participation. This stronger relation will be called performance. Performance is a kind of participation. Endurants that perform social perdurants also participate in them, but not all participants are performers.

Consider the ceremony of conferring knighthood upon a squire. There are several participants in the ceremony. The squire participates in his own knighting. The lord dubbing the squire participates. A priest may bless the arms and armor of the squire the night before and administer religious rites to the squire, and thus participate in the ceremony. There might be many spectators to witness the dubbing, who also participate in that regard. Both the lord and the squire seem to be necessary participants in the ceremony since it could have taken place on the battlefield and therefore be conducted without the priest and the religious rites, or the ceremony could have been conducted privately so there were no spectators. Other participants even include the squire's shoulder, since the squire's shoulder is being touched with the sword during the dubbing, and the sword itself, since it is used to do the dubbing. Intuition suggests that the lord is unlike the others in a very specific way, in that it is the lord who actually *performs* the knighting.

The performer is the participant whose physical action actually carries the social action. If the social action requires joint action on the part of two of more agents, there may be more than one performer. Only agents may perform actions. Non-agents may participate in them (as is the case with the squire's shoulder and the sword), but only an agent may perform an action. Of course, it is also possible for an agent merely to participate in an event as well.

Both participation and performance are different from merely being present at the particular time or location (or both) at which a social action is going on. Being present may still be very important, since someone who was present at a social event could verify its occurrence. In certain circumstances, a participant may even be required to play the role of "witness" for the social event to occur.

Some social perdurants are of a kind that can be performed, whereas others are not. Why can one perform the play *Henry V*, or a knighting ceremony, but not a war, or a battle? There is no entity that performs the war. The belligerent states participate in the war, but World War II is not a perdurant that can be performed. One qualification appears to be that a performer must always be a social individual.[10] Two actors might be said to perform a play (if there are only two roles), but this is because together the actors form a single social individual – the cast – and the cast performs the play. The belligerents of a war do not have any unity criteria by which they are one. Furthermore, perdurants that can be performed seem to be repeatable in a very specific sense. The play *Henry V* can be repeated, the ceremony to knight

a squire can be repeated with new squires and is performed each time, but wars are not repeatable in the same way. World War II cannot be repeated in the way *Henry V* can.

Smith and Grenon (2004) discuss a number of formal ontological relations related to the ones being put forward here, but different in important respects. For instance, when discussing participation, they list a number of ways in which participation can vary. These variations included an active/passive distinction and a direct/mediated distinction. The active/passive distinction is based on whether or not the participating entity is agentive. Agentive participation is called perpetration, whereas non-agentive participation is called patiency.[11] Perpetration is "direct and agentive participation in a process" (p. 290), whereas with patiency "a substance is being acted on by a process" (p. 291). Smith and Grenon's perpetration is different from the performance relationship described here in at least the sense that performing entities can be acting indirectly in a process.

Their article also includes "mediation," which considers indirect participation, but not in the sense of representation discussed here. Rather, they consider mediation to occur when a "substance plays an indirect role in the unfolding of a process relating other participants" (p. 291). The given examples are "the Norwegians mediate the discussions between the warring parties" and "the mailman brings Mary's letter to John" (p. 291). Their article also includes a brief mention of a performance relation, but as a specific variant of the realization relation.

Parallels can be drawn between the performance relation given here and the *is-agent-of* relation given in Trypuz (2008). Trypuz (2008) uses *is-agent-of* as "the main relation between an agent and an action" and indicates that "for any action there is always an agent which is an agent of action" (p. 19). Later, when integrated with DOLCE, *is-agent-of* is interpreted as participation and dependency. While participation and dependency are necessary for performance, it is the intention for performance to have a stronger meaning than merely those two relationships. This is because even though knighting a squire does depend upon the participation of the squire as well as the lord, the lord is still further distinguished as being the performer of the knighting, since it is his actions that carry the social action of bestowing the accolade of knighthood.

Possible Restrictions on the Performance of Social Actions

Physical agents can perform physical actions, and they can do so directly without the need of representation. Physical agents can perform social actions and can do so directly. Social agents can indirectly perform social actions by virtue of representatives. A more difficult question is whether social agents can perform physical actions. Clearly they cannot do so directly, due to their immaterial nature, but can an *Agentive Social Object*, through the use of a representative, perform a physical action?

In the context of DOLCE, the answer would seem to be "yes." The Roman Empire may destroy the city of Jerusalem, al Qaeda may detonate a bomb, and the U.S. Air Force may attack a Taliban troop position. All of these are social entities taking physical action. As a descriptive ontology, DOLCE would seem to need to be able to account for such situations. It may also be that social acts can cause physical acts. The cause of a person's death (a physical act) may have been a war (a social act) or even the declaration of the war (another social act) as well as the sword stroke of the enemy soldier (a physical act), but the purpose of this article is not to analyze causation or responsibility from either a legal or moral perspective. Further, D18 does not describe mechanisms by which DOLCE might handle causation. Developing such mechanisms is left for future research.

PRELIMINARY FORMALIZATION OF THE PROPOSED ONTOLOGY

In this section, some preliminary axioms for the proposed revision to DOLCE's structure and theory of social action are provided.

Introduction of Basic Predicates

Following the notation given in D18, x, y, and z will be used as variables that range over particulars. DOLCE's notation for the predicates of endurant, perdurant, agentive physical object, agentive social object, participation, parthood, proper parthood, specific constant dependence, one-sided constant dependence, being present, and time interval are all adopted here. Further, the category description $(DS(x)$ is a description) and the definition relation $(DF(x, y) x$ defines $y)$ is adopted from Bottazzi and Ferrario (2009). The basic predicates introduced in this article are as follows:

- *PPD(x)* standing for "*x is a physical perdurant*".
- *NPPD(x)* standing for "*x is a nonphysical perdurant*".
- *PEV(x)* standing for "*x is a physical event*".
- *NPEV(x)* standing for "*x is a nonphysical event*".
- *SACH(x)* standing for "*x is a social achievement*".
- *SACC(x)* standing for "*x is a social accomplishment*".
- *PACC(x)* standing for "*x is a physical accomplishment*".

Construction of the Revised DOLCE is-a Tree

The division of perdurants into physical and nonphysical varieties occurs at the same ontological level as the endurants are so divided. Figure 4 shows the original DOLCE is-a tree and Figure 5 shows the suggested revision. As has been noted previously, DOLCE's original distinctions regarding cumulativity, homeomericity, and atomism are preserved, despite the introduction of the physical and nonphysical divide. See definition Dd57 for the definition of cumulatively, Dd59 for the definition of homeomerous, and Dd61 for the definition of atomic in Wonderweb Deliverable D18.

Introduction of Formal Axioms Regarding "Carrying"

The carry relationship is used to describe how through one action (either a physical action or another social action), a social action can take place. The predicate CARRY(x, y, t) standing for "perdurant x carries the perdurant y at time t" is now introduced formally.

One action can only carry another when it is performed in the correct context. This context must be defined in a description. The circumstances under which an event occurred can be compared with the description to determine whether or not the action a further action was carried. This makes it important to understand how the context fits within the underlying ontology. The context of an action is the collection of all the facts or conditions related to that action. This means the context surrounding an event is a kind of collective, and unfortunately "there is little support for them in DOLCE" (Wood & Galton, 2009, p. 269). While DOLCE can classify the members of collectives, "one searches in vain for any category to place the collectives themselves" (p. 269). This means that the underlying ontology is not expressive enough with regard to its ability to describe collectives. DOLCE requires further development in this area, but for present purposes, the variable c will be used to indicate a context, a collective which with currently no place in the DOLCE *is-a* hierarchy.

However, using this context variable c, one can define what it means for one action to carry another. One action carries another at a certain time, if and only if there exists a description that defines the context under which that action is carried and that context is present at that time (1D).

$$\text{CARRY}(x, y, t) := \exists z(DS(z)) \wedge DF(z, c) \wedge$$
$$\text{PRE}(c, t) \tag{1D}$$

Only *Social Achievements*, *Social Accomplishments*, and *Social Processes* can be carried (1A). *Social States* may be the result of other social activities, but they do not need other actions to carry them. For example, the process of declaring war is carried by physical action, but the result of the process, a country being in a state of war, requires no other perdurant to carry it.

$$\text{CARRY}(x, y, t) \rightarrow (PPD(x) \vee NPPD(x)) \wedge$$
$$(SACH(y) \vee SACC(y) \vee SPRO(y)) \wedge T(t) \tag{1A}$$

CARRY is transitive (2A). It is also asymmetric (3A) and antireflexive (4A).

$$\text{CARRY}(x, y, t) \wedge \text{CARRY}(y, z, t) \rightarrow \text{CARRY}(x, z, t) \tag{2A}$$

$$\text{CARRY}(x, y, t) \rightarrow \neg\, \text{CARRY}(x, y, t) \tag{3A}$$

$$\text{CARRY}(x, y, t) \rightarrow \neg\, \text{CARRY}(x, x, t) \tag{4A}$$

When one action carries another at time t, and t' is a part of t and both the carrying and carried perdurants are nonatomic events (i.e., *Physical Achievements* or *Social Achievements*), then part of the carrying event carries part of the carried event during that part of the time interval (5A).

$$\text{CARRY}(x, y, t) \wedge \exists t'(P(t', t) \wedge (PACC(x) \vee$$
$$SACC(x)) \wedge (PACC(y) \vee SACC(y)) \rightarrow \exists x'(P(x', x)) \wedge \exists y'(P(y', y)) \wedge \text{CARRY}(x', y', t') \tag{5A}$$

Because CARRY is transitive, there are two different ways that a social action can be carried: directly (DCARRY) or indirectly (ICARRY). An action is directly carried when there is no intermediate action between the starting action and the carried action. The definition of DCARRY is as follows:

$$DCARRY(x, y, t) := CARRY(x, y, t) \wedge \neg \exists z(CARRY(x, z, t) \wedge CARRY(z, y, t)) \quad (2D)$$

Similarly, the definition of ICARRY is as follows:

$$ICARRY(x, y, t) := CARRY(x, y, t) \wedge \exists z(CARRY(x, z, t) \wedge CARRY(z, y, t)) \quad (3D)$$

If an action is directly carried, it is not indirectly carried, and vice versa (6A)

$$ICARRY(x, y, t) \leftrightarrow \neg DCARRY(x, y, t) \quad (6A)$$

From 1D and 2D, it can be determined that if an action is carried, then it is either directly or indirectly carried (T1).

$$CARRY(x, y, t) \rightarrow (DCARRY(x, y, t) \vee ICARRY(x, y, t)) \quad (1T)$$

If x carries y at t, and y' is part of y at t, then there exists an x' such that x' is part of x at t and x' carries y' at t (7A). By using the parthood relation, rather than the stronger proper parthood relation, the possibility that y' may equal y and x' may equal x is preserved. Thus, this axiom holds even in the case of atomic achievements, since atomicity is defined through proper parthood and not simple parthood (see Ao5 in D18).

$$CARRY(x, y, t) \wedge P(y', y, t) \rightarrow \exists x'(P(x', x, t) \wedge CARRY(x', y', t)) \quad (7A)$$

However, 7A could be strengthened by the use of proper parthood instead of mere parthood (8A). For instance, in the case where a woman takes the physical action of waving her hand, which carries the social action of saying hello, the first part of her saying hello is carried by the first part of the wave of the hand. The inclusion of this axiom

makes it impossible for a y that has proper parts to be carried by an x that has no proper parts.

$$CARRY(x, y, t) \wedge PP(y', y, t) \rightarrow \exists x'(PP(x', x, t) \wedge CARRY(x', y', t)) \quad (8A)$$

If x carries y at time t, then x is present at t and y is present at t (9A)

$$CARRY(x, y, t) \rightarrow (PRE(x, t) \wedge PRE(y, t)) \quad (9A)$$

CARRY is not parthood. If x carries y at time t, then x is not a part of y at time t (10A). This means the physical action of the emperor pointing his thumb downward is not part of the condemnation of the gladiator.

$$CARRY(x, y, t) \rightarrow \neg P(x, y) \quad (10A)$$

Following 1A and DOLCE's axiom Ad33 in D18, CARRY is not participation (2T). CARRY is a relation between perdurants (1A), whereas participation is a relation between an endurant and a perdurant (DOLCE axiom Ad33).

$$CARRY(x, y, t) \rightarrow \neg PC(x, y, t) \quad (2T)$$

Specific Constant Dependence (SD) is a relation that can hold between particulars or properties. "A particular x is specifically constantly dependent on another particular y iff, at any time t, x can't be present at t unless y is also present at t" (Masolo et al., 2003, p. 21). Furthermore, "This notion is naturally extended to properties by defining that a property ϕ is specifically constantly dependent on a property ψ iff every ϕer is specifically constantly dependent on a ψer" (p. 21). If x carries y at time t, then y is *one-sidedly specifically constantly dependent* (OSD) on x (11A). In the action of waving hello, communicating hello is the social action and it is dependent upon the waving of the hand.

$$CARRY(x, y, t) \rightarrow OSD(y, x) \quad (11A)$$

See DOLCE definition Dd69 for the definition of *specific constant dependence* and Dd74 for the definition of *one-sided specific constant dependence*.

DOLCE includes the constitution relation K(*x*, *y*, *t*), and it can hold between perdurants (DOLCE axiom Ad20), if and only if both its *x* and *y* terms are perdurants (DOLCE axiom Ad23). If perdurant *x* is carried by perdurant *y*, is *y* constituted by *x*? D18 does not use perdurants to illustrate the constitution relation, but rather endurants (the lump of clay LUMPL, and the statue GOLIATH). While recognizing that additional study on perdurant constitution may be required in the future, for now, if *x* carries *y*, then *x* is considered to constitute *y* (12A)

$$\text{CARRY}(x, y, t) \rightarrow \text{K}(x, y, t) \qquad (12A)$$

Formalization of Performance

The predicate PER(x, y, t) standing for "*the endurant x performs the perdurant y at time t*" is now introduced. If an entity performs a perdurant, then it participates in it (13A) and the perdurant is dependent upon the performing entity.

$$\text{PER}(x, y, t) \rightarrow \text{PC}(x, y, t) \wedge \text{OSD}(y, x) \wedge T(t) \ (13A)$$

Of course, the reverse is not true. An entity can participate in an event without performing it. In order to perform an action, the entity in question must be agentive (either a member of the class *Agentive Social Object* or *Agentive Physical Object*), and the action it is performing must be a perdurant, specifically, either a *Physical Event* or a *Non-Physical Event* (14A).

$$\text{PER}(x, y, t) \rightarrow (APO(x) \vee ASO(x)) \wedge (PEV(y) \vee NPEV(y)) \wedge T(t) \qquad (14A)$$

DPER(*x*, *y*, *t*) will stand for "*the endurant x directly performs the perdurant y at time t*." IPER(*x*, *y*, *t*) will stand for "*the endurant x indi-*

rectly performs the perdurant y at time t." If an agent directly or indirectly performs an action, it has performed that action (15A and 16A). Direct and indirect performance are different relations (17A), and all performances are either direct or indirect (18A).

$$\text{DPER}(x, y, t) \rightarrow \text{PER}(x, y, t) \qquad (15A)$$

$$\text{IPER}(x, y, t) \rightarrow \text{PER}(x, y, t) \qquad (16A)$$

$$\text{DPER}(x, y, t) \rightarrow \neg \text{IPER}(x, y, t) \qquad (17A)$$

$$\text{PER}(x, y, t) \rightarrow \text{DPER}(x, y, t) \vee \text{IPER}(x, y, t) \qquad (18A)$$

Agentive Social Objects can only perform actions indirectly (19A)

$$\text{PER}(x, y, t) \wedge ASO(x) \rightarrow \text{IPER}(x, y, t) \qquad (19A)$$

It can also be noted that entities can indirectly participate in activities that they do not perform. For example, the state of Latvia might send a representative to a state funeral being held by the state of Estonia. The Latvian representative and thus the state of Latvia participate in the funeral (as observers), but do not perform it. DPC(*x*, *y*, *t*) will stand for "*endurant x directly participates in a perdurant y at time t*." IPC(*x*, *y*, *t*) will stand for "*endurant x indirectly participates in a perdurant y at time t*."

Both are kinds of participation (20A and 21A), but direct and indirect participation are different relations (22A).

$$\text{DPC}(x, y, t) \rightarrow \text{PC}(x, y, t) \qquad (20A)$$

$$\text{IPC}(x, y, t) \rightarrow \text{PC}(x, y, t) \qquad (21A)$$

$$\text{DPC}(x, y, t) \rightarrow \neg \text{IPC}(x, y, t) \qquad (22A)$$

If perdurant x carries action y and an agent performs the action x, then the agent has performed the action y (23A).

$$\text{CARRY}(x, y, t) \wedge \text{PER}(z, x, t) \rightarrow \text{PER}(z, y, t)\, (23A)$$

Formalization of Representation

The predicate REP(x, y, p, t) standing for "the endurant x represents the endurant y for purpose p at time t" is now introduced. Both the representative and the represented must be agents (24A).

$$\text{REP}(x, y, p, t) \rightarrow (ASO(x) \vee APO(x)) \wedge (ASO(y) \vee APO(y)) \wedge NASO(p) \wedge T(t) \qquad (24A)$$

If x represents y (either directly or indirectly) and x performs a physical action on behalf of y that carries a particular social action, then y has performed that social action (25A and 26A).

$$\text{REP}(x, y, p, t) \wedge \text{PER}(x, z, t) \wedge \text{CARRY}(z, w, t) \rightarrow \text{PER}(y, w, t) \qquad (25A)$$

$$\text{REP}(x, y, p, t) \wedge \text{REP}(z, x, t) \wedge \text{PER}(z, w, t) \wedge \text{CARRY}(w, a, t) \rightarrow \text{PER}(y, a, t) \qquad (26A)$$

THE THEORY IN USE

The information on the semantic web will be designed for computers to manipulate meaningfully (Berners-Lee, Hendler, & Lassila 2001). Through the theory articulated above, a system could derive knowledge of social entities and social actions that is not explicitly found on the web. It also could understand the potential consistency between statements that might appear contradictory in an initial evaluation. For instance, if it were known that a certain Navy SEAL killed Osama bin Laden, the physical killing carried the social action of bringing bin Laden to justice,[12] and that this SEAL represented the United States for the purpose of that operation, then the United States must have brought Osama bin Laden to justice.

The system could reason in reverse. If it were known that the United States brought bin Laden to justice, then the system would know that the United States, being a nonphysical geopolitical entity, must have been represented by some physical entity which performed a physical action that carried the social action of bringing bin Laden to justice, given the context in which it occurred. Thus, the statement that United States brought bin Laden to justice would not be incompatible with the statement that a certain Navy SEAL brought bin Laden to justice. Likewise, the statement that the United States killed bin Laden need not be regarded as in contradiction with the statement that a certain Navy SEAL killed bin Laden. Instead, these statements could be understood to be consistent and the system could better understand the social situation, thereby allowing information about social entities and social actions to be more meaningfully manipulated.

CONCLUSION

The purpose of this article has been to solve some of the problems of social agentivity within DOLCE, a descriptive ontology where natural language and "commonsense" are intended to have ontological relevance. It has proposed a system by which both physical and social objects are agentive, but which also recognizes the different ways in which they act. It has elucidated a theory by which physical objects can take social action, and then by which social objects can take action as well. A system based on this theory could simultaneously and in a noncontradictory manner handle statements and queries where both nonphysical social agents and physical agents take action. In order to encode this information into DOLCE, a revision of its taxonomic structure regarding perdurants was proposed, in which a division between physical and social is recognized.

Through this system, some nonphysical social entities can be regarded as agentive, as they are in natural language, while the "behind-the-scenes" activities that must take place in order for a social entity to take an action are still recognized. It also allows the actions of social entities to be coded into the ontology without explicit knowledge of what process was undertaken by physical agents in order to bring about the social act, while still recognizing that there must have been one. For example, one can know that Germany or France declared war at a certain time and encode that information into the ontology without having to know anything about the physical actions that were required in either country for that declaration to have been made. Nevertheless, the ontology still recognizes that some physical actions must have taken place. Likewise, one could encode specific physical actions that physical agents undertook, even though it might not be known at the time what social acts those physical acts might have carried.

This also allows the ontology to handle multiple levels of granularity in a single system. For those individuals who are interested in the social actions undertaken by legal persons, organizations, or social groups, the ontology can encode that information. Those interested in particular physical or social actions underlying higher-level social action will find that information encoded as well.

ACKNOWLEDGMENT

This article is based upon work supported by the National Science Foundation's Integrative Geographic Information Science Traineeship Program (Grant No. DGE 0333417) awarded to the University at Buffalo. Thanks go to Thomas Bittner, David Mark, Jessie Poon, and Barry Smith, who provided helpful commentary on earlier versions of this manuscript. Special thanks also go the anonymous reviewers, whose thoughtful commentary helped to improve the article.

REFERENCES

Berners-Lee, T., Hendler, J., & Lassila, O. (2001). The Semantic Web. *Scientific American, 284*, 34–43. doi:10.1038/scientificamerican0501-34 PMID:11396337.

Bickhard, M. H. (2008). The social ontology of persons. In Carpendale, J., & Müller, U. (Eds.), *Social interaction and the development of knowledge* (pp. 111–132). Mahwah, NJ: Lawrence Erlbaum.

Boella, G., & van der Torre, L. (2004). An agent oriented ontology of social reality. In *Proceedings of the International Conference on Formal Ontology in Information Systems*, Torino, Italy.

Bottazzi, E., Catenacci, C., Gangemi, A., & Lehmann, J. (2006). From collective intentionality to intentional collectives: An ontological perspective. *Cognitive Systems Research, 7*, 192–208. doi:10.1016/j.cogsys.2005.11.009.

Bottazzi, E., & Ferrario, R. (2009). Preliminaries to a DOLCE ontology of organisations. *International Journal of Business Process Integration and Management, 4*(4), 225–238. doi:10.1504/IJBPIM.2009.032280.

Fitzpatrick, D. (2003). Searle and collective intentionality: The self-defeating nature of internalism with respect to social facts. *American Journal of Economics and Sociology, 62*(1), 45–66. doi:10.1111/1536-7150.t01-1-00002.

Frawley, W. (1992). *Linguistic semantics*. Mahwah, NJ: Lawrence Erlbaum.

Hornsby, J. (1997). Collectives and Intentionality. *Philosophy and Phenomenological Research, 57*(2), 429–434. doi:10.2307/2953732.

Johansson, I. (2004). *Ontological investigations: An inquiry into the categories of nature, man and society* (2nd ed.). Frankfurt, Germany: Verlag.

Kemke, C. (2001). *About the ontology of actions* (Tech. Rep. No. MCC-01-328). University Park, NM: Computing Research Laboratory, New Mexico State University.

Lee, A. S. (2004). Thinking about social theory and philosophy for information systems. In Mingers, J., & Willcocks, L. (Eds.), *Social theory and philosophy for information systems*. Chichester, UK: John Wiley & Sons.

Masolo, C., Borgo, S., Gangemi, A., Guarino, N., & Oltramari, A. (2003). *WonderWeb Deliverable D18: Ontology Library*. Trento, Italy: Laboratory for Applied Ontology – ISTC-CNR.

Masolo, C., Guizzardi, G., Vieu, L., Bottazzi, E., & Ferrario, R. (2005). *Relational roles and qua-individuals*. Paper presented at the AAAI Fall Symposium on Roles, an Interdisciplinary Perspective.

Masolo, C., Vieu, L., Bottazzi, E., Catenacci, C., Ferrario, F., Gangemi, A., et al. (2004, June 2-5). *Social roles and their descriptions*. Paper presented at the Ninth International Conference on the Principles of Knowledge Representation and Reasoning, Whistler, BC, Canada.

Popper, K. (1945). *The open society and its enemies*. London, UK: Routledge.

Robinson, E. H. (2010). An ontological analysis of states: Organizations vs. legal persons. *Applied Ontology*, *5*(2), 109–125.

Rowe, W. (1999). Agent causation. In Audi, R. (Ed.), *The Cambridge dictionary of philosophy* (2nd ed., pp. 14–15). Cambridge, UK: Cambridge University Press.

Ryan, M. (2005). Social action. In Ritzer, G. (Ed.), *Encyclopedia of social theory* (*Vol. 2*, pp. 714–715). Thousand Oaks, CA: Sage.

Schalley, A. C. (2004). Representing verbal semantics with diagrams an adaptation of the UML for lexical semantics. In *Proceedings of the 20th International Conference on Computational Linguistics*, Geneva, Switzerland.

Searle, J. R. (1983). *Intentionality: An essay in the philosophy of mind*. Cambridge, UK: Cambridge University Press.

Searle, J. R. (1995). *The construction of social reality*. New York, NY: Free Press.

Searle, J. R. (2008). Social ontology and political power. In Smith, B., Mark, D. M., & Ehrlich, I. (Eds.), *The mystery of capital and the construction of social reality* (pp. 19–34). Chicago, IL: Open Court.

Searle, J. R. (2010). *Making the social world: The structure of human civilization*. New York, NY: Oxford University Press.

Smith, B. (2003). Ontology. In Floridi, L. (Ed.), *The Blackwell guide to the philosophy of computing and information* (pp. 155–166). Malden, MA: Blackwell.

Smith, B. (2008). Searle and de Soto: The new ontology of the social world. In Smith, B., Mark, D. M., & Ehrlich, I. (Eds.), *The mystery of capital and the construction of social reality* (pp. 35–51). Chicago, IL: Open Court.

Smith, B., & Grenon, P. (2004). The cornucopia of formal ontological relations. *Dialectica*, *58*(3), 279–296. doi:10.1111/j.1746-8361.2004.tb00305.x.

Smith, B., & Searle, J. (2003). The construction of social reality: An exchange. *American Journal of Economics and Sociology*, *62*(1), 285–309. doi:10.1111/1536-7150.t01-1-00012.

Stoutland, F. (2008). The ontology of social agency. *Analyse & Kritik*, *30*, 533–551.

Tomasello, M., & Rakoczy, H. (2003). What makes human cognition unique? From individual to shared to collective intentionality. *Mind & Language*, *18*(2), 121–147. doi:10.1111/1468-0017.00217.

Trypuz, R. (2008). *Formal ontology of action: A unifying approach*. Poland: Wydawnictwo KUL.

Ware, R. (1988). Group action and social ontology. *Analyse & Kritik*, *10*, 48–70.

Weber, M. (1978). *Economy and society*. Berkeley, CA: University of California Press. (Original work published 1968).

Wight, C. (2004). State agency: Social action without human activity? *Review of International Studies*, *30*, 269–280. doi:10.1017/S0260210504006060.

Wood, Z., & Galton, A. (2009). A taxonomy of collective phenomena. *Applied Ontology*, *4*, 267–292.

ENDNOTES

[1] However, it is possible that the physical blows between the two cyclists might also involve a social component. For instance, the exchange of blows might carry the social action of assault and battery according to a system of laws. The point is that the physical exchange of blows is not regarded as a social action in this article merely because more than one human being is involved.

[2] This distinction can result in a different classification for nonvolitional "agents" (such as the brick breaking the window). Instigation of an action can either be volitional or nonvolitional. Volitional instigators are agents, whereas nonvolitional instigators are called effectors (Frawley, 1992; Schalley, 2004).

[3] A distinction between a physical and legal person is not always made. Sometimes the distinction is blurred, as with Bickhard (2008), who writes that "Persons are biological beings who participate in social environments" (p. 111).

[4] DOLCE's appeal to commonsense for the structure of its ontology is not new, especially in social ontology. For instance, Ware (1988) made an appeal to commonsense in his investigation of social ontology. He wrote, "Ordinary perceptions and a lot of commonsense can also tell us much about what there is" (p. 49). He wrote that these two sources argue strongly in favor of groups and other social entities.

[5] Intentionality from the perspective of individuals and groups is an important part of social reality, but the move from a single person's intentions to a group's intentions is not particularly straightforward. In this article, intentionality is not discussed in detail, but for deeper expositions on intentionality as it relates to the construction of social reality, see Searle (1983, 1995, 2010), Hornsby (1997), Tomasello and Rakoczy (2003), Fitzpatrick (2003), Johansson (2004), and Bottazzi, Catenacci, Gangemi, and Lehmann (2006).

[6] An element of this theory, which will not be explored here, but may be the focus of additional research, is the power dynamic involved in deciding which context takes precedence. In the case of the secret handshake, the context of the private club is overruled by the context imposed by the government. The ability of an entity to decide in what context a physical event took place, or impose a context, may be a key element of power in some situations.

[7] The question remains open as to whether the insurgents in this situation are actually representatives of the organization for the

purposes of violence, or if they are merely affiliated with the organization. Affiliation is a very broad relation between an agent or a social individual and another social individual. "If an agent or a social individual is affiliated to another social individual at a certain time then at that time (s)he plays a role that is institutionalised for the social individual" (Bottazzi & Ferrario, 2009, p. 232). Thus, representatives of an organization are affiliated with the organization, but all affiliates of the organization may not be able to represent it.

[8] While it would be desirable to refer back to DOLCE's documentation regarding the distinguishing *Agentive Social Object* from *Non-Agentive Social Object*, D18 provides no axioms to make such a determination. There, and in other literature, the distinction between these two categories seems to be made largely through example, leaving it up the intuition of the user of the ontology to sort other entities into the categories. A law, an economic system, a currency, and an asset are *Non-Agentive Social Objects*, whereas Fiat, Apple, the Bank of Italy, a (legal) person, and a contractant are *Agentive Social Objects*. Ultimately, a far more concrete methodology for distinguishing these two categories will be required.

[9] It can also be questioned whether or not having direct spatial qualities or not is the best way to divide endurants into the physical and nonphysical. Perhaps it would be more intuitive for a descriptive ontology to use whether or not the entity is "made of" matter as the distinction between the physical and the nonphysical. Discussion of this subject is left to further research.

[10] Social individuals were informally introduced in Masolo et al. (2004) and used formally in Bottazzi and Ferrario's (2009) preliminary ontology of organizations.

[11] The related term "undergoer" refers to the participant that is most affected by an action (van Valin & LaPolla, 1997).

[12] The proposition that the killing of bin Laden carried the social action of bringing him to justice may or may not be true. The purpose of this article is not to argue conclusively either way, but rather to use it as an example whereby a physical action may carry a social action. This article does provide a framework through which the truth-value of the proposition can be evaluated, namely through the evaluation of 1D. The killing of Osama bin Laden carried the social action of bringing him to justice if and only if there is a description of a context in which a killing results in the social action of bring Osama bin Laden (or someone in general) to justice and that context was present when the killing occurred. The context under which the CARRY relationship holds between those two actions is certainly complex. It must consider international law, the motivation of the killing, the guilt of the individual regarding the action for which he must be brought to justice, the authority under which the agent doing the killing acted, and so on.

This work was previously published in the International Journal on Semantic Web and Information Systems, Volume 7, Issue 4, edited by Amit P. Sheth,, pp. 62-86, copyright 2011 by IGI Publishing (an imprint of IGI Global).

Chapter 3
AL–QuIn:
An Onto–Relational Learning System for Semantic Web Mining

Francesca A. Lisi
Università degli Studi di Bari "Aldo Moro", Italy

ABSTRACT

Onto-Relational Learning is an extension of Relational Learning aimed at accounting for ontologies in a clear, well-founded and elegant manner. The system $\mathcal{AL}$ - $Q\text{u}\textsc{In}$ supports a variant of the frequent pattern discovery task by following the Onto-Relational Learning approach. It takes taxonomic ontologies into account during the discovery process and produces descriptions of a given relational database at multiple granularity levels. The functionalities of the system are illustrated by means of examples taken from a Semantic Web Mining case study concerning the analysis of relational data extracted from the on-line CIA World Fact Book.

INTRODUCTION

Semantic Web Mining is an application area which aims at combining the two areas of Semantic Web and Web Mining from a twofold perspective (Stumme, Hotho, & Berendt, 2006). On one hand, the new semantic structures in the Web can be exploited to improve the results of Web Mining. On the other hand, the results of Web Mining can be used for building the Semantic Web. Most work in Semantic Web Mining simply extends previous work to the new application context, e.g., Maedche and Staab (2000) apply a well-known algorithm for association rule mining to discover conceptual relations from text. Indeed, we argue that Semantic Web Mining can be considered as

DOI: 10.4018/978-1-4666-3610-1.ch003

Data Mining (DM) for/from the Semantic Web. Current DM systems could serve the purpose of Semantic Web Mining if they were more compliant with, e.g., the standards of representation for ontologies in the Semantic Web and/or interoperable with well-established tools for Ontological Engineering (Gómez-Pérez, Fernández-López, & Corcho, 2004), e.g., Protégé (Knublauch, Fergerson, Noy, & Musen, 2004), that support these standards. In particular, those Knowledge Representation (KR) formalisms known as *Description Logics* (DLs) which collectively form a family of decidable fragments of First Order Logic (FOL) (Baader, Calvanese, McGuinness, Nardi, & Patel-Schneider, 2007) have been the starting point for the W3C recommended Ontology Web Language (OWL) (Horrocks, Patel-Schneider, & van Harmelen, 2003).

Algorithms for *Relational Learning* try to avoid the limitation of classical Machine Learning (ML) in describing the relationships between more than one object by using a richer representation language, such as (fragments of) FOL (De Raedt, 2008). This logic-based approach to Relational Learning is also known under the name of Inductive Logic Programming (ILP) (Nienhuys-Cheng & de Wolf, 1997). ILP has been historically concerned with concept learning from examples and background knowledge within the representation framework of Horn Clausal Logic (HCL) (underlying the Logic Programming paradigm) and with the aim of prediction, e.g., the system FOIL learns classification rules from examples expressed in the form of relations (Quinlan, 1990). More recently the ILP community has developed an interest in applications for relational databases, thus giving rise to the field of Relational Data Mining (Džeroski & Lavrač, 2001). Systems like WARMR (Dehaspe & Toivonen, 1999) adopt DATALOG (Ceri, Gottlob, & Tanca, 1990) (a logical language for relational databases which corresponds to a function-free fragment of HCL) as representation language and support tasks of description rather

than prediction in challenging applications, such as trying to understand the structure of proteins and designing pharmaceuticals. Though ILP is widely recognized as a major approach to Relational Learning, ILP as such cannot face the challenges of the Semantic Web, notably the availability of ontologies to deal with. This inadequacy of Relational Learning is due to the following KR issue: DLs are incomparable with HCL as regards the expressive power (Borgida, 1996) and the semantics (Rosati, 2005). Yet, since DLs and HCL can be combined according to some limited forms of hybridization (Rosati, 2005), the adoption of hybrid KR systems such as $\mathcal{AL}$-log (Donini, Lenzerini, Nardi, & Schaerf, 1998) can help overcome the current difficulties in accommodating ontologies in ILP (Lisi & Esposito, 2009). We claim that this paves the way to an extension of Relational Learning, called Onto-Relational Learning, to account for ontologies in a clear, well-founded and elegant manner.

In this paper we present an Onto-Relational Learning system, named $\mathcal{AL}$-QuIn[1], that adopts ILP as a methodological apparatus and $\mathcal{AL}$-log as a KR formalism. The system solves a variant of the popular DM problem of frequent pattern discovery which takes *taxonomic*[2] ontologies into account during the discovery process and produces descriptions of a given relational database at multiple granularity levels. The functionalities of the system are illustrated by means of examples taken from a Semantic Web Mining case study concerning the analysis of relational data extracted from the on-line CIA World Fact Book.

The paper is structured as follows. First we shall provide a motivation for Onto-Relational Learning by showing the limits of systems like WARMR in dealing with prior knowledge in the form of taxonomic ontologies, and the necessary background information to readers not acquainted with reasoning and learning in $\mathcal{AL}$-log. Then we shall present the techniques and the algorithms employed in $\mathcal{AL}$-QuIn and describe how $\mathcal{AL}$-

QuIn has been used as an inferential engine in a Semantic Web Mining platform. Finally, we shall discuss related work and draw conclusions.

Motivation

As a motivating case study for Onto-Relational Learning we choose the DM task of Frequent Pattern Discovery because it has been investigated also in Relational Data Mining. Furthermore it is the most representative product of the cross-fertilization among Databases, Machine Learning and Statistics that has given rise to DM. Indeed it is central to an entire class of DM descriptive tasks among which Association Rule Mining (Agrawal, Imielinski, & Swami, 1993) is the most popular.

In DM a *pattern* is considered as an intensional description (expressed in a given language $\mathcal{L}$) of a subset of a data set **r**. The *support* of a pattern is the relative frequency of the pattern within **r** and is computed with the evaluation function *supp*. The task of *frequent pattern discovery* aims at the extraction of all *frequent* patterns, i.e., all patterns whose support exceeds a user-defined threshold of *minimum support*. The blueprint of most algorithms for frequent pattern discovery, notably APRIORI (Agrawal & Srikant, 1994) and it variants, is the *levelwise search* method (Mannila & Toivonen, 1997). It is based on the following assumption: If a generality order $\succeq$ for the language $\mathcal{L}$ of patterns can be found such that $\succeq$ is monotonic w.r.t. *supp*, then the resulting space $(\mathcal{L}, \succeq)$ can be searched breadth-first starting from the most general pattern in $\mathcal{L}$ and by alternating *candidate generation* and *candidate evaluation* phases. In particular, candidate generation consists of a refinement step followed by a pruning step. The former derives candidates for the current search level from patterns found frequent in the previous search level. The latter allows some infrequent patterns to be detected and discarded prior to evaluation thanks to the monotonicity of $\succeq$. Though both are based on the levelwise method, WARMR and APRIORI differ in many aspects as shown in Table 1.

Briefly, WARMR adopts the ILP approach to Relational Data Mining, i.e., it follows the practice of upgrading DM algorithms to the KR framework of HCL. Conversely, systems like FARMER (Nijssen & Kok, 2001, 2003) represent patterns and rules as tree data structures to improve the performance of the resulting Relational Data Mining algorithms.

Taxonomic relations are commonly used in domain knowledge ranging from the simpler concept hierarchies to the more expressive ontologies. Variants of APRIORI have been proposed which take taxonomic prior knowledge into account during the discovery process, e.g., concept hierarchies are exploited to mine multiple-level association rules (Han & Fu, 1995, 1999) or generalized association rules (Srikant & Agrawal, 1995). Both extend the levelwise search method so that patterns can refer to multiple levels of description granularity. They differ in the strategy used in visiting the concept hierarchy: the former visits the hierarchy top-down, the latter bottom-up. Conversely, neither WARMR nor FARMER can exploit the semantic information conveyed by concept hierarchies because both adopt a syntactic generality relation for patterns and rules. Condensed representations are proposed in order to discard semantic redundancies of the computation w.r.t. the domain knowledge in the ILP system C-ARMR (De Raedt & Ramon, 2004). Yet, C-ARMR cannot be considered a system for

Table 1. Warmr versus Apriori

	Warmr	**Apriori**
Search space	DATALOG query lattice	itemset lattice
Generality relation	θ-subsumption relation	subset relation
Loading unit from database	sub-database	tuple
Candidate evaluation technique	coverage test	subset check

multiple-level association rule mining. Indeed, it could in principle discover patterns at multiple levels of description granularity but it was not conceived to explore systematically the taxonomic relations according to the original Han and Fu's problem formulation. A first attempt aimed at incorporating taxonomies in Relational Data Mining has been the ILP system SPADA (Lisi & Malerba, 2004) which can be considered as an upgrade of Han & Fu's work on multiple-level association rule mining to a multi-relational representation though specifically designed for geographic knowledge discovery in spatial databases. The system $\mathcal{AL}$ - QuIn being presented in this paper is an evolution of SPADA. It keeps the same problem statement and the search strategy of SPADA but implements several optimizations and includes novel features.

Background

In this section we shall provide the necessary background information to readers not acquainted with reasoning and learning in $\mathcal{AL}$ -log.

$\mathcal{AL}$ - log from the KR Viewpoint

The system $\mathcal{AL}$ - log is a KR framework for the integration of the DL $\mathcal{ALC}$ and DATALOG (Donini et al., 1998). Indeed, in $\mathcal{AL}$ - log one can define DATALOG clauses enriched with *constraints* of the form *s:C* where *s* is either a constant or a variable, and *C* is an $\mathcal{ALC}$ concept. Note that the usage of concepts as typing constraints applies only to variables and constants that already appear in the clause. The symbol & separates constraints from DATALOG atoms in a clause. A *constrained DATALOG clause* is an implication of the form

$$\alpha_0 \leftarrow \alpha_1, \ldots, \alpha_m \ \& \ \gamma_1, \ldots, \gamma_n$$

$$\alpha_i \quad \gamma_j \quad \Pi$$

An $\mathcal{AL}$ *-log knowledge base* $\mathcal{B}$ is the pair $\langle \Sigma, \Pi \rangle$ where Σ is an $\mathcal{ALC}$ knowledge base and Π is a constrained DATALOG program. For a knowledge base to be acceptable, it must satisfy the following conditions:

- The set of DATALOG predicate symbols appearing in Π is disjoint from the set of concept and role symbols appearing in Σ.
- The alphabet of constants in Π coincides with the alphabet $\mathcal{O}$ of the individuals in Σ.
- Every constant occurring in Π appears also in Σ.
- For every clause in Π, every variable occurring in the constraint part occurs also in the DATALOG part.

These properties allow for the extension of terminology and results related to the notion of *substitution* from DATALOG to $\mathcal{AL}$ - log in a straightforward manner. In particular, the last condition makes $\mathcal{AL}$ - log a *safe* integration scheme between DLs and DATALOG (Rosati, 2005). Indeed it allows solving the semantic mismatch between the Open World Assumption (OWA) holding in DLs (and ontologies) and the Closed World Assumption (CWA) holding in DATALOG (and databases) because it forbids the reference to unknown individuals. Due to the safety condition, a model-theoretic semantics can be defined for $\mathcal{AL}$ - log.

The main reasoning service for $\mathcal{AL}$ - log knowledge bases is *hybrid deduction* which is based on *constrained SLD-resolution*, i.e., SLD-resolution extended with a tableau calculus to deal with constraints. Constrained SLD-resolution is *decidable* and runs in single non-deterministic exponential time. Also it is a complete and sound method for answering *ground* queries by refutation: Given a ground query Q to an $\mathcal{AL}$ - log knowledge base $\mathcal{B}$, it holds that $\mathcal{B} \vdash Q$ if and only if $\mathcal{B} \vDash Q$ (Donini et al., 1998). Given *any* query Q, the success set of Q in $\mathcal{B}$ coincides with the answer set of Q in $\mathcal{B}$. This provides an operational means for computing correct answers to queries.

Example 1

As an illustrative case, we consider an $\mathcal{AL}$ -log *knowledge base* $\mathcal{B}_{CIA}$ *that integrates an* $\mathcal{ALC}$ *ontology* Σ_{CIA} *and a* DATALOG *database* Π_{CIA}. *The ontology* Σ_{CIA} *encompasses axioms such as*

```
AsianCountry⊑Country.
MiddleEasternEthnicGroup⊑EthnicGro
up.
MiddleEastCountry≡AsianCountry⊓∃Hos
ts.MiddleEasternEthnicGroup.
IndoEuropeanLanguage⊑Language.
IndoIranianLanguage⊑IndoEuropeanLang
uage.
MonotheisticReligion⊑Religion.
PolytheisticReligion⊑Religion.
ChristianReligion⊑MonotheisticReligi
on.
MuslimReligion⊑MonotheisticReligion.
```

that define four taxonomies rooted in the concepts Country, EthnicGroup, Language, and Religion, and involving 24 concepts in total. Note that Middle East countries (concept MiddleEastCountry) have been defined as Asian countries that host at least one Middle Eastern ethnic group. Assertions like

```
'ARM':AsianCountry.
'IR':AsianCountry.
'Arab':MiddleEasternEthnicGroup.
'Armenian':MiddleEasternEthnicGroup.
<'ARM','Armenian'>:Hosts.
<'IR','Arab'>:Hosts.
'Armenian':IndoEuropeanLanguage.
'Persian':IndoIranianLanguage.
'Armenian
```

```
Orthodox':ChristianReligion.
'Shia':MuslimReligion.
'Sunni':MuslimReligion.
```

belong to the extensional part of Σ_{CIA}. In particular, Armenia ('ARM') and Iran ('IR') are two of the 15 Asian countries that are classified as Middle Eastern.

The database Π_{CIA} consists of 1,434 facts extracted from the on-line 1996 CIA World Fact Book (http://www.odci.gov/cia/publications/factbook) *such as*

```
language('ARM','Armenian',96).
language('IR','Persian',58).
religion('ARM','Armenian Ortho-
dox',94).
religion('IR','Shia',89).
religion('IR','Sunni',10).
```

where numbers are treated like individuals.[3] Also Π_{CIA} contains rules (Listing 1).

that define views (or derived relations) on the relations language and religion. Note that the constraint ReligionName:MonotheisticReligion in the body of the rule defining believesOneGod(CountryID, ReligionName) reduces the number of admissible values for the variable ReligionName.

Suppose now that we want to compute the correct answers to the query

$Q = \leftarrow$ believes('ARM',Y)

w.r.t. $\mathcal{B}_{CIA}$. It can be proved by constrained SLD-refutation that $answerset(Q, \mathcal{B}_{CIA})$ =({Y/'ArmenianOrthodox'}). Indeed the fact believes('ARM','Armenian Orthodox') is logically entailed by and can be derived from $\mathcal{B}_{CIA}$.

Being considered as the progenitor of the family of hybrid KR systems with safe integration schemes, $\mathcal{AL}$ -log is a framework which can be

Listing 1.

```
speaks(CountryID, LanguageName) ←
     language(CountryID,LanguageName,Percent) &
     CountryID:Country, LanguageName:Language
believes(CountryID, ReligionName) ←
     religion(CountryID,ReligionName,Percent) &
     CountryID:Country, ReligionName:Religion
believesOneGod(CountryID, ReligionName) ←
     religion(CountryID,ReligionName,Percent) &
     CountryID:Country, ReligionName:MonotheisticReligion
```

instantiated and implemented. OWL-log is an implementation of $\mathcal{AL}$-log where the DL component is extended to OWL DL (Ruckhaus, Kolovski, Parsia, & Cuenca Grau, 2006). One such approach to $\mathcal{AL}$-log is of high interest to us because it enables the possibility of incorporating more expressiveness into the DL part, e.g., datatypes that are necessary to deal properly with numbers.

$\mathcal{AL}$-**log from the ML Viewpoint**

While defining a framework for learning in $\mathcal{AL}$-log (Lisi, 2008) we follow the 'generalization as search' approach proposed in the seminal work of Mitchell on concept learning (Mitchell, 1982) and adopted in the ILP methodological approach. In this approach the mechanism of *generalization*, which is central to many concept learning problems, was formalized as a search process through a partially ordered space of hypotheses.

A relevant yet underestimated aspect in this formalization is that the space of hypotheses is strongly biased by the hypothesis representation. Indeed, by selecting a hypothesis representation, the designer of the learning algorithm implicitly defines the space of all hypotheses that the program can ever represent and therefore can ever learn. In our framework for learning in $\mathcal{AL}$-log we represent hypotheses as constrained DATALOG

clauses that fulfill the restrictions of linkedness, connectedness, and Object Identity (OI) conformancy. A clause H is *linked* if each literal $l_i \in H$ is linked. A literal l_i is linked if at least one of its terms is linked. A term t in some literal $l_i \in H$ is linked with linking-chain of length 0, if t occurs in *head(H)*, and with linking-chain of length $d+1$, if some other term in l_i is linked with linking-chain of length d. The link-depth of a term t in l_i is the length of the shortest linking-chain of t. A clause H is *connected* if each variable occurring in *head(H)* also occur in *body(H)*. The OI bias yields to a restricted form of substitution whose bindings avoid the identification of terms: A substitution σ is an *OI-substitution* w.r.t. a set of terms T iff $\forall t_1, t_2 \in T: t_1 \neq t_2$ yields that $t_1\sigma \neq t_2\sigma$ (Semeraro, Esposito, Malerba, Fanizzi, & Ferilli, 1998). Also, the OI can be considered as an extension of the Unique Names Assumption (UNA) holding for DLs from the semantic level to the sintactic one of $\mathcal{AL}$-log. The relation of $\mathcal{B}$-subsumption, inspired by generalized subsumption (Buntine, 1988), is proposed as the starting point for a generality order, denoted as $\succeq_B$, which allows the space of constrained DATALOG clauses to be better organized for search. Let H_1, H_2 be two constrained DATALOG clauses and $\mathcal{B}$ an $\mathcal{AL}$-log knowledge base. We say that H_1 is *at least as general as H_2 under $\mathcal{B}$-subsumption, $H_1 \succeq_B H_2$,* iff H_1 $\mathcal{B}$-subsumes H_2. Furthermore, H_1 is *more general than* H_2 under $\mathcal{B}$-subsumption, $H_1 \succ_\mathcal{B} H_2$, iff $H_1 \succeq_\mathcal{B} H_2$ and $H_2 \not\succeq_\mathcal{B} H_1$. Finally, H_1 is *equivalent* to H_2 under $\mathcal{B}$-subsumption, $H_1 \sim_\mathcal{B} H_2$, iff $H_1 \succeq_\mathcal{B} H_2$ and $H_2 \succeq_\mathcal{B} H_1$. It can be easily shown that $\succeq_\mathcal{B}$ is a quasi-order (i.e., it is a reflexive and transitive relation) for constrained DATALOG clauses. Also it can be proved that $\succeq_\mathcal{B}$ relies on constrained SLD-resolution: Given two constrained DATALOG clauses H_1, H_2 standardized apart[4], an $\mathcal{AL}$-log knowledge base $\mathcal{B}$, and a Skolem substitution[5] σ for H_2 with respect to $\{H_1\} \cup \mathcal{B}$, we say that $H_1 \succeq_\mathcal{B} H_2$ iff there exists a substitution θ for H_1 such that (i) $head(H_1)\theta = head(H_2)$ and (ii) $\mathcal{B} \cup body(H_2)\sigma \vdash body(H_1)\theta\sigma$ where $body(H_1)\theta\sigma$ is ground (Lisi & Malerba, 2003a). This provides a decidable procedure for checking $\mathcal{B}$-subsumption.

Example 2

Let us consider the following two constrained DATALOG clauses:

$H_1 = q(X) \leftarrow believes(X,Y)$ & *X:MiddleEastCountry, Y:Religion*

$H_2 = q(X) \leftarrow believes(X,Y)$ & *X:MiddleEastCountry, Y:MonotheisticReligion*

and the $\mathcal{AL}$-log knowledge base introduced in Example 1. It can be proved that $H_1 \succeq_\mathcal{B} H_2$ and $H_2 \not\succeq_\mathcal{B} H_1$, therefore $H_1 \succ_\mathcal{B} H_2$.

Note that this framework for learning in $\mathcal{AL}$-log is valid whatever the scope of induction (prediction/description) is. The system $\mathcal{AL}$-QuIn implements the framework in the case of description.

The System $\mathcal{AL}$-QuIn

The system $\mathcal{AL}$-QuIn solves a variant of the frequent pattern discovery problem which takes taxonomic ontologies into account during the discovery process, thus yielding multi-grained descriptions of a relational data set. More formally:

Definition 1

Given

- *A relational data set* Π
- *A taxonomic ontology* Σ
- *A multi-grained language* $\mathcal{L} = \{\mathcal{L}^l\}_{1 \leq l \leq maxG}$
- *A set* $\{minsup^l\}_{1 \leq l \leq maxG}$ *of support thresholds*

The problem of frequent pattern discovery in Π at l levels of description granularity w.r.t. Σ, $1 \leq l \leq maxG$, is to find the set $\mathcal{F}$ of all the patterns $P \in \mathcal{L}^l$ frequent in $\mathcal{B} = (\Pi, \Sigma)$, namely P's with support s such that (i) $s \geq minsup^l$ *and (ii) all ancestors of P w.r.t.* Σ *are frequent.*

In $\mathcal{AL}$-QuIn the data set **r** is represented as an $\mathcal{AL}$-log knowledge base $\mathcal{B} = (\Pi, \Sigma)$ because we assume that Π and Σ share the same set of constants.

The language $\mathcal{L} = \{\mathcal{L}^l\}_{1 \leq l \leq maxG}$ allows for the generation of unary conjunctive queries, called $\mathcal{O}$-queries, that relate individuals of a reference concept to individuals of the task-relevant concepts. Note that these concepts must occur in Σ and must be named. Furthermore the language $\mathcal{L}$ is *multi-grained*, i.e., it contains expressions at multiple levels of description granularity. The level of description granularity for an expression is uniquely determined by the position that all the task-relevant concepts occurring in the expression share in Σ. Therefore the generation of so-called cross-level patterns is not possible with $\mathcal{AL}$-QuIn. The language is implicitly defined by a *declarative bias specification* which consists of a finite alphabet A of DATALOG predicate names and finite alphabets Γ^l (one for each level l of description granularity) of $\mathcal{ALC}$ concept names. We impose $\mathcal{L}$ to be finite by specifying some bounds, mainly *maxD* for the maximum depth of search and *maxG* for the maximum level of granularity. More formally, given a reference concept C_{ref}, an $\mathcal{O}$-*query* Q to an $\mathcal{AL}$-log knowledge base $\mathcal{B}$ is a (linked and connected) constrained DATALOG clause of the form

$$Q = q(X) \leftarrow \alpha_1, \ldots, \alpha_m \,\&\, X : C_{ref}, \gamma_2, \ldots, \gamma_n$$

where X is the *distinguished variable* and the remaining variables occurring in the body of Q are the *existential variables*. Note that the α_i's are taken from A and γ_j's are taken from Γ^l. The $\mathcal{O}$-query

$$Q_t = q(X) \leftarrow \,\&\, X : C_{ref}$$

is called *trivial* for $\mathcal{L}$ because it only contains the constraint for the distinguished variable. Other restrictions, such as the maximum number of unconstrained variables, are imposed on the form of admissible $\mathcal{O}$-queries via declarative bias.

Example 3

Suppose that we are interested in discovering frequent patterns in $\mathcal{B}_{CIA}$ that describe Middle East countries (individuals of the reference concept) with respect to the religions believed and the languages spoken (individuals of the task-relevant concepts) at three levels of granularity (maxG=3). To this aim we define $\mathcal{L}_{CIA}$ as the set of $\mathcal{O}$-queries with C_{ref}=MiddleEastCountry that can be generated from the alphabet

A= {believes/2, speaks/2}

> *Γ^1= {Language, Religion}*
> *Γ^2 = {IndoEuropeanLanguage,…, MonotheisticReligion,…}*
> *Γ^3 = {IndoIranianLanguage,… ,MuslimReligion,…}*

of $\mathcal{ALC}$ concept names for $1 \leq l \leq 3$, up to maxD=5. Examples of $\mathcal{O}$-queries in $\mathcal{L}_{CIA}$ are the following (Listing 2)

In particular Q_0 is the trivial $\mathcal{O}$-query for $\mathcal{L}_{CIA}$, Q_1 and Q_2 are valid for any l, $Q_3 \in \mathcal{L}^1_{CIA}$, $\{Q_4, Q_5\} \in \mathcal{L}^2_{CIA}$, and $Q_6 \in \mathcal{L}^3_{CIA}$.

Minimum support thresholds are set to the following values: $minsup^1$=20%, $minsup^2$=13%, and $minsup^3$=10%. After maxD=5 search stages, $\mathcal{AL}$-QuIn returns 53 frequent patterns out of 99 candidate patterns compliant with the parameter settings.

The *support* of an $\mathcal{O}$-query $Q \in \mathcal{L}$ w.r.t. $\mathcal{B}$ is defined as

$$supp(Q, \mathcal{B}) = \frac{|\, answerset(Q, \mathcal{B}) \,|}{|\, answerset(Q_t, \mathcal{B}) \,|}$$

where $answerset(Q, \mathcal{B})$ is the set of correct answers to Q w.r.t. $\mathcal{B}$, i.e., the set of substitutions θ_i for the distinguished variable of Q such that there exists a correct answer to $body(Q)\theta$ w.r.t. $\mathcal{B}$. In other words $answerset(Q, \mathcal{B})$ lists the individuals of C_{ref} that satisfy Q. Therefore the support is the percentage of individuals of C_{ref} that satisfy Q. Condition (i) of Definition 1 relies on the notion of support. As for condition (ii), a pattern Q is considered to be an ancestor of P w.r.t. Σ if it is a coarser-grained version of P. The link between a pattern and its ancestors is determined via $\mathcal{B}$-subsumption (see next subsection).

Example 4

From Example 1 it follows that θ ={X/'ARM'} is a correct answer to Q_4 w.r.t. $\mathcal{B}_{CIA}$. Furthermore, since $|\, answerset(Q_4, \mathcal{B}_{CIA}) \,| = 14$ and $|\, answerset(Q_0, \mathcal{B}_{CIA}) \,| = |$ MiddleEastCountry $| = 15$, then $supp(Q_4, \mathcal{B}_{CIA}) = 93\%$. The $\mathcal{O}$-query Q_4 decorated with its support value has to be read as '93% of Middle East countries believes a monotheistic religion'.

Listing 2.

Q_0 = q(X) ← & X:MiddleEastCountry

Q_1 = q(X) ← believes(X,Y) & X:MiddleEastCountry

Q_2 = q(X) ← speaks(X,Y) & X:MiddleEastCountry

Q_3 = q(X) ← believes(X,Y) & X:MiddleEastCountry, Y:Religion

Q_4 = q(X) ← believes(X,Y) & X:MiddleEastCountry, Y:MonotheisticReligion

Q_5 = q(X) ← believes(X,Y), speaks(X,Z) &
                X:MiddleEastCountry, Y:MonotheisticReligion,
Z:IndoEuropeanLanguage

Q_6 = q(X) ← believes(X,Y), speaks(X,Z) &
                X:MiddleEastCountry, Y:MuslimReligion, Z:IndoIranianLanguage

The system $\mathcal{AL}$ - QuIn implements the afore-mentioned levelwise search method. In particular, candidate patterns of a certain level k (called *k-patterns*) are obtained by refinement of the frequent patterns discovered at level $k-1$. In $\mathcal{AL}$ - QuIn patterns are ordered according to $\mathcal{B}$ - subsumption (which has been proved to fulfill the abovementioned condition of monotonicity (Lisi & Malerba, 2004)). As shown in Figure 1, the search starts from the trivial $\mathcal{O}$ - query in $\mathcal{L}$ and iterates through the generation-evaluation cycle (procedures generateCandidates() and evaluateCandidates()) for a number of times that is bounded with respect to both the granularity level l (*maxG*) and the depth level k (*maxD*).

We need now to prove that the main algorithm of $\mathcal{AL}$ - QuIn (shown in Figure 1) terminates returning a correct solution to the problem stated in Definition 1.

Theorem 1

$\mathcal{AL}$ - QuIn works correctly.

Proof

The algorithm consists of two nested loops: the outer one is a cycle on levels of description granularity whereas the inner one is a cycle on levels of search depth. First we concentrate on the inner loop (steps (9)-(14)) because it properly corresponds to the levelwise search for frequent pattern discovery.

Given a fixed l, we prove that in step (9) the following properties hold invariantly at the beginning of each iteration:

R_1: $\mathcal{F}$ contains the frequent O-queries $Q \in \mathcal{L}^l$ up to depth level k−1.

R_2: $\mathcal{C}_k^l$ is the superset of frequent $\mathcal{O}$-queries $Q \in \mathcal{L}^l$ at depth level k.

R_3: Frequent $\mathcal{O}$ - queries $Q \in \mathcal{L}^l$ from depth level k+1 onwards are specializations of queries in $\mathcal{F}_k^l$.

Figure 1. The levelwise search in $\mathcal{AL}$ - QuIn

```
𝒜ℒ-QuIn(ℬ, maxG, maxD,{ℒ^l, minsup^l}_{1≤l≤maxG})
1.  ℱ ← ∅;
2.  Q_t ← {generateTrivialPattern(ℒ)};
3.  l ← 1;
4.  while l ≤ maxG do
5.       𝓘^l ← ∅;
6.       k ← 1;
7.       𝒞_k^l ← {Q_t};
8.       ℱ_k^l ← ∅;
9.       while k ≤ maxD and 𝒞_k^l ≠ ∅ do
10.          ℱ_k^l ← evaluateCandidates(ℬ, 𝒞_k^l, 𝓘^l, minsup^l);
11.          ℱ ← ℱ ∪ ℱ_k^l;
12.          k ← k + 1;
13.          𝒞_k^l ← generateCandidates(ℱ_{k-1}^l, ℒ^l, 𝓘^l);
14.      endwhile
15.      l ← l + 1;
16.  endwhile
return ℱ
```

R_4: *All* $\mathcal{O}$ - queries in $\mathcal{I}^l$ are infrequent.

It is easy to verify that R_1, R_2, R_3, and R_4 hold at the beginning of the first iteration, i.e., after initialization (steps (1) and (5)-(8)). Let us now assume that R_1, R_2, R_3, and R_4 hold up to the n-th iteration, n<maxD and prove that these relations still hold at the beginning of the (n+1)-th iteration.

- *After step (10), R_2 and R_4 are still valid, since the* $\mathcal{O}$ - *queries added to* $\mathcal{I}^l$ *are infrequent, and* $\mathcal{F}_k^l$ *is equal to the set of frequent* $\mathcal{O}$ - *queries at depth level k. Also R_3 still holds, since, due to the monotonicity of* $\succeq_B$ *w.r.t. frequency of* $\mathcal{O}$ - *queries none of the frequent* $\mathcal{O}$ - *queries from depth level k+1 onwards are specializations of the infrequent* $\mathcal{O}$ - *queries moved to* $\mathcal{I}^l$. *Finally, R_1 is valid since neither* $\mathcal{F}$ *nor k have been modified.*
- *After step (11),* $\mathcal{F}$ *contains the frequent* $\mathcal{O}$ - *queries up to depth level k, and R_2, R_3, and R_4 still hold.*
- With the increment of k in step (12) R_1, R_2, R_3, and R_4 again hold.
- *In step (13), the* $\mathcal{O}$ - *queries of depth level k+1 are generated, and since R_3 holds at that moment,* $\mathcal{C}_{k+1}^l$ *is the superset of frequent* $\mathcal{O}$ - *queries at depth level k+1.*

The loop terminates if either the depth bound maxD has been reached or $\mathcal{C}_k^l$ *is empty.* If the latter is the case, then it follows from R_2 and R_3 that language $\mathcal{L}^l$ contains no frequent $\mathcal{O}$ - queries at depth level k or from level k+1 onwards. Since $\mathcal{F}$ contains all frequent $\mathcal{O}$-queries in the language up to depth level k−1, $\mathcal{F}$ at that moment contains all frequent $\mathcal{O}$ - queries in the language $\mathcal{L}^l$ as required. The depth bound assures termination of $\mathcal{AL}$ - QuIn in case of infinite languages.

The outer loop also terminates because step (15) makes the level l of description granularity converge to maxG.

Candidate Generation

Candidate generation consists of a refinement step followed by a pruning step. The former derives new patterns from patterns previously found frequent by preserving the properties of linkedness and connectedness. The pruning step allows some infrequent patterns to be detected and discarded prior to evaluation by testing the following conditions: A k-pattern Q in $\mathcal{L}^l$, $1 \leq l \leq maxG$, is infrequent if it is $\mathcal{B}$ - subsumed w.r.t. an $\mathcal{AL}$ - log knowledge base $\mathcal{B}$ by either (i) an infrequent (k−1)-pattern in $\mathcal{L}^l$ or (ii) an infrequent k-pattern in $\mathcal{L}^{l-1}$ (Lisi & Malerba, 2004). Note that these pruning conditions arise from the monotonicity of $\succeq_B$ w.r.t. *supp*. Other pruning conditions concern the admissible form for patterns according to the languages bias specification, e.g., the number of unconstrained variables.

The algorithm for candidate generation in $\mathcal{AL}$ - QuIn is shown in Figure 2. For a given level l of description granularity, $1 \leq l \leq maxG$, the procedure generateCandidates() builds the set $\mathcal{C}_k^l$ of candidate k-patterns starting from the set $\mathcal{F}_{k-1}^l$ of frequent (k−1)-patterns and the language $\mathcal{L}^l$ by taking the set $\mathcal{I}^l$ of infrequent patterns into account. It consists of two computation branches.

The former concerns the case of search in $\mathcal{L}^l$. It applies either the refinement rule $\langle AddA \rangle$ or $\langle AddC \rangle$ (procedure intraRefine() presented in Figure 3) and checks the pruning conditions (procedure prune()). Furthermore it updates a complementary data structure, called the *graph of backward pointers*, by inserting an edge (*backward pointer*) from any retained candidate Q to the frequent pattern P from which Q has been derived by refinement (procedure setIntraSpaceEdge()). These edges are called *intra-space* because they keep track of search stages that do not cause a shift of description granularity. The advantages of using this complementary data structure will be illustrated later on in this section.

Figure 2. Candidate generation in $\mathcal{AL}$ -QuIn

```
Procedure generateCandidates(F_{k-1}^l, L^l, var I^l)
1.  C_k^l ← ∅;
2.  if l = 1 then /* search in L^1 */
3.     foreach pattern P in F_{k-1}^l do
4.        Q ← intraRefine(P, L^l);
5.        Q ← prune(Q, I^l);
6.        foreach pattern Q in Q do
             /* set the intra-space edge from Q to P */
7.           setIntraSpaceEdge(Q, P)
8.        endforeach
9.        C_k^l ← C_k^l ∪ Q
10. endforeach
11. else /* search in L^l, l > 1 */
12. foreach pattern P in F_{k-1}^l do
13.    P' ← getInterSpaceParent(P);
14.    Q' ← getIntraSpaceChildren(P');
15.    foreach pattern Q' in Q' do
16.       Q ← interRefine(Q', L^l);
17.       Q ← prune(Q, I^l);
18.       foreach pattern Q in Q do
            /* set the inter-space edge from Q to Q' */
19.          setInterSpaceEdge(Q, Q');
            /* set the intra-space edge from Q to P */
20.          setIntraSpaceEdge(Q, P);
21.       endforeach
22.       C_k^l ← C_k^l ∪ Q
23.    endforeach
24. endforeach
return C_k^l
```

Example 5

As an illustrative example of candidate generation at the first level of description granularity we report the computation of $\mathcal{C}_2^1$ with reference to $\mathcal{L}_{\text{CIA}}$ (See Example 3). The set $\mathcal{F}_1^1$ contains the trivial query Q_0 only. The procedure call intraRefine $(Q_0, \mathcal{L}_{\text{CIA}}^1)$ returns the set of possible refinements of Q_0 according to directives of $\mathcal{L}_{\text{CIA}}^1$ namely the queries Q_1 and Q_2 obtained by adding

the atoms believes(X,Y) and speaks(X,Y) to the body of Q_0 respectively. Furthermore the procedure call prune $(\mathcal{Q}, \mathcal{I}^1)$ does affect neither $\mathcal{Q}$ nor $\mathcal{I}^1$ Before returning control to the main procedure of $\mathcal{AL}$ - QuIn, generateCandidates $(\mathcal{F}_1^1, \mathcal{L}_{\text{CIA}}^1, \mathcal{I}^1)$ inserts intra-space edges for Q_1 and Q_2 into the graph of backward pointers. Assuming that $\mathcal{F}_2^1$ contains Q_1 we carry on this example by focusing on the generation of candidate patterns starting from Q_1 Possible refinements of Q_1 according to directives of $\mathcal{L}_{\text{CIA}}^1$ *are the queries:*

$Q_{1.1}$ = q(X) ← believes(X,Y), believes(X,Z) & X:MiddleEastCountry

$Q_{1.2}$ = q(X) ← believes(X,Y), speaks(X,Z) & X:MiddleEastCountry

$Q_{1.3}$ = q(X) ← believes(X,Y) & X:MiddleEastCountry, Y:Religion

$Q_{1.4}$ = q(X) ← believes(X,Y) & X:MiddleEastCountry, Y:Language

In particular, $Q_{1.1}$ *and* $Q_{1.2}$ *are generated by applying* $\langle AddA \rangle$ *whereas* $Q_{1.3}$ *and* $Q_{1.4}$ *are generated by applying* $\langle AddC \rangle$ *Since* $Q_{1.1}$ *and* $Q_{1.2}$ *do not fulfill the requirement on the maximum number of unconstrained variables, they are gen-*

Figure 3. Intra-space refinement in $\mathcal{AL}$ - QuIn

```
Procedure intraRefine(P, L^l)
Input:
• P = q(X) ← α_1,...,α_m & X : C_ref, γ_1,...,γ_n in L^l
• L^l = A ∪ Γ^l
Output:
The set Q of all Q ∈ L^l that can be obtained from P by applying one of the following
refinement rules:

⟨AddA⟩ atoms(Q) = atoms(P) ∪ {α_{m+1}}, where α_{m+1} is an instantiation of an atom tem-
       plate in A such that α_{m+1} ∉ body(P).

⟨AddC⟩ constraints(Q) = constraints(P) ∪ {γ_{n+1}} where γ_{n+1} is an instantiation of a
       constraint template in Γ^l such that γ_{n+1} constrains an unconstrained variable in
       body(P).
```

erated then pruned. So $Q_{1.3}$ namely Q_3, and $Q_{1.4}$ are the only to pass the pruning step. Actually $Q_{1.4}$ will not pass the evaluation phase, thus it will not appear as child of Q_1 in $\mathcal{F}_3^1$.

The other branch of generateCandidates() concerns the case of search at deeper levels of description granularity, i.e., for $l > 1$. Note that searching $\mathcal{L}^l$ with only $\langle AddA \rangle$ or $\langle AddC \rangle$ implies to restart from scratch. Therefore we have tried to capitalize on the computational effort made when searching $\mathcal{L}^{l-1}$ and minimize the number of $\mathcal{B}$-subsumption checks performed during the pruning step. Our solution requires that is computed taking both $\mathcal{F}_{k-1}^l$ and $\mathcal{F}_k^{l-1}$ into account. Also it assumes that each pattern P in $\mathcal{F}_{k-1}^l$ is linked to its ancestor pattern in $\mathcal{F}_k^{l-1}$ by means of an edge (called *inter-space backward pointer*) in the graph of backward pointers. In particular, the expansion of a node P in $\mathcal{F}_{k-1}^l$ is done as follows:

- Retrieve the parent node P' of P by following the inter-space backward pointer (step (13)).
- Retrieve the set $\mathcal{Q}' \subseteq \mathcal{F}_k^{l-1}$ of child nodes of P' by navigating intra-space backward pointers in reverse sense (step (14)).
- Generate the set $\mathcal{Q}$ of $\mathcal{O}$-queries obtained by applying the refinement rule $\langle StrengthenC \rangle$ to each Q' in $\mathcal{Q}'$ (step (16)).

In particular, $\langle StrengthenC \rangle$ replaces old constraints with new constraints that are as strict as $\left(\trianglerighteq \right)$ the old ones (procedure interRefine() presented in Figure 4). In order to get a proper refinement, at least one of the new constraints must be stricter $\left(\triangleright \right)$ than the corresponding old one. The relation of strictness for constraints derives from the relation of subsumption for concepts.

Example 6

Again with reference to Example 3 we report some of the computation of C_3^2. Assuming that $\mathcal{F}_2^2$ contains Q_1, we concentrate on the generation of candidate patterns starting from Q_1. The expansion of Q_1 in the case of Q_1 considered as belonging to $\mathcal{L}_{CIA}^2$ is done indirectly by accessing search stages of success in $\mathcal{L}_{CIA}^1$ departing from Q_1. In Example 5 we have seen that Q_3 is the only child of Q_1. By applying $\langle StrengthenC \rangle$ to Q_3 we obtain the queries:

$Q_{3.1} = $ q(X) ← believes(X,Y) & X:MiddleEastCountry, Y:MonotheisticReligion

$Q_{3.2} = $ q(X) ← believes(X,Y) & X:MiddleEastCountry, Y:PolytheisticReligion

where both Y:MonotheisticReligion and Y:PolytheisticReligion are stricter than Y:Religion. Note that the expansion of Q_3 by means of $\langle AddA \rangle$ and $\langle AddC \rangle$ would have generated patterns such as

$Q_{3.3} = q(X) \leftarrow believes(X,Y), believes(X,Z)$ & *X:MiddleEastCountry*
    that are not valid for $\mathcal{L}_{CIA}^2$ or patterns like

$Q_{3.4} = $ q(X) ← believes(X,Y) & X:MiddleEastCountry, Y:IndoEuropeanLanguage

that are certainly infrequent in $\mathcal{L}_{CIA}^2$.

Note that the refinement operator implemented in $\mathcal{AL}$-QuIn is slightly different from the one implemented in SPADA (see Def. 4.5 in Lisi & Malerba, 2004). It consists of three rules instead of only two. Notably it distinguishes between DATALOG atoms and $\mathcal{ALC}$ constraints when adding new literals to the body of $\mathcal{O}$-queries ($\langle AddA \rangle$ and $\langle AddC \rangle$ vs $\langle Lit \rangle$). Also it generates proper refinements when strengthening $\mathcal{ALC}$

Figure 4. Inter-space refinement in $\mathcal{AL}$ - QUIN

Procedure interRefine($P, \mathcal{L}^l$)
Input:
- $P = q(X) \leftarrow \alpha_1, \ldots, \alpha_m \& X : C_{ref}, \gamma_1, \ldots, \gamma_n$ in $\mathcal{L}^{l-1}$
- $\mathcal{L}^l = \mathcal{A} \cup \Gamma^l$

Output:
The set $\mathcal{Q}$ of all $Q \in \mathcal{L}^l$ that can be obtained from P by applying the following refinement rule:

$\langle StrengthenC \rangle$ $constraints(Q) = \{\gamma'_1, \ldots, \gamma'_n\}$ where for each j, $1 \le j \le n$, γ'_j is an instantiation of a constraint template in Γ^l such that $\gamma'_j \unrhd \gamma_j$ and there exists at least one γ_k, $1 \le k \le n$, such that $\gamma'_k \rhd \gamma_k$.

---

constraints ($\langle StrengthenC \rangle$ vs $\langle \forall C \rangle$). Thus the new refinement operator introduces some optimizations in the search for patterns (see Lisi & Malerba, 2003b, for further details of candidate generation in $\mathcal{AL}$ - QUIN).

Candidate Evaluation

Candidate evaluation phases are responsible for filtering out those candidate patterns with insufficient support. The algorithm for candidate evaluation in $\mathcal{AL}$ - QUIN is shown in Figure 5. For a given level l of description granularity and a given level k of search depth, the procedure evaluateCandidates() computes the set $\mathcal{F}^l_k$ of frequent patterns by starting from the set $\mathcal{C}^l_k$ of candidate patterns.

The procedure computeAnswerSet() is reported in Figure 6. It also benefits from the graph of backward pointers because the $\mathcal{B}$ - subsumption relations captured in it have the following desirable side effects from the viewpoint of query answering: Given P, Q two $\mathcal{O}$ -queries to an $\mathcal{AL}$ - log knowledge base $\mathcal{B}$, if $P \succeq_{\mathcal{B}} Q$ then $answerset(Q, \mathcal{B}) \subseteq answerset(P\gamma, \mathcal{B})$ for some renaming substitution γ of the distinguished variable of P (Lisi & Esposito, 2004).

Example 7

Following Example 3, it can be proved that $Q_5 \succeq_{\mathcal{B}} Q_6$ and $\theta = \{X / \text{ARM}\}$ is an answer to Q_5 but not to Q_6.

Therefore we store the answer set of frequent patterns and, when evaluating new candidates, we use backward pointers to access this data quickly. This is analogous to a well-known database practice: P is usually a *view* (i.e., a query

Figure 5. Candidate evaluation in $\mathcal{AL}$ - QUIN

Procedure evaluateCandidates($\mathcal{B}, \mathcal{C}^l_k, minsup^l, var \mathcal{I}^l$)
1. $\mathcal{F}^l_k \leftarrow \emptyset$;
2. foreach pattern Q in $\mathcal{C}^l_k$ do
3. $answerset(Q, \mathcal{B}) \leftarrow$ computeAnswerSet($Q, \mathcal{B}$);
4.   if $supp(Q, \mathcal{B}) \ge minsup^l$
5.   then $\mathcal{F}^l_k \leftarrow \mathcal{F}^l_k \cup \{Q\}$
6.   else $\mathcal{I}^l \leftarrow \mathcal{I}^l \cup \{Q\}$
7.   endif
8. endforeach
return $\mathcal{F}^l_k$

Figure 6. Computation of the answer set of an $\mathcal{O}$ - query in $\mathcal{AL}$ - QUIN

Procedure computeAnswerSet($Q, \mathcal{B}$)
1. if $intraSpaceEdge(Q) = null$ /* case of trivial pattern */
2.   then $answerset(Q, \mathcal{B}) \leftarrow$ listRefIndividuals($Q, \mathcal{B}$);
3. else
4. $P \leftarrow$ getIntraSpaceParent(Q);
5. $answerset(Q, \mathcal{B}) \leftarrow \emptyset$;
6.   foreach substitution θ_i in $answerset(P, \mathcal{B})$ do
7.   if θ_i is a correct answer to Q w.r.t. $\mathcal{B}_i$
8.   then $answerset(Q, \mathcal{B}) \leftarrow answerset(Q, \mathcal{B}) \cup \{\theta_i\}$;
9.   endforeach
10. endif
return $answerset(Q, \mathcal{B})$

---

whose answers are pre-computed, stored and maintained up-to-date) and the relation of query containment for a query Q in P is exploited to speed up query answering by filtering the answers of P instead of computing the answers of Q from scratch. In particular the procedure compute-AnswerSet() uses the intra-space backward pointers. Note that the computation of the answer set of the trivial $\mathcal{O}$ - query Q_t for a given language $\mathcal{L}$ needs a special branch in the procedure computeAnswerSet() since the intra-space backward pointer for Q_t is null. In this case the answer set is trivially the list of individuals belonging to the reference concept (returned by the function listRefIndividuals()).

Note that candidate evaluation in $\mathcal{AL}$ - QuIn does not follow the levelwise method's dictate of evaluating the candidates of each depth level in one single pass through the database. Indeed it makes as many passes through the database as the number of $\mathcal{O}$ - queries in $\mathcal{C}_k^l$ (see Lisi & Esposito, 2004, for further details of candidate evaluation in $\mathcal{AL}$ - QuIn).

Semantic Web Mining with $\mathcal{AL}$ - QuIn

In order to enable $\mathcal{AL}$ - QuIn to Semantic Web applications we have developed a software component, SWing, that assists users of $\mathcal{AL}$ - QuIn in the design of Semantic Web Mining sessions. As illustrated in Figure 7, SWing interoperates with Protégé-OWL (release 3.4) (Stanford University, 2011) via API to benefit from its facilities for browsing OWL ontologies, and with Pellet (release 1.4) (Clark & Parsia, 2011) via DIG interface[6] for reasoning on OWL ontologies. Also it relies on Graphviz (release 2.24) (http://www.graphviz.org/) for the graphical rendering of Semantic Web Mining results.

The screenshots reported in Figure 8, 9, and 10 refer to a Semantic Web Mining session with SWing for the task introduced in Example 3. In SWing a wizard provides guidance for:

- The selection of the relational database to be mined and the taxonomic ontology to be consulted during the discovery process,
- The selection of the reference concept and the task-relevant concepts from the chosen ontology (Figure 8).
- The selection of the relations among the ones appearing in the chosen database (Figure 9) or derived from them (Figure 10).
- The setting of minimum support thresholds for each level of description granularity and of several other parameters required by $\mathcal{AL}$ - QuIn.

Different files are produced and shown in preview to the user for confirmation at the end of this assisted procedure. The file *.lb contains the declarative bias specification for the language of patterns and other directives. The file *.db contains

Figure 7. SWing system architecture and I/O

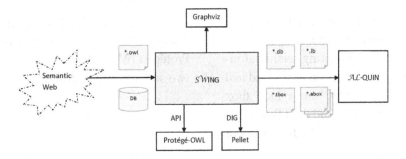

Figure 8. Selection of concepts with SWING

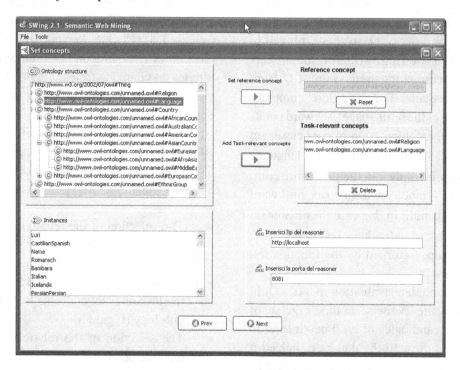

Figure 9. Selection of relations with SWING

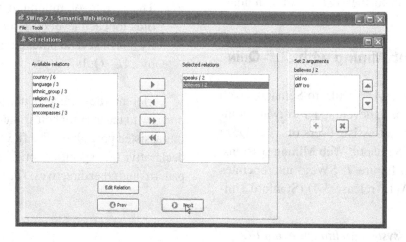

the chosen database represented with DATALOG and eventually enriched with an intensional part. A suite of wrappers for extracting relational information from the Web has been developed and integrated in SWING. The files *.abox and *.tbox contain portions of the ABox and the TBox of the chosen ontology, respectively. The fragments of interest are determined during the step of concept selection by invoking appropriate services of Protégé-OWL and Pellet. Indeed, this step triggers two supplementary computations:

1. Levelwise retrieval w.r.t. Σ,

Figure 10. Editing of derived relations with SWING

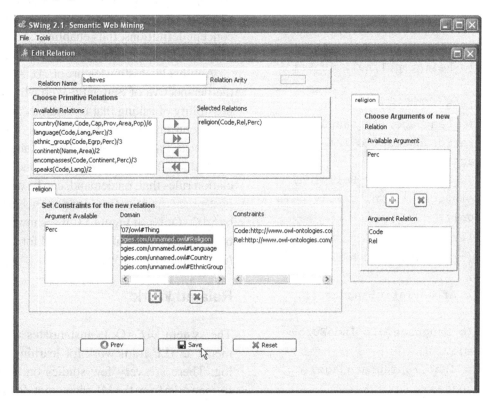

2. Translation of both (asserted and derived) concept assertions and subsumption axioms of Σ to DATALOG^{OI} facts.

aimed at making an OWL ontology Σ usable by $\mathcal{AL}$ - QuIn. The latter relies on the former, meaning that the results of the levelwise retrieval are exported to DATALOG^{OI}. The *retrieval* problem is known in DL literature as the problem of retrieving all the individuals of a concept C (Baader et al., 2003). Here, the retrieval is called *levelwise* because it follows the layering of the TBox $\mathcal{T}$: Individuals of concepts belonging to the l-th layer $\mathcal{T}^l$ of $\mathcal{T}$ are retrieved all together. This makes SLD-refutations of queries in $\mathcal{L}$ work only on extensional structural knowledge at the level l of description granularity (*levelwise saturation*).

Example 8

The step of concept selection with SWING *on* Σ$_{CIA}$ produces four files: cia.tbox, cia.abox_1, cia.abox_2, and cia.abox_3. The file cia.tbox contains a DATALOG^{OI} rewriting of the taxonomic relations of $\mathcal{T}_{CIA}$ such as in Listing 3.

The files cia.abox_1, cia.abox_2, and cia.abox_3 contain the result of the levelwise instance retrieval, e.g., the file cia.abox_2 stores facts like in Listing 4.

that are the result of the DATALOG^{OI} *rewriting of the concept assertions derived for* $\mathcal{T}_{CIA}^2$. The files cia.abox_1 and cia.abox_3 are produced analogously.

Note that the translation from OWL to DATALOG^{OI} is possible because we assume that *all* the concepts are named. This means that an equivalence axiom is required for each complex concept in the ontology. Equivalence axioms help keep

Listing 3.

```
hierarchy(c_Language,1,null,[c_Lan-
guage]).
hierarchy(c_Religion,1,null,[c_Reli-
gion]).
 for the layer T¹ and
hierarchy(c_Language,2,c_Language,
[c_AfroAsiaticLanguage, c_IndoEuro-
peanLanguage, …]).
hierarchy(c_Religion,2,c_Religion,
[c_MonotheisticReligion, c_Polythei-
sticReligion]).
 for the layer T²_CIA and
hierarchy(c_Language,3,c_AfroAsiati-
cLanguage,
        [c_AfroAsiaticLanguage]).
…
hierarchy(c_Language,3,c_IndoEuro-
peanLanguage,
        [c_IndoIranianLanguage, c_
SlavicLanguage]).
hierarchy(c_Language,3,c_UralAlta-
icLanguage,
        [c_TurkicLanguage]).
hierarchy(c_Religion,3,c_Monotheisti-
cReligion,
        [c_ChristianReligion, c_
JewishReligion, c_MuslimReligion]).
 for the layer T³_CIA.
```

Listing 4.

```
c_AfroAsiaticLanguage('Arabic').
…
c_IndoEuropeanLanguage('Persian').
…
c_UralAltaicLanguage('Kazak').
…
c_MonotheisticReligion('ShiaMuslim').
c_MonotheisticReligion('SunniMusl
im').
…
c_PolytheisticReligion('Druze').
…
```

concept names (to be used in the body of constrained DATALOG clauses) independent from concept definitions, thus enabling $\mathcal{AL}$ - QuIn to deal with DLs more expressive than $\mathcal{ALC}$.

Another interesting feature of $\mathcal{AL}$ - QuIn from the perspective of Semantic Web Mining is the possibility of asking that its findings are formatted according to the XML syntax for SWRL (Horrocks, Patel-Schneider, Boley, Tabet, Grosof, & Dean, 2004). This possibility concerns association rules that, on demand, can be obtained by post-processing the frequent patterns discovered by $\mathcal{AL}$ - QuIn. In Figure 11, it is shown how one of the association rules generated for the task in hand looks like in SWRL.

Related Work

The system $\mathcal{AL}$ - QuIn instantiates and implements an ILP framework for learning in $\mathcal{AL}$ - log. There are very few studies on hybrid KR frameworks from the ML viewpoint. In Rouveirol and Ventos (2000), CARIN- $\mathcal{ALN}$ - an instantiation of the unsafe KR framework CARIN (Levy & Rousset, 1998) - is chosen as representation formalism in an ILP algorithm for classification. Unfortunately, this algorithm has been neither implemented nor motivated by and/or aimed at a specific application. Following Rouveirol and Ventos (2000), Kietz studies the learnability of CARIN- $\mathcal{ALN}$, thus providing a pre-processing method which enables ILP systems to learn CA-RIN- $\mathcal{ALN}$ rules (Kietz, 2003). In Lisi (2010), $\mathcal{DL}$ +LOG$^{\neg\vee}$ (Rosati, 2006) - a weakly-safe KR framework which integrates any DL and disjunctive DATALOG - is adopted for the induction of view definitions and integrity theories in relational databases with ILP. In Józefowska, Lawrynowicz, and Lukaszewski (2010), DL knowledge bases extended with DL-safe rules (Motik, Sattler, & Studer, 2005) are considered in an algorithm for frequent pattern discovery inspired by SPADA, FARMER and C-ARMR. This work is the closest to ours though differs from ours in several aspects.

Figure 11. SWRL formatting of rules discovered by $\mathcal{AL}$ - QuIn

Notably, it supports the task of frequent pattern discovery in the original formulation of WARMR and not in the variant at multiple description granularity levels proposed first in SPADA and then further extended in $\mathcal{AL}$ - QuIn. Globally speaking, the actual added value of $\mathcal{AL}$ - QuIn in comparison with Józefowska et al. (2010) is the continuity with respect to the tradition of Relational Data Mining. Indeed, it can work with but also without ontologies as prior conceptual knowledge.

The platform SWING supplies several facilities to $\mathcal{AL}$ - QuIn, primarily facilities for compiling OWL down to DATALOG. Note that DATALOG is the usual KR setting for ILP. In this respect, the pre-processing method proposed by Kietz (2003)

is related to ours but it lacks an application. Analogously, the method proposed in Hustadt, Motik, and Sattler (2004) for translating OWL to disjunctive DATALOG is far too general with respect to the specific needs of our application. Rather, the proposal of interfacing existing reasoners to combine ontologies and rules (Assmann, Henriksson, & Maluszynski, 2006) is more similar to ours in the spirit.

CONCLUSION

Onto-Relational Learning has been conceived to overcome the limits of Relational Learning in dealing with ontologies. In this paper we have shown that the applicability of Relational Learning in the Semantic Web context suffer from these limits. More precisely, we have considered the DM task of frequent pattern discovery in relational databases at multiple levels of description granularity as a showcase of the inadequacy of Relational Learning systems like WARMR. Our proposal, $\mathcal{AL}$ - QuIn, is an Onto-Relational Learning system. It can be considered as an upgrade of WARMR towards KR frameworks more expressive than DATALOG and ILP techniques more powerful than θ - subsumption. Indeed, it adopts $\mathcal{AL}$ - log as KR framework and generalized subsumption[7] as ILP technique. In particular, the choice of a semantic generality order allows $\mathcal{AL}$ - QuIn to actually exploit the semantic information conveyed by ontologies during the search for frequent patterns in relational databases. Thanks to these features, $\mathcal{AL}$ - QuIn turns out to be better equipped to face some of the challenges of the Semantic Web to ML and DM, notably the availability of an increasing amount of conceptual knowledge in the form of ontologies. Note that, since ontologies are taken as input to the learning process, $\mathcal{AL}$ - QuIn cannot be considered a system for Ontology Learning (Maedche & Staab, 2004) where ontologies are the output of the learning process. Nevertheless the system discovers knowledge that can be used to make the given ontology evolve (Ontology Refinement). Indeed each $\mathcal{O}$ - query describes a subset of the individuals of the reference concept. A frequent $\mathcal{O}$ - query could be therefore interpreted by the ontology engineer as a suggestion that the set of individuals satisfying the $\mathcal{O}$ - query should form a new concept (more precisely, a *conceptual cluster*) which is subsumed by the reference concept and can be added to the original ontology. Further details of one such application of $\mathcal{AL}$ - QuIn to Ontology Refinement can be found in Lisi (2008). Also the possibility of returning association rules formatted according to the XML syntax for SWRL makes $\mathcal{AL}$ - QuIn able to enrich the given ontology with further useful knowledge that can be exchanged with other applications accessing the ontology. Note that both the conceptual clustering and the SWRL formatting are novel features of $\mathcal{AL}$ - QuIn wrt its predecessor SPADA.

The platform SWING follows engineering principles because it promotes the reuse of existing systems ($\mathcal{AL}$ - QuIn, Protégé-OWL, Pellet and GraphViz) and the adherence to standards (either normative - see OWL for the Semantic Web - or *de facto* - see DATALOG for ILP). The resulting artifact overcomes the capabilities of these systems when considered stand-alone. In particular, $\mathcal{AL}$ - QuIn was originally conceived to deal with $\mathcal{ALC}$ ontologies but is enabled to cope with more expressive DL ontologies thanks to SWING. Clearly, there are restrictions on the kind of ontologies that SWING can process. An absolute requirement for Semantic Web Mining applications is that the ontology is populated, possibly with instances distributed over leaf classes rather than over high-level classes. Other assumptions in SWING pose issues from the Ontological Engineering viewpoint. First, all the concepts in the ontology are named. The construction of meaningful names for unnamed classes is not yet automated in SWING. Second, the hierarchical structure of the ontology is 'layered'. SWING automatically assigns a level of description granularity to concepts on the basis of the internal representation of ontologies in Protégé-OWL. The case of differently long branches in the hierarchy is dealt with by 'lengthening' the shorter branches, e.g., a leaf concept at level 2 is considered also for the instance retrieval at subsequent levels up to the maximum description granularity level set for the Semantic Web Mining task in hand. Third, the predicate spaces for the OWL ontology and the DATALOG database are disjoint according to the $\mathcal{AL}$ - log framework. Therefore, if it happens that a predicate occurs in both knowledge sources, we need to change the name of one of the two occurrences. This task is also not yet automated in SWING.

As a final remark, we would like to point out that Onto-Relational Learning is not alternative but complementary to Statistical Relational Learning. A first step from Statistical Relational Learning towards dealing with formal ontologies is testified by Rettinger, Nickles, and Tresp (2009). We deem the investigation of solutions for uncertainty reasoning in Onto-Relational Learning an equally interesting direction of future research.

REFERENCES

Agrawal, R., Imielinski, T., & Swami, A. (1993). Mining association rules between sets of items in large databases. In *Proceedings of the ACM SIGMOD International Conference on Management of Data* (pp. 207-216). New York, NY: ACM Press.

Agrawal, R., & Srikant, R. (1994). Fast algorithms for mining association rules in large databases. In *Proceedings of the 20th International Conference on Very Large Data Bases* (pp. 487-499). San Francisco, CA: Morgan Kaufmann.

Assmann, U., Henriksson, J., & Maluszynski, J. (2006). Combining safe rules and ontologies by interfacing of reasoners. In J. Alferes, J. Bailey, W. May, & U. Schwertel (Eds.), *Proceedings of the 4th International Conference on Principles and Practice of Semantic Web Reasoning* (LNCS 4187, p. 33-47).

Baader, F., Calvanese, D., McGuinness, D., Nardi, D., & Patel-Schneider, P. (Eds.). (2007). *The description logic handbook: Theory, implementation, and applications* (2nd ed.). Cambridge, UK: Cambridge University Press. doi:10.1017/CBO9780511711787.

Borgida, A. (1996). On the relative expressiveness of description logics and predicate logics. *Artificial Intelligence*, 82(1-2), 353–367. doi:10.1016/0004-3702(96)00004-5.

Buntine, W. (1988). Generalized subsumption and its application to induction and redundancy. *Artificial Intelligence*, 36(2), 149–176. doi:10.1016/0004-3702(88)90001-X.

Ceri, S., Gottlob, G., & Tanca, L. (1990). *Logic programming and databases*. New York, NY: Springer.

Clark & Parsia. (2011). *Pellet: OWL 2 reasoner for Java*. Retrieved from http://clarkparsia.com/pellet/

De Raedt, L. (2008). *Logical and relational learning*. New York, NY: Springer. doi:10.1007/978-3-540-68856-3.

De Raedt, L., & Ramon, J. (2004). Condensed representations for inductive logic programming. In Dubois, D., Welty, C. A., & Williams, M. A. (Eds.), *Principles of knowledge representation and reasoning* (pp. 438–446). Menlo Park, CA: AAAI Press.

Dehaspe, L., & Toivonen, H. (1999). Discovery of frequent DATALOG patterns. *Data Mining and Knowledge Discovery*, 3, 7–36. doi:10.1023/A:1009863704807.

Donini, F., Lenzerini, M., Nardi, D., & Schaerf, A. (1998). -log: Integrating datalog and description logics. *Journal of Intelligent Information Systems*, 10(3), 227–252. doi:10.1023/A:1008687430626.

Džeroski, S., & Lavrač, N. (Eds.). (2001). *Relational data mining*. New York, NY: Springer.

Gómez-Pérez, A., Fernández-López, M., & Corcho, O. (2004). *Ontological engineering*. New York, NY: Springer.

Han, J., & Fu, Y. (1995). Discovery of multiple-level association rules from large databases. In *Proceedings of the 21st International Conference on Very Large Data Bases* (pp. 420-431). San Francisco, CA: Morgan Kaufmann.

Han, J., & Fu, Y. (1999). Mining multiple-level association rules in large databases. *IEEE Transactions on Knowledge and Data Engineering*, 11(5).

Horrocks, I., Patel-Schneider, P., Boley, H., Tabet, S., Grosof, B., & Dean, M. (2004). *SWRL: A semantic web rule language combining OWL and RuleML.* Retrieved from http://www.w3.org/Submission/SWRL/

Horrocks, I., Patel-Schneider, P., & van Harmelen, F. (2003). From $\mathcal{SHIQ}$ and RDF to OWL: The Making of a Web Ontology Language. *Journal of Web Semantics*, *1*(1), 7–26. doi:10.1016/j.websem.2003.07.001.

Hustadt, U., Motik, B., & Sattler, U. (2004). Reducing -Description Logic to Disjunctive Datalog Programs. In D. Dubois, C. Welty, & M. A. Williams (Eds.), Principles of knowledge representation and reasoning (pp. 152–162). Menlo Park, CA: AAAI Press.

Józefowska, J., Lawrynowicz, A., & Lukaszewski, T. (2010). The role of semantics in mining frequent patterns from knowledge bases in description logics with rules. *Theory and Practice of Logic Programming*, *10*(3), 251–289. doi:10.1017/S1471068410000098.

Kietz, J. (2003). Learnability of description logic programs. In S. Matwin & C. Sammut (Eds.), *Proceedings of the International Conference on Inductive Logic Programming* (LNCS 2583, pp. 117-132).

Knublauch, H., Fergerson, R. W., Noy, N. F., & Musen, M. A. (2004). The Protégé OWL Plugin: An open development environment for semantic web applications. In S. A. McIlraith, D. Plexousakis, & F. van Harmelen (Eds.), In *Proceedings of the Semantic Web Conference* (LNCS 3298, p. 229-243).

Levy, A., & Rousset, M. C. (1998). Combining Horn rules and description logics in CARIN. *Artificial Intelligence*, *104*, 165–209. doi:10.1016/S0004-3702(98)00048-4.

Lisi, F. (2008). Building rules on top of ontologies for the semantic web with inductive logic programming. *Theory and Practice of Logic Programming*, *8*(03), 271–300. doi:10.1017/S1471068407003195.

Lisi, F. (2010). Inductive logic programming in databases: From Datalog to $\mathcal{DL}$ +log. *Theory and Practice of Logic Programming*, *10*(3), 331–359. doi:10.1017/S1471068410000116.

Lisi, F., & Esposito, F. (2004). Efficient evaluation of candidate hypotheses in $\mathcal{AL}$ -log. In R. Camacho, R. King, & A. Srinivasan (Eds.), *Proceedings of the 14th International Conference on Inductive Logic Programming* (LNCS 3194, pp. 216-233).

Lisi, F., & Esposito, F. (2009). On ontologies as prior conceptual knowledge in inductive logic programming. In Berendt, B., Mladenic, D., de Gemmis, M., Semeraro, G., Spiliopoulou, M., & Stumme, G., et al. (Eds.), *Knowledge discovery enhanced with semantic and social information* (*Vol. 220*, pp. 3–18). New York, NY: Springer. doi:10.1007/978-3-642-01891-6_1.

Lisi, F., & Malerba, D. (2003a). Bridging the gap between horn clausal logic and description logics in inductive learning. In A. Cappelli & F. Turini (Eds.), *Proceedings of the 8th Congress of the Italian Association for Artificial Intelligence on Advances in Artificial Intelligence* (LNCS 2829, pp. 49-60).

Lisi, F., & Malerba, D. (2003b). Ideal refinement of descriptions in $\mathcal{AL}$-log. In T. Horvath & A. Yamamoto (Eds.), *Proceedings of the 13th International Conference on Inductive Logic Programming* (LNCS 2835, pp. 215-232).

Lisi, F., & Malerba, D. (2004). Inducing multi-level association rules from multiple relations. *Machine Learning, 55*, 175–210. doi:10.1023/B:MACH.0000023151.65011.a3.

Maedche, A., & Staab, S. (2000). Discovering conceptual relations from text. In *Proceedings of the 14th European Conference on Artificial Intelligence* (pp. 321-325). Amsterdam, The Netherlands: IOS Press.

Maedche, A., & Staab, S. (2004). Ontology learning. In Staab, S., & Studer, R. (Eds.), *Handbook on ontologies*. New York, NY: Springer.

Mannila, H., & Toivonen, H. (1997). Levelwise search and borders of theories in knowledge discovery. *Data Mining and Knowledge Discovery, 1*(3), 241–258. doi:10.1023/A:1009796218281.

Mitchell, T. (1982). Generalization as search. *Artificial Intelligence, 18*, 203–226. doi:10.1016/0004-3702(82)90040-6.

Motik, B., Sattler, U., & Studer, R. (2005). Query Answering for OWL-DL with Rules. *Journal of Web Semantics, 3*(1), 41–60. doi:10.1016/j.websem.2005.05.001.

Nienhuys-Cheng, S., & de Wolf, R. (1997). *Foundations of inductive logic programming (Vol. 1228)*. New York, NY: Springer.

Nijssen, S., & Kok, J. (2001). Faster association rules for multiple relations. In *Proceedings of the 17th International Joint Conference on Artificial Intelligence* (pp. 891-896). San Francisco, CA: Morgan Kaufmann.

Nijssen, S., & Kok, J. N. (2003). Efficient frequent query discovery in FARMER. In N. Lavrac, D. Gamberger, H. Blockeel, & L. Todorovski (Eds.), *Proceedings of the 7th European Conference on Knowledge Discovery in Databases* (LNCS 2838, pp. 350-362).

Quinlan, J. (1990). Learning logical definitions from relations. *Machine Learning, 5*, 239–266. doi:10.1007/BF00117105.

Rettinger, A., Nickles, M., & Tresp, V. (2009). Statistical relational learning with formal ontologies. In W. L. Buntine, M. Grobelnik, D. Mladenic, & J. Shawe-Taylor (Eds.), *Proceedings of the European Conference on Machine Learning and Knowledge Discovery in Databases, Part II* (LNCS 5782, pp. 286-301).

Rosati, R. (2005). Semantic and computational advantages of the safe integration of ontologies and rules. In F. Fages & S. Soliman (Eds.), *Proceedings of the Third International Workshop on Principles and Practice of Semantic Web Reasoning* (LNCS 3703, pp. 50-64).

Rosati, R. (2006). $\mathcal{DL}$+log: Tight integration of description logics and disjunctive datalog. In *Proceedings of the 10th International Conference on Principles of Knowledge Representation and Reasoning* (pp. 68-78). Menlo Park, CA: AAAI Press.

Rouveirol, C., & Ventos, V. (2000). Towards Learning in CARIN-$\mathcal{ALN}$. In J. Cussens & A. Frisch (Eds.), *Proceedings of the 10th International Conference on Inductive Logic Programming* (LNCS 1866, pp. 191-208).

Ruckhaus, E., Kolovski, V., Parsia, B., & Cuenca Grau, B. (2006). Integrating Datalog with OWL: Exploring the $\mathcal{AL}$-log Approach. In S. Etalle & M. Truszczynski (Eds.), *Proceedings of the 22nd International Conference on Logic programming* (LNCS 4079, p. 455-456).

Semeraro, G., Esposito, F., Malerba, D., Fanizzi, N., & Ferilli, S. (1998). A logic framework for the incremental inductive synthesis of Datalog theories. In N. Fuchs (Ed.), *Proceedings of 7th International Workshop on Logic Program Synthesis and Transformation* (LNCS 1463, pp. 300-321).

Srikant, R., & Agrawal, R. (1995). Mining generalized association rules. In *Proceedings of the 21st International Conference on Very Large Data Bases* (pp. 407-419). San Francisco, CA: Morgan Kaufmann.

Stanford University. (2011). *What is protégé-OWL?* Retrieved from http://protege.stanford.edu/overview/protege-owl.html

Stumme, G., Hotho, A., & Berendt, B. (2006). Semantic Web Mining: State of the art and future directions. *Journal of Web Semantics, 4*(2), 124–143. doi:10.1016/j.websem.2006.02.001.

ENDNOTES

1. Acronym of $\mathcal{AL}$-log QUERY INduction.
2. DL-based ontology languages like OWL can only represent hierarchies based on is-a relations, i.e. *taxonomies*. Conversely, *meronomies* are hierarchies based on part-of relations.
3. We remind the reader that datatypes are not allowed in the $\mathcal{ALC}$ DL.
4. Two clauses are said to be *standardized apart* if they have no variables in common.
5. Let $\mathcal{B}$ be a clausal theory and H a clause. Let $X_1, \ldots, X_n$ be all the variables appearing in H, and $a_1, \ldots, a_n$ be distinct constants (individuals) not appearing in $\mathcal{B}$ or H. Then the substitution $\{X_1 / a_1, \ldots, X_n / a_n\}$ is called a *Skolem substitution* for H w.r.t. $\mathcal{B}$.
6. The DIG Interface is a standardised XML interface to Description Logics systems developed by the DL Implementation Group (DIG).
7. The extension of generalized subsumption to the $\mathcal{AL}$-log KR framework, though formally proved, is only partially implemented in $\mathcal{AL}$-QUIN where it is basically used only to reason over DL constraints.

This work was previously published in the International Journal on Semantic Web and Information Systems, Volume 7, Issue 3, edited by Amit P. Sheth,, pp. 1-22, copyright 2011 by IGI Publishing (an imprint of IGI Global).

Section 2
Reasoning and Ontology Development

Chapter 4
Semi–Automatic Ontology Construction by Exploiting Functional Dependencies and Association Rules

Luca Cagliero
Politecnico di Torino, Italy

Tania Cerquitelli
Politecnico di Torino, Italy

Paolo Garza
Politecnico di Milano, Italy

ABSTRACT

This paper presents a novel semi-automatic approach to construct conceptual ontologies over structured data by exploiting both the schema and content of the input dataset. It effectively combines two well-founded database and data mining techniques, i.e., functional dependency discovery and association rule mining, to support domain experts in the construction of meaningful ontologies, tailored to the analyzed data, by using Description Logic (DL). To this aim, functional dependencies are first discovered to highlight valuable conceptual relationships among attributes of the data schema (i.e., among concepts). The set of discovered correlations effectively support analysts in the assertion of the Tbox ontological statements (i.e., the statements involving shared data conceptualizations and their relationships). Then, the analyst-validated dependencies are exploited to drive the association rule mining process. Association rules represent relevant and hidden correlations among data content and they are used to provide valuable knowledge at the instance level. The pushing of functional dependency constraints into the rule mining process allows analysts to look into and exploit only the most significant data item recurrences in the assertion of the Abox ontological statements (i.e., the statements involving concept instances and their relationships).

DOI: 10.4018/978-1-4666-3610-1.ch004

INTRODUCTION

The outstanding growth of both context-aware environments and user-generated content coming from social network communities prompted the investigation of new ways to represent domain knowledge and its relationships. Semantic Web tools provide the instruments to significantly enrich the knowledge representation through a wide range of semantics-based models. These models, often called ontologies, support users in understanding the meaning of a resource and the related domain. Ontologies are fully comprehensive models for describing domain-specific knowledge. Knowledge representation entails (i) shared agreement of meaning, (ii) term disambiguation, and (iii) domain description through concepts and relationships. The contribution of both advanced data mining algorithms and semantics-based knowledge representation may enhance the knowledge discovery process in a broad range of application contexts, such as social behavior analysis, knowledge discovery from user-generated content, and Web service personalization.

Useful ontologies for a given application domain can be either provided by domain experts or (semi-)automatically inferred from the data of interest. Although the Semantic Web already provides a full technological stack to access semantics-based resources, most of the existing approaches, such as the creation of ontologies in a Web Ontology Language like the OWL (World Wide Web Consortium, 2009), still heavily rely on the human intervention. Hence, the machine-driven construction of meaningful ontologies is becoming an increasingly appealing target in several research fields, including information retrieval, data mining, and data summarization. For example, the exponential growth of social media like blogs and social network services has significantly increased the need of useful ontologies to efficiently support the analysis of large data volumes. Thus, novel and more efficient approaches to automatically construct useful ontologies tailored to the analyzed data are desirable.

This paper presents a novel and effective semi-automatic approach to construct ontologies tailored to structured data. Structured datasets are data collections whose content is organized by means of a schema that describes the relevant data features of interest. For instance, a relational dataset schema is characterized by a set of attributes which describes the main data features. Similarly, an XML dataset is characterized by a set of tags (elements). For the sake of simplicity, we will denote the data features belonging to the dataset schema as attributes in the rest of this paper for both relational and XML data. Ontology construction commonly entails a two-level analysis: (i) an intensional data analysis, to represent shared data concepts and their relationships, and (ii) an extensional data analysis, to represent instances of concepts (i.e., the individuals) and their associations. Different approaches can be used to model and represent ontologies. For instance, Description Logic (DL) (Baader, Calvanese, McGuinness, Nardi, & Patel-Schneider, 2003) can be profitably used to represent ontologies. Ontology representation based on Description Logic relies on two main components: (i) the Tbox component, which includes intensional statements about general concepts, and (ii) the Abox component, which includes both extensional statements about the individuals of those concepts and membership statements, which bind instances with their concepts.

To support domain experts in constructing meaningful ontologies, expressed by using the Description Logic and tailored to the input structured data, the DOnG (Dependency-driven Ontology Generator) framework has been designed and developed. It exploits two well-founded database and data mining techniques, i.e., functional dependency discovery and association rule mining. These techniques provide valuable correlations hidden in both the data schema and content. Although these correlations have not the semantic expressiveness of formal ontological statements, they may be used, in conjunction with a formal knowledge base representation (e.g., the Description Logic) to effectively support experts in ontology construction. Given a structured dataset, DOnG infers a Schema Ontology Graph, denoted as SOnG, through the discovery of functional dependencies holding in the schema of the analyzed data. The SOnG provides a graph-based representation of some of the hidden correlations among the attributes of the schema. Attributes are considered as the main concepts at the intensional level over which experts may assert meaningful Tbox ontological statements concerning the analyzed data (Baader et al., 2003). Since functional dependencies (Tan, Steinbach, & Kumar, 2006) represent tight correlations among sets of attributes, we exploit them to represent conceptual relationships among attributes (i.e., concepts). A functional dependency, written as $S_1 \Rightarrow S_2$, states that if, in a structured dataset characterized by a set of attributes $T=\{t_1, ..., t_n\}$, two data instances agree on the value of a set of attributes $S_1 \subseteq T$, then they must agree on the value of a set of attributes $S_2 \subseteq T$. We argue that a functional dependency models a conceptual relationship that is worth considering during the Tbox statement assertion. Next, driven by the analyst-validated dependencies, the DOnG framework analyzes the data content to discover the Schema Ontology Instance Graphs, denoted as SOnIG. A SOnIG is a graph composed of data item, i.e., pairs (attribute, value), linked by association rules. Association rules represent relevant but hidden correlations among data at the instance level. Among the set of discovered rules, the analyst may select and exploit most valuable ones to assert Abox ontological statements, i.e., assertions about individuals and their relationships. Individuals are represented by data items and rules suggest possibly relevant relations. Furthermore, the recurrent data items, i.e., the pairs (attribute, value), may suggest to the expert significant membership assertion (e.g., an individual is an instance of a given concept). The pushing of functional dependency constraints into

the rule mining step enables the efficient inference of an ontology instance graph at the data item granularity as well as eases domain expert validation by focusing the investigation on the most relevant item recurrences.

Experimental results, performed on both relational and XML datasets, show the effectiveness and the efficiency of the DOnG framework in supporting the semi-automatic construction of high-quality ontologies from the input data. Furthermore, to evaluate the usefulness of the generated ontologies, we exploited the discovered ontologies to drive the generalized itemset extraction process (Baralis, Cagliero, Cerquitelli, D'Elia, & Garza, 2010) that, otherwise, relies on a (wasteful) user-provided domain knowledge representation to discover high level patterns among data.

The paper is organized as follows. The section *Definitions and related notation* formalizes the problem addressed in this paper, while the section *The dependency-driven ontology generator* presents an overview of the DOnG framework and describes the main features of its building blocks. The section *Experimental results* discusses the experiments performed to validate the proposed approach. The section *Previous work* discusses related works and compares our approach with previous ones, while the section *Conclusions and Future work* draws conclusions and discusses future works.

DEFINITIONS AND RELATED NOTATION

In a given domain, an ontology is a formal knowledge representation that highlights the main concepts and the relationships among those concepts. In this paper, we focus on ontology construction from structured data.

A structured dataset is characterized by a schema (i.e., a set of conceptual features, also called attributes in the following) and a content (i.e., a set of instances). Let $T=\{t_1, ..., t_n\}$ be a set of attributes and $\Omega=\{\Omega_1, ..., \Omega_n\}$ be the corresponding attribute domains. An item is a pair $(t_i, value_i)$ which assigns value $value_i \in \Omega_n$ to attribute t_i. A structured dataset D is a collection of instances, where each instance is a set of items.

The process of ontology construction may be effectively supported by two database and data mining techniques, i.e., functional dependency discovery and association rule mining. In the following, we formally introduce both association rules and functional dependencies.

Association Rules

Itemsets and association rules describe the co-occurrence of data items in large data collections (Agrawal & Srikant, 1994). An itemset is a set of items. An itemset of length k is also called k-itemset. Furthermore, each itemset is usually characterized by the support quality index, which is its observed frequency in the source dataset.

Association rules (Agrawal & Srikant, 1994) are usually represented as implications $X \rightarrow Y$, where X and Y are arbitrary itemsets such that $X \cap Y = \varnothing$. The rule length is the length of $X \cup Y$. The quality of the rule is typically measured in terms of support and confidence quality indexes. The support of rule $X \rightarrow Y$ is equal to the support of the itemset $X \cup Y$ in the source dataset, while its confidence is the conditional probability of finding Y having found X and is given by

$\sup(X \cup Y)/\sup(X)$ where $\sup(X \cup Y)$ and $\sup(X)$ denote, respectively, the support of itemsets $X \cup Y$ and X.

Functional Dependencies

Different relationships may hold among data attributes. Functional dependencies, formally stated in the following definition, are a notable and widely established kind of attribute relationships.

Definition 1: *Functional dependency.* Let D be a structured dataset and let $T=\{t_1, ..., t_n\}$ be its attributes. Let $S_1 \subseteq T$ and $S_2 \subseteq T$ be two

subsets of attributes. D satisfies the functional dependency $S_1 \Rightarrow S_2$ if the following condition holds for every pair of instances r_1 and r_2 in D:

If $r_1.S_1 = r_2.S_1$, then $r_1.S_2 = r_2.S_2$

For example, consider a zoological dataset for biological classification storing all the information (e.g., the class, the discovery date) about all the species belonging to the animal kingdom discovered in the last five centuries. A functional dependency may hold from the specie (e.g., lions) to class (e.g., mammals) attributes as it holds a is-a relationship among these concepts. In Kivinen and Mannila (1995), approximate functional dependencies have been also proposed. They represent functional dependencies that almost hold. Their definition is based on the minimum number of records that needs to be removed from the relation D for the dependency $S_1 \Rightarrow S_2$ to hold in D. The number of records that needs to be removed is represented by the error measure (or by the opposite measure, called strength). The error $\epsilon(S_1 \Rightarrow S_2)$ (Huhtala, Karkkainen, Porkka, & Toivonen, 1999) should be defined as in Definition 2.

Definition 2: *Dependency error.* Let D be a structured dataset and $T=\{t_1, ..., t_n\}$ be its attributes. Let $S_1 \subseteq T$ and $S_2 \subseteq T$ be two subsets of attributes in D. The dependency error $\epsilon(S_1 \Rightarrow S_2)$ of the dependency $S_1 \Rightarrow S_2$, is defined as:

$\epsilon(S_1 \Rightarrow S_2) = \min\{|R| \mid R \subseteq D \wedge S_1 \Rightarrow S_2 \text{ holds in } D \backslash R\}/|D|$

Corollary 1: *Dependency strength.* Let D be a structured dataset and let $S_1 \subseteq T$ and $S_2 \subseteq T$ be two sets of attributes in D. The dependency strength $st(S_1 \Rightarrow S_2)$ of a dependency $S_1 \Rightarrow S_2$ is defined as:

$st(S_1 \Rightarrow= 1 - \epsilon(S_1 \Rightarrow S_2) \text{ S2})$

The dependency error $\epsilon(S_1 \Rightarrow S_2)$ has a natural interpretation as the fraction of records with exceptions affecting dependency $S_1 \Rightarrow S_2$. The strength measure represents the opposite information with respect to dependency error. When the strength measure is equal to 100% the dependency holds on the whole dataset, i.e., a functional dependency holds.

The definition of approximate functional dependency (Huhtala et al., 1999; Kivinen & Mannila, 1995) follows.

Definition 3: *Approximate functional dependency.* Let D be a structured dataset and $T=\{t_1, ..., t_n\}$ be its attributes. Let $S_1 \subseteq T$ and $S_2 \subseteq T$ be two sets of attributes in D. An approximate functional dependency is an implication in the form $S_1 \Rightarrow S_2$, such that

1. $S_1 \subseteq T$ and $S_2 \subseteq T$
2. $S_1 \cap S_2 = \varnothing$
3. $st(S_1 \Rightarrow S_2) < 1$

An approximate dependency satisfies a minimum strength threshold *min_st* if its strength is higher than *min_st*. Usually, only functional dependencies and approximate functional dependencies satisfying *min_st* are considered. The dependencies characterized by a dependency strength value lower than the threshold are usually not of interest as they do not represent schema correlations holding on the majority of the data.

Dependencies and association rules can be exploited to provide to analysts information useful for semi-automatic ontology construction. In this paper, two graph-based representations of the most significant correlations holding among the schema and the content of the analyzed data, i.e., the schema ontology graph and the schema ontology instance graph, are proposed and exploited to support the expert in ontology construction. Their definitions follow.

Schema Ontology Graph

A schema ontology O is a graph-based representation of the (approximate) dependencies holding in a structured dataset and their strengths. Its definition follows.

Definition 4: *Schema Ontology Graph (SOnG).* Let D be a structured dataset and $T=\{t_1, ..., t_n\}$ be its attributes. Let *min_st* be a minimum dependency strength threshold. A SOnG O is an oriented graph $\Gamma=<T, E^*>$, whose nodes are $t_i \in T$. An oriented edge $e_{ik} = (t_i, t_k) \in E^*$ represents a functional dependency or an approximate functional dependency satisfying *min_st* that holds from t_i to t_k and is labeled with a weight $w_{ik} = st(t_i \Rightarrow t_k)$.

Graph nodes are attributes while edges represent dependencies, eventually approximate, holding among couples of attributes. Edge weights take values in the range (0,1] and represent the attribute dependency strength, i.e., the fraction of instances for which each dependency holds. Figure 1 shows an example of a simplified SOnG obtained by enforcing a minimum dependency strength equal to 95%, i.e., only the edges that correspond to dependencies characterized by a dependency strength higher than 95% are included in the SOnG reported in Figure 1. It concerns a portion of the (simplified) DBLP XML dataset (Ley, 2005), which collects information about conference proceedings. For instance, the concept *Author name* may be meaningfully associated with the author *Affiliation* (each authors is related to an affiliation or a set of affiliations in some cases).

Schema Ontology Instance Graph

Given a SOnG built over the data schema, the corresponding graph at the data item level could be defined. We propose a graph-based representation, namely the SOnIG (Schema Ontology Instance Graph), of the correlations holding among couples

Figure 1. A simplified SonG built over the example DBLP XML attributes

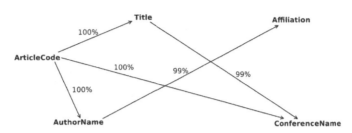

of items, belonging to the structured dataset D, such that their corresponding attributes are (approximately) functionally dependent in D. A more formal definition follows.

Definition 5: *Schema Ontology Instance Graph (SOnIG).* Let $T=\{t_1, …, t_n\}$ be the attributes which describe a structured dataset D and let I be the set of all data items in D. Let $O = <T, E^*>$ be a SOnG built over D. Let Φ: $E^* \to R$ be an application that maps each oriented edge $e_{ik} = (t_i, t_k) \in E^*$ to the set R_{ij} of 2-length association rules $(t_i, value_i) \to (t_j, value_j)$ holding from items belonging to attribute t_i to items belonging to attribute t_j. The schema ontology instance graph is an oriented graph $\Theta= <I, \Phi(E^*)>$ whose nodes are distinct data items in D and the oriented edges represent association rules holding between couples of items. An oriented edge from item $(t_i, value_i)$ to item $(t_j, value_j)$ is weighted by the confidence of the corresponding association rule $(t_i, value_i) \to (t_j, value_j)$.

Starting from the structured dataset D and a SOnG O (cf. Definition 4), the SOnIG is constructed by representing data items in D and the association rules involving couples of items belonging to (approximately) functionally dependent attributes. The SOnIG edge weight, i.e., the rule confidence, represents the strength of the correlations among data items. To extract the SOnIG we exploit the association rule mining (Agrawal &

Srikant, 1994) without enforcing any mining constraint (i.e., absolute minimum support threshold = 1 and minimum confidence = 0%). Since we are looking for association rules between couples of items we only mine 2-length rules.

Figure 2 shows a portion of SOnIG built over the example DBLP XML dataset (Figure 4). The edge between {(*Author name, Rossi*)} and {(*Affiliation, Politecnico di Torino*)} is weighted by 78% because the confidence of the rule {(*Author name, Rossi*)} → {(*Affiliation, Politecnico di Torino*)} is 78%. Notice that, according to Definition 5, an oriented edge between two data items is omitted if the attributes of the corresponding items are not dependent, e.g., the edge directed from {(*Author name, Rossi*)} to (*Title, A performance evaluation for …*).

In this paper, we propose a novel framework, namely DOnG, that extracts both SOnGs (cf. Definition 4) and SOnIGs (cf. Definition 5) from structured datasets to support analysts in the construction of meaningful ontologies.

THE DEPENDENCY-DRIVEN ONTOLOGY GENERATOR

This section describes the DOnG (Dependency-driven Ontology Generator) framework, which entails ontology construction from structured data supported by a two-step mining process, which entails: (i) approximate functional dependency discovery, and (ii) association rule mining.

Figure 2. An example of the SOnIG over some DBLP XML records enriched with confidence values

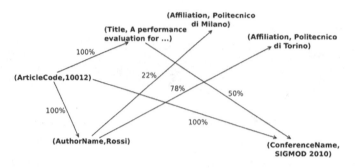

Figure 3. The DOnG framework

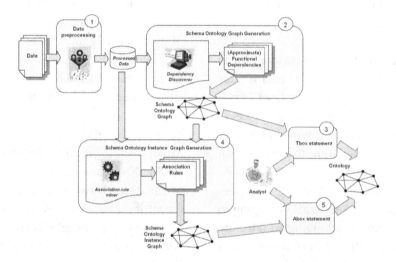

Figure 4. A simplified labeled tree of a portion of the example DBLP XML document

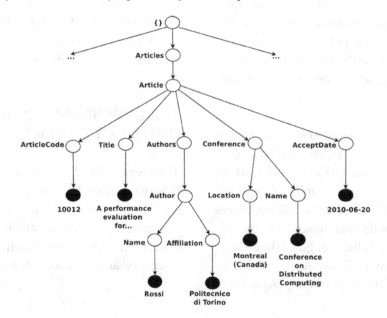

Figure 3 shows the building blocks of the DOnG framework, which addresses the semi-automatic construction of a meaningful ontology, expressed by the Description Logic, tailored to the input data. Description Logic (Baader et al., 2003) formalizes the ontology representation in terms of a set of shared concepts and their relationships. It includes two distinct parts: (i) the Tbox, which includes a finite set of assertions about shared primitive concepts, inferred from the data of interest, and the binary relations among them, and (ii) the Abox, which includes membership assertions (e.g., an individual is an instance of a given concept) as well as extensional statements about the concept instances (belonging to the analyzed data) and their relationships.

In DOnG, the Tbox and Abox statement assertion steps are fully supported by an ad-hoc mining process. The mining process makes use of a two-step analysis: (i) functional dependency discovery from the data schema (i.e., the attribute level), and (ii) association rule mining from the data instances (i.e., the item level). The first step of the mining process supports the construction of the Tbox part of the ontology representation, while the second one supports the Abox construction step. Functional dependencies and approximate functional dependencies are discovered and represented in a graph-based model, i.e., the SOnG (cf. Definition 4). The generated model is validated by the analyst and it is used to semi-automatically generate the Tbox component of the description logic based ontology representation. In particular, the analyst selects the dependencies that are worth considering in the Tbox construction phase. Validated dependencies are then used to drive the rule mining process at the item level. This enables the generation of a reduced amount of relevant rules, thus, easing the analyst validation of the extracted recurrences. Association rules and related data items are represented in a graph-based model, i.e., SOnIGs (cf. Definition 5), which effectively support the analysts during the Abox generation phase. In particular, each rule is a potential statement in the defined Abox.

Data Preprocessing

The DOnG addresses ontology construction from structured data. A structured dataset is a dataset characterized by a schema, which describes its main data features. Most common examples of structured data are the relational and the XML data. A relational dataset is described by a set of attributes, while an XML dataset is organized by a set of tags. To enable both functional dependency discovery and association rule mining from generic structured data, the DOnG framework requires a preprocessing step to make data suitable for the mining process. Since the application of the aforementioned data mining techniques to relational data is straightforward (Agrawal & Srikant, 1994; Huhtala et al., 1999), in this section we mainly focus on describing how to make XML data suitable for both functional dependency and association rule discovery.

Most of the well-founded models proposed in the past, for example, OEM (Papakonstantinou, Garcia-Molina, & Widom, 1995), UnQL (Buneman, Davidson, Hillebrand, & Suciu, 1996), GraphLog (Consens & Mendelzon, 1990), and G-Log (Paredaens, Peelman, & Tanca, 1995), lend themselves to represent XML data by graphs whose nodes denote either objects (i.e., abstract entities) or values (i.e., primitive values), while edges represent relationships between them. According to Damiani, Oliboni, Quintarelli, and Tanca (2003), we represent an XML document as a labeled tree, as stated in Definition 6. Note that XML documents are here tree-like structures (and not generic graphs) because, following the so-called literal semantics, we do not interpret referencing attributes as pointers.

Definition 6: *XML document.* An XML document is a labeled tree $<N, E, r>$, such that:

- N is the set of nodes;
- $r \in N$ is the root of the tree (i.e., the root of the XML document);
- E is the set of undirected edges.

Figure 4 reports a portion of the DBLP XML document represented as a tree-based structure (with the considered labels for nodes and edges). It will be used as running example in the rest of the paper. The XML document reports information about a number of conference proceedings. Each article is characterized by its code, title, authors' name and affiliation, acceptance date, conference name, and location. Attributes and elements are characterized by empty circles, whereas the textual content of the elements and the attribute values are reported as black-filled circles. The node labeled as { } is the root of the XML document. The labeled tree rooted in the Article node is an example of conference proceeding. In general, the elements may be connected to either their sub-elements, attributes, or leaf node, while the attribute nodes may be connected to leaf nodes that represent their corresponding attribute values.

Moreover, the following two properties regarding graph nodes and edges hold: (1) Each node n_i has a tuple of labels $NL_i = <Ntag_i, Ntype_i, Ncontent_i>$. The label type $Ntype_i$ indicates whether the node is a root, an element, a text, or an attribute, whereas the label $Ncontent_i$ can assume as value a PCDATA (PCDATA is a reserved keyword which stands for Parsed Character Data and indicates a generic plain text) or $\perp$ (undefined, for nonterminals). (2) Each edge $e_j = <(n_h, n_k), EL_j>$, with n_h and n_k in N, has a label $EL_j = <Etype_j>$, $Etype_j \in$ {*attribute of*, *sub-element of*}.

Since our focus is to find correlations among elementary values of the XML documents, and such values may occur as either textual content of leaf elements or attribute values, we only consider a single node type and we do not specify any type label. In the following, we define the notion of item in the XML data format.

Definition 7: *XML document item.* Let $<N, E, r>$ be an XML document and $r_r \in N$ be the root of the corresponding document. An item is a couple (*attribute, value*) that could be represented in the XML document $<N, E,$

$r>$ as a path connecting a direct descendant $n_{dr} \in N$ of the root r_r to a leaf, i.e., a terminal node $n_n \in N$. The path corresponds to an item such that:

1. *Attribute* is the label of the element with a content rooted in n_{dr} and defined as a sub-path from n_{dr} to the element.
2. *Value* is the content of the considered element.

Consider again the example DBLP XML dataset reported in Figure 4. Suppose to set the node labeled as Articles as root of the dataset instances. An example of item is the couple (*Article Title, A performance evaluation of ...*) which identifies a sub-path connecting node labeled as *Article* to the element node labeled as *Title*.

XML documents can be analyzed by different data mining techniques, such as association rule extraction (Augurusa, Braga, Campi, & Ceri, 2003) and taxonomy inference (Clifton, Cooley, & Rennie, 2004), and data summarization (Baralis, Garza, Quintarelli, & Tanca, 2007), to discover interesting recurrences among data items. To exploit well-known techniques proposed for relational datasets, the XML document is usually transformed in a relational dataset as stated by the following definition.

Definition 8: *XML in the relation data format.* Let $<N, E, r>$ be an XML document and $r_r \in N$ be a root of the corresponding document. Let $T=\{t_1, ..., t_n\}$ be the set of attributes. A relational representation of the XML document is a collection of instances, where each instance r is a set of items $\{(t_1, value_1), ..., (t_n, value_n)\}$ in $<N, E, r>$.

To transform an XML document into the corresponding relational format, we follow an approach similar to that proposed in Baralis et al. (2007). However, we generate a relational representation while the authors of Baralis et al.

(2007) transform each XML document into a transactional dataset. We first select as instance root n_{dr} the appropriate node in the labeled tree representing the XML document. Items are couples of $(t_i, value_i)$, where the attribute t_i is the label of an element with a content rooted in the instance root and defined as a complete sub-path from the root to the element, while $value_i$ is the content of the considered element. Each subtree, rooted in n_{dr}, defines an instance in the XML dataset.

Consider again the example DBLP XML dataset. The corresponding relational dataset is a set of per-author article records, each one composed of a set of items describing, for a specific author, a published proceeding. The corresponding relation achieved by tailoring the XML data to the relational data format is the following.

DBLP(Article code, Author name, Title, Conference name, Conference location, Author affiliation)

in which the pair (*Article code, Author name*) represents the primary key of the relation.

The $(t_i, value_i)$ representation for data items yields a single item when the XML element contains a single data value and when it has a textual content. Even in the case in which the textual content can be considered as a multiple value element (e.g., the article author may assume multiple values), data preprocessing yields a single data value to preserve the relational data schema (cf. Definition 8). The presence of multiple value elements may produce a set of records each one involving distinct single item values. To reduce side effects due to multiple values and textual data noise, textual elements may be preprocessed by performing stopword elimination (i.e., elimination of very frequent and noisy words such as articles) and stemming (i.e., reduction of words to their semantic stem) (Porter, 1980, 1997). Both operations are commonly performed in textual data management.

Schema Ontology Graph Generation

The aim of this block is to build a SOnG based on the schema of the input structured dataset to effectively support the analyst in the Tbox ontological statement assertion. Since our challenge is to figure out shared data concepts and their relationships we exploit data attributes belonging to the schema as potentially relevant concepts and the notion of approximate functional dependencies (Tan, Steinbach, & Kumar, 2006) (cf. Definition 3) to highlight tight correlations among attributes.

The SOnG generation block of the DOnG framework takes in input both the preprocessed structured dataset and a minimum dependency strength (cf. Definition 1), and generates a schema ontology graph (cf. Definition 4) over the schema of the analyzed data. To this aim, three main steps are performed:

- **Functional Dependency and Approximate Functional Dependency Discovery:** To discover functional and approximate functional dependencies we exploit the traditional TANE algorithm (Huhtala et al., 1999), which is a level-wise algorithm in which, at the k-th iteration, dependencies involving attribute sets of size at most equal to k are considered. A brief overview of the adopted approach (Huhtala et al., 1999) is reported in the following. Nevertheless, the proposed DOnG framework enables users to easily integrate diverse algorithms as well.

- **Analyst Validation:** The analyst validates the inferred dependencies and selects the most relevant ones for the ontology Tbox construction process. The domain expert is in charge of discriminating among relevant data attributes and functional dependencies holding among them and, eventually, pruning uninteresting ones.

- **SOnG Building:** This step generates a SOnG (Schema Ontology Graph) according to Definition 4. It includes each validated dependency as an edge connecting two data attributes (i.e., the SOnG nodes). Nodes are the selected attributes while the oriented edges represent dependencies among schema concepts that are worth considering from the analyst's point of view. An edge connecting two arbitrary nodes is weighted by the strength of the approximate functional dependency between the corresponding nodes. The higher is the dependency strength (cf. Definition 1) the higher is the correlation strength in the source dataset.

Consider again the previous example, and suppose that, by enforcing a minimum dependency strength threshold equal to 80%, the set of approximate dependencies reported in Table 1 is discovered from the example dataset. Remember that a dependency strength equal to 100% implies that the approximate dependencies always holds in the source dataset (i.e., it is a functional dependency).

Consider now the last approximate dependency *Title ⤳ Author affiliation* with strength equal to 90% reported in Table 1. It highlights a correlation that might be of minor interest from the domain expert point of view. Expert pruning may discard the uninteresting dependency *Title ⤳ Author affiliation* discovered from *D*. Since an early dependency filtering based on minimum dependency strength threshold *min_st* has been enforced, the analyst may also vary the mining constraint (e.g., by setting a higher minimum strength threshold) to tailor the discovered dependency set to his actual needs. An experimental analysis on the impact of the maximum dependency strength threshold is reported in the section *Experimental results*.

Table 1. Discovered dependencies from a portion of DBLP XML dataset

Num	Dependency	Strength (%)
1	*Article code ⤳ Title*	100
2	*Article code ⤳ Conference name*	100
3	*Article code ⤳ Author name*	100
4	*Author name ⤳ Author affiliation*	99
5	*Title ⤳ Conference name*	99
6	*Title ⤳Author affiliation*	90

The schema ontology graph obtained after the expert validation of the approximate dependencies in Table 1 is reported in Figure 1.

The TANE algorithm (Huhtala et al., 1999), whose pseudo code is reported in Algorithm 1, searches for approximate dependencies that (i) Satisfy the minimum strength threshold *min_st*, and (ii) are minimal (i.e., the right-hand side attribute set is not functional dependent with any subset of the left-hand side set). TANE is a level-wise algorithm in which, at iteration k, dependencies having the left-hand size in L_{k-1} are computed (line 5). A level L_k is a collection of attribute sets of size k. Then, the minimality property and the minimum strength threshold are exploited to prune L_k and, thus, avoid exhaustive lattice exploring. Finally, level L_{k+1} is generated starting from L_k (line 7).

To discover functional dependencies that involve just single attributes at both the left-hand and the right-hand dependency side, the iterative procedure described above is stopped when iteration $k = 2$ is completed. Thus, the redundant knowledge extraction is prevented.

Schema Ontology Instance Graph Generation

The last step of the DOnG framework entails the generation of the SOnIG (Schema Ontology Instance Graph) built over the analyzed data (cf.

Algorithm 1. The TANE algorithm

Require: relation D over schema R, minimum strength threshold *min_st*
Ensure: minimum not trivial approximate functional dependencies that hold in D 1: $L_0 = \varnothing$
2: $L_1 = \{\{A\} \mid A \in R\}$
3: $k = 1$
4: **while** $L_k \neq \varnothing$ **do**
5: compute Dependencies(L_k, D)
6: prune(L_k, *min_st*)
7: $L_{k+1} =$ generate Next Level(L_k, D)
8: $k = k + 1$
9: end while

10: return L

Definition 5), which might be profitably exploited to drive both the Abox ontological statement assertion and the data mining and knowledge discovery process (see the section *Application scenario*). To this aim, it takes in input the preprocessed structured dataset D (see the section *Data preprocessing*), and the SOnG (Schema Ontology Graph) O. It produces a SOnIG (cf. Definition 5) by performing 2-length association rule mining driven by the previously extracted and validated schema dependencies.

Algorithm 2 reports the pseudo-code of the SOnIG mining step of the DOnG framework. It adopts an Apriori-like approach to frequent itemset mining (Agrawal & Srikant, 1994). The traditional Apriori-like miner iteratively generates

Algorithm 2. Schema Ontology Instance Graph extraction

Require: SOnG O, structured dataset D
Ensure: SOnIG Θ
1: $L_1 =$ set of items in D
2: $L_2 =$ itemset generation(L_1, O) {/* 2-itemset generation */}
3: scan D and count support for each $c \in L_2$
4: *Rules* = rule generation(L_1, L_2)
5: **for all** r in *Rules* **do**
6: **if** expertvalidation(r) = 'discard rule' **then**
7: remove r from *Rules*
8: end if
9: end for
10: $\Theta =$ buildSchemaOntologyInstanceGraph(*Rules*, O)

11: return Θ

---

frequent itemsets by following a level-wise approach. First, it extracts itemsets of length k and then itemsets of length $k + 1$ by combining frequent k-itemsets. Finally, association rules are mined from the set of frequent itemsets.

Since only rules that involve couples of items are needed to generate the SOnIG, and in particular only those rules that are instances of the SOnG (cf. Definition 5), Algorithm 2 extracts only items (line 1) and 2-itemsets (lines 2-3). Hence, differently from traditional Apriori-like algorithms (Agrawal & Srikant, 1994), a constraint on the maximum length of the mined itemsets is enforced. By exploiting 1-itemsets and 2-itemsets, only those 2-length rules that are instances of SOnG are mined (line 4).

To check their semantic soundness, the analyst may look into the content of the extracted rules and, possibly, discard uninteresting ones (lines 5-9).

For instance, suppose now that both rules $X = \{(Article\ code, 10012)\} \rightarrow \{(Title, A\ performance\ evaluation\ for ...)\}$ and $Z = \{(Author\ name, Rossi)\} \rightarrow \{(Author\ affiliation, Politecnico\ di\ Torino)\}$ are frequent and their corresponding dependencies have been validated by the analyst. Since they are both instances of the SOnG (Figure 1), they are extracted and validated by the analyst.

After the expert validation step, only validated rules are included into Rules. Selected rules are exploited to represent the output SOnIG Θ related to SOnG O and the source dataset D. The SOnIG building phase (line 10) generates a valid SOnIG, according to Definition 5. It includes each validated rule as an instance of a relationship (i.e., an oriented edge) among data items belonging to the rules (i.e., SOnG nodes). Consider again rule $X = \{(Article\ code, 10012)\} \rightarrow \{(Title, A\ performance\ evaluation\ for ...)\}$. By looking into the SOnG reported in Figure 1, the attribute node *Article code* is connected to node *Title* through an oriented edge. Thus, the corresponding edge is included into the SOnIG as reported in Figure 2, and represents the rule X.

The generated SOnIG is used by the expert during the Abox ontology construction. More specifically, data items belonging to the SOnIG may suggest to the expert possibly relevant membership statements (e.g., *10012* is an instance of the *article code*) while validated association rules may prompt the assertion of extensional statements (e.g., the article code 10012 is associated with the article title "A performance evaluation for ...").

EXPERIMENTAL RESULTS

To evaluate the proposed approach, we addressed the following issues: (i) the quality of the extracted knowledge through domain expert validation, (ii) the effect of the minimum functional dependency strength on the ontology construction process, and (iii) the applicability of the proposed approach to a business-oriented application context.

Experiments have been performed on 3.0 GHz Pentium IV system with 4 GB RAM, running Ubuntu 2.6. For rule mining we exploited our implementation of the Apriori mining algorithm (Agrawal & Srikant, 1994), while for the approximate dependency discovery we exploited a public available version of Tane (Huhtala et al., 1999).

Both relational and XML datasets have been used to validate the proposed approach. Table 2 describes the five datasets considered in our experiments. The first dataset has been generated by means of the TPC-H synthetic generator (TPC, 2005). It consists of a suite of business oriented ad-hoc queries tailored to the relational data format. By varying the scale factor parameter, datasets with different sizes can be generated. We generated a dataset with scale factor equal to 1.0 and we focused our analysis on the Part table. Furthermore, we considered two real-life XML datasets coming from an American research project (American University Courses Datasets, http://www.cs.washington.edu/research/projects/xmltk/xmldata/www/repository.html). Finally, two real-life relational datasets have been retrieved from the UCI Machine Learning Repository (Blake & Merz, 2010).

Domain Expert Validation

The assessment of the quality of the extracted knowledge is in charge of domain experts. In this section, we evaluate discovered dependencies and rules through expert validation.

Consider the UCI Zoo dataset (Blake & Merz, 2010) firstly. It is a simple database which contains 17 boolean-valued attributes about 7 classes of animals. The 18-th *type* attribute is typically exploited as class attribute for classification. By enforcing a minimum dependency strength equal to 85% the TANE algorithm comes by a relevant set of meaningful approximate dependencies. Table 3 reports a selection of the 14 most interesting approximate dependencies among the 39 ones discovered from Zoo. They have been selected by the expert as valuable dependencies to consider during the ontological Tbox statement assertion.

Nevertheless, some misleading dependencies are discovered as well. Domain experts are in charge of checking the soundness of the discovered dependencies and prune the uninteresting ones.

Table 2. Dataset characteristics

Source Name	Dataset	File Size	Description
TPC-H	Part	59 MB	Part table (1.0 scale factor), 12 attributes, 100,000 instances
UCI	Zoo Breast Cancer	10 KB 20 KB	18 attributes, 101 instances 32 attributes, 569 instances
University XML	Reed Wsu	278 KB 1.6 MB	12 attributes and 13,359 instances 16 attributes and 90,254 instances

Table 3. Discovered dependencies from the UCI Zoo dataset

Num	Dependency	Strength (%)
1	Type ↝ Milk	100
2	Type ↝ Backbone	100
3	Type ↝ Feathers	100
4	Animal name ↝ Type	99
5	Type ↝ Toothed	98
6	Milk ↝ Eggs	97
7	Eggs ↝ Milk	97
8	Type ↝ Eggs	97
9	Type ↝ Fins	96
10	Type ↝ Breathes	96
11	Legs ↝ Backbone	95
12	Type ↝ Hair	94
13	Type ↝ Tail	92
14	Tail ↝ Backbone	90

For instance, although the dependency *Milk ↝ Hair* is characterized by a dependency strength equal to 97%, it highlights a dependency between the animal characteristics of being hairy and milk-producing that seems to be not semantically relevant. Similarly, both the dependencies *Tails ↝ Backbone* and *Backbone ↝ Tail* are discovered. However, since the tail could be considered as a backbone extension, only the first one highlights a meaningful relationship. This dependency may prompt the expert to assert the following two Tbox statements "An animal with the backbone is-a an animal with the tail" and "An animal without the backbone is-a an animal without the tail".

A portion of a simplified schema ontology graph generated from the UCI Zoo dataset is reported in Figure 5.

Once the SOnG is generated, the corresponding SOnIG is generated by means of association rule mining. Frequent rules matching the selected functional dependencies are validated by the analyst. Consider, for example, the following representative rules conformed to the functional dependency *Type ↝ Tail*.

1. $\{(Type, Insect)\} \rightarrow \{(Tail, False)\}$, sup=7.9%, conf=100%
2. $\{(Type, Mammals)\} \rightarrow \{(Tail, True)\}$, sup=34.6%, conf=85.3%
3. $\{(Type, Mammals)\} \rightarrow \{(Tail, False)\}$, sup=5.9%, conf=14.7%

By analyzing rule (1), which is characterized by a confidence equal to 100%, the analyst could argue that aggregate insects, i.e., the item (*Type, Insect*), in the higher level set of the animals without the tail, i.e., the item (*Tail, False*), is sound as all insects are, actually, without tail. Thus, the relationship between the two individuals suggests the meaningful Abox assertion "Animals of type insects is-a Animals with no tail". Furthermore, the meaningful membership assertion "Insect is an instance of Animal Type" should be stated as well. Differently, the analyst will probably remove the last two rules, since they do not provide relevant domain knowledge. In fact, it is not reasonable to associate mammals with either the class of animals with tail or the class of animals without tail. In fact, 85.3% of mammals have a tail, while the remaining 14.7% have not. By removing the last two rules, the schema ontology instance graph does not include any edge between the items (*Type, Mammals*) and (*Tail, True*) or between (*Type, Mammals*) and (*Tail, False*) anymore.

By enforcing a minimum dependency strength equal to 90%, also the other tested datasets produce relevant domain knowledge. In Tables 4 and 5 a selection of the most interesting approximate dependencies discovered, respectively, from Breast Cancer Wisconsin, Reed, and Wsu datasets, is reported.

The UCI Breast Cancer Wisconsin dataset attributes are computed from a digitized image of a fine needle aspirate (FNA) of a breast mass. They describe the characteristics of the cell nuclei shown by the image. The class attribute assigns each image to a tumor class (malignant or benign). Since some peculiar characteristics of the tumor cell (e.g., the uniformity of the cell size and shape)

Figure 5. A simplified SonG over some Zoo attributes

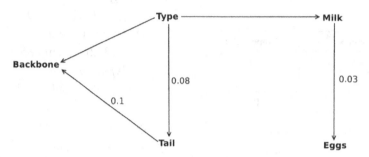

are relevant indicators of membership to a tumor class, they have been selected as relevant dependencies by the domain expert (Table 4).

The Reed and Wsu datasets collect information about university courses. Dependency 1 in Table 5 has been discovered from both Reed and Wsu dataset, dependency 2 from the Wsu dataset only, while dependencies 3 and 4 from the Reed dataset only. Dependencies selected by the analyst allow binding the concept of course code to a specific course title, which, in turn, may be further aggregated in the (more general) subject. The course title may be associated with a specific learning unit, in which lectures of different subjects may be given, or, alternatively, with a specific credit amount.

Consider now the TPC-H Part dataset. By enforcing a minimum dependency strength equal to 99% the approximate dependencies reported in Table 6 are discovered. The exact functional dependency *Brand ⤳ Manufacturer* (i.e., dependency strength equal to 100%) suggests the sound relationship between the product brand and its manufacturer. The analyst may deduce the meaningful Tbox ontological assertion "A product brand is relative to a manufacturer" and their corresponding Abox assertions about its instances. Even the approximate dependency *Partname ⤳ Type* may highlight an interesting correlation since the type values may recall the product name. The expert validation step is performed before the schema ontology instance graph generation. If the soundness of the corresponding instances is

Table 4. Discovered dependencies from the UCI Breast Cancer dataset

Num	Dependency	Strength (%)
1	*Cell size uniformity ⤳ Tumor class*	93
2	*Cell shape uniformity ⤳ Tumor class*	92
3	*Bland chromatin ⤳ Tumor class*	91

Table 5. Discovered dependencies from the Reed and Wsu datasets

Num	Dependency	Strength (%)
1	*Registration number ⤳ Course title*	99 (Reed), 95 (Wsu)
2	*Course title ⤳ Credits*	95 (Wsu)
3	*Course title ⤳ Subject*	94 (Reed)
4	*Course title ⤳ Learning unit*	94 (Reed)

Table 6. Discovered dependencies from the TPC-H Part dataset

Num	Dependency	Strength (%)
1	*Brand ⤳ Manufacturer*	100
2	*Partname ⤳ Manufacturer*	99
3	*Partname ⤳ Brand*	99
4	*Partname ⤳ Type*	99
5	*Partname ⤳ Size*	99
6	*Partname ⤳ Container*	99
7	*Partname ⤳ Price*	99
8	*Partname ⤳ Comment*	99

verified all over the input dataset, the discovered dependency is validated accordingly. The remaining dependencies in Table 6 are considered as less interesting by the domain expert and, thus, they are discarded.

Effect of the Minimum Dependency Strength

To investigate the performance of the schema ontology generation algorithm, we analyzed the impact of the minimum dependency strength threshold on the number of discovered dependencies. Figure 6 reports, for each considered dataset, the corresponding curve.

The analyzed datasets (cf. Table 2) are representatives of different dataset sizes and item distributions. All the tested datasets highlight a manageable amount of approximate dependencies. As expected, though a reduced number of exact dependencies (i.e., dependency strength 100%) is discovered, in most cases the dependency set

cardinality scales more linearly with the minimum dependency strength (Figures 6(b), 6(c), and 6(e)). However, in a few cases the cardinality of the mined set is weakly affected by the minimum dependency strength threshold (Figures 6(a) and 6(d)). The impact of the minimum dependency strength actually depends on the data item distribution.

Domain experts may look into the discovered dependencies and, possibly, tune the minimum dependency strength threshold with the aim at tailoring the mined set to their actual needs.

Application Scenario

An ontology is a knowledge representation that models the main concepts and their relationships.

In the following, we propose an application scenario in which the DOnG framework may be profitably exploited in a business-oriented environment. A data mining algorithm that heavily relies on a user-provided domain knowledge representation

Figure 6. Number of discovered approximate dependencies by varying the minimum dependency strength threshold

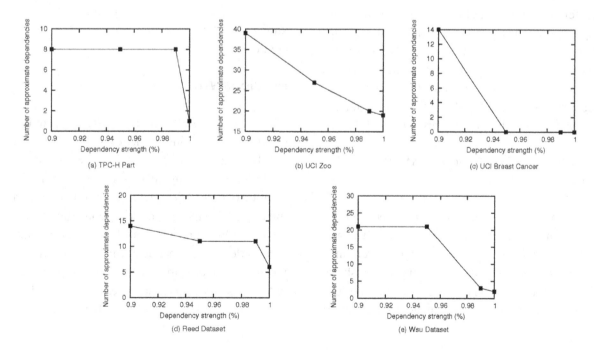

has been recently proposed in Baralis et al. (2010). It addresses generalized itemset mining (Srikant & Agrawal., 1995), which extends the traditional frequent itemset mining proposed in Agrawal and Srikant (1994) by exploiting a high level abstraction of the mined patterns to prevent relevant knowledge pruning. By evaluating a hierarchical set of aggregations built over data items (i.e., a tree-based schema ontology instance graph), items can be aggregated based on different granularity concepts (generalized items). Each generalized itemset, which is a high level representation of a set of lower level itemsets, can be used both to (i) give a higher level view of patterns hidden in the analyzed data, and (ii) represent knowledge pruned by discarding infrequent lower level itemsets.

However, domain experts are typically asked to build meaningful hierarchical aggregations over the data items from scratch. Hierarchies among data items are examples of simplified ontologies. Manual generation of ad-hoc aggregation hierarchies (ontologies) is often subject to errors and inconsistencies (Maedche & Staab, 2001) due to (i) data sparsity, (ii) limited analyst experience, or (iii) limited time available for context learning and data processing. Indeed, the semi-automatic generation of meaningful hierarchies of data item aggregations is desirable. Hierarchical aggregations may be discovered by the DOnG framework. The analyst could exploit part of the generated SOnIG to drive the generalization process over data items. Consider the following 3-itemset extracted from the TPC-H Part dataset (Table 2):

$$X = \{(Brand, 13), (Container, SM\_PKG), (Size, 1)\}, \text{sup}=0.03\%$$

It provides relevant business-oriented information concerning transport of products of a specific brand. However, mining such a pattern may require enforcing a very low support threshold. This task may become unfeasible or could lead to the extraction of an unmanageable amount of patterns. Suppose to enforce a minimum support threshold $min\_sup=0.05\%$. Since the above pattern is infrequent, it is not extracted. By considering the exact functional dependency *Brand ⇝ Manufacturer* extracted from the TPC-H Part dataset (Table 6) the DOnG framework may generate the corresponding schema ontology instance graph over data items, which, in turn, can be exploited to drive the generalization process over item (*Brand*, *13*). The soundness of the generated SOnIG is validated by a domain expert. The generalization process over itemset X produces the following generalized patterns Y:

$$Y = \{(ManufacturerID, 1), (Container, SM\_PKG), (Size, 1)\}, \text{sup}=0.08\%$$

The brand is generalized into its corresponding manufacturer. Since the pattern is a higher level aggregation of the knowledge represented by itemset X, it is characterized by a higher support. Note that the generalized itemset becomes frequent with respect to the minimum support threshold.

The semi-automatic generation of data item hierarchies selected from the generated SOnIG may effectively drive the process of generalized itemset mining. The generated pattern may enable knowledge discovery in a number of different application contexts.

Previous Work

Ontologies support users and systems in understanding the meaning of the resources of interest and the related domain. Hence, they are frequently exploited by intelligent systems. However, the creation of ontologies heavily relies on the human intervention. Hence, ontology construction remains a tedious and hard task that can easily result in a bottleneck (Maedche & Staab, 2001). Thus, the automatic or semi-automatic construction of ontologies is becoming an increasingly appealing target in several research fields. However, to the best of our knowledge, a few approaches have been proposed to address automatic, or semi-automatic, ontology construction.

Maedche and Staab (2001) proposed a generic architecture to extract and maintain ontologies from Web data. The construction process is semi-automatic and requires a heavy participation of the ontology engineer to complete and/ or refine the output of some of the steps of the automatic ontology construction algorithm. The ontology is learnt by exploiting formal concept analysis, clustering, and generalized association rules extraction. In particular, taxonomic concept classification is performed by means of a hierarchical clustering algorithm, while binary relations among relevant concepts are learnt by analyzing frequent generalized association rules. However, to extract the latter knowledge, an ontology engineer (domain expert) needs to manually identify all pairs of syntactically related concepts, which are the input to the algorithm. Finally, to refine the extracted knowledge, a multi-strategy learning and result combination approach is exploited. As in Maedche and Staab (2001) we proposed a framework (DOnG) to easily address ontology learning, tailored to structured data, by means of a semi-automatic approach. Differently from Maedche and Staab (2001), we exploited (approximate) functional dependencies to automatically discover potential conceptual relationships among attributes. The inferred dependencies are graphically represented by means of a Schema Ontology Graph. The analyst in charge of semi-automatically constructing the ontology, supported by the generated Schema Ontology Graph, asserts the Tbox statements of the ontology. The selected (approximate) functional dependency constraints are pushed into the association rule mining algorithm to infer, by exploiting association rules, a schema ontology instance graph (SOnIG) at the data item granularity as well as eases domain expert validation by focusing the investigation on the most relevant item recurrences. The generated SOnIG is the building block used by analysts to

assert the Abox statements of the ontology. Our approach extends the work proposed in Maedche and Staab (2001) by reducing the human intervention towards a more automatic approach.

Many approaches have been proposed to either construct or semi-automatically infer taxonomies, which are particular kind of ontologies. A taxonomy is a hierarchical organization of concepts, topics, and keywords in which only is-a relationships among concepts hold. Hence, taxonomy construction is simpler than ontology construction. Several works address taxonomy construction by exploiting well-known data mining techniques. Mostly proposed algorithms exploited clustering techniques to provide a well-founded structuring of concepts of interest (Dhillon & Modha, 2001; Clifton et al., 2004; Gates, Teiken, & Cheng, 2005; Ienco & Meo, 2008). The mostly used techniques are based on hierarchical clustering, which produces a set of nested clusters organized as a hierarchical tree, called dendrogram. The most relevant application context in which clustering techniques have been adopted to address taxonomy construction is the context of textual data analysis (Dhillon & Modha, 2001; Clifton et al., 2004; Gates et al., 2005; Ienco & Meo, 2008; Hofmann, 1999; Hatzivassiloglou, Gravano, & Maganti, 2000). However, the focus of our approach is different from the aforementioned one. We propose a framework for semi-automatic construction of ontologies. Hence, we try to address a more general case with respect to taxonomy construction. Furthermore, many of the proposed taxonomy construction approaches have been developed for a specific domain, while our approach can be effectively exploited in different application domains, for example, context-aware user and service profiling (Baralis, Cagliero, Cerquitelli, Garza, & Marchetti, 2009) and network traffic analysis (Baldi, Baralis, & Risso, 2005; Baralis et al., 2010).

Database and data mining techniques, such as functional dependency discovery and association rule mining, may provide knowledge valuable for looking into the analyzed data. While correlations hidden in the schema of a structured dataset may be discovered and represented as functional dependencies among data attributes, data recurrences at the instance level may be represented as association rules. Although these correlations have not the semantic expressiveness of formal ontological statements, they may be used, in conjunction with a formal knowledge base (e.g., the Description Logic), to effectively support the analysts in the process of ontology construction. Hence, functional dependencies and association rules provide useful knowledge about the characteristics of the analyzed data. However, they must be opportunely combined by an analyst to construct an ontology used to represent a domain of interest. The framework proposed in this paper shows how (approximate) functional dependencies and associations rules can be used to construct ontologies by means of a semi-automatic approach.

CONCLUSION AND FUTURE WORK

Ontologies are fully comprehensive models for describing domain knowledge. Since a reliable domain knowledge representation is desirable in a wide range of application contexts (e.g., biological domain, context-aware applications, social network modeling), a novel and effective approach to support domain experts in the construction of domain-specific ontology tailored to structured data has been presented. The proposed approach focuses on exploiting both the schema and the content of the analyzed data. To this aim, both functional dependencies and association rules have been exploited by the DOnG framework to suggest hidden and relevant correlations valuable for ontology construction from data. Experimental results show the effectiveness of the DOnG framework in supporting ontology construction.

Furthermore, an application scenario, in which the constructed ontologies have been exploited to drive the mining activity, has been presented and discussed.

Future developments of this work will address two main issues: (i) the investigation of the ontology evolution over time by incrementally updating the generated model, and (ii) the exploitation of the devised approach to user-generated content coming from different application contexts (e.g., social media, online communities).

REFERENCES

Agrawal, R., & Srikant, R. (1994). Fast algorithms for mining association rules in large data-bases. In J. B. Bocca, M. Jarke, & C. Zaniolo (Eds.), *Proceedings of the International Conference on Very Large Data Bases* (pp. 487-499). San Francisco, CA: Morgan Kaufmann.

Augurusa, E., Braga, D., Campi, A., & Ceri, S. (2003). Design and implementation of a graphical interface to XQuery. In G. B. Lamont, H. Haddad, G. A. Papadopoulos, & B. Panda (Eds.), *Proceedings of the ACM Symposium on Applied Computing* (pp. 1163-1167). New York, NY: ACM Press.

Baader, F., Calvanese, D., McGuinness, D. L., Nardi, D., & Patel-Schneider, P. F. (Eds.). (2003). *The description logic handbook: Theory, implementation, and applications*. Cambridge, UK: Cambridge University Press.

Baldi, M., Baralis, E., & Risso, F. (2005). Data mining techniques for effective and scalable traffic analysis. In A. Clemm, O. Festor, & A. Pras (Eds.), *Proceedings of the IEEE International Symposium on Integrated Network Management* (pp. 105-118). Washington, DC: IEEE Computer Society.

Baralis, E., Cagliero, L., Cerquitelli, T., D'Elia, V., & Garza, P. (2010). Support driven opportunistic aggregation for generalized itemset extraction. In *Proceedings of the IEEE Conference on Intelligent Systems* (pp. 102-107). Washington, DC: IEEE Computer Society.

Baralis, E., Cagliero, L., Cerquitelli, T., Garza, P., & Marchetti, M. (2009). Context-aware user and service profiling by means of generalized association rules. In J. D. Velasquez, S. A. Rios, R. J. Howlett, & L. C. Jain (Eds.), *Proceedings of the International Conference on Knowledge-Based and Intelligent Information & Engineering Systems* (pp. 50-57). Berlin, Germany: Springer.

Baralis, E., Garza, P., Quintarelli, E., & Tanca, L. (2007). Answering XML queries by means of data summaries. *ACM Transactions on Information Systems, 25*(3), 1–33. doi:10.1145/1247715.1247716.

Blake, C., & Merz, C. (2010). *UCI repository of machine learning databases.* Retrieved July 25, 2011, from http://archive.ics.uci.edu/ml

Buneman, P., Davidson, S., Hillebrand, G., & Suciu, D. (1996). A Query Language and Optimization Techniques for Unstructured Data. In H. V. Jagadish & I. S. Mumick (Eds.), *Proceedings of the ACM SIGMOD International Conference on Management of Data* (pp. 505-516). New York, NY: ACM Press.

Clifton, C., Cooley, R., & Rennie, J. (2004). TopCat: Data mining for topic identification in a text corpus. *IEEE Transactions on Knowledge and Data Engineering, 16*(8), 949–964. doi:10.1109/TKDE.2004.32.

Consens, M. P., & Mendelzon, A. O. (1990). Graphlog: a Visual Formalism for Real Life Recursion. In D. J. Rosenkrantz & Y. Sagiv (Eds.), *Proceedings of the ACM SIGACT-SIGMOD-SIGART Symposium on Principles of Database Systems* (pp. 404-416). New York, NY: ACM Press.

Damiani, E., Oliboni, B., Quintarelli, E., & Tanca, L. (2003). *Modeling Semistructured Data by using graph-based constraints* (Tech. Rep. No. 27/03). Milano, Italy: Politecnico di Milano, Dipartimento di Elettronica e Informazione.

Dhillon, I. S., & Modha, D. S. (2001). Concept decompositions for large sparse text data using clustering. *Machine Learning, 42*(1-2), 143–175. doi:10.1023/A:1007612920971.

Gates, S. C., Teiken, W., & Cheng, K.-S. F. (2005). Taxonomies by the numbers: building high-performance taxonomies. In O. Herzog, H.-J. Schek, N. Fuhr, A. Chowdhury, & W. Teiken (Eds.), *Proceedings of the ACM International Conference on Information and Knowledge Management* (pp. 568-577). New York, NY: ACM Press.

Hatzivassiloglou, V., Gravano, L., & Maganti, A. (2000). An investigation of linguistic features and clustering algorithms for topical document clustering. In N. J. Belkin, P. Ingwersen, & M.-K. Leong (Eds.), *Proceedings of the ACM SIGIR Conference on Research and Development in Information Retrieval* (pp. 224-231). New York, NY: ACM Press.

Hofmann, T. (1999). The cluster-abstraction model: Unsupervised learning of topic hierarchies from text data. In T. Dean (Ed.), *Proceedings of the International Joint Conference on Artificial Intelligence* (pp. 682-687). San Francisco, CA: Morgan Kaufmann.

Huhtala, Y., Karkkainen, J., Porkka, P., & Toivonen, H. (1999). TANE: An efficient algorithm for discovering functional and approximate dependencies. *The Computer Journal, 42*(2), 100–111. doi:10.1093/comjnl/42.2.100.

Ienco, D., & Meo, R. (2008). Towards the automatic construction of conceptual taxonomies. In I.-Y. Song, J. Eder, & T. M. Nguyen (Eds.), *Proceedings of the International Conference on Data Warehousing and Knowledge Discovery* (pp. 327-336). Berlin, Germany: Springer.

Kivinen, J., & Mannila, H. (1995). Approximate inference of functional dependencies from relations. *Theoretical Computer Science, 149*(1), 129–149. doi:10.1016/0304-3975(95)00028-U.

Ley, M. (2005). *DBLP bibliography server.* Retrieved July 25, 2011, from http://dblp.uni-trier.de/xml

Maedche, A., & Staab, S. (2001). Ontology learning for the semantic web. *IEEE Intelligent Systems, 16*(2), 72–79. doi:10.1109/5254.920602.

Papakonstantinou, Y., Garcia-Molina, H., & Widom, J. (1995). Object Exchange across Heterogeneous Information Sources. In P. S. Yu & A. L. P. Chen (Eds.), *Proceedings of the International Conference on Data Engineering* (pp. 251-260). Los Alamitos, CA: IEEE Computer Society Press.

Paredaens, J., Peelman, P., & Tanca, L. (1995). G–Log: A Declarative Graphical Query Language. *IEEE Transactions on Knowledge and Data Engineering, 7*(3), 436–453. doi:10.1109/69.390249.

Porter, M. F. (1980). An algorithm for suffix stripping. *Program, 14*(3), 130–137. doi:10.1108/eb046814.

Porter, M. F. (1997). An algorithm for suffix stripping. In Sparck Jones, K., & Willett, P. (Eds.), *Readings in information retrieval* (pp. 313–316). San Francisco, CA: Morgan Kaufmann.

Srikant, R., & Agrawal, R. (1995). Mining generalized association rules. In U. Dayal, P. M. D. Gray, & S. Nishio (Eds.), *Proceedings of the International Conference on Very Large Data Bases* (pp. 407-419). San Francisco, CA: Morgan Kaufmann.

Tan, P.-N., Steinbach, M., & Kumar, V. (2006). *Introduction to Data Mining.* Boston, MA: Addison-Wesley.

TPC. (2005). *The TPC benchmark H. Transaction Processing Performance Council.* Retrieved July 25, 2011, from http://www.tpc.org/tpch/default.asp

World Wide Web Consortium. (W3C). (2009). *OWL 2 Web Ontology Language.* Retrieved July 25, 2011, from http://www.w3.org/TR/owl-overview/

This work was previously published in the International Journal on Semantic Web and Information Systems, Volume 7, Issue 2, edited by Amit P. Sheth,, pp. 1-22, copyright 2011 by IGI Publishing (an imprint of IGI Global).

Chapter 5
Concept Induction in Description Logics Using Information-Theoretic Heuristics

Nicola Fanizzi
University of Bari, Italy

ABSTRACT

This paper presents an approach to ontology construction pursued through the induction of concept descriptions expressed in Description Logics. The author surveys the theoretical foundations of the standard representations for formal ontologies in the Semantic Web. After stating the learning problem in this peculiar context, a FOIL-like algorithm is presented that can be applied to learn DL concept descriptions. The algorithm performs a search through a space of candidate concept definitions by means of refinement operators. This process is guided by heuristics that are based on the available examples. The author discusses related theoretical aspects of learning with the inherent incompleteness underlying the semantics of this representation. The experimental evaluation of the system DL-FOIL, which implements the learning algorithm, was carried out in two series of sessions on real ontologies from standard repositories for different domains expressed in diverse description logics.

1 INTRODUCTION

Formal ontologies are likely to play a key role in the next generation information systems moving from legacy to (linked) open data whose semantics is intended to be formalized and shared across the Web (Staab & Studer, 2009). One of the bottlenecks of this process is certainly represented by the construction (and evolution) of the ontologies since it involves different actors: *domain experts* contribute their knowledge but this is to be formalized by *knowledge engineers* so that it can be mechanized for the machines.

As the gap between these roles likely makes the process slow and burdensome, this problem may be tackled by resorting to *machine learning*

DOI: 10.4018/978-1-4666-3610-1.ch005

techniques. *Ontology learning* (Cimiano, Mädche, Staab, & Völker, 2009) is intended to provide solutions to the problem of (semi-) automated ontology construction. Cast as an *information extraction* subtask, ontology learning has focused on learning from text corpora (Buitelaar & Cimiano, 2008). The main drawback of this approach is that the elicited concepts and relations are represented with languages of limited expressiveness. A different approach can be based on *relational learning* (see De Raedt, 2008, for a recent survey), which requires a limited effort from domain experts (labeling individual resources as instances or non instances of the target concepts) and which leads to the construction of concepts even in very expressive languages (Lehmann, 2010).

If the concept learning problem is tackled as a search through a space of candidate descriptions in the reference representation guided by exemplars of the target concepts, then the same algorithms can be adapted to solve also *ontology evolution* problems. Indeed, while normally the semantics of change operations for this task has been considered from the logical and deductive point of view of automated reasoning, a relevant part of information lying in the data that populates ontological knowledge bases is generally overlooked or plays a secondary role.

Description Logics (DLs) is a family of languages supporting the standard ontology languages designed for knowledge bases in the context of the Semantic Web. These logics constitute specific fragments of First Order Logic (FOL) that differ from the standard clausal languages employed in *relational learning*, namely they have a different syntax and especially very different semantics (Borgida, 1996; Baader, Calvanese, McGuinness, Nardi, & Patel-Schneider, 2007). This motivates the growing interest in investigating inductive methods for such new formalisms.

1.1 Related Work

Early work on the application of machine learning to DLs essentially focused on demonstrating the PAC-learnability for various terminological languages derived from CLASSIC. In particular, Cohen and Hirsh investigate the CORECLASSIC DL proving that it is not PAC-learnable (Cohen & Hirsh, 1992) as well as demonstrating the PAC-learnability of peculiar classes among its sub-languages, such as C-CLASSIC (Cohen & Hirsh, 1994), through the bottom-up LCSLEARN algorithm starting from lifted representatives of the instances obtained with another language-specific operator.

These approaches tend to cast supervised concept learning as performed through a structural generalizing operator working on equivalent graph representations of the concept descriptions. It is also worth mentioning unsupervised learning methodologies for DL concept descriptions, whose prototypical example is KLUSTER (Kietz & Morik, 1994), a polynomial-time algorithm for the induction of BACK terminologies, which exploits the tractability of the standard inferences in this DL language (Baader, Calvanese, et al., 2007).

More recently, approaches have been proposed that adopt the idea of *generalization as search* (Mitchell, 1982) performed through suitable operators that are specifically designed for DL languages (Badea & Nienhuys-Cheng, 2000; Fanizzi, Esposito, Ferilli, & Semeraro, 2003; Fanizzi, Ferilli, Iannone, Palmisano, & Semeraro, 2005; Esposito, Fanizzi, Iannone, Palmisano, & Semeraro, 2004; Iannone, Palmisano, & Fanizzi, 2007; Lehmann, 2010; Lehmann & Hitzler, 2010) on the grounds of the previous experience in the context of ILP which have been implemented in supervised (resp., unsupervised) learning systems, such as YINYANG (Iannone et al., 2007) and DL-LEARNER (Lehmann, 2009; Lehmann, Auer, Bühmann, & Tramp, 2011) (resp., CSKA) (Fanizzi, Iannone, Palmisano, & Semeraro, 2004).

In particular, the OCEL algorithm (Lehmann & Hitzler, 2010) contained in the new releases of DL-LEARNER is able to learn class expressions in very expressive DL languages.

Learning alternative models such as logical decision trees offers another option for concept induction. The introduction of *terminological decision trees* (Fanizzi, d'Amato, & Esposito, 2010), i.e., logical decision trees with test-nodes represented by DL concept descriptions, and algorithms for their conversion into disjunctive descriptions, allows the combination of a *divide-and-conquer* learning strategy together with the standard *separate-and-conquer* strategy followed by most of the algorithms mentioned previously (Boström & Asker, 1999).

In other cases, combined refinement operators have been proposed for learning in hybrid representations, integrating clausal and description logics (Grosof, Horrocks, Volz, & Decker, 2003). While Kietz investigated the learnability of the *DL programs*, exploiting *ad hoc* transformations from DLs to LP (Kietz, 2002), other related studies propose learning methods for hybrid languages, such as CARIN-$\mathcal{ALN}$ (Rouveirol & Ventos, 2000), and $\mathcal{SHIQ}$-log (Lisi & Esposito, 2008) that allow expressive DLs to be combined with DATALOG.

1.2 Contributions

We focus on learning concepts in expressive concept languages, seeking for a trade-off between expressiveness, efficiency and completeness of the resulting algorithm. In our vision, inductive inference should be employed to help the knowledge engineer construct new concept definitions, that can possibly be further refined, by means of other semi-automatic tools. This would save the engineer from finding trivial regularities in the examples so that he/she could concentrate the efforts in refining the induced definition.

The paper extends our preliminary work (Fanizzi et al., 2008a). A specific new version of the FOIL algorithm (Quinlan, 1990) has been devised and implemented, resulting in the DL-FOIL system (Fanizzi et al., 2008a), that is adapted to learning the DL representations supporting the OWL-DL language. The main components of these new systems are represented by a set of refinement operators borrowed from other similar systems (Iannone et al., 2007; Lehmann, 2010) proposed in the literature and by a specific *information-gain function* which must take into account the open-world assumption, namely, many instances may be available which cannot be ascribed to the target concept nor to its negation. This requires a different setting, similar to learning with unknown class attributes (Goldman, Kwek, & Scott, 2003), requiring a special treatment of the unlabeled individuals.

In the experimental sessions the DL-FOIL system is applied to real ontologies which represent a real testbed w.r.t. the synthetic datasets employed for testing YINYANG (Iannone et al., 2007) and DL-Learner (Lehmann et al., 2011) which limit their scope to $\mathcal{ALC}$ concepts. This also demonstrates the usage of the method as a means for performing approximations of concepts across ontologies described with different languages (Brandt, Küsters, & Turhan, 2002).

The outcomes in terms of precision and recall were satisfactory, despite of the employment of incomplete refinement operators. However these outcomes are not as meaningful as they might be in a standard (closed-world) setting. Namely, since many test instances might not be proved to be examples or counter-examples, we resort to different performance metrics, measuring the alignment of the classification decided by the concept descriptions induced by DL-FOIL with the classification derived deductively by a DL reasoner. This allows measuring the amount of unlabeled instances that may be ascribed to the newly induced concepts (or to their negations), which may constitute a real added value brought by the inductive method. Actually these abductive conclusions should be evaluated by the expert who helped during the construction of the ontology. However, this is not always possible. Even more adopting such indices allows also for a comparison with the results obtained with other learning algorithms described in previous and current works.

1.3 Summary

The remainder of the paper is organized as follows. After the next section introducing the basics of the DL representations and related reasoning tasks, in Section 3 we give a formal definition of the learning/refinement problem in DLs and propose refinement operators to be exploited in suitable algorithms. In particular Section 4 presents the adaptation of the FOIL algorithm exploiting some of the proposed refinement operators. In Section 5 two experimental sessions are reported discussions their outcomes. Finally, possible developments are reported in Section 6.

2 REPRESENTATION ESSENTIALS

We assume the reader is familiar with the syntax and semantics of the DL representation. For the sake of self-containment, we briefly recall the basic notions which are needed for this paper. A thorough reference can be found in the DL handbook (Baader, Calvanese, et al., 2007).

2.1 DL Knowledge Bases

DL languages define their axioms on the ground of a basic vocabulary $\langle N_C, N_R, N_I \rangle$, where (atomic) *concept* names $N_C = \{A, B, ...\}$ are meant to represent sets of objects and (atomic) *roles* names $N_R = \{R, S, ...\}$ denote binary rela-

tionships between them. Individuals represent the objects of some domain (resources) through names chosen from $N_I = \{a, b, ...\}$.

Many different DL languages can be defined based on these building blocks. In the following we will focus on the DL language $\mathcal{ALC}$ (*Attributive Language with Complement*) will be considered as prototypical. This logic allows for building complex concepts from a vocabulary by means of specific constructors applied to the atomic concepts and roles in the vocabulary. These constructors can be defined inductively through the grammar shown in Figure 1.

The meaning of the concept descriptions is formalized in terms of interpretations:

Definition 2.1 (Interpretation): *An* interpretation $\mathcal{I}$ is a couple $(\Delta^{\mathcal{I}}, \cdot^{\mathcal{I}})$, where $\Delta^{\mathcal{I}}$ is the non-empty domain *of the interpretation and the functor* $\cdot^{\mathcal{I}}$ stands for the interpretation function, *mapping the intension of concepts and roles names to their extensions: each individual name* $a \in N_I$ *corresponds[1] to an element of the domain* $a^{\mathcal{I}} \in \Delta^{\mathcal{I}}$, *each atomic concept name* $A \in N_C$ *corresponds to a set* $A^{\mathcal{I}} \subseteq \Delta^{\mathcal{I}}$ *and each primitive role name* $R \in N_R$ *corresponds to a set* $R^{\mathcal{I}} \subseteq \Delta^{\mathcal{I}} \times \Delta^{\mathcal{I}}$.

An interpretation $\mathcal{I}$ is easily extended to complex concept descriptions as follows. The *top* concept symbol $\top$ is interpreted as the whole

Figure 1. Syntactic rules and examples of the concept constructors of the $\mathcal{ALC}$ DL

$C, D \rightarrow \top$	top concept	Thing
$\mid \bot$	bottom concept	Nothing
$\mid A$	primitive concept	Human
$\mid \neg C$	(full) concept negation	¬Parent
$\mid C \sqcap D$	concept conjunction	Person⊓Male
$\mid C \sqcup D$	concept disjunction	Father⊔Mother
$\mid \exists R.C$	existential restriction	∃hasChild.Male
$\mid \forall R.C$	universal restriction	∀hasChild.Female

domain $\Delta^{\mathcal{I}}$, while the *bottom* concept $\perp$ corresponds to the empty set of objects $\varnothing$. Given any concept description C, the *full negation* $\neg C$ is interpreted as $\Delta^{\mathcal{I}} \setminus C^{\mathcal{I}}$. The *conjunction* of concepts $C_1 \sqcap C_2$, corresponds to the extension $C_1^{\mathcal{I}} \cap C_2^{\mathcal{I}}$; dually, concept *disjunction* $C_1 \sqcup C_2$, corresponds to $C_1^{\mathcal{I}} \cup C_2^{\mathcal{I}}$. Finally, there are two kinds of restrictions on the role domains: the *existential restriction* $\exists R.C$ is interpreted as $\{x \in \Delta^{\mathcal{I}} \mid \exists y \in \Delta^{\mathcal{I}}: (x,y) \in R^{\mathcal{I}} \wedge y \in C^{\mathcal{I}}\}$, i.e., the subset of individuals in the domain of R that are related to individuals that are known to belong to C; conversely the *value restriction* $\forall R.C$, has the extension $\{x \in \Delta^{\mathcal{I}} \mid \forall y \in \Delta^{\mathcal{I}}: (x,y) \in R^{\mathcal{I}} \rightarrow y \in C^{\mathcal{I}}\}$, which is fulfilled also in case of absence of such an individual.

Terminologies will be defined in terms of specific terminological axioms which are statements on the relationships between concepts (or even roles in more complex DLs):

Definition 2.2 (Axioms, Assertions):

- **Terminological Axioms:** *Have the form* $C \sqsubseteq D$ (concept inclusion*) or* $C \equiv D$ (concept equality*), where C and D are (complex) concepts. An interpretation* $\mathcal{I}$ *satisfies (is a* model *for) the inclusion* $C \sqsubseteq D$ *iff* $C^{\mathcal{I}} \subseteq D^{\mathcal{I}}$ *and it satisfies (is a* model *for) the equality* $C \equiv D$ *iff* $C^{\mathcal{I}} = D^{\mathcal{I}}$.

- **The Assertions:** *Are ground atomic formulæ concerning, respectively, the membership of individuals w.r.t. some concept, denoted C(a), or their relationship through some role R(a,b). An interpretation* $\mathcal{I}$ *is a model of the concept (resp. role) assertion prior if* $a^{\mathcal{I}} \in C^{\mathcal{I}}$ (resp. $(a^{\mathcal{I}}, b^{\mathcal{I}}) \in R^{\mathcal{I}}$).

Given a set $\mathcal{S}$ of terminological axioms (resp. assertions), an interpretation $\mathcal{I}$ which satisfies all of them is a *model* for $\mathcal{S}$.

An equality whose left hand side is an atomic concept is called a *concept definition*. Definitions introduce symbolic names for concept descriptions, e.g.,

```
Father ≡ Man ⊓ ∃hasChild.Person.
```

Now we can formally define knowledge bases as made up of intensional and extensional components:

Definition 2.3 (Knowledge Base): *A knowledge base is a couple* $\mathcal{K} = \langle \mathcal{T}, \mathcal{A} \rangle$, *where the TBox* $\mathcal{T}$ *is a finite set of terminological axioms and the ABox* $\mathcal{A}$ *contains assertions regarding the individuals[2].*

A model of the knowledge base $\mathcal{K}$ is an interpretation which satisfies both its TBox $\mathcal{T}$ and its ABox $\mathcal{A}$.

For the sake of simplicity, we will consider only *acyclic* axioms[3] in the form of definitions which lead naturally to definitorial TBoxes. Dividing the atomic concept names into *primitive*, those occurring only on the right-hand side of the axioms, and *defined* ones, those that occur on the left-hand side an axiom, a definitiorial TBox is satisfied by models of the primitive concepts that admit an extension to a unique interpretation of the defined concept names (Baader, Calvanese, et al., 2007).

Further constructors extend the expressiveness of the $\mathcal{ALC}$ language. We are interested in the languages that constitute the decidable fragment of OWL named OWL-DL, $\mathcal{SHOIQ}(\mathbf{D})$ that, roughly, extends $\mathcal{ALC}$ with number restrictions, individual classes, inverse roles and inclusion or transitivity axioms for roles. Besides, representing relations that involve concrete domains[4] (**D**) for the fillers is also possible.

In the definition of refinement operators (See Section 3) the notion of a *normal form* for $\mathcal{ALC}$ concept descriptions will be required. Preliminarily, a concept is in *negation normal form* iff negation only occurs in front of concept names. Now, some notation is needed to name the different parts of an $\mathcal{ALC}$ description in this form: $\text{prim}(C)$ is the set of all the concepts at the top-level conjunction of C; if there exists a universal restriction $\forall R.D$ on the top-level of C then $\text{val}_R(C)=\{D\}$ (a single description because a conjunction of universal restrictions is equivalent to a single one with a conjunctive filler concept) otherwise $\text{val}_R(C)=\{\top\}$. Finally, $\text{ex}_R(C)$ is the set of the concept descriptions E appearing in existential restrictions $\exists R.E$ at the top-level conjunction of C.

Definition 2.4 ($\mathcal{ALC}$ normal form): *A concept description D is in $\mathcal{ALC}$ normal form iff D is $\bot$ or $\top$ or if $D = D_1 \sqcup \cdots \sqcup D_n$ with*

$$D_i = \bigsqcap_{A \in \text{prim}(D_i)} A \sqcap \bigsqcap_{R \in N_R} \left[\bigsqcap_{V \in \text{val}_R(D_i)} \forall R.V \sqcap \bigsqcap_{E \in \text{ex}_R(D_i)} \exists R.E \right]$$

where, for all $i = 1,...,n$, $D_i \not\equiv \bot$ and for any R, every sub-description in $\text{ex}_R(D_i)$ and $\text{val}_R(D_i)$ is in normal form.

2.2 Deductive Inference with DL Knowledge Bases

A knowledge base $\mathcal{K}$ is *consistent* if it admits a model. In the following, we will consider reasoning w.r.t. the models of consistent knowledge bases.

Given a concept C, it is *satisfiable* w.r.t. $\mathcal{K}$ if $C^{\mathcal{I}} \neq \varnothing$ for some model $\mathcal{I}$ of $\mathcal{K}$. We have seen that subsumption $\sqsubseteq$ is the most important relationship between concepts (roles), determining the underlying hierarchy of concepts in terms of the models of the knowledge base. Checking concept subsumption, say $C \sqsubseteq D$, through satisfiability is possible since it is semantically equivalent to checking whether $C \sqcap \neg D$ is unsatisfiable. It is easy to show that also other

standard inferences such as *equivalence*, and *disjointness* can be reduced to the others. They are implemented in DL reasoners recurring to *tableaux algorithms* (Baader, Calvanese, et al., 2007).

Analogously, the most important inference service involving ABoxes is checking their satisfiability (especially w.r.t. the models of the TBox). From an inductive point of view, another key inference is *instance checking* (Baader, Calvanese, et al., 2007), that amounts to ascertain concept-membership assertions:

Definition 2.5 (Instance Checking): *Given a knowledge base $\mathcal{K}$, a concept C and an individual $a \in N_I$, determine whether a is an instance of C w.r.t. $\mathcal{K}$: $\mathcal{K} \models C(a)$.*

An important difference with other FOL fragments is the *open-world assumption* (OWA) which makes answering class-membership queries different from the common settings of knowledge discovery methods (which target databases). Database instances are meant to represent a single model giving a complete knowledge about the world state. Conversely ABoxes may have infinitely many models, for knowledge is assumed to be incomplete. Absence of information is interpreted negatively for databases while it is just lack of knowledge. Hence while query answering from databases is a form of finite model checking, things are different with ABoxes which require logical reasoning. Indeed it may happen that an object that cannot be proved to belong to a certain concept is not necessarily a counterexample for that concept. That would only be interpreted[5] as a case of insufficient (incomplete) knowledge for proving that assertion. Note that to denote that a is not an instance of C with respect to $\mathcal{K}$ one should write $\mathcal{K} \not\models C(a)$, which means that there is an interpretation that satisfies $\mathcal{K}$ but not $C(a)$. A different meaning is assigned to the instances of the complement: $\mathcal{K} \models \neg C(a)$.

Another important inference service provided by DL reasoners, given a concept, amounts to find all the individuals that can be logically proven to belong to it:

Definition 2.6 (retrieval) *Given a knowledge base $\mathcal{K}$ and a concept C, the retrieval of a concept C w.r.t. $\mathcal{K}$ is the set, denoted $R_{\mathcal{K}}(C)$, of all individuals that are instances of C w.r.t. $\mathcal{K}$:*

$$R_{\mathcal{K}}(C) = \{a \in N_I \mid \mathcal{K} \models C(a)\}$$

3 LEARNING AS SEARCH IN DESCRIPTION LOGICS

Concept learning from examples can be cast as a search problem in a space of candidate definitions (Mitchell, 1982). In this section we formalize some possible definitions for learning problems in the reference representation and exploit the natural ordering relationship between DL concept descriptions induced by subsumption to (re-) propose operators that can be used to solve the learning problems by traversing the search space.

3.1 Learning Problem

We can formally define the learning problem in this setting as follows:

Definition 3.1 (Learning Problem in DLs): *Let $\mathcal{K} = (\mathcal{T}, \mathcal{A})$ be a DL knowledge base.*

Given

- A new concept name $C \notin N_C$
- A set of assertions for C:

$$\mathcal{A}_C = \mathcal{A}_C^+ \cup \mathcal{A}_C^-$$

with

$$\mathcal{A}_C^+ = \{C(a) \in \mathcal{A}_C \mid a \in N_I\}$$

(positive assertions)

$$\mathcal{A}_C^- = \{\neg C(b) \in \mathcal{A}_C \mid b \in N_I\}$$

(negative assertions)

Find a concept description D defining C, *so that* $\mathcal{K}' = \langle \mathcal{T}', \mathcal{A}' \rangle$ is satisfiable and $\forall \alpha \in \mathcal{A}_C \colon \mathcal{K}' \models \alpha$, *with* $\mathcal{T}' = \mathcal{T} \cup \{C \equiv D\}$ and $\mathcal{A}' = \mathcal{A} \cup \mathcal{A}_C$.

This definition is deliberately general and does not favor any specific solution over others. Adding further constraints can help better circumscribing also the methods to solve the problem.

Note that entailing negative assertions as required by the constraint $\mathcal{K}' \models \neg C(b)$ is stronger w.r.t. other settings, yet it seems more coherent with a scenario where information is assumed to be inherently incomplete[6] (because of the OWA); then one must consider as negative examples only those individuals that are explicitly indicated as such. A weaker form considered in other works like $\mathcal{K}' \not\models C(b)$, leads naturally to assuming binary classification problems, putting together the actual counterexamples with individuals that may not be recognized as positive only because of the current (partial) state of knowledge represented by the ABox. This may be a source of further problems in the perspective of following the dynamics (http://www.ontologydynamics.org/) of evolving ontologies.

A different learning problem (not considered in the following) is when $C \in N_C$, with a definition for C, say $C \equiv D$, that is already available in $\mathcal{T}$, yet some (new) assertions on individuals to be included in the ABox may fail to be entailed (or even lead to inconsistency):

$$\exists C(a) \in \mathcal{A}_C^+ \colon \quad \mathcal{K} \not\models C(a)$$

or

$$\exists \neg C(b) \in \mathcal{A}_C^- : \quad \mathcal{K} \not\models \neg C(b)$$

the problem can be cast as a *refinement problem* which would amount to searching for a solution D starting from the approximation D'. This can be considered as a form of *ontology evolution* (Bloehdorn, Haase, Sure, & Voelker, 2006).

3.2 Refinement Operators

The solution of the learning problem stated before can be cast as a search for a correct concept definition in an ordered space $(\Sigma, \preceq)$. In such a setting, one can define suitable operators in order to traverse the search space. Refinement operators can be formally defined as follows:

Definition 3.2 (Refinement Operator): *Given a quasi-ordered[7] search space $(\Sigma, \preceq)$*

- **A Downward Refinement Operator:** *Is a mapping $\rho : \Sigma \to 2^{\Sigma}$ such that*

$$\forall \alpha \in \Sigma \quad \rho(\alpha) \subseteq \{\beta \in \Sigma \mid \beta \preceq \alpha\}$$

- **An Upward Refinement Operator:** *Is a mapping $\delta : \Sigma \to 2^{\Sigma}$ such that*

$$\forall \alpha \in \Sigma \quad \delta(\alpha) \subseteq \{\beta \in \Sigma \mid \alpha \preceq \beta\}$$

In the following, we will consider a space of concept definitions ordered by the subsumption relationship $\sqsubseteq$ which induces a quasi-order on the space of all the possible concept descriptions (Badea & Nienhuys-Cheng, 2000; Esposito et al., 2004). In particular, given a space of concept definitions in the reference DL language, say $(\mathcal{L}, \sqsubseteq)$, ordered by subsumption, there is an infinite number of generalizations and specializations. Usually one tries to devise operators that can traverse efficiently throughout the space in pursuit of one of the correct definitions (w.r.t. the examples that have been provided).

We will consider two theoretical refinement operators[8] that, given a starting incorrect definition (too weak or too strong) for the target concept in the search space, can compute one (or some) of its generalizations/specializations. Both are defined (w.l.o.g.) for $\mathcal{ALC}$ descriptions in normal form (see Def. 2.4).

Definition 3.3 (Downward Operator ρ): *Let ρ be a downward refinement operator that assumes two forms $\rho_{\sqcup}$ and $\rho_{\sqcap}$, where:*

$[\rho_{\sqcup}]$ *given a description in $\mathcal{ALC}$ normal form* $D = D_1 \sqcup \cdots \sqcup D_n$:

$$D' \in \rho_{\sqcup}(D) \text{ if } D' = \bigsqcup_{\substack{1 \le i \le n \\ i \ne j}} D_i$$

for some $j \in \{1, \ldots, n\}$

$$D' \in \rho_{\sqcup}(D) \text{ if } D' = D_i' \sqcup \bigsqcup_{\substack{1 \le i \le n \\ i \ne j}} D_i$$

for some $j \in \{1, \ldots, n\}$ and $D_j' \in \rho_{\sqcap}(D_j)$

$[\rho_{\sqcap}]$ *given a conjunctive description* $C = C_1 \sqcap \cdots \sqcap C_m$:

$$C' \in \rho_{\sqcap}(C) \text{ if } C' = C \sqcap C_{m+1}$$

for some C_{m+1} such that $\bot \sqsubset C' \sqsubseteq C \bot$

$$C' \in \rho_{\sqcap}(C)$$

if $C' = \displaystyle\bigsqcap_{\substack{1 \le i \le m \\ i \ne k}} C_i \sqcap C_k'$

for some $k \in \{1, \ldots, m\}$, where:

$$C_k' \sqsubseteq C_k$$

if $C_k \in \mathsf{prim}(C)$ or

$$C'_k = \exists R.D'$$

if $C_k = \exists R.D$ and $D' \in \rho_\sqcup(D)$ or

$$C'_k = \forall R.D' \,'$$

if $C_k = \forall R.D$ and $D' \in \rho_\sqcup(D)$

Note that a difference operator for concepts is used to single out the sub-concepts to be refined. Further possibilities may be explored using the operator defined $C - D = C \sqcup \neg D$ (Teege, 1994).

The operator for disjunctive concepts $\rho_\sqcup$ simply drops one top-level disjunct or replaces it with a downward refinement obtained with $\rho_\sqcap$. $\rho_\sqcap$ adds new conjuncts or replaces one with a refinement obtained by specializing a primitive concept or the sub-concepts in the scope of a universal or existential restriction (again through $\rho_\sqcup$). Note that successive applications of the operator may require intermediate normalization steps.

Definition 3.4 (Upward Operator δ) : *Let* δ be a downward refinement operator that assumes two forms $\delta_\sqcup$ *and* $\delta_\sqcap$, where:

$[\delta_\sqcup]$ *given a description in $\mathcal{ALC}$ normal form*

$$D = D_1 \sqcup \cdots \sqcup D_n :$$

$D' \in \delta_\sqcup(D)$ if $D' = D \sqcup D_{n+1}$

for some D_{n+1} *such that* $D_{n+1} \not\sqsubseteq D$

$$D' \in \delta_\sqcup(D) \text{ if } D' = D'_j \sqcup \bigsqcup_{\substack{1 \le i \le n \\ i \ne j}} D_i$$

for some $j \in \{1,\dots n\}$, $D'_j \in \delta_\sqcap(D_j)$

$[\delta_\sqcap]$ given a conjun*ctive description*

$$C = C_1 \sqcap \cdots \sqcap C_m :$$

$$C' \in \delta_\sqcap(C) \text{ if } C' = \bigsqcap_{\substack{1 \le i \le m \\ i \ne k}} C_i$$

for some $k \in \{1,\dots m\}$

$$C' \in \delta_\sqcap(C) \text{ if } C' = \bigsqcap_{\substack{1 \le i \le m \\ i \ne k}} C_i \sqcap C'_k$$

for some $k \in \{1,\dots,m\}$, where:

$$C'_k \sqsupseteq C_k$$

if $C_k \in \mathsf{prim}(C)$ or

$$C'_k = \exists R.D'$$

if $C_k = \exists R.D$ and $D' \in \delta_\sqcup(D)$ *or*

$$C'_k = \forall R.D'$$

if $C_k = \forall R.D$ and $D' \in \delta_\sqcup(D)$

$\delta_\sqcup$ and $\delta_\sqcap$ simply perform dual operations w.r.t. $\rho_\sqcup$ and $\rho_\sqcap$, respectively. Some examples of their application can be found in Iannone et al. (2007).

These operators follow the definition of the $\mathcal{ALC}$ normal form. Hence they cannot be complete for more expressive DLs (for an analysis of refinement operators in DLs, see Lehmann, 2010).

However, instead of such operators that likely lead to overfit the data (e.g., a generalizing operator based on the LCS operator would amount to a simple union of the input descriptions in $\mathcal{ALC}$) (Cohen & Hirsh, 1994), it may be preferable to search the space (incompletely) using the non-$\mathcal{ALC}$ restrictions as atomic features (concepts).

Moreover, other operators have been designed to exploit also the knowledge conveyed by the positive and negative examples in order to prune the possible candidate refinements yielded by a single generalization/specialization step and to better direct the search for suitable problem solutions (Iannone et al., 2007). Even more so, instead of using the examples in a mere *generate-and-test* strategy based on these operators, they could be exploited more directly[9], in order to influence the choices made during the refinement process.

The next step is embedding these simple operators in a learning algorithm based on sequential covering.

4 THE LEARNING ALGORITHM

The main aim of this work was conceiving a learning algorithm that could overcome two limitation of (some of) the current DL concept learning systems, namely avoiding the computation of the most specific concepts (which is also language-dependent) and the excessive (syntactic) complexity of the resulting generalizations. For instance, the algorithm presented in (Iannone et al., 2007) requires lifting the instances to the concept level through a suitable approximations of their most specific concept and then start learning from such extremely specific concept descriptions. This setting has the disadvantages of approximation and language-dependency.

Various other search strategies have been experimented as well as evaluation measures. In algorithms implemented in early versions (Lehmann, 2007) of DL-LEARNER these drawbacks are

partly mitigated: e.g., adopting a learning procedure based on a genetic programming based on refinement operators, whose fitness is computed on the grounds of the covered instances (retrieval). More heuristics and approximated retrieval procedures are further investigated in (Lehmann, 2010; Hellmann, Lehmann, & Auer, 2011).

The algorithm proposed in this paper, DL-FOIL, essentially adapts the original FOIL algorithm (Quinlan, 1990) to the specificities of the learning problem with DL knowledge bases, as previously defined. Together with the sequential covering procedure, it exploits the (downward) refinement operators previously defined and a heuristic similar to the *information gain* to select among candidate specializations. A sketch of the main routine of the learning procedure is reported as Figure 2.

Like in the original FOIL algorithm, the generalization routine computes (partial) generalizations as long as they do not cover any negative example. If this occurs, the SPECIALIZE routine is invoked for solving these specialization problems. This routine applies the idea of specializing using the (incomplete) refinement operator defined in the previous section. The specialization continues until no negative example is covered (or a very limited amount[10] of them). The partial generalizations built on each outer loop are finally grouped together in a disjunction which is an allowed constructor for more expressive logics than (or equal to) $\mathcal{ALC}$. Also the outer while-loop can be exited before covering all the positive examples for avoiding overfitting generalizations.

The specialization function SPECIALIZE (reported as Figure 3) is called from within the inner loop of the generalization procedure in order to specialize an overly general partial generalization. The function searches for proper refinements that provide at least a minimal gain fixed with a threshold (*MINGAIN*). Specializations are randomly generated using the operator ρ defined in the previous section, especially $\rho_\sqcap$ is exploited with the addition of new conjuncts or the special-

Figure 2. Algorithm 1

Algorithm 1 GENERALIZE(*Positives, Negatives, Unlabeled*): *Generalization*

Input:
> *Positives, Negatives, Unlabeled*: positive, negative and unlabeled individuals

Output:
> *Generalization*: concept definition solving the learning problem

1: *Generalization* ← ⊥
2: *PositivesToCover* ← *Positives*
3: **while** *PositivesToCover* ≠ ∅ **do**
4:   *PartialDef* ← ⊤
5:   *CoveredNegatives* ← *Negatives*
6:   **while** *CoveredNegatives* ≠ ∅ **do**
7:     *PartialDef* ← SPECIALIZE(*PartialDef, PositivesToCover, CoveredNegatives, Unlabeled*)
8:     *CoveredNegatives* ← {$n \in Negatives \mid \mathcal{K} \models PartialDef(n)$}
9:   **end while**
10:   *CoveredPositives* ← {$p \in PositivesToCover \mid \mathcal{K} \models PartialDef(p)$}
11:   *Generalization* ← *Generalization* ⊔ *PartialDef*
12:   *PositivesToCover* ← *PositivesToCover* \ *CoveredPositives*
13: **end while**
14: **return** *Generalization*

Figure 3. Algorithm 2

Algorithm 2 SPECIALIZE(*PartialDef, Positives, Negatives, Unlabeled*): *Refinement*

Input:
> *PartialDef*: concept definition
> *Positives, Negatives, Unlabeled*: (positive, negative and unlabeled) individuals

Output:
> *Refinement*: concept definition

1: **const:**
> *MINGAIN*: minimal acceptable gain;
> *NUMSPECS*: number of specializations to be generated

2: *bestGain* ← 0
3: **while** *bestGain* < *MINGAIN* **do**
4:   **for** $i \leftarrow 1$ **to** *NUMSPECS* **do**
5:     *Specialization* ← GETRANDOMREFINEMENT(ρ, *PartialDef*)
6:     *CoveredPositives* ← {$p \in Positives \mid \mathcal{K} \models Specialization(p)$}
7:     *CoveredNegatives* ← {$n \in Negatives \mid \mathcal{K} \models Specialization(n)$}
8:     *thisGain* ← GAIN(*CoveredPositives, CoveredNegatives, Unlabeled, Positives, Negatives*)
9:     **if** *thisGain* > *bestGain* **then**
10:       *bestConcept* ← *Specialization*
11:       *bestGain* ← *thisGain*
12:     **end if**
13:   **end for**
14: **end while**
15: **return** *Refinement*

---

ization of primitive concepts or role restrictions. This is similar to the original FOIL algorithm, where new random literals are appended to clauses' antecedents. A first random choice is made between atomic concepts or role restrictions. In the latter case another random choice is made between existential and universal restriction. In all cases the required concept and roles names are also randomly selected. This may give a way to impose some further bias to the form of the concept descriptions to be induced.

4.1 Heuristics

As regards the heuristic employed to guide the search, it was shown in the paper on the FOIL-I system (Inuzuka, Kamo, Ishii, Seki, & Itoh, 1997), that the gain function has to take into account incomplete examples. Similarly to a semi-supervised learning setting, the gain value g that is computed in GAIN for selecting the best refinement is obtained as follows:

$$g = p_1 \cdot \left[\log \frac{p_1 + u_1 w_1}{p_1 + n_1 + u_1} - \log \frac{p_0 + u_0 w_0}{p_0 + n_0 + u_0} \right]$$

where p_1, n_1 and u_1 represent, resp., the number of positive, negative and unlabeled examples covered by the specialization D_1 and p_0, n_0 and u_0 stand for the number of positive, negative and unlabeled examples covered by the former definition D_0, while the weights w_0,w_1 can determined by an estimate of the prior probability of the positive examples, resp., in the current and former concept definition. In order to avoid the case of null numerators, a further correction of the probabilities is performed by resorting to an *m*-estimate procedure.

Further heuristics based on the number of false positives and negatives can be found in (Lehmann, 2010). Since in the problem setting considered in this work the algorithm should induced D such that $\mathcal{K} \models D(a)$ for all positive examples a and $\mathcal{K} \models \neg D(b)$ for all negative examples b, a better score function should be devised. A proposal may be the following

$$s_{D_0}^{D_1} = tp_1 \cdot \left[\log \frac{tp_1 + tn_1}{pos + neg} - \log \frac{tp_0 + tn_0}{pos + neg} \right]$$

which is based on the gain in terms of the number of true positive and negative examples (resp. $tp_{0/1}$ and $tn_{0/1}$) observed adopting the specialized concept D_1 or the previous version D_0. Of course using this score would require changes in the conditions controlling the loops. Indeed in this case the algorithm should accommodate both positive and negative examples simultaneously. Note that specializing a concept, while narrowing its extension (causing some positive examples not to be covered), at the same time broadens the extension of its complement so that also previously unlabeled instances may be included in its extension and they should be treated as false negatives.

4.2 Discussion

Despite of its simplicity, the overall complexity of the algorithm is largely determined by the calls to reasoning services, namely subsumption (satisfiability) and especially instance-checking (see Section 2.2), whose complexity is not less than subsumption, depending on the underlying DL language. For example, considering exclusively concepts expressed in $\mathcal{ALC}$ logic, the complexity of this inference is P-space. Given this inference service as an oracle, the complexity of the algorithm does not increase w.r.t. the original FOIL.

However, should the considered knowledge base contain definitions expressed in more expressive languages, which, in turn, require more complex reasoning procedures, the inductive algorithm can be thought as a means for building (upper) $\mathcal{ALC}$ - approximations of the target concepts. Indeed the specializing routine may diverge in case the refinement sought cannot be expressed in terms of the considered language. To avoid such cases the implementation of the algorithm limits the number of attempts of refinement. Another such case may be caused by the choice of the *MINGAIN* value for the problem at hand (checked at line 3).

The number of nodes of the *refinement tree* that may be visited during the traversal of the search space grows with richness of the vocabulary, yet not with the expressiveness of the underlying DL, because the algorithm searches a sub-space of the actual search space induced by the language.

As discussed in Iannone et al. (2007) and more recently in Lehmann and Hitzler (2010) and Lehmann (2010), (weakly) complete, finite and proper refinement operators cannot be defined for the space of $\mathcal{ALC}$ concepts (and also more expressive languages).

The problem of handling noisy data is also not considered in the algorithm. As in the original system (Quinlan, 1990), a post-*pruning* stage of the induced concepts can be considered to avoid overfitting the data.

5 EMPIRICAL EVALUATION

In order to perform an experimental evaluation of DL-FOIL on real ontologies, it was applied to a number individual classification problems w.r.t. a number of randomly generated target concepts.

5.1 Experimental Settings

Three OWL ontologies regarding various domains were selected, namely:

- NEWTESTAMENTNAMES (NTN): From the Protégé library (http://protege.stanford. edu/plugins/owl/owl-library) accounting for characters and places mentioned in the book.
- **The BioPax Glycolysis Ontology:** (BioPax, http://www.biopax.org/ Downloads/Level1v1.4/biopax-example-ecocyc-glycolysis.owl) Describing the glycolysis pathway from the EcoCyc database, translated into BioPax format; it is intended to show what a pathway from an existing database might look like after being translated into BioPAX format.
- **The FINANCIAL Ontology:** (http://www. cs.put.poznan.pl/alawrynowicz/financial. owl) Built for eBanking applications, deals with accounts, holders, loans and related events.

Table 1 summarizes important details concerning these ontologies.

Since these ontologies have been selected also in the evaluation of other systems with similar settings (d'Amato, Fanizzi, & Esposito, 2008; Fanizzi et al., 2009a, 2010), this gives the chance for a comparison with the results obtained through other inductive approaches. In particular, some results obtained with the *terminological decision tree* learner TERMITIS will be reported for the comparison, as also this system is able to induce logical trees and then also DL concepts.

For the sake of reproducibility, we did not employ artificially populated the ontologies, an option used in other works, because the generation of the training examples could bias the learning process. Rather, ontologies were used as they can be found in the Web. For each ontology, 30 (satisfiable) target concepts were randomly generated[11] by composition of 2 through 8 primitive or defined concepts from each knowledge base by means of the concept constructors: intersection, union, and simple universal or existential restrictions (only atomic concepts in their scope were allowed). Given the overall set of individuals occurring in the ABox $\mathsf{Ind}(\mathcal{A})$, this was split in a training and a test set according to the ten-fold *cross-validation* procedure. A standard reasoner[12] was employed to decide the class-membership (and non-membership) of the training and test individuals w.r.t. the target concepts. The performance of the DL-FOIL system was evaluated assessing the accuracy of the definitions of the concepts induced by the system using the training examples, determining the class-membership of the individuals test examples (in the given fold), and using the original target concepts as a gold standard.

Note that the constant *NUMSPECS* that determines the maximum number of specializations evaluated per turn was set to 15 (larger numbers yield better results but may decrease the overall efficiency).

5.2 Results

5.2.1 Standard Measures

Initially the standard indices of *precision*, *recall*, and F_1-*measure* were employed to evaluate the system performance. To this purpose, a two-way classification was taken into account where relevance coincides with class-membership and the rest of instances are considered irrelevant (negative or unknown membership information).

Table 1. Facts concerning the ontologies employed in the experiments

ontology	DL language	#concepts	#object properties	#datatype properties	#individuals
BioPax	$\mathcal{ALCHF}(\mathbf{D})$	28	19	30	323
NTN	$\mathcal{SHIF}(\mathbf{D})$	47	27	8	676
Financial	$\mathcal{ALCIF}$	60	17	0	1000

The outcomes are reported in Table 2. For each knowledge base, we report the average values obtained over the 30 target concepts as well as their standard deviation.

It is possible to note that precision and recall are generally good but not very high which is also reflected by the F-measure. This happens because these parameters are taken on the grounds of the positive instances which are likely to be in a limited amount w.r.t. the overall number of individuals, especially when random concepts are considered. This is also the cause for the variance to be quite high over all of the experiments. Of course more largely populated ontologies would help assess more stable results. Actually for the FINANCIAL ontology, a reduced number of individuals were employed for the experiments. With larger numbers of individuals, of course better and more stable results (not presented here) were observed.

The reason for precision being less than recall is probably due to the OWA. Indeed, in many cases it was observed that the inductive classification deemed some individuals as instances of the given target concept while the DL reasoner was not able

to assess the membership and this was considered as a mistake, while it may likely turn out to be a correct inference when judged by a human agent (a domain expert). Because of this issue with the OWA, different indices would be needed in this context to help make explicit the cases of individuals of unknown membership that may receive an inductive classification and the cases (and nature) of wrong classification.

5.2.2 Alternative Measures

Due to the OWA, unknown membership cases are frequently observed in which the reasoner cannot ascertain that an individual is definitively either a member of the given target concept or of its complement. Indeed, a more natural and preferable setting would require a three-way classification. Hence, for a better insight, we introduced new evaluation indices (d'Amato et al., 2008) that essentially measure the correspondence between the classification provided by the reasoner for the test instances w.r.t. the original target concept and the definition induced from training examples by a learning system:

- **Match Rate:** Cases of individuals that got exactly the same classification with both definitions.
- **Omission Error Rate:** Cases of individuals of unknown class-membership w.r.t. the induced definition, which actually belong (resp. do not belong) to the target concept.

Table 2. Experimental results in terms of standard measures: averages ± standard deviations

ontology	precision	recall	F_1-measure
BioPax	**66.0** ± 24.1	**76.5** ± 21.7	**69.6** ± 21.0
NTN	**59.0** ± 36.8	**64.9** ± 25.7	**59.1** ± 30.0
Financial	**62.1** ± 40.7	**64.8** ± 37.0	**63.3** ± 39.1

- **Commission Error Rate:** Cases of individuals that received opposite classifications w.r.t. the original and the induced definition of the target concept.
- **Induction Rate:** Cases of individuals of unknown class-membership w.r.t. the target concept, that can be proven to actually belong (resp. not belong) to the induced definition of the concept.

The experiments were performed measuring the quality of the induced concept definitions in terms of these new indices. Table 3 reports the outcomes. Preliminarily, we found that the search procedure was accurate enough: it made few critical mistakes (commission error) especially when the considered concepts are known to have many examples (and counterexamples) in the ontology. However, it is important to note that, in each experiment, the commission error rate was limited but not absent, as in the experiments with other classification methods (d'Amato et al., 2008). The cases of target concepts for which this measure was high were due to the limited amount of examples available (too narrow concepts in terms of their *retrieval*). Even few mistakes provoked high error rates. This is also due to the insufficiency or absence of axioms stating explicitly the disjointness of some concepts.

Also the observed omission error rates were quite low. They are comparable with the rates of definitive (non-)membership cases that could be assessed employing the induced concept definitions. Again these figures are variable as a consequence of the presence or absence of knowledge about the disjunction of (sibling) concepts in the subsumption hierarchies.

In an ontology population perspective, the cases of induction are interesting because they may suggest new assertions which cannot be logically derived using the original concept definition yet they might correspond to the intended meaning and be used to complete a knowledge base (Baader, Ganter, Sertkaya, & Sattler, 2007), e.g., after being validated by an ontology engineer. Better results were obtained on the same task with different inductive methods providing alternative classification models and procedures (e.g., similarity-based classification) (d'Amato et al., 2008; Fanizzi et al., 2009a). However, using DL concept learners like DL-FoIL there is the added value of having a definition of the target concepts, which can be directly integrated in the ontology.

The elapsed time (not reported here) was very limited: about 0.5 hour for a whole ten-fold cross validation experiment including the time consumed by the reasoner to make the judgments. Moreover, this is a typical activity that can be kept off-line, when weaker time constraints may allow for different setting of the parameters which would induce the algorithm to span broader regions of the search space, thus improving the accuracy of the definitions returned. Another option would require the employment of the refinement operators in their complete version (esp. as regards the sub-concepts nested in role restriction). This will be the focus of further experiments presented in Section 5.4

5.3 Learned Definitions

In order to appreciate the quality of the concepts induced by DL-FoIL, for each ontology, we report examples in concrete LISP-like syntax of the

Table 3. Results with alternative indices: averages ± standard deviations

ontology	match rate	commission error rate	omission error rate	induction rate
BioPax	**76.9** ± 15.7	**19.7** ± 15.9	**07.0** ± 20.0	**07.5** ± 23.7
NTN	**78.0** ± 19.2	**16.1** ± 04.0	**06.4** ± 08.1	**14.0** ± 10.1
Financial	**75.5** ± 20.8	**16.1** ± 12.8	**04.5** ± 05.1	**03.7** ± 07.9

concept descriptions that were learned during the experiments and compare them to the random concept that was used generated the examples and counterexamples.

BioPax

```
induced:
    (or (and physicalEntity protein)
dataSource)
original:
    (or (and (and dataSource external-
ReferenceUtilityClass)
    (forall ORGANISM (forall CON-
TROLLED phys icalInteraction)))
protein)
NTN
induced:
    (or EvilSupernaturalBeing (not
God))
original:
    (not God)
```

Financial

```
induced:
    (or (not Finished) NotPaidFinish-
edLoan Weekly)
original:
    (or LoanPayment (not NoProblems-
FinishedLoan))
```

Note that the original and induced concepts shown prior totally overlap in terms of their retrieval sets.

Of course for a correct qualitative interpretation of the value of these concepts some familiarity is assumed with the domains of the ontologies.

5.4 Further Sessions

Further experimental sessions extended the previous experimental settings along various dimensions, namely the adoption of more complete refinement operators, an increased number of the ontologies, the design of the procedure for evaluating the system performance.

As regards the first point, a more complete downward refinement operator is adopted for obtaining specializations of the current candidate concept description. Indeed, while in the former sessions the concept descriptions in the scope of existential and universal restrictions were limited to (primitive or defined) concept names ($\forall R.C$ or $\exists R.C$ with $C \in N_C$), in the latter sessions the descriptions were allowed to span over the entire (infinite) set of descriptions that can be built using the language, thus allowing for complex ones. However, as this is performed randomly, nested restrictions are discouraged by making their selection more unlikely with the depth of the nesting level. Moreover, it should also pointed out that candidate concept descriptions are only considered for the inclusion as new conjuncts when they are satisfiable and actually have at least one instance occurring the in ABox.

Together with the ontologies employed in the previous sessions, three further ontologies have been considered for testing the method accuracy:

- **MDM0.37:** Is an OWL ontology, that can be found also in the Protégé library, for describing some features of the breast cancer prognosis (http://acl.icnet.uk/~mw/MDM0.73.owl).
- **the WINE ontology:** (http://www.w3.org/TR/owl-guide/wine.rdf) Is a popular ontology used as a benchmark for many applications related to the Semantic Web.

- **HUMANDISEASE (shortly hDisease):** (http://www.jalojavier.es/humandisease. owl) Is one of the ontologies developed for the *Open Biomedical Ontologies* project (http://www.obofoundry.org).

Basic information about them can be found in Table 4. For further details the reader is referred to the respective websites.

In these new sessions the system performance was evaluated using the same indices, yet using the .632-bootstrap procedure instead of the 10-fold cross validation so that a greater number of repetitions led to better estimates of the indices values.

The average outcomes of these sessions are summed up in Table 5. Comparing the match rates observed in the cases of BIOPAX, NTN and FINANCIAL to those observed in the previous sessions, it is immediately evident a growth of about 5%. This is likely due to the increased complexity of the computed refinements which allowed for better defining the induced concepts during the training phase. As regards the other three ontologies, results are slightly lower (for the match rate) with the special case of the WINE ontology were it went below 70%. However on a more careful inspection of the of the experiment outcomes, two facts have to be taken into account. Firstly, this case presents the largest variability w.r.t. all others. This is explained by the peculiar sparseness of data in the ontology, that made some of the target concepts particularly hard to approximate using an inductive method. This is confirmed also by the hight error rates. Secondly, part of the mass of total tests resulted in a relevant induction rate (over 16%) which means that, likely, reasoning with the induced concept descriptions turned out to be especially less *cautious* than with the original concepts (this may also depend of the availability of disjunction axioms). Hence, tests on some individuals which had an unknown membership w.r.t. the original concepts, turned out to be negative or positive w.r.t. the concept descriptions induced by the system on the grounds of examples and counter examples.

Table 4. Facts concerning the ontologies employed in the additional experiments

ontology	DL language	#concepts	#object properties	#datatype properties	#individuals
MDM0.37	$\mathcal{ALCROF}(\mathbf{D})$	196	22	3	103
Wine	$\mathcal{SHOIN}(\mathbf{D})$	140	21	1	206
hDisease	$\mathcal{ALCIN}(\mathbf{D})$	1449	10	10	639

Table 5. Results of the extended sessions: averages ± standard deviations

ontology	match rate	commission error rate	omission error rate	induction rate
BioPax	82.48 ± 03.84	17.20 ± 03.75	00.25 ± 00.24	00.08 ± 00.05
NTN	81.13 ± 01.76	00.99 ± 00.36	08.90 ± 01.01	08.98 ± 01.42
Financial	84.15 ± 03.17	10.35 ± 02.41	02.19 ± 01.02	03.30 ± 00.96
Wine	67.37 ± 14.65	01.01 ± 01.72	15.37 ± 07.32	16.24 ± 10.45
MDM0.37	86.78 ± 08.13	05.67 ± 05.04	03.52 ± 03.75	04.04 ± 03.12
hDisease	78.38 ± 07.76	00.15 ± 00.25	12.33 ± 02.10	09.14 ± 09.14

The considerations about the lower variability of the outcomes (w.r.t. the previous sessions) can be extended to all cases but, as mentioned, this may depend on the number of repetitions in the bootstrap procedure. As regards the error rates, differently from the behavior of other inductive classification methods (d'Amato et al., 2008; Fanizzi et al., 2008b, 2009a), which clearly show nearly null commission rates and a limited number of omission cases, the presented method showed a diverse behavior which again can be explained with the availability of disjointness axioms contained in the ontologies (and partly also to the number of individuals with a known membership w.r.t. the query concepts).

These results can be further compared with those obtained using another concept learner (Table 6). The table immediately shows a certain superiority of the newer algorithm in terms of increase of match rate and decrease of the error rates (especially omission cases). The new results also show more stability except for the ontologies with the hardest concepts (e.g., WINE). An explanation for the improvement comes from the algorithm, implementing a divide-and-conquer strategy, seems more suitable for the problem setting that requires partitioning both positive and negative instances. The algorithm and heuristic implemented in DL-Foil is more separate-and-conquer, and tends to favor the separation of positives from negative and unlabeled instances.

6 CONCLUSION AND OUTLOOK

In this work, we investigated the task of learning concept descriptions expressed in the representations that support the standard ontology languages.

The concept learning problem was formally defined so that its (approximate) solutions could be searching the space of possible definitions of the target concept. This search is operated within a sequential covering algorithm by suitable refinement operators for DLs and guided by the positive and negative training examples labeled by some expert.

The algorithm, that is an adaptation of FOIL to the issues related to the different representation, was implemented in the DL-FOIL system whose components feature a set of refinement operators and a different gain function which takes into account the open-world semantics that requires a special treatment of the unlabeled individuals.

Some experiments have been presented in the paper, applying the DL-FOIL system to learning from individuals in real ontologies which represent a harder testbed w.r.t. the datasets employed for testing other learning systems which aimed at concepts (Fanizzi et al., 2010) or statistical models (d'Amato et al., 2008; Fanizzi et al., 2008b, 2009a). The outcomes in terms of precision and recall were satisfactory. However, these results do not appear as meaningful because in a standard (two-way) setting where uncertainty on the test data is not treated specially, we resorted to different performance metrics, measuring the alignment of the

Table 6. Results obtained using terminological decision trees: averages ± standard deviations

ontology	match rate	commission error rate	omission error rate	induction rate
BioPax	96.51 ± 06.03	01.30 ± 05.72	02.19 ± 00.51	00.00 ± 00,00
NTN	91.65 ± 15.89	00.01 ± 00.09	00.36 ± 01.58	07.98 ± 14.60
Financial	96.21 ± 10.48	02.14 ± 10.07	00.16 ± 00.55	01.49 ± 00.16
Wine	74.36 ± 25.63	00.67 ± 04.63	12.46 ± 14.28	12.13 ± 23,49
MDM0.37	93.96 ± 05.44	00.39 ± 00.61	03.50 ± 04.16	02.15 ± 01.47
hDisease	78.60 ± 39.79	00.02 ± 00.10	01.54 ± 06.01	19.82 ± 39.17

classification decided using the concept descriptions induced by DL-Foil with the classification assigned by the DL reasoner using the original concepts. This allowed assessing the amount of cases of unknown-membership instances that may be ascribed to the newly induced concepts (or to their negations), which constituted an added value brought by the inductive classification method. Actually these conclusions may be considered as *abductive* and their actual relevance should be evaluated by the expert who helped during the construction of the ontology which is very difficult when real ontologies are employed. This may be exploited also in algorithms that aim at detecting hidden disjointness relationships between concepts (Völker, Vrandecic, Sure, & Hotho, 2007).

Especially the second experimental sessions, carried out on various ontologies, showed that the method is quite effective, and its performance depends on the number (and distribution) of the available training instances. Besides, the procedure appears stable and also robust since commission errors were limited in the experiments carried out so far.

The method could be extended along different directions. It may be used for approximating concepts in languages with lower expressiveness (and likely allowing for more efficient reasoning). It may be also the basis for an incremental algorithm that may be able to detect defective concept definitions (e.g., with the availability of new individuals and assertions or as a consequence of some form of *drift*) and employ the refinement operators for finding better definitions (an *ontology evolution* task). Another extension is related to the employment of suitable similarity measures that could influence the chosen generalization strategy as well as example ordering in the training set. Such measures might be exploited also in (hierarchical) clustering algorithms where clusters would be formed grouping instances on the grounds of their similarity (Fanizzi et al., 2004, 2009b). Different groups would be then assimilated to disjoint concepts whose definitions could be learned by means of DL-Foil or similar algorithms.

ACKNOWLEDGMENT

The author is very grateful to Claudia d'Amato and Floriana Esposito for their help and support shown during fruitful discussions.

REFERENCES

Baader, F., Calvanese, D., McGuinness, D., Nardi, D., & Patel-Schneider, P. (Eds.). (2007). *The Description Logic Handbook* (2nd ed.). Cambridge, UK: Cambridge University Press. doi:10.1017/CBO9780511711787.

Baader, F., Ganter, B., Sertkaya, B., & Sattler, U. (2007). Completing description logic knowledge bases using formal concept analysis. In M. Veloso (Ed.), *Proceedings of the 20th International Joint Conference on Artificial Intelligence,* Hyderabad, India (pp. 230-235).

Badea, L., & Nienhuys-Cheng, S.-H. (2000). A refinement operator for description logics. In J. Cussens & A. Frisch (Eds.), *Proceedings of the 10th International Conference on Inductive Logic Programming* (LNAI 1866, pp. 40-59).

Bloehdorn, S., Haase, P., Sure, Y., & Voelker, J. (2006). Ontology evolution. In Davies, J., Studer, R., & Warren, P. (Eds.), *Semantic Web Technologies: Trends and Research in Ontology-based Systems.* New York, NY: Wiley. doi:10.1002/047003033X.ch4.

Borgida, A. (1996). On the relative expressiveness of description logics and predicate logics. *Artificial Intelligence, 82*(1-2), 353–367. doi:10.1016/0004-3702(96)00004-5.

Boström, H., & Asker, L. (1999). Combining divide-and-conquer and separate-and-conquer for efficient and effective rule induction. In S. Dzeroski & P. Flach (Eds.), *Proceedings of the 9th International Workshop on Inductive Logic Programming (ILP-99)* (LNCS 1634, pp. 33-43).

Brandt, S., Küsters, R., & Turhan, A.-Y. (2002). Approximation and difference in description logics. In D. Fensel et al. (Eds.), *Proceedings of the International Conference on Knowledge Representation* (pp. 203-214). San Francisco, CA: Morgan Kaufmann.

Buitelaar, P., & Cimiano, P. (Eds.). (2008). *Ontology Learning and Population: Bridging the Gap between Text and Knowledge*. Amsterdam, The Netherlands: IOS Press.

Cimiano, P., Mädche, A., Staab, S., & Völker, J. (2009). Ontology learning. In Staab, S., & Studer, R. (Eds.), *Handbook on Ontologies* (pp. 245–267). Berlin, Germany: Springer. doi:10.1007/978-3-540-92673-3_11.

Cohen, W., & Hirsh, H. (1992). Learnability of description logics. In *Proceedings of the 4th Annual Workshop on Computational Learning Theory*. New York, NY: ACM Press.

Cohen, W., & Hirsh, H. (1994). Learning the CLASSIC description logic. In P. Torasso, J. Doyle, & E. Sandewall (Eds.), *Proceedings of the 4th International Conference on the Principles of Knowledge Representation and Reasoning* (pp. 121-133). San Francisco, CA: Morgan Kaufmann.

d'Amato, C., Fanizzi, N., & Esposito, F. (2008). Query answering and ontology population: An inductive approach. In S. Bechhofer et al. (Eds.), *Proceedings of the 5th European Semantic Web Conference (ESWC2008)* (LNCS 5021, pp. 288-302).

De Raedt, L. (2008). *Logical and Relational Learning*. Berlin, Germany: Springer. doi:10.1007/978-3-540-68856-3.

Esposito, F., Fanizzi, N., Iannone, L., Palmisano, I., & Semeraro, G. (2004). Knowledge-intensive induction of terminologies from metadata. In F. van Harmelen et al. (Eds.), *Proceedings of the 3rd International Semantic Web Conference (ISWC2004)* (LNCS 3298, pp. 441-455).

Fanizzi, N., d'Amato, C., & Esposito, F. (2008a). DL-FOIL: Concept learning in description logics. In F. Zelezný & N. Lavrač (Eds.), *Proceedings of the 18th International Conference on Inductive Logic Programming (ILP2008)* (LNAI 5194, pp. 107-121).

Fanizzi, N., d'Amato, C., & Esposito, F. (2008b). Statistical learning for inductive query answering on OWL ontologies. In A. Sheth (Eds.), *Proceedings of the 7th International Semantic Web Conference (ISWC2008)* (LNCS 5318, pp. 195-212).

Fanizzi, N., d'Amato, C., & Esposito, F. (2009a). Inductive classification of semantically annotated resources through reduced coulomb energy networks. *International Journal on Semantic Web and Information Systems*, 5(4), 19–38. doi:10.4018/jswis.2009100102.

Fanizzi, N., d'Amato, C., & Esposito, F. (2009b). Metric-based stochastic conceptual clustering for ontologies. *Information Systems*, 34(8), 792–806. doi:10.1016/j.is.2009.03.008.

Fanizzi, N., d'Amato, C., & Esposito, F. (2010). Induction of concepts in web ontologies through terminological decision trees. In J. L. Balcázar et al. (Eds.), *Proceedings of the ECML PKDD 2010 Conference: Part I* (LNAI 6321, pp. 442-457).

Fanizzi, N., Esposito, F., Ferilli, S., & Semeraro, G. (2003). A methodology for the induction of ontological knowledge from semantic annotations. In F. Turini & A. Cappelli (Eds.), *Proceedings of the 8th Conference of the Italian Association for Artificial Intelligence (AI*IA2003)* (LNAI 2829, pp. 65-77).

Fanizzi, N., Ferilli, S., Iannone, L., Palmisano, I., & Semeraro, G. (2005). Downward refinement in the $\mathcal{ALN}$ description logic. In *Proceedings of the 4th International Conference on Hybrid Intelligent Systems (HIS2004)* (pp. 68-73). Washington, DC: IEEE Computer Society.

Fanizzi, N., Iannone, L., Palmisano, I., & Semeraro, G. (2004). Concept formation in expressive description logics. In Boulicaut, J.-F. et al., (Eds.), *Proceedings of the 15th European Conference on Machine Learning (ECML2004)* (LNAI 3201, pp. 99-113).

Goldman, S. A., Kwek, S., & Scott, S. D. (2003). Learning from examples with unspecified attribute values. *Information and Computation, 180*(2), 82–100. doi:10.1016/S0890-5401(02)00030-5.

Grosof, B., Horrocks, I., Volz, R., & Decker, S. (2003). Description logic programs: combining logic programs with description logic. In *Proceedings of the 12th International Conference on World Wide Web (WWW03)* (pp. 48-57). New York, NY: ACM.

Hellmann, S., Lehmann, J., & Auer, S. (2011). Learning of OWL class expressions on very large knowledge bases and its applications. In Sheth, A. (Ed.), *Semantic Services, Interoperability and Web Applications: Emerging Concepts* (pp. 104–130). Hershey, PA: IGI Global.

Iannone, L., Palmisano, I., & Fanizzi, N. (2007). An algorithm based on counterfactuals for concept learning in the semantic web. *Applied Intelligence, 26*(2), 139–159. doi:10.1007/s10489-006-0011-5.

Inuzuka, N., Kamo, M., Ishii, N., Seki, H., & Itoh, H. (1997). Tow-down induction of logic programs from incomplete samples. In S. Muggleton (Ed.), *Selected Papers from the 6th International Workshop on Inductive Logic Programming (ILP96)* (LNAI 1314, pp. 265-282).

Kietz, J.-U. (2002). Learnability of description logic programs. In S. Matwin & C. Sammut (Eds.), *Proceedings of the 12th International Conference on Inductive Logic Programming* (LNAI 2583 pp. 117-132).

Kietz, J.-U., & Morik, K. (1994). A polynomial approach to the constructive induction of structural knowledge. *Machine Learning, 14*(2), 193–218. doi:10.1023/A:1022626200450.

Lehmann, J. (2007). Hybrid learning of ontology classes. In P. Perner (Ed.), *Proceedings of the 5th International Conference on Machine Learning and Data Mining in Pattern Recognition (MLDM2007)* (LNCS 4571, pp. 883-898).

Lehmann, J. (2009). DL-Learner: Learning concepts in description logics. *Journal of Machine Learning Research, 10,* 2639–2642.

Lehmann, J. (2010). *Learning OWL Class Expressions*. Heidelberg, Germany: AKA Heidelberg.

Lehmann, J., Auer, S., Bühmann, L., & Tramp, S. (2011). Class expression learning for ontology engineering. *Journal of Web Semantics, 9*(1), 71–81. doi:10.1016/j.websem.2011.01.001.

Lehmann, J., & Hitzler, P. (2010). Concept learning in description logics using refinement operators. *Machine Learning, 78*(1-2), 203–250. doi:10.1007/s10994-009-5146-2.

Lisi, F. A., & Esposito, F. (2008). Learning $\mathcal{SHIQ}$ +log rules for ontology evolution. In A. Gangemi et al. (Eds.), *Proceedings of the 5th Workshop on Semantic Web Applications and Perspectives (SWAP2008)* (Vol. 426). CEUR-WS.org.

Mitchell, T. (1982). Generalization as search. *Artificial Intelligence, 18*(2), 203–226. doi:10.1016/0004-3702(82)90040-6.

Quinlan, R. (1990). Learning logical definitions from relations. *Machine Learning, 5,* 239–266. doi:10.1007/BF00117105.

Rouveirol, C., & Ventos, V. (2000). Towards learning in CARIN-$\mathcal{ALN}$. In J. Cussens & A. Frisch (Eds.), *Proceedings of the 10th International Conference on Inductive Logic Programming* (LNAI 1866, pp. 191-208).

Staab, S., & Studer, R. (Eds.). (2009). *Handbook on Ontologies* (2nd ed.). Berlin, Germany: Springer. doi:10.1007/978-3-540-92673-3.

Teege, G. (1994). A subtraction operation for description logics. In P. Torasso et al. (Eds.), *Proceedings of the 4th International Conference on Principles of Knowledge Representation and Reasoning* (pp. 540-550). San Francisco, CA: Morgan Kaufmann.

Völker, J., Vrandecic, D., Sure, Y., & Hotho, A. (2007). Learning disjointness. In E. Franconi et al. (Eds.), *Proceedings of the 4th European Semantic Web Conference (ESWC 2007)* (LNCS 4519, pp. 175-189).

ENDNOTES

[1] Note that $\cdot^{\mathcal{I}}$ restricted to N_I is not necessarily injective, that is the unique names assumption is not made by default in this context, hence it must be asserted explicitly if necessary.

[2] The set of the individuals occurring in the assertions of the ABox $\mathcal{A}$ is denoted with $\mathsf{Ind}(\mathcal{A})$.

[3] Dealing with TBoxes with cyclic axioms would require a suitable different (fix-point) semantics (Baader et al., 2007a).

[4] Concrete domains include data types such as numerical types, but also more elaborate domains, such as tuples of the relational calculus, spatial regions, or time intervals.

[5] A model could be constructed for both the membership and non-membership case (Baader et al., 2007a).

[6] This has an impact also on the indices used to assess the quality of the induced concept definition (see Section 5).

[7] A quasi-ordering is a reflexive and transitive relation.

[8] Differently from more complex definitions given in previous works (Iannone et al., 2007), examples do not influence the operators directly.

[9] E.g., using the most specific concepts (Baader et al., 2007a) as their representatives to the concept level. But their exact computation is feasible only for very simple DLs.

[10] The actual exit-condition for the inner loop (line6)being: $1 - \dfrac{\mid CoveredNegatives \mid}{\mid Negatives \mid} < \varepsilon$ for some small constant ε.

[11] A snippet of the code used for query concept generation can be found at: http://lacam.di.uniba.it:8000/~nico/research/snippet1.html.

[12] PELLET (v. 2, publicly available at: http://www.clarkparsia.com/pellet) was adopted for performing instance-checking and the other required reasoning services.

This work was previously published in the International Journal on Semantic Web and Information Systems, Volume 7, Issue 2, edited by Amit P. Sheth,, pp. 23-44, copyright 2011 by IGI Publishing (an imprint of IGI Global).

Chapter 6
Using Similarity–Based Approaches for Continuous Ontology Development

Maryam Ramezani
SAP Research, Germany

ABSTRACT

This paper presents novel algorithms for learning semantic relations from an existing ontology or concept hierarchy. The authors suggest recommendation of semantic relations for supporting continuous ontology development, i.e., the development of ontologies during their use in social semantic bookmarking, semantic wiki, or other Web 2.0 style semantic applications. This paper assists users in placing a newly added concept in a concept hierarchy. The proposed algorithms are evaluated using datasets from Wikipedia category hierarchy and provide recommendations.

INTRODUCTION

Ontologies are known in computer science as consensual models of domains of discourse, usually implemented as formal definitions of the relevant conceptual entities (Hepp, 2007). There are two broad schools of thought on how ontologies are created: the first views ontology development akin to software development as a - by and large - one off effort that happens separate from and before ontology usage. The second view is that ontolo-gies are created and used at the same time, that ontologies are continuously developed throughout their use. The second view is exemplified by the Ontology Maturing model (Braun, Kunzmann, & Schmidt, 2010; Braun, Schmidt, & Walter, 2007) and by the ontologies that are developed in the course of the usage of a semantic wiki (Krótzsch, Vrandecic, Vólkel, Haller, & Studer, 2007).

Machine learning, data mining and text mining methods to support ontology development have so far focused on the first schools of thought;

DOI: 10.4018/978-1-4666-3610-1.ch006

have focused on creating an initial ontology from large sets of text or data that is refined in a manual process before it is then used. For example, recently, many researchers have tried to apply data mining techniques to create ontologies from folksonomies (Heymann & Garcia-Molina, 2006; Balby Marinho, Buza, & Schmidt-Thieme, 2008).

In our work, however, we focus on using machine learning techniques to support continuous ontology development. In particular, we focus on one important decision: given the current state of the ontology, the concepts already present and the sub/super concept relations between them - where should a given new concept be placed? Which existing concept(s) can be considered as the super concept(s) of the new concept?

We investigate this question on the basis of applications that use ontologies to aid in the structuring and retrieval of information resources (as opposed to for example the use of ontologies in an expert system). These applications associate concepts of the ontology with information resources, e.g., a concept "Computer Science Scholar" is associated to a text about Alan Turing. Such system can use the background knowledge about the concept to include Alan Turing page in responses to queries like "important British scholars". Important examples for such systems are:

- **The Floyd Case Management System:** Developed at SAP. In that system, cases and other objects (that are attached to cases, such as documents) can be tagged freely with terms chosen by the user. These terms can also be organized in a semantic network and this can be developed by the users. The Floyd system is usually deployed with a semantic network initially taken from existing company vocabulary.
- **The SOBOLEO System:** (Zacharias & Braun, 2007) Uses a taxonomy developed by the users for the collaborative organization of a repository of interesting web pages.

- **The (Semantic) Media Wiki system:** (Krötzsch et al., 2007) Uses a hierarchy of categories to tag pages. We can view categories as akin to concepts and support the creation and placement of new categories by proposing candidate super-categories.

All these system are "Web 2.0" style semantic applications; they enable users to change and develop the ontology during their use of the system. The work presented in this paper assists users in this task by utilizing machine learning algorithms. The algorithms suggest potential super-concepts for any new concept introduced to the system.

RELATED WORK

According to one of the most cited definitions of the Semantic Web literature, an ontology is a formal, explicit specification of a shared conceptualization (Gruber, 1993). Guarino clarifies Gruber's definition by adding that the AI usage of the term refers to "an engineering artifact, constituted by a specific vocabulary used to describe a certain reality, plus a set of explicit assumptions regarding the intended meaning of the vocabulary words".

John Sowa (Sowa, 2009) classifies ontologies into three kinds. A *formal ontology* is a conceptualization in which categories are described by axioms and definitions. They are stated in logic or in some computer-oriented language that could be automatically translated to logic. In contrast, in *prototype-based ontologies*, categories are distinguished by typical instances or prototypes rather than by axioms and definitions in logic. Categories are formed by collecting instances rather than describing the set of all possible instances in an intensional way, and the most typical members are selected for description. The third kind of ontology is *terminological ontology* which is partially specified by subtype-supertype relations. The concepts are described by concept labels or synonyms rather than prototypical instances (Biemann, 2005). A well known example for a terminological ontology is WordNet (Miller, Beckwith, Fellbaum, Gross, & Miller, 1990). In this work, we focus on terminological ontologies specifically on subtype-supertype relations among concepts.

Ontologies can be learnt from various sources, structured and unstructured documents, databases or more recently from folksonomies. Ontology learning techniques can be divided in two groups: those that construct ontologies from scratch and those that extend existent ontologies. The former includes various clustering techniques (unsupervised learning) and the latter can be viewed as a classification task (supervised learning) (Biemann, 2005) such as machine learning algorithms introduced in Iannone, Palmisano, and Fanizzi (2007), Lehmann and Hitzler (2010), and Fanizzi, d'Amato, and Esposito (2008)

Hierarchical clustering for ontology learning allocates sets of terms in a hierarchy that can be transformed directly into a prototype-based ontology. A distance or similarity measure on terms is defined, and the terms with higher similarity than a specified threshold are merged into one cluster. An overview of clustering methods for obtaining ontologies from different sources is presented in Cimiano, Mдdche, Staab, and Voelker (2009). Here, we review several approaches on ontology learning specifically from folksonomies.

Heymann and Molinay (Heymann & Garcia-Molina, 2006) suggest creating a hierarchical taxonomy of tags. Their algorithm calculates the similarity between tags using the cosine similarity between tag vectors and each new tag added to the system will be categorized as the child of the most similar tag. If the similarity value is less than a pre-defined threshold then the new tag will be added as a new category, which is a new child for the root. The problem with this algorithm is that there is no heuristic to find the parent-child relation. Any new similar tag will be considered as a child of the most similar tag previously added to the system although it might be more general than the other tag.

Marinho et al. (Balby Marinho et al., 2008) use frequent itemset mining for learning ontologies from Folksonomies. In this work, a folksonomy is enriched with a domain expert ontology and the output is a taxonomy which is used for resource recommendation. Authors use two major heuristic to create the taxonomy. First, more popular tags are considered more general and second, a tag x is a super-concept of a tag y if there are frequent itemsets containing both tags such that $support(x) > support(y)$.

Hotho et al. suggest using association rules for discovering semantic relations between tags (Hotho, Jäschke, Schmitz, & Stumme, 2006). Wu et al. use probabilistic EM algorithms to estimate the probability of co-occurrences of folksonomy elements to obtain the emergent semantics contained in the data (Zhang, Wu, & Yu, 2006; Wu, Zhang, & Yu, 2006). The discovered semantic relations are then applied for semantic search and resource discovery. Similarly, Zhou et al. (Zhou, Bao, Wu, & Yu, 2007) propose a probabilistic clustering approach named Deterministic Annealing (DA) for extracting hierarchical semantics from social annotations.

The above mentioned approaches focus on constructing ontologies from folksonomies using unsupervised learning. On the other hand, extension of an existing ontology can often be viewed as a classification task. Features of the existing data can be used as a training set to design a classifier for new instances. Our work in this paper is an extension of such approach in a Web 2.0 environment.

Researchers have explored different machine learning algorithms for learning semantic relations from an existing ontology. Alfonseca and Manandhar (Alfonseca & Manandhar, 2002) propose enrichment of WordNet with new concepts learnt from general purpose texts. For each new concept, the algorithm performs a top-down search along the ontology, and stops at the synset that is most similar to the new concept. The ontology is traversed top-down from the root until an appropriate position is found. The largest problem with this approach is the general nature of top-level concepts that leads to taking the wrong path in the beginning of the process. Similar work is presented in (Witschel, 2005) in which decision trees are used for extending lexical taxonomies. Co-occurrence statistics is used to discover the relations among concepts and the semantic descriptions are propagated iteratively upwards to the root.

Fleischman and Hovy (Fleischman & Hovy, 2002) focus on one specific category of named entities, *persons*, and describe a method for automatically classifying person instances into eight sub-categories, e.g politician, entertainer, etc. A supervised learning method is suggested that considers the local context surrounding the entity as well as more global semantic information derived from topic signatures and WordNet. An unsupervised algorithm is presented in (Widdows, 2003) for placing unknown words into Wordnet taxonomy. The algorithm first finds semantic neighbors of an unknown word by applying latent semantic analysis with part-of-speech information. Then, the unknown word is placed in the part of the taxonomy where these neighbors are most concentrated, using a class-labeling algorithm.

Our approach is similar to the classification tasks described above with several differences. First, all the above mentioned techniques are appropriate for a taxonomic relationship where each concept has only one super-concept while our approach does not have this limitation. Our algorithms can propose several potential super-concepts ordered by the associated confidence. Second, the core algorithm proposed in this work is adaptable for learning any kind of semantic relations including sub-concept, synonym, etc. Finally, our approach suggests a recommendation algorithm to support end users for continuous ontology development collaboratively (Braun et al., 2010, 2007) in a Web 2.0 environment, i.e. where anybody can add a new element to the ontology, and refine or modify existing ones in a work-integrated way. That means the ontology is

continuously evolving and gradually built up from social tagging activities and it is not derived once at a specific time. Our work provides a supporting tool for such ontology building by helping users with recommendation of semantic relationships.

ALGORITHMS

We propose three algorithms for the recommendation of super-concepts for a new concept. First, we presume that a seed hierarchy is not available or if there is one, it is not populated enough to be used for learning purpose. Second, we assume to have an existing concept hierarchy and our goal is to assist users to place a new concept in the right place in the hierarchy. Finally, we present a hybrid recommendation algorithm which combines the first two algorithms.

Algorithm 1: Recommendation of Super-Concepts Without An Existing Seed Hierarchy

We propose Algorithm 1 for cases where little data and (almost) no existing hierarchy is present (for example for cases where a system is just starting to be used). For these cases we propose to use a string-based approach inspired by Hippisley, Cheng, and Ahmad (2005); an approach focusing on compound terms. There are different approaches to find the similarity of two concepts only based on string-based attributes. The common approaches included edit-distance, token-based, and hybrid distance functions. For an overview of different approaches refer to Moreau, Yvon, and Cappé (2008). These approaches are pretty well-established in the literature and our goal is not to contribute to string-based similarity functions but just use them as a first step for our recommendation. We use two of the string-based approaches: Soft-TFIDF and Jaccard similarity. We selected Jaccard similarity for its simplicity and Soft-TFIDF since it has been shown to be the most successful algorithm for string name matching in comparison with other approaches (Cohen, Ravikumar, & Fienberg, 2003).

- **Jaccard Similarity:** Two strings $S1$ and $S2$ can be considered as multi-sets (or bags) of words or tokens). The Jaccard similarity between the word sets $S1$ and $S2$ is simply defined as:

$$J(S1, S2) = \frac{|S1 \cap S2|}{|S1 \cup S2|} \qquad (1)$$

where $S1$ and $S2$ are the sets of words in the concept names being compared. According to this definition, Jaccard similarity of two strings is non-zero only if one string is a compound and contains the other string. For example the Jaccard similarity between two concepts "Computer" and "Computer Science" is 1/2.

- **Soft-TFIDF:** *TFIDF* is a measure widely used in information retrieval and can be also used to compute string similarity between bags of words in a corpus. According to (Moreau et al., 2008), the TFIDF value represents the importance of each feature w (e.g. word) for an entity S belonging to the set E of entities:

$$tf(w, S) = \frac{n_{w,S}}{\sum_{w'} n_{w',S}}, idf(w)) = log \frac{|E|}{|S \in E \mid w \in S|} \qquad (2)$$

$$TFIDF(w, S) = tf(w, S) \times idf(w) \qquad (3)$$

where $n_{w,x}$ is the number of times w appears in S. The TFIDF similarity between S1 and S2 is defined as the COS similarity between the TFIDF vector representations of the S1 and S2.

Soft-TFIDF is a hybrid similarity measure introduced by Cohen et al. (2003) which is designed to take advantage of the good performance of TFIDF, without automatically discarding words which are not strictly identical. Soft-TFIDF combines TFIDF with Jaro-Winkler distance (Winkler, 1999) which is a measure based on the number and order of the common characters between two strings. We have used the available java implementation provided by Cohen et al. (2003). For more details of the algorithm, please refer to Cohen et al. (2003).

- **Super-Concept Recommendation:** We first compute the similarity between the name of the new concept and the names of concepts already known to the system (the candidate super-concepts) as described above. The super-concept recommendation is then based on the observation that the head of a compound is often a super-concept of the compound itself (Hippisley et al., 2005). Therefore, we can observe that sub-concepts generally consist of more terms than their super-concepts, and – if they are formed out of super-concepts by adding so-called modifiers – usually also have significant string overlap with their super-concepts. For example "Computer Science" is a sub-concept of "science".

Thus, we define recommendation confidence as $W(S,T)=Sim(S,T)$ if S has fewer terms than T and 0 otherwise. More formally:

$$W(S,T) = \begin{cases} Sim(S,T) & \text{If } \sum_{w \in S} n_{w,S} < \sum_{w' \in T} n_{w',T} \\ 0 & \text{otherwise} \end{cases} \qquad (4)$$

where $Sim(S,T)$ is the string-based similarity and $n_{w,S}$ is the number of times w appears in S.

To find the super concepts for a new concept C_t, we find $W(C_i, C_t)$ where $C_i \in E$ represents all existing concepts in the existing concept-hierarchy E.

Concepts with the highest W can be recommended as possible super concept for the new concept. We can recommend a list of top n concepts with highest W where n is a pre-fixed number or we can use a threshold value and only recommend concepts with W higher than the threshold.

This algorithm though useful, has several weaknesses. First, it does not work when two words are syntactically very similar but semantically different (or opposite), i.e., "science" and "non science". Second, it does not make a distinction between different parts of the words. For instance, both terms "computer" and "science" get the same confidence for being the super-concept of "computer science". Third, this algorithm is only applicable for taxonomic relations and is not easily adaptable for other types of relations in an ontology.

Other imaginable algorithms for this task could build on data distribution properties such as entropy or co-occurrence. However, we do not consider those approaches here because our main goal in this paper is to learn from an existing hierarchy. We only suggest Algorithm 1 for cases that there is not enough data to learn from, and in such cases, statistical approaches are also not practical. Our main contribution in this paper will be presented in the next section, in Algorithm 2, in which we assume to have a seed hierarchy to start with.

Algorithm 2: Recommendation of Super-Concepts by Learning from an Existing Concept Hierarchy

We propose Algorithm 2 for cases where already a sizeable hierarchy exists. The abstract idea for the proposed algorithm is to place a new concept at a location in the hierarchy where it is most similar to its siblings; most similar to other concepts in the same neighborhood of the concept hierarchy. We first present a simple approach to measure the degree of sub-super relationship between

concepts in a concept hierarchy. Then, we present our algorithm which predicts this value for any newly introduced concept based on its similarity to the existing concepts.

- **Degree of Sub-Super Relationship in a Concept Hierarchy:** There are various approaches to calculate the semantic similarity between concepts in a concept hierarchy. The simplest approach is probably the edge-counting which goes back to Quillian's semantic memory model (Collins & Quillian, 1969). Later, more factors including depths of concept nodes, the density of the hierarchy, link type, and link strength were considered to enhance the path length approach (Xu, Huang, Wan, & Jiang, 2008, Yang & Powers, 2005, Rodrнguez, Rodrguez, Egenhofer, & Egenhofer, 2003).

In this work, we are interested in measuring the degree of sub-super relationship between two concepts rather than the semantic similarity between them since our goal is to find the super-concepts for a particular new concept. For this purpose, we adopt the simple edge-counting approach by considering one-directional edges between super and sub-concepts. We define "super-sub affinity" (SSA) as following.

Definition 1: *SSA(A,B) is the reverse of the shortest path distance between two concepts A and B, starting from the concept B allowing only upward edges to arrive to A. We define SSA(A,A)=1.*

To clarify how we find SSA, consider the concept hierarchy in Figure 1. In this example the SSA(Computer Science,Algorithms)=1 since the shortest path distance between "computer science" and "computer vision" is 1, SSA(Computer Science, Computer Vision)=1/2 since the short-

Figure 1. An example from a part of concept Hierarchy from Wikipedia. We define "SSA" as the reverse of shortest path distance between the super-sub concept.

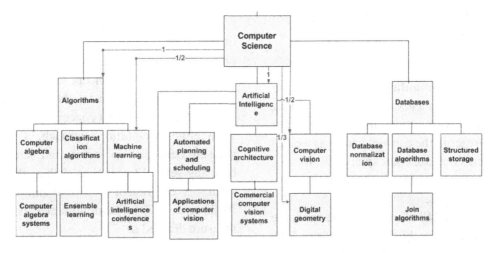

est path distance between the two concepts is 2. SSA(Algorithms, Structured Storage)=0 since we only consider the upward edges starting from concept "Structured Storage". Note that SSA is not a symmetric relation, considering that if *A* is super-concept of *B*, then *B* can not be a super-concept of *A*. In fact, the definition of SSA would entail "if SSA(A,B)≠0 then SSA(B,A)=0".

We can store all SSA values of a concept hierarchy in an $n \times m$ matrix where n is the number of concepts which have at least one sub-concept, m is the total number of concepts in the hierarchy, and the matrix diagonal is always 1. We will use this matrix in our recommendation algorithm for discovering super-concepts. The transpose of this matrix can be used for suggesting sub-concepts

using the same algorithm. However, in this work, we focus only on recommending super-concepts.

- **General Architecture:** Figure 2 shows the general architecture of our system. Generally, we assume that users interact with a Web 2.0 application. While they do so, the database gets updated with new concepts that they enter, for example, tags in a social tagging system, categories or pages in a Wiki. The new concepts are then introduced to the maturing engine, which recommends potential super-concepts to the user once it has enough information about the new concept. If the user accepts the recommendation, the new sub-super relationship will be added to the concept

Figure 2. Recommender Architecture

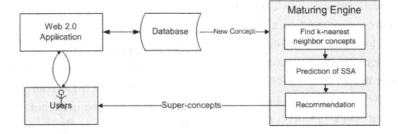

hierarchy. The maturing engine executes three main steps to compute the potential super-concepts: Similarity computation, SSA prediction, and recommendation.

- **Similarity Computation:** To find the similarity between a new concept and existing concepts, we consider measures that use similarities in the concept names as well as measures that use contextual cues. We discuss details of either approach in the coming paragraphs.

- **String-Based Similarity:** we use the same approaches already described in previous section, Jaccard and Soft-TFIDF. We define $Sim_s(C_t, C_i)$ as the string-based similarity between two concepts C_t and C_i. We also define the set of k most similar concepts to the target concept C_t and call this set N_s.

- **Context-Based Similarity:** uses the context that the new concept has been used in to find similar concepts. Context has been defined by Dey (Dey, 2001) as any information that can be used to characterize the situation of an entity. In a social tagging system, for example, the context of a new tag entered into the system can be determined by the related resources, links between the resources, users who enter the tag, time, language and geographical information. In this work, we assume that the new concept is added to the system by associating it to several resources. The resources can be Web pages (such as in social bookmarking systems or Wikipedia pages), documents, images, music, etc. We use the resources associated to a concept as a feature set to determine the context of the concept. We represent each concept, C, as a vector over the set of resources, where each weight, $w(r_i)$, corresponds to the importance of a particular resource, r_i.

$$\vec{C} = \langle w(r_1), w(r_2) w(r_{|R|}) \rangle \quad (5)$$

In calculating the vector weights, a variety of measures can be used. The weights may be binary, merely showing that one or more users have associated that concept to the resource, or it may be finer grained using the number of users that have associated that concept to the resource. With either weighting approach, a similarity measure between two vectors can be calculated by using several techniques such as the Jaccard similarity coefficient or Cosine similarity (Van Rijsbergen, 1979). Cosine similarity is a popular measure defined as

$$Cosine(C1, C2) = \frac{C1.C2}{\|C1\|\|C2\|} \quad (6)$$

In this work, we use binary weighting for representing concepts as a vector of pages and Cosine similarity to find similar concepts. Thus, the similarity between each concept C_i and the new target concept C_t is defined as $sim_c(C_t, C_i) = Cosine(C_t, C_i)$. Using this similarity measure, we find the set of k most similar concepts to the target concept C_t and we call this set N_c.

We define a *hybrid similarity measure* by combining the string-based and contextual-based similarity measures. For that purpose, we use a linear combination of the similarity values found in each approach.

$$Sim_h(C_i, C_t) = \alpha Sim_s(C_i, C_t) \\ +(1-\alpha)Sim_c(C_i, C_t) \quad (7)$$

where $Sim_h(C_i, C_t)$ is the hybrid similarity value, and α is a combination parameter specifying the weight of string-based approach in the combined measure. If $\alpha = 1$, then $Sim_h(C_i, C_t) = Sim_s(C_i, C_t)$, in other words the neighbors are calculated only based on string-similarity. On the other hand, if

$\alpha = 0$, then only the contextual information is used for finding similar concepts. We choose the proper value of alpha by performing sensitivity analysis in our experimental section.

- **Prediction Computation:** Based on the Super-Sub Affinity and the similarity measures defined above, we can now predict the degree of sub-super relationship (SSA) between the new concept and every other concept in the hierarchy. Our proposed algorithm is inspired by the popular weighted sum approach for item-based collaborative filtering (Sarwar, Karypis, Konstan, & Reidl, 2001).

Formally, we predict the SSA between the target concept C_tC_t and all other concepts C_iC_i in the hierarchy as follows.

$$SSA_p(C_i,C_t) = \frac{\sum\limits_{C_n \in N} SSA(C_i,C_n) * sim(C_t,C_n)}{\sum\limits_{C_n \in N} sim(C_t,C_n)} \quad (8)$$

where $SSA_p(C_i,C_t)$ stands for the predicted SSA value for the pair (C_i,C_t), $SSA(C_i,C_n)$ stands for the actual SSA for (C_i,C_n), and $sim(C_t,C_n)$ is the similarity value between the target concept and neighbor concept which can be either string-based (Sim_s), contextual (Sim_c) or the hybrid (Sim_h) similarity. Thus, N can be either N_s, N_c or N_h as described previously. Basically, SSA_p is predicted based on the location of the existing concepts that are similar to C_tC_t; it becomes large when many of C_t's neighbors are close to the current candidate concept C_i in terms of SSA. Hence, the best candidates for becoming a super-concept of C_t are those C_i for which $SSA_p(C_i,C_t)$ is maximal. The weighted sum is scaled by the sum of the similar-

ity terms to make sure the prediction is within the predefined range. In this work we have defined the direct sub-super affinity as 1. Thus, the nearer the prediction of $SSA(C_i,C_t)$ to 1, the more probable that C_i is a good super-concept of C_t.

Recommendation: Once the SSA values for all existing concepts and the new concept are calculated, the concept(s) with the highest SSA can be recommended as super-concept(s) for the new concept. We can recommend a list of top n n concepts with highest SSA prediction or we can use a threshold value and only recommend concepts with predicted SSA higher than the threshold. The threshold value (between 0 and 1) represents the "confidence" of the algorithm in recommendations. If there are no similar concepts found in step 1 or the predicted SSA values are lower than the threshold, the system does not make a recommendation which might mean that the new concept should be added as a new independent concept in top of the hierarchy or that the system is not able to find the right place for the new concept.

Algorithm 3: Hybrid Recommendation

As Algorithm 3 we propose a combination of the two algorithms presented above based on the well known idea of hybrid recommender systems that combine two or more recommendation techniques to gain better performance with fewer of the drawbacks of any individual one (Burke, 2002). We combine Algorithm 1 and Algorithm 2 using a linear combination approach:

$$\begin{aligned} W_h(C_i,C_t) &= \beta W(C_i,C_t) \\ &+ (1-\beta)SSA_p(C_i,C_t) \\ \beta \quad &\beta = 1, \quad \beta = 0, \quad \beta \end{aligned} \quad (9)$$

EVALUATION

In this section, we describe the data sets used for evaluation, our evaluation methodology, and our experimental metrics.

DATA SETS

Wikipedia: To test our algorithms we need a Web 2.0 application where users can easily add new concepts and create semantic relations. We decided to use Wikipedia which is the most suitable Web 2.0 application at hand. Hepp (Hepp, Siorpaes, & Bachlechner, 2007) theoretically proves Wikipedia as a reliable and large living ontology. We treat the categories of Wikipedia as concepts and the existing relationships between "Sub-categories" as the seed concept hierarchy. Each category in Wikipedia has several associated pages, which we use as a context vector for the category. Thus, each category is represented as a binary vector over the set of pages. The weight of each page r_i for category C_j is 1 if page r_i is associated to category C_j and 0 otherwise.

For running our experiments, we focused on a small part of the English Wikipedia. We started from the category "Computer Science" as the root concept and extracted the sub-categories by traversing with breadth first search through the category hierarchy. Our final data set has over 80,000 categories. For our experiments we created three smaller data sets to compare how the size and properties of the seed concept hierarchy impact the results. Table 1 shows the properties of each data set from Wikipedia.

Floyd: As second data set we utilize data from the use of the prototypical Floyd system at SAP. This data set provides a seed ontology in the sense that 241 known hierarchical relations between term concepts are defined in the semantic network.

Unfortunately, the user base for the Floyd system is still too small to yield any significant

Table 1. Properties of the Wikipedia category data for different sizes

Data Properties	Large	Medium	Small
Number of Concepts	24,024	9931	3016
Number of Pages	209,076	107,41	47,523
Average depth of the hierarchy	9	6	3

context data and the semantic network which is to be used as the seed concept hierarchy is still under development. So, only Algorithm 1 could be evaluated on this data. It is still interesting to investigate this data set, especially because of its differences with the Wikipedia data since it is used within the marketing domain. The system contains mainly named entities – names of products, competitors, and also terms describing the market addressed by the company. These terms are quite different from Wikipedia categories and are from a rather specialized vocabulary.

EVALUATION METHODOLOGY

We divided each data set into a training set and a test set. Since we were interested to know how the density of the seed ontology affects the results, we introduced a variable that determines what percentage of data is used as training and test sets; we call this variable x. A value of $x = 20\%$ would indicate 80% of the data was used as training set and 20% of the data was used as test set. The test cases are selected randomly from the data. We remove all information of test cases from the data set to evaluate the performance of the algorithm. For each experiment, we calculate the SSA values before and after removing the test cases. If the test case has sub-concept and super-concept, after removing the test case, its sub-concepts will be directly connected to its super-concepts. Since Algorithm 1 does not need training, we expect no change in performance of the algorithm with different test/train ratio and we can use leave one out methodology for experiments of Algorithm 1.

EXPERIMENTAL METRICS

For the evaluation we adopt the common recall and precision measures from the Information Retrieval community. Recall is a common metric for evaluating the utility of recommendation algorithms. It measures the percentage of items in the test set that appear in the recommendation set. Recall is a measure of completeness and is defined as:

$$Recall = \frac{\mid relevantitems \mid \cap \mid recommendeditems \mid}{\mid allrelevantitems \mid} \quad (10)$$

Precision measures the percentage of items in the recommendation set that appear in the test set. Precision measures the exactness of the recommendation algorithm and is defined as:

$$Precision = \frac{\mid relevantitems \mid \cap \mid recommendeditems \mid}{\mid allrecommendeditems \mid} \quad (11)$$

In order to be able to compare the performance of the algorithms, we use the F-measure defined as following:

$$F - Measure = \frac{2 \times Precision \times Recall}{Precision + Recall} \quad (12)$$

EXPERIMENTAL RESULTS

In this section we present our experimental results of applying the proposed recommendation algorithms to the data sets described above. In all experiments, we change the threshold value from 0 to 0.95 and record the values of precision and recall. As the threshold value increases, we expect precision to increase and recall to decrease since

we recommend less items with higher confidence. In addition, to get a better view of performance of the algorithms, we use the notion of recall at N. The idea is to establish a window of size N at the top of the recommendation list and find recall for different number of recommendations. As the number of recommendations increases, we expect to get higher recall.

EXPERIMENTAL RESULTS FROM ALGORITHM 1

We applied the mentioned string-based techniques for recommendation of super-concepts for both data sets. The results of those experiments are shown in Figures 3 and 4. The charts show the precision and recall as we increase the threshold value. The maximum threshold value for each case is the maximum possible string-similarity in the data set which is not necessarily 1. We can observe a similar trend for both data sets which can confirm that our evaluation with Wikipedia data set is applicable to an actual real data set. From these charts, we can also observe that while Jaccard similarity seems to deliver better precision, TFIDF similarity provides better recall for almost all threshold values.

EXPERIMENTAL RESULTS FROM ALGORITHM 2

Similar to Algorithm 1, we change the threshold value from 0 to .95 and record the values of precision and recall. Before we compare the performance of different similarity measures, we run several experiments to find the sensibility of different parameters including the data size, the neighborhood size, and the combination factor for the hybrid similarity.

Effect of the Neighborhood Size: To determine the influence of neighborhood size, we

Figure 3. Result of Algorithm 1 for Wikipedia data set

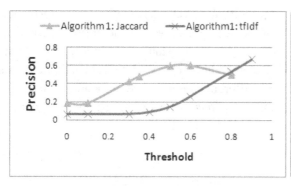 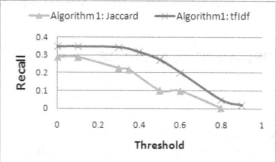

Figure 4. Result of Algorithm 1 for Floyd data set

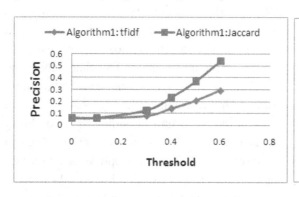 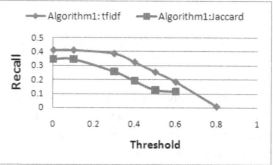

Figure 5. Precision and Recall for different threshold values for different neighborhood values (k)

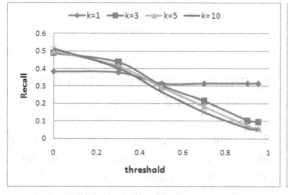 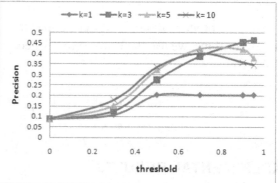

performed an experiment where we varied the number of neighbors to be used and computed precision and recall. The results of this experiment for the medium data set is shown in Figure 5. From this figure, we can observe that there is a trade-off between better precision or better recall depending on the neighborhood size. We select $k=3$ as our neighborhood size which gives better precision for high threshold values assuming that precision is more important for users. In a real scenario, depending on the goal of the system, the neighborhood size can be tuned for the optimum performance which can be high precision, high recall or a middle point with acceptable values for both.

Note that k=1 can be considered as a baseline algorithm since it simply finds the most similar concept to the new concept and recommends its super-concepts.

Effect of Data Set Size: To determine the effect of the size of the data in our results, we conducted experiments with differently sized data sets. We recorded the values of precision and recall for different threshold values for our three data sets with 10% test data (x=10%). We can observe from the results shown in Figure 6 that the differences between the values are not significant. While the small data set seems to create slightly better results, the large data set shows slightly better precision and recall than the medium data set. Thus, the algorithm is not really sensitive to the data size. For that reason and also because of need of more computation time for larger data set, we used the small data set for the further experiments.

Effect of comb*ination factor* α : To determine the sensitivity of the value of α for combining different similarity cues, we conducted experiments with different values of α. The result of this experiments is shown in the left chart of Figure 8. From this chart we select the value of $\alpha = .4$.

Comparison of Similarity Measures and Comparison with Baseline: Once we obtain the

optimal values of the parameters, we compare the performance of the algorithm when using different similarity computation techniques. In addition, we compared our approach with a baseline algorithm suggested in Heymann and Garcia-Molina (2006). The results of these comparisons are shown in Figure 7. The baseline algorithm uses the cosine similarity between concepts and recommends the concepts with highest cosine similarity. Basically, the baseline algorithm is similar to similarity computation step of our algorithm where we find the k-nearest neighbors based on contextual cues. Even though our approach show extremely better results that the baseline, we have to note that the results from our algorithm is not really comparable with this baseline or other ontology learning approaches from folksonomies in the literature since previous approaches similar to Heymann and Garcia-Molina (2006) focus on creating an ontology from folksonomy while our approach focuses on extension of existing ontologies. Other previous algorithms suggested for extension of existing ontologies such as Alfonseca and Manandhar (2002) and Widdows (2003) focus on ontology learning from text rather than Web 2.0 and are not exactly comparable with our method. So, we did not implement those approaches in our work.

Our results show that the hybrid similarity outperforms other approaches for both precision and recall for all threshold and x values. We can observe from Figure 7 that while contextual cues result in less precision than the string-based techniques, they produce slightly higher recall. That

Figure 6. Precision and Recall for different threshold values in three data sets with different sizes

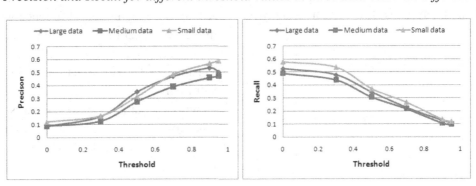

Figure 7. Comparison of Precision and Recall of Algorithm 2 when using different similarity measures

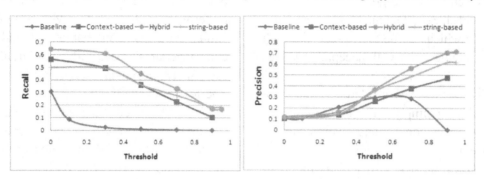

Table 2. An example: Output of recommendation Algorithm 2 using different similarity cues. Recommendations are predicted super-concepts for the new concept "Botnets"

Wikipedia	Contextual-based	String-based	Hybrid Similarity
Multi-agent systems	Artificial intelligence	Multi-agent systems	Multi-agent systems
Computer network security	Multi-agent systems	Computer network security	Artificial intelligence
	Computer architecture	Computer security organizations	Computer architecture
	Network architecture	Artificial intelligence	Computer network security
	Distributed computing	Computer architecture	Distributed computing

shows that string-based techniques can suggest more accurate recommendations but they do not have as much coverage as the contextual cues.

An Example: Table 2 shows one such sample from the actual recommendation results. The example shows the five top recommendation for potential super concepts of the new concept "Botnets", when using different similarity measures. The most right column shows the actual super-concepts in Wikipedia. We can observe that even though the system considers the recommendations that do not appear in Wikipedia as incorrect and counts them as miss in calculating the precision and recall, in many cases they might actually make sense.

EXPERIMENTAL RESULTS FROM ALGORITHM 3

We applied the hybrid recommendation algorithm by combining the results from the hybrid similarity approach of Algorithm 2 and TFIDF string-based technique from Algorithm 1. The right chart of Figure 8 shows the result of the sensitivity analysis for selecting the optimum β. We selected the combination factor, $\beta = .3$ from this chart.

The precision and recall values shown in Figure 9 show that the performance of Algorithm 3 does not have significant difference with Algorithm 2 in respect to recall while it can result in considerably higher precision. We can achieve precision of 90% when the threshold value is set accordingly.

Figures 10 and 11 show comparison of performance of different algorithms. Figure 10 shows the F-measure for each algorithm as threshold

Figure 8. Selection of the optimum combination factor

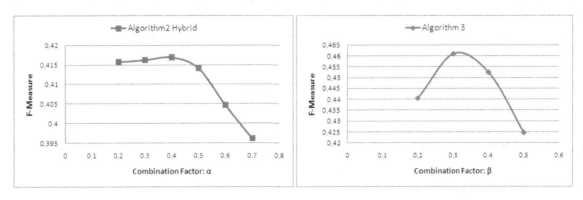

Figure 9. Comparison of precision and recall values for Algorithm 2 and Algorithm 3

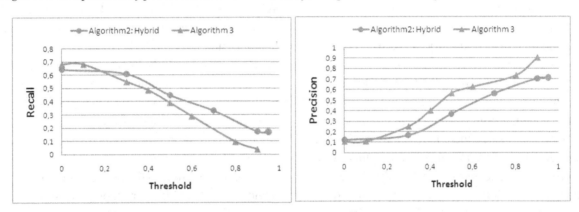

Figure 10. Comparison of F-measure for different approaches by changing the threshold value

Figure 11. Comparison of recall at N for different algorithms

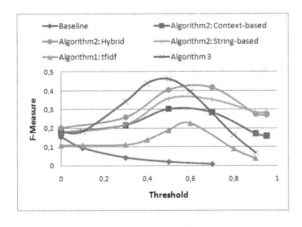
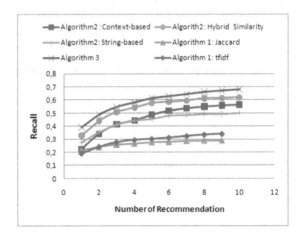

value changes and Figure 11 shows recall at N. Basically, we count the correct answers as we recommend N super-concepts.

We can observe from both charts that Algorithm 3 obviously outperforms all other techniques. In addition, it is clear from the charts that the hybrid similarity outperforms each individual similarity cue. However, it is not trivial to determine if string-based similarity performs better in Algorithm 2 than the contextual one. The contextual cues outperform string-based ones when looking at the Recall at N while based on F-measure the string-based techniques outperform contextual ones.

Impact of the Seed Hierarchy Density. To determine the effect of density of the seed concept hierarchy, we carried out an experiment where we varied the value of x from 20% to 80%. Our results are shown in Figure 12. As expected, the quality of recommendations of Algorithm 2 decreases as we increase x since there is less information for the algorithm to learn from the existing hierarchy. However, the performance of Algorithm 1 does not change as we increase x since Algorithm 1 does not need training. Algorithm 3 benefits from this feature of Algorithm 1 and its performance does not drastically decrease as the seed hierarchy gets smaller. Thus, Algorithm 3 can perform well when the system is almost new and there is not much

existing hierarchy information to learn from. The performance would increase as more information is entered into the system by the users.

EXPERT EVALUATION

Table 3 shows an example of the potential super-concepts suggested by each algorithms for the concept "Computer hardware researchers". We can see that the actual super concepts for this concept in Wikipedia are "Computer scientists by field of research" and "Computer architecture". While only these two concepts are considered as correct answer, we can see that some of the recommendations might be even more relevant than these two concepts. For example, "Computer scientists" and "Computer systems researchers", recommended by Algorithm 2 and Algorithm 3 are certainly more relevant to be the super-concept of "Computer hardware researchers" than "Computer architecture".

To gain insight into the quality of the recommendation created by our algorithm, we further performed an expert evaluation by exploring sample recommendation results from Algorithm 3. We extracted 100 examples from the data set and asked 10 computer science experts (senior PhD students and postdocs) to evaluate if the

Figure 12. Impact of the test/train ratio (the density of the seed hierarchy)

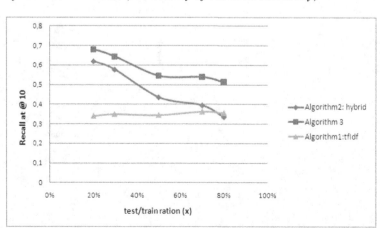

Table 3. An example: Output of different recommendation algorithms. Recommendations are predicted super concepts of the new concept "Computer hardware researchers"

Wikipedia	Algorithm 1: Jaccard Similarity	Algorithm 2: Hybrid Similarity	Algorithm 3
Computer scientists by field of research	Computer vision	Computer scientists by field of research	Computer scientists by field of research
Computer architecture	Computer architecture	Computer scientists	Computer scientists
	Database researchers	Computer systems researchers	Computer architecture
	Graphics hardware	Computer graphics	Computer systems researchers
	Computer scientists	Computer graphics researchers	Graphics hardware

recommended super-concepts are appropriate. We provided the experts with two sets of potential super-concepts for each concept. The first set consists of the super categories directly extracted from Wikipedia and the other set consists of the results of our algorithm. Thus, the experts have evaluated our algorithm as well as the Wikipedia category hierarchy. The results from the expert evaluation is shown in Table 4. The Wikipedia category hierarchy has precision of 82% which means that in some cases, the experts found the super-categories in the Wikipedia inappropriate. Since our algorithm learns from existing relations in Wikipedia, we do not naturally expect to get better results than Wikipedia. However, we can see that based on expert evaluation reported in Table 4, our algorithm performs even better than the reported values in the charts. For example, in Figure 9, the precision is equal to 58% when the threshold is set to .5 while in Table 4, the precision for this threshold is 89%.

We report the average number of super-concepts instead of recall since it is only possible to measure recall if the correct super-concepts are clearly defined in advance. The average number of super-concepts for each concept in Wikipedia is 1.7. We can see that to get similar coverage from our algorithm (average number of super-concepts=1.65), we should set the threshold to .4 which results in precision of 77%. We also looked at the precision when exactly one super-concept

is recommended for each new concept independent of the threshold value. In this case, the average number of super-concept is obviously 1 and it results in precision of 81%.

DISCUSSION

From the experimental evaluation of the algorithms, we make some important observations. Each of the proposed algorithms has certain pros and cons. Algorithm 1 does not require a seed hierarchy and this feature makes it applicable to any kind of system. However, the algorithm is very basic and does not learn or get better as more data enters to the system. Thus, this algorithm might only be appropriate at start phase of a system. On the other hand, Algorithm 2 requires a seed hierarchy to start with but it has the advantage that it can learn from the existing hierarchy and also

Table 4. Expert evaluation results

Threshold	Precision	Average number of super-concepts
.9	100%	.16
.7	97%	.45
.5	89%	.87
.4	77%	1.65
–	81%	1
Wikipedia Hierarchy	82%	1.7

considers the contextual information. Therefore, it results in considerably higher accuracy and coverage. Algorithm 3 can benefit from both Algorithms 1 and 2 without having the limitations of each individual algorithm. We can conclude from the overall results that the hybrid algorithm (Algorithm 3) can be used as a strong algorithm for recommendation of potential super-concepts independent of the properties of the seed hierarchy.

The qualitative results from expert evaluations shows that our algorithm can produce results which are almost as accurate as the existing Wikipedia hierarchy. Thus, the system can also be used directly in Wikipedia for improving the coverage of the category hierarchy.

In this work, we have focused on recommendation of super-concepts. An important feature of our proposed algorithm, is that it is not only limited to super-concepts. Other types of semantic relations such as sub-concepts, synonymy, antonymy, polysemy, etc. can be recommended by defining the SSA value in the right way. For example, to recommend sub-concepts, it is enough to define the $SSA(C1,C2)=1$ when C1 is sub-concept of C2. Similarly, for any other type of semantic relations, it is enough to define the SSA accordingly.

CONCLUSION AND FUTURE WORK

In this paper, we presented machine learning algorithms to support continuous ontology development. We proposed recommendation of semantic relations to assist end users to continuously develop the ontology. Our core algorithm learns from existing relations of a concept hierarchy and uses similarity cues to place newly added concepts into the existing hierarchy. We suggested a hybrid algorithm to increase the performance of the algorithm in cases where the hierarchy is not

yet populated enough. Our extensive experiments on data sets from Wikipedia category hierarchy and our expert evaluation show excellent results. Even though we have concentrated on learning taxonomic relations, the algorithm can easily be adapted for learning other kinds of relations in an ontology.

Future work can evaluate the algorithm for prediction of other types of semantic relations. In addition, exploring other contextual cues such as links between pages, user information, etc. can be considered for finding the most similar concepts. Using more sophisticated string-based algorithms that can solve the problems of Algorithm 1 is also a matter of future work.

Evaluation of the algorithms in an actual interactive social semantic bookmarking application can help us answer the question whether the generated recommendations are actually perceived as useful by the user.

ACKNOWLEDGMENT

This paper is an extension of conference paper, "Using Machine Learning to Support Continuous Ontology Development" presented at the 17th International Conference on Knowledge Engineering and Knowledge Management, EKAW 2010 (Ramezani, Friedrich Witschel, Braun, & Zacharias, 2010). Thanks to Valentin Zacharias, Hans Friedrich Witschel and Simone Braun for their contributions to this work. This work was supported in part by the MATURE Project co-funded by the European Commission.

REFERENCES

Alfonseca, E., & Manandhar, S. (2002). Extending a lexical ontology by a combination of distributional semantics signatures. In *Proceedings of the 13th International Conference on Knowledge Engineering and Knowledge Management, Ontologies and the Semantic Web* (pp. 1-7). Berlin, Germany: Springer-Verlag.

Balby Marinho, L., Buza, K., & Schmidt-Thieme, L. (2008). Folksonomy-based collabulary learning. In *ISWC '08: Proceedings of the 7th International Conference on the Semantic Web* (pp. 261-276). Berlin, Germany: Springer-Verlag.

Biemann, C. (2005). Ontology learning from text: A survey of methods. *LDV Forum, 20*(2), 75–93.

Braun, S., Kunzmann, C., & Schmidt, A. (2010). People tagging & ontology maturing: Towards collaborative competence management. In Randall, D., & Salembier, P. (Eds.), *From CSCW to Web2.0: European Developments in Collaborative Design Selected Papers from COOP08*. Berlin, Germany: Springer-Verlag. doi:10.1007/978-1-84882-965-7_7.

Braun, S., Schmidt, A., & Walter, A. (2007). Ontology maturing: a collaborative web 2.0 approach to ontology engineering. In *Proceedings of the Workshop on Social and Collaborative Construction of Structured Knowledge (CKC) at the 16th International World Wide Web Conference*.

Burke, R. (2002). Hybrid recommender systems: Survey and experiments. *User Modeling and User-Adapted Interaction, 12*(4), 331–370. doi:10.1023/A:1021240730564.

Cimiano, P., Mädche, A., Staab, S., & Voelker, J. (2009). Ontology learning. In Staab, S., & Studer, R. (Eds.), *Handbook on Ontologies* (2nd ed.). Berlin, Germany: Springer. doi:10.1007/978-3-540-92673-3_11.

Cohen, W. W., Ravikumar, P., & Fienberg, S. E. (2003). A Comparison of String Distance Metrics for Name-Matching Tasks. In *Proceedings of the IJCAI'03 Workshop on Information Integration on the Web* (pp. 73-78).

Collins, A. M., & Quillian, M. R. (1969). Retrieval time from semantic memory. *Journal of Verbal Learning and Verbal Behavior, 8*, 240–248. doi:10.1016/S0022-5371(69)80069-1.

Dey, A. K. (2001). Understanding and using context. *Personal and Ubiquitous Computing, 5*(1), 4–7. doi:10.1007/s007790170019.

Fanizzi, N., d'Amato, C., & Esposito, F. (2008). Conceptual clustering and its application to concept drift and novelty detection. In *Proceedings of the 5th European Semantic Web Conference on the Semantic Web: Research and Applications* (pp. 318-332). Berlin, Germany: Springer-Verlag.

Fleischman, M., & Hovy, E. (2002). Fine grained classification of named entities. In *Proceedings of the 19th International Conference on Computational Linguistics* (pp. 1-7).

Gruber, T. R. (1993). Toward principles for the design of ontologies used for knowledge sharing. *International Journal of Human-Computer Studies, 43*(5), 907–928. doi:10.1006/ijhc.1995.1081.

Hepp, M. (2007). Possible ontologies: How reality constrains the development of relevant ontologies. *IEEE Internet Computing, 11*, 90–96. doi:10.1109/MIC.2007.20.

Hepp, M., Siorpaes, K., & Bachlechner, D. (2007). Harvesting wiki consensus: Using Wikipedia entries as vocabulary for knowledge management. *IEEE Internet Computing, 11*, 54–65. doi:10.1109/MIC.2007.110.

Heymann, P., & Garcia-Molina, H. (2006, April). *Collaborative creation of communal hierarchical taxonomies in social tagging systems* (Tech. Rep. No. 2006-10). Palo Alto, CA: Stanford University.

Hippisley, A., Cheng, D., & Ahmad, K. (2005). The head-modifier principle and multilingual term extraction. *Natural Language Engineering*, *11*(2), 129–157. doi:10.1017/S1351324904003535.

Hotho, A., Jäschke, R., Schmitz, C., & Stumme, G. (2006). Emergent Semantics in BibSonomy. In *Proceedings of the Workshop on Applications of Semantic Technologies*.

Iannone, L., Palmisano, I., & Fanizzi, N. (2007). An algorithm based on counterfactuals for concept learning in the semantic web. *Applied Intelligence*, *26*, 139–159. doi:10.1007/s10489-006-0011-5.

Krótzsch, M., Vrandecic, D., Vólkel, M., Haller, H., & Studer, R. (2007). Semantic Wikipedia. *Journal of Web Semantics*, *5*, 251–261. doi:10.1016/j.websem.2007.09.001.

Lehmann, J., & Hitzler, P. (2010). Concept learning in description logics using refinement operators. *Machine Learning*, *78*, 203–250. doi:10.1007/s10994-009-5146-2.

Miller, G. A., Beckwith, R., Fellbaum, C., Gross, D., & Miller, K. (1990). Wordnet: An on-line lexical database. *International Journal of Lexicography*, *3*, 235–244. doi:10.1093/ijl/3.4.235.

Moreau, E., Yvon, F., & Cappé, O. (2008). Robust similarity measures for named entities matching. In *COLING '08: Proceedings of the 22nd International Conference on Computational Linguistics* (pp. 593-600). Morristown, NJ: Association for Computational Linguistics.

Ramezani, M. FriedrichWitschel, H., Braun, S., & Zacharias, V. (2010). Using machine learning to support continuous ontology development. In *EKAW 2010: 17th International Conference on Knowledge Engineering and Knowledge Management*.

Rodrиguez, M. A., Rodrguez, M. A., Egenhofer, M. J., & Egenhofer, M. J. (2003). Determining semantic similarity among entity classes from different ontologies. *IEEE Transactions on Knowledge and Data Engineering, 15*, 442-456.

Sarwar, B., Karypis, G., Konstan, J., & Reidl, J. (2001). Item-based collaborative filtering recommendation algorithms. In *WWW '01: Proceedings of the 10th International Conference on World Wide Web* (pp. 285-295). New York, NY: ACM.

Sowa, J. F. (2009). *Building, Sharing, and Merging Ontologies*. Retrieved from http://www.jfsowa.com/ontology/ontoshar.htm

Van Rijsbergen, C. (1979). *Information Retrieval*. Newton, MA: Butterworth-Heinemann.

Widdows, D. (2003). Unsupervised methods for developing taxonomies by combining syntactic and statistical information. In *Proceedings of the 2003 Conference of the North American Chapter of the Association for Computational Linguistics on Human Language Technology* (Vol. 1, pp. 197-204). Morristown, NJ: Association for Computational Linguistics.

Winkler, W. E. (1999). The state of record linkage and current research problems (Tech. Rep.). Suitland, MD: Statistical Research Division, U.S. Census Bureau.

Witschel, H. F. (2005). Using decision trees and text mining techniques for extending taxonomies. In *Proceedings of the Workshop on Learning and Extending Lexical Ontologies by Using Machine Learning (ONTOML)*, Bonn, Germany.

Wu, X., Zhang, L., & Yu, Y. (2006). Exploring social annotations for the semantic web. In *WWW '06: Proceedings of the 15th International Conference on World Wide Web* (pp. 417-426). New York, NY: ACM.

Xu, X., Huang, J., Wan, J., & Jiang, C. (2008). A method for measuring semantic similarity of concepts in the same ontology. In *IMSCCS '08: Proceedings of the 2008 International Multi-symposiums on Computer and Computational Sciences* (pp. 207-213). Washington, DC: IEEE Computer Society.

Yang, D., & Powers, D. M. W. (2005). Measuring semantic similarity in the taxonomy of wordnet. In *ACSC '05: Proceedings of the 28th Australasian Conference on Computer Science* (pp. 315-322). Australian Computer Society, Inc.

Zacharias, V., & Braun, S. (2007). Soboleo- social bookmarking and lightweight ontology engineering. In *Proceedings of the WWW '07 Workshop on Construction of Structured Knowledge.*

Zhang, L., Wu, X., & Yu, Y. (2006). Emergent Semantics from Folksonomies: A Quantitative Study. *Journal of Data Semantics on Emergent Semantics,* 168-186.

Zhou, M., Bao, S., Wu, X., & Yu, Y. (2007). An unsupervised model for exploring hierarchical semantics from social annotations. In *Proceedings of the 6th International Semantic Web Conference and 2nd Asian Semantic Web Conference (ISWC/ASWC 2007), Busan, South Korea* (LNCS 4825, pp. 673-686).

This work was previously published in the International Journal on Semantic Web and Information Systems, Volume 7, Issue 2, edited by Amit P. Sheth,, pp. 45-64, copyright 2011 by IGI Publishing (an imprint of IGI Global).

Chapter 7
A Modal Defeasible Reasoner of Deontic Logic for the Semantic Web

Efstratios Kontopoulos
Aristotle University of Thessaloniki, Greece

Nick Bassiliades
Aristotle University of Thessaloniki, Greece

Guido Governatori
NICTA, Australia

Grigoris Antoniou
FORTH, Greece

ABSTRACT

Defeasible logic is a non-monotonic formalism that deals with incomplete and conflicting information, whereas modal logic deals with the concepts of necessity and possibility. These types of logics play a significant role in the emerging Semantic Web, which enriches the available Web information with meaning, leading to better cooperation between end-users and applications. Defeasible and modal logics, in general, and, particularly, deontic logic provide means for modeling agent communities, where each agent is characterized by its cognitive profile and normative system, as well as policies, which define privacy requirements, access permissions, and individual rights. Toward this direction, this article discusses the extension of DR-DEVICE, a Semantic Web-aware defeasible reasoner, with a mechanism for expressing modal logic operators, while testing the implementation via deontic logic operators, concerned with obligations, permissions, and related concepts. The motivation behind this work is to develop a practical defeasible reasoner for the Semantic Web that takes advantage of the expressive power offered by modal logics, accompanied by the flexibility to define diverse agent behaviours. A further incentive is to study the various motivational notions of deontic logic and discuss the cognitive state of agents, as well as the interactions among them.

DOI: 10.4018/978-1-4666-3610-1.ch007

INTRODUCTION

Defeasible Logic, originally introduced by Nute (1994), is a non-monotonic formalism that deals with incomplete and conflicting information. Compared to other more mainstream non-monotonic approaches (Gottlob, 1992; Kautz & Selman, 1991; Soininen & Niemela, 1998), this approach offers enhanced representational capabilities and low computational complexity. Defeasible reasoning can represent facts, rules, priorities and conflicts among rules. Such conflicts usually emerge in the case of rules with exceptions, which are a natural representation for policies and business rules (e.g., Rissland & Skalak, 1991; Schild & Herzog, 1993). In these cases priority information is often used in resolving conflicts among rules.

Modal Logic (Blackburn, de Rijke, & Venema, 2001), on the other hand, is a system of formal logic that deals with *modalities*, namely, expressions that are associated with the notions of *possibility* and *necessity*. However, modal logic is not restricted to these concepts, but can assume a variety of interpretations, depending on meaning, context and various other factors. Thus, according to the different interpretations, there exist diverse categories of modal logics, like *epistemic logic* that deals with the certainty of sentences (Meyer, 2001), *deontic logic*, which deals with the notions of obligation and permission (Hilpinen, 2001), *temporal logic*, which deals with temporal notions (Venema, 2001) and *doxastic logic* that deals with reasoning about beliefs (Meyer, 2003).

Modal logics are usually deployed as extensions to classical propositional logic with intentional operators. However, classical propositional logic requires complete, consistent and reliable information, requirements that are rarely met in real-life scenarios, which are by default defeasible in nature. Additionally, reasoning about motivational notions like beliefs, intentions or obligations, displays a significant degree of defeasibility. Consequently, instead of extending propositional logic, it is more appropriate to extend defeasible logic with modal logic elements and recent work confirms this trend (Governatori & Rotolo, 2004; Governatori, Hulstijn, Riveret, & Rotolo, 2007; Riveret, Rotolo, & Governatori, 2007).

The above types of logics are extremely suitable in the *Semantic Web*, which aims at enriching the available information on the Web with meaning, leading to better cooperation between end-users and applications (Berners-Lee, Hendler & Lassila, 2001). Defeasible and modal logics, in general, and deontic logic, in particular, can assist towards this direction, by providing means for modeling *multi-agent systems* (*MAS*), where each agent is characterized by its own cognitive profile and normative system, as well as *policies*, which define privacy requirements for a user, access permissions for a resource, individual rights, etc. Already, defeasible logic is applied in a number of related fields, like *semantic brokering* (Antoniou, Skylogiannis, Bikakis, & Bassiliades, 2007), *security policies* (Ashri, Payne, Marvin, Surridge, & Taylor, 2004), *e-contracting* (Governatori, 2005) and *agent negotiations* (Skylogiannis, Antoniou, Bassiliades, Governatori, & Bikakis, 2007) and, as the article argues, extending defeasible logic with deontic logic operators significantly improves our ability to model applications, naturally using concepts and notions similar to those we find in applications.

This article is based on previous work by the authors (Kontopoulos, Bassiliades, Governatori, & Antoniou, 2008) and reports on extending the *DR-DEVICE* first-order defeasible logic reasoner (Bassiliades, Antoniou, & Vlahavas, 2006) with reasoning capabilities on modal defeasible logic rule bases. Notice that in this work we focus mainly on deontic logic operators, without loss of generality, even if the techniques proposed can be applied to any modal logic. More specifically, the system has been extended to introduce rule modes that determine the modalities of the derived conclusions, as well as modalized literals that can serve as facts or premises of rule bodies. The aim is to develop a practical defeasible logic reasoner that will take advantage of the expressive power of modal logics, accompanied by the flexibility to define various agent types and behaviors. The motivation behind this work is two-fold, since we wish to: (1) study the various motivational notions, especially those of deontic logic, and (2) discuss the cognitive state of agents as well as the interactions among them, focusing mainly on deontic logic.

The rest of the article is organized as follows: The following section outlines the basics of defeasible logic, focusing mainly on its knowledge representation and inference mechanism, followed by a description of the fundamental notions of modal and deontic logics. The next section summarizes the core notions of extending defeasible logics with modal and deontic logic operators and focuses on two important aspects of modal interactions, namely conflict resolution and rule conversions. The section that follows comprises the backbone of the article and addresses the theoretical and practical issues of extending the DR-DEVICE defeasible logic reasoner with modal and deontic operators, accompanied by a complete use case scenario in the Semantic Web. In our discussion of the implementation we include a proof of the correctness and completeness of the transformation algorithm from a modalized defeasible rule base to an non-modalized equivalent one, along with a discussion on the efficiency of the implementation, which is proved to be in the same order of magnitude in complexity with that of the underlying first-order defeasible reasoning system. Finally, an outline of related ongoing work in the area is presented, as well as concluding remarks and directions for future improvements.

DEFEASIBLE LOGIC

A *defeasible theory* D (i.e., a knowledge base or a program in defeasible logic) consists of three basic elements: a set of *facts* (F), a set of *rules* (R) and a *superiority relationship* ($>$). Therefore, D can be represented by the triple (F, R, $>$). We assume a function-free first-order language.

In defeasible logic, there are three distinct types of rules: strict rules, defeasible rules and defeaters. *Strict rules* are interpreted in the typical sense: whenever the premises are indisputable, then so is the conclusion. Strict rules are denoted by $A \rightarrow p$, where A is a set of literals and p is a (positive or negative) literal. An example of a strict rule is: "E-books are books", which can be formalised as: r_s: ebook(X) $\rightarrow$ book(X).

Contrary to strict rules, *defeasible rules* can be defeated by contrary evidence and are denoted by $A \Rightarrow p$. Two examples are: r_{d1}: book(X) $\Rightarrow$ printed(X) ("*Books are typically printed*") and r_{d2}: ebook(X) $\Rightarrow \neg$printed(X) ("Ebooks are not printed").

Defeaters, denoted by $A \hat{I} p$, are rules that do not actively support conclusions, but can only defeat conflicting defeasible conclusions, by producing evidence to the contrary. An example of a defeater is: r_f: cheap(X) $\hat{I} \neg$printed(X), which reads as: "Cheap books might not be printed". This defeater can defeat, for example, rule r_{d1} mentioned above, eventually preventing the derivation of its conclusion.

Finally, the *superiority relationship* among the rule set R is an acyclic relation $>$ on R, used to resolve conflicts among rules. For example, given defeasible rules r_{d1} and r_{d2}, no conclusive decision can be made about whether an e-book is eventually printed or not, because rules r_{d1} and r_{d2} contradict each other. But, if the superiority relationship $r_{d2} > r_{d1}$ is introduced, then r_{d2} overrides r_{d1} and we can indeed conclude that e-books are not printed. In this case rule r_{d2} is called *superior* to r_{d1} and r_{d1} *inferior* to r_{d2}.

A *conclusion* of D is a tagged literal and can have one of the following forms:

- $+\Delta q$, i.e., q is definitely provable in D (i.e., using only facts and strict rules).

- $-\Delta q$, i.e., we have proved that q is not definitely provable in D.
- $+\P q$, i.e., q is defeasibly provable in D.
- $-\P q$, i.e., we have proved that q is not defeasibly provable in D.

If q can be proved definitely, then q is also defeasibly provable.

MODAL AND DEONTIC LOGIC

Modal logic deals with the notions of *possibility* ("it is possible that") and *necessity* ("it is necessary that"). In other words, it not only considers truth and falsity, as normal logic does, but also considers what it would be like, if things were different in a possible alternative world. In this sense, something is *necessary* in a world, if it can be proved in all alternative worlds, and it is *possible* in a world, if it can be proved in at least one of all alternative worlds.

Modal logic extends classical logic (either propositional or predicate calculus) by adding two monadic operators that introduce the corresponding modal notions:

- **The Necessity Operator:** Written as $\Box$: $\Box p$ ("necessarily p")
- **The Possibility Operator:** Written as $\diamond$: $\diamond p$ ("possibly p")

The interpretation of these operators often covers a wider range of concepts with similar rules and a variety of different symbols that can handle an array of other ideas. Thus, modal logic has been applied as the means for establishing the foundations of analyzing epistemic and doxastic notions, like knowledge and belief, paving the way for agents and MAS; modal operators are very useful in expressing the internal cognitive states of agents, as well as interactions among different agents.

A member of the family of logics that stem from modal logic is *deontic logic* that is concerned with permissions, obligations and related concepts. The term "deontic" stems from the Greek corresponding term for "duty". Deontic logic introduces three operators: O for "it is obligatory that", P for "it is permitted that" and F for "it is forbidden that". P and F are defined in terms of O:

$$Pq \equiv \sim O \sim q \quad Fq \equiv O \sim q$$

Deontic logics can also be built upon propositional logic and can assume an elegant Kripke-style semantics, similarly to standard modal logics. The result is known as *Standard Deontic Logic* (often referred to as *SDL*) and can be axiomatized by adding the following axioms to a standard axiomatization of classical propositional logic:

$O(p \rightarrow q) \rightarrow (Op \rightarrow Oq)$ (if it is obligatory to be that p implies q, then, if p is obligatory, then q is obligatory)

$Oq \rightarrow Pq$ (if q is obligatory, then q is permissible)

Deontic logic is heavily used in expressing policies (Bieber & Cuppens, 1993; Kolaczek, 2002), which are rule sets used in defining access permissions, security and privacy requirements, individual rights, etc. for government, private sector organizations and groups, and individuals. Especially for the Semantic Web domain, policies and automated trust negotiation are two highly appealing applications (Bonatti, Duma, Fuchs, Nejdl, Olmedilla, Peer, & Shahmehri, 2006; Kagal, Berners-Lee, Connolly, & Weitzner, 2006).

MODAL DEFEASIBLE LOGIC

First-order logic has also been used to represent deontic notions (Lokhorst, 1996) leading to formal theories that can be implemented in logic programming systems. Our implementation is one of them, incorporating deontic logic theories in a first-order defeasible logic programming system, called DR-DEVICE. The idea behind this combination is to have a modal framework expressive enough to model certain kinds of deontic defeasibility, in particular by taking into account preferences on norms (Artosi et al., 1996).

In the rest of this article the following modal operators are considered:

- **Belief (K):** Represents the agent's theory of the world.
- **Intention (I):** Corresponds to the agent's intentions (policies).
- **Obligation (O):** Captures the agent's obligations.
- **Agency (Z):** Represents the agent's intentional actions.
- **Permission (P):** Corresponds to what the agent is permitted to do.

The permission operator was adopted from Antoniou, Dimaresis, and Governatori (2009), allowing the representation of (and reasoning with) business rules and policies. Permissions and obligations form the agent's *normative system* and allow studying the interaction between internal and external factors.

As Governatori and Rotolo (2008a) suggest, there are two potential ways of extending defeasible logics with modal logic operators: (1) adopt explicit predicates that represent the effect of modal operators, or (2) introduce new rule types for modal operators. Thus, the rule "We intend to go to Rome for the summer" can be represented in the following two forms respectively:

$$r_1: \text{summer} \Rightarrow I\_\text{weGoToRome} \qquad (1)$$

$$r_2: \text{summer} \Rightarrow_I \text{weGoToRome} \qquad (2)$$

Option 1 might seem preferable, since it imposes no need for introducing new rule types. Nevertheless, explicit predicates need to be ac-companied each time by formal semantics. On the other hand, option 2 enriches the expressiveness of the language and permits interactions among modal operators. The main idea behind this option is to have one defeasible consequence relation for each modal operator. Defeasible logic is able to handle different, and somehow incompatible, intuitions of non-monotonic reasoning. Thus this choice allows us (a) to have modal operators with different properties, and (b) to have a more fine grained control on how a proposition can be derived and can be used to derive other conclusions. This is not possible if one adopts Option 1.

The second difference between the two options is about the interactions among the various modal operators. To illustrate this difference, suppose, for example, that we have two modal operators $\Box_1$ and $\Box_2$, and the interaction between these two is $\{a: \Box\Box_1 a\} \subseteq \{a: \Box\Box_2 a\}$, or in other terms that the two modal operators are related by the axiom $\Box_1 a \rightarrow \Box_2 a$. To capture this, according to the first option, for each proposition/predicate a we need to introduce the propositions/predicates $\Box_1\_a$ and $\Box_2\_a$ and the rule $\Box_1\_a \Rightarrow \Box_2\_a$. For the second option, as we shall see in details in the rest of the paper, we can capture the relationship at the logic level. This means that we can define appropriate derivability conditions. In addition, if we do not want the property to hold for all predicates but only for a few instances, we can capture this at the theory level by introducing rules like $\Box_1 a \Rightarrow_{\Box_2} a$ for the specific predicates. The above discussion illustrates the advantages of the second option over the first, and shows also that the second option is more general and conceptually better, therefore, it is seemingly more appropriate to adopt Option 2 to extend defeasible logics with modal logic operators.

A *modalized literal* is represented by a literal accompanied by a modal operator prefix. For example, the application of rule r_2 above would produce the conclusion $I(\text{weGoToRome})$. A K-modalized literal belongs to the knowledge of the environment and is equivalent to the same literal without any prefix. Thus, K(summer) and summer are equivalent. Consequently, rules with K as their mode produce un-prefixed conclusions, if their antecedents are derived. Finally, since rules are meant to introduce modalities, modalized literals appear only in the rule body and not in the head.

With the exception of the belief operator K, the rest of the modal operators treated by the system are modeled as *non-reflexive*, meaning that, if X is a modal operator, a does not follow from $X(a)$: $X(a) \nrightarrow a$. Also, *iterated modalities*, like $I(O(a))$ or $O(I(a))$, that feature iterations of modalities, are not considered in this paper, in order to keep the system manageable (in first-order logic) and because their semantics would be too complicated for the casual Semantic Web end-user. The interested reader can refer to the work by Governatori and Rotolo (2008b) for a better insight into how iterated modalities can be handled. Also *modal interaction axioms*, like $Z(O(a)) \rightarrow I(a)$ and $I(O(a)) \rightarrow I(a)$ are not treated in this paper because there is no general consensus among the researchers on how many and which such axioms should be included in a normative system. However, any modal interaction axiom can be easily handled through the rule conversion technique used in our system that is presented later in the article.

A conclusion in modal defeasible logic is represented with a tagged literal, similarly to the proof theory of defeasible logics (see previous section), but augmented with information regarding the modality, in which each conclusion is (or is not) proved. Thus, such a conclusion can have one of four forms:

- $+\Delta_X q$: q is definitely provable in modality X in the defeasible theory D.
- $-\Delta_X q$: q is not definitely provable in modality X in the defeasible theory D.
- $+\P_X q$: q is defeasibly provable in modality X in the defeasible theory D.
- $-\P_X q$: q is not defeasibly provable in modality X in the defeasible theory D.

An example that illustrates all of the above is the well-known "prisoner's dilemma" borrowed from game theory (Hofstadter, 1983):

Two suspects are arrested by the police. The police have insufficient evidence for a conviction, and, having separated both prisoners, visit each of them to offer the same deal: if one testifies against the other and the other remains silent, the betrayer goes free and the silent accomplice receives the full 10-year sentence. If both remain silent, both prisoners are sentenced to only six months in jail for a minor charge. If each betrays the other, they receive a 5-year sentence. However, the "criminal code of honour" designates not to betray fellow criminals. Each prisoner must make the choice of whether betraying the other or remaining silent. The best individual outcome for each prisoner is to confess the crime, while the best mutual outcome is to stay silent.

The above can be formalized in defeasible deontic logic as follows (Governatori & Rotolo, 2004):

f_1: committedCrime

f_2: arrested

p_1: committedCrime $\land$ arrested $\Rightarrow_Z$ confess

p_2: committedCrime $\land$ arrested $\Rightarrow_O \neg$confess

The dilemma represents a typical conflict between an agent's intentions and normative system (obligations and permissions). According to the agent type, various conclusions can be drawn; for example one can conclude $+\P_Z confess$ and $-\P_O \sim confess$ if the agent is *deviant* (intentions and intentional actions override obligations). More details regarding the language and inference of modal defeasible logic can be found in work by Governatori and Rotolo (2004, 2008a).

Conflict Resolution

In the modal extension of defeasible logics a rule is attacked by another rule when the two conclusions are complementary and the two rule modes are different. This conflict resolution scheme is more flexible than the superiority relationship encountered in classical defeasible logics; depending on the modes of the attacking and attacked rules, a set of criteria is designated that determines whether a rule (and which one) eventually prevails. Interestingly, there exist *basic attacks*, which always apply, as well as attacks that depend on the agent type.

In general, beliefs override all other modes, with the exception of agency (i.e., intentional actions). Since beliefs represent an agent's knowledge of the world, they are considered rationally superior to its policies and normative system. Actions, on the other hand, can attack beliefs; because they can have a contradicting effect on the agent's knowledge of the world (i.e., actions can alter the status of the world). As Table 1 shows, no conclusion can be made on the truth of either the belief or the intentional action. This means that knowledge is lost when the agent wants to act in order to change something in the world it believes in. In an actual agent implementation after this conclusion was drawn, the agent would have re-observed the world in order to recover its knowledge.

Intention and agency are mutually attacked; this means that they block each other's proof, since agency (action) is intentional by definition. Mutual attacks also exist among obligation and

permission. Agents that encompass this "basic attacks" conflict resolution scheme are often called *realistic* (Broersen, Dastani, Hulstijn, Huang, & van der Torre, 2001; Governatori & Rotolo, 2004). Table 1 displays the basic attacks and the corresponding results. For each pair of cells, the first one describes the attack; e.g., the top-left cell features a rule in mode "K" that is attacked by a rule in mode "O". The second cell displays the resulting conclusions; e.g., in the second top-left cell, the results of the previous attack are $+\P_K p$ and $-\P_O \sim p$, meaning that conclusion p is proved defeasibly, while its complement is not defeasibly provable.

Nevertheless, as the table exhibits, the conflicts among intentions, obligations and actions are resolved, depending on the agent type. Thus, agent types are used in establishing conflict resolution schemes, by determining the way that rules of various modes interact with each other. Table 2 displays the way agent types assist in resolving these conflicts.

The table features six common agent types. The two most "extreme" types are the *independent* agent that can freely adopt intentions and actions that disagree with its normative system and the *pragmatic* agent, which does not allow for any derivation at all. The *selfish saint* has conflicting intentions and obligations, but no intentional action can be derived, while the *social sinner* does not proceed to any action contrary to its obligations, but remains with the intentions to the contrary. Finally, for a *social* agent, obligations override all intentions and actions to the contrary, while *deviant* agents represent the opposite, where

Table 1. Basic attacks and corresponding results

$\Rightarrow_K p / \Rightarrow_O \sim p$	$+\P_K p / -\P_O \sim p$	$\Rightarrow_I p / \Rightarrow_P \sim p$	$+\P_I p / +\P_P \sim p$
$\Rightarrow_K p / \Rightarrow_I \sim p$	$+\P_K p / -\P_I \sim p$	$\Rightarrow_P p / \Rightarrow_Z \sim p$	$+\P_P p / +\P_Z \sim p$
$\Rightarrow_K p / \Rightarrow_Z \sim p$	$-\P_K p / -\P_Z \sim p$	$\Rightarrow_P p / \Rightarrow_O \sim p$	$-\P_P p / -\P_O \sim p$
$\Rightarrow_K p / \Rightarrow_P \sim p$	$+\P_K p / -\P_P \sim p$	$\Rightarrow_O p / \Rightarrow_I \sim p$	*type of agent*
$\Rightarrow_I p / \Rightarrow_Z \sim p$	$-\P_I p / -\P_Z \sim p$	$\Rightarrow_O p / \Rightarrow_Z \sim p$	*type of agent*

Table 2. Resolving conflicts among obligations/intentions/actions, depending on agent type

$\Rightarrow_O p\ /\ \Rightarrow_I \sim p$		$\Rightarrow_O p\ /\ \Rightarrow_Z \sim p$		agent type
$+\P_O p$	$+\P_I \sim p$	$+\P_O p$	$+\P_Z \sim p$	independent
$+\P_O p$	$+\P_I \sim p$	$+\P_O p$	$-\P_Z \sim p$	selfish saint
$+\P_O p$	$-\P_I \sim p$	$+\P_O p$	$-\P_Z \sim p$	social
$-\P_O p$	$+\P_I \sim p$	$-\P_O p$	$+\P_Z \sim p$	deviant
$-\P_O p$	$+\P_I \sim p$	$-\P_O p$	$-\P_Z \sim p$	social sinner
$-\P_O p$	$-\P_I \sim p$	$-\P_O p$	$-\P_Z \sim p$	pragmatic

obligations are overridden by opposing intentions and intentional actions. Note that our implementation currently includes only the latter two agent types, accompanied by the *realistic* type, but the variety can easily be extended, as explained later.

Rule Conversion

There are certain cases where the conclusion does not "inherit" the rule mode, but it adopts a different modality. This feature, called *rule conversion*, allows for various rational side effects to be derived and is required in capturing certain aspects of the rationality of agents. Rule conversions offer the possibility to convert the rule mode, depending on the modalities, in which the corresponding rule premises have been proved. For example, if we have rule weGoToRome $\Rightarrow_K$ weGoToItaly, and we intend to go to Rome, then should we conclude $+\P_K weGoToItaly$ or $+\P_I weGoToItaly$? The latter seems more intuitive; thus, the rule can be converted into a rule for intentions. Generally speaking, conversions are a means for deriving rational side effects.

In some cases rule conversion is a debatable principle, and for some combination of modalities and applications it might not be appropriate. Governatori and Rotolo (2004, 2008a) and Governatori, Padmanabhan, Rotolo, and Sattar (2009) argue that conversion from beliefs to intention allows us to model the notion of intentionality and that this is essential if one wants to model normative reasoning. In some jurisdiction, the concept of (legal) responsibility depends on that on intentionality, that is if one is aware of the consequences of an intended action (and carries it out), then one intends the consequences as well, unless there are some reasons not to do so. This should be contrasted by the infamous dentist example of Cohen and Levesque (Cohen & Levesque, 1990). The example runs as follows: "If I intend to the dentist's and I know that if I go to the dentist, I will have pain, it should not follow that I intend to have pain." Thus, it seems that subscribing to the conversion principle for belief and intentions leads to counterintuitive conclusions. Let us go back to the example, and let us suppose that I go to the dentist to have a (painful) root canal procedure. Now, let us ask, what are the reasons for going to the dentist to have the procedure? If no further information is given, then, it is reasonable to conclude that I go the dentist to suffer some pain, but if the reasons is that I had a bad cavities that causes some very painful abscess, then the reason is to cure my tooth and this implies that I have the intention not to have pain (Governatori & Rotolo, 2008a).

Conflicts and conversions are not directly related to each other, but they both help portray the cognitive profile of an agent. Nevertheless, similarly to conflicts, there exist rule conversions that apply to all agent types, but there also exist type-dependant conversions.

Table 3 displays the rule conversions supported by the extended DR-DEVICE. The first column indicates the permitted modality of the rule premises. Note that a rule can of course have more than one antecedent; all of them, however, have to share

Table 3. Supported rule conversions

X	⇒	Y	agent type	X	⇒	Y	agent type
O	*K*	*O*	*all types*	*O*	*Z*	*O*	*all types*
I	*K*	*I*	*all types*	*I*	*O*	*I*	*social*
Z	*K*	*Z*	*all types*	*Z*	*O*	*Z*	*social*
P	*K*	*P*	*all types*	*O*	*I*	*O*	*deviant*
I	*Z*	*I*	*all types*	*O*	*Z*	*O*	*deviant*

the same modality. Currently, rule conversions for rules with more than one modality in their body are not supported, since they can potentially lead to a combinatorial explosion of cases and also increase the computational complexity of reasoning. The second column indicates the rule mode, while the third one displays the resulting modality of the conclusion. The final column indicates the agent types, for which the specific conversion holds. The selection of agent types can, nevertheless, be extended, as described later.

As a final remark, notice that the contents of the tables (attacks/corresponding results as well as agent types and rule conversions) merely comprise axioms, which are (philosophically) debatable and with subjective applicability. Of course, each user (developer/knowledge engineer, etc.) can designate different conflict resolution and conversion schemes that better reflect his/her view of the notions at hand.

IMPLEMENTATION

This section describes the extension of DR-DEVICE, which is called *DR-DEVICE$_M$* and handles modal and deontic logic operators, rule conversions and conflict resolution schemes.

The DR-DEVICE Defeasible Logic Reasoner

DR-DEVICE (Bassiliades et al., 2006) is a defeasible logic reasoner that employs an object-oriented RDF data model, which is different from the established triple-based data model for RDF. The main difference is that the system treats properties as normal encapsulated attributes of resource objects. This way, properties of resources are not scattered across several triples, as in most other RDF inference systems, resulting in increased query performance due to less joins. The most important features of DR-DEVICE are the following:

- It supports multiple rule types of defeasible logic, such as strict rules, defeasible rules, and defeaters.
- It supports two types of negation (strong, negation-as-failure) and conflicting (mutually exclusive) literals.
- It supports RuleML (Boley, 2006), a mainstream standardization effort for rules in the Semantic Web.
- It supports direct import from the Web and processing of RDF data and RDF Schema ontologies.
- It supports direct export to the Web of the results (conclusions) of the logic program as an RDF document.
- It is built on-top of a CLIPS-based implementation of deductive rules (Bassiliades & Vlahavas, 2006). The core of the system consists of a translation of defeasible knowledge into a set of deductive rules, including derived and aggregate attributes.

As a result of the above, DR-DEVICE is a powerful declarative system supporting: rules, facts and ontologies; major Semantic Web standards: RDF, RDFS, RuleML; monotonic and non-monotonic rules and reasoning with inconsistencies. More details can be found in Bassiliades et al. (2006) and Bassiliades and Vlahavas (2006).

DR-DEVICE supports two types of syntax for defeasible logic rules: a native CLIPS-like syntax and a RuleML-compatible one, called *DR-RuleML*. While DR-RuleML utilizes as many features of the official RuleML as possible, several of the features of defeasible logic cannot be expressed by the existing RuleML specifications. For this reason the modularization scheme of RuleML was applied and new XML Schema documents (up to v.0.91-compatible) were developed. The performed extensions deal with rule types, superiority relations among rules and conflicting literals, as well as with constraints on predicate arguments and functions.

Figure 1 displays the following rule in DR-RuleML (v. 0.91):

r_{d2}: novel(X) $\Rightarrow$ ¬hardcover(X) ("Novels are typically not hard-covered")

The names (Rel elements) of the operator (op) elements of atoms are class names, since atoms actually represent CLIPS objects (Bassiliades et al., 2006). RDF class names used as base classes in the rule condition are referred to through the uri attribute of the Rel element (e.g., novel in the figure), while derived class names are text values of the Rel element. Atoms have named arguments (slots), which correspond to object/RDF properties. Since RDF resources are represented as CLIPS objects, atoms in the rule body correspond to queries over RDF resources of a certain class with certain property values, while atoms in the rule head correspond to templates of materialized derived objects, which are exported as RDF resources at the end of the inference process (Bassiliades et al., 2006; Bassiliades & Vlahavas, 2006).

Rule Language Extensions for Modal Logic

The DR-DEVICE RuleML-like syntax (DR-RuleML) described previously was further extended, in order to embrace essential modal logic elements. The language has to describe rule modes as well as a "modalization" mechanism for expressing the modal operator of each literal.

To support these features, two attributes are introduced: ruleMode that is appended to the attribute list of the Implies element and modality that is attached to the Atom element. Both attributes can assume only one of five values: bel (belief – K), int (intention – I), obl (obligation – O), age (agency – Z) and per (permission – P). The use of the two attributes is optional; thus, when the

Figure 1. Representing rule r_{d2} in the DR-DEVICE RuleML-compatible syntax

```
<Implies ruletype="defeasiblerule" superior="rd1">
    <oid> <Ind uri="rd2">rd2</Ind> </oid>
    <head>
        <Neg>
            <Atom>
                <op> <Rel>hardcover</Rel> </op>
                <slot> <Ind>name</Ind> <Var>x</Var> </slot>
            </Atom>
        </Neg>
    </head>
    <body>
        <Atom>
            <op> <Rel uri="books:novel"/> </op>
            <slot> <Ind uri="books:name"/> <Var>x</Var> </slot>
        </Atom>
    </body>
</Implies>
```

attribute is absent, the corresponding rule or atom is assigned bel (belief) as its mode or modality, respectively.

Finally, the notion of agent type is represented by an agentType attribute, attached to the rule base element (element RuleML). As already mentioned, the currently permitted agent types are *realistic*, *social* and *deviant*, but the selection can be extended by adding more agent types to the schema. Figure 2 displays a fragment of a "social prisoner's" rule base, detailing on rule p_1 below, which states that the intention of an arrested prisoner is to confess the crime to achieve the best individual outcome for him:

$$p_1: \text{committedCrime} \land \text{arrested} \Rightarrow_z \text{confess}$$

A similar approach to the rule language presented here was proposed by Pham, Governatori, Raboczi, Newman, and Thakur (2008), which is also an extension to the DR-DEVICE RuleML-like syntax. In essence, the two approaches attack the problem similarly, with the difference being that the approach by Pham et al. gives a way to define the agent types in the rule language, whereas in DR-DEVICE we use "preconfigured" types.

DR-DEVICE$_M$ – Overview

Before proceeding to more specific implementation details regarding DR-DEVICE$_M$, this subsection gives an overview of the system functionality. As displayed in Figure 3, the system accepts as input the address of a modal defeasible logic rule base (Step 1 in the Figure), written in DR-RuleML. The rule base is submitted to DR-DEVICE$_M$ (Step 2) and the theory transformation (described subsequently) commences. During the process, the system deploys an external parameterized modality interaction schema (Step 3) and an equivalent non-modal defeasible logic theory is produced (Step 4). The latter is then fed to the core reasoner (Step 5).

DR-DEVICE downloads the input RDF documents, including their schemas (Step 6) and translates RDF descriptions into CLIPS objects. Rule conclusions are also materialized as objects (Step 7) and the instances of designated derived classes are exported as an RDF document (Step 8), which includes the RDF Schema definitions for the exported derived classes and those instances of the exported derived classes, which have been proved, either positively or negatively, either defeasibly or definitely. Finally, the user

Figure 2. Extending DR-RuleML with modal capabilities

```
<RuleML ... agentType="social">
    <Assert>
        <Implies ruletype="defeasiblerule" ruleMode="age">
            <oid> <Ind uri="r1">r1</Ind> </oid>
            <head>
                <Atom modality="bel">
                    <op> <Rel>confess</Rel> </op>
                </Atom>
            </head>
            <body>
                <And>
                    <Atom modality="bel">
                        <op> <Rel>committedCrime</Rel> </op>
                    </Atom>
                    <Atom modality="bel">
                        <op> <Rel>arrested</Rel> </op>
                    </Atom>
                </And>
            </body>
        </Implies>
        ...
    </Assert>
</RuleML>
```

Figure 3. Modal DR-DEVICE overall functionality

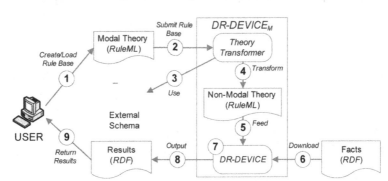

can access the results through a web browser or through specialized software that can customize the visualization (Step 9). Notice, that DR-DE-VICE can also provide explanations about non-proved objects. More details regarding the functionality and architecture of the system can be found in Bassiliades et al. (2006).

Theory Transformation

DR-DEVICE$_M$ applies a rule-rewriting transformation to the input modal defeasible logic theory (like the one in Figure 2) that moves modalities from rules to conclusions and takes care of modal interactions. The transformation is based on the following two binary anti-symmetric relations, introduced subsequently, that define how pairs of modalities interact in *rule conflicts* $(\prec)$ and *rule conversions* (a).

Definitions: In both the following definitions, as well as the subsequent sections, $R_Y^X[E(q)]$ will denote the set of rules with mode X, with antecedents that all share the same modality Y and with q as the rule consequent that is modalized under modality E. Note, however, that the above notation is generic and is presented here for representation reasons; it is not possible to concurrently have a rule mode and a modalized conclusion. More specifically, the following distinctions exist:

- When consequent modality E is absent (e.g., $R_Y^X[q]$), then the modality of the consequent is not yet designated.
- When the notation lacks q (e.g., R_Y^X), then the consequent is irrelevant to the expression at hand.
- When index X is absent (e.g., $R_Y[E(q)]$), the rule set consists of modeless rules.
- When index Y is absent (e.g., $R^X[q]$), then the modality of antecedents is irrelevant.

Definition 1 (Rule Conflicts): The relation $\prec$ between two modalities defines how conflicts among conclusions with different modalities are resolved.

$\prec Í M x M, X \in M, Y \in M$:

$$Y \prec X \Rightarrow (\text{``}q \text{``}r \text{``}r', r Î R^X[q] \wedge r' Î R^Y[\sim q] \wedge X \neq Y \rightarrow r > r')$$

In the above definition, M is the set of all modality types (in our current implementation $M \equiv \{K, I, O, Z, P\}$) and $R^Y[q] \subseteq R$ denotes the set of rules with mode $Y \in M$ and literal q as their consequent (R is the set of all rules). The definition implies that, for every pair $Y \prec X$, where $X \in M$ and $Y \in M$, if there is an attack $\Rightarrow_X q / \Rightarrow_Y \sim q$, for any literal q in the rule base, the rule with mode

X is defined as superior and its conclusion will indeed be derived $(+\P_X q)$. The inferior rule conclusion will not be provable $(-\P_Y \sim q)$, thus, mode X prevails over Y.

The above definition can be extended to consider agent types, as well, meaning that certain conflicts between modalities occur only for specific agent types only and not for others. The relation is augmented with the agent type α:

Definition 1a (Rule Conflicts with Agent Types):

$$\prec_a \hat{I} M \times M \times G, X \in M, Y \in M, a \in G:$$

$$Y \prec_a X \Rightarrow (\text{``}r\text{ ``}r'\text{ ``}q, r \,\hat{I}\, R^X[q] \wedge r' \,\hat{I}\, R^Y[\sim q] \wedge X \neq Y \to r > r')$$

In the above expression, G is the set of all implemented agent types (currently, $G \equiv \{$realistic, deviant, social$\}$).

Each instantiation of the conflict relation $A \prec_a B$, where $A \in M$ and $B \in M$, is represented by a tuple $<a, A, B>$. Note that the absence of index a referring to the agent type (e.g., $\prec$) indicates that the specified conflict belongs to the basic conflicts set and is present in all agent schemes; actually, agents that adopt the basic conflicts scheme are called *realistic* (the realistic type is the most generic agent type).

Definition 2 (Rule Conversions): The relation a between two modalities defines how a rule mode is converted into a different conclusion modality when the modality of the condition is different than the modality expected in the original rules.

$$a\hat{I} M \times M, U \in M, Y \in M:$$

$$UaY \Rightarrow (\text{``}r, r \,\hat{I}\, R_Y^U \to \$r', r' \,\hat{I}\, R_Y^Y)$$

In the above definition, $R_Y^U \subseteq R$ denotes the set of all rules with mode $U \in M$ and with $Y \in M$ as the modality of all rule antecedents.

Definition 2 implies that, for every pair YaX, where $X \in M$ and $Y \in M$, if a rule r exists with mode U and Y as the modality of all antecedents, then a new rule r' is added to the rule base with the same mode as the antecedents of rule r. Notice that relation a is reflexive, i.e., $\forall X \in M$ it is true that XaX.

The above definition can be extended to consider agent types, as well, meaning that certain modality conversions occur only for specific agent types only and not for others. The relation is augmented with the agent type α:

Definition 2a (Rule Conversions with Agent Types):

$$a_a \hat{I} M \times M \times G, U \in M, Y \in M, a \in G:$$

$$Ua_a Y \Rightarrow (\text{``}r, r \,\hat{I}\, R_Y^U \to \$r', r' \,\hat{I}\, R_Y^Y)$$

In the above expression, G is the set of all implemented agent types (currently, $G \equiv \{$realistic, deviant, social$\}$).

Each instantiation of the conversion relation $Aa_a B$, where $A \in M$ and $B \in M$, is represented by a tuple $<a, A, B>$. Similarly to definition 1a, the absence of index a (e.g., a) indicates that the specified conversion belongs to the basic conversions set and is present in all agent schemes (i.e., realistic agents).

Transformation Steps: The transformation from a modal defeasible theory D_m to a non-modal defeasible theory D_f is influenced by the object-oriented philosophy, on which the system is built (see previous sections). The process consists of three distinct steps that augment theory D_m, so that the resulting defeasible theory D_f is semantically equivalent. Each step takes as input the theory produced by the previous step and produces as output a modified theory to be fed to the next step. The input of the first step is D_m and the output of the last step is D_f.

Before executing the transformation, an initial step that handles a necessary syntactical transformation is performed: for every rule r that belongs to the rule set R_m of D_m, a rule r^o is generated in the rule set R_o of D_o that has the modality of every rule body atom of r transformed from an XML attribute into an argument of the element atom of rule r^o. Since atoms in DR-DEVICE are treated as objects, the modality becomes an object slot (or property) with the same name, which is added to the corresponding object definition. This initial step is defined formally as follows:

$R_o = \{ r^o(r) \mid r \text{ Î } R_m \wedge a_i \text{ Î } r.body.atom \wedge r^o.ID = r.ID \wedge r^o.head = r.head \wedge$

$r^o.body.atom = r.body.atom \cup slot(name(\text{"modality"}), value(a_i.modality)) \}$

Here, we assume a dot-notation, where the expression *e1.e2* delivers the child element or attribute value *e2* of (parent) element *e1*. Functions *name* and *value* are predefined properties of a *slot* element and refer to the slot name and slot value, respectively.

Figure 4 displays an example of the above process: the left-hand-side excerpt, expressed in the DR-RuleML modal extension described earlier, is the original rule body (rule p_1 from the prisoner's dilemma example seen previously), while the right-hand-side excerpt shows the output body, where modalities have been transformed from atom attributes into object slots (i.e., core DR-RuleML syntax).

To better understand this transformation, rule p_1 is the following:

p_1: committedCrime $\wedge$ arrested $\Rightarrow_Z$ confess

The literals of body of the rule are all under the knowledge or belief modality K (committedCrime$_K$ $\wedge$ arrested$_K$) and during this initial syntactical transformation the modality is transformed into an extra argument of each atom: committedCrime(K) $\wedge$ arrested(K).

Then, the actual transformation commences. More specifically, the theory transformation process involves the following steps:

Step 1: This step takes as input the transformed defeasible theory D_o and the corresponding rule set R_o and produces as output the defeasible theory D_1 that contains the rule set R_1. During this step, the mode of each rule (which is an attribute) becomes a slot of the head atom:

$R_1 = \{ r^1(r^o) \mid r^o \text{ Î } R_o \wedge r^1.ID = r^o.ID \wedge r^1.body.atom = r^o.body.atom \wedge$

$r^1.head.atom = r^o.head.atom \cup slot(name(\text{"modality"}), value(r^o.mode)) \}$

Figure 4. Example of the initial syntactical transformation

```
<body>
  <And>
    <Atom modality="bel">
      <op>
        <Rel>committedCrime</Rel>
      </op>
    </Atom>
    <Atom modality="bel">
      <op>
        <Rel>arrested</Rel>
      </op>
    </Atom>
  </And>
</body>
```

```
<body>
  <And>
    <Atom>
      <op><Rel>committedCrime</Rel></op>
      <slot><Ind>modality</Ind>
        <Ind>bel</Ind></slot>
    </Atom>
    <Atom>
      <op><Rel>arrested</Rel></op>
      <slot><Ind>modality</Ind>
        <Ind>bel</Ind></slot>
    </Atom>
  </And>
</body>
```

Figure 5 displays an example of the above process: the left-hand-side excerpt is the original rule head (again, rule p1 from the prisoner's dilemma example), while the right-hand-side excerpt shows the output head, where rule modes have been transferred to head atoms as object slots.

To better understand this transformation step, rule p_1 is the following (after the initial syntactical transformation):

p_1: committedCrime(K) $\wedge$ arrested(K) $\Rightarrow_Z$ confess

After the transformation step 1, the rule looks as follows:

p_1: committedCrime(K) $\wedge$ arrested(K) $\Rightarrow$ confess(Z)

Step 2: This step takes as input the transformed defeasible theory D_1 and the corresponding rule set R_1 and produces as output the defeasible theory D_2 that contains the rule set R_2. During this step, rule conversions are considered and as a result additional rules are added to the rule base. According to rule conversions, the modality of a rule conclusion depends both on the rule mode and on the modalities of the body atoms. So, the rule set R_2 contains all rules of R_1 and the additional rules that take care of rule conversion.

$$R_2 = R_1 \cup \bigcup_{\forall r \in R_1} C(r)$$

The set $C(r)$ contains all additional rules needed for each original rule r. Indeed, many such additional rules could be required (for each rule r), because there can be many qualifying modalities E for conversion.

$$C(r) = \bigcup_{\forall E \in M} \left\{ r' \mid r \in R^X[q] \wedge X \mapsto E \wedge r' \in R_E[E(q)] \right\}$$

The additional rules $r'\hat{I}R_E[E(q)]$ assess whether a rule satisfies the necessary qualifications for rule conversion and are "transparent" to the user, since they are appended during the transformation of the initially submitted theory D_m. Since relation XaE may hold for several Es for each X, one rule for each E is appended to the theory.

Actually, in order not to clutter the rule base with many rules, instead of appending multiple such conversion rules for each qualifying E, in our implementation we just add one rule whose condition is satisfied for every qualified E. So the previous expression for $C(r)$ is modified as follows:

$$C(r) = \left\{ r' + +X \mapsto E \mid r \in R^X[q] \wedge r' \in R_E[E(q)] \right\}$$

Figure 5. Example of transformation step 1

```
<Implies ruleMode="int"
    ruletype="defeasiblerule">
..........
  <head>
    <Atom modality="bel">
      <op>
        <Rel>confess</Rel>
      </op>
    </Atom>
  </head>
..........
</Implies>
```

```
<Implies
    ruletype="defeasiblerule">
..........
  <head>
    <Atom>
      <op><Rel>confess</Rel></op>
      <slot><Ind>modality</Ind>
        <Ind>int</Ind></slot>
    </Atom>
  </head>
..........
</Implies>
```

In the previous expression, $r'++XaE$ defines a rule r' as previously and concatenates the condition XaE to the rule condition (E is a new universally quantified variable). So, now set $C(r)$ contains just one rule for each r.

Figure 6 displays an example of a rule added to theory D_f during step 2. The rule (labelled p1-conv) is based on rule p_1, but has variable modalities for its body and head atoms in the form of random 4-character strings, like mt98 and sw64. These modalities are checked for their compatibility with the rule mode (function compatible-modality) and, if the check is passed, the convert-modality function proceeds with the rule conversion (the head modality is converted accordingly).

To better understand this transformation step, rule p_1 is the following (after transformation step 1):

p_1: committedCrime(K) $\wedge$ arrested(K) $\Rightarrow$ confess(Z)

After the transformation step 2, the following rule is added to the rule base:

p_1-conv: committedCrime(X) $\wedge$ arrested(Y) $\wedge$ compatible-modality(X,Y,Z) $\Rightarrow$ confess(convert-modality(X,Y,Z))

that checks in the condition if X, Y modalities are compatible with Z and if this is true, then they are converted to a compatible with Z modality in the rule head using the convert-modality function.

Step 3: This step takes as input the transformed defeasible theory D_2 and the corresponding rule set R_2 and produces as output the final defeasible theory D_f that contains the rule set R_f. During this step, the issue of rule attacks (conflicts) has to be tackled with. Typically in DR-DEVICE, two modalized literals (actually objects), such as $I(p)$ and $O(\sim p)$, are not conflicting, since they are treated by the system as different literals/

Figure 6. Example of step 2 addition

```
<Implies ruleMode="int" ruletype="defeasiblerule">
  <oid><Ind uri="p1-conv">p1-conv</Ind></oid>
  <head>
    <Atom>
      <op><Rel>confess</Rel></op>
      <slot><Ind>modality</Ind>
      <Var>sw64</Var></slot>
    </Atom>
    <Equal>
      <Var>sw64</Var>
      <Expr>
        <Fun in="yes">convert-modality</Fun>
        <Ind>social</Ind> <Ind>int</Ind>
        <Var>mt98</Var> <Var>yl14</Var>
      </Expr>
    </Equal>
  </head>
  <body>
    <And>
      <Atom>
        <op><Rel>committedCrime</Rel></op>
        <slot><Ind>modality</Ind>
        <Var>mt98</Var></slot>
      </Atom>
      <Atom>
        <op><Rel>arrested</Rel></op>
        <slot><Ind>modality</Ind>
        <Var>yl14</Var></slot>
      </Atom>
      <Equal>
        <Expr>
          <Fun in="yes">compatible-modality</Fun>
          <Ind>social</Ind> <Ind>int</Ind>
          <Var>mt98</Var> <Var>yl14</Var>
        </Expr>
        <Ind>true</Ind>
      </Equal>
    </And>
  </body>
</Implies>
```

objects (because of the different values in the modality slot). In order to allow the reasoner to indeed consider the literals/objects as conflicting, extra rules are added to the rule base, which are also "transparent" to the user. These additional rules realize the so-called *modality inclusion* that deals with the associations among modalities. The results of the attacks are determined by the "basic attacks" scheme (Table 1) as well as the agent type (Table 2), represented by the rule conflicts relation $\prec$. A modality inclusion is denoted by $T_B^A[q] \in T$, where $B \prec A$ (independently of agent type; i.e., the agent type is irrelevant for handling modality inclusions) and T is the modality inclusion set of theory D_f. Each modality inclusion $T_B^A[q]$ results in two defeater rules being added into the rule set R_f: $A(q) \hat{I} B(q)$ and $A(\neg q) \hat{I} B(\neg q)$.

Modality inclusions are formulated as defeaters, since they do not aim at deriving new knowledge, but are only used for defeating rules with contrary conclusions. More specifically, for every conclusion q in the rule base, the following modality inclusions have to be incorporated:

$$T_X^Y[q] = \{\ Y(q)\ \hat{I}\ X(q),\ Y(\neg q)\ \hat{I}\ X(\neg q)\ \}$$

$$R_f = R_2 \cup \bigcup_{\forall q} \bigcup_{\forall X \forall Y, X \prec Y} T_X^Y[q]$$

Notice that the previous definition handles all cases of modality conflicts:

- If $Y \prec X$, i.e., when $+\P_X q\ /\ -\P_Y \sim q$, then $T_Y^X[q]$ is included in R_f.
- If both $Y \prec X$ and $X \prec Y$ hold, i.e., when $-\P_X q\ /\ -\P_Y \sim q$, then both $T_Y^X[q]$ and $T_X^Y[q]$ are included in R_f.

As for the remaining two cases of conflicts ($X \prec Y$ and $Y \nprec X \wedge X \nprec Y$), the former is the inverse of the first case and is treated similarly, while the latter does not result in the addition of extra rules to the rule base, since both conclusions ($+\P_X q$, $+\P_Y \sim q$) are derived.

Figure 7 displays an example of the modality inclusion addition: for conclusion confess and for modes K and O, where $O \prec K$, the two following defeaters will be appended to the rule base:

confess-bel-obl-pos: confess(K) $\hat{I}$ confess(O)

confess-bel-obl-neg: ¬confess(K) $\hat{I}$ ¬confess(O)

Transformation Correctness/Completeness: Proving the correctness and completeness of the theory transformation will ensure that the latter always achieves the intended result, i.e., every transformed non-modal defeasible theory is se-

mantically equivalent to the original modal theory, namely, the inferred conclusions are the same. In essence, the aim is to have a transformation from a domain-independent rule base into a domain-dependent theory.

The transformation process comprises an algorithm consisting of three distinct steps plus an initialization step (see previous section). At each step an input rule set is transformed into an output rule set. The input of the initial step is the original, modal rule set R_m, while the output of the last step is an equivalent non-modal rule set R_f. In order to prove that R_f is equivalent to R_m it suffices to prove that each step produces at its output a rule set that is equivalent to its input rule set.

Step 0:

Input: R_m
Output: R_o

Description: Transforms the original rule set R_m into rule set R_o that has the modality of every rule body atom transformed from an XML attribute into an argument of the atom (XML element).

Proof: This step is a trivial syntactical transformation. Thus $|R_o|=|R_m|$ and there is "1-1" correspondence between rules in the two sets. Furthermore, rules are interpreted similarly. Thus, the two sets are semantically equivalent.

Step 1:

Input: R_o
Output: R_1

Description: Transforms the rule set R_o into rule set R_1 assigning rule modes of rules in R_o to rule head atom modalities in R_1.

Proof: Rule set R_o contains rules r^o of type $Y(a_1) \wedge Y(a_2) \wedge \ldots \wedge Y(a_n) \Rightarrow_X q$ that all have a mode. Even modeless rules have by default mode K (belief). During this step for each rule r^o in R_o one rule rule r^1: $Y(a_1) \wedge Y(a_2) \wedge \ldots \wedge Y(a_n) \Rightarrow X(q)$ is generated in R_1. There exists a "1-1" association among the rule sets of the two theories

Figure 7. Example of modality inclusion addition during step 3

```
<Implies ruleMode="bel" ruletype="defeater">        <Implies ruleMode="bel" ruletype="defeater">
  <oid>                                               <oid>
    <Ind uri="confess-bel-obl-pos">confess-             <Ind uri="confess-bel-obl-neg">confess-
    bel-obl-pos</Ind>                                   bel-obl-neg</Ind>
  </oid>                                               </oid>
  <head>                                              <head>
    <Atom>                                              <Neg>
      <op><Rel>confess</Rel></op>                         <Atom>
      <slot>                                                <op><Rel>confess</Rel></op>
        <Ind>modality</Ind>                                 <slot><Ind>modality</Ind>
        <Ind>obl</Ind>                                      <Ind>obl</Ind></slot>
      </slot>                                            </Atom>
    </Atom>                                            </Neg>
  </head>                                            </head>
  <body>                                             <body>
    <Atom>                                             <Neg>
      <op><Rel>confess</Rel></op>                        <Atom>
      <slot>                                               <op><Rel>confess</Rel></op>
        <Ind>modality</Ind>                                 <slot><Ind>modality</Ind>
        <Ind>bel</Ind>                                      <Ind>bel</Ind></slot>
      </slot>                                           </Atom>
    </Atom>                                           </Neg>
  </body>                                            </body>
</Implies>                                          </Implies>
```

$(|R_l|=|R_o|=|R_m|)$, and, since the corresponding conclusions from the two rules $(+\P_X q$ and $+\P X(q))$ are semantically equivalent, step 1 is proved to be correct and complete.

Step 2:

Input: R_1
Output: R_2
Description: Transforms the rule set R_1 into rule set R_2 by adding new rules that assess, whether a rule qualifies for rule conversion.

Proof: For each rule r^l: $Y(a_1) \wedge Y(a_2) \wedge \ldots \wedge Y(a_n) \Rightarrow X(q)$ in R_1, and for each E, such that XaE, a new rule $E(a_1) \wedge E(a_2) \wedge \ldots \wedge E(a_n) \Rightarrow E(q)$ should be appended to the theory. However, in order not to clutter the rule base with many rules, instead of appending multiple such conversion rules for each qualifying E, we add just one such rule that its condition is satisfied for every qualified E, namely the following rule is added to the rule base for each rule r^l: $E(a_1) \wedge E(a_2) \wedge \ldots \wedge E(a_n) \wedge XaE \Rightarrow E(q)$. Thus, $|R_2|=2 \cdot |R_1|=2 \cdot |R_m|$. Furthermore, according to formal modal defeasible logics, applying rule conversion on a rule such as $E(a_1) \wedge E(a_2) \wedge \ldots \wedge E(a_n) \Rightarrow_X q$ would result in concluding $+\P_E q$. Following our approach, the appended rule $E(a_1) \wedge E(a_2) \wedge \ldots \wedge E(a_n) \wedge XaE \Rightarrow E(q)$ results in $+\P E(q)$, which is semantically

equivalent to $+\P_E q$; therefore, correctness and completeness of step 2 are proven.

Step 3:

Input: R_2
Output: R_f
Description: Transforms the rule set R_2 into the final rule set R_f by adding new rules that tackle modality inclusion, namely rule attacks (conflicts).

Proof: During this step a number of defeater rules are added to rule set R_2. For every pair of conflicting heads $X(q)$ and $Y(\neg q)$, where $Y \prec X$, two new defeater rules are appended to the rule set R_2. Thus, if $a\hat{I}N$ is the number of $\prec$ relation instances (actually, the number of modality attacks) occurring in D_m and c is the number of distinct (non-modalized) literals occurring at rule heads in R_m, then $|R_f|=|R_2|+2 \cdot a \cdot c = 2 \cdot |R_m|+2 \cdot a \cdot c$. In the worst case $c=|R_m|/2$, i.e., each conflicting rule pair has a distinct conclusion; therefore $|R_f| = 2 \cdot |R_m|+a \cdot |R_m| = |R_m| \cdot (a+2)$, which is always finite. Also, according to formal modal defeasible logics, if there exists a pair of rule consequents $\Rightarrow_X p / \Rightarrow_Y \neg p$ with $Y \prec X$, then we conclude $+\P_X p$ and $-\P_Y \neg p$. Similarly, according to our approach, the addition of modality inclusion $T_Y^X[p]$ will result in defeaters $X(p) \hat{I} Y(p)$ and $X(\neg p) \hat{I} Y(\neg p)$ being added to theory D_f. Consequently, these defeaters result in concluding $-\P_Y \sim p$ and allowing the eventual inference of $+\P_X p$. Thus, step 3 is also correct and complete.

Implementing Modality Interactions

As studied previously in the article, each type of agent is accompanied by its own modality interaction schema, namely, a distinct set of conflicts and conversions. In order to represent modality interactions in DR-DEVICE$_M$, in a simple yet expressive way that could facilitate re-use and evolution, a generic XML-Schema-based representation is adopted. The representation allows defining agent types along with the respective sets of conflicts and conversions, with the help of the relations $\prec$ and a, described earlier.

More specifically, for the case of attacks we define the set L of all attacks as:

$$L = T_B \cup \bigcup_{\forall a} T_a$$

where T_B is the set of basic attacks (Table 1), which is common for all agent types and T_a is the set of attacks that are specific for agent type $a \in A$. Similarly, the set V of conversions is defined as:

$$V = N_B \cup \bigcup_{\forall a} N_a$$

where N_B is the set of basic rule conversions (Table 3), which is common for all agent types, and N_a is the set of rule conversions that are specific for agent type a. Therefore, for each agent type $a \in A$, its conflict and conversion sets (L_a and V_a respectively) are defined as follows:

$$L_a = T_B \grave{\mathrm{E}} T_a, T_a \equiv \{ <a, X, Y> \mid Y \prec_a X \}$$

$$V_a = N_B \grave{\mathrm{E}} N_a, N_a \equiv \{ <a, Y, U> \mid U \; a_a \; Y \}$$

The schema is illustrated as a DTD (for simplicity) in Figure 8. The figure also depicts a sample XML excerpt that defines the *social* agent type.

Figure 8. Modality interaction schema and excerpt defining the social agent type

```
<!-- root element -->
<!ELEMENT agents (agent*)>

<!--
Each agent is characterized by a conflict
and a conversion set
-->
<!ELEMENT agent (conflicts?, conversions?)>
<!ATTLIST agent type ID #REQUIRED>

<!-- agent conflict set -->
<!ELEMENT conflicts (conflict*)>

<!--
The 1st mode is the superior rule mode
The 2nd mode is the inferior rule mode
The superior rule always prevails
-->
<!ELEMENT conflict (mode, mode)>

<!-- agent conversion set -->
<!ELEMENT conversions (conversion*)>

<!--
The 1st mode occurs in the body
The 2nd mode is the rule mode
-->
<!ELEMENT conversion (mode, mode)>

<!-- element representing mode/modality -->
<!ELEMENT mode (#PCDATA)>
```

```
<agent type="social">
    <conflicts>
        <conflict>
            <mode>BEL</mode>
            <mode>OBL</mode>
        </conflict>
        <conflict>
            <mode>BEL</mode>
            <mode>INT</mode>
        </conflict>
        <conflict>
            <mode>OBL</mode>
            <mode>INT</mode>
        </conflict>
    </conflicts>
    <conversions>
        <conversion>
            <mode>OBL</mode>
            <mode>BEL</mode>
        </conversion>
        <conversion>
            <mode>INT</mode>
            <mode>BEL</mode>
        </conversion>
        <conversion>
            <mode>OBL</mode>
            <mode>INT</mode>
        </conversion>
    </conversions>
</agent>
```

Implementation Efficiency

In this subsection we briefly discuss the efficiency of our implementation in reference to the computational complexity of the underlying logic and that of the transformed rule base. We claim that the reasoning computational complexity of the transformed rule base is $O(n^2)$, where n is the number of rules in the original rule base. In order to prove this, we need to have as input:

- The computational complexity of the underlying logic, which is a first-order defeasible reasoning system.
- The computational complexity of the transformed rule base.

Our underlying defeasible reasoning system is DR-DEVICE (Bassiliades et al., 2006). DR-DEVICE has undergone extensive testing with scalable knowledge bases which showed that the system can handle inferences with thousands of rules within few seconds. Its performance scalability is $O(n^2)$, where n is the size of the theory, i.e., the total number of defeasible rules.

As shown in the previous subsection, the transformed rule base (the one with non-modalized literals) contains $m \cdot (\alpha + 2)$ rules, where m is the number of rules in the modalized rule base and α is the number of modality attacks (namely $|L_a|$, the cardinality of the L_a set, for each agent type a). Upon scaling, the number of rules tends to grow quite larger than α. For example in Bassiliades et al. (2006) m scaled up to 10^3, whereas α is usually less than 10 (for example, in our implementation the "social" agent type has 3 modality attacks, see Figure 8). If we replace this in the complexity of the DR-Device system we can conclude that the complexity of our implementation is $O(m^2 \cdot a^2)$, therefore assuming that $m >> \alpha$ the complexity is $O(m^2)$, i.e., it is quadratic to the number of rules of the original modalized rule base, as our initial claim was.

Example: Prisoner's Dilemma

To illustrate all of the above, we use an example that features the prisoner's dilemma rule base. Notice that, although DR-DEVICE$_M$ is a first-order system, this example is in propositional logic for the sake of simplicity for the demonstration. In the next subsection we include a predicate logic example.

Initially, the rule base contains two facts (f_1 and f_2) and two rules (p_1 and p_2):

f_1: committedCrime

f2: arrested

p1: committedCrime $\wedge$ arrested $\Rightarrow_Z$ confess

p2: committedCrime $\wedge$ arrested $\Rightarrow_O$ ¬confess

Let's suppose that we deal with a *social* agent. The initial rule base undergoes the transformation described previously, before being submitted to the defeasible logic reasoner of the system. As already outlined, the transformation includes turning predicate modalities into atom slots and assigning modalities to rule heads, depending on the corresponding rule modes (step 1). Predicates with no modality assume modality K (knowledge). As a result, at this stage the transformed rule base will be as follows:

f1-CONV: K(committedCrime)

f2-CONV: K(arrested)

p1-CONV: K(committedCrime) $\wedge$ K(arrested) $\Rightarrow$ Z(confess)

p2-CONV: K(committedCrime) $\wedge$ K(arrested) $\Rightarrow$ ¬O(confess)

Then, the issue of rule conversion, i.e., the conversion of rule conclusion modality according to the condition modality, is handled by the addition of two rules at step 2:

p1-CONV-VAR: $M(committedCrime) \land M(arrested) \land Z$ a $M \Rightarrow M(confess)$

p2-CONV-VAR: $M(committedCrime) \land M(arrested) \land O$ a $M \Rightarrow \neg M(confess)$

The above rules (e.g., $p_{1\text{-CONV-VAR}}$) indicate that if the modality of all condition literals is M and M is a modality that is compatible with the original rule mode Z, then it is indeed possible to derive the conclusion of the rule with modality M.

Finally, the issue of rule attacks has to be dealt with. In the rule base there is only a single conclusion (confess) and a single attack ($\Rightarrow_z confess / \Rightarrow_o \sim confess$). Therefore, two defeaters are added in step 3 for the specific agent type (any obligation is also the agent's intentional action), as seen below:

pO-Z-POS: $O(confess) \hat{I} Z(confess)$

pO-Z-NEG: $\neg O(confess) \hat{I} \neg Z(confess)$

Rule $p_{1\text{-CONV}}$ is defeated by $p_{O\text{-Z-NEG}}$ and it is eventually concluded that $+_o \sim confess$ and $-_z confess$, which implies that the social agent's obligation to confess overpowers its intention not to confess.

A slight variation of the example that demonstrates rule conversion would include facts f_1' and f_2' instead of f_1 and f_2:

f1': $Z(committedCrime)$

f2': $Z(arrested)$

· In this case no conclusion is derived, because rule $p_{2\text{-CONV-VAR}}$ tries to conclude $\neg Z(confess)$, since the agent is *social* and OaZ, while rule $p_{1\text{-CONV-VAR}}$ tries to conclude Z(confess), because ZaZ. Thus, no conclusion on the confession can be derived, even though the agent is social and this would incline to its cooperativeness. Although the rationality of this last example is dubious, cases like this are useful in studying the "side-effects problem" (Governatori & Rotolo, 2008a; Governatori et al., 2009) (i.e., results from agent's actions that are not among its intentions, at least not *all* of them), which is one of the most interesting topics of discussion regarding the *rationality* and *awareness* of agents.

A Semantic Web Example: Apartment Renting

This subsection describes a more sophisticated example, in predicate (first-order) logic, that is oriented towards the Semantic Web paradigm. The example is adopted from Antoniou and van Harmelen (2004) and is applied as a use case scenario for the DR-DEVICE defeasible reasoner (Bassiliades et al., 2006). In its original form the scenario involves two parties: (1) A potential renter, who assigns his/her personal agent to discover an apartment to rent that suits his/her specifications (e.g., location, floor) and personal preferences (e.g., price, size), and (2) a broker, who possesses a list of available apartments and has to match the client's requirements with the features of the available apartments and eventually propose suitable flats.

In the Semantic Web environment, the broker's list of available apartments along with their specifications is materialized as an RDF document (Figure 9) that complies with a corresponding RDF Schema ontology (http://lpis.csd.auth.gr/systems/dr-device/carlo/carlo.rdf). Actually, this piece of data (also known as "fact" in logic programming terminology), is equivalent to the following in POSL notation:

apartment(name->a1, bedrooms->1, central->yes, floor->1, gardenSize->0, lift->no, pets->yes, price->300, size->50).

Figure 9. RDF fragment representing available apartments

```
<ex:apartment rdf:about="&ap;a1">
    <ex:name>a1</ex:name>
    <ex:bedrooms rdf:datatype="&xsd;integer">1</ex:bedrooms>
    <ex:central>yes</ex:central>
    <ex:floor rdf:datatype="&xsd;integer">1</ex:floor>
    <ex:gardenSize rdf:datatype="&xsd;integer">0</ex:gardenSize>
    <ex:lift>no</ex:lift>
    <ex:pets>yes</ex:pets>
    <ex:price rdf:datatype="&xsd;integer">300</ex:price>
    <ex:size rdf:datatype="&xsd;integer">50</ex:size>
</ex:apartment>
...
```

POSL (positional-slotted language) notation (Boley, 2004) is an ASCII language that integrates Prolog's positional and F-logic's slotted syntaxes for representing knowledge (facts and rules) in the Semantic Web. For representing defeasible rule bases in a concise syntax, we proposed the d-POSL notation in Kontopoulos, Bassiliades, Governatori, and Antoniou (2010) and we use this notation to concisely present rules of this example in this paper. When compared to RuleML-based types of syntax (e.g., DR-RuleML, Figure 2), d-POSL is considered more compact and human-readable, since it is faster to write and easier to read. Variables in d-POSL are denoted with a preceding "?", rule types ("strict", "defeasible", "defeater") are expressed via binary infix functors (":-", ":=", ":~"), while the extension also deals with other essential features in defeasible logic, like rule labels, rule superiorities and conflicting literals. More details regarding the application of d-POSL in an agent-based brokering scenario can be found in Kravari, Kontopoulos, and Bassiliades (2010b).

Assuming that the schema is publicly available, the renter's requirements and preferences are based on it as well and are expressed in defeasible logic, in the DR-RuleML syntax (Figure 10 – left). The rule r_1 is expressed as follows in d-POSL notation:

r_1: acceptable(apartment->?x):= apartment(name->?x).

The final conclusion regarding the most appropriate apartment for rental is derived via inference by the DR-DEVICE reasoner over the rule set and the RDF list of available apartments (Figure 10 – right). Suppose that the final conclusion is rent(apartment->a5) (in d-POSL), where a5 is the id of the most appropriate apartment. Notice that in the OO-RDF model of DR-DEVICE properties, like apartment, are encapsulated inside their domains, such as rent class.

The above example can be extended with deontic defeasible logic elements, in order to illustrate the applicability of this type of logic in pragmatic Semantic Web scenarios. According to a "deontic" point of view, since the renter has used a specific broker's services, he/she is "morally obliged" to make an offer for one of the broker's apartments (specifically for apartment a5, which is the most appropriate one for him). This obligation is expressed via rule:

r_{M1}: make_offer(apartment->?x):=$_O$ rent(apartment->?x).

Continuing the "deontic" version of the apartment renting scenario, let's suppose that the renter has conducted on the Web another market research by himself/herself and has formed a list of advertised apartments, expressed via predicate advertised_apartment(name->?x,price->?y).

Figure 10. DR-RuleML fragment of the renter's requirements (left) and DR-DEVICE derived conclusions (right)

Let's also suppose that he/she has performed the selection process himself/herself on the latter list (and not on the broker's apartment list), retrieving his/her favorite apartment expressed, e.g., as my_rent(apartment->b2). If the renter's agent discovers a cheaper favorite apartment than the one proposed by the broker (apartment a5), his/her intention is to *not* make an offer for the broker's apartment (and maybe later make an offer to the apartment he/she found on the web):

r_{M2}: ¬make_offer(apartment->?x):=$_I$

rent(apartment->?x), apartment(name->?x, price->?y),

my_rent(apartment->?z), advertised_ apartment(name->?z, price->?w),

?x ≠ ?z, ?w < ?y.

Considering rules r_{M1} and r_{M2} above, a deviant agent's intentions prevail over its obligations to the contrary and the agent will eventually avoid making an offer for apartment a5. Contrasted, a social agent would prefer to obey to the moral obligation of preferring the broker's suggestion and would eventually make an offer for apartment a5.

To demonstrate the effect of rule conversions, an initial precondition of *I*(rent(apartment->a5)) would produce via rule r_{M1} (supposing that the renter's agent is *social*) the corresponding rule

conversion $+\P_I$ make_offer(apartment->a5). Supposing also that the rule's r_{M2} prerequisites hold as well, the second conclusion would be $+\P_I$ ¬make_offer(apartment->a5). The two conclusions are conflicting and none of them prevails, if no superiority relationship is explicitly expressed in the rule base.

RELATED WORK

The work presented here relies heavily on work by Governatori and Rotolo (2004, 2008a), where a detailed account on extending defeasible logics with modal logic operators is given. The main differentiation among the two lines of research lies in the fact that the work by Governatori and Rotolo is based on the meta-program formalization presented by Maher and Governatori (1999), while our approach adopts a theory transformation for turning a modal defeasible theory into a non-modal one. Other secondary differences involve the permission operator (which, however, is included in the ideas for future work by the other authors) and the definition of the agent type.

An implementation approach with similar functionality to ours is proposed by Antoniou, Dimaresis and Governatori (2009). The proposed system is based on *DR-Prolog* (Antoniou & Bikakis, 2007), a Prolog-based defeasible reasoner for the Semantic Web. The approach extends the meta-program for simulating modal defeasible logic (Antoniou, Billington, Governatori, & Maher, 2006) and the corresponding inference mechanism. Similarly to DR-DEVICE$_M$, the proposed system also deals with rule conflicts and rule conversions and can also describe various agent types. The main difference among the two implementations lies in the superior centralization and modularization offered by our system. The type of the agent can be declared centrally in each rule base, while modality interactions (attacks and conversions) are dealt with parametrically (i.e., via easily-parameterized external agent-type definition files), as described in this work. Also, the RuleML-like language for describing a modal defeasible logic rule base is quite easy to grasp, since the extensions to the language are limited.

Another similar paradigm is *SPINdle* (Lam & Governatori, 2009), a propositional defeasible logic reasoner that covers both the standard and modal extensions to defeasible logics. Regarding efficiency, when compared to DR-DEVICE$_M$, the system demonstrates low computational complexity during reasoning coupled with low memory consumption. In *SPINdle*, agent types can be defined by specifying the conversion and conflict relationships using the rule language, while in DR-DEVICE$_M$ there are predefined agent types in a separate configuration file. This may be more user-friendly and less error-prone than the approach of *SPINdle*, but could be less flexible. Finally, DR-DEVICE$_M$ and the modal extension of DR-Prolog are more RuleML-compatible and they are more expressible than *SPINdle*, since they are first-order. On the other hand, the modal extension of DR-Prolog is query based while DR-DEVICE$_M$ and *SPINdle* are extension based.

Taking into consideration more traditional approaches, the approach presented in this article has a lot of common points with the *BOID* architecture (Broersen et al., 2001), where the conflicts among agents' informational and motivational attitudes are explored. The BOID calculation scheme is similar to the one proposed here; e.g.,

it is possible to state general orders of overruling but also local preferences involving single rules. However, our system also deals with agency and permission, a factor that largely differentiates our approach from the BOID architecture, and is also designed to take care of modalized literals and modal conversions. This is due to the rule-based approach of introducing modalities.

Also, Nute (1998) proposed a *Deontic Defeasible Logic* which, in some respect, is similar to the framework presented here. Besides some minor differences in the way rules are handled at the propositional level, the main difference is that he uses only one type of rule. In proof theory operators are traditionally introduced for giving meaning to rules. Thus, using only one type of rule both for obligation and factual conclusion does not reveal the real meaning of the operators involved. Moreover, it is not clear whether and how complex conversions and reductions can be dealt with in a system with only a single type of rule.

CONCLUSION AND FUTURE WORK

This article discusses the extension of defeasible logics with modal logic operators and reports on the implementation of a modal defeasible logic reasoner, focusing mainly on deontic logic operators. The implementation is based on DR-DEVICE, a defeasible logic reasoner over RDF metadata in the Semantic Web. The system was extended, so that it can handle modal logic operators, while testing the implementation with deontic logic operators. More specifically, five operators are included: knowledge, intention, obligation, agency and permission. The article also demonstrated how the RuleML-like language of DR-DEVICE, called DR-RuleML, was extended to incorporate the necessary modal logic aspects. Besides modal operators and modalization of literals, the system also deals with modal interactions, like conflict resolution and rule conversion. The submitted defeasible theory undergoes a transformation, imposed by the object-oriented philosophy, on which the system is built, so that the modal defeasible reasoning can be successfully performed.

Nevertheless, there is still plenty of room for improvement. More specifically, the system currently handles only three types of agents, realistic, social and deviant, but the selection can easily be extended to include other agent types as well, starting with the ones in Table 2. Defining new agent types will consequently allow the enrichment of the available rule conversions, which will lead to a more expressive rule language but also to a more thorough study of the "side-effects problem". Furthermore, we would like to test our implementation by introducing more operators from other modal logics, such as temporal, epistemic, doxastic, etc. Finally, more complicated features of modal logics, such as iterated modalities and modal interaction axioms, will be incorporated in our implementation by extending the existing transformation mechanisms. Overall, the aim of this line of work is to observe and explore the interactions among agents of various cognitive profiles.

A more ambitious goal, though, is to utilize a multi-agent system, such as *EMERALD* (Kravari, Kontopoulos & Bassiliades, 2010a), for deploying argumentation scenarios among agents, each one of which will possess its own agenda and normative system. EMERALD is a knowledge-based framework for interoperating intelligent agents in the Semantic Web. It is built on top of the JADE (http://jade.tilab.com/) multi-agent development framework and features trusted, third party reasoning services, a reusable agent prototype for knowledge-customizable agent behavior, as well as a reputation mechanism for ensuring trust in the framework.

REFERENCES

Antoniou, G., & Bikakis, A. (2007). DR-Prolog: A System for Defeasible Reasoning with Rules and Ontologies on the Semantic Web. *IEEE Transactions on Knowledge and Data Engineering, 19*(2), 233–245. doi:10.1109/TKDE.2007.29.

Antoniou, G., Billington, D., Governatori, G., & Maher, M. J. (2006). Embedding Defeasible Logic into Logic Programming. *Theory and Practice of Logic Programming, 6*(6), 703–735. doi:10.1017/S1471068406002778.

Antoniou, G., Dimaresis, N., & Governatori, G. (2009). A Modal and Deontic Defeasible Reasoning System for Modelling Policies and Multi-Agent Systems. *Expert Systems with Applications, 36*(2), 4125–4134. doi:10.1016/j.eswa.2008.03.009.

Antoniou, G., Skylogiannis, T., Bikakis, A., & Bassiliades, N. (2007). DR-BROKERING: A Semantic Brokering System. *Knowledge-Based Systems, 20*(1), 61–72. doi:10.1016/j.knosys.2006.07.006.

Antoniou, G., & van Harmelen, F. (2004). *A Semantic Web Primer*. Cambridge, MA: MIT Press.

Artosi, A., Governatori, G., & Sartor, G. (1996). Towards a computational treatment of deontic defeasibility. In M. Brown & J. Carmo (Eds.), *Deontic Logic Agency and Normative Systems: Workshop on Computing* (pp. 27-46). Berlin, Germany: Springer-Verlag.

Ashri, R., Payne, T., Marvin, D., Surridge, M., & Taylor, S. (2004). Towards a Semantic Web Security Infrastructure. In *Proceedings of the AAAI Spring Symposium on Semantic Web Services* (pp. 84-91). Menlo Park, CA: AAAI Press.

Bassiliades, N., Antoniou, G., & Vlahavas, I. (2006). A Defeasible Logic Reasoner for the Semantic Web. *International Journal on Semantic Web and Information Systems*, *2*(1), 1–41. doi:10.4018/jswis.2006010101.

Bassiliades, N., & Vlahavas, I. (2006). R-DEVICE: An Object-Oriented Knowledge Base System for RDF Metadata. *International Journal on Semantic Web and Information Systems*, *2*(2), 24–90. doi:10.4018/jswis.2006040102.

Berners-Lee, T., Hendler, J., & Lassila, O. (2001). The Semantic Web. *Scientific American*, *284*(5), 34–43. doi:10.1038/scientificamerican0501-34.

Bieber, P., & Cuppens, F. (1993). Expression of Confidentiality Policies with Deontic Logic. In Meyer, J. C., & Wieringa, R. J. (Eds.), *Deontic Logic in Computer Science: Normative System Specification* (pp. 103–123). Chichester, UK: John Wiley & Sons.

Blackburn, P., de Rijke, M., & Venema, Y. (2001). *Modal Logic*. Cambridge, UK: Cambridge University Press.

Boley, H. (2004). *An Integrated Positional-Slotted Language for Semantic Web Knowledge*. Retrieved from http://www.ruleml.org/submission/ruleml-shortation.html

Boley, H. (2006). The RuleML Family of Web Rule Languages: Invited talk. In *Proceedings of 4th Workshop on Principles and Practice of Semantic Web Reasoning,* Budva, Montenegro (LNCS 4187, pp.1-15).

Bonatti, P. A., Duma, C., Fuchs, N., Nejdl, W., Olmedilla, D., Peer, J., & Shahmehri, N. (2006). Semantic Web Policies - a Discussion of Requirements and Research Issues. In *Proceedings of the 3rd European Semantic Web Conference,* Budva, Montenegro (LNCS 4011, pp. 712-724).

Broersen, J., Dastani, M., Hulstijn, J., Huang, Z., & van der Torre, L. (2001). The BOID Architecture: Conflicts between Beliefs, Obligations, Intentions and Desires. In *Proceedings of the 5th International Conference on Autonomous Agents,* Montreal, QC, Canada (pp. 9-16). New York, NY: ACM.

Cohen, P. R., & Levesque, H. J. (1990). Intention is Choice with Commitment. *Artificial Intelligence*, *42*(2-3), 213–261. doi:10.1016/0004-3702(90)90055-5.

Gottlob, G. (1992). Complexity Results for Nonmonotonic Logics. *Journal of Logic and Computation*, *2*, 397–425. doi:10.1093/logcom/2.3.397.

Governatori, G. (2005). Representing Business Contracts in RuleML. *International Journal of Cooperative Information Systems*, *14*(2-3), 181–216. doi:10.1142/S0218843005001092.

Governatori, G., Hulstijn, J., Riveret, R., & Rotolo, A. (2007). Characterising Deadlines in Temporal Modal Defeasible Logic. In *Proceedings of the 20th Australian Joint Conference on Artificial Intelligence (AI 2007)* (pp. 486-496).

Governatori, G., Padmanabhan, V., Rotolo, A., & Sattar, A. (2009). A Defeasible Logic for Modelling Policy-based Intentions and Motivational Attitudes. *Logic Journal of the IGPL*, *17*(3), 227–265. doi:10.1093/jigpal/jzp006.

Governatori, G., & Rotolo, A. (2004). Defeasible Logic: Agency, Intention and Obligation. In *Proceedings of the 7th International Workshop on Deontic Logic in Computer Science,* Madeira, Portugal (pp. 114-128).

Governatori, G., & Rotolo, A. (2008a). BIO Logical Agents: Norms, Beliefs, Intentions in Defeasible Logic. *Journal of Autonomous Agents and Multi Agent Systems*, *17*(1), 36–69. doi:10.1007/s10458-008-9030-4.

Governatori, G., & Rotolo, A. (2008b). A Computational Framework for Institutional Agency. *Artificial Intelligence and Law*, *16*(1), 25–52. doi:10.1007/s10506-007-9056-y.

Hilpinen, R. (2001). Deontic Logic. In Goble, L. (Ed.), *The Blackwell Guide to Philosophical Logic* (pp. 159–182). Oxford, UK: Blackwell.

Hofstadter, D. R. (1983). Metamagical Themas: Computer Tournaments of the Prisoner's Dilemma Suggest How Cooperation Evolves. *Scientific American*, *248*(5), 16–26. doi:10.1038/scientificamerican0583-16.

Kagal, L., Berners-Lee, T., Connolly, D., & Weitzner, D. (2006, July 16-20). Using Semantic Web Technologies for Open Policy Management on the Web. In *Proceedings of the 21st National Conference on Artificial Intelligence (AAAI 2006)*. Menlo Park, CA: AAAI Press.

Kautz, H. A., & Selman, B. (1991). Hard Problems for Simple Default Theories. *Artificial Intelligence*, *28*, 243–279. doi:10.1016/0004-3702(91)90011-8.

Kolaczek, G. (2002). Application of Deontic Logic in Role-based Access Control. *International Journal of Applied Mathematics and Computer Science*, *12*(2), 269–275.

Kontopoulos, E., Bassiliades, N., Governatori, G., & Antoniou, G. (2008). Extending a Defeasible Reasoner with Modal and Deontic Logic Operators. In *Proceedings of the Workshop on Logics for Intelligent Agents and Multi-Agent Systems (WLIAMAS 2008), IEEE/WIC/ACM International Conference on Web Intelligence and Intelligent Agent Technology,* Sydney, NSW, Australia (pp. 626-629). Washington, DC: IEEE Computer Society.

Kontopoulos, E., Bassiliades, N., Governatori, G., & Antoniou, G. (2011). Visualizing Semantic Web Proofs of Defeasible Logic in the DR-DEVICE System. *Knowledge-Based Systems*, *24*(3), 406–419. doi:10.1016/j.knosys.2010.12.001.

Kravari, K., Kontopoulos, E., & Bassiliades, N. (2010a, May 4-7). EMERALD: A Multi-Agent System for Knowledge-based Reasoning Interoperability in the Semantic Web. In *Proceedings of the 6th Hellenic Conference on Artificial Intelligence (SETN 2010)*, Athens, Greece (pp. 173-182).

Kravari, K., Kontopoulos, E., & Bassiliades, N. (2010b). Trusted Reasoning Services for Semantic Web Agents. *Informatica: International Journal of Computing and Informatics*, *34*(4), 429–440.

Lam, H., & Governatori, G. (2009). The Making of SPINdle. In G. Governatori, J. Hall, & A. Paschke (Eds.), *Proceedings of the 2009 International Symposium on Rule Interchange and Applications* (LNCS 5858, pp. 315-322).

Lokhorst, G.-J. C. (1996). Reasoning about actions and obligations in first-order logic. *Studia Logica*, *57*(1), 221–237. doi:10.1007/BF00370676.

Maher, M. J., & Governatori, G. (1999). A Semantic Decomposition of Defeasible Logics. In *Proceedings of the 16th National Conference on Artificial Intelligence*, Orlando, FL (pp. 299-305). Menlo Park, CA: AAAI Press.

Meyer, J.-J. C. (2001). Epistemic Logic. In Goble, L. (Ed.), *The Blackwell Guide to Philosophical Logic*. Oxford, UK: Blackwell.

Meyer, J.-J. C. (2003). Modal Epistemic and Doxastic Logic. In Gabbay, D., & Guenthner, F. (Eds.), *Handbook of Philosophical Logic* (2nd ed., Vol. 10, pp. 1–38). Dordrecht, The Netherlands: Kluwer.

Nute, D. (1994). Defeasible logic. In Gabbay, D. (Ed.), *Handbook of Logic and Artificial Intelligence* (Vol. 3, pp. 353–395). Oxford, UK: Oxford University Press.

Nute, D. (1998). Norms, Priorities, and Defeasible Logic. In McNamara, P., & Prakken, H. (Eds.), *Norms, Logics and Information Systems* (pp. 201–218). Amsterdam, The Netherlands: IOS Press.

Pham, D. H., Governatori, G., Raboczi, S., Newman, A., & Thakur, S. (2008). On Extending RuleML for Modal Defeasible Logic. In N. Bassiliades, G. Governatori, & A. Paschke (Eds.), *Proceedings of the International Symposium on Rule Representation, Interchange and Reasoning on the Web (RuleML 2008)*, Orlando, FL (LNCS 5321, pp. 89-103).

Rissland, E. L., & Skalak, D. B. (1991). CABARET: Rule Interpretation in a Hybrid Architecture. *International Journal of Man-Machine Studies*, *34*(6), 839–887. doi:10.1016/0020-7373(91)90013-W.

Riveret, R., Rotolo, A., & Governatori, G. (2007). Interaction between Normative Systems and Cognitive Agents in Temporal Modal Defeasible Logic. In G. Boella, L. van der Torre, & H. Verhagen (Eds.), *Proceedings of the Normative Multi-Agent Systems (NorMAS) Conference*, Dagstuhl, Germany.

Schild, U. J., & Herzog, S. (1993). The Use of Meta-rules in Rule Based Legal Computer Systems. In *Proceedings of the 4th International Conference on Artificial Intelligence and Law (ICAIL'93)* (pp. 100-109). New York, NY: ACM Press.

Skylogiannis, T., Antoniou, G., Bassiliades, N., Governatori, G., & Bikakis, A. (2007). DR-NEGOTIATE – A System for Automated Agent Negotiation with Defeasible Logic-Based Strategies. *Data & Knowledge Engineering*, *63*(2), 362–380. doi:10.1016/j.datak.2007.03.004.

Soininen, T., & Niemela, I. (1998). Developing a Declarative Rule Language for Applications in Product Configuration. In G. Gupta (Ed.), *Proceedings of International Symposium on Practical Aspects of Declarative Languages (PADL)* (pp. 305-319). Berlin, Germany: Springer-Verlag.

Venema, Y. (2001). Temporal Logic. In Goble, L. (Ed.), *The Blackwell Guide to Philosophical Logic* (pp. 203–223). Oxford, UK: Blackwell.

This work was previously published in the International Journal on Semantic Web and Information Systems, Volume 7, Issue 1, edited by Amit P. Sheth,, pp. 18-43, copyright 2011 by IGI Publishing (an imprint of IGI Global).

Section 3
Web of Data and Applications

Chapter 8
Data Linking for the Semantic Web

Alfio Ferraram
Università degli Studi di Milano, Italy

Andriy Nikolov
The Open University, UK

François Scharffe
University of Montpellier, France

ABSTRACT

By specifying that published datasets must link to other existing datasets, the 4th linked data principle ensures a Web of data and not just a set of unconnected data islands. The authors propose in this paper the term data linking to name the problem of finding equivalent resources on the Web of linked data. In order to perform data linking, many techniques were developed, finding their roots in statistics, database, natural language processing and graph theory. The authors begin this paper by providing background information and terminological clarifications related to data linking. Then a comprehensive survey over the various techniques available for data linking is provided. These techniques are classified along the three criteria of granularity, type of evidence, and source of the evidence. Finally, the authors survey eleven recent tools performing data linking and we classify them according to the surveyed techniques.

INTRODUCTION

In the Semantic Web and in the Web in general, a fundamental problem is the comparison and matching of data and the capability of resolving the multiplicity of data references to the same real-world objects, by defining correspondences among data in form of data links. The data linking task is becoming more and more important as the number of structured and semistructured data available on the Web is growing. The transformation of the Web from a "Web of documents" into a "Web of data", as well as the availability of large collections of sensor generated data ("internet of

DOI: 10.4018/978-1-4666-3610-1.ch008

things"), is leading to a new generation of Web applications based on the integration of both data and services. At the same time, new data are published every day out of user generated contents and public Web sites.

In general terms, *data linking* is the task of determining whether two object descriptions can be linked one to the other to represent the fact that they refer to the same real-world object in a given domain or the fact that some kind of relation holds between them[1]. Quite often, this task is performed on the basis of the evaluation of the degree of similarity among different data instances describing real-world objects across heterogeneous data sources, under the assumption that the higher is the similarity between two data descriptions, the higher is the probability that the two descriptions actually refer to the same object. From an operative point of view, data linking includes also the task of defining methods, techniques and (semi-) automated tools for performing the similarity evaluation task. We call this specific subtask *instance matching*.

In this context, one of the most important initiatives in the Semantic Web field is the Linked Open Data project, which promotes the idea of improving interoperability and aggregation among large data collections already available on the Web (Berners-Lee et al., 2008). The example of Linked Data shows how the data linking task is crucial on the Web nowadays. Fortunately, there is a lot of work done in other fields that can be used to provide solutions, methods, and techniques to address data linking on the Semantic Web. Moreover, there are important works describing research fields that are very close to data linking (Euzenat & Shvaiko, 2007; Koudas et al., 2006; Bleiholder & Naumann, 2009). However, there are specific features of semantic data which require specific solutions both in terms of new techniques and in terms of original combinations of techniques that have been originally proposed in different fields. For example, on one side, data linking requires dealing with the semantic complexity which is typical of ontology matching, but, on the other side,

the large amount of data available on the "Web of data" requires to deal with scalability issues that are typical of record linkage. This situation leads to the development of new approaches, addressing problems that are typical of the data linking field on the Semantic Web. In this paper, we provide a general definition of this field, in order to underline problems and to describe solutions. In particular, in the next section, we will better define the data linking problem, by discussing also the terminology used in the field. After that, we present the main families of techniques proposed for the most relevant subtask of data linking, that is instance matching, then we survey the most relevant tools in the field by comparing them. Finally, we discuss the main open problems and directions of work in the field.

PROBLEM FORMULATION

Data linking can be formalized as an operation which takes two collections of data as input and produces a collection of mappings between entities of the two collections as output. Mappings denote binary relations between entities corresponding semantically one to another. The data linking task is articulated in steps as shown in Figure 1.

The input of the process is given by one or more datasets. Each dataset is a collection of data representing object descriptions to be linked. The output of the process is a *mapping set* that is a collection of binary relations (usually referred as *mappings* or *links*) between the object descriptions in the input dataset(s)[2]. The data linking task also involves a user, who has the responsibility of configuring the process and, optionally, interacting with the predicate selection, pre-processing, matching and post-processing steps in case of a semi-automatic procedure. Another optional component is provided by external resources such as lexical databases and thesauri, reasoning systems or pre-defined mappings that can be used both in the matching and in the post-processing steps as a support for the main process. A typical

Figure 1. The data linking tasks

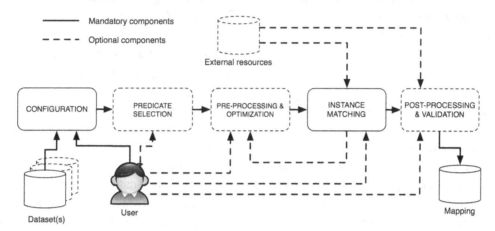

external resource used for the comparison is a schema level mapping that is used to determine which data must be compared. The main steps of the process are more extensively described in the following:

Configuration

The configuration step has the goal of setting up the parameters used during the instance matching step in order to compare object descriptions. In particular, it is very common to evaluate similarity between object descriptions as a value in the range [0,1] and to set a threshold that denotes the minimum value of similarity needed in order to consider a pair of object descriptions as similar one to the other. Another parameter in some systems is the choice of similarity metrics combination that has to be used in the matching step as well as the list of external resources that may be needed for similarity evaluation.

Predicate Selection (Optional)

The general goal of the whole data linking task is to retrieve a set of links between two collections of data. The term "links" is generic and, in fact, the choice of the predicates used to represent the meaning of the linking relation is an important step of the data linking task configuration. Usually, the default option is to intend data linking as the task of retrieving links between data that refer to the same real objects, i.e., *identity* links. However, data linking techniques and tools can be used (and actually are often used) in order to retrieve more generic similarity relations among data, in order, for example, to exploit these links for approximate query answering. Since the goal of data linking depends on the assumptions and goals of users and it affects the nature of matching techniques that are enforced, predicate selection is part of the data linking configuration, even if some work exists about the problem of *a posteriori* mapping interpretation (see next section).

Pre-Processing and Optimization (Optional)

Pre-processing of data is an optional step that can be executed for two main purposes. The first is to transform the original representation of data according to a reference format used for the comparison. A second goal is to minimize the number of comparisons that have to be executed in order to produce the final mapping set. To this end several kinds of blocking techniques can be adopted to compare each object description only against those descriptions that have a high probability to be considered similar to it.

Matching

In the instance matching step, the object description comparison is executed according to the metrics chosen in the configuration step. In many cases, more than one type of matching techniques are combined, including for example string/value matching, learning-based matching, similarity propagation. If required, external resources are used in this step to optimize the matching with respect to a pre-defined mapping or to determine the similarity between property values according to existing lexical resources or ontologies (e.g., WordNet, SKOS, OpenCyC). In case of a semi-automatic process, the user interaction is needed in the matching step in order to select the correct mappings or to validate the system result.

Post-Processing and Validation (Optional)

The post-processing step is optional and has the goal of refining the matching result according to specific domain or application requirements. A typical post-processing goal is to validate the mappings with respect to a formal definition of consistency for the mapping set, that may include, for example, the fact that two object descriptions classified in disjoint classes cannot be mapped onto the same entity (Meilicke et al., 2008). Another kind of validation is executed with respect to the required mapping set cardinality. In some cases, a mapping set cannot include more than one matching counterpart for each object description. This requirement can be taken into account either in the instance matching step or in the post-processing step, by defining appropriate heuristics for the deletion of multiple mapping rules and the selection of the best ones (Castano et al., 2008).

Terminological Hints and Related Problems

The problem of data linking is directly related to many similar problems, and this causes confusion about the appropriate terminology. Problems similar to data linking can be grouped in two main categories: the first category describes the problems related to the proper activity of *data linking* (Alexander et al., 2009), i.e., connecting together different data provided by heterogeneous data sources. In this field, we often talk about *entity matching*, *coreference resolution* or *entity resolution* to denote the activities of evaluating the degree of similarity between pairs of entities with the goal of finding a common reference to a single real-world object (Cudré-Mauroux et al., 2009; Köpcke et al., 2010; Köpcke & Rahm, 2010). On the other side, a second category of problems is related to the comparison of data records especially for data cleaning and duplicate detection purposes. In this field, we often talk about *duplicate identification*, *record linkage* or *merge/purge problem*. For both the categories of problems many solutions have been proposed. Recent surveys and contributions on this field include for example Koudas et al. (2006), Bleiholder and Naumann (2009), and Batini and Scannapieco (2006). The main differences between these two categories of problems and their related solutions can be described according to three main dimensions of analysis: i) the *goal* of the comparison; ii) the *object* of the comparison, and iii) the *meaning* of the resulting mappings, as graphically shown in Figure 2.

Goal of the Comparison

Some of the problems mentioned above have the goal for example of detecting duplicate records in order to clean a collection of data by capturing errors. This is the case for example of the merge/purge problem in the context of data cleaning. Another goal is data integration. In this case, the

Figure 2. A map of the terminology in the field of data linking

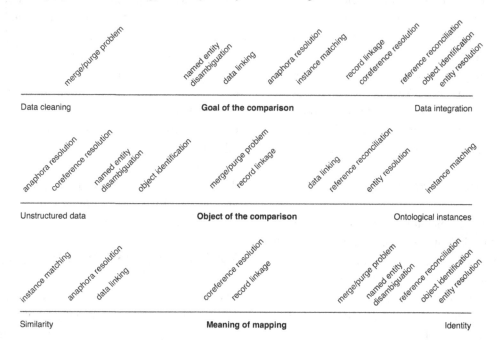

final purpose is to provide a unique description for each real-world object mentioned in different data sources, by exploiting object identification and entity reconciliation/resolution techniques. Between these two options, a third goal is the linkage of data. In this case, we admit the presence of different and heterogeneous descriptions of real-world objects, but we want to create links and relations among these descriptions in order to make explicit their correspondence. To this end, several techniques may be used referred with terms such as "coreference resolution", "record linkage", and "instance matching".

Object of the Comparison

By object of the comparison we mean the kind of data that are taken into account for the data linking task. A general but useful distinction concerns techniques and solutions mainly focused on unstructured data, such as plain text or Web pages, on one side, and those mainly focused on richly structured ontology instances on the other

side. Between these two sides of the comparison, it is very important to recall several methods and techniques that have been aimed at other types of structured data (relational or XML database instances). On the side of unstructured data, we collocate approaches mainly derived from the natural language processing field, such as anaphora resolution, named entity disambiguation, and coreference resolution (this last term is used also in the context of ontology instances). In the database community, the terms mainly used are record linkage and merge/purge. Terms like entity resolution, data linking, reference resolution are more typical of the Semantic Web and the ontology fields. The main difference between these kinds of solutions is that the assumptions that can be made on unstructured and relational data are different from those that are valid in case of ontological data. For example, in case of relational data we usually do not deal with multi-valued attributes and class hierarchy, and the structure of data is explicit. On the contrary, the structure of ontological data is implicit and must be inferred from the ontology.

Moreover, the structure of ontological instances is often not rigid and can provide multi-valued or structured attributes. Finally, when dealing with relational data, the attribute values of records often consist in atomic data, and references to other records through foreign keys are not so frequent. On the contrary, in linked data it is very common to provide attribute values in form of references to other objects inside or across datasets.

Meaning of the Mappings

Finally, about the meaning of mappings produced as a result of the comparison, we can distinguish between two main approaches. On one side, mappings are interpreted as "same-as" relations, where the two mapped object descriptions are intended to denote the same real-world object. On the other side, a mapping may be intended just as a generic relation of similarity between object descriptions. In those cases where the terminology mainly refers to the idea of connecting data more than finding a common reference to a real-world object, we have classified the terms in the category of similarity, such as in case of the terms instance matching, data linking, and anaphora resolution. Instead, terms like object identification, (named) entity resolution, reference reconciliation are used to stress the fact that the meaning of mappings found by the comparison task is to denote an identity relation between objects described by data. Other terms like coreference resolution and record linkage are used in both senses according to different approaches in the literature. More details about the interpretation of mappings meaning is given.

Other Relevant Terminology and Fields

The problem of data linking and its associated techniques of instance matching and object description comparison is very pervasive also in fields other than the Semantic Web and for purposes other than the linking of data. For example,

the expression *reference reconciliation* has been used with reference to ontological data in Dong et al. (2005) and Säis et al. (2007). The problem of comparing different object descriptions has been addressed also in the natural language processing research community, where linguistic descriptions of objects like names of sentences are compared for disambiguation purposes. In this case we talk about *anaphora resolution* or *named entity disambiguation* (Elmagarmid et al., 2007). In the database and data mining fields, the problem is also addressed as *object identification*.

MAPPINGS AND THEIR MEANING

The data linking task produces a collection of mappings that are used to define links between object descriptions in different data sources. In this context, a relevant issue is to determine the meaning of these mappings. Usually, the mappings are interpreted as binary relations between two object descriptions that could be considered *identical* in the sense that they refer to the same real-world object. The notion of identity in itself, however, is ambiguous and is a subject of philosophical discussions. In the literature about ontologies and the Semantic Web, identity has been described as the problem of distinguishing a specific instance of a certain class from other instances (Guarino & Welty, 2002). Thus, the identity criterion is linked to the class to which an instance belongs and depends on the assumptions made by the ontology designer. In this way, identity mappings between instances should, in principle, follow the identity criterion associated with the corresponding classes. However, instance matching usually deals with datasets originating from different sources, and the assumptions of their creators may be potentially different. Moreover, the design practices in the Semantic Web are always not explicitly declared and do not follow a standard approach. On the Web of Data, identity is commonly expressed using the standard *owl:sameAs* property. In OWL, two individuals connected by the *owl:sameAs* property are considered identical in the sense that the subject and object of this statement share all their properties. Such interpretation of identity, however, appears too strong in many cases and it is not always compatible with the evaluation of mappings, which is based on similarity. In order to understand the practices of the usage of *owl:sameAs* links by existing repositories, Halpin et al. (2010) distinguished five weaker varieties of identity beyond the canonical one. The idea of providing more than a single notion of identity is also adopted by the UMBEL and the SKOS vocabularies (http://umbel.org) (W3C, 2004), which provide weaker relations of correspondence such as *umbel:isLike* or the family of "Match" properties of SKOS.

More generally, the problem of having a sound and well founded notion of identity is often ignored in the data linking process. As a consequence, the interpretation of mapping can shift among three very different notions of identity:

1. **Ontological Identity:** The idea behind ontological identity is that the real-world and existing object denoted by two identical object descriptions is the same. In other terms, we ask whether two "identical" object descriptions denote the same real-world object. For example, the expressions "Bard of Avon" and the name "William Shakespeare" denote the same real-world person.

2. **Logical Identity:** What we call "logical identity" is the idea that two descriptions are identical when they can be substituted one to the other in a logical expression without changing the meaning of the expression. This kind of identity depends on the context where the expression is used and the fact that an object description is used to denote the reality of just to mention the term. For example, we can say "The Bard of Avon wrote A Midsummer Night's Dream" instead of "William Shakespeare wrote A Midsummer Night's Dream". But, we cannot substitute the expression "The Bard of Avon" with "William Shakespeare" in a sentence like "William Shakespeare is often called the Bard of Avon".

3. **Formal Identity:** In case of formal identity, we refer to the fact that identity is superimposed to the data. This happens for example when some organization sets a unique identifier for something with the goal of providing a standard tool for the identification of the object, such as for example the ISBN code for publications.

The main problem with the notion of identity in the field of data linking is that the process of matching is always based on the notion of similarity and that the relation between similarity and identity is not clear. This can be shown by the following example: suppose we need to compare two object descriptions referred to different editions of the same book. Now, two descriptions are probably similar, but they can be considered identical only if we are interested in the book, seen as a work and not as the edition. But if we look for the manifestation of the book (i.e., the edition) or even for a physical volume in a library, these two descriptions have to be considered different. Thus, identity is not "internal" to the data and it is not directly dependent on the relation of similarity, but depends on the reference to something else than data (e.g., in this case the kind of object we are interested in). However, despite the fact that the identity problem is widely recognized and discussed in the research community and that ontologies defining weaker degrees of identity exist (e.g., SKOS or the ontology proposed in Halpin et al., 2010), *owl:sameAs* remains the most popular representation of identity links between Semantic Web repositories. In literature, there is a variety of predicates proposed for denoting the general notion of "correspondence"[3]. Of course, having a canonical set of properties would be useful and might help in clarifying the task of mapping interpretation, but it is also an interesting research direction to work on the definition of semi-automatic approaches to mapping interpretations based on the nature of matching operations that are enforced during the linking task. At the moment, existing matching systems do not explicitly operate with different interpretations of matching results: instead the choice of interpretation is left to the user of the system.

INSTANCE MATCHING TECHNIQUES

As was discussed in the previous section, the problem of data linking is closely related both to the problem of database record linkage and the problem of ontology schema matching. Data linking systems processing semantic data utilize many techniques originating from both these communities. Thus, in order to determine suitable classification criteria for data linking techniques, we considered both the techniques themselves and existing classification schemas proposed in the literature on database record linkage (Elmagarmid et al., 2007; Winkler, 2006; Köpcke & Rahm, 2010) and schema matching (Rahm & Bernstein, 2001; Euzenat & Shvaiko, 2007). Based on this analysis, we have chosen the following dimensions for classifying linked data resolution techniques and approaches.

The first dimension we included in our classification schema is *Granularity*, which is also commonly used in the literature on adjacent topics. In the record linkage research there is a distinction between *field matching* and *record matching* techniques, which focus on two different stages of the linkage process (Elmagarmid et al., 2007). The former concentrate on identifying equivalent values for the same field in two records. This requires resolving the cases of different representation for the same data, such as misspellings, format variations, and synonymy (e.g., "Smith, John" and "J. Smith" or "Yangtze River" vs. "Chang Jiang"). The latter focus on deciding whether two records (possibly contain-

ing several fields) refer to the same real-world object. A similar distinction exists in the schema matching research community: e.g., as discussed by Rahm and Bernstein (2001) and Euzenat and Shvaiko (2007), matching algorithms are classified into *element-level* and *structure-level* ones. When analyzing existing data linking techniques with respect to the granularity criterion, we identified three main categories:

1. **Value Matching:** Similarly to the field matching task in record linkage, this step focuses on identifying equivalence between property values of instances. In the simplest cases (e.g., when equivalence of two individuals is decided based on equivalence of their labels), no further steps are performed.

2. **Individual Matching:** The goal of this stage is to decide whether two individuals represent the same real-world object or not. Individual matching techniques compare two individuals and utilize the results of the value matching stage applied to properties of these individuals. At this stage, two individuals are considered in separation from all other individuals in two datasets.

3. **Dataset Matching:** This step takes into account all individuals in two datasets and tries to construct an optimal alignment between these whole sets of individuals. The techniques handling this stage take as their input the results of the individual matching and further refine them. At this level, mutual impact of pairwise individual matching decisions can be taken into account: e.g., if we know that both datasets do not contain duplicates, then one individual cannot be mapped to two individuals from the other dataset.

As the second classification criterion, we use *Type of Evidence* used by the matching method. Based on this criterion, we distinguish between two categories of methods:

- **Data-Level:** These methods rely on information defined at the level of individuals and their property values. In case of ontologies based on description logic, this information corresponds to ontological A-Box.
- **Knowledge-Level:** These methods utilize knowledge defined by the ontological schema (e.g., subsumption relations, property restrictions) as well as in external sources. External sources can include, for example, third-party ontologies as well as linguistic resources which specify the meaning of terms based on their relations with other terms (such as WordNet (Miller, 1995).

Finally, we distinguished algorithms based on the *Source of Evidence*:

- **Internal:** These techniques only utilize information contained in the datasets being matched.
- **External:** These techniques exploit information contained in external sources.

To select the techniques for this section, we reviewed different relevant tools and algorithms described in the literature, which included the instance matching task in their process. We use the following criteria for considering a tool or an algorithm as a relevant one:

- It has to operate on semantic data expressed in RDF. Thus, various record linkage tools, which assume relational data representation are not included and the methods used in these tools are not mentioned. However, we consider also techniques developed for other types of data, if those techniques were later adopted by the tools processing semantic data.
- It has to include the instance matching task in its workflow. We primarily focused on the systems dedicated to data linking (see next section). However, we also included

the techniques used by tools, which performed instance matching as an auxiliary task. In particular, these include generic ontology matching systems which match instance data in addition to schemas, e.g., RiMOM (Li et al., 2009) or ASMOV (Jean-Mary et al., 2009), semantic search tools, e.g., PowerAqua (Lopez et al., 2009), and identity management servers, e.g., OKKAM (Bouquet et al., 2008).

With respect to the data linking workflow shown in Figure 1, most systems implement these techniques as a part of the *instance matching* stage. However, some of the techniques (primarily, dataset matching ones) are sometimes applied during the *post-processing & validation* step.

Table 1 summarizes the main categories of techniques and knowledge resources used by Semantic Web tools. In the rest of the section, we discuss each category of techniques in more detail.

VALUE MATCHING

Sometimes two individual descriptions contain the same property value expressed in different ways, e.g., because of different formatting conventions of two repositories or the use of synonyms. Resolving these discrepancies and determining that two values are equivalent constitutes the value matching task. As their output, value matching techniques often produce a score denoting the degree of similarity between two values, e.g., that "J. Smith" and "Smith, John" are likely to be two representations of the same name. Although equivalence of values does not necessarily imply equivalence of entities (e.g., there can be many people with the name "John Smith"), value matching techniques serve as building blocks in the instance matching process: their output is aggregated and serves as evidence for making decisions about equivalence of individuals.

Table 1. Categories of techniques applied in the Semantic Web domain

	Data-level		Knowledge-level	
	Internal	**External**	**Internal**	**External**
Value Matching	string similarity	keyword search services	-	linguistic resources formal domain models multi-lingual dictionaries
Individual Matching	attribute-based similarity	external mapping sets	schema restrictions	schema mappings external ontologies
Dataset Matching	belief propagation	external mapping sets	belief propagation (enhanced with ontological reasoning) linear programming	schema mappings

Data-Level Techniques

Data-level value matching techniques primarily involve various *string similarity* measures widely used in both record linkage and schema matching. These measures often serve as basic components for more sophisticated methods operating at individual matching and dataset matching levels. External data-level methods are less frequent and include, in particular, standard *keyword search services* such as Google.

Internal Approaches

To perform value matching, data linking systems widely adopt methods developed for database record linkage, in particular, various string similarity measures. There are several survey papers reviewing these measures (e.g., Cohen et al., 2003; Elmagarmid et al., 2007; Winkler, 2006) and we refer the reader to these papers for the detailed description of different similarity functions. Given that there is no single best string similarity measure for all domains, data linking tools usually allow selection among several measures. In particular, existing tools use the following similarity functions:

- **String Equality:** The basic similarity function, which returns 1 if two values are equal and 0 otherwise. It has the highest precision, but does not accept slight varia-

tions caused by typos or minor formatting differences. Nevertheless, it is used, in particular, by the popular Silk data linking tool as one of the options (Volz, Bizer, Gaedke, & Kobilarov, 2009).

- **Edit Distance (Levenshtein):** Character-based similarity function which measures the number of primitive change operations needed to transform one string value into another. Examples of systems employing this metrics are described by Volz, Bizer, Gaedke, and Kobilarov (2009), Li et al. (2009), and Lopez et al. (2009).

- **Jaro:** The measure designed to take into account common spelling deviations. It is also employed in the Silk system (Volz, Bizer, Gaedke, & Kobilarov, 2009).

- **Jaro-Winkler:** A modification of the Jaro measure adjusted to give a higher score to values which share a common prefix. It is commonly used to compare person names. Examples of usage are given by Udrea et al.(2007), Säis et al. (2008), Volz, Bizer, Gaedke, and Kobilarov (2009), Nikolov et al. (2008a), and Ioannou et al. (2008).

- **Monge-Elkan:** This similarity function first involves dividing input strings into a set of substrings and then computing the maximal aggregated similarity between pairs of tokens. In the comparison study described by Cohen et al. (2003), this function achieved the best average performance. Among data linking systems, its use is reported by Volz, Bizer, Gaedke, and Kobilarov (2009) and Nikolov et al. (2008a).

- **Soundex:** This is a phonetic similarity function, which tries to determine string values which are pronounced similarly despite being different at the character level. The approach proposed by Ioannou et al. (2008) uses Soundex similarity as part of their algorithm.
- **Token Set Similarity:** This function involves tokenizing the input strings and then comparing resulting sets of tokens using a common set similarity function (such as Jaccard score or overlap distance). It is employed by Volz, Bizer, Gaedke, and Kobilarov (2009) and Jean-Mary et al. (2009).
- **I-Sub:** This function proposed by Stoilos et al. (2005) specifically for the ontology matching task calculates similarity between two strings as a function of both their commonalities and their differences. For the purpose of instance matching, this technique is employed in ObjectCoref (Hu et al., 2011).

In order to optimize the use of value matching techniques and reduce the number of comparisons needed to match two datasets, the LIMES framework (Ngomo & Auer, 2011) implements an approach which allows estimating the similarity or a pair of values based on the known similarity between each of two values and an exemplar point in a metric space. This technique uses the properties of metric spaces such as symmetry ($s(x, y) = s(y, x)$) and triangle inequality ($s(x, z) \leq s(x, y) + s(y, z)$), so it can be used with the similarity functions which satisfy these properties: e.g., Levenshtein, but not Jaro-Winkler.

We can distinguish two common usage patterns of string similarity measures depending on the purpose of the system:

Semi-automated tools, which must be pre-configured by the user often include a wide range of similarity functions. The user can select suitable similarity functions depending on the task at hand. This particularly applies to data linking frameworks designed to deal with RDF data such as Silk (Volz, Bizer, Gaedke, & Kobilarov, 2009) or KnoFuss (Nikolov et al., 2008a).

The tools that implement an automated workflow usually employ a single function or an aggregation of several measures applicable to a wide range of domains. This approach is usually implemented in ontology matching tools which also deal with instance matching, e.g., RiMOM (Li et al., 2009), ASMOV (Jean-Mary et al., 2009), or ILIADS (Udrea et al., 2007) and semantic search tools, e.g., PowerAqua (Lopez et al., 2009).

Existing tools usually do not implement the similarity functions but reuse public API libraries containing these implementations, such as Simmetrics (Reverend Sam, 2010) or SecondString (Cohen, Ravikumar, Fienberg, & Rivard, 2003).

External Approaches

Standard keyword-based Web search engines provide an additional source of evidence available to matching tools. Normalized Google distance (Cilibrasi & Vitanyi, 2007) uses the sets of hits returned by Google for two labels being compared as an indication of semantic similarity between these terms. The distance is defined as:

$$NGD(x,y) = \frac{\max(\log(f(x)), \log(f(y))) - \log(f(x,y))}{\log(M) - \min(\log(f(x)), \log(f(y)))}$$

- **f(t):** Is the number of Google hits for the search term t
- **f(x,y):** Is the number of Google hits for the tuple of search terms x and y,
- **M:** Is a total number of pages indexed by Google.

This distance measure is adopted for the generic ontology matching task by Gligorov et al. (2007). One disadvantage of this measure is the time cost of the Web search operations, which complicates its use for data linking tasks potentially involving large number of value comparisons.

Knowledge-Level Techniques

Knowledge-level techniques try to discover similarity between property values based on some semantic relations between them. In order to obtain this information, the tools involve external knowledge sources. These sources can be classified into two main categories: *Linguistic resources* and *Formal domain models*.

Linguistic resources provide relations between words used in the property values. WordNet (Miller, 1995) is the most commonly used thesaurus which contains such relations as synonymy and hyponymy, which are used directly for value matching. In particular, it is employed by Castano et al. (2006), Gracia and Mena (2008), Scharffe et al. (2009), and Lopez et al. (2009). Similarity between terms is computed using distance measures based on the length of path between two entities in the graph. For example, the term affinity function which is used in HMatch (Castano et al., 2006) is defined as

$$A(t,t') = \begin{cases} \max_{i=1..k} W_{t \to_i^i t'} & if(k \geq 1) \\ 0 & otherwise \end{cases}$$

where k is the number of paths between t and t' in the graph, $t \to_i^i t'$ is the i-th path of length n, $Wt \to_i^i t' = W_{1tr} \cdot W_{2tr} \cdot ... \cdot W_{ntr}$ is the aggregated weight of the i-th path, which is equal to the product of weights associated with each edge in the path. Weights of edges are set depending on the type of the corresponding relation (hyponymy, synonymy, and so on).

In a specific case where the datasets contain field values expressed in different languages, multi-lingual dictionaries are used to pre-process values and translate them into a default language (e.g., English). Translation procedures are applied, for example, by the OKKAM server (Bouquet et al., 2008).

More specialized relations between terms are represented in publicly available ontologies. High-level vocabularies such as SUMO (http://www. ontologyportal.org) and OpenCYC (http://www. opencyc.org) contain terms from a wide range of domains; others, like SKOS (W3C, 2004), provide a vocabulary for relating other domain vocabularies. In particular, taxonomic distance based on SKOS is used in RDF-AI (Scharffe et al., 2009). The approaches based on formal domain models, however, are less commonly used for the instance matching task than in the schema matching community. This is due to the fact that these models mainly cover common terms, which correspond to classes in the ontologies, rather than entity names, which denote labels of individuals.

Summary

The choice of value matching techniques depend the domain and type of data values. Performance of different string similarity functions is influenced by the formatting conventions of labels and acceptable degrees of variance (e.g., changing order of tokens and abbreviations). For example, Jaro-Winkler similarity is better suited for person names, while Levenshtein is more appropriate for cases where variance is not expected, and only typos must be recognized. Thus, two approaches are possible: choosing appropriate functions for specific tasks or employing an ensemble of similarity functions. The use of external resources can substantially improve the performance, but the scope of tasks in which these resources is limited: commonly used external resources mainly cover common terms rather than entity names.

INDIVIDUAL MATCHING

Establishing links between individuals which refer to the same real-world objects constitutes the main goal of the matching process. Individuals are described using their properties as well as relations to other individuals in the dataset. Individual matching techniques decide whether two individuals taken from different datasets should be linked or not using descriptions of these individuals as evidence.

Data-Level Techniques

Data-level individual matching normally involves aggregating the results of value matching methods over the values of properties belonging to two individuals being compared. Different *attribute-based similarity functions* have been proposed to perform such aggregation. In addition, existing *external mapping sets* are utilized to infer mappings between individuals in the context of Linked Data cloud.

Internal Approaches

The classical approach to individual matching includes aggregating the results produced by value matching techniques. This model for solving the record linkage problem was proposed in a seminal paper by Fellegi and Sunter (1969). The model assumes that there exist two lists of records (A and B) describing some real-world objects. The task of record linkage is to classify each pair of records from the set $A \times B$ into two sets: M (set of matched pairs) and U (set of non-matched pairs). Given that each real-world object a or b is described using records $\alpha(a)$ and $\beta(b)$, the classification decision is based on a comparison of two records expressed as a vector function $\gamma(\alpha(a), \beta(b)) = \gamma(a,b)$ (distance function). The authors propose a probabilistic model introducing conditional probabilities

$$m(\gamma) = P\left(\gamma\big[\alpha(a), \beta(b)\big]\big|(a,b) \in M\right)$$
$$= \sum\nolimits_{(a,b) \in M} P\left(\gamma\big[\alpha(a), \beta(b)\big]\right) \cdot P\left((a,b)\big|M\right)$$

The obtained value $m(\gamma)/u(\gamma)$ is used to make a decision about the equivalence of two entities. Possible decisions are denoted as A_1 (positive link), A_2 (possible (uncertain) link), and A_3 (positive non-link). The decision is chosen by comparing the value $m(\gamma)/u(\gamma)$ with thresholds $T\mu$, such that if $m(\gamma)/u(\gamma) > T\mu$ then $P(A_1|U) < \mu$, and $T\lambda$, such as if $m(\gamma)/u(\gamma) < T\lambda$ then $P(A_3|M) < \lambda$, where μ and λ are desired error levels. The challenges in this classical model include calculating $m(\gamma)$ and $u(\gamma)$, threshold values $T\mu$ and $T\lambda$, and the form of the comparison function γ. In the original method proposed by Fellegi and Sunter (1969), components of the vector $\gamma = (\gamma_1, \gamma_2, ..., \gamma_K)$ are the results of pairwise field values comparison produced by value matching techniques.

This model serves as the base for the majority of algorithms developed in the record linkage domain (see Elmagarmid et al., 2007, for a survey) and was re-used in several tools developed in the Semantic Web community. The aggregation methods adopted by these tools include the following:

Weighted Average: $\gamma = \dfrac{\sum_{i=1}^{K} w_i \gamma_i}{K}$, where w_i denotes the weight of the ith element of the attribute comparison vector.

Picking Maximal (Minimal) Value: $\gamma = \max_{i=1}^{K}(\gamma_i)$.

Euclidean Distance: $\gamma = \sqrt{\sum_{i=1}^{K} \gamma_i^2}$.

Weighted Product: $\gamma = \prod_{i=1}^{K} w_i \gamma_i$.

Group Linkage: $\gamma = \dfrac{\sum_{i=1}^{K} s_i}{|Q| + |C| - |M|}$, where

$s_i = \{\gamma_i, if \gamma_i > t, 0\ otherwise\}$, $\{Q, C\}$ are the sets of predicated of two individuals, and M is the set of elements for which $\gamma_i > t$

Log-based tempered geometric mean.

$$\gamma = \exp \frac{\sum_{i=1}^{K} w_i \log(\gamma_i + \varepsilon)}{\sum_{J=1}^{K} w_j} - \varepsilon.$$

In particular, the Silk system (Volz, Bizer, & Gaedke, 2009) assumes a supervised matching scenario where the user selects an aggregation approach (weighted average, max(min), Euclidean distance, or weighted product) for her task. Similarly, the the ODDLinker system (Hassanzadeh et al., 2009) used to discover interlinks for the LinkedMDB repository represented RDF individuals as relational tuples and employed aggregated attribute-based similarity to decide on equivalence of individuals.

In contrast, the OKKAM Entity Naming Service (Bouquet et al., 2008) is targeted at the unsupervised matching scenario in an open environment and employs automatic selection of an aggregation function. In order to achieve high precision, more involved functions (such as group linkage or geometric mean) are utilized (Ioannou, Niederée et al., 2010). The SERIMI system (Araujo et al., 2011) uses a two-step approach: first, it selects potentially matching candidates using string similarity applied to their labels, and then utilizes the specially designed CRDS similarity function over the complete set of instances properties to discriminate between several candidate matching pairs with similar labels. An alternative approach to the choice of a suitable attribute-based similarity function utilizes unsupervised learning using a genetic algorithm (Nikolov et al., 2011): the system uses assumptions about the matched datasets (e.g., the need for 1-to-1 mappings) and incorporates them into a fitness function, which is used by the genetic algorithm to propose an optimal parameters of the composite matching function: pairs of attributes to compare, specific value matching functions, weights, and the threshold.

External Approaches

While internal data-level individual matching techniques are largely adopted from traditional record linkage research, external approaches often utilize the features specific for the Web environment, and, in particular, Semantic Web. Sets of pre-existing identity links between individuals declared in distributed Linked Data repositories constitute one such feature. Using the transitivity of the *owl:sameAs* property, these identity links can be aggregated to infer the equivalence between individuals connected via a chain of *owl:sameAs* links. This approach is directly exploited by the authors of *sameas.org* portal (http://www.sameas.org), which aggregates equivalent Linked Data resources into "coreference bundles" using both explicit *owl:sameAs* links and inferred ones. The idMesh algorithm (Cudré-Mauroux et al., 2009) employs this method as its first step to construct the graphs connecting potentially equivalent RDF individuals, which it later refines using the graph analysis techniques. The ObjectCoref system (Hu et al., 2011) also uses existing sets of individuals linked via the *owl:sameAs* property to bootstrap learning of discriminative properties which are later used to infer new equivalence mappings.

Knowledge-Level Techniques

The main source of knowledge which can be utilized by individual matching algorithms are *ontological restrictions* defined by domain ontologies used to structure the data in the matched repositories. In cases where the repositories are structured using different schema ontologies, *ontology mappings* obtained from external sources can be exploited to establish correspondences between schema terms and align the structure of individual descriptions in both repositories.

Internal Approaches

The main sources of information used by internal knowledge-level approaches are the domain ontologies which define the structure of individuals in the input repositories. Logical axioms defined in the ontologies can provide both "positive" evidence from which new equivalence mappings can be inferred as well as "negative" evidence which can be used to filter out spurious mappings. Because of this, methods based on the use of ontological constraints are often applied to refine an initial set of candidate equivalence mappings obtained using other methods (such as attribute-based similarity).

In particular, the following ontological constructs are valuable for the individual matching task and are often directly utilized by matching systems:

- **owl:FunctionalProperty:** (*owl:Inverse FunctionalProperty*) These properties essentially define the key attributes for individuals similarly to database keys. Equivalent values of inverse functional properties imply the equivalence of the subjects of properties. Functional properties, in a similar way, allow equivalence of objects to be inferred if they are connected to the same subject. Functionality provides a strong restriction which can be useful both for inferring the new *sameAs* links between instances and for detecting spurious existing links: if two individuals were initially considered as equivalent and connected by a *owl:sameAs* mapping but have two different values for the same functional property, this can indicate that the mapping was incorrect.
- **owl:maxCardinality:** Similarly to the functionality restriction, cardinality violation can also point out to an incorrect mapping (although, according to its definition, it does not directly imply equivalence of property objects).

- **owl:disjointWith:** As another type of negative evidence, disjointness between classes can be used to reject candidate mappings if they connect instances belonging to different classes.

Among the existing systems, Sindice (Tummarello et al., 2007) implements a method for instance matching using explicitly defined inverse functional properties as positive evidence to infer equivalence between instances. The L2R algorithm (Säis et al., 2007) utilizes all relevant ontological schema constraints mentioned above and uses them as both positive and negative evidence. ObjectCoref (Hu et al., 2011) also employs ontological restrictions together with explicit *owl:sameAs* links to create the initial "kernel" mappings. These "kernel" mappings are used as a training set to learn discriminative properties, which in turn help to infer more individual mappings.

While logical restrictions are valuable in the data linking task, it is difficult to exploit them if the datasets are structured using different schema ontologies: precise translation of ontological axioms is problematic for automatic ontology matching systems. ILIADS (Udrea et al., 2007) is an ontology matching system, which performs schema- and data-level matching in iterations. After each data-level matching iteration, restrictions defined in both ontologies being matched are used to check the validity of obtained mappings between instances. Then, at the schema-level iteration, these mappings are used as evidence to infer mappings between classes (by applying set similarity metrics over the sets of their instances).

External Approaches

External knowledge sources are particularly valuable in the data linking tasks involving repositories structured using different ontologies. Such tasks are common in the Linked Data environment, and existing *schema mappings* and *schema restrictions* represent a commonly used knowledge resource.

In the approach described by Nikolov et al. (2010) schema mappings are inferred using existing *owl:sameAs* links between Linked Data repositories. In case where instances of two repositories are not linked to each other directly, but there exist connections to the same external repositories, such links are used as evidence for instance-based ontology matching.

For example, both instances *movie:music_contributor* from LinkedMDB (http://www.linkedmdb.org) and *dbpedia:Ennio_Morricone* from DBpedia (http://dbpedia.org) are connected to *music:artista16e47f5-aa54-47fe-87e4-bb8a-f91a9fdd* from MusicBrainz (http://dbtune.org/musicbrainz). Aggregating sets of such composite mappings and using set similarity functions, the system can derive mappings between corresponding classes *movie:music_contributor* and *dbpedia:MusicalArtist*. Schema-level mappings obtained in this way present an additional input to the KnoFuss system (Nikolov et al., 2008a). They are used to determine subsets of two repositories which are likely to contain identical instances and to perform instance matching in the same way as in a single-ontology scenario.

An extension to the CIDER ontology matching system (Gracia & Mena, 2008) described in Gracia et al. (2009) uses ontological context to disambiguate ontological entities (both classes and individuals), e.g., to disambiguate the country name "Turkey" from the name of the bird. Ontological context consists of all neighboring ontological terms and is obtained by querying the Watson ontology search service (http://watson.kmi.open.ac.uk). This ontological context is then used to cluster different senses of the same term available on the Semantic Web as a whole and to assign the ontological entities being compared into appropriate clusters. This approach, however, is primarily targeted at the schema level and has a limited applicability to instance matching. For instance, it is difficult to distinguish between two individuals belonging to the same class as there would be little difference in their ontological context.

Moreover, external knowledge bases available on the Web provide useful evidence for disambiguating data instances. For example, Wikipedia (http://www.wikipedia.org) provides a generic source of information used, in particular, for disambiguating data instances extracted from text (e.g., Bryl et al., 2010). For restricted domains examples of such knowledge bases include, e.g., UniProt (Swiss Institute of Bioinformatics, 2011) (for proteins) and KEGG GENES (2010) (for genomics).

Summary

Individual matching techniques implement the core functionality of a data linking system: producing mappings between pairs of individuals. While these mappings can be further refined by dataset matching techniques, these techniques strongly rely on the output of individual matching and, in particular, confidence degrees associated with mappings. The choice of appropriate individual matching techniques must be motivated by several factors, among them:

- **Degree of Semantic Heterogeneity:** In a scenario involving datasets structured using the same ontology or two aligned ontologies, correspondences between properties must be utilized: it makes sense only comparing values of corresponding properties, as envisaged by the Fellegi-Sunter model. In the absence of such mappings, the system can either try to establish them (Hu et al., 2011; Nikolov et al., 2011) or rely on "bag-of-words" techniques.
- **Availability of External Reference Sources:** The advantages of using trusted data sources (e.g., DBpedia, Freebase, or

GeoNames) are the possibilities to involve additional information describing individuals, as well as to estimate the ambiguity of a particular description: e.g., whether a certain label (such as "Paris") denotes a unique entity ("Yangtze River") or is ambiguous ("Cambridge").

- **Availability of Additional Information Exploitable by Dataset Matching Algorithms:** The dataset matching stage can refine initial mappings produced by individual matching. If dataset matching is applicable, then recall of individual matching becomes particularly important: incorrect initial mappings can still be filtered out, while omissions are more difficult to recognize.

DATASET MATCHING

Individual matching techniques analyze a pair of individuals taken from two datasets together with their attributes and produce a decision on whether these two individuals are matching or not. However, it is often the case that comparing individual descriptions alone is not sufficient and misses relevant additional information. In particular, this information includes:

- **A-Priori Knowledge about the Matched Datasets:** For example, knowing that one of the datasets does not contain duplicates gives an indication that out of several mappings linking to the same instance only one can be correct.
- **Information about Relations between Individuals in Corresponding Datasets:** For example, deciding that two publication references in two citation datasets refer to the same paper also implies that the references to their authors are also matching.

Such information can only be utilized by analyzing the whole set of potential mappings

between two datasets. This is the focus of different dataset matching techniques, which are applied to the initial set of candidate mappings provided by the individual matching stage and refine it. In the domain of linked data, dataset matching techniques can be particularly valuable when matching against a trustable reference source (such as DBpedia or GeoNames). In this case, a-priori information about such a source can be exploited: for instance, that all instances in such sources are distinct, and that some relations are in fact functional even when not declared as such in the ontology (e.g., birth place of a person).

Data-Level Techniques

Data-level dataset matching techniques involve the analysis of graphs formed by both relations between individuals within repositories and identity mappings across repositories. Internal matching techniques perform this on the basis of two datasets being matched while external ones involve information from third-party sources, in particular, Linked Data repositories containing links to the input datasets. To reason about the data statements and individual mappings in these graphs, various *belief propagation frameworks* are used.

Internal Approaches

Existing systems commonly employ various similarity propagation techniques. These techniques exploit the principle that the similarity between two nodes in the graph depends on the similarity between their adjacent nodes. A generic graph matching algorithm called similarity flooding (Melnik, 2002) is used both in schema- and data-level ontology matching (in particular, in the RiMOM system) (Li et al., 2009). Similarity flooding includes the following stages:

1. Transforming datasets into a directed graph in which pairs of entities (potential matches) correspond to nodes. Edges between two

nodes exist in both directions if in both datasets there is a relation between the corresponding entities.

2. Assigning weights to the edges. Usually, $w_{ij} = 1/n$, where w_{ij} is the weight of the edge from the node i to the node j and n is the number of outgoing edges of the source node i.

3. Assigning initial similarity σ^0 to nodes. The value of σ^0 is usually taken from the output of the individual matching stage.

4. Computing σ^{i+1} using a weighted linear aggregation function. The default function is defined as

$$\sigma^{i+1}(x, x') = \sigma^0(x, x') + \sum_{e_p} \sigma^i(y, y') \times w(e_p),$$

5. The procedure stops if no similarity value changes more than a particular threshold ε or after a pre-defined number of iterations.

In the algorithm proposed by Dong et al. (2005), another propagation algorithm is used where the graph includes not only individual matching nodes but value matching nodes as well. Nodes corresponding to pairs of individuals are connected by edges to nodes corresponding to pairs of their property values: e.g., a node representing a potential mapping between two publications *{a_1, a_2}* has edges from the node representing the similarity between titles {"Title_1", "Title_2"} and publication years {1978, 1979}, expressing the dependency of the individual similarity from value similarities. In this way, the propagation algorithm combines the value matching, individual matching, and dataset matching stages in a single workflow. At each iteration, the algorithm makes a decision about whether a pair of individuals should be merged. Each individual in a merged pair is assumed to contain all the properties of its counterpart, and the graph is updated accordingly. Impact factors which specify how a similarity between a pair of nodes influences similarities

between pairs of their neighbors are chosen on the basis of the type of property corresponding to the edge and the class of instances included in the node. These parameters are set by human users.

In a similar way, the RDF-AI system (Scharffe et al., 2009) implements an algorithm which propagates similarities from value similarity nodes to resource similarity ones. This algorithm does not assume the use of the same schema ontology by two datasets. The procedure first selects pairs of matching property values. At each iteration, a pair of values with the highest similarity is selected as potentially matching and other candidate pairs containing the same values are discarded. Then, similarities are propagated from value matching nodes to individual matching ones. The aggregation function chosen by the authors calculates a new resource similarity as average of the neighboring value similarity nodes.

The approach presented by Ioannou et al. (2008) is based on the interpretation of similarities as Bayesian probabilities. Accordingly, Bayesian networks are used as the framework for belief propagation in graphs. The propagation is performed by the standard message passing algorithm described by Pearl (1988).

External Approaches

External data-level dataset matching approaches aggregate mutual impact of individual matching decisions in a set of several repositories rather than only two at a time. This method is particularly relevant in the Linked Data environment which represents a network of distributed interconnected repositories. These interconnections are usually created by applying data linking to a pair of repositories. In the idMesh algorithm (Cudré-Mauroux et al., 2009), these sets of mappings between individuals are combined over the whole network of data repositories and refined by analyzing mutual impact of these mappings. In this way, idMesh can be considered a meta-level data linking algorithm. idMesh builds graphs based only on equivalence and non-equivalence relations between entities and uses factor-graph message passing to compute marginal probabilities. As mentioned in next section, ObjectCoref (Hu et al., 2011) uses a set of mappings between individuals collected from the whole network of distributed semantic repositories as a training set to learn discriminative data patterns.

Knowledge-Level Techniques

Dataset matching techniques often rely on relations between individuals as evidence. These relations can either be declared or assumed: e.g., having a hypothesis that all individuals within a repository are different from each other. To decide how a specific relation impacts a matching decision, data-level techniques utilize various statistic-based heuristics (e.g., number of incoming/outgoing properties in similarity flooding). One disadvantage of the purely data-level techniques is ignoring explicit definitions of relations provided by the domain ontologies. Knowledge-level methods aim at improving the dataset matching results by utilizing this information. These methods usually enrich the *belief propagation algorithms* operating at the data level. However, one of the proposed approaches also implements dataset matching as a standard *linear programming* problem.

Internal Approaches

Internal knowledge-level dataset matching techniques utilize information defined in the domain ontologies which describe the structure of data in the repositories.

LN2R system (Säis et al., 2008) employs similarity propagation as a part of the "numerical" matching algorithm N2R, which is combined with the "logical" one (L2R). Unlike the algorithms described in next section, this procedure is schema-aware. It employs the aggregation function

$$\sigma^{i+1}(x,x') = \max(\sigma_f^{i+1}(x,x'), \sigma_{nf}^{i+1}(x,x')),$$

where $\sigma_f^{i+1}(x,x')$ is the aggregated similarity function over the edges representing functional properties and $\sigma_{nf}^{i+1}(x,x')$ corresponds to non-functional ones. Similar to Melnik (2002), the impact of non-functional attributes is reduced proportionally to the number of edges corresponding to the same property.

In the method described by Nikolov et al. (2008b) the results of value matching, ontological axioms, and relations between individuals are combined together using valuation networks (Shenoy, 1992). Valuation networks are graphs containing two kinds of nodes. Variable nodes correspond to the confidence degrees of individual matching decisions and data statements[4]. Valuation nodes represent the rules that determine the valid combinations of states of the neighbor variable nodes and correspond to ontological axioms and weak relations. Confidence degrees are interpreted as Dempster-Shafer belief distributions (Shafer, 1976).

Unlike the majority of dataset matching approaches which are based on various algorithms for belief propagation on the graph, Noessner et al. (2010) implement the procedure for global optimization of the whole set of mappings. They use class subsumption relations in addition to property restrictions. Their method measures the impact of non-strict ontological relations relevant for a particular mapping between instances. For example, having two potential instance mappings (a, b_1) and (a, b_2) and the concept C defined in the ontology such that $a, b_1 \in C$, but $b_2 \notin C$, the first mapping is preferred because it better fits the semantics of the domain ontology. They define the A-Box similarity measure, which quantifies the degree of similarity between two ontological A-Boxes described in terms of the same ontological T-Box. This similarity metrics relies on the value of the overlap function $overlap_T(A_1, A_2, M)$ between A-Boxes A_1 and A_2 induced by an instance alignment M. The weighted overlap function measures the aggregated "compatibility" of all pairwise mappings included in M.

$$overlap_T^w(A_1, A_2, M) = overlap_c + overlap_p + overlap_{\neg c} + overlap_{\neg p},$$

where

$$overlap_c = \sum_{(<a,b>)} \sum_{(C(a) \wedge C(b))} \sigma(a,b),$$

where $<a,b> \in M$ and $C \in T$ - the aggregated confidences $(\sigma(a,b))$ of mappings connecting instances belonging to the same class,

$$overlap_p = \sum_{(<a,b>,<a',b'>)} \sum_{(P(a,a') \wedge P(b,b'))} \frac{\sigma(a,b) + \sigma(a',b')}{2},$$

where $<a,b>, <a',b'> \in M$ and $P \in T$ – impact of mappings between pairs of individuals connected by the same property in both repositories,

$$overlap_{\neg c} = \sum_{(<a,b>)} \sum_{(\neg C(a) \wedge \neg C(b))} \sigma(a,b),$$

and

$$overlap_{\neg p} = \sum_{(<a,b>,<a',b'>)} \sum_{(P(a,a') \wedge P(b,b'))} \frac{\sigma(a,b) + \sigma(a',b')}{2}$$

impact of corresponding negated concept and property assertions.

At the next step, weighted A-Box similarity has to be maximized, in other words the value of $\arg\max_M(A_1, A_2, M)$ has to be determined. The authors propose two alternative approaches to achieve this. The first one involves transforming the problem into an integer linear programming problem (Schrijver, 1998) and solving it using standard methods. However, the disadvantage of these methods is their computational complexity, which makes it difficult to apply them to large-scale repositories. In order to reduce the computational cost, the authors included an alternative approach which involves applying a generic algorithm for inexact graph matching (Cour et al., 2006). This algorithm reduces execution time with some loss of precision.

External Approaches

External knowledge sources can contribute with additional information of the same kind as utilized by internal techniques, namely ontological restrictions, subsumption and equivalence relations between schema terms, information about properties valuable for determining identity and so on. Relevant knowledge sources include, among others:

- Schema-level mappings obtained using third-party services. Such mappings can be used to translate ontological restrictions from the terminology of one ontology into another.
- Existing interlinked data repositories. These repositories can be used to infer schema-level mappings using instance-based ontology matching (as described by Nikolov et al., (2010) and to mine common data patterns such as discriminative properties for matching (as described by Hu et al., 2011).

Summary

As we can see, dataset matching techniques are primarily targeted at exploiting additional information about processed datasets. Although such additional information can be unavailable in the general case, the Semantic Web domain and linked data environment in particular possess specific features, which can be exploited by dataset matching methods. Such specific features include:

- Rich structure and additional expressivity provided by ontological schema definition languages (especially OWL) in comparison with relational database schemas. Advanced schema constructs (e.g., class hierarchy, disjointness relations) can be used to refine the mappings produced by individual matching and dataset matching methods.

- Availability of large volumes of publicly available data and existing mappings between them. In the Linked Data cloud, data linking systems can consider a whole network of repositories instead of only two as in classical record linkage and ontology matching scenarios.

DATA LINKING SYSTEMS

Data linking systems implement a number of the techniques identified in the previous section in order to interlink Web data described in RDF.

In the following analysis, we study 11 systems performing both automated and semi-automated data linking. While many ontology matching systems are also able match instance sets or use instance matching techniques in the ontology matching process (Castano et al., 2006; Li et al., 2009; Gracia & Mena, 2008; Jean-Mary et al., 2009; Noessner et al., 2010; Udrea et al., 2007), we focus here on systems whose primary focus is to perform data linking. A few other systems dealing with Web data use data linking techniques while not focusing on linking data and are thus not included in this section (Lopez et al., 2009; Bouquet et al., 2008; Tummarello et al., 2007).

More generally, many ad-hoc matchers are designed when interlinking a specific dataset on the Web of data. Semi-automated data linking

systems typically use configuration files that need to be adapted for each pair of datasets. Parameters such as matching techniques, properties to be compared and thresholds need to be entered by the user. This manual input is in most cases needed if a high link quality has to be reached. Automated matching with high quality links can be achieved if the domain of the tool is well defined, such as for LD Mapper (Raimond et al., 2008) for the music domain.

Tools are described below; then we specify which of the techniques we presented in the previous section have been implemented by each tool.

LN2R

LN2R (Säis et al., 2008) is an unsupervised instance matching system. It uses two approaches: one logical (L2R) and one numerical (N2R). L2R exploits the axioms of the ontologies describing instances. Functional and inverse functional properties, as well as disjoint classes axioms are considered. Matches and non-matches found by L2R are then used as input for the numerical similarity method N2R. N2R uses equations modeling dependencies between similarities of entities. This capture the intuition that if two pairs of instances are related in two datasets and two of these instances are similar across datasets, then the two other instances are likely to be similar as well. Similarity between attributes is computed using an external thesaurus or string similarity algorithms. Then an iterative algorithm computes the similarity of instances based on the attributes similarities and the dependencies equations.

ObjectCoref

ObjectCoref (Hu et al., 2011) aims at building a searchable repository of identity links between resources on the Web of data. The data linking system is based on a self-training network, a semi-supervised learning framework. The system thus needs a training set before being able to interlink two datasets. ObjectCoref uses ontological axioms to further discover equivalences between resources: existing *owl:sameAs* links, functional and inverse functional, as well as cardinality restrictions. A discriminating factor is then computed for pairs of properties belonging to matching resources in the training set. The system then performs an analysis of property-value pairs in order to ascertain which properties have a similar value for resources in the training set. In fact the system performs on the fly matching of properties used in the two datasets. The matching properties are then used to link the two datasets in an iterative process.

Okkam

Okkam (Ioannou, Niederée et al., 2010) proposes an architecture based on the use of distributed servers maintaining sets of equivalent resources. They are named Entity Name Servers (ENS). Each equivalent resource set is assigned a identifier. ENS store entity descriptions on the form of key/property values. New entities are added based on a matching algorithm constructing a similarity measure between the candidate resource and the ENS entity. The similarity measure uses a string matching algorithm between the key/property pairs. The similarity measure is then weighted according to the likelihood of the key to indicate a name for the entity. A small vocabulary of naming properties is thus maintained in the system. Finally similarities are aggregated by computing the sum of maximal similarities between the features of the two entities.

RKB-CRS

The co-reference resolution system of RKB (Glaser et al., 2008; Jaffri et al., 2008) consists of resource equivalence lists. These lists are constructed using ad-hoc Java code on the specific conference/university domain. Domain heuristics are provided such as co-authorship analysis. New

code needs to be written for each dataset. It consists in selecting resources to be matched and performs string similarity matching on relevant attributes.

LD Mapper

LD Mapper (Raimond et al., 2008) is a Prolog based dataset interlinking tool. The tool is based on a similarity aggregation algorithm taking into account the similarity of neighbor resources. The tool requires little user configuration and has been tested on music related datasets. The current implementation works with the Music Ontology, but the algorithm can be used on datasets working with any ontology.

Silk

Silk (Volz, Bizer, Gaedke, & Kobilarov, 2009) is a framework and tool for interlinking datasets and maintaining the links. It consists of a tool and a link specification language: the Silk Link Specification Language. Before matching two datasets, the user specifies entities to link in a LSL file. The tool uses various string matching methods, but also numeric equality, date equality, taxonomical distance similarity, and sets similarity measure. All these similarity measures are parameterized by the user using a specific format. Preprocessing transformations can be specified by the user in order to improve the quality of the matching. Matching algorithms can be combined using a set of operators (MAX, MIN, AVG). Also, literals can be transformed before the comparison by specifying a transformation function, concatenating or splitting resources. Silk takes as input two datasets by specifying SPARQL endpoints. It is able to output *sameAs* triples or any other predicate between the matched entities. Silk was tested on diverse datasets available on its project Web page (Isele, 2011).

LIMES

LIMES (Ngomo & Auer, 2011) is a semi-automatic interlinking tool that can be configured using a XML specification format. Its originality lies in the usage of the properties of metric spaces in order to optimize the use of matching techniques and to reduce the number of comparisons needed to match two datasets. The tool needs user input formatted using a link specification language. The tool is available online as a Web service (http://aksw.org/Projects/limes) and a graphical user interface to a Web service is also available (http://limes.aksw.org).

KnoFuss

The KnoFuss architecture (Nikolov et al., 2008a) is designed for the fusion of heterogeneous knowledge sources. One particularity of KnoFuss is its ability to match datasets described under heterogeneous ontologies. The matching process is driven by an ontology specifying resources to be matched, and the adequate matching techniques to use for these resources. For each type of resource to be matched, an *application context* is defined, specifying a SPARQL query for this type of resource. A variety of string similarity algorithms are available. When datasets described by heterogeneous ontologies are used, it is possible to specify an ontology alignment in the alignment format (http://alignapi.gforge.inria.fr/format.html), thus allowing using any matcher outputting this format. The tool is primarily meant to perform fusion of two input dataset. The input fusion ontologies thus also specify how the resources should be fused. A post-processing step is performed to verify and enforce the consistency of the new dataset resulting from the fusion operation with regards to the ontologies. The tool works with local copies of the datasets and is implemented in Java.

RDF-AI

RDF-AI (Scharffe et al., 2009) is an architecture and prototype implementation for datasets matching and fusion. The tool generates an alignment that can be further used to either fuse the two matched datasets or produce a set of links containing the *owl:sameAs* triples. The system takes as input XML files specifying the preprocessing parameters: name reordering, property strings translation, datasets ontological structure, and matching techniques for each kind of resource. The datasets structure and the resources to be matched are described in two files. This descriptions in fact corresponds to a small ontology containing only resources of interest and the properties to be used in the matching process. Another configuration file describes post-processing parameters such as the threshold for generating links, as well the fusion parameters in case of a fusion. The tool works with local copies of the datasets and is implemented in Java.

Zhishi.links

Zhishi.links (Niu et al., 2011) is a general purpose data linking tool using a distributed framework to reduce the time complexity when matching large datasets. Resources are therefore indexed before similarity calculations are performed. Two similarity comparisons are available, based on entities names (RDFS and SKOS labels, aliases) and based on geographical location. Then a semantic matching technique is used to increase the similarity of instances sharing same property-value pairs. Candidates are finally sorted by their similarity value score, using an eventual new computation on their default label to disambiguate candidates having the same score. The system also uses abbreviations list for persons, locations and organizations (i.e., "Jr" for junior).

Serimi

Serimi (Araujo et al., 2011) interlinking tool use a two phases approach. In a first phase, traditional information retrieval strategies are applied to select candidate resource to be linked. More precisely, entity labels of the source dataset are used to search for entities in the target dataset. In a second phase, candidates matches sharing same labels are disambiguated using an algorithm that identifies which of the candidates is more likely to be the correct one. This technique is based on an analysis of resources descriptions, by identifying property sets shared by instances. *Classes of interest* are thus formed. Instances of the same class in the source dataset are finally linked to instances of the same class of interest in the target dataset.

Summary

As we can see in Tables 2, 3, and 4, varying data linking techniques are implemented by the studied systems.

It seems obvious that internal data level techniques are implemented in every system for value matching as they are the basic operation for comparing instances values. Only two systems use translation services to translate strings before comparing them. This can surely be explained by the fact a large majority of the data available on the Web of data is in English. External knowledge sources are commonly used to compute similarity between instances values.

Most tools use similarity aggregation in order to combine similarity over many attributes of the matched instances, but few tools make use of existing links (data level, external techniques). As the density of links on the Web of data increase, reusing existing links or computing transitivity closures might be useful. It is however crucial to consider links quality in order to prevent the propagation of incorrect links. Three tools only consider the ontology axioms when computing the similarity of two instances. One reason behind this is that few vocabularies on the Web of data actually have these axioms. As more work will

Table 2. Systems value matching techniques

System	Data Level		Knowledge Level
	Internal	*External*	
LN2R	String matching	-	WordNet Synonyms dictionary
ObjectCoref	String matching	-	-
OKKAM ENS	String matching	Translation service	Entity names vocabulary
RKB-CRS	String matching	-	-
LD Mapper	String lookup search	-	-
Silk	String matching Numerical similarity	-	-
LIMES	String matching on metric spaces	-	-
KnoFuss	String matching	-	-
RDF-AI	Fuzzy string matching	Translation service	WordNet Taxonomic distance
Zhishi.links	String matching	-	Abbreviations list
Serimi	String matching	-	-

Table 3. Systems individual matching techniques

System	Data Level		Knowledge Level
	Internal	*External*	
LN2R	*Maximum weighed average*	*-*	*sameAs InverseFunctional FunctionalProperty cardinality maxCardinality*
ObjectCoref	*attribute-based similarity (learned)*	*Existing links*	*sameAs InverseFunctional FunctionalProperty cardinality maxCardinality*
OKKAM ENS	*similarity combination techniques (listed in paper)*	*-*	*-*
RKB-CRS	*domain-specific metrics for citations*	*Existing links*	*-*
LD Mapper	*Sum*	*-*	*-*
Silk	*Many*	*-*	*-*
LIMES	*-*	*-*	*-*
KnoFuss	*Weighted average*	*sameAs transitive closure*	*Cardinality Disjointness Functionality*
RDF-AI	*Weighted average*	*-*	*-*
Zhishi.links	*Geographical distance*	*-*	*Functional Inverse functional*
Serimi	*-*	*-*	*-*

Table 4. Systems dataset matching techniques

System	Data Level	Knowledge Level	
		Internal	*External*
LN2R	Iterative similarity	"Schema aware" similarity propagation	-
ObjectCoref	Existing links between web datasets	-	-
OKKAM ENS	-	-	-
RKB-CRS	-	-	-
LD Mapper	-	-	-
Silk	-	-	-
LIMES	-	-	-
KnoFuss	-	Dempster-Shafer similarity propagation	Third-party schema mappings
RDF-AI	Similarity propagation	-	-
Zhishi.links	-	-	-
Serimi	Classes of interest	-	-

be done on increasing vocabularies quality, data linking using ontological axioms will become more and more important.

Dataset matching techniques are the least used ones. Indeed they rely on the previous set of techniques and thus are the most advanced ones. One tool only makes use of third-party schema mappings. This can be seen as very low given that reconciling schemas greatly facilitates the matching task. Semi automated tools actually solve this problem by implicitly letting the user to specify the schema alignment when configuring the tool for a specific matching task.

Table 5 shows that the tools require different levels of manual input. While most of the tools require manual input, two tools only are fully automated: LN2R and LD Mapper. These two tools can only be used on datasets sharing a same ontology, with LD Mapper being specialized for the MusicOntology. Another tool, ObjectCoref, does not need to be configured but instead takes as input a training set that it will use to find the best appropriated configuration. The other tools

require a user specification that varies in syntax, but have similar content: what kind of entities are linked, which properties are compared and which similarity computation methods are used. RKB CRS follows this scheme but includes built-in heuristics making it more efficient for linking university and conferences related datasets.

We will next discuss techniques that could be used to make tools more efficient and more automated.

OPEN PROBLEMS AND CONCLUDING REMARKS

In the Semantic Web domain, data linking represents a relatively new direction, which largely follows the research conducted in generic ontology matching and especially in the database research community. Thus, we can say that many open problems currently considered in these areas are also relevant for data linking: for example, such issues as scalability (Rastogi et al., 2011), unreliable data sources (Dong et al., 2009), erroneous data values (Guo et al., 2010), and the need to take links into account when processing queries (Ioannou, Nejdl, et al., 2010). However, the task of semantic data linking has its unique features: the use of ontologies for data structuring and the availability of large volumes of distributed data published using the Linked Data principles. These features lead to several research problems, which are primarily relevant for the data linking task.

As discussed in the previous sections, in the field of data linking a clear and widely accepted definition of the meaning of mappings is still missing. On one side, we have a wide spectrum of different techniques, capable of discovering different kinds of possible links between object descriptions, ranging from weak correspondences to strong relations of identity. On the other side, we still use (or abuse) the *owl:sameAs* relation for

Table 5. Systems usability and manual input

LN2R	Automated, works only if datasets share the same ontology
ObjectCoref	Needs a training set, then automated
OKKAM ENS	Must be run on one entity type at a time (e.g., Persons, places)
RKB-CRS	A Java class has to be implemented for each pair of datasets
LD Mapper	Automated, works only for datasets described using the MusicOntology
Silk	Link specification language: used techniques, implicit schema alignment, aggregations need to be described
LIMES	Link specification language, Web service and Web GUI
KnoFuss	Dataset description ontology needs to be written; ontology alignments can be reused
RDF-AI	Dataset, techniques, pre- and post- processing configuration files need to be written
Zhishi.links	Information not available
Serimi	Automated, command line parameters

representing all these different links, in spite of the original meaning of this specific OWL relation.

Concerning this point, a lot of work is possible towards a finer definition of the relation of identity and a richer vocabulary for representing it. Both UMBEL and SKOS can be seen as useful starting points for the definition of a shared vocabulary concerning identity and mappings. However, covering the range of possible meanings for a mapping is just part of the problem: in fact, we also need to clarify and study the correspondence between the different techniques available for instance matching and the possible meanings of their resulting mappings. To this end, some preliminary work has been proposed by McCusker and McGuinness (2010), where the authors discuss a solution that allows the extraction of isomorphic statements from data without requiring their direct assertion and propose a Identity Ontology for the representation of identity. However, an analytic inquiry about the formal properties of instance matching techniques with respect to identity is still missing.

Currently, published identity links between individuals indicate equivalent instances. However, it is also important to maintain information about pairs of individuals, which represent distinct entities, especially if these individuals have similar descriptions which can be misleading for data linking tools. Providing the means to state and maintain such distinction relations represents another research problem, for which existing solutions can be insufficient: e.g., using explicit *owl:differentFrom* statements between each pair of distinct individuals would lead to very large amount of auxiliary data.

Besides the ones chosen for this work, there are other dimensions of analysis that can taken into account for presenting the data linking problem, such as for example the degree of automation, the human contribution.

Our approach was to concentrate not on the engineering aspects of the tools (e.g., pre-processing,

post-processing, programming language, human contribution) but on the underlying techniques. About this point, there are several potentially promising research directions concerning the development of novel matching techniques. We can particularly point out two of them. First, the growth of the Linked Data cloud provides unique possibility to use large volumes of already existing data as information sources. Moreover, the task of data linking itself becomes transformed from the traditional scenario, which focuses on finding sets of mappings between two datasets to the more open task of discovering mappings within a network of many datasets. This makes the dataset matching techniques particularly important. Two examples of tools targeting these issues are idMesh (Cudré-Mauroux et al., 2009) and ObjectCoref (Hu et al., 2011). Second, given the variety of used schema vocabularies, methods able to overcome semantic heterogeneity and deal with information expressed using different ontologies are especially valuable.

With regards to the tools, we see that there is still room for improving their automation. Most tools are semi-automated and require an extensive amount of configuration for each data linking task, while automatic tools work only in predefined domains. We identify three types of input: i) schema alignments, ii) matching techniques, and iii) key properties.

We can envisage three possible improvements to automate existing tools. Schema alignments could be shared using a server, such as the R2R framework (Bizer & Schultz, 2010). By doing so they could be reused for every data linking task involving the aligned schemas. The selection of matching techniques is depending on the kind of data needed to be matched as some techniques are better working than others on specific data types. Information about the techniques to use could be directly attached to the schemas and thus would not need to be specified for each data linking task. Finally, data has to be analyzed in order to specify what properties need to be compared for determining the identity of two instances. This set of discriminative properties ensure that there are no two instances sharing the same combination of values for these properties: in other words, they have the same role as a key in a relational database. Statistical analysis could be used in order to automatically mine such key properties in RDF datasets.

In conclusion, after defining the data linking problem, we have presented a comprehensive survey of techniques helping to solve it. We have classified these techniques according to the criteria of granularity, type of evidence, and source of the evidence. We have presented eleven data linking systems and classified them according to which technique they use. We observed that the studied systems leave room for improvement, particularly at the dataset level of granularity.

REFERENCES

W3C. (2004). *SKOS: Simple knowledge organization system*. Retrieved from http://www.w3.org/2004/02/skos

Alexander, K., Cyganiak, R., Hausenblas, M., & Zhao, J. (2009). Describing linked datasets - on the design and usage of void, the "vocabulary of interlinked datasets". In *Proceedings of the Linked Data on the Web Workshop and the 18th International World Wide Web Conference*, Madrid, Spain.

Araujo, S., de Vries, A., & Schwabe, D. (2011). *Serimi results for OAEI 2011*. Paper presented at the Ontology Matching Workshop on Ontology Alignments Evaluation Initiative.

Batini, C., & Scannapieco, M. (2006). *Data quality: Concepts, methodologies and techniques (data-centric systems and applications)*. New York, NY: Springer.

Berners-Lee, T., Hollenbach, J., Lu, K., Presbrey, J., Prud'hommeaux, E., & Schraefel, M. (2008). Tabulator Redux: Browsing and Writing Linked Data. In *Proceedings of the WWW International Workshop on Linked Data on the Web*, Beijing, China.

Bizer, C., & Schultz, A. (2010). The r2r framework: Publishing and discovering mappings on the web. In *Proceedings of the 1st International Workshop on Consuming Linked Data*, Shanghai, China.

Bleiholder, J., & Naumann, F. (2009). Data fusion. *ACM Computing Surveys*, *41*(1), 1–41. doi:10.1145/1456650.1456651.

Bouquet, P., Stoermer, H., & Bazzanella, B. (2008). An entity name system (ens) for the semantic web. In *Proceedings of the 5th European Semantic Web Conference on the Semantic Web: Research and Applications*, Tenerife, Spain (pp. 258-272).

Bryl, V., Giuliano, C., Serafini, L., & Tymoshenko, K. (2010). Supporting natural language processing with background knowledge: Coreference resolution case. In *Proceedings of the 9th International Semantic Web Conference*, Shanghai, China (pp. 80-95).

Castano, S., Ferrara, A., Lorusso, D., Näth, T. H., & Möller, R. (2008). Mapping validation by probabilistic reasoning. In *Proceedings of the 5th European Semantic Web Conference on the Semantic Web: Research and Applications*, Tenerife, Spain (pp. 170-184).

Castano, S., Ferrara, A., & Montanelli, S. (2006). Matching ontologies in open networked systems: Techniques and applications. *Journal on Data Semantics*, *5*, 25–63.

Cilibrasi, R., & Vitanyi, P. (2007). The Google similarity distance. *IEEE Transactions on Knowledge and Data Engineering*, *19*(3), 370–383. doi:10.1109/TKDE.2007.48.

Cohen, W. W., Ravikumar, P., & Fienberg, S. E. (2003). A comparison of string metrics for matching names and records. In *Proceedings of the KDD Workshop on Data Cleaning and Object Consolidation*.

Cohen, W. W., Ravikumar, P., Fienberg, S. E., & Rivard, K. (2003). *Second string project*. Retrieved from http://secondstring.sourceforge.net

Cour, T., Srinivasan, P., & Shi, J. (2006). Balanced graph matching. *Advances in Neural Information Processing Systems*, *19*, 313–320.

Cudré-Mauroux, P., Haghani, P., Jost, M., Aberer, K., & de Meer, H. (2009). idMesh: Graph-based disambiguation of linked data. In *Proceedings of the 18th International World Wide Web Conference*, Madrid, Spain (pp. 591-600).

Dong, X., Berti-Equille, L., & Srivastava, D. (2009). Integrating conflicting data: The role of source dependence. In *Proceedings of the 35th International Conference on Very Large Databases*, Lyon, France (pp. 550-561).

Dong, X., Halevy, A., & Madhavan, J. (2005). Reference reconciliation in complex information spaces. In *Proceedings of the ACM SIGMOD International Conference on Management of Data* (pp. 85-96).

Elmagarmid, A., Ipeirotis, P., & Verykios, V. (2007). Duplicate record detection: A survey. *IEEE Transactions on Knowledge and Data Engineering*, *19*(1), 1–16. doi:10.1109/TKDE.2007.250581.

Euzenat, J., & Shvaiko, P. (2007). *Ontology matching*. Heidelberg, Germany: Springer-Verlag.

Fellegi, I. P., & Sunter, A. B. (1969). A theory for record linkage. *Journal of the American Statistical Association*, *64*(328), 1183–1210. doi:10.2307/2286061.

Glaser, H., Millard, I., & Jaffri, A. (2008). Rkbexplorer.com: a knowledge driven infrastructure for linked data providers. In *Proceedings of the 5th European Semantic Web Conference on the Semantic Web: Research and Applications*, Tenerife, Spain (pp. 797-801).

Gligorov, R., Aleksovski, Z., ten Kate, W., & van Harmelen, F. (2007). Using Google distance to weight approximate ontology matches. In *Proceedings of the 16th International World Wide Web Conference*, Banff, AB, Canada (pp. 767-775).

Gracia, J., d'Aquin, M., & Mena, E. (2009). Large scale integration of senses for the Semantic Web. In *Proceedings of the 18th International World Wide Web Conference*, Madrid, Spain.

Gracia, J., & Mena, E. (2008). Matching with CIDER: Evaluation report for the OAEI 2008. In *Proceedings of the 3rd Ontology Matching Workshop and the 7th International Semantic Web Conference*, Karlsruhe, Germany.

Guarino, N., & Welty, C. (2002). Identity and subsumption. In Green, R., Bean, C. A., & Myaeng, S. H. (Eds.), *The semantics of relationships: An interdisciplinary perspective* (pp. 111–125). Dordrecht, The Netherlands: Kluwer Academic.

Guo, S., Dong, X., Srivastava, D., & Zajac, R. (2010). Record linkage with uniqueness constraints and erroneous values. In *Proceedings of the 36th International Conference on Very Large Databases*, Singapore (pp. 417-428).

Halpin, H., Hayes, P. J., McCusker, J. P., McGuinness, D. L., & Thompson, H. S. (2010). When owl:sameas isn't the same: An analysis of identity in linked data. In *Proceedings of the 9th International Semantic Web Conference*, Shanghai, China (pp. 305-320).

Hassanzadeh, O., Lim, L., Kementsietsidis, A., & Wang, M. (2009). A declarative framework for semantic link discovery over relational data. In *Proceedings of the 18th International Conference on World Wide Web* (pp. 1101-1102).

Hu, W., Chen, J., & Qu, Y. (2011). A self-training approach for re- solving object coreference on the semantic web. In *Proceedings of the 20th International World Wide Web Conference*, Hyderabad, India (pp. 87-96).

Ioannou, E., Nejdl, W., Niederée, C., & Velegrakis, Y. (2010). On-the-fly entity-aware query processing in the presence of linkage. In *Proceedings of the 36th International Conference on Very Large Databases*, Singapore (pp. 429-438).

Ioannou, E., Niederée, C., & Nejdl, W. (2008). Probabilistic entity linkage for heterogeneous information spaces. In *Proceedings of the 20th International Conference on Advanced Information Systems Engineering*, Montpellier, France (pp. 556-570).

Ioannou, E., Niederée, C., Velegrakis, Y., Bonvin, N., Mocan, A., Papadakis, G., et al. (2010). *Intelligent entity matching and ranking* (Tech. Rep. No. D3.1). Brussels, Belgium: OKKAM.

Isele, R. (2011). *Link specification language*. Retrieved from http://www4.wiwiss.fu-berlin.de/bizer/silk/spec

Jaffri, A., Glaser, H., & Millard, I. (2008). URI disambiguation in the context of Linked Data. In *Proceedings of the WWW International Workshop on Linked Data on the Web*, Beijing, China.

Jean-Mary, Y., Shironoshita, E., & Kabuka, M. (2009). Ontology matching with semantic verification. *Web Semantics: Science. Services and Agents on the World Wide Web*, 7(3), 235–251. doi:10.1016/j.websem.2009.04.001.

KEGG. (2010). *Genes database*. Retrieved from http://www.genome.jp/kegg/genes.html

Köpcke, H., & Rahm, E. (2010). Frameworks for entity matching: A comparison. *Data & Knowledge Engineering*, 69, 197–210. doi:10.1016/j.datak.2009.10.003.

Köpcke, H., Thor, A., & Rahm, E. (2010). Evaluation of entity resolution approaches on real-world match problems. *Proceedings of the Very Large Data Base Endowment*, 3(1-2), 484–493.

Koudas, N., Sarawagi, S., & Srivastava, D. (2006). Record linkage: similarity measures and algorithms. In *Proceedings of the ACM SIGMOD International Conference on Management of Data*, Chicago, IL (pp. 802-803).

Li, J., Tang, J., Li, Y., & Luo, Q. (2009). RiMOM: A dynamic multistrategy ontology alignment framework. *IEEE Transactions on Knowledge and Data Engineering*, 21(8), 1218–1232. doi:10.1109/TKDE.2008.202.

Lopez, V., Nikolov, A., Fernandez, M., Sabou, M., Uren, V., & Motta, E. (2009). Merging and ranking answers in the Semantic Web: The wisdom of crowds. In *Proceedings of the 4th Asian Semantic Web Conference*, Shanghai, China (pp. 135-152).

McCusker, J., & McGuinness, D. (2010). Towards identity in linked data. In *Proceedings of the OWL Experiences and Directions Seventh Annual Workshop*, Karlsruhe, Germany.

Meilicke, C., Völker, J., & Stuckenschmidt, H. (2008). Learning disjointness for debugging mappings between lightweight ontologies. In *Proceedings of the 16th International Conference on Knowledge Engineering: Practice and Patterns* (pp. 93-108).

Melnik, S. (2002). Similarity flooding: a versatile graph matching algorithm. In *Proceedings of the 18th International Conference on Data Engineering*, San Jose, CA (pp. 117-128).

Miller, G. (1995). WordNet: a lexical database for English. *Communications of the ACM*, *38*(11), 39–41. doi:10.1145/219717.219748.

Ngomo, A.-C. N., & Auer, S. (2011). LIMES - a time-efficient approach for large-scale link discovery on the web of data. In *Proceedings of the International Joint Conference on Artificial Intelligence*, Barcelona, Spain.

Nikolov, A., d'Aquin, M., & Motta, E. (2011). *Unsupervised instance coreference resolution using a genetic algorithm (Tech. Rep. No. kmi-11-02)*. Milton Keynes, UK: Knowledge Media Institute.

Nikolov, A., Uren, V., & Motta, E. (2010). Data linking: Capturing and utilising implicit schema-level relations. In *Proceedings of the 3rd Workshop on Linked Data on the Web*, Raleigh, NC.

Nikolov, A., Uren, V., Motta, E., & de Roeck, A. (2008a). Integration of semantically annotated data by the KnoFuss architecture. In *Proceedings of the 16th International Conference on Knowledge Engineering and Knowledge Management*, Acitrezza, Italy (pp. 265-274).

Nikolov, A., Uren, V., Motta, E., & de Roeck, A. (2008b). Refining instance coreferencing results using belief propagation. In *Proceedings of the 3rd Asian Semantic Web Conference*, Bangkok, Thailand (pp. 405-419).

Niu, X., Rong, S., Zhang, Y., & Wang, H. (2011). Zhishi.links results for oaei 2011. In *Proceedings of the 10th International Semantic Web Conference*, Bonn, Germany.

Noessner, J., Niepert, M., Meilicke, C., & Stuckenschmidt, H. (2010). Leveraging terminological structure for object reconciliation. In *Proceedings of the 7th Extended Semantic Web Conference*, Crete, Greece (pp. 334-348).

Pearl, J. (1988). *Probabilistic reasoning in intelligent systems: networks of plausible inference*. San Francisco, CA: Morgan Kaufmann.

Rahm, E., & Bernstein, P. A. (2001). A survey of approaches to automatic schema matching. *The Very Large Data Base Journal*, *10*(4), 334–350. doi:10.1007/s007780100057.

Raimond, Y., Sutton, C., & Sandler, M. (2008). Automatic interlinking of music datasets on the semantic web. In *Proceedings of the Linking Data on the Web Workshop*, Beijing, China.

Rastogi, V., Dalvi, N., & Garofalakis, M. (2011). Large-scale collective entity matching. *Proceedings of the Very Large Data Base Endowment*, *4*(4), 208–218.

Reverend Sam. (2010). *SimMetrics*. Retrieved from http://sourceforge.net/projects/simmetrics

Säis, F., Pernelle, N., & Rousset, M.-C. (2007). L2R: A logical method for reference reconciliation. In *Proceedings of the Twenty-Second Conference on Artificial Intelligence*, Vancouver, BC, Canada (pp. 329-334).

Säis, F., Pernelle, N., & Rousset, M.-C. (2008). Combining a logical and a numerical method for data reconciliation. *Journal of Data Semantics*, *12*, 66–94.

Scharffe, F., Liu, Y., & Zhou, C. (2009). RDF-AI: an architecture for RDF datasets matching, fusion and interlink. In *Proceedings of the Workshop on Identity and Reference in Knowledge Representation*, Pasadena, CA

Schrijver, A. (1998). *Theory of linear and integer programming*. New York, NY: John Wiley & Sons.

Shafer, G. (1976). *A mathematical theory of evidence*. Princeton, NJ: Princeton University Press.

Shenoy, P. P. (1992). Valuation-based systems: a framework for managing uncertainty in expert systems. In Zadeh, L., & Kacprzyk, J. (Eds.), *Fuzzy logic for the management of uncertainty* (pp. 83–104). New York, NY: John Wiley & Sons.

Stoilos, G., Stamou, G., & Kollias, S. (2005). A string metric for ontology alignment. In *Proceedings of the 4th International Semantic Web Conference*, Galway, Ireland (pp. 624-637).

Swiss Institute of Bioinformatics. (2011). *UniProt knowledgebase: SwissProt protein knowledge knowledgebase: TrEMBL protein database (user manual)*. Retrieved from http://web.expasy.org/docs/userman.html

Tummarello, G., Delbru, R., & Oren, E. (2007). Sindice.com: Weaving the open linked data. In *Proceedings of the 6th International Semantic Web Conference*, Busan, Korea (pp. 552-565).

Udrea, O., Getoor, L., & Miller, R. J. (2007). Leveraging data and structure in ontology integration. In *Proceedings of the ACM SIGMOD International Conference on Management of Data*, Beijing, China (pp. 449-460).

Volz, J., Bizer, C., & Gaedke, M. (2009). *Web of data link maintenance protocol (Technical Report)*. Berlin, Germany: Frei Universität Berlin.

Volz, J., Bizer, C., Gaedke, M., & Kobilarov, G. (2009). Discovering and maintaining links on the web of data. In *Proceedings of the 8th International Semantic Web Conference* (pp. 650-665).

Winkler, W. (2006). *Overview of record linkage and current research directions* (Tech. Rep. No. 2006-2). Washington, DC: Statistical Research Division, U.S. Census Bureau.

ENDNOTES

[1] In this context, we use the term real-world object in order to denote the intended referent of an object description.

[2] Sometimes, the term *mapping* is used in order to denote the collection of binary relations between object descriptions and the term *mapping rule* is used in order to denote the single correspondence between two object descriptions. This terminology is more common in the field of ontology matching, where mappings often represent more than a simple correspondence between entities, but a transformation rule holding between two entities (Euzenat & Shvaiko, 2007). Another terminological choice is to use the term *alignment* in order to denote the mapping set and the term *correspondence* to denote the mapping.

[3] For an interesting discussion on this point see http://www.mkbergman.com/935/the-nature-of-connectedness-on-the-web.

[4] Since the approach is aimed at processing annotations extracted from text, data statements are not considered 100% reliable.

This work was previously published in the International Journal on Semantic Web and Information Systems, Volume 7, Issue 3, edited by Amit P. Sheth,, pp. 46-76, copyright 2011 by IGI Publishing (an imprint of IGI Global).

Chapter 9

ACRONYM:
Context Metrics for Linking People to User–Generated Media Content

Fergal Monaghan
SAP Research, UK

Siegfried Handschuh
National University of Ireland, Galway, Ireland

David O'Sullivan
National University of Ireland, Galway, Ireland

ABSTRACT

With the advent of online social networks and User-Generated Content (UGC), the social Web is experiencing an explosion of audio-visual data. However, the usefulness of the collected data is in doubt, given that the means of retrieval are limited by the semantic gap between them and people's perceived understanding of the memories they represent. Whereas machines interpret UGC media as series of binary audio-visual data, humans perceive the context under which the content is captured and the people, places, and events represented. The Annotation CReatiON for Your Media (ACRONYM) framework addresses the semantic gap by supporting the creation of a layer of explicit machine-interpretable meaning describing UGC context. This paper presents an overview of a use case of ACRONYM for semantic annotation of personal photographs. The authors define a set of recommendation algorithms employed by ACRONYM to support the annotation of generic UGC multimedia. This paper introduces the context metrics and combination methods that form the recommendation algorithms used by ACRONYM to determine the people represented in multimedia resources. For the photograph annotation use case, these result in an increase in recommendation accuracy. Context-based algorithms provide a cheap and robust means of UGC media annotation that is compatible with and complimentary to content-recognition techniques.

DOI: 10.4018/978-1-4666-3610-1.ch009

1. INTRODUCTION

"User-Created Content" (UCC) or "User-Generated Content" (UGC) (Wunsch-Vincent & Vickery, 2006) is paving the way towards a Web of "object-centred sociality" (Cetina, 1997; Bojārs, Heitmann, & Oren, 2007): a collaborative knowledge management platform built around documents or other objects of interest that goes beyond unidirectional publication and consumption. As well as user profiles, blogs, and other information manually input as text media by users, a significant proportion of UGC now consists of multimedia such as photographs, video and music. With the proliferation of cheap storage and affordable recording devices, interaction with digital multimedia has become a major activity for computer users. Furthermore, fast broadband network connections and ubiquitous, network-ready, sensor-laden mobile devices have facilitated the shift of this interaction to the global stage on the increasingly-available Internet.

Users create, store, upload, download, tag, rate, review, browse, search and share text, photograph, video and audio resources using a myriad of hardware and software tools on their personal computers, local networks, mobile devices and the Internet. This UGC multimedia is the currency of popular object-centered social network services like Flickr (photographs), YouTube (video) and Last.fm (music).

The spread of peer-to-peer distribution on the Internet and between mobile devices via Personal Area Networking (PAN) allows users to share raw multimedia directly with each other, increasing throughput over the network by cutting out centralised "middle-men" such as Web servers. However, users of social networking services often find their profiles, preferences, tags and other meta-content locked into the proprietary repository of the service that they used to create the content. Every time a user wants to join another online social network hosted by a different social network service, they must leave their existing content behind and recreate or re-upload their user profile and all other UGC. This repetitive process can be extremely tedious and leads to the current situation where social networking services hoard UGC in isolated and disjointed islands of data.

Standards can bridge the gaps between these islands by providing best-practice means of storing and sharing UGC as portable, reusable data. Advocates of data portability -such as the Data Portability project (http://www.dataportability. org/) -believe that users should be able to move, share, and control their identity, photographs, videos and all other forms of personal data independently. This can be done by separating the user's content from the social network service's functionality; in this way social network services can still compete for membership based on the value added to the user's content by their functionality. Data portability can be enabled by the widescale adoption of reusable and extensible standards that allow users to control, share, and move their data from one system to another. Such standards are in fact at the heart of the Semantic Web vision, which has data portability as one of its key features.

Due to the dependence of the Semantic Web on ontology-based metadata, an important question is how to support the creation of this semantic metadata. As online social networking and the Semantic Web converge, a social Semantic Web is emerging which may help kickstart this process: a Web of collaborative knowledge management which is able to provide useful information based on human contributions and which becomes more useful as more people participate.

Instead of relying entirely on automated semantics with formal ontology processing and inferencing, the idea behind the social Semantic Web is to complement the formal Semantic Web vision by adding a pragmatic approach relying on heuristic classification and tagging to create semantic metadata in standard description languages. This requires a continuous process of eliciting crucial knowledge of a domain through semi-formal ontologies and emphasises the importance of manually-created, loose semantics as a means to initialise the vision of the Semantic Web. While the Semantic Web enables integration of domain-specific processing with precise automatic logic inference computing across domains, the social Semantic Web offers a more social interface to semantics, allowing interoperability between objects of interest, actions and users.

To increase the relevancy of metadata, there have been efforts to expose, share, and connect Resource Description Framework (RDF) (Klyne & Carroll, 2004) metadata as Linked Data on the Web (Berners-Lee, 2006; Bizer, Cyganiak, & Heath, 2007). Linked Data refers to a style of publishing and interlinking structured data on the Web; the basic assumption behind Linked Data is that the value and usefulness of data increases the more it is interlinked with other data.

While much research has focused on managing and publishing existing knowledge as portable, semantic metadata, we identify a need to support the initial supply of valuable, relevant, linked metadata to the Semantic Web. Indeed, principles, standards and tools are now emerging to support the creation of metadata that capture knowledge about community- and user-generated content (Breslin, Harth, Bojars, & Decker, 2005; Adida, Birbeck, McCarron, & Pemberton, 2008). However, most of these approaches revolve around capturing metadata from text or XHTML content; less focus on creating metadata describing UGC multimedia.

The complex activities that occur between UGC generation and sharing are receiving increased attention (management, retrieval, recommendation, etc.) (Rodden & Wood, 2003; Kirk, Sellen, Rother, & Wood, 2006; Lindley, Durrant, Kirk, & Taylor, 2009). The work reported in this paper focuses on one such activity: annotation. Annotation enhances the media collections with metadata which facilitates consequent organisation, retrieval and sharing. While multimedia resources are now the subject of major knowledge management activity

for Web users, the rates of metadata creation or annotation have fallen behind the rate at which multimedia data are created:

- 95B photos on Flickr and Facebook alone (Pingdom, 2011; Mitchell, 2011).
- 152M blog posts on the Internet (Pingdom, 2011).
- 20B tweets on Twitter during 2010 (Pingdom, 2011).
- 3B photos uploaded to Facebook per month (Pingdom, 2011).
- 35hrs of new video every minute on YouTube (Pingdom, 2011).

It is further speculated that the rapid adoption of camera phones worldwide generated an additional 200 billion digital photographs in 2008 alone, with camera phones set to take 89% of the mobile market by 2009 (InfoTrends/CAP Ventures, 2004). This situation is set to further deteriorate in the future: forecasted mobile phone user and retail trends are reflected in Figure 1 (Euromonitor International, 2010; US Census Bureau, 2010).

With such an enormous amount of multimedia data, a user manually looking for a particular media resource may feel like they are looking for the proverbial "needle in a haystack"; the result is that the user suffers from a particularly acute branch of information overload as their attempts to find relevant resources are frustrated. The problem presented by the gap between audio-visual data and personal knowledge has been termed the "semantic gap".

Smeulders, Worring, Santini, Gupta, and Jain (2000) first defined the semantic gap specifically for visual media as "the lack of coincidence between the information that one can extract from the visual data and the interpretation that the same data have for a user in a given situation" while (Dorai & Ventakesh, 2003) refine and generalise it to "the gulf between the rich meaning and interpretation that users expect systems to associate with their queries for searching and browsing media and the

Figure 1. Forecasted user and retail volume trends 2003-2013: (a) Internet & mobile phone users; (b) Camera & mobile phone retail volumes (Euromonitor International, 2010; US Census Bureau, 2010)

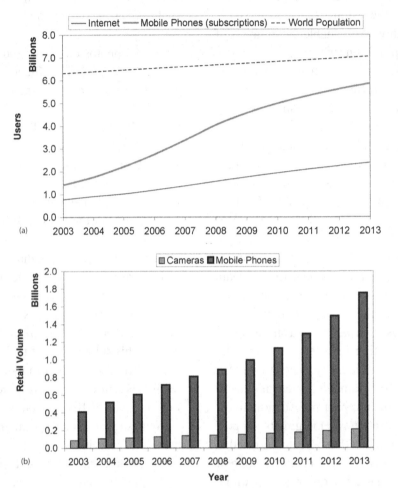

shallow, low level features (content descriptions) that the systems actually compute". Smeulders, Worring, Santini, Gupta, and Jain (2000) further elaborate that while "the user seeks semantic similarity, the database can only provide similarity on data processing".

Whereas text or structured data such as XHT-ML may yield some explicit content that can be extracted using natural language processing or keyword extraction, it is more difficult to bridge the semantic gap with audio-visual data due to the analogue nature and high bit-rates involved. Useful metadata describing media resources bridges the semantic gap between what a resource means to a

user and what it means to computers. This enables applications to perform the hard work of finding resources for the user and thereby alleviates the audio-visual data overload.

To enable the machine to retrieve media resources for the user, however, we must first analyse how users themselves mentally recall the resources: this is covered next in Section 2. Section 3 highlights key related work. Then Section 4 outlines the ACRONYM annotation framework for context-aware UGC media annotation. Since photographs are the most ubiquitous, most prolific and therefore most urgent form of UGC media to address, the initial use case for ACRONYM has been personal photograph annotation as outlined in previous work (Monaghan & O'Sullivan, 2007) and with more recent results summarised in the following Section 5. The underlying recommendation algorithms used, however, may be used to annotate general UGC multimedia, as will be shown in Section 6. Section 7 presents an evaluation of the recommendation algorithms before Section 8 concludes the paper.

2. MOTIVATION: USEFUL RECALL CUES

To organise and search through large digital multimedia collections it is necessary to extract recognisable features that can be stored as metadata and used as memory cues and filters when browsing the collections, especially as these collections grow into the tens of thousands and span dozens of years. For example, tracks in music collections may be filtered according to artist, album, genre, melody or lyrics while movies may be navigated by actors, directors, genres or parental guidance level. Meanwhile, digital image libraries of artwork such as paintings may be organised by artist, period, style or patron in the same way that catalogue images such as stock photography may be organised by dominant colour, theme or subject. Likewise, (UGC) media resources may be organised by where they were created, when they were created or who is represented.

A user study and a survey conducted by Stanford University (Naaman, Harada, Wangy, Garcia-Molina, & Paepcke, 2004) expose the most useful cue categories for recalling and finding photographs. The results of the study indicate that users recall photographs primarily by the following cues:

- Who is depicted in the photograph.
- Where the photograph was taken.
- What event the photograph covers.

The conclusions of the Stanford study generally agree with Wagenaar (1986) who stated that the most important categories for recall in general are 'who', 'where' and 'when' in that order, and with the more recent survey by Hasan and Jameson (2008). The importance of the chronological ordering of photographs had previously also been highlighted in a preceding study (Rodden & Wood, 2003). The Stanford study delved deeper into the important 'who' category and revealed that the most important cues for photographs in this category in descending order of importance were (Naaman, Harada, Wangy, Garcia-Molina, & Paepcke, 2004):

1. The identity of subjects in the photograph.
2. The number of subjects in the photograph regardless of identity.
3. The identity of people who were present at the time of capture, but not necessarily as subjects in the photograph.

A key challenge is how to create this useful description metadata. Manual annotation of multimedia is tedious and consumes large amounts of time. Content-based approaches attempt to directly address the semantic gap by using content-based tools that try to extract semantic information from the audio-visual content of multimedia (Veltkamp & Tanase, 2002). For example, low-level visual features such as dominant colour, brightness and even simple shapes can be easily extracted from images. However, the semantic gap between identifying the low-level features and recognising important semantic themes are still wide and error-prone (Suh & Bederson, 2007).

For example, off-the-shelf software like iPhoto and Picasa make use of face recognition to recommend the identities of people present in photographs. However, traditional face recognition methods cannot satisfy the requirement of "reliable automatic face annotation" for the case of personal photographs (Choi, Yang, Ro, & Plataniotis, 2008). Robust and reliable face recognition is still not available as it depends on: (1) large training sets; (2) direct alignment of faces to the camera; and (3) the illumination conditions at the scene of capture (O'Toole, Phillips, Jiang, Ayyad, Penard, & Abdi, 2007).

This is especially true when considering media recorded by multi-purpose mobile devices: not only is the quality produced by the hardware lower but often media resources are 'snapped' in unposed and active situations (Davis, Smith, Canny, Good, King, & Janakiraman, 2005). Even more complex is the ability to identify semantic themes (such as events or activities) by analysing audio-visual features.

Alternatively, context-based approaches present a lightweight, robust and scalable option to both support the abstract way in which users actually think about media resources and to compliment content-based approaches. To clarify context in the scope of this paper, we now adopt the following definition formulated by Dey and Abowd (2000).

Definition 1. Context is any information that can be used to characterise the situation of an entity. An entity is a person, place, or object that is considered relevant to the interaction between a user and an application, including the user and applications themselves.

Context-based approaches attempt to automatically organise multimedia collections using context metadata provided by the recording device, e.g., the timestamps of photographs (Girgensohn, Adcock, Cooper, Foote, & Wilcox, 2003; Naaman, Yeh, Garcia-Molina, Paepcke, 2005). Context-based tools often suffer from a lack of useful context metadata from the source device. To combat this, they often supply an interface and tools for the user to also enhance and improve the organisation manually, in which case they can be considered semi-automatic (Suh & Bederson, 2007). Additionally, context can be combined with content to provide a hybrid solution, e.g., by taking into account the visual content of faces and clothes depicted over the context of a short

space of time or event (Zhao, Teo, Liu, Chua, & Jain, 2006; Choi, Yang, Ro, & Plataniotis, 2008), or by mining existing sources of context (Tuffield et al., 2006).

3. RELATED WORK

There is a significant amount of research into multimedia annotation and related areas: here we limit our review to context-aware photograph annotation approaches for the sake of comparison within the photograph annotation use case.

Davis, Smith, Canny, Good, King, and Janakiraman (2005) use a statistical factor analysis approach to combine face recognition with context information such as detected Bluetooth devices, GPS coordinates and previous photograph annotations to suggest people for annotation to camera phone photographs. This previous work uses binary-valued statements about photographs as their observed variables: a disadvantage of only taking into account direct properties of a photograph is that it ignores direct relationships that instances may have with each other independent of any photographs, e.g., people may state that they know each other.

A further disadvantage arises from the use of binary data. For example, the binary model cannot use the geographic proximity of photographs, only the Boolean value of whether a photograph belongs to an artificially created geographic cluster or not. The binary approach requires photographs to be clustered geographically into an arbitrary number of clusters (100 in their case), the granularity of which may be too coarse for many applications and which does not scale well. For example, photographs taken in Ireland and Germany may be indistinguishable geographically under this model and may well both be included in the arbitrary 'Europe' cluster.

Finally, Davis, Smith, Canny, Good, King, and Janakiraman (2005) do not describe the use of any metadata standard to capture the annotations. The evaluation of their approach is further discussed in Section 7.5.

PhotoCompas combines temporal and geographic data with existing Web services to automatically provide higher level context metadata on several temporal, geographic and event recall cues (Naaman, 2005). They use GPS-enabled digital cameras to stamp photographs taken with time and geographical coordinates of capture. Given manual annotations from previous photographs in a local database, PhotoCompas can also suggest the probable identity of subjects in consequent photographs by monitoring previous manual annotations of subjects and maintaining a history of their whereabouts (Naaman, 2005). Suggestions for subject annotation are made for subsequent photographs by checking their time and location metadata.

ZoneTag is a prototype for Nokia S60 smartphones that allows the user to upload images to the Flickr website (Ahern, King, Naaman, Nair, & Yang, 2007; Naaman & Nair, 2008). ZoneTag leverages the location and time captured by the smartphone to find a location tag and to suggest other tags based on those previously entered by the user and their social network in similar contexts, offering valuable automation. The proprietary keyword tags employed allow minimal expressivity and limited interoperability, and since they are stored and transmitted to Flickr as separate XML data their portability is limited.

Photocopain focuses on using what the authors call "low value" information from cheaply available sources such as the user's calendar, Flickr tags, EXIF metadata and GPS logs to support domain-independent annotation automation (Tuffield et al., 2006). Content analysis provides further estimates, e.g., whether a photograph depicts natural or artificial objects. They create expressive, interoperable annotations by reusing Semantic Web standards and metadata. They plan to construct narratives to let users make better sense of digital data.

Zhao, Teo, Liu, Chua, and Jain (2006) propose an automated method to annotate people to family photographs based on face, content and social context information. They adopt an adaptive event clustering method to cluster photos based on time and then location to support "social" context-based recommendations. They report that while their social context analysis improves the recall of content recognition, it only makes minor improvements to precision. Body content information is used to identify other instances of known people and to improve face recognition accuracy as it can reject falsely recognised faces. While they state that their current body clustering technique is still preliminary and is far from ideal performance, future work includes improving its performance, as well as adding the ability to detect bodies without detected faces, and better use of social context information.

Similarly, Choi, Yang, Ro, and Plataniotis (2008) use person clustering methods based on the time and space context of photographs in combination with clothes recognition to improve face recognition performance. The two approaches do not mine or make use of existing data sources independent of the photographs nor do they generate reusable metadata. Conversely, an additional source of context that has been proposed for exploitation is the medium through which people communicate in relation to photographs: this could be the digital medium that is used to send or share a photograph (Lieberman, Rosenzweig, & Singh, 2001) or audible conversation (Barthelmess, Kaiser, & McGee, 2007).

The following section presents the ACRONYM annotation framework, which takes a robust, scalable, context-based approach towards automating UGC multimedia annotation.

4. ACRONYM ANNOTATION FRAMEWORK

The ACRONYM annotation framework enables the capture of data from the user's real-world, ambient environment via mobile device sensors and the mining of data from the user's information space where they may have already expended effort creating data about themselves. To this end, the framework essentially comprises two independent processes:

1. Mobile device-based process to capture data from the real world (optional).
2. Web-based annotation process with more processing and information resources at its disposal to perform mining and further computation on the real world data.

Note that the latter may annotate any UGC media on the Web and that the former is optional and not strictly necessary, although it increases annotation automation. The mobile-and Web-based processes each gather context data from their respective space:

1. **Ambient Space:** Context of the user in the real world.
2. **Information Space:** Context of the user in the digital world.

4.1. Harvesting Context from Ambient Spaces

The first source of context data is the user's ambient space, or the space they occupy in the real world. A number of technologies may be exploited to harvest data from the user's ambient space. The inherent connectivity of mobile devices can be exploited to automate mundane tasks for the user.

Firstly, auto-synchronisation of mobile device clocks with a network provider's global clock eliminates the need for them to be manually set, regardless of power depletion and consequent cold restart.

Secondly, an increasing number of mobile devices are inherently location-aware. This location can be provided either by a GPS receiver (either built-in or via a wireless connection), via the network provider or through other means such as tracking nearby cell towers or devices. Crucially, the underlying means of location detection is becoming increasingly unimportant as it is further abstracted by middleware on phones that can accept input from various sources. Hybrid positioning systems such as Skyhook XPS (http://www.skyhookwireless.com/howitworks/xps.php) combine several sources to provide geographic context that is more accurate than that of any single source alone.

Thirdly, mobile devices can use their PAN connectivity to detect nearby objects. This detection provides further context as to the ambient situation in which media resources are created. Blue-tooth is practically ubiquitous amongst mobile devices and with a range of approximately 10 metres it can provide a new technological context surrounding the user (Davis, Smith, Canny, Good, King, & Janakiraman, 2005; Lavelle, Byrne, Gurrin, Smeaton, & Jones, 2007). With Wireless Local Area Network (WLAN) protocols gaining a foothold on mobile devices, we envisage that it is a matter of time until the actual underlying means of detecting nearby devices will become unimportant as technological context is abstracted in a similar way to that of geographical context.

Lastly, the user interface of a mobile device can be used for direct input from the user. Context-aware annotation systems such as ZoneTag adopt this user interface to allow the user to manually input valuable, reusable context in the form of tags (Ahern, King, Naaman, Nair, & Yang, 2007; Naaman & Nair, 2008).

4.2. Gathering Context from Information Spaces

The second source of context is the user's information space, or the space they occupy in the digital world, e.g., on their computer, social network or the Web. A number of sources may be mined to access data in the user's information space:

- The user's social network.
- The user's calendar.
- Data manually loaded or input by the user via a user interface.
- Web services that provide access to online datasets. Note that even if the user has no digital presence and no inclination to enter data manually that at least public information from Web services and linked open data sources such as GeoNames (http://www.geonames.org/) are still available for mining.

5. USE CASE: PHOTOGRAPH ANNOTATION

With the ACRONYM framework's two annotation processes in mind, we implemented two applications for the use case of photograph annotation:

1. Mobile device-based camera application.
2. Web-based photograph annotation application.

5.1. Mobile Device-Based Camera Application

ACRONYM's mobile device-based camera application harvests context from the ambient scene at the time of photograph capture. This was implemented as a downloadable Java Midlet (http://acronym.deri.org/downloads/midlet/acronym.jar) to be platform-independent and to take advantage of Java Microedition's abstraction interface lay-

ers that provide access to a device's services and sensors. When the user takes a photograph, this Java MIDlet runs in the background to exploit the increasingly ubiquitous sensors available in mobile devices to capture contextual metadata from the ambient environment. As illustrated in Figure 2, parallel processing threads simultaneously capture:

1. The time of creation via the network provider.
2. The coordinates of capture if a location service (e.g., GPS) is available.
3. The unique physical addresses of nearby devices at the time of creation via PAN transceivers.
4. The email address of the creator via a once-off login.

Once these threads have completed gathering information from the ambient environment, an initial RDF graph describing a created photograph is created using these contextual metadata which is in turn encoded in XML. While a discussion about the nature of this graph and the ontologies used is outside the scope of this paper, further details are available in Monaghan (2008) (Ch. 4). It is suffice to say here that in the spirit of Semantic Web reuse over reinvention, the ontology used is integrated from elements of existing popular ontologies where possible. Figure 3 shows key classes and properties of the integrated ontology.

The RDF/XML is next wrapped in an eXtensible Metadata Platform (XMP) (Adobe Developer Technologies, 2005) packet which is in turn embedded in a JPEG file along with the image data as already illustrated in Figure 2. The resulting JPEG file can be shared through normal means with another device, user or indeed uploaded to the Web while preserving its descriptive metadata. Later this initial RDF description will come into play to help automate the creation of annotations for the photograph that are actually useful

Figure 2. Harvesting context metadata from the user's ambient space

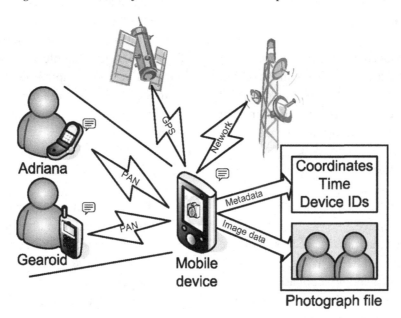

Figure 3. Key classes and properties of integrated ontology for context-aware photograph annotation

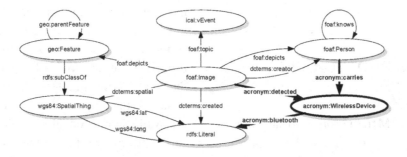

to users for recalling the photograph from a query engine.

5.2. Web-Based Photograph Annotation Application

ACRONYM's Web-based photograph annotation application mines context from the user's information space, combines it with that from their ambient space and supports the reuse of the combined contextual knowledge for context-aware photograph annotation. This was implemented as a lightweight Java Servlet; an online demo is available (http://acronym.deri.org/). This annotation application allows the user to login and annotate any JPEG photograph that is accessible by HTTP; the only requirement is that the photograph must at least have an EXIF timestamp. In the background, the annotation application exploits the contextual knowledge available to it to support the user in their annotation task by recommending particular annotations. These recommendations are in the form of a ranked list for each of the three most useful recall cues for photograph management:

1. People depicted.
2. Geographical features depicted.
3. Events covered.

Note that annotations and recommendations for each of people, places and events are placed side by side to ease comparison; these are all presented as simple "tags" with human-readable labels, familiar to users of contemporary popular photograph annotation tools such as Flickr or Facebook. The machine-readable semantics and ontology are hidden from the user, who simply selects from the list of recommendations to annotate the photograph.

The current Web-based application supports the semi-automatic annotation of places and events using fairly straightforward approaches based on spatial and temporal proximity respectively. However, a set of novel algorithms have been developed to support the annotation of the people represented, which is both one of the most useful recall cue to users as well as the most difficult to automate. Therefore, the remainder of this paper considers the place and event annotation algorithms outside of scope, and now focuses on the context-aware recommendation algorithms used to recommend people. Furthermore, while the use case in this section has demonstrated an application to personal photographs, the recommendation approach is generalised and can recommend the people represented in any UGC multimedia resource, be it a text post, a photograph, a video or an audio clip.

6. RECOMMENDATION ALGORITHMS

To inform the recommendation of the recall cues represented in UGC multimedia resources, context metrics may be defined to measure the strength of certain relationships between instances of recall cues (e.g., people, places, events) and individual UGC media resources. The hypothesis is that there exist latent relationships (social, geographical, temporal, etc.) between instances of recall cues and individual time-stamped UGC media resources in the ambient space that have observable repre-

sentations in the form of contextual knowledge in the information space. The context metrics use statistical dataset analysis of these observations to provide a measure of the strength of the individual latent relationships.

In practice, the contextual knowledge is given domain-specific meaning by a media annotation ontology, e.g., the integrated ontology referred to in Section 5 for the domain of photographs. We also define combination methods that combine the measurements of several context metrics to present an aggregated result with the aim to provide more accurate and robust recommendations.

6.1. Context Metrics

While the set of context metrics may be extended without change to the combination methods, we define here several specific context metrics to specifically inform the recommendation of people represented in UGC media resources. In particular, these metrics measure the strength of several relationships between individual people and UGC media resources.

For a dataset, let P be the set of all people, R the set of all media resources and D the set of all wireless devices. Then let $p \in P$ be an individual person, $r \in R$ be an individual media resource and $d \in D$ be an individual device. Then, to enable the description of the context metrics themselves, we predefine the following important sets and properties:

- Let *rep'tations*$(p) \subset R$ be the subset of resources representing a person p.
- Let *represents*$(r) \subset P$ be the subset of people a resource r represents.
- Let *knows*$(p) \subset P$ be the subset of people a person p knows.
- Let *detections*$(d) \subset R$ be the subset of resources created with a device d detected nearby.

- Let *detected*(*r*) ⊂ *D* be the subset of devices detected nearby when a resource r was created.
- Let *carries*(*p*) ⊂ *D* be the subset of devices a person p carries.
- Let *created*(*r*) be the time when a resource r was created.
- Let *creator*(*r*) ∈ P be the creator of resource r.
- Let *createdBy*(*p*) ⊂ *R* be the subset of resources created by person p.
- Let *creations*(*r*) ⊂ *R* be the subset of resources created by the creator of resource *r*, *createdBy*(*creator*(*r*)).
- Let *spatial*(*r*) be the spatial coordinates where a resource r was created.

These definitions are used by the context metrics, which each calculate a value between 0 and 1 which gives that metric's confidence that a person is represented in a given media resource. Furthermore, several of the metrics give the conditional probability that a person is represented given the existing contextual knowledge (Figure

4). To this end, they use the mathematical concept of set containment to measure what proportion of one set is contained within another (Broder, 1997). There are six context metrics based on:

1. Spatio-temporal proximity.
2. Person acquaintance containment.
3. Person corepresentation containment.
4. Device carriage containment.
5. Device copresence containment.
6. Creator containment.

6.1.1. Spatio-Temporal Proximity

This metric measures how close person p is estimated to have been to the scene of creation of resource *r*, at the time the resource was created, *created*(*r*). First, the location of the person at time *created*(*r*) is estimated. Let $r1 \in represents(p)$ be the previous resource - in chronological order - that *p* is represented in and $r_1 \in represents(p)$ be the next. The estimated location of p at *created*(*r*) is then estimated by interpolating $spatial(r_{-1})$ and

Figure 4. Screenshot of ACRONYM web-based annotation application user interface

spatial(r_1) at time *created*(r); this interpolation assumes a spherical coordinate system such as that used on Earth (Vincenty, 1975). Note that if r is the oldest resource and therefore r-1 is unavailable, *spatial*(r_1) and *spatial*(r_2) are extrapolated instead; interpolation and extrapolation are handled identically. Likewise, in the case that r is the most recent resource and so r_1 is unavailable, *spatial*(r_{-2}) and *spatial*(r_{-1}) are extrapolated instead.

Definition 2: *Let intcoords(p, t) be the interpolated coordinates of person p at time t, assuming a spherical coordinate system.*

Definition 3: *Let gcd(coords$_1$, coords$_2$) be the great-circle (shortest path) distance between two points on a sphere with radius equal to that of the Earth's.*

This allows the distance between the interpolated co-ordinates of person p and the co-ordinates of creation of resource r to be defined:

$$dist(p,r) = gcd(intcoords(p, created(r)), spatial(r))$$

Then the final metric gives the spatio-temporal proximity of person p to resource r as a value between 0 and 1:

$$metric_1(p, r) = e^{-dist(p,r)} \qquad (1)$$

For example, $metric_1(p, r)$ might give a 10% confidence that p is depicted and/or audible in video r due to their estimated spatial proximity at the time.

6.1.2. Person Acquaintance Containment

The person acquaintance containment metric is a measure of how much of a person's social network is represented in a resource. The measurement taken is the containment (Broder, 1997) of the set of people that person p is asserted to know within the set of people represented. For resource r, it

measures the containment of the set of p's acquaintances within the set of those people represented:

$$metric_2(p,r) = \frac{\left|knows(p) \cap represents(r)\right|}{\left|knows(p)\right|} \qquad (2)$$

6.1.3. Person Corepresentation Containment

Many people may not create social networking profiles or explicitly assert statements about themselves. Therefore, we also define a person corepresentation containment metric which aims to implicitly measure how often p is represented with those people already represented in r, without requiring them to assert their acquaintances (Figure 5). First the containment of the set of resources representing another person $q \in P$ within that of p is calculated using the *PeopleRank*$_{photo}$ single-resource variant (Naaman, Yeh, Garcia-Molina, & Paepcke, 2005):

$$PeopleRank(q, p) = \frac{\left|rep'tations(q) \cap rep'tations(p)\right|}{\left|rep'tations(q)\right|}$$

For example, *PeopleRank*(q,p) could calculate that p is mentioned in 20% of all blog posts q is mentioned in. Then the containment of the sets of representations of each person represented in

Figure 5. Corepresentation of people with other people

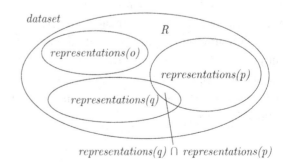

r within that of p can be used to calculate the final person corepresentation containment metric:

$$metric_3(p,r) = \sum_{q \in represents(r)} \frac{PeopleRank(q,p)}{|represents(r)|} \quad (3)$$

For example, $metric_3(p, r)$ might give a 15% confidence that p is mentioned in blog post r due to their usually being co-mentioned with those mentioned.

6.1.4. Device Carriage Containment

Similarly to the person acquaintance containment metric, the device carriage containment metric is a measure of how many of a person's wireless devices were detected nearby to the scene of resource creation. The measurement taken is the containment of the set of devices that person p is asserted to carry within the set of devices detected. For resource r, it measures the containment of the set of p's devices within the set of those detected:

$$metric_4(p,r) = \frac{|carries(p) \cap detected(r)|}{|carries(p)|} \quad (4)$$

6.1.5. Device Copresence Containment

While the ACRONYM Ontology (http://acronym.deri.org/schema#) allows people to explicitly assert which devices they carry, it must be assumed that many people will not. Therefore we also define a device copresence containment metric which aims to implicitly measure how often p is present with those devices detected near to the creation of r, without requiring users to state the devices they carry (Figure 6). First the containment of the set of resources for which device $d \in D$ was detected within the set of resources representing p must be defined:

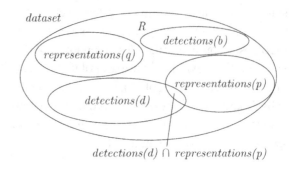

Figure 6.Copresence of people with devices

$$prescon(d,p) = \frac{|detections(d) \cap rep'tations(p)|}{|detections(d)|}$$

Then the containment of the set of detections of each device detected in r within the set of representations of p can be used to calculate the final device copresence containment metric:

$$metric_5(p,r) = \sum_{d \in detected(r)} \frac{|prescon(d,p)|}{|detected(r)|} \quad (5)$$

6.1.6. Creator Containment

The creator containment metric is a measure of how often a person has been represented in resources created by the creator of resource r. The measurement taken is the containment of the set of resources created by the creator of r within the set of resources that represent person p. For resource r, it measures the containment of the set of the creator's resources within the set of resources representing p:

$$metric_6(p,r) = \frac{|creations(r) \cap rep'tations(p)|}{|creations(r)|} \quad (6)$$

For example, $metric_6(p, r)$ might give a 35% confidence that p is depicted in photograph r

due to their usually being photographed by the photographer.

6.2. Combination Methods

While recommendations may be made based on any single context metric alone, if metrics are combined they may provide more accurate and more robust recommendations. This section explores methods to combine the context metrics to provide robust recommendation algorithms. Two combination methods are presented:

1. Correlation-weighted-mean CombSUM.
2. Factor analysis.

Importantly, the combination methods presented here are chosen so as to model people as individuals with unique usage/data profiles, instead of averaging over a generic profile. This means that each combination method can simultaneously handle people with widely varying usage and available data. For example, one extreme person may be very sociable -appearing in lots of photos with friends - and may travel a lot, but may not use computers, gadgets or social networking at all. For this "travelling socialite technophobe" user, the spatio-temporal proximity and person corepresentation metrics may be the most accurate at recommending them in photos they appear in, whereas the person acquaintance and device carriage metrics may be the least accurate since the user has provided no data whatsoever for them to function. Therefore this person's model should reflect a higher weighting for those more accurate metrics.

Conversely, the opposite may be true for a user on the other end of the spectrum, who may never leave home nor appear in many photos with others, but who may be a heavy user of gadgets and social networking, keeping their digital presence up to date meticulously. For this "anti-social agoraphobic technophile" user, there may not be many photos to use as historical observations, but

still the explicit data provided for the person acquaintance, device carriage and device copresence metrics may provide accurate recommendations for photos they do appear in. Obviously, between these two extreme profiles (and any other combination of extremes) may lie any number of unique individuals. Both combination methods presented here model this individuality.

6.2.1. Correlation-Weighted-Mean CombSUM

The first combination method is a weighted-mean CombSUM method (Fox & Shaw, 1994) which combines the context metric confidence scores, giving a single representation confidence value between 0 and 1 for individual person-resource pairs. Once a metric has been used to calculate the confidence for the representation of p in every resource $r \in R$, these scores form a vector of confidence scores for each resource.

Definition 4: *Let $metric_i(p, r)$ denote context metric i's score for person p and resource r. Then the variable $metric_i(p)$ contains p's confidence scores for all resources $r \in R$.*

Definition 5: *This variable is compared with the vector rep' tations(p) containing either a 0 or 1 for each previously annotated resource depending on whether p is asserted as represented or not. The Pearson correlation between these two variables is then taken as the weight to use for that metric. Definition 5 Let corr(x, y) denote the Pearson correlation between any variables x and y.*

$$w_i(p) = corr(metric_i(p), rep' \, tations(p))$$

When the weights for all metrics have been calculated for p, they are applied to their corresponding metric. The mean of the weighted metrics is then calculated using Equation 7 and is taken as the final confidence metric that a person p is represented in r. Let m be the number of context metrics being used; in our case this is six, but this may be extended:

$$confidence_{cs}(p, r) = \sum_{i=1}^{m} \frac{w_i(p) \cdot metric_i(p, r)}{m} \quad (7)$$

For example, $confidence_{cs}(p, r)$ could return 18% combined confidence that singer p is audible in audio clip r. Once the confidences for each person have been calculated for a resource, they may be used to rank recommendations to the user to support their task of annotating people to resources. The correlation-based weighting deals with missing data for each person by assigning low weights to metrics that over the dataset do not correlate with actual depictions of that person. For example, for a user who is not part of an online social network (or indeed does not have a digital presence at all), the personalised weights would suppress the useless output of the acquaintance containment and device carriage metrics and allow the algorithm to function purely on data from the recording device and previous annotations.

6.2.2. Factor Analysis

The second combination method uses factor analysis to combine the context metric confidence scores in an unbiased way. Factor analysis refers to a variety of statistical techniques whose common objective is to represent a set of variables in terms of a smaller number of hypothetical variables. A factor analytic approach may be used to address whether there are positive correlation relationships between observed metrics that may be explained by a smaller number of latent, unobserved variables (Kim & Mueller, 1978). For example, the implicit, abstract, unobserved relationship of "social proximity" between people in the real world may cause those people to be explicitly stated as being both acquainted and corepresented in the digital world more often than not.

Such a latent variable may be detected by several metrics; hence it is a common factor shared by those metrics. If more metrics measure one latent variable than another, the purely correlation-based weights used in the CombSUM method produce biased results; in effect, they may lend more weight to certain latent variables simply because there are more metrics available to measure them. Meanwhile, factor analysis has been shown to be the most accurate method on standard collaborative filtering data (Canny, 2002).

In factor analysis, each metric is assumed to be influence by a unique component (assumed to be random noise) and one or more common factors; this is illustrated in the path model in Figure 7. In our approach we determine a separate factor model for each individual person $p \in P$. Factor analysis is described in Kim and Mueller (1978) and Davis, Smith, Canny, Good, King, and Janakiraman (2005) and we will now use notation prevalent in the literature.

X is a vector of n (partially) observed variables. F is a latent vector representing the $k \le n$ factor variables underlying the observed variables. U is a noise function. Here W is the factor structure matrix: a 2-dimensional matrix of size $n \times k$ giving the scalar influence weight values of the latent factors on the observed variables. The factor model for a person p is then formally described as:

$$X = WF + U \quad (8)$$

In factor analysis, X and F are assumed to be real-valued vectors. U is assumed to be multivariate, independent Gaussian noise. F is assumed to have a Gaussian prior distribution. The $n = m + 1$ fields of the X vector encode all observed variables: there is a continuous variable (between 0 and 1) for each metric plus a discrete binary variable (either 0 or 1) stating whether p is actually represented or not.

With the general factor model for a person formally defined, the factor analytic method requires two phases. In the training phase, standard factor analysis techniques as described in Kim and Mueller (1978) are used on a training set of complete

Figure 7. Path model for a multivariate multi-common factor model

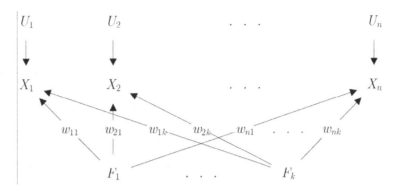

X vectors to determine the most likely values for the set of F vectors and for the factor structure matrix W for person p. The training data includes all metrics and whether p is represented or not.

In the test phase, the algorithm will receive just the metric scores (without the representation values) from a new media resource r. From these partial observations X and from the previously-trained W, F is determined for the case of r. With W and F determined, they are plugged directly back into Equation 8 to predict the missing X value. This predicted value gives a single continuous confidence value $confidence_{fa}(p, r)$ between 0 and 1 that person p is represented in resource r.

Once again, with the confidences for each person $p \in P$ calculated for resource r, they may be used to rank recommendations to the user. The factor analysis deals with missing data and allows the algorithm to function optimally with the data available.

7. EVALUATION

The recommendation algorithms were evaluated for the use case task of personal photograph annotation presented in Section 5.

7.1. Datasets

We evaluate each recommendation algorithm using training and testing datasets through a commonly applied technique of evaluating prediction of deleted values from existing data (Herlocker, Konstan, Terveen, & Riedl, 2004). The difficulty here is in obtaining a large dataset with all the test features needed for an approach that makes use of multiple context metrics (including Bluetooth, social network connections, etc.). Large US government-sponsored photo datasets are traditionally content-focused, e.g., CMU-PIE (http://vasc.ri.cmu.edu/idb/html/face/index.html) and FERET (http://www.itl.nist.gov/iad/humanid/feret/feret_master.html) and do not have all the features needed for a comprehensive evaluation of context metrics. In particular, an evaluation of our context-based approach requires a dataset including the following features:

- Captured Bluetooth/wireless device addresses.
- Social networking connections.
- GPS co-ordinates.
- Photographer (linked to OSN).
- Located and identified faces (linked to OSN).
- (Optional) Device ownership (linked to OSN).

This kind of combined dataset is only emerging now alongside the emergence of linked data on the social Semantic Web (http://linkeddata.org/), and previously this kind of work would have been limited to the realm of computer vision (http://www.cs.cmu.edu/~cil/v-images.html). It would require several years of community i) participation and ii) co-operation/sharing to generate large quantities of usable test data with all the context features needed. As with so much concerning Semantic Web research, the chicken-and-egg problem rears its ugly head: what should come first, large-scale data acquisition to evaluate approaches or new approaches to generate data? Inevitably the answer is that to make progress we must attempt a bit of both.

So in the meantime, since we are unaware of any publically available evaluation datasets that include all of the above features, we undertook to collect data with all the features needed to prove the concept. This has obvious budgetary issues (devices, people, time, etc.) which limit its size, compared to the aforementioned government-sponsored datasets of faces. We use several datasets gathered from three users (one of which is an author) who each annotated their own personal photograph collections using the ACRONYM Web-based annotation application outlined in Section 5:

- Datasets 1, 2 and 3 were each annotated by their respective owners; all photographs in 2 and 3 and the majority in 1 were taken with regular digital cameras.
- Dataset Σ is the result of merging and consolidating datasets 1, 2 and 3; this simulates a situation where several users of a social network may benefit from each other's annotations.
- Dataset 1a is a subset of dataset 1 that consists only of photographs captured using the ACRONYM mobile device-based camera application outlined in Section 5.
- An anonymised version of dataset Σ (which contains all data and may be split by cre-

ator to recreate the other datasets) is publically available online (http://acronym.deri.org/datasets/).

Due to the private nature of the personal photographs and their metadata to the evaluation users, the dataset had to be anonymised before publication to remove "human-readable" personal names and faces. In this regard, public research is faced with the same restrictions that large OSNs like Facebook encounter: they also do not publish private user data, instead allowing each user to choose their own personalised privacy settings.

While we cannot fit a research paper on multimedia annotation and simultaneously, within the same short article, solve the general problem of data acquisition and publication that somehow sidesteps but does not break privacy laws, in this article we do our utmost to ensure and encourage the repeatability, comparability and extensibility of our work in Section 7.6. There's a whole other branch of "Web Science" emerging on the social, legal, etc., side dealing with this in general. That's a story for another article, and more likely another entire journal issue full of articles.

The anonymisation procedure has two main consequences. Initially, the actual photographic content has been removed. Furthermore, all attempts have been made to purge the metadata of personally-identifying strings as well as URIs to linked data about people: these have been replaced by unique but meaningless and non-dereferenceable strings. All other non-person concepts, e.g., geographical locations retain their

Figure 8. Resources and predicates in evaluation dataset Σ

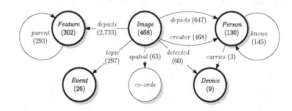

Table 1. Resources, predicates and faces in each evaluation dataset

Dataset	Image	Person	Feature	Event	Device	creator	depicts$_p$	depicts$_f$	topic	spatial	knows	carries	detected	$\|T\|$	$\|T_{trml}\|$
1	267	64	97	10	9	267	267	1,695	191	63	61	3	60	260	63
2	101	21	47	11	1	101	212	476	101	0	18	1	0	208	74
3	100	67	188	5	0	100	168	562	5	0	66	0	0	168	93
Σ	468	130	302	26	9	468	647	2,733	297	63	145	3	60	636	295
1a	82	64	97	10	9	82	129	468	9	63	61	3	60	125	25

Table 2. Statistics for number of people depicted in each photograph

Dataset	Depict	Minimum	Maximum	Mean	Median
1	137	1	6	1.95	2
2	99	1	6	2.14	2
3	93	1	6	1.81	1
Σ	329	1	6	1.97	2
1a	59	1	6	2.19	2

identifying strings and original URIs dereferencing more information and integrating them into the Linked Data Web.

Figure 8 illustrates the structure of each evaluation dataset along with the numbers of resources and predicates present in the dataset for collection Σ. Table 1 elaborates with a summary of the number of resources and predicates by class in each collection's dataset; note that depicts predicates that are used to state that people are depicted are denoted with *depicts$_p$* while those used similarly for features are denoted with *depicts$_f$*.

Table 2 gives further statistics for the numbers of people annotated as depicted in some way in each photograph (whether their faces appear or not). The first column gives the total number of photographs in the dataset that actually depict people. The remaining columns give the minimum, maximum, mean and median statistics for the number of people depicted in each photograph. For example, it can be seen that of the 329 photographs in dataset Σ that depict people, each

depicts between 1-6 people. The mean is 1.97 people per photograph. Figure 9 shows the frequency distribution of people depictions for all datasets.

Additionally, the 3D scatter plot in Figure 10 gives the distribution of photographs in datasets 1, 2 and 3 in both space (horizontal axes) and time (vertical axis). The transparency of each data point is set to 0.05 opacity, so that closely clustered photographs are illustrated as overlapping clouds of increased opacity (i.e., clusters of 20+ overlapping photographs appear fully opaque). The size of the data points was aesthetically chosen for visibility and holds no meaning. The data points in each dataset are connected by a line that shows their ordering in time. It can be seen that the "bursty" nature of personal photographs Naaman (2005, Ch. 3) holds true for datasets 1 and 2 which have photographs densely clustered around discrete spatio-temporal events with empty gaps between events. Dataset 3 presents an alternate scenario where the photographs are sparsely

Figure 9. Frequency distribution of people per photograph

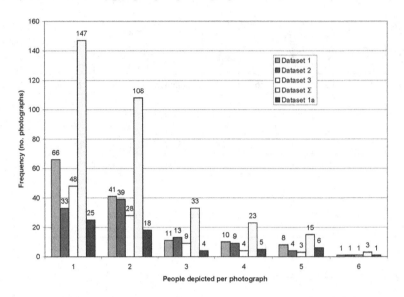

Figure 10. Spatio-temporal distribution of photographs

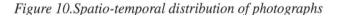
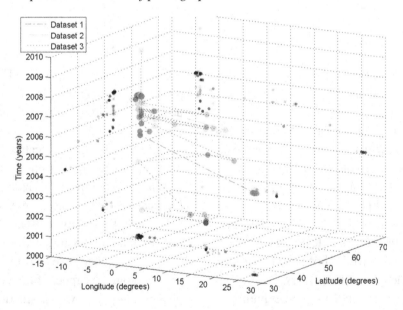

distributed with many events scattered throughout space and time with few photographs per event (several events are represented by a single photograph), made evident by the voluminous but low-density clouds of blue data points.

7.2. Experimental Setup

In the evaluation, we emulated the process of users annotating their photographs (Naaman, 2005). Having obtained the annotations in advance, we do not require interaction with human subjects. Rather, we "hide" the depicted people annotations from the algorithm; the process of users annotating photographs is simulated by revealing the annotations to the system. In other words, we have a "virtual user" who adds annotations to the system. In this paper we consider a "casual user" mode for the virtual user only (Naaman, 2005): for an extended evaluation please see Monaghan (2008, Ch. 6).

Casual users (Naaman, 2005) annotate a certain percentage of the people represented in media resources: this helps to evaluate how accurate an algorithm's recommendations are when only a fixed percentage of represented people have been annotated. Thus, in the beginning of the process, the algorithm is trained by randomly selecting resources and pre-annotating some of the people that are represented, such that after initialisation 75% of the annotations are known to the algorithm (e.g., for dataset Σ we randomly pre-annotate 485 of its 647 person depiction statements).

After initialisation, the casual user selects one random media resource to fully annotate; at each annotation step, the casual user then annotates one person to the current resource, supported by the algorithm's recommendations. At each annotation step, however, the algorithm starts with the same initial state and the casual user randomly selects a person to annotate to the resource who was not selected before, until all the people represented in that resource have been selected.

The casual user then repeats this for all media resources that were not fully annotated during initialisation, until all resources have been selected. Due to the dependence on the random nature of the initialisation, the entire evaluation run is then repeated 10 times to yield 10-set cross-validated results.

The primary evaluation technique is prediction of deleted values. However, a requirement of recommender systems is to rank recommendations according to their relevance instead of just returning them as a set of results (Herlocker, Konstan, Terveen, & Riedl, 2004). Since in practice not all recommendations can be displayed or will be considered by the user, for each annotation step we analyse at which rank position the removed statements are recommended.

At each annotation step the algorithm being evaluated returns a ranked recommendation list of people for which we calculate the accuracy using precision and recall. Regular precision and recall are measures for the entire list: they do not account for the quality of ranking the recommendations in the list. Relevance ranking is measured by computing precision at different cut-off points (Manning, Raghavan, & Schütze, 2008, Sec. 8.3; therefore if the first correct recommendation is returned at position n in the list, we calculate the precision at n. Similarly we calculate the recall at n: the actual number of relevant recommendations up to the first correct recommendation in the list. Plotting the trend of precision over recall for the list then yields the precision-recall plot. Averaged over all annotation steps during the virtual user's annotation of a given dataset, this plot gives an impression of information retrieval accuracy.

7.3. Comparison with Face Recognition

The evaluation includes comparison and combination with a face recognition method. While Choi, Yang, Ro, and Plataniotis (2008) shows that a Bayesian face recognition method (Moghaddam, Jebara, & Pentland, 2000) is shown to perform slightly better than the Principal Component Analysis (PCA/eigenfaces) method (Turk & Pentland, 1991) on the manually selected face images from the CMU-PIE and FERET face datasets, (Davis, Smith, Canny, Good, King, & Janakiraman, 2005) has shown PCA to be the more robust method on real-world personal photographs. These images may be noisy, may not have well-aligned faces nor favourable illumination conditions and may have been captured on lower-resolution capture devices like camera phones. Subsequently, while there has been recent enhancements to state-of-the-art face recognition attempting to circumvent the pose, illumination and expression problem, as well as to use body and clothing recognition to boost performance (Zhao, Teo, Liu, Chua, & Jain, 2006; Anguelov, Lee, Gokturk, & Sumengen, 2007; O'Hare & Smeaton, 2009), PCA face recognition is chosen here as a reasonable baseline content analysis approach for comparison and combination on the task of user-generated photograph annotation.

To this end, we reuse the face distance metric used by Davis, Smith, Canny, Good, King, and Janakiraman (2005) as our face proximity content metric. During training for a given evaluation run, the face proximity metric uses all known training faces of a given person to build a single face class for them, as described in Turk and Pentland (1991). During testing, we first assume perfect detection. This is due to contemporary face detection (as opposed to recognition) being well-solved, accurate and trainable on generic human faces elsewhere (Viola & Jones, 2001). We therefore give the face proximity metric the location of all faces in each photograph during testing, only hiding the identities of the located faces to test recognition alone. The face proximity metric handles multiple faces identically to that of Davis, Smith, Canny, Good, King, and Janakiraman (2005): since there may be multiple faces in a photograph - each giving a distance measurement from a given trained face class - we use the minimum of those distances when considering that face class for recommendation.

For the evaluation of the face proximity metric, each test collection owner manually identified the faces present in their personal photographs by dragging squares and identities across them.

They also manually indicated which of those faces were clear enough to be used as profile pictures for training purposes. Table 1 gives the size $|T|$ of the set of faces T and the size of the subset of those that are also training faces $T_{trn} \subset T$ for each dataset.

Table 3 gives further statistics for face appearances of people in each dataset. The first column gives the number of distinct people whose faces are actually depicted in at least one photograph in the dataset. The second column gives the number of those annotated who have no training faces visible, with the number of those who also have no face visible whatsoever given in brackets. The remaining columns give the minimum, maximum, mean and median statistics for the number of training faces per person, with the figures for the total number of faces per person in brackets.

For example, it can be seen that each of the 98 distinct people annotated to photographs in dataset Σ has their face appear between 0-71 times: 1 person present in the photographs does not have their face appear at all. The mean is 6.54 face appearances per person. Each person has between 0-29 training faces: 17 annotated people had no training face at all. The mean is 3.13 training faces per person. Figure 11 shows the frequency distribution of all face appearances for all datasets. The face proximity content metric was then added to the set of context metrics for both comparison and combination during the evaluation.

Table 3. Statistics for number of face appearances for each person

Dataset	Depict	No face	Min.	Max.	Mean	Median
1	32	7(1)	0(0)	17(46)	2.66(8.25)	2(2.5)
2	18	7(0)	0(1)	16(30)	4.11(11.61)	3(10.5)
3	67	4(0)	0(1)	8(19)	1.40(2.51)	1(2)
Σ	98	17(1)	0(0)	29(71)	3.13(6.54)	1(2)
1a	12	3(1)	0(0)	9(24)	2.42(10.58)	1.5(9.5)

Figure 11. Frequency distribution of faces per person

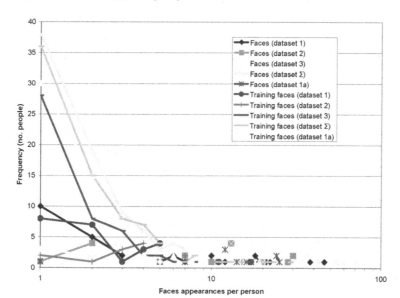

Figure 12. Precision-recall plot for recommendations to casual annotator of dataset Σ

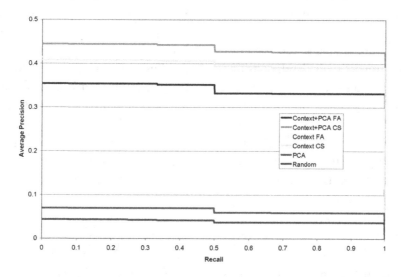

7.4. Results

Figure 12 shows the trend of precision over recall of recommendations given to a casual user for the consolidated dataset Σ. The results for each algorithm are averaged across all annotation steps of each evaluation repetition, and averaged again across all 10 random repetitions. The plot shows the results for the following algorithms - the ran-

dom metric presents recommendations in random order and acts as a control to show how "easy" each dataset is to recommend for:

1. Random metric (Random).
2. PCA face proximity content metric (PCA).
3. Context metrics combined by CombSUM (Context CS).

4. Context metrics combined by factor analysis (Context FA).
5. Context and PCA metrics combined by CombSUM (Context+PCA CS).
6. Context and PCA metrics combined by factor analysis (Context+PCA FA).

It can be seen that while PCA performed rather poorly on the data, Context FA and Context CS performed similarly, both with initial average precision above 40%. PCA has boosted Context+PCA CS while pulling Context+PCA FA down: this shows that, for this selection of metrics at least, CombSUM can perform at least as well if not better than factor analysis, even if for metrics in general it may be a biased approach.

This disparity in performance could be due to the number of factors selected by the factor analytic approach for each person. While factor analysis texts warn against trying to label the common factors (Kim & Mueller, 1978) at a glance two factors loosely emerged for most people: one with strong "social" relationships to the corepresentation and creator metrics, the other with a strong "geographic" relationship to the spatio-temporal metric. On the other hand, some people with stronger "technological" device copresence relationships had three. However, these comments are not founded on rigorous analysis and in fact contravene the intention of factor analysis by attributing too much meaning to the emergent factors: this is identified as an area that deserves further study.

While the average precision of all algorithms stays fairly flat across recall, there are noticeable drops in precision where recall is 1/6, 1/5, 1/4, 1/3, 2/5, ½, etc. This is intuitive due to there being between 1-6 people depicted in each image in the dataset (See Table 2, Section 7.1). The most severe drop at 1/2 recall has significance since the sharpest accuracy drop is likely to occur between the first and second recommendations. This drop also has a trivial element since there are significantly more photographs with one or two people in the dataset than three or more (Figure 9, Section 7.1), and therefore most incorrect (as well as most correct) recommendations were made on these photographs.

Figure 13 further summarises the results for all recommendation algorithms for the remaining evaluation datasets. The figure displays Mean Average Precision (MAP) of each evaluation run; this is simply the area under each precision-recall plot, as seen in Figure 12 for the plots for dataset Σ. As well as the mean, the standard deviation of the average precision across the 10 repetitions is given by the thin errors bars.

In general, CombSUM slightly outperformed factor analysis. Dataset 1 gave the best results; as seen in Section 7.1, this dataset contained the most observations (photographs), and therefore a larger pre-annotated training set as described in Section 7.2. Dataset 3 gave the worst results; as seen in Section 7.1, this dataset consists of photographs split over several distinct events, many events having just a single photograph. This demonstrates that the context-aware recommendation algorithms perform poorly in the absence of a certain amount of training data from each event. The results for the largest, consolidated dataset Σ suggest that overall and on a larger scale CombSUM outperformed factor analysis and that PCA did not significantly improve either algorithm's accuracy.

Finally, we analysed which of the individual metrics were the most accurate when used on their own. This evaluation may additionally help implementers to choose which individual metrics to use given constrained resources. To provide an unbiased view of the performance of the device carriage and device copresence metrics, this evaluation was only carried out on photographs from dataset 1a; these were taken by a camera phone with the ACRONYM mobile device-based camera application installed and so support the full range of context metrics. The breakdown of the MAP and standard deviation for each metric

Figure 13. Mean average precision of recommendations to casual annotator across datasets

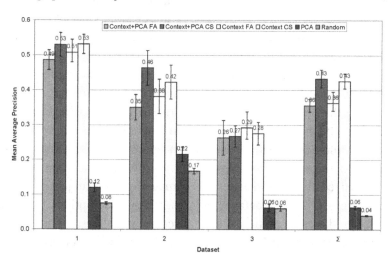

Figure 14. Breakdown of the mean average precision of the individual context metrics for dataset 1a

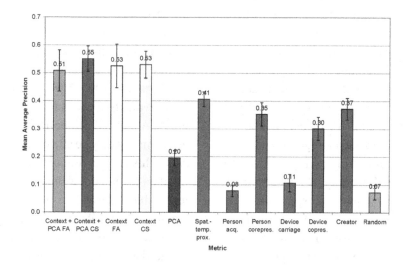

is compared in Figure 14 along with the combinations and random control for comparison.

The MAP results for individual context metrics suggest that the spatio-temporal proximity, person corepresentation and creator based ones are the most accurate. It is noteworthy that the implicit person corepresentation and device copresence metrics were more accurate than their explicit person acquaintance and device carriage counterparts; this may well be due to a lack of social networking and device ownership statements in the dataset. Either way this demonstrates the robust

nature of these implicit, real-world metrics over their explicit, digital world counterparts. The results also suggest that both combinations of context metrics are indeed more accurate than any single context metric alone. These results suggest that CombSUM is again the slightly more accurate combination method when ambient space context is available to the given context metrics and face recognition is used, with a MAP of 55% compared to 51% for factor analysis.

7.5. Discussion

Factor analysis has already been used to combine context-based and content-based cues to support the prediction of faces in photographs (Davis, Smith, Canny, Good, King, & Janakiraman, 2005). The major difference is that this previous work uses binary-valued statements about photographs as their observed variables while we use continuous-valued metrics taking into account relationships between various contextual recall cues. As detailed in Section 3, their approach has 2 disadvantages. First, by only considering direct properties of a photograph, it ignores direct relationships that instances may have with each other independent of any photographs, e.g., people may state that they know each other. By using context metrics derived from the user's information space, we take advantage of the rich contextual knowledge that is available for mining on the social Semantic Web.

The second disadvantage of the approach of Davis, Smith, Canny, Good, King, and Janakiraman (2005) arises from their binary modelling of data. For example, the binary model cannot use the geographic proximity of photographs, only the boolean value of whether a photograph belongs to an artificially created geographic cluster or not. The binary approach requires photographs to be clustered geographically into an arbitrary number of clusters (100 in their case), the granularity of which may be too coarse for many applications and which does not scale well. For example, photographs taken in Ireland and Germany may be indistinguishable geographically under this model and may well both be included in the arbitrary 'Europe' cluster.

Importantly, the authors of Davis, Smith, Canny, Good, King, and Janakiraman (2005) report some significantly more accurate results than this paper: they report 60% initial precision for a combined PCA+context method. As well as using a larger training set, it is important to note that in their evaluation the authors report that they manually tailored the training set in several ways with constraints that introduce several assumptions (Davis, Smith, Canny, Good, King, & Janakiraman, 2005, Sec. 4): "For each face, 8 photos were taken at random and 4 photos were selected manually for the training set. Manual selection was done to insure a sufficient number of visible faces in the training set. We will automate this process in future work. Each photo contained images of 1 to 4 people. The training gallery contained 2-4 images of each subject on average."

These assumptions would tend to boost the accuracy of all results, but specifically face recognisers. While the dataset used in Davis, Smith, Canny, Good, King, and Janakiraman (2005) is not publically available, the boosts provided by the larger size and manual selection of the training set can be measured by comparing the results of the PCA recogniser: while this algorithm was included in both evaluations, it achieved 43% accuracy in Davis, Smith, Canny, Good, King, and Janakiraman (2005) but a maximum of only 22% in the evaluation presented here (dataset 2). Since the PCA method is identical, this 20%+ boost in performance may be attributed to the training/test data. This assumption of manually chosen training data is outside of the original algorithm, not repeatable in the real-world without universal user labour and contributes to a smudging of the performance of the algorithm with the performance of the data. Since these assumptions cannot be guaranteed in actual use, we did not introduce similar assumptions to our evaluation but rather allowed the algorithms to be compared on a robust and realistic playing field of randomly selected, 10-set cross-validated training sets, as described in Section 7.2

Furthermore, it should be noted that throughout their evaluation, Davis, Smith, Canny, Good, King, and Janakiraman (2005) only give the best results numbers: initial precision. They do not average their results for entire lists of recommendations using MAP, as we do here. Finally, to conclude a direct comparison with Davis, Smith, Canny, Good, King, and Janakiraman (2005), their context-only approach (without content/face recognition) achieves sub-50% MAP (initial precision 50%, dropping off for further hits), whereas our context-only approach achieves 53% MAP (dataset 1a).

Similarly to Davis, Smith, Canny, Good, King, and Janakiraman (2005), the context analysis approaches of Naaman (2005) have been combined with content analysis and extended by O'Hare and Smeaton (2009). In particular, they also extend the PeopleRank algorithm, and their spatial and temporal proximity metrics take a similar manually-chosen window approach to the spatial proximity method of Naaman (2005) and Davis, Smith, Canny, Good, King, and Janakiraman (2005). While the naming of their separate temporal proximity and spatial proximity metrics may appear similar to our single spatio-temporal proximity metric, they in fact operate quite differently. As detailed in Section 6.1.1, we use continuous spatial interpolation over time to calculate a single proximity value estimating how close a person was at a given time, whereas Naaman (2005) and Davis, Smith, Canny, Good, King, and Janakiraman (2005) use time and space windows of arbitrarily-chosen granularity to come up with two different scores which they later attempt to combine.

O'Hare and Smeaton (2009) extend this latter approach with Jelinek-Mercer smoothing over layered windows. For example, for spatial proximity, they use 100km windows layered on top of 1km windows layered on top of cooccurrence within single photographs. Our patented spatio-temporal proximity approach is shown in our evaluation to be our most successful individual metric, which complements the conclusion of O'Hare and Smeaton (2009) where their best performing individual metric was the one that incorporated temporal proximity.

Of note, O'Hare and Smeaton (2009) report relatively better results than reported here for face recognition when compared against context-based approaches (reporting 1-hit rates of 45% compared to 55% respectively in their approach while we report MAP of 20% compared to 53% in our approach). However, this is only after a substantial amount of dataset and evaluation method tweaking. Initially, in their face recognition approach they "position, scale, and rotate each face to create a normalized face image" before running PCA/ICA (O'Hare & Smeaton, 2009, Sec. IV.B.1). We do not, reusing the approach of Davis, Smith, Canny, Good, King, and Janakiraman (2005) to let PCA perform on its own on the original faces as seen in the photographs. This would contribute significantly to any relative disparity in results reported for face recognition.

Furthermore, while the dataset used in O'Hare and Smeaton (2009) is not publically available, they describe several major ways in which they manually tailor it for the evaluation of their approach. Since these would again tend to blur the line between dataset and evaluation method and significantly impact any evaluation results, we detail each below. It should be noted that since our approach is intended to work at Web scale with UGC data, and not on curated data, we must be able to deal with (and therefore should evaluate on) real untampered data. For a detailed discussion of the non-trivial problems with data cleanliness on the Semantic Web, see Hogan, Harth, Passant, Decker, and Polleres (2010).

Firstly, and similar to Davis, Smith, Canny, Good, King, and Janakiraman (2005) as described, (O'Hare & Smeaton, 2009, Sec. V) manually tailor their dataset to be a sample of good training data from the real-world population: "The MediAssist personal photo archive contains 23,774 geotagged photos from 29 users, taken as part of their private personal photo collections. Of these, nine users have collections suitable for evaluation of person identification, with the other user collections not containing enough known people. Table 1 summarizes the nine individual personal photo collections used."

Secondly, they further manually tailor the dataset by only including in the test set those people with the most available training data, introducing the following unfounded and uncited assumption: "Since a user is generally only interested in annotating the most popular identities in their collection, we use the top 20-most popular people in each collection for evaluation, assuming the user is not interested in less popular faces.". Based on our own observations, this would have a major impact on performance. Since it is completely unsupported by evidence from the real world, and is non-repeatable in actual use, we cannot and do not make such an assumption.

Thirdly, they continue to bias their results with weights learned specifically for each user's dataset, never providing an evaluation of their approach over their dataset as a whole (O'Hare & Smeaton, 2009, Sec. V): "The weights are learned separately for each user collection and are biased, 'oracle', weights and cannot be said to represent weights that we could expect a system to learn automatically." On the other hand, our approach is intended from the ground up to automatically learn its weights for each person represented in multimedia on the social Semantic Web, and does not require an artificial ringfence to be erected around any one users' collection.

Fourthly, in their evaluation of their smoothing methods, (O'Hare & Smeaton, 2009, Sec. VI.A) make trial-and-error manual optimisations in the arbitrary sizing of their smoothing layer window sizes and in the arbitrary number of layers. This is outside of their presented algorithms and again is not repeatable in actual use without human intervention: "For MLE, Smoothing and Hierarchical Smoothing language models a large number of alternative variations were evaluated, with varying window sizes and hierarchical structures explored, and the best-performing variation for each is shown here."

When considering these latter points on manual blurring of the actual approach with the dataset and with the evaluation method, it can be reasonably inferred that the approach of O'Hare and Smeaton (2009) would fare significantly worse on an even playing field of untampered data from the real world using a consistent and repeatable evaluation method. In particular, this would help to explain any relative disparity in results for content-based approaches - which require plenty of good training data (Section 2) reported between this paper and O'Hare and Smeaton (2009).

Similarly, Zhao, Teo, Liu, Chua, and Jain (2006) take several measures to circumvent the face pose, illumination and expression problems for their content-based approach: "Face detection is first applied to detect the near frontal faces. To alleviate the pose problem, eye detection is used to rotate the faces so that the two eye[s] are horizontal. The eye detector is trained with AdaBoost, which has been used successfully in face detection. To overcome the illumination problem, we employ the generalized quotient image for delighting. Finally to tackle the pose problem, we use translation and rotation to generate more training faces for three views, i.e., left-view, front-view and right-view, for each person." They then use pseudo 2DHMM models for each of the three views to recognise faces. They also add body recognition to their content-based approach.

Zhao, Teo, Liu, Chua, and Jain (2006) also support their content-based approach with social context using (1) the PeopleRank algorithm amongst their own algorithms based on (2) global popularity (a rude probability for each person, identical for each photo), (3) event co-occurrence (based on clustering of events) and (4) temporal reoccurrence (based on temporal clustering of photos). While they do not provide an evaluation of their context-based approach standing alone, they report that it improves the recall of their content-based approach when used in combination, but it does not improve precision noticeably.

Finally, while Zhao, Teo, Liu, Chua, and Jain (2006) report 70% initial precision results for their combined Face+Body(A)+Context approach, they also encounter sharp drop-offs across recall. They do not report overall performance numbers for MAP, but these can still be estimated from the PR plot in their Figure 4. They achieve about 30%, 20% lower than our best context-based approach's MAP results. This can be roughly calculated by taking the area under their plot: 0.70 (precision) * 0.82 (recall) / 2 (rough triangle shape) = 0.29.

7.6. Repeatability

This section summarises a strategy to help the community have a reusable and extensible suite of data so that evaluations are repeatable and comparable. The strategy aims to convince that this, related and future work can be evaluated with relevance to Web-scale (in the context of UGC). In the spirit of linked open data we have gone above and beyond the state of the art in making our data as well as our approach available for others. Below, we clearly address the issue of repeatability of our approach and evaluation giving our best view on:

- How the data is reusable.
- How others can compare the results.
- How others can build upon or participate in developing a larger evaluation set.

7.7. Data Reusability

We have made every attempt possible to publish as much data as we are legally allowed to with the permission of the data owners. We provide our entire dataset of metadata, minus "human-readable" personally identifying content like names and faces as is required practice for personal data. This goes beyond efforts from state of the art related work which mostly (including those cited) do not even attempt to share the data used for repetition. The data retains all other strings, e.g., placenames and all anonymised Person concepts retain unique

identifiers as well as links to other concepts. This dataset is valid RDF, classifies as Linked Data as it reuses URIs dereferencable to existing data out there and is ready to go into any RDF store as-is.

We provide a detailed description in Section 7 of the makeup of the dataset including a detailed statistical breakdown of concepts and relationships, along with distribution of faces per person and photo. This includes graphical representations of the data. This gives the reader deep insight into the dataset, before they have even clicked the link to download it into their RDF store.

7.8. Result Comparability

Our zero-assumption evaluation approach is completely repeatable without human intervention, and involves no tailoring of the data for our or any one approach. We also use the completely repeatable and directly-comparable evaluation technique of Mean Average Precision. See Section 7.5 for a discussion and comparison with related work in this regard.

7.9. Data Extensibility

We have reused and integrated popular existing ontologies like FOAF, GeoNames and iCal where possible. See Section 5.1 for an overview and Monaghan (2008, Ch. 4) for a detailed description of the integrated ontology used. We also go beyond any related work and actually provide free of charge the same mobile device app we use to capture sensor data in Section 5.1. A detailed description of our algorithms is provided for anyone who wants to repeat or extend our work.

8. CONCLUSION

We have proposed an approach to media annotation that is social Semantic Web-aware and which taps the rich contextual data available thereon. This is a novel dimension beyond existing approaches that comes with its own implications, and has resulted in the following contributions of this paper:

- **Robust Recommendation Algorithms:** Novel context-aware recommendation algorithms that require no manual tweaking or dataset tailoring.
- **Factor Analytic Combination Method:** Unique application of personalised, continuous-valued factor analysis to combine metrics without bias. This alternative approach to handling sparse media annotation data automatically tailors itself to annotated individuals and is an innovation beyond Davis, Smith, Canny, Good, King, and Janakiraman (2005) or any other work we are aware of.
- **Media Agnostic:** Our approach is designed from the ground up to be media-agnostic, and is generically reusable beyond any one media (e.g., photographs) and applicable to UGC multimedia at large (video, text posts, e.g., tweets, audio clips, etc.).
- **Dataset of Context-Aware Photo Metadata:** The first publically available RDF dataset for context-aware media annotation evaluation.
- **Evaluation of Algorithms for Reuse:** An analysis highlighting the most useful of the metrics and combination methods presented for the personal photograph annotation use case.

The automation provided by these contributions to multimedia annotation can alleviate the audiovisual data overload on users searching for or managing UGC multimedia. Face recognition and other content-recognition techniques can be supported by context-aware, data mining and social techniques. More specifically, the social Semantic Web domain provides powerful tools for mining and integrating distributed information to create new knowledge on the context surrounding multimedia resources and the people represented by them.

Mobile devices can be used to gather ground truth data about the ambient environment at the time of capture which can be reused to infer higher level contextual information. This information can help automate the annotation of media resources with cues useful for knowledge recall by users. This paper defines several context metrics which measure the strength of relationships between some of the key recall cues people use for managing UGC multimedia.

In particular, the context-aware ACRONYM approach can support the semi-automatic annotation of the people depicted in personal photographs with 53% mean average precision based on context alone. The same approach can increase the accuracy of state of the art face recognition from 20% to 55%. Additionally, it has been shown that implicitly measured context allows robust recommendations to be made when explicitly asserted statements are sparse. Furthermore, the context metrics can be combined to make recommendations that are more accurate than any that could be made by a single metric alone. The knowledge represented in completed annotations can then be integrated into the Semantic Web as portable, linked data describing the ever-increasing amount of UGC content.

ACKNOWLEDGMENT

The authors would like to thank Robert Engels for his key input to the context metrics. The work presented in this paper has been funded in part by Science Foundation Ireland under Grants No. SFI/02/CE/I131 (Líon) and SFI/08/CE/I1380 (Líon-2) and the European Union under Grants

No. FP6-2004-IST-NMP-2-17120 (AmI4SME) and FP6-027705 (Nepomuk).

REFERENCES

Adida, B., Birbeck, M., McCarron, S., & Pemberton, S. (2008). *RDFa in XHTML: Syntax and processing*. Retrieved from http://www.w3.org/TR/rdfa-syntax/

Adobe Developer Technologies. (2005). *Extensible Metadata Platform (XMP) specification*. San Jose, CA: Adobe Systems Incorporated. Retrieved from http://partners.adobe.com/public/developer/en/xmp/sdk/XMPspecification.pdf

Ahern, S., King, S., Naaman, M., Nair, R., & Yang, J. H.-I. (2007). ZoneTag: Rich, community-supported context-aware media capture and annotation. In *Proceedings of the Mobile Spatial Interaction Workshop at the SIGCHI Conference on Human Factors in Computing Systems*, San Jose, CA. New York, NY: ACM.

Anguelov, D., Lee, K.-C., Gokturk, S. B., & Sumengen, B. (2007). Contextual identity recognition in personal photo albums. In *Proceedings of the International Conference on Computer Vision and Pattern Recognition*, Minneapolis, MN (pp. 1-7). Washington, DC: IEEE Computer Society. Retrieved from http://robotics.stanford.edu/~drago/Papers/cvpr2007.pdf

Barthelmess, P., Kaiser, E., & McGee, D. R. (2007). Toward content-aware multimodal tagging of personal photo collections. In *Proceedings of the 9th International Conference on Multimodal Interfaces*, Nagoya, Aichi, Japan (pp.122-125). New York, NY: ACM. Retrieved from http://home.comcast.net/~pbarthelmess/Publications/Photos/icmi259-barthelmess.pdf

Berners-Lee, T. (2006). *Linked data* (Tech. Rep.). Retrieved from http://www.w3.org/DesignIssues/LinkedData.html

Bizer, C., Cyganiak, R., & Heath, T. (2007). *How to publish linked data on the web* (Tech. Rep.). Berlin, Germany: Freie Universität Berlin. Retrieved from http://www4.wiwiss.fu-berlin.de/bizer/pub/LinkedDataTutorial/20070727/

Bojārs, U., Heitmann, B., & Oren, E. (2007). A prototype to explore content and context on social community sites. In *Proceedings of the International Conference on Social Semantic Web* (pp. 47-58). Retrieved from http://www.eyaloren.org/pubs/cssw2007.pdf

Breslin, J. G., Harth, A., Bojars, U., & Decker, S. (2005). Towards semantically interlinked online communities. In A. Gómez-Pérez & J. Euzenat (Eds.), *Proceedings of the 2nd European Semantic Web Conference: Research and Applications*, Heraklion, Greece (LNCS 3532, pp. 71-83). Retrieved from http://sw.deri.org/2004/12/sioc/index.pdf

Broder, A. Z. (1997). On the resemblance and containment of documents. In *Proceedings of the International Conference on Compression and Complexity of Sequences*, Salerno, Italy (pp. 21-29). Washington, DC: IEEE Computer Society. Retrieved from http://www.cs.princeton.edu/courses/archive/spr05/cos598E/bib/broder-97resemblance.pdf

Canny, J. (2002). Collaborative filtering with privacy via factor analysis. In *Proceedings of the 25th Annual International ACM SIGIR Conference on Research and Development in Information Retrieval*, Tampere, Finland (pp. 238-245). New York, NY: ACM. Retrieved from http://www.cs.berkeley.edu/~jfc/'mender/sigir.pdf

Cetina, K. K. (1997). Sociality with objects: Social relations in postsocial knowledge societies. *Theory, Culture & Society*, *14*(4), 1–30. doi:10.1177/026327697014004001.

Choi, J.-Y., Yang, S., Ro, Y. M., & Plataniotis, K. N. (2008). Face annotation for personal photos using context-assisted face recognition. In *Proceedings of the 1st ACM International Conference on Multimedia Information Retrieval*, Vancouver, BC, Canada (p. 44). New York, NY: ACM.

Davis, M., Smith, M., Canny, J., Good, N., King, S., & Janakiraman, R. (2005). Towards context-aware face recognition. In *Proceedings of the 13th Annual ACM International Conference on Multimedia*, Singapore (pp. 483-486). Retrieved from http://fusion.sims.berkeley.edu/GarageCinema/pubs/pdf/pdf_89FB89A7-2534-412F-A815230DFDB32CDC.pdf

Dey, A. K., & Abowd, G. D. (2000). Towards a better understanding of context and context-awareness. In *Proceedings of the Workshop on The What, Who, Where, When, and How of Context-Awareness at the Conference on Human Factors in Computing Systems*, The Hague, The Netherlands.

Dorai, C., & Ventakesh, S. (2003). Bridging the semantic gap with computational media aesthetics. *IEEE MultiMedia*, *10*(2), 15–17. doi:10.1109/MMUL.2003.1195157.

Euromonitor International. (2010). *Global Market Information Database (GMID)*. Retrieved January 19, 2010, from http://www.portal.euromonitor.com

Fox, E. A., & Shaw, J. A. (1994). Combination of multiple searches. In *Proceedings of the 2nd Text Retrieval Conference TREC2 NIST SP 500215* (pp. 243-252). Gaithersburg, MD: NIST.

Girgensohn, A., Adcock, J., Cooper, M., Foote, J., & Wilcox, L. (2003). Simplifying the management of large photo collections. In *Proceedings of the Ninth IFIP TC13 International Conference on Human-Computer Interaction*. Amsterdam, The Netherlands: IOS Press.

Hasan, T., & Jameson, A. (2008). Bridging the motivation gap for individual annotators: What can we learn from photo annotation systems? In *Proceedings of the 1st Workshop on Incentives for the Semantic Web at the 7th International Semantic Web Conference*, Karlsruhe, Germany. Retrieved from http://km.aifb.uni-karlsruhe.de/ws/insemtive2008/hasan2008insemtive.pdf

Herlocker, J. L., Konstan, J. A., Terveen, L. G., & Riedl, J. T. (2004). Evaluating collaborative filtering recommender systems. *ACM Transactions on Information Systems*, *22*(1), 5–53. doi:10.1145/963770.963772.

Hogan, A., Harth, A., Passant, A., Decker, S., & Polleres, A. (2010). Weaving the pedantic web. In *Proceedings of the Linked Data on the Web World Wide Web Workshop*, Raleigh, NC. Retrieved from http://sw.deri.org/~aidanh/docs/pedantic_ldow10.pdf

InfoTrends/CAP Ventures. (2004). *Mobile imaging: Technology trends, consumer behavior, and business strategies* (Tech. Rep.). Retrieved from http://www.capv.com/home/Multiclient/MobileImaging.html

Kim, J.-O., & Mueller, C. W. (1978). *Introduction to factor analysis: what it is and how to do it* (10th ed.). Thousand Oaks, CA: Sage.

Kirk, D., Sellen, A., Rother, C., & Wood, K. (2006). Understanding photowork. In *Proceedings of the SIGCHI Conference on Human Factors in Computing Systems* (pp. 761-770). New York, NY: ACM.

Klyne, G., & Carroll, J. J. (2004). *Resource Description Framework (RDF): Concepts and abstract syntax*. Retrieved from http://www.w3.org/TR/2004/REC-rdf-concepts-20040210/

Lavelle, B., Byrne, D., Gurrin, C., Smeaton, A. F., & Jones, G. J. F. (2007). Bluetooth familiarity: Methods of calculation, applications and limitations. In *Proceedings of the 9th International Conference on Human Computer Interaction with Mobile Devices and Services Mobile Interaction with the Real World*, Singapore. Retrieved from http://www.medien.ifi.lmu.de/mirw2007/papers/MIRW2007_Lavelle.pdf

Lieberman, H., Rosenzweig, E., & Singh, P. (2001). Aria: An agent for annotating and retrieving images. *IEEE Computer, 34*(7), 5762. doi:10.1109/2.933504.

Lindley, S. E., Durrant, A., Kirk, D., & Taylor, A. (2009). Collocated social practices surrounding photos. *International Journal of Human-Computer Studies, 67*(12), 995–1004. Retrieved from http://research.microsoft.com/pubs/115365/IJHCS_Editorial.pdf doi:10.1016/j.ijhcs.2009.08.004.

Manning, C. D., Raghavan, P., & Schütze, H. (2008). *Introduction to information retrieval*. Cambridge, UK: Cambridge University Press. Retrieved from http://nlp.stanford.edu/IR-book/pdf/irbookonlinereading.pdf

Mitchell, J. (2011). *How many photos are uploaded to Facebook each day?* Retrieved June 26, 2011, from http://www.quora.com/How-many-photos-are-uploaded-to-Facebook-each-day

Moghaddam, B., Jebara, T., & Pentland, A. (2000). Bayesian face recognition. *Pattern Recognition, 33*(11), 1771–1782. doi:10.1016/S0031-3203(99)00179-X.

Monaghan, F. (2008). *Context-aware photograph annotation on the social Semantic Web* (Doctoral dissertation, National University of Ireland). Retrieved from http://sw.deri.org/~ferg/publications/thesis.pdf

Monaghan, F., & O'Sullivan, D. (2007). Leveraging ontologies, context and social networks to automate photo annotation. In B. Falcidieno, M. Spagnuolo, Y. S. Avrithis, I. Kompatsiaris, & P. Buitelaar (Eds.), *Proceedings of the 2nd International Conference on Semantics and Digital Media Technologies*, Genoa, Italy (LNCS 4816, pp. 252-255).

Naaman, M. (2005). *Leveraging geo-referenced digital photographs* (Doctoral dissertation, Stanford University). Retrieved from http://infolab.stanford.edu/~mor/research/naamanthesis.pdf

Naaman, M., Harada, S., Wangy, Q., Garcia-Molina, H., & Paepcke, A. (2004). Context data in georeferenced digital photo collections. In *Proceedings of the 12th International Conference on Multimedia* (pp. 196-203). New York, NY: ACM.

Naaman, M., & Nair, R. (2008). Zonetag's collaborative tag suggestions: What is this person doing in my phone? *IEEE MultiMedia, 15*(3), 34–40. doi:10.1109/MMUL.2008.69.

Naaman, M., Yeh, R. B., Garcia-Molina, H., & Paepcke, A. (2005). Leveraging context to resolve identity in photo albums. In *Proceedings of the 5th ACM/IEEE-CS Joint Conference on Digital Libraries*. (pp. 178-187). New York, NY: ACM.

O'Hare, N., & Smeaton, A. F. (2009). Context-aware person identification in personal photo collections. *IEEE Transactions on Multimedia, 11*(2).

O'Toole, A. J., Phillips, P. J., Jiang, F., Ayyad, J., Penard, N., & Abdi, H. (2007). Face recognition algorithms surpass humans matching faces over changes in illumination. *IEEE Transactions on Pattern Analysis and Machine Intelligence, 29*(9), 1642–1646. doi:10.1109/TPAMI.2007.1107 PMID:17627050.

Pingdom. (2011). *Internet 2010 in numbers* [Web log post]. Retrieved June 26, 2011, from http://royal.pingdom.com/2011/01/12/internet-2010-in-numbers/

Rodden, K., & Wood, K. R. (2003). How do people manage their digital photographs? In *Proceedings of the ACM Conference on Human Factors in Computing Systems*, Fort Lauderdale, FL (pp. 409-416). New York, NY: ACM. http://www.rodden.org/kerry/chi2003.pdf

Smeulders, A. W. M., Worring, M., Santini, S., Gupta, A., & Jain, R. (2000). Content-based image retrieval at the end of the early years. *IEEE Transactions on Pattern Analysis and Machine Intelligence*, 22(12), 1349–1380. doi:10.1109/34.895972.

Suh, B., & Bederson, B. B. (2007). Semi-automatic photo annotation strategies using event based clustering and clothing based person recognition. *Interacting with Computers*, 19(4), 524–544. doi:10.1016/j.intcom.2007.02.002.

Tuffield, M. M., Harris, S., Dupplaw, D. P., Chakravarthy, A., Brewster, C., & Gibbins, N. Wilks, Y. (2006). Image annotation with photocopain. In *Proceedings of the First International Workshop on Semantic Web Annotations for Multimedia*, Edinburgh, UK. Retrieved from http://www.image.ntua.gr /swamm2006/resources/paper09.pdf

Turk, M. A., & Pentland, A. P. (1991). Eigenfaces for recognition. *Journal of Cognitive Neuroscience*, 3(1), 71–86. doi:10.1162/jocn.1991.3.1.71.

US Census Bureau. (2010). *International Data Base (IDB)*. Retrieved January 19, 2010, from http://www.census.gov/ipc/www/idb/

Veltkamp, R. C., & Tanase, M. (2002). *Content-based image retrieval systems: A survey* (Tech. Rep. No. TR UUCS-2000-34). Utrecht, The Netherlands: Utrecht University. Retrieved from http://www.aa-lab.cs.uu.nl/cbirsurvey/cbir-survey/

Vincenty, T. (1975). Direct and inverse solutions of geodesics on the ellipsoid with application of nested equations. *Survey Review*, 23(176), 88–93.

Viola, P., & Jones, M. (2001). Robust real time object detection. In *Proceedings of the IEEE ICCV Workshop on Statistical and Computational Theories of Vision*, Vancouver, BC, Canada. Washington, DC: IEEE Computer Society. Retrieved from http://research.microsoft.com/en-us/um/people/viola/Pubs/Detect/violaJones_IJCV.pdf

Wagenaar, W. A. (1986). My memory: A study of autobiographical memory over six years. *Cognitive Psychology*, 18, 225–252. doi:10.1016/0010-0285(86)90013-7.

Wunsch-Vincent, S., & Vickery, G. (2006). *Participative web: User-created content* (Report No. DSTI/ICCP/IE(2006)7/FINAL). Paris, France: OECD. Retrieved from http://www.oecd.org/dataoecd/57/14/38393115.pdf

Zhao, M., Teo, Y. W., Liu, S., Chua, T.-S., & Jain, R. (2006). Automatic person annotation of family photo album. In H. Sundaram, M. Naphade, J. R. Smith, & Y. Rui (Eds.), *Proceedings of the 5th International Conference on Image and Video Retrieval* (LNCS 4071, pp. 163-172).

This work was previously published in the International Journal on Semantic Web and Information Systems, Volume 7, Issue 4, edited by Amit P. Sheth,, pp. 1-35, copyright 2011 by IGI Publishing (an imprint of IGI Global).

Chapter 10
An Enhanced Semantic Layer for Hybrid Recommender Systems:
Application to News Recommendation

Iván Cantador
Universidad Autónoma de Madrid, Spain

Pablo Castells
Universidad Autónoma de Madrid, Spain

Alejandro Bellogín
Universidad Autónoma de Madrid, Spain

ABSTRACT

Recommender systems have achieved success in a variety of domains, as a means to help users in information overload scenarios by proactively finding items or services on their behalf, taking into account or predicting their tastes, priorities, or goals. Challenging issues in their research agenda include the sparsity of user preference data and the lack of flexibility to incorporate contextual factors in the recommendation methods. To a significant extent, these issues can be related to a limited description and exploitation of the semantics underlying both user and item representations. The authors propose a three-fold knowledge representation, in which an explicit, semantic-rich domain knowledge space is incorporated between user and item spaces. The enhanced semantics support the development of contextualisation capabilities and enable performance improvements in recommendation methods. As a proof of concept and evaluation testbed, the approach is evaluated through its implementation in a news recommender system, in which it is tested with real users. In such scenario, semantic knowledge bases and item annotations are automatically produced from public sources.

DOI: 10.4018/978-1-4666-3610-1.ch010

1. INTRODUCTION

The growing volume and complexity of digital information (news, blogs, music, movies, etc.) of potential value to our daily activities challenge the limits of human processing capabilities in a wide array of information seeking and e-commerce tasks. Users need help to cope with a wealth of readily available information, in order to reach the most interesting items in online retrieval spaces. The problem is not just to find the needle in the haystack, but to select the best among thousands of needles. In such information overload scenarios, recommender systems become particularly appealing as a means to help users make choices, by proactively finding items or services on their behalf, taking into account or predicting their tastes, priorities or goals.

Recommender systems came forth by the early nineties as an emerging area at the confluence of Artificial Intelligence and Information Retrieval, to address the essential research problem of predicting or estimating the relevance of items that a user has not seen or searched for. The way in which the estimation is computed raises the distinction of two main recommendation strategies (Adomavicius & Tuzhilin, 2005): *content-based filtering* (CBF) strategies, which predict the relevance of an item for a user according to the relevance that other similar items seemed to have for him in the past, and *collaborative filtering* (CF) strategies, which predict the relevance of an item for a user by considering the relevance that other items had in the past for similar people.

It has been generally observed that combining CBF and CF methods, known as *hybrid recommendation*, is usually the best approach to mitigate the limitations CBF and CF approaches suffer separately (Adomavicius & Tuzhilin, 2005). Hybrid recommendation approaches are becoming an integral part of a large number of important e-commerce and leisure Web sites like *Amazon*, *Netflix*, and many online retailers, where recommendation models have proved successful.

Nonetheless, ample room and need for further improvements remains in the current generation of recommender systems to achieve more effective algorithms, in a wider variety of applications. These improvements include, among others:

- Better coping with low data density situations in the available evidence of user preference, e.g., user input scarcity in initial situations (*cold-start problem*). When a new user enters a recommender system, no personal profile is yet available for him, and no proper recommendations can be made. Similarly, until a new item is rated by a substantial number of users, a CF recommender is not able to recommend it, as observed user preference for specific items is the data CF relies upon. This problem is particularly prevalent in *sparse* domains such as the News, where there is a constant stream of new items, and each user only rates a few.

- The consideration of *contextual information* in the recommendation strategies. Traditional recommenders operate on the two-dimensional Users×Items space, i.e., they make recommendations based solely on user and item information, and do not take into consideration additional contextual information that may be crucial in some applications. In many situations, the utility of a certain item to a user may largely depend on the circumstances under which the item would be utilised, or the temporary purpose and changing goals of users with respect to the items. Using multidimensional settings, the inclusion of knowledge about the user's task, goals, environment, etc., into the recommendation algorithm can lead to better recommendations.

Among other directions, the enhancement of the semantics representation of user preferences and item contents is being identified as a key outlook to achieve qualitative steps forward on the above problems (Anand & Mobasher, 2007; Mobasher & Burke, 2007). Classic techniques usually describe user and item profiles in terms of identifiers and numerical preference values, plain keywords, and/or attribute/value pairs with controlled vocabularies. The latent semantic meanings underneath the user and item spaces involved in recommendations, and the semantic relations between their elements, are largely underexploited when building recommendations.

Following this direction, and aiming to address the aforementioned limitations of current recommendation technologies, we propose a three-folded knowledge model, in which a space for interrelated semantic concepts is incorporated between the user and item spaces. The concepts are defined by ontology classes and instances, describing one or several domains. On top of this, user and item profiles are described by vectors consisting of weighted concepts from the ontology space. In this respect, our contribution is the definition of a formal knowledge representation of user preferences and item contents, which is not ambiguous, and takes into account arbitrary (i.e., not pre-established) semantic relations between concepts.

In order to address the *cold-start* and *sparsity* problems, we propose a strategy that spreads the weights of the ontological concepts available in user and item profiles towards other concepts that are connected through semantic relations of the domain ontologies. The semantic propagation strategy proposed herein is based on Constrained Spreading Activation techniques (Cohen & Kjeldsen, 1987; Crestani, 1997), considering the attenuation of weights as the expansion grows away from the initial set, with loop control in the propagation paths, and the possibility to bound the expansion distance. Our contribution is the design of a novel mechanism that extends the semantic descriptions of user preferences and item contents through the ontological relations of the involved concepts.

Based on the proposed ontology-based user and item profile models, we define a personalised recommendation approach based on an adaptation of the vector-space information retrieval model (Baeza-Yates & Ribeiro-Neto, 1999), which exploits the semantic extension technique mentioned above. Analogously, we also define the notion of *semantic context* as the set of ontological concepts present in the annotations of the items recently browsed or evaluated by the user. The context is described by a vector representation, so it can be easily combined with the basic personalised model.

Furthermore, alternatively to global comparisons of profiles made by state of the art recommenders, we propose a diversity-aware approach that leverages partial yet meaningful similarities between users even if they are not globally alike, but share strongly similar preferences in focused areas of interest. The hypothesis is that since user interests are not made of a single piece, an approach that deals with them as such would have inevitable limitations. We realize this principle by splitting user profiles according to meaningful groups/layers of preferences shared among users, and establishing user similarities based on the sub-profiles rather than the global profiles. Thus, coincidences of unusual preferences have further chances of being found when dealing with smaller profiles, focused on specific semantic areas of interest and taste. The semantic information plays a key role in this strategy, as a basis to relate preference data together, and determine meaningful interest layers. The relations between users at the different semantic layers represent different latent communities of interest, and are used to provide recommendations in more focused or specialised conceptual areas, even when the whole user profiles are globally fairly dissimilar. Our contribution can be expressed as building hybrid recommendation models that combine user profiles collaboratively at various semantic levels, in response to different groups of shared preferences.

In this paper, we present an evaluation of the above approaches in a controlled yet live and open setting, enabling a realistic evaluation of context-aware recommendation with interactive user feedback. Framing our scientific contributions within a consistent connection to the perspective of a feasible working application, the evaluation is conducted on a news recommender prototype, News@hand, in which all the proposed methods are integrated. As the implementation and evaluation of our methods require the availability of appropriate semantic resources, not readily available today from public sources, automatic knowledge base creation (i.e., ontology population) and semantic annotation techniques have been developed and evaluated as part of the work presented here.

The rest of the paper is organised as follows. Section 2 presents an overview and discussion of works that are related to our research. Section 3 describes the proposed ontology-based representation for recommender systems. Section 4 explains the recommendation methods we have built upon that enhanced semantic representation. Section 5 describes News@hand, the news recommender system that integrates the recommendation methods, and is been used as an evaluation platform. Section 6 presents the experiments performed with News@hand and results thereof. Finally, Section 7 provides conclusions and future work.

2. RELATED WORK: SEMANTICS IN RECOMMENDER SYSTEMS

One of the trends of work in the introduction of semantics for recommendation has been oriented towards the exploitation of social information in the recommendation methods. Approaches have been proposed that automatically collect explicit or implicit social network information from the Web and other sources, in order to apply Semantic Network Analysis methods for the study of online communities. Flink (Mika, 2005) is a system for the extraction, aggregation and visualisation of online social networks. It employs semantic tech-

nologies for reasoning with personal information extracted from a number of electronic information sources including Web pages, emails, publication archives, and FOAF profiles. Extending the traditional bipartite model of ontologies (classes and instances) with the social dimension leads to a tripartite model of the Semantic Web, namely the layer of communities and their relations (users), the layer of semantics (ontologies and their relations), and the layer of content items and their relations (the hypertext Web).

Aside from explicit social relations, further research works have focused their attention on finding implicit relations among people. Hence, for example, Liu, Maes, and Davenport (2006) present an implementation of "taste fabrics", a semantic mining approach to model personal tastes for different topics of interests. The taste fabric affords a flexible representation of a user in the taste-space, enabling a keyword-based profile to be relaxed by a spreading activation pattern. An evaluation of taste-based recommendation shows it compares favourably to classic CF methods, and whereas CF is an opaque mechanism, recommendation using taste fabrics can be effectively visualised, thus enhancing transparency and user trust.

In addition to the explicit and implicit definition of social relations (and the subsequent discovery of communities) to be exploited by recommender systems, other works have studied the incorporation of semantic-based knowledge representations to describe user and/or item profiles, and making enhanced, more understandable recommendations. An adaptation of the item-based CF method integrating semantic similarities for items with rating- or usage-based similarities is presented in Mobasher, Jin, and Zhou (2004). The reported experimental results demonstrate the integrated approach yields significant advantages both in terms of improving accuracy, as in dealing with sparse datasets. An approach to ontological user profiling in recommender systems is presented in Middleton, Roure, and Shadbolt (2004). Working on the problem of recommending on-line academic research papers, the authors present two systems, Quickstep and Foxtrot, which create user profiles monitoring the behaviour of the users, and gathering relevance feedback from them. The obtained profiles are represented in terms of a research topic ontology. Research papers are classified using ontological classes, and the proposed recommenders suggest documents seen by similar people on their current topics of interest. In this scenario, ontological inference is shown to ease user profiling, external ontological knowledge seems to successfully improve the recommendations, and the profile visualisation is used to enhance profiling accuracy.

More recently, Anand and Mobasher (2007) take up again the issue that most currently available recommender systems still tend to use very simplistic user models to generate recommendations. The authors contend for a fundamental shift in terms of how a user is modelled in a recommender. Specifically, they distinguish between a user's long term and short term memories, and propose a recommendation process that uses these two memories. Context-based retrieval cues are obtained to retrieve relevant preference information stored in the long term memory, and the identified relevant preferences are used in conjunction with the information stored in the short term memory to make recommendations. The paper introduces three types of contextual cues: collaborative, behavioural and semantic, and provides empirical evidence that the approach improves recommendation quality. An implementation of the semantic contextualisation proposed in the previous work is described in Sieg, Mobasher, and Burke (2007). In this case, the authors present a strategy for personalised search that involves building models of user contexts as ontological profiles by assessing implicitly derived interest scores to concepts defined in a domain ontology. A spreading activation algorithm is used to maintain the interest scores based on the user's ongoing behaviour. The conducted experiments show that re-ranking search results based on the interest scores and the semantic evidence in an ontological user profile are effective in presenting the most relevant results

to the user. Finally, Shoval, Maidel, and Shapira (2008) propose the incorporation of a common ontology that enables describing both the users' and items' profiles with concepts taken from the same vocabulary. Based on this representation approach, and utilising the ontology hierarchy, the authors present a content-based method for filtering items for a given user. The active user's profile is compared with the item profiles using a similarity measure that takes into account the occurrence of common concepts in both profiles, as well as the existence of "related" items according to their position in the ontology hierarchy. Based on the computed similarities, items are ranked for the user. At the time of this writing, the method is being implemented in ePaper, a personalised electronic newspaper, using an ontology that mirrors the two first levels of the IPTC news taxonomy (http://www.iptc.org/NewsCodes).

Our semantic-based knowledge representation and recommendation proposals, and their integrated implementation in a news recommender system, are related to the works outlined in this section.

- **Ontology-Based Knowledge Representation:** Similarly to Mika (2005), we base and focus our research on a tripartite knowledge model, where user and item spaces are connected through a semantic one. As done in Shoval, Maidel, and Shapira (2008), we propose to build this layer in terms of concepts available in domain ontologies. In our case, domain ontologies and items are respectively populated and annotated in an automatic way.
- **Spreading of Semantic Preferences:** The extension of ontology-based user profiles through the semantic relations of the domain ontologies (Mobasher, Jin, & Zhou, 2004; Sieg, Mobasher, & Burke, 2007) is also studied in this work. We show that this strategy is beneficial to mitigate the cold-start and sparsity problems in a user study.

- **Implicit Communities of Interest:** Like Liu, Maes, and Davenport (2006), we discover implicit user relations (communities) from the similarities existing among semantic user preferences. Differently, in our approach, the identification of such communities is carried out at different semantic interest layers, laying the ground for building what we shall call multilayered Communities of Interest.

- **Personalised and Context-Aware Recommendations:** Personalisation (Anand & Mobasher, 2007) and contextualisation (Sieg, Mobasher, & Burke, 2007) of content retrieval exploiting an ontological knowledge representation are proposed and evaluated in this work.

- **Hybrid Recommendations:** Explicit item-based collaborative recommendation from ontological user profiles was presented in Middleton, Roure, and Shadbolt (2004). Here, we propose the exploitation of the underlying multilayered communities found by our approach, for making hybrid recommendations.

- **A Prototype Recommender System:** The integration and evaluation of our content-based and collaborative recommendation strategies in a news recommender system is reported herein. Similarly to ePaper system (Shoval, Maidel, & Shapira, 2008), our prototype will make use of the IPTC news codes ontology to describe both user and item profiles, but will extend such taxonomy with concepts obtained from news contents.

3. KNOWLEDGE REPRESENTATION

Our general recommendation approaches make use of explicit user profiles (as opposed to for example sets of preferred items). User preferences are represented as vectors $\mathbf{u} = (u_1, u_2, ..., u_K) \in [-1,1]^K$ where the weight $u_k \in [-1,1]$ measures the intensity of the interest of user $u \in U$ for concept $c_k \in O$ (a class or an instance) in a domain ontology O, K being the total number of concepts in the ontology. A positive value indicates that the user is interested in the concept, while a negative one reflects a user's dislike for the concept. Similarly, items $i \in I$ are assumed to be described (annotated) by vectors $\mathbf{i} = (i_1, i_2, ..., i_K) \in [0,1]^K$ of concept weights, in the same space as user preferences. The recommendation approaches we shall develop upon this basis (which are described later in Section 4) do not prescribe a particular granularity for the semantic representation, the domain ontology, or the user profiles. This is largely generic in the representation and recommendation approaches, and left for the application to instantiate it. Section 5 will illustrate the instantiation of the framework by the integration of a medium-sized domain ontology in a news recommender prototype.

An ontology-based representation is richer and less ambiguous than a keyword-based or item-based model, providing a number of benefits:

- **Semantic Detail:** A concept-driven representation of user preferences is generally more meaningful for and useful for personalisation. It enables more precise specifications of users' tastes, with less ambiguity than is involved in plain keyword terms. For instance, if the system just knows about a user interest involving the keyword "java", without further information the system cannot tell whether the user is interested in the programming language or the Pacific island. Stating the preference in terms of a concept such as "ProgrammingLanguage:Java" (the instance *Java* of the *Programming Language* class) is not ambiguous in that sense, and further, allows the exploitation of any known semantics associated with the concept (e.g., Java is object-oriented), its class (e.g., related to computers), etc., which may be available in a domain knowledge base.

- **Hierarchical Representation:** Ontology concepts are represented in a hierarchical way, through different hierarchy properties, such as *subClassOf, instanceOf* or *partOf*. Parents, ancestors, children and descendants of a concept give valuable information about the semantics of the concept. For instance, the concept *leisure* might be highly enriched by the semantics of each leisure activity, which would be described by the taxonomy that the concept could subsume.

- **Inference:** Ontology standards, such as RDF and OWL, support inference mechanisms that can be used to enhance the representation of user tastes and interests, so that, for instance, a user keen on *animals* (superclass of *dog*) could be also interested in items about dogs. Inversely, a user interested in *skiing, snowboarding* and *ice hockey* can be inferred with a certain confidence to be globally interested in *winter sports*. Also, a user keen on *Spain* could be assumed to like *Madrid*, through the *locatedIn* transitive relation, assuming that this relation had been seen as relevant for inferring previous underlying user's interests.

Figure 1 shows an example of conceptualised preferences. Circles indicate ontology classes and instances, solid lines represent hierarchical relations between pairs of classes (*subclassOf* property) or between classes and instances (*instanceOf* property), and dotted lines are associated to other arbitrary semantic properties. Having a set of three ontologies with information about art works, institutions and regions, let us suppose a user indicates an interest for the topic "visual art works", which is represented in the ontologies as a class *Visual Art Work* inheriting from the main class *Art Work*. The system is then able to infer preferences for *Visual Art Work* subtopics (trough the general property *subClassOf*), obtaining finer grain details about the user's preferences, such as potential interests in "paintings" and "photographs". Note that original and more specific preferences will prevail over the system's inference. In this case, as highlighted in the figure, the user is not interested in the concept "movie", whose negative weight prevails over the higher-level topic inference. Other arbitrary semantic relations can be exploited for preference extension, as shown in the figure (relations *exibitedAt, locatedIn*).

In addition to the above benefits, this kind of knowledge representation provides advantages in recommendation scenarios thanks to the use of semantic-based technologies.

- **Portability:** Based on XML standards, the domain knowledge, user profile, and item annotation information could be easily distributed, adapted and integrated in different recommender systems for different applications.

- **Domain Independence:** Using a semantic-based knowledge representation, recommendation algorithms can be designed independently from the domain of discourse. Ontology hierarchies, concepts and relations are the elements to be taken into consideration for the definition of new recommenders. In principle, no domain-dependent restrictions would affect the implementation and reuse of such systems. This is not feasible for example in model-based recommender systems, where probabilistic models are built from the available data, and cannot be used in different domains, unless the entire model is rebuilt with new data.

- **Multi-Source Annotation:** Assuming the existence of manual or automatic mechanisms to semantically annotate any type of content (text, images, audio, video, etc.),

Figure 1. Representation of user preferences as concepts of domain ontologies

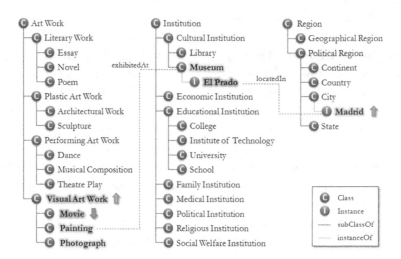

ontology-based recommenders could suggest items from multiple different sources without the need of changing their inner recommendation algorithms.

The use of ontology-based knowledge frameworks in recommender systems may also provide a series of advantages with respect other techniques, such as a better comprehension and explainability of the user's preferences and recommendations, an easy adaptation and extension of further personalization and recommendation models, and a potential integration of several sources of user information, which may be used to perform cross-domain recommendations. These represent promising research issues to address in the future.

3.1. Semantic Extension of User Preferences

To overcome cold-start and sparsity in user profiles, we propose a semantic preference spreading mechanism that expands the initial set of preferences stored in user profiles through explicit semantic relations with other concepts in the ontology. The activation of user preferences is based on an approximation to conditional probabilities.

Let $u_k \in [-1,1]$ be the preference (dislike/interest) of the user u for the ontology concept $c_k \in O$. The probability that c_x is relevant for the user can be expressed in terms of the probability that c_x and each concept $c_y \in O$ directly related to c_x in the ontology belong to the same interest topic, and the probability that c_y is relevant for the user. A similar formulation could be given for non-relevant concepts.

Let R be the set of all relations in O. The spreading strategy is based on weighting each relation $r \in R$ with a measure $w(r, c_x, c_y)$ that represents the probability that given the fact that $r(c_x, c_y)$ holds, c_x and c_y belong to the same topic. This is used for estimating the relevance of c_y when c_x is relevant for the user. With this measure, concepts are expanded through the relations of the ontology using a Constrained Spreading Activation (CSA) mechanism over the semantic network defined by these relations. As a result, the initial user profile $\mathbf{P}_u = \{c_x \in O \mid u_{c_x} \neq 0\}$ is extended to a larger vector $\mathbf{EP}_u$, which is computed as:

$$\mathbf{EP}_u[c_y]$$
$$= \begin{cases} \mathbf{P}_u[c_y] & \text{if } \mathbf{P}_u[c_y] > 0 \\ R\left(\{\mathbf{EP}_u[c_x] \cdot power(c_x)\}_{c_x \in O, r(c_x, c_y)}\right) & \text{otherwise} \end{cases}$$

where $power\left(c_x\right) \in [0,1]$ is a propagation power assigned to each concept c_x (1 by default), and

$$R\left(\mathbf{X}\right) = \sum_{S \subset \mathbb{N}_n} \left\{ (-1)^{|S|+1} \times \prod_{i \in S} x_i \right\},$$

having $\mathbf{X} = \{x_i\}_{i=0}^n, x_i \in [0,1]$.

The above formula is an adaptation of CSA (Cohen & Kjeldsen, 1987; Crestani, 1997) to an ontology-based personalized retrieval setting developed in Vallet et al. (2007). Figure 2 shows a simple example of the preference extension process, where three concepts are involved. The user has preferences for two of these concepts, which are related to a third through two different ontology relations. The extension shows how a third preference is inferred, accumulating the evidence of relevance from the original two preferences.

The relation weights in our experiments are different for each semantic relation type, and could in fact be different depending on the concepts being related, though in our experiments we used fixed values for each relation type, that is, $w\left(r, c_x, c_y\right) = w(r)$. Relation weighting is a modular problem in our approach, which can be addressed by several methods (co-occurrence analysis, etc.). In our experiments, we used manual values taken from prior work (Vallet et al., 2007).

Our constrained spreading activation technique can reach any concept which is connected through a semantic path (formed by semantic relations of the ontology) with the current concepts of the user's profile and context (see Sections 4.1 and 4.2). The pseudocode of the technique is shown in Figure 3. The spreading mechanism is characterised not only by the propagation decay factors (i.e., the multiplying values $w(r)$ in [0, 1]) of the semantic relations between concepts, but also by several constraints such as (1) the minimum threshold weight value å a concept has to have in order to propagate its activation to related

Figure 2. Example of semantic preference extension computation

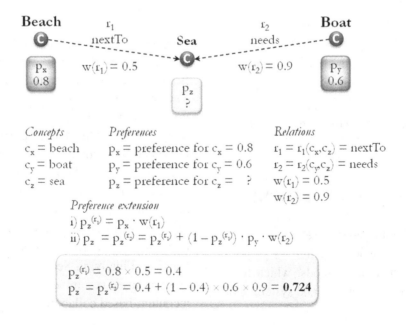

Figure 3. Pseudocode of the semantic spreading algorithm

```
function expand(P, EP, w) {
   // Init the expanded concept weights with the input ones
   for ( c_x ∈ O ) {
      EP[c_x] = P[c_x]
   }

   // Create a priority queue based on concept weights (initially null)
   Q ← buildPriorityQueue(O ×{prev=0,hierarchyLevel=0,expansionLevel=0})

   while ( Q.isEmpty() == false ) {
      // Extract the next concept to expand
      (c_x, prev_x, hierarchyLevel, expansionLevel) ← Q.pop()

      // Check the minimum concept weight constraint
      if ( EP[c_x] < ε ) {
         exit          // The remaining concept weights are also below ε
      }

      // Check the maximum expansion constrain
      if(expansionLevel ≥ n_e){
         goto while
      }

      // Expand the neighbourhood of the current concept
      for({r, c_y} ∈ c_x.getNeighbourhood()){
         prev_y = EP[c_y]

         // Check the hierarchical level expansion constrain
         if(EP[c_y] = 1 OR (r.isHierarchical() AND hierarchyLevel ≥ n_h)){
            goto for
         }

         // "Undo" the last update from c_x
         EP[c_y] ← (EP[c_y] - w(r,c_x,c_y)*power(c_x)*prev_x) /
                   (1 - EP[c_y]*w(r,c_x,c_y)*w_f(c_x,n_f)*power(c_x)*prev_x

         // Do the propagation taking into account the fan-out factor
         EP[c_y] ← EP[c_y] + (1 - EP[c_y])*w(r,c_x,c_y)*w_f(c_x,n_f)*power(c_x)*EP[c_x]

         if(r.isHierarchical()){
            hierarchyLevel++;
         }

         Q.push(c_y,prev_y,hierarchyLevel,expansionLevel)
      }

      expansionLevel++
   }
}
```

concepts, (2) the maximum distance (number of propagation steps) n_e to be reached by the spreading algorithm, and (3) the maximum fan-out (i.e., the number of outgoing links) n_f a concept can propagate its activation through, to reduce the "hub effect" in concepts with many relations to other concepts.

4. RECOMMENDATION METHODS

Building upon the knowledge representation model presented in the previous section, we propose several recommendation methods, which have been integrated in the News@hand system. Our evaluation methodology foresees an experimental design supporting the analysis of the specific effect of each of these techniques in the overall system performance, as will be reported in Section 6. The first method, explained in Section 4.1, suggests items to a single user considering only the preferences described in his profile. The second, presented in Section 4.2, incorporates semantic contextual information into the above content-based recommendation method. Specifically, we define the notion of semantic context as the set of ontological concepts present in the annotations of items recently browsed or evaluated by the user. Finally, in Section 4.3, we extend our content-based recommendation method through a content-based collaborative (i.e., hybrid) strategy, which establishes and exploits user relations according to semantic similarities between user and item profiles.

4.1. Personalised Recommendation

Our notion of personalised recommendation is based on the definition of a matching algorithm that provides a personal relevance measure $pref(u, i)$ of an item i for a user u. This measure is set according to the semantic preferences $\mathbf{u}$ of the user and the semantic annotations $\mathbf{i}$ of the item, and is based on the cosine function for vector similarity computation:

$$pref\left(u, i\right) = \cos\left(\mathbf{u}, \mathbf{i}\right) = \frac{\mathbf{u} \cdot \mathbf{i}}{\mathbf{u} \times \mathbf{i}} \ .$$

The formula matches two weighted-concept vectors and produces a value in $[0, 1]$. Values close to 0 are obtained when the two vectors are dissimilar, and indicate that user preferences negatively match the content metadata. On the other hand, values close to 1 indicate that user preferences significantly match the content metadata, which means a potential interest of the user for the item.

In Section 6, we empirically show that this and subsequent recommendation models perform better when they are used with user profiles extended through the semantic extension mechanism introduced in Section 3.1.

4.2. Context-Aware Recommendation

Context is a difficult notion to capture in a recommender system (Adomavicius & Tuzhilin, 2011; Dey, 2001), and the elements that can be considered under the notion of context are manifold: user tasks/goals, recently browsed/rated items, physical environment and location, time, social environment, etc. As representative examples, the reader is referred to Ahn et al. (2007), Billsus and Pazzani (2000), Räck, Arbanowski, and Steglich (2006), Sujiyama, Hatano, and Yoshikawa (2004). Complementarily to these, we propose a particular notion of context for semantic content retrieval: the *semantic runtime context*, which we define as the background topics $\mathbf{C}_u^t$ under which activities of a user u occur within a given unit of time t. A runtime context is represented in our approach as a set of weighted concepts from a domain ontology O. This set is obtained by collecting the concepts that have been involved in user's actions (e.g., accessed items) during a session. Similarly to Middleton, Roure, and Shadbolt (2004), the context is built in such a way that the importance of concepts $c_k \in O$ fades away with time (number of steps back when the concept occurred) by a decay factor $\hat{\imath} \in [0, 1]$:

$$\mathbf{C}_u^t\left[c_k\right] = \hat{\imath} \cdot \mathbf{C}_u^{t-1}\left[c_k\right] + (1 - \hat{\imath}) \cdot \mathbf{Req}_u^t\left[c_k\right]$$

$\mathbf{Req}_u^t \in [0, 1]^{|O|}$ c_k t $\hat{\imath}$ Once the context is built, a contextual activation of preferences is achieved by finding semantic paths linking preferences to context. These paths are made of existing relations between concepts in the ontology, following the CSA technique explained in Section 3.1. This process can be understood as finding an intersection between user preferences and the semantic context, where the final computed weight of each concept represents the degree to which it belongs to each set (Figure 4). The perceived effect of contextualisation is that user interests that are out of focus, under a given context, are disregarded, and those that are in the semantic scope of the ongoing user activity are considered for recommendation.

After the semantic user profile $\mathbf{P}_u^t = \mathbf{u}$ and context $\mathbf{C}_u^t$ are propagated through the ontology relations, a combination of their expanded versions $\mathbf{EP}_u^t$ and $\mathbf{EC}_u^t$ is exploited for making context-aware recommendations using the following expression:

Figure 4. Extension and contextualisation of user preferences

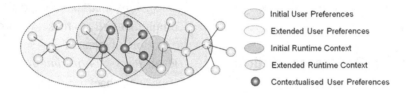

Initial User Preferences
Extended User Preferences
Initial Runtime Context
Extended Runtime Context
Contextualised User Preferences

$$pref_C(u,i)$$
$$= \lambda \cdot pref\left(\mathrm{EP}_u, i\right) + \left(1 - \lambda\right) \cdot pref\left(\mathrm{EC}_u, i\right)$$

$$= \lambda \cdot \cos\left(\mathbf{EP}_u, \mathbf{i}\right) + \left(1 - \lambda\right) \cdot \cos\left(\mathbf{EC}_u, \mathbf{i}\right)$$

where $\lambda \in [0,1]$ measures the strength of the personalisation component with respect to the current context. This parameter can be manually established by the user, or dynamically adapted by the system according to multiple factors, such as the current size of the context, and the automatic detection of a change in the user's search focus.

4.3. Hybrid Recommendation

Complementarily to the two previous methods, which apply to single users, we explore the potential of the ontology-based representation to enhance collaborative recommendation techniques. Of all three approaches this is the one which more deeply explores the conjunction and joint processing of complex hybrid networks involving users, items and concepts. In the approach, links among concepts (semantic networks), between users and items (ratings), and between items and concepts (annotations) are explicit, where as relations between users are implicitly (collaboratively) derived from their links to concepts and items.

We propose to exploit the links between users and concepts to extract relations among users and derive semantic Communities of Interest (CoI) according to common preferences. Analysing the

structure of the ontologies, and taking into account the preference weights of the user profiles, we cluster the domain concept space generating groups of interests shared by several users. Thus, those users who share interests of a specific concept cluster are connected in the community, and their preference weights measure their degree of membership to each cluster.

Specifically, a vector $\mathbf{c}_k = (c_{k,1}, c_{k,2}, \ldots, c_{k,M}) \in [-1,1]^M$ is assigned to each ontology concept c_k present in the preferences of at least one user, where $c_{k,m} = u_{m,k}$ is the weight of concept c_k in the profile of user u_m. Based on these vectors, a classic hierarchical clustering strategy is applied. The obtained clusters represent the groups of preferences (topics of interests) in the concept-user vector space shared by a significant number of users.

Once the concept clusters are created, each user can be assigned to a specific cluster. The similarity between a user's preferences $\mathbf{u} = (u_1, u_2, \ldots, u_K) \in [-1,1]^K$ and a cluster C_q is computed by: $sim\left(u, C_q\right) = \dfrac{\sum_{c_k \in C_q} u_k}{\left|C_q\right|}$, where c_k represents the concept that corresponds to the u_k component of the user preference vector, and $\left|C_q\right|$ is the number of concepts included in the cluster.

Taking into account the concept clusters, user profiles are partitioned into semantic segments. Each of these segments corresponds to a concept cluster, and represents a subset of user interests shared by the users who contributed to the clustering process. By thus introducing further structure in user profiles, it is now possible to define relations among users at different levels, obtaining a multilayered network of users.

Using our semantic multilayered CoI proposal, we present two recommendation models that generate ranked lists of items taking into account the obtained links between users. The first model, which is labelled as *UP* (i.e., user profile based), generates a unique ranked list based on the similarities between the items and all the existing semantic clusters. The second model, labelled *UP-q,* provides a ranking for each semantic cluster C_q. The strategies are formalised next. In the following, for a user profile $\mathbf{u}$, an information item vector $\mathbf{i}$, and a cluster C_q, we denote by $\mathbf{u}^q$ and $\mathbf{i}^q$ the projections of the corresponding concept vectors onto cluster C_q, i.e., the k-th components of $\mathbf{u}^q$ and $\mathbf{i}^q$ are u_k and i_k respectively if $c_k \in C_q$, and 0 otherwise.

Model UP

The semantic profile of a user u is used by the system to return a unique ranked list. The preference score of an item i is computed as a weighted sum of the indirect preference values based on similarities with other users in each cluster. The sum is weighted by the similarities with the clusters, as follows:

$$pref\left(u,i\right) = \sum_q \mathrm{nsim}(i,C_q)\sum_{v \neq u}\mathrm{nsim}_q\left(u,v\right)\cdot \mathrm{sim}_q\left(v,i\right),$$

where

$$\mathrm{sim}\left(i,C_q\right)$$
$$= \frac{\sum_{c_k \in C_q} i_k}{\mathbf{i}\sqrt{\left|C_q\right|}}, \mathrm{nsim}\left(i,C_q\right) = \frac{\mathrm{sim}\left(i,C_q\right)}{\sum_{C \in C}\mathrm{sim}\left(i,C\right)}$$

are the single and normalised similarities between the item i and the cluster C_q, C being the set of all clusters,

$$\mathrm{sim}_q\left(u,v\right) = \cos\left(\mathbf{u}^q, \mathbf{v}^q\right)$$
$$= \frac{\mathbf{u}^q \cdot \mathbf{v}^q}{\mathbf{u}^q \times \mathbf{v}^q}, \mathrm{nsim}_q\left(u,v\right) = \frac{\mathrm{sim}_q\left(u,v\right)}{\sum_{w \neq u}\mathrm{sim}_q\left(u,w\right)}$$

layer between item and user q between users u and v, and

$$\mathrm{sim}_q\left(u,i\right) = \cos\left(\mathbf{u}^q, \mathbf{i}^q\right) = \frac{\mathbf{u}^q \cdot \mathbf{i}^q}{\mathbf{u}^q \times \mathbf{i}^q}$$

is the similarity at layer q between item i and user u.

The idea behind this first model is to compare the current user's interests with those of the others users, and, taking into account the similarities among them, weight all their complacencies about the different items. The comparisons are done for each concept cluster measuring the similarities between the items and the clusters. We thus attempt to recommend an item in a double way. First, according to the item characteristics, and second, according to the connections among user interests, in both cases at different semantic layers.

Model UP-q

The preferences of the user are used by the system to return one ranked list per cluster, obtained from the similarities between users and items at each cluster layer. The ranking that corresponds to the cluster for which the user has the highest membership value is selected. The expression is analogous to *UP* model equation, but does not include the term that connects the item with each cluster C_q:

$$pref\left(u,i\right) = \sum_{v \neq u}\mathrm{nsim}_q\left(u,v\right)\cdot \mathrm{sim}_q\left(v,i\right),$$

where q maximises $\mathrm{sim}(i, C_q)$.

Analogously to the previous model, this one makes use of the relations among the user interests, and the user satisfactions with the items. The difference here is that recommendations are done separately for each layer. If the current semantic cluster is well identified for a specific item, we expect to achieve better precision/recall results than those obtained with the overall model.

5. NEWS@HAND

Specific aspects of the recommendation methods described in the previous section were evaluated in prior studies with artificial datasets created from external sources and standard collections (Cantador, Bellogín, & Castells, 2008a). The experiments with standard datasets are needed to isolate and focus on specific aspects of our approaches, and adhere to established methodologies and benchmarks. At the same time, these experiments require simplifications and adaptations of our approaches to the constraints and limitations of the collection data, which restricts the scope of techniques that can be evaluated. In particular, standard datasets do not properly support the evaluation of contextual methods involving dynamic interaction with users, in a fair enough approximation of the conditions of a real setting. Also, we aim to study the combined effect of the different methods, which in standard experiments would require different datasets.

To meet these aims, we have implemented News@hand, a news recommender system in which all the proposed recommendation strategies are integrated, and where textual contents of news are annotated with concepts belonging to a set of ontologies covering various domains. With this system, users can interact with the methods for longer periods of time, and further information can be captured as required to measure the effectiveness of the proposed techniques.

Besides this integrative evaluation, the experience with News@hand has been useful to uncover the difficulties involved in the transition of the presented ontology-based models and strategies to a real application. While building the system, a number of research challenges emerged, for which additional solutions have been developed. Specifically, we needed to implement a technique to populate (i.e., create instances in) the domain ontologies, and an automatic mechanism to semantically annotate the news articles.

In the following, we describe News@hand, highlighting the important aspects of its architecture (Section 5.1), and explaining the followed ontology population (Section 5.2), and item annotation (Section 5.3) strategies.

5.1. Architecture

Like in other systems (Ahn et al., 2007; Jones, Quested, & Thomson, 2000; Nadjarbashi-Noghani et al., 2005), in News@hand, news are automatically and periodically retrieved from several on-line news services via RSS feeds. Using Natural Language Processing (NLP) and indexing tools, the title and summary of the retrieved news are annotated with concepts (classes and instances) of the domain ontologies available to the system. Thus, for example, all the news about actors, actresses and similar terms may be annotated with the concept "actor". News@hand ontologies contain concepts of multiple domains such as education, politics, science, technology, business, entertainment, sports, etc. As done in Ahn et al. (2007) and Billsus and Pazzani (1999), a TF-IDF technique is applied to assign weights to the annotated concepts, measuring their importance (informativeness) to the news contents in the document repository.

News@hand has a client/server architecture, where users interact with the system through a Web interface in which they receive on-line news recommendations, and update their semantic profiles. A dynamic graphical interface (Figure 5) allows the system to automatically store all the

Figure 5. A typical news recommendation page in News@hand

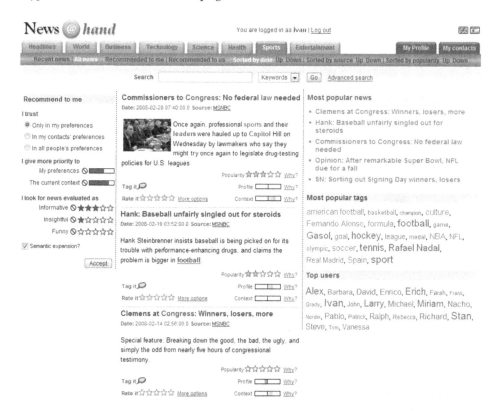

users' inputs, analyse their behaviour with the system, update their semantic preferences, and adjust the recommendations in real time. Similarly to Claypool et al. (1999), Das et al. (2007), and Chu and Park (2009), implicit and explicit user preferences are taken into account, via manual ratings and tags, and via automatic learning from the users' actions. News@hand has a preference learning module that identifies concepts annotating recent consumed (browsed, rated, tagged) items which are susceptible of being included in the long term user profile. We do not explain News@hand preference learning mechanism since it is out of the scope of the paper. The reader is referenced to Cantador et al. (2008) and Picault et al. (2011) for further details. On the other hand, the system integrates specific facilities for manual user profile building, such as an ontology browser,

and an ontology concept search engine for instant ontology class and instance suggestion, in the form of a query completion facility in the search box.

Leveraging the semantically annotated news items, the defined ontology-based user profiles, and the knowledge represented by the domain ontologies, a set of recommendation algorithms is executed. Specifically, News@hand integrates all the recommendation models explained in Section 4, i.e., personalised, context-aware, and multilayer recommenders. Figure 6 shows a detailed schema of the system modules which are directly involved in the domain-independent semantic-based recommendation and user profiling processes. In the figure, the arrows indicate dependency relationships from a source to a target component. Three main layers of related modules can be distinguished:

Figure 6. Architecture of News@hand

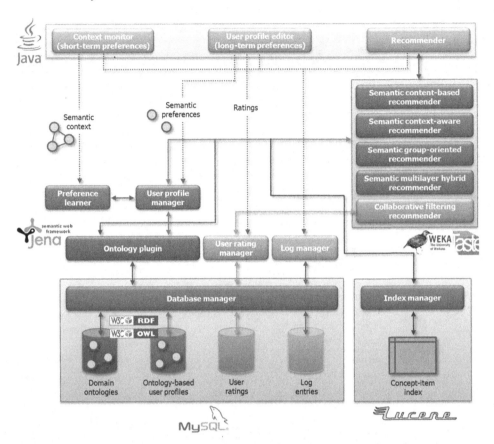

- **The Server-Side Access Layer:** (top part of the figure) Is composed by those modules that receive requests from a client interface, and return the corresponding results: short- and long-term preference reads/updates, and recommendation responses.

- **The Recommendation Layer:** (right part of the figure) Contains and combines the proposed semantic-based personalised, context-aware and hybrid recommenders.

- **The Data Access Layer:** (bottom part of the figure) Provides functionalities to manage the domain, user preference, user rating, log, and item annotation information exploited by the system using ontologies, databases and indices.

5.2. Knowledge Base

In this section, we describe the Knowledge Base (KB) creation methods developed as part of the addressed research problem. A total of 17 ontologies have been used. They are adaptations of the IPTC ontology (http://ir.ii.uam.es/news-at-hand/iptc-ontology_v01.rdfs), which contains concepts of multiple domains. They have been populated with semantic information extracted from news contents and social tags, applying an automatic population mechanism that exploits Wikipedia, and is explained below. A total of 137,254 Wikipedia entries were used to populate 744 classes with 119,497 instances. Table 1 gathers the characteristics of the generated KB. In Cantador, Bellogín, and Castells (2008b), we present a manual evaluation in which the ontology population process obtained 69.9% and 84.4% average accuracy values for class and ontology assignments respectively (Table 1), according to 8,500 assessments provided by 20 subjects.

The ontologies are populated with semantic concepts associated to noun terms extracted from the news contents to be annotated and recommended, and tags manually introduced by users (Szomszor et al., 2008). These terms are categorised as common nouns (e.g., *actor*) and proper nouns (e.g., *Brad Pitt*). The terms belonging to the first category are easily processable because their corresponding semantic concepts are the terms themselves. In this case, with simple morphological transformations, the concepts can be found in English dictionaries like WordNet (Miller, 1995). The terms of the second category may result in a complex processing. In order to

infer their semantic concepts, general multi-domain semantic knowledge is needed. For News@ hand, we propose to extract that information from Wikipedia. We have implemented an automatic mechanism that creates ontology instances using, among other things, the Wikipedia categories of the terms. We explain in detail the whole population process in the following.

5.2.1. Semantic Information Extraction

Many of the entities are ambiguous, having several meanings for different contexts. For instance, the same term "java" could be assigned to a picture of the Pacific island, or a Web page about the programming language. One approach to address disambiguation is by using the information available in Wikipedia.

Table 1. Number of classes and instances available in News@hand KB, and average accuracy of class/ontology assignments

Ontology	#classes	#instances	Avg. #instances/class	Memory (KB)	Avg. accuracy
Arts, culture, entertainment	87	33,278	383	5,347	78.7 / 93.3
Crime, law, justice	22	971	44	444	62.7 / 73.3
Disasters, accidents	16	287	18	358	74.7 / 84.0
Economy, business, finance	161	25,345	157	8,468	69.3 / 80.0
Education	20	3,542	177	649	57.5 / 76.7
Environmental issues	41	20,581	502	692	72.0 / 85.3
Health	26	1,078	41	967	65.3 / 89.3
Human interests	6	576	96	288	64.0 / 84.0
Labour	6	133	22	688	70.7 / 78.7
Lifestyle, leisure	29	4,895	169	820	72.0 / 90.7
Politics	54	3,206	59	2,989	60.0 / 81.3
Religion, belief	31	3,248	105	711	84.0 / 90.7
Science, technology	50	7,869	157	1,591	68.0 / 86.7
Social issues	39	8,673	222	2,649	70.7 / 85.3
Sports	124	5,567	45	6,454	72.0 / 86.7
Unrests, conflicts, wars	23	1,820	79	355	61.3 / 80.0
Weather	9	66	7	92	69.7 / 89.5
	744	**119,497**	**134.3** (avg.)	**33,562**	**69.9 / 84.4** (avg.)

A Wikipedia article is fairly structured: the title of the page is the entity name itself, the content is divided into well delimited sections, and a first paragraph is dedicated to possible disambiguation for the corresponding term. For example, the page of the entry "apple" starts with sentences such as "This article is about the fruit...", "For the Beatles multimedia corporation, see...", "For the technology company, see...".

Apart from these elements, every article contains a set of collaboratively generated categories. Hence, for example, the categories created for the concept "Teide" are: world heritage sites in Spain, Tenerife, mountains of Spain, volcanoes of Spain, national parks of Spain, stratovolcanoes, hotspot volcanoes, and decade volcanoes. Processing the previous information, we could infer that "Teide" is a volcano located in Spain.

Disambiguation and categorisation information have been therefore extracted from Wikipedia for every concept appearing in our news item and social tag datasets.

5.2.2. Categorisation of Terms Into Ontology Classes

The assignment of an ontology class to a Wikipedia entry is based on a morphological matching measure between the name and the categories of the entry, and the "names" of the ontology classes. The ontology classes with most similar names to the name and categories of the entry are chosen as the classes whereof the corresponding individual (instance) is to be created. The created instances are assigned a URI containing the entry name, and RDFS labels with the Wikipedia category names.

To better explain the proposed matching method, let us consider the following example. Let "Brad Pitt" be the concept we want to instantiate. If we look for this concept in Wikipedia, a page with information about the actor is returned. At the end of the page, several categories are shown: "action film actors", "American film actors", "American

television actors", "best supporting actor Golden Globe (film)", "living people", "Missouri actors", "Oklahoma (state) actors", etc.

After retrieving that information, all the terms (tokens) appearing in the name and categories of the entry (which we will henceforth refer to as entry terms) are morphologically compared with the names of the ontology classes (by the name of a class we mean all the possible textual forms of the class, assuming a class-label mapping is available, as is usually the case). Applying singularisation and stemming, and computing the Levenshtein distance, only the entry terms that match some class name above a certain similarity threshold (set to 2 in the experiments) are kept. For instance, suppose that "action", "actor", "film", "people", and "television" are the entry terms sufficiently close to some ontology class names, e.g., "Actions", "Actors", "Films", "People" and "Television", respectively.

To select the most appropriate ontology class among the matching ones, we firstly create a vector whose components correspond to the filtered entry terms, taking as values the numbers of times each term appears in the entry and category names together. In the example, the vector might be as follows: {(action, 1), (actor, 6), (film, 3), (people, 1), (television, 1)}, assuming that "actor" appears in six categories of the Wikipedia entry "Brad Pitt", and so forth. Once this vector has been created, one or more ontology classes are selected by the following heuristic:

- If a single component holds the maximum value in the vector, we select the ontology class that matches the corresponding term. Here, we are assuming that in Wikipedia, a concept belongs to several categories that are semantically related through hierarchical relations (i.e., there are subcategories or sibling categories between them), and are morphologically similar, sharing main terms, e.g., subcategories of "Actors" are

"Female actors", "Male actors", "Ancient actors", "Child actors", "Fictional actors", etc.

- In case of a tie between several components having the maximum value, a new vector is created, containing the matched classes plus their taxonomic ancestor classes in the ontologies. Then, the weight of each component is computed as the number of times the corresponding class is found in this step. Finally, the original classes that have the highest valued ancestor in the new vector are selected.

In our example, the weight for the term "actor" is the highest, so we select its matching class as the category of the entry. Thus, assuming that the class matching this term was *Actor*, we finally define *Brad Pitt* as an instance of *Actor*.

Now suppose that, instead, the vector for *Brad Pitt* was {(actor, 1), (film, 1), (people, 1)}. In this case, there would be a tie in the matching classes, and we would apply the second case of the heuristic. We take the ancestor classes, which could be for example "cinema industry" for "actor", "cinema industry" for "film", and "mammal" for "person", and create a weighted list with the original and ancestor classes. Then, we count the number of times each class appears in the previous list, and create the new vector: {(actor, 1), (film, 1), (person, 1), (cinema industry, 2), (mammal, 1)}. Since the class *Cinema industry* has the highest weight, we finally select its sub-classes *Actor* and *Film* as the classes of the instance *Brad Pitt*.

We must note that our ontology population mechanism does not necessarily generate individuals following an "is-a" schema, but a more relaxed, fuzzier semantic association principle. This is not a problem for our final purposes, since the annotation and recommendation methods are themselves rooted on models of inherently approximated nature, for example regarding the relationships between concepts and item contents.

Nonetheless, there is a wide range of works on ontology population, and alternative techniques could be investigated in the future.

5.3. Item Annotation

News@hand periodically retrieves news items from websites of well-known news and media sources. These items are obtained via RSS feeds, and contain information of published news articles: their title, summary of contents, publication date, hyperlinks to the full texts, and related on-line images. The system analyses and automatically annotates the textual information (title and summary) of the RSS feeds with concepts (classes and instances) existing in the domain ontologies, and have been previously indexed.

Using Wraetlic NLP tools (Alfonseca et al., 2006), an annotation module removes stop words, and extracts relevant (simple and compound) terms, categorised according to their Part of Speech (PoS): nouns, verbs, adjectives, etc. Then, nouns are morphologically compared with the names of the classes and instances of the domain ontologies. The comparisons are done using an ontology index created with Lucene, and according to fuzzy metrics based on the Levenshtein distance. For each term, if similarities above a certain threshold are found, the most similar semantic concepts are chosen and added as annotations of the news items. After all the annotations are created, a TF-IDF technique computes and assigns weights to them. Figure 7 shows a more detailed view of the annotation mechanism, which takes as input the HTML document to annotate, and the system ontology indices, and returns as output new entries for the annotation database.

The steps illustrated in Figure 7 are:

- A Web document is parsed removing HTML tags and meaningless textual parts (in terms of not having or being related to news contents).

Figure 7. Semantic annotation mechanism

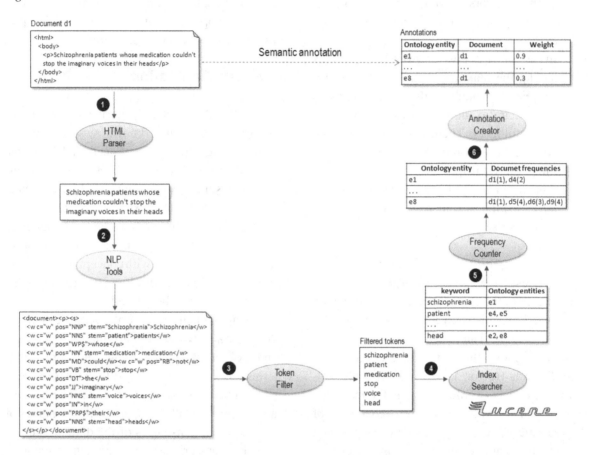

- The remaining text is analysed by the Wraetlic tools to extract the PoS and the stem of each term.

- The information provided by the linguistic analysis is used to filter the less meaningful terms (determinants, prepositions, etc.), and to identify those sets of terms that can operate as individual information units.

- The filtered terms are searched in the ontology indices, obtaining the subset of semantic entities to annotate.

- The annotations are weighted according to the semantic entity frequencies within individual documents and the whole collection.

- The annotations are added to a relational database.

The next subsections explain in more detail the previous steps and provide information about the gathered and annotated news contents. We run our semantic annotator on a set of 9,698 news items daily retrieved during two months. The ontological KB from which we obtained the semantic concepts appearing in the annotations is the one explained in Section 5.3. A total of 66,378 annotations were created. Table 2 describes the information gathered and annotated for each news section. In Cantador, Bellogín, and Castells (2008b), we present a manual evaluation in which the semantic annotation process of news items obtained an average accuracy of 74.8% (Table 2), according to 800 assessments provided by 20 subjects.

Table 2. Average number of annotations per news item, and average accuracy of the annotation process for each news section

News section	#news items	#annotations	Avg. #annotations/item	Avg. accuracy
Headlines	2,660	18,210	7	71.4
World	2,200	17,767	8	72.7
Business	1,739	13,090	8	79.2
Technology	303	2,154	7	76.3
Science	346	2,487	7	74.1
Health	803	4,874	6	73.1
Sports	603	2,453	4	75.8
Entertainment	1,044	5,343	5	76.0
	9,638	**66,369**	**6.5** (avg.)	**74.8** (avg.)

5.3.1. Natural Language Processing of News Contents

The NLP of news contents is performed by means of the Wraetlic linguistic-processing tools, an XML suite for processing texts which performs the following tasks:

- **Segmentation:** Identification of lexical units in the texts. It is done by two components: a *tokeniser* which finds word boundaries, and a sentence splitter which locates the sentence boundaries.
- **Part-of-Speech (PoS) Tagging:** Assignment of a PoS to each token. A *PoS tagger* labels each token with its corresponding PoS. Wraetlic tools utilise the PoS tags of the Penn Treebank corpus (http://www.cis.upenn.edu/~treebank), and take into consideration the grammatical context of a word (i.e., its surrounding terms) to infer its PoS.
- **Morphological Analysis:** Study of the inner structure of the words. For each token, a morphological analyser identifies the root (stem), which contains the basic meaning of the word, and the bound morphemes (prefixes and suffixes), which vary

the basic meaning, e.g., by pluralizing a noun (e.g., "parent" and "parents"), or by changing an adjective into a noun (e.g., "wide" and "width").

5.3.2. Semantic Annotation

The semantic annotator identifies ontology entities (classes and instances) within the text documents, and generates links between the identified ontology entities and the documents using index structures.

Semantic annotations are assigned weights that reflect how well the ontology entities represent the meaning of the document. Weights are computed by an adaptation of the TF-IDF algorithm, and based on the frequency of the occurrences of each ontology entity within the document. Initially, the frequency of occurrences of an entity in a document was defined as the number of times any of its associated "mappings" appears in the document text. In preliminary experiments; however, we realised that quite a number of occurrences were missed, since we were not considering pronouns as entity occurrences. To slightly overcome this limitation, we included a modification in the algorithm to also count pronoun occurrences in a sentence if an entity was previously identified. This modification does not help to increase the annotation accuracy or incorporate new annotations, but enhances the preciseness of the annotation weights that will be later used during the recommendation processes.

The weight $w_{k,n}$ in the annotation of a document i_n with an ontology entity c_k is computed as:

$$w_{k,n} = TF - IDF_{k,n} = \frac{freq_{k,n}}{\max_j freq_{j,n}} \times log \frac{N}{N_k},$$

where $freq_{k,n}$ is the number of occurrences in i_n of the keywords attached to c_k, $\max_j freq_{j,n}$ is the frequency of the most repeated ontology entity in i_n, N_k is the number of documents annotated with c_k, and N is the total number of documents.

On the other hand, we exploit the PoS information provided by Wraetlic tools to identify and discard those words that typically do not provide significant semantic information, and to group sets of words that can operate as individual semantic information units. The following are some examples of the considered word group patterns.

- *Noun + noun*, e.g., "tea cup".
- *Proper noun + proper noun*, e.g., "San Francisco".
- *Proper noun + proper noun + proper noun*, e.g., "Federico García Lorca".
- *Abbreviation + proper noun + proper noun*, e.g., "F. García Lorca".
- *Abbreviation + abbreviation + proper noun*, e.g., "F. G. Lorca".
- *Participle + preposition*, e.g., "located in", "stored in".
- *Modal verb + participle + preposition*, e.g., "is composed by", "is generated with".

6. EXPERIMENTS

The News@hand system was implemented to support comparative evaluations of the proposed recommendation models with real users, without the inherent restrictions that previous isolated (offline) experiments with public datasets imposed (Cantador, Bellogín & Castells, 2008a). The integration of the recommendation models in a single evaluation framework enables A/B tests in which each particular recommendation functionality is activated/deactivated for comparison. Specifically, we aim to evaluate and empirically compare the effect of semantic preference expansion and contextualization on our personalized recommender, and assess the potential improvements resulting from the proposed hybrid recommendation approach. By alternately activating/deactivating these functionalities, we discriminate, observe and measure the effect of each other separate from the rest. In our experiments, we state the following hypotheses:

- Extending the semantic descriptions of user preferences through the ontological relations of the involved concepts will mitigate sparsity and cold-start user situations. By applying semantic preference expansion, user profiles become larger, covering more areas of the conceptual space, and resulting in a higher likelihood of finding user and item similarities and correlations.
- Adding semantic context into the personalised recommendation process allows casting the user's preferences into the scope of the ongoing user activity, and obtaining more accurate recommendations.
- Building hybrid models that combine user profiles collaboratively at various semantic levels, in response to different groups of shared preferences, will enhance personalised recommendations, and would help to address the grey-sheep effect.

In this section, we present the conducted experiments, but before that, we identify the evaluation cases we should investigate in order to cover the validation of the above recommendation functionalities. We also list general steps that should be followed in the identified evaluation cases.

Activation/Deactivation of Functionalities

The following are identified as the significant comparisons to be investigated in order to properly assess the performance of the personalisation and recommendation functionalities.

- **Test 1:** *Evaluation of the semantic preference extension mechanism*, by activating and deactivating it in the personalised recommendation model. When no semantic expansion is applied, the above model reduces to a keyword vector space model, which is analogous to our semantic-based approach but performing exact matching between keyword vectors.
- **Test 2:** *Evaluation of the effect of semantic contextualisation*, by activating and deactivating it in the personalised recommendation model. In this case, the semantic preference extension mechanism is activated to better find intersections between the extended versions of the user profile and context.
- **Test 3:** *Evaluation of the hybrid recommendation approach against the personalised recommender*. In this case, the semantic preference extension mechanism is also activated since it enhances the semantic clustering process (Cantador et al., 2008).
- **Test 4:** *Evaluation of the hybrid recommendation approach against a rating-based CF strategy* (Konstan et al., 1997)

in order to measure the quality of provided recommendation. In this case, it is important to note that our aim is not no conduct an exhaustive empirical comparison of our hybrid recommender with state of the art CF strategies (Koren & Bell, 2011), but to show the feasibility of our approach in terms of obtaining performance values of comparable magnitude with respect to widely used standard recommendation approaches. In order to conduct more precise experiments, a significant amount of rating data would be needed, and issues such as the ontology population and semantic annotation processes would have to be improved.

Table 3 shows the functionalities in each of the four proposed testing cases. We consider the basic ontology-based approach without semantic preference extension as a form of simple keyword-based content retrieval technique. Since, in this case, we do not perform any semantic inference, concept vectors are treated as plain keyword vectors.

Execution of Evaluation Tasks

We propose an experimental protocol where every subject performs several tasks. Each pair of tasks is aimed to evaluate a specific testing case. A user does not have to deal with all the testing cases, but only a subset evenly distributed (according to a *Latin square* design) so that users and tasks do not introduce any bias in the performance of the different configurations. An average result is finally obtained for each evaluation case from the corresponding tasks performed by the users.

The following is a general scheme about how the experimentation has to be conducted.

- T specific search tasks are defined. We set $T = 6$.

Table 3. Functionalities to be evaluated (activated) in each testing case

		Personalisation functionalities			Recommendation Functionalities	
		Keyword-based personalisation	*Ontology-based personalisation*	*Context-aware personalisation*	*Collaborative filtering*	*Hybrid recommen-dation*
Evaluation of personalisation	*1*	X	X			
	2		X	X		
Evaluation of recommendation	*3*		X			X
	4				X	X

- Each user performs 2*S* tasks (with $S \leq T/2$). We set $S = 2$ (i.e., 4 search tasks per user).
- The tasks of each user will be used to evaluate *S* testing cases: a pair of tasks addresses a specific testing case activating or deactivating the involved functionalities.
- The first task for each user is used to make the user familiar with the system functionalities and experiment tasks. Thus, the evaluation of the results obtained in this task is omitted.
- Average precision/recall results are measured for each testing case and all users involved in the testing case.

The experiments described in the next subsections have been designed following the previous evaluation methodology. The definition of the tasks and the computation of the precision/recall values will be different depending on which functionality is tested.

6.1. Evaluating Personalised and Context-Aware Recommendations

We conducted an experiment to evaluate the precision of the personalisation and contextualisation functionalities. With this experiment we also wanted to investigate the influence of each mechanism in the integrated system, measuring the precision of the recommendations when a combination of both models is used.

The experiment was done with sixteen subjects, recruited among members of our department. They were PhD students and academics staff members. The experiment consisted of two phases, each composed of two different tasks.

- In the first phase, only the personalisation module was active, and its tasks were different in having the semantic preference extension enabled or disabled. The baseline in this phase is the keyword-based recommender, and the goal is to evaluate the effect of semantic expansion of user preferences.
- In the second phase, the semantic preference extension was activated, and the contextualisation was alternately activated and deactivated. On its second task, we also enabled the personalised recommendation in order to compare the effect of combining personalisation and contextualisation.

Search Tasks

A task was defined as finding out and evaluating those news items that were relevant to a given goal. Each goal was framed in a specific domain. We considered three domains: *telecommunications*, *banking* and *social care* issues. For each domain, a user profile and two search goals were manually defined (see next). Table 4 shows a summary of the involved tasks. To simplify the searching tasks, they are defined for pre-established sections and queries. For example, the task goal of finding news items about software piracy, illegal downloads and file sharing, $Q_{1,2}$, was reduced to evaluate those articles existing in *Entertainment* section that were retrieved from the query "music".

The configuration and assignment of the tasks were set according to the following principles:

- A user should not repeat a query during the experiment.
- The domains should be equally covered by each experiment phase.
- A user has to manually define a user profile once in the experiment.

For each phase, the combination of personalised and context-aware recommendations was established as a linear combination of their results using two weights $w_p, w_c \in [0,1]$:

$$score(u,i) = w_p \cdot pref(u,i) + w_c \cdot pref_C(u,i).$$

As explained before, in the personalisation phase, the contextualisation was disabled (i.e., $w_c = 0$). Its first tasks were performed without semantic extension, and its second tasks had the semantic extension activated. In the contextualisation phase, w_c was set to 1, and the extension was enabled. Its first tasks were done without personalisation ($w_p = 0$), and its second tasks were a bit influenced by the corresponding profiles ($w_p = 0.5$).

User Profiles

Static user profiles were used for each domain. Some of them were common predefined profiles, and others were created by the users during the experiment using the profile editor of News@ hand. In addition, some tasks were done with user profiles containing concepts belonging to all the three domains.

Table 5 lists those concepts included in the predefined domain-driven user profiles. Each domain was described with six semantic concepts, appearing in a significant number of item annotations. Note that each domain may be described by concepts belonging to different ontologies, and may be covered with news items of different news sections.

Analogously to the predefined user profiles, those manually created by the evaluators using the profile editor of News@hand contained semantic concepts of the above three domains. In this case, the evaluators were free to select their preferences from concepts available in the entire KB. No restriction was placed on the number, type (classes or instances) and ontology of the concepts. Table 6 shows the concepts included

Table 4. Summary of the search tasks performed in the experiment

Domain	Section	Query		Task goal
Telecommunications	*World*	$Q_{1,1}$	pakistan	News about media: TV, radio, Internet
	Entertainment	$Q_{1,2}$	music	News about software piracy, illegal downloads, file sharing
Banking	*Business*	$Q_{2,1}$	dollar	News about oil prices
	Headlines	$Q_{2,2}$	fraud	News about money losses
Social care	*Science*	$Q_{3,1}$	food	News about cloning
	Headlines	$Q_{3,2}$	internet	News about children, young people, child safety, child abuse

Table 5. Topics and concepts allowed for the predefined user profiles in the evaluation of personalised and context-aware recommenders

Domain	Concepts
Telecommunications	internet, network, satellite, technology, telecommunications, website
Banking	bank, banking, business, economy, euro, dollar
Social care	drug, health, immigration, safety, social abuses, terrorism

for each domain, and the average size of the sixteen profiles. For instance, in *Telecommunication* domain, 55 preferences were declared using 30 different semantic concepts, producing an average of 3.4 preferences per user. On average, each profile contained 3.2 preferences of each domain.

Steps for the Evaluation of the Personalised Recommendation

The objective of the two tasks performed in the first experiment phase was to assess the importance of activating the semantic extension in our recommendation models. The following are the steps the users had to do in these tasks.

- Launch the query with the personalisation module deactivated.
- Rate the top 15 news items. The allowed rating values were: 1 if the item was not relevant to the task goal, 2 if the item was relevant to the task goal, and 3 if the item was relevant to the task goal and the user profile. These ratings are considered as our baseline case.
- Launch the query with the personalisation module activated (and the semantic extension enabled/disabled depending on the case).
- Rate the new top 15 news items as explained before.

Steps for the Evaluation of the Context-Aware Recommendation

The objective of the two tasks performed for the second experiment phase was to assess the quality of the results when the contextualisation functionality is activated and combined with personalisation. The steps done in this phase are the following:

Table 6. Topics and concepts of the manually-defined user profiles in the evaluation of personalised and context-aware recommenders

Domain	Concepts	#pref.	Avg. #pref./user
Telecommunications (30 concepts)	blackberry, cell phone, computer programming, computer sciences, computing and information technology, digital voice, email, encryption, file sharing, free downloads, internet, internet history, mobile network operator, network theory, networks, router, search engine, signal processing, social search, software, technology, telecommunications, television, tfidf, video arcade, video call, video game, voice over internet, web crawler, web search	55	3.4
Banking (25 concepts)	bank, bank charges, bank machine, bank of america, banker, banking, business, cash, credit card, dollar, economy, euribor, euro, euro interbank offered rate, finance, foreign exchange market, funds, ibank, macroeconomics, microfinance, money, payment system, stock, stock broking, trade policy	46	2.9
Social care (26 concepts)	abstinence, abuse, adoption, charity, children, civil society, drug, drug trafficking, family, gay, health, homophobia, homosexuality, immigration, pornography, safety, sexuality, smoking, social abuses, social change, social development, social groups, teenagers, terrorism, victims, volunteerism	51	3.2

- Launch the query with the contextualisation deactivated.
- Rate the top 15 news items as explained before, and evaluate as relevant (clicking the title) the first two items which are related to the task goal. Doing this the current semantic context is updated.
- Launch the query with the contextualisation activated (semantic extension enabled, and personalisation enabled/disabled depending on the case).
- Rate again the top 15 news items as explained before.

Results

Once the two evaluation phases were finished, we computed the precision values for the top $N = 5$, 10, 15 news items as follows:

$$P @ N = \frac{\#\{relevant\ items\ in\ the\ top\ N\ news\ items\}}{N}.$$

Figure 8 shows the average results for the sixteen users, taking into account those items evaluated as relevant to the task goal, and also the user profile. In both cases, the recommendation models outperformed the baseline case (except some, for P@15), especially for the five top items. The P@5 values increased from 20% of the baseline case to almost 40% and 50% when contextualisation and personalisation functionalities were enabled. The semantic extension seemed to be an essential component. It accounts for a 10% improvement in the personalisation precision in this experiment. This is in line with results we obtained in previous studies (Cantador, Bellogín, & Castells, 2008a; Cantador, Castells, & Bellogín, 2007) for different domains and applications of our semantic extension approach, thus adding empiric evidence on the benefits of the semantic user preference expansion in our content-based recommender. Finally, the combination of personalised and context-aware recommendations (plus semantic extension) gave the best results, achieving a P@5 value of 80%. The results in P@10 showed a similar trend, slightly less far above the baseline, and only for P@15 two configurations perform the same as or very slightly below the baseline, namely semantic personalisation and contextualisation alone. We performed a two paired sample Wilcoxon signed rank test, comparing (1) the baseline against the rest of the algorithms, (2) the personalised recommender with and without semantic preference expansion, and (3) the effect of enabling and disabling semantic contextualisation, obtaining respectively p values $p \leq 0.002$, $p \leq 0.05$ ($p = 0.049$ for results marked as relevant to the task goal, $p = 0.040$ for results marked as relevant to the task goal and the user's profile), and $p \leq 0.006$ ($p = 0.006$ for results marked as relevant to the task goal, $p = 0.005$ for results marked as relevant to the task goal and the user's profile). For all the recommendation models, no significant differences were found in the recommendation performance when using pre-defined and manually created user profiles. We think that this was due to the fact that the average numbers of preferences in both types of profiles were quite similar (Tables 5 and 6).

Apart from the computation of the precision values, we also asked the evaluators to provide comments and suggestions about the system. The most remarkable feedback we obtained can be summarised in the following points:

- *The contextualisation of recommendations is a useful functionality.* The users noticed and positively assessed how news items relevant to the current search goal move up to the top positions of the ranked lists when the context-aware recommender is activated.

Figure 8. Average precision values for the top 5, 10 and 15 news items, taking into account those items evaluated as relevant to the task goal and the user profile

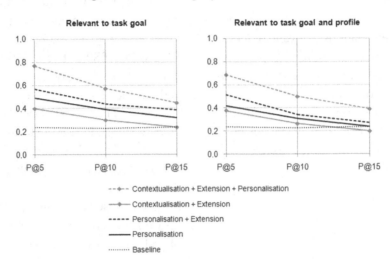

- *A disambiguation mechanism should be included within the annotation process.* The users found out annotations whose terms appeared in their profiles but having different meanings. This not only worsened the generated recommendations, but also the users' evaluations.
- *A content-based collaborative approach to enrich the semantic profiles may be beneficial.* Several users declared some preferences assuming that related ones (e.g., synonyms) were going to be implicitly taken into account. A mechanism to exploit co-occurrences among preferences of different users could be useful to automatically add related semantic concepts into the profiles.
- *The incorporation of a user preference recommender would be helpful.* Despite the facilities offered by the ontology browser and the auto-complete concept search boxes of News@hand, several users missed the fact of having concept suggestions (e.g., in the form of "related preferences are...") when they had to create their profiles.

6.2. Evaluating Content-Based Collaborative Recommendations

A second experiment was conducted with News@hand to evaluate the multilayer hybrid recommenders. The objective of this experiment was to compare the recommendations provided by our hybrid models with those obtained using a classic CF approach. Again, an off-line execution of the recommendation strategies over a set of user profiles and ratings was performed in order to compute accuracy measures.

The sixteen members of our department who participated in the previous experiment were again requested to take part of the evaluation presented herein. Three phases were followed by each user, assessing news recommendations for three news sections: *Business*, *Sports* and *World* (see below why we selected these sections). For each phase, two tasks were defined:

- In the first task, the users had to rate a number of news items from a random list. The goal of this task was to obtain a significant amount of personal rating data, with which collaborative filtering approaches could be executed in an offline process.

- In the second task, the users had to rate several news items from a list generated with the personalisation functionality activated. The goal of this task was to ensure obtaining a set of user ratings with which content-based, collaborative filtering and hybrid approaches could be compared.

Search Tasks

A task was defined as finding out and rating those news items that were "related to" a personal user profile. By "related to" we mean that a news item contains semantic annotations whose concepts appear in the user's profile. Note that a concept could be assigned negative or positive weights within a profile, so the evaluation of an item might have a low (close or equal to 1 star) or a high (close or equal to 5 stars) rating values.

User Profiles

Similarly to the experiment described in Section 6.1, the evaluators were asked to choose their preferences. However, in this case, they could only select preferences from a given list of semantic concepts. They were provided a form with a list of 128 concepts, classified in 8 different domains. From this list, the users had to select a subset of concepts, and assign them negative/positive weights according to personal interests. Table 7 shows the concepts available for each domain, and the average number of preferences per user. On average, each profile was created with 7.8 preferences per domain, duplicating the preferences introduced by the users when they had to manually search the concepts in the ontology browser (see Section 5.2).

Once the user profiles were created, we identified which news sections contained news items annotated with the most popular (i.e., the most used) preferences. The goal was to define an item set from which the recommenders could provide a significant number of personalised recommendations. Finally, we selected the news sections mentioned previously: *Business*, *Sports* and *World*.

Steps for the Evaluation of the Collaborative Filtering and Hybrid Recommendations

The users had to perform three tasks, each of them in one of the following news sections: *Business*, *Sports* and *World*. Successively, for each section, a user had to:

- Deactivate the personalisation functionality, and display the news items of the section. The goal is to present to all the users the same set of news items, in order to obtain a "shared" group of rated items.
- Rate 20 news items that are related (with negative or positive weights) to the user profile. Taking into account the similarities between item annotations with user preferences, assign a 1-5 start rating to the selected news items. No restriction is placed on which items have to be rated.
- Activate the personalisation functionality, and display again the news items of the section. This time the order (ranking) of the news items is different to the one shown previously. The goal here is to present to each user a set of news items that might be related to his semantic profile. Thus, content-based similarities could be found among profiles of different users.
- Rate (as explained before) 50 news items not evaluated previously.

Table 7. Topics and concepts allowed for the user profiles in the evaluation of the hybrid recommenders

Domain	Concepts	#preferences	Avg. #pref./user
Computers Technology Telecommunications	computer, digital, ebay, google, ibm, internet, mass, media, microsoft, networking, online, satellite, software, technology, video, website	135	8.4
Wars Armed conflicts	al-qaeda, army, battle, combat, crime, kidnapping, kill, memorial, military, murder, peace, prison, strike, terrorism, war, weapons	104	6.5
Social issues	aids, assassination, babies, children, death sentence, divorce, drugs, family, health, hospital, immigration, love, obesity, smoking, suburb, suicide	115	7.2
Television Cinema Music	actor, bbc, cinema, cnn, film, grammy, hollywood, movie, music, musician, nbc, radio, rock, oscar, singer, television	129	8.1
Sports	baseball, cricket, football, lakers, nascar, nba, new england patriots, new york giants, nfl, olympics, premier league, running, sports, soccer, super bowl, tennis	168	10.5
Politics	george bush, condolezza rice, congress, democracy, elections, government, hillary clinton, john maccain, barack obama, parliament, politics, president, senate, senator, voting, white house	104	6.5
Banking Economy Finance	banking, business, cash, companies, earnings, economy, employment, finance, fraud, gas price, industry, marketing, markets, money, oil price, wall street	120	7.5
Climate Weather Natural disasters	air, climate, earth, earthquake, electricity, energy, fire, flood, forecast, fuel, gas, pollution, sea, storm, weather, woods	128	8.0

With this strategy, the sixteen users provided a total of 3,360 ratings for 859 different news items.

Results

The purpose of the experiment was to compare the accuracy values obtained with our multilayer hybrid recommendation model UP-q, with those achieved by a classic item-based CF strategy (Konstan et al., 1997).

We computed the accuracy of the recommendations using different percentages of the user ratings to build (train) and evaluate (test) off-line the models. For comparative purposes, we computed the Root Mean Squared Error (RMSE) between the actual ratings $r_{u,i}$ introduced by the users u for items i belonging to the test set T, and the ratings $\hat{r}_{u,i}$ predicted by the above recommenders:

$$RMSE = \sqrt{\frac{1}{|T|} \sum_{(u,i) \in T} \left(r_{u,i} - \hat{r}_{u,i}\right)^2}.$$

Figure 9 shows separately the average results for the items belonging to the three considered news sections. In *Business* and *World* sections, the accuracy values of both models seem to be very similar. For the *World* section, the UP-q strategy performs slightly better than CF when 10% to 50% of the ratings were used to build the recommenders. In the *Sports* section, the UP-q model provides better recommendations at all sparsity levels. The user profiles created with concepts of this domain were rich, enabling the discovery of similarities among the user interests. However, for the *Business* section, there is no significant difference. Checking the news items profiles, we noticed that there was a relatively small number of annotations about banking, economy and fi-

Figure 9. Average Mean Squared Error of item-based collaborative filtering (CF) and semantic multilayer hybrid (UP-q) recommendation strategies using 10%, 20%, ..., 90% of the available ratings for building (training) the models, and the rest for testing

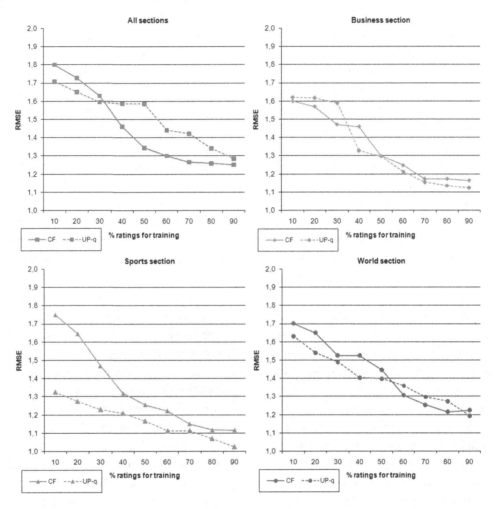

nance. As one might expect, our semantic-based approach is sensitive to the availability of semantic information. In the general case where items of the three sections were taken into account, the hybrid model seems again to give more accurate recommendations when few ratings are available. Specifically, utilising 10%, 20% and 30% of the rating information, the UP-q error is lower than the error obtained with the CF strategy.

The observed results show that the semantic approach enhances the recommendation performance as soon as the semantic data provides a fair coverage. Further research might be worth on

this point to more closely study the dependence between recommendation accuracy and semantic data sparsity. On the other hand, we see that the hybrid recommender improves the performance of the baseline in cold-start and sparsity situations. However, when enough user data is available, CF becomes better than our approach. This motivates further research to find an optimal point up to which our hybrid approach should be applied, after which CF should take over.

Apart from the computation of accuracy metrics, we gathered more subjective assessments of the system. We asked the evaluators to provide us comments about the recommendations obtained during the experiment. The most remarkable observations were the following:

- *Very similar news items were closely shown.* The non-diversity problem has not been addressed in this work. In the current version of the system, a certain news item can be retrieved from different RSS sources, and might be recommended to the user several times. Various users did not rate some items because they had already evaluated very similar ones.

- *A disambiguation mechanism should be included within the annotation process.* As noticed in the evaluation of the personalised and context-aware recommenders, the users found out semantic annotations with wrong meanings.

- *The contextualisation of recommendations is a desirable functionality even when collaborative item suggestions are provided.* Several users missed the activation of the context-aware recommender for this experiment. They also suggested us to consider additional sources of context, such as the semantics of news items linked through spatial (location) and temporal relations.

- *The rating of news items according to the user profile seemed to be difficult in some cases.* Several users found difficult to rate some news items because they could not easily distinguish between interesting and pleasant-reading articles.

7. CONCLUSION AND FUTURE WORK

Our research elaborates on the incorporation of a conceptual space describing and connecting user preferences and item contents, as a means to enhance recommendations. The specific results of our research are:

- The definition of a formal (ontology-based) knowledge model, supporting the expression of explicit semantic relations between concepts.
- The design of flexible semantic content-based recommenders, allowing the contextualisation of the recommendations.
- The design of semantic-layered hybrid recommenders, drawing further benefit from content-based and collaborative filtering approaches.
- The integration and joint evaluation of the proposed approaches with end users in a news recommender system. The semantic recommendation methods are executed in parallel in the system, and their outputs are combined in different configurations.

The results confirm previous observations from partial, separate evaluations of the methods, within the restrictions of standard datasets, and provide additional findings which cannot be obtained in the isolated experiments. The personalised recommendations help users find relevant news articles, and the semantic extension of user preferences supports a richer matching between user and item profiles, improving precision for the top suggested items, and mitigating the cold-start and sparsity problems. The incorporation of contextualisation in the personalisation mechanism got positive subjective feedback from the users, and supported faster discovery of items related to current search goals. Finally, layered hybrid recommendations enhance content-based collaborative approaches in the experiments when partial (interest-focused) comparisons of user profiles are computed. In this context, the detection of relations among users at multiple interest layers may be reducing the effect of the grey sheep problem, as shown in the reported results. This issue has to be investigated in depth in future work.

The implementation of a recommender system based on a semantic representation of user preferences and item features raised interesting additional challenges which we addressed as well. First, we had to build a knowledge base from scratch comprising different domains. For that purpose, we developed an automatic ontology population mechanism that extracts semantic information from several public information sources such as WordNet and Wikipedia. Next, we annotated news contents with classes and instances from the domain ontologies. To this end, we developed an automatic semantic annotator that makes use of NLP tools to analyse and process texts, retrieving their semantic concepts. Finally, we provided easy to use interactive facilities for users to edit their semantic profiles. The experimental work has produced valuable feedback from the users about system functionalities and outputs. Among other issues, user comments evidenced the need for a more elaborated semantic disambiguation step in the annotation process. Preliminary results in this direction are reported in Cantador et al. (in press). The users also noticed the need of addressing the non-diversity problem, as very similar (or even the same) items were presented closely in the recommendation sets. Moreover, they suggested additional improvements in the personal profile editor, such as the integration of a real-time preference recommender which takes into account concepts related to the already introduced ones (synonyms, co-occurrences, etc.).

REFERENCES

Adomavicius, G., & Tuzhilin, A. (2005). Toward the Next Generation of Recommender Systems: A Survey of the State-of-the-Art and Possible Extensions. *IEEE Transactions on Knowledge and Data Engineering*, *17*(6), 734–749. doi:10.1109/TKDE.2005.99.

Adomavicius, G., & Tuzhilin, A. (2011). Context-Aware Recommender Systems. In Ricci, F., Rokach, L., Shapira, B., & Kantor, P. B. (Eds.), *Recommender Systems Handbook* (pp. 217–253). doi:10.1007/978-0-387-85820-3_7.

Ahn, J., Brusilovsky, P., Grady, J., He, D., & Syn, S. Y. (2007). Open User Profiles for Adaptive News Systems: Help or Harm? In *Proceedings of the 16th International World Wide Web Conference* (pp. 11-20).

Alfonseca, E., Moreno-Sandoval, A., Guirao, J. M., & Ruiz-Casado, M. (2006). The Wraetlic NLP Suite. In *Proceedings of the 5th International Conference on Language Resources and Evaluation*.

Anand, S. S., & Mobasher, B. (2007). Contextual Recommendation. In Berendt, B., Hotho, A., Mladenic, D., & Semeraro, G. (Eds.), *From Web to Social Web: Discovering and Deploying User and Content Profiles* (pp. 142–160). doi:10.1007/978-3-540-74951-6_8.

Baeza-Yates, R., & Ribeiro-Neto, B. (1999). *Modern Information Retrieval*. Reading, MA: Addison-Wesley.

Billsus, D., & Pazzani, M. J. (1999). A Personal News Agent that Talks Learns and Explains. In *Proceedings of the 3rd International Conference on Autonomous Agents* (pp. 268-275).

Billsus, D., & Pazzani, M. J. (2000). User Modeling for Adaptive News Access. *User Modeling and User-Adapted Interaction*, *10*(2), 147–180. doi:10.1023/A:1026501525781.

Cantador, I., Bellogín, A., & Castells, P. (2008a). A Multilayer Ontology-based Hybrid Recommendation Model. *AI Communications*, *21*(2-3), 203–210.

Cantador, I., Bellogín, A., & Castells, P. (2008b). Ontology-based Personalised and Context-aware Recommendations of News Items. In *Proceedings of the 2008 IEEE/WIC/ACM International Conference on Web Intelligence and Intelligent Agent Technology* (pp. 562-565).

Cantador, I., Bellogín, A., Fernández-Tobías, I., & López-Hernández, S. (in press). Semantic Contextualization of Social Tag-based Item Recommendations. In *Proceedings of the 12th International Conference on E-Commerce and Web Technologies*.

Cantador, I., Fernández, M., Vallet, D., Castells, P., Picault, J., & Ribière, M. (2008). A Multi-Purpose Ontology-Based Approach for Personalised Content Filtering and Retrieval. In Wallace, M., Angelides, M., & Mylonas, P. (Eds.), *Advances in Semantic Media Adaptation and Personalization* (pp. 25–51). doi:10.1007/978-3-540-76361_2.

Cantador, I., Szomszor, M., Alani, H., Fernández, M., & Castells, P. (2008). Enriching Ontological User Profiles with Tagging History for Multi-Domain Recommendations. In *Proceedings of the 1st International Workshop on Collective Semantics: Collective Intelligence and the Semantic Web* (pp. 5-19).

Chu, W., & Park, S. T. (2009). Personalized Recommendation on Dynamic Content Using Predictive Bilinear Models. In *Proceedings of the 18th International World Wide Web Conference* (pp. 691-700).

Claypool, M., Gokhale, A., Miranda, T., Murnikov, P., Netes, D., & Sartin, M. (1999). Combining Content-Based and Collaborative Filters in an Online Newspaper. In *Proceedings of the SIGIR 1999 Workshop on Recommender Systems: Algorithms and Evaluation*.

Cohen, P. R., & Kjeldsen, R. (1987). Information Retrieval by Constrained Spreading Activation in Semantic Networks. *Information Processing & Management*, *23*(4), 255–268. doi:10.1016/0306-4573(87)90017-3.

Crestani, F. (1997). Application of Spreading Activation Techniques in Information Retrieval. *Artificial Intelligence Review*, *11*(6), 453–482. doi:10.1023/A:1006569829653.

Das, A., Datar, M., Garg, A., & Rajaram, S. (2007). Google News Personalisation: Scalable Online Collaborative Filtering. In *Proceedings of the 16th International World Wide Web Conference* (pp. 271-280).

Dey, A. K. (2001). Understanding and Using Context. *Personal and Ubiquitous Computing*, *5*(1), 4–7. doi:10.1007/s007790170019.

Haake, J. M., Hussein, T., Joop, B., Lukosch, S., Veiel, D., & Ziegler, J. (2010). Modeling and Exploiting Context for Adaptive Collaboration. *International Journal of Cooperative Information Systems*, *19*(1-2), 71–120. doi:10.1142/S0218843010002115.

Jones, G. J., Quested, D. J., & Thomson, K. E. (2000). Personalised Delivery of News Articles from Multiple Sources. In *Proceedings of the 4th European Conference on Research and Advanced Technology for Digital Libraries* (pp. 340-343).

Konstan, J. A., Miller, B. N., Maltz, D., Herlocker, J. L., Gordon, L. R., & Riedl, J. (1997). GroupLens: Applying Collaborative Filtering to Usenet News. *Communications of the ACM*, *40*(3), 77–87. doi:10.1145/245108.245126.

Koren, Y., & Bell, R. B. (2011). Advances in Collaborative Filtering. In Ricci, F., Rokach, L., Shapira, B., & Kantor, P. B. (Eds.), *Recommender Systems Handbook* (pp. 145–186). doi:10.1007/978-0-387-85820-3_5.

Liu, H., Maes, P., & Davenport, G. (2006). Unravelling the Taste Fabric of Social Networks. *International Journal on Semantic Web and Information Systems*, *2*(1), 42–71. doi:10.4018/jswis.2006010102.

Middleton, S. E., Roure, D. D., & Shadbolt, N. R. (2004). Ontology-based Recommender Systems. In Staab, S., & Studer, R. (Eds.), *Handbook on Ontologies* (pp. 477–498). Berlin, Germany: Springer-Verlag.

Mika, P. (2005). Flink: Semantic Web Technology for the Extraction and Analysis of Social Networks. *Journal of Web Semantics*, *3*(2-3), 211–223. doi:10.1016/j.websem.2005.05.006.

Miller, G. (1995). WordNet: A Lexical Database for English George. *Communications of the ACM*, *38*(11), 39–41. doi:10.1145/219717.219748.

Mobasher, B., Jin, X., & Zhou, Y. (2004). Semantically Enhanced Content-based Collaborative Filtering on the Web. In Berendt, B., Hotho, A., Mladenic, D., Van Someren, M., & Spiliopoulou, M. (Eds.), *Web Mining: From Web to Semantic Web* (pp. 57–76). doi:10.1007/978-3-540-30123-3_4.

Nadjarbashi-Noghani, M., Zhang, J., Sadat, H., & Ghorbani, A. A. (2005). PENS: A Personalised Electronic News System. In *Proceedings of the 3rd Annual Communication Networks and Services Research Conference* (pp. 31-38).

Picault, J., Ribière, M., Bonnefoy, D., & Mercer, K. (2011). How to Get the Recommender Out of the Lab? In Ricci, F., Rokach, L., Shapira, B., & Kantor, P. B. (Eds.), *Recommender Systems Handbook* (pp. 333–365). doi:10.1007/978-0-387-85820-3_10.

Räck, C., Arbanowski, S., & Steglich, S. (2006). Context-aware, Ontology-based Recommendations. In *Proceedings of the 2006 International Symposium on Applications and the Internet Workshops* (pp. 98-104).

Shoval, P., Maidel, V., & Shapira, B. (2008). An Ontology- Content-based Filtering Method. *International Journal of Information Theories and Applications*, *15*, 303–318.

Sieg, A., Mobasher, B., & Burke, R. (2007). Ontological User Profiles for Personalized Web Search. In *Proceedings of the AAAI 2007 Workshop on Intelligent Techniques for Web Personalization* (pp. 84-91).

Sujiyama, K., Hatano, K., & Yoshikawa, M. (2004). Adaptive Web Search Based On User Profile Constructed Without Any Effort From Users. In *Proceedings of the 13th International World Wide Web Conference* (pp. 675-684).

Szomszor, M., Alani, H., & Cantador, I. OHara, K., & Shadbolt, N. R. (2008). Semantic Modelling of User Interests based on Cross-Folksonomy Analysis. In *Proceedings of the 7th International Semantic Web Conference* (pp. 632-648).

Vallet, D., Castells, P., Fernández, M., Mylonas, P., & Avrithis, Y. (2007). Personalized Content Retrieval in Context Using Ontological Knowledge. *IEEE Transactions on Circuits and Systems for Video Technology*, *17*(3), 336–346. doi:10.1109/TCSVT.2007.890633.

This work was previously published in the International Journal on Semantic Web and Information Systems, Volume 7, Issue 1, edited by Amit P. Sheth,, pp. 44-78, copyright 2011 by IGI Publishing (an imprint of IGI Global).

Chapter 11
Numeric Query Answering on the Web

Steven O'Hara
University of Texas at San Antonio, USA

Tom Bylander
University of Texas at San Antonio, USA

ABSTRACT

Query answering usually assumes that the asker is looking for a single correct answer to the question. When retrieving a textual answer this is often the case, but when searching for numeric answers, there are additional considerations. In particular, numbers often have units associated with them, and the asker may not care whether the raw answer is in feet or meters. Also, numbers usually denote a precision. In a few cases, the precision may be explicit, but normally, there is an implied precision associated with every number. Finally, an association between different reliability levels to different sources can be made. In this paper, the authors experimentally show that, in the context of conflicting answers from multiple sources, numeric query accuracy can be improved by taking advantage of units, precision, and the reliability of sources.

MOTIVATION

Suppose you wanted to know the answer to a specific question, such as "What is the atomic mass of Copper?" or "What is the diameter of Pluto?" Certainly, you could Google (www.google.com) it and get many different answers. You could also ask experts, or go to specific websites that you expect to know an answer, or run software to get an answer. Now, suppose you were able to ask all of these sources at the same time, and wanted to consolidate those answers into a single answer. You'd probably find some answers that are incorrect; and some answers that are more precise than others; and there may even be multiple "correct" answers.

DOI: 10.4018/978-1-4666-3610-1.ch011

Expecting any single source to have the best answers for a wide range of questions is quite unreasonable. Sources like Wikipedia (www.wikipedia.org), Google Calculator, Yahoo! Answers (answers.yahoo.com), Wolfram Alpha (www.wolframalpha.com) and others are viable sources, but not to the exclusion of the other possible sources. One of the major tenets of this research is that having a range of sources for answers is likely to increase overall accuracy.

Many questions follow this same form: given an object, what is the value of a specified attribute? What is the radius of Mars? What is the population of Rome? What is the length of the Nile River? How tall is Mt. Everest? And so forth. The literature uses the term "factoid" for these types of questions (Lin & Katz, 2003).

With the immense amount of information available on the internet, and the advent of systems like GROK (described herein), it is possible to send a single question and receive many different answers quickly. The GROK architecture provides the mechanism for broadcasting questions to multiple agents (Singh & Huhns, 2005), which in turn search websites for answers. Next, those answers are consolidated into a "best" answer and returned back to the user.Natural Language processing (such as understanding, paraphrasing or generation) is beyond the scope of this project. See the Text Retrieval Conference website (trec.nist.gov) for some recent research.

HYPOTHESIS

Numeric query answering is different than ordinary query answering (Katz et al., 2002; Kwok, Etzioni, & Weld, 2001; Lin & Katz, 2003; Roussinov, Fan, & Robles-Flores, 2008) in two fundamental ways: unit conversions and implied precision. Query accuracy can be improved by taking advantage of these distinct differences. It can also take advantage of source reliability, which is considered in this paper.

Numeric Values Often Have Units

When searching for numeric values, many of them will be expressed in units, such as feet or meters. When a candidate value is found, the units can be converted automatically. So, if you are searching for the radius of Mars, some answers may come back in meters, some in miles, and some in kilometers. If the search is expecting only miles, it may miss some good answers that were expressed in kilometers, for example.

Numbers Have Implicit Precision

In a few cases, numbers have explicit precision. Wikipedia, for example, often shows values in the form "2100 $\pm$ 40 grams" which means 2060 to 2140 grams. However, most resources will report values like "2100 grams" or "2110 grams", etc. Based on common interpretation of numbers ending in zeros, we assume that the 2100 value has an implied precision of 2050 to 2150, and that the 2110 value means 2105 to 2115. These interval values can be compared against each other to see if they reinforce each other.

Naturally, this assumption can fail in both directions. One might find a value such as "1000 meters" that really means exactly 1000.000 meters. And one might find a value such as "123.45 miles" that is not really accurate to one hundredth of a mile. Part of this research is testing to see if overall accuracy improves with this assumption, even knowing that it will occasionally fail.

Sources Have Different Reliability

Sources like NASA are tightly controlled and very likely to have accurate answers to most astronomy-related questions. Wikipedia is loosely controlled (for a discussion on reliability, see en.wikipedia.org/wiki/Reliability_of_Wikipedia); information is often entered by non-experts and is often invalid. Google, in general, is completely uncontrolled. When comparing answers, it seems reasonable to consider the reliability of the source.

RELATED WORK

The annual Text Retrieval Conference (TREC) has been the mainstay of question answering systems for many years. Many serious academic efforts have participated, although the majority of the work assumes a finite corpus of documents that can be pre-processed, unlike the web which is virtually unbounded.

Note that, to the knowledge of the authors, none of the efforts consider the implicit precision associated with numbers, and hence none of them have a concept like Interval Support at described in the Statistical Foundation section, later in this paper.

Academic Efforts

Numeric query answering has been identified as a different type of problem for some time. For example, Ferret, Grau, Hurault-Plantet, Illouz, and Jacquemin (2001) categorize answer types as Named Entities, such as person, organization, location (city or place), number (a time expression or a number expression).

The earliest web-based question answering system is START (Katz, 1997) which has been in continuous operation since 1993. It has its own knowledge base and is able to search online for answers in sources like the CIA World Fact Book.

The KnowItAll (Cafarela, Downey, Soderland, & Etzioni, 2005) system uses a variety of natural language techniques to collect triples with very high accuracy, although it does require some human guidance. TextRunner (Yates, Banko, Broadhead, Cafarella, Etzioni, & Soderland, 2007) crawls the web looking for object-relationship-object triples that it collects for answering queries. It has a big focus on complete automation – no human input needed to tune rules. Both of these systems share the problem of how to generate the right query for Google, and how to identify extract the candidate answer.

Clarke, Cormack, and Lynam (2001) use an iterative algorithm to validate source reliability, based on candidate answer redundancy and term frequencies. White, Cardie, and Ng (2002) create summaries of multiple websites to highlight discrepancies between them; their focus is on tracking events in which the known facts can change on a daily basis (e.g., the damage and loss of life from an earthquake). TruthFinder (Yin, Han, & Yu, 2007) is based on the idea that a web site is reliable if it provides many pieces of true information, and a piece of information is likely to be true if it is provided by many reliable web sites.

FACTO (Yin, Tan, & Liu, 2011) is intended as part of Microsoft's Bing search engine. It also crawls the web looking for object-attribute-value triples and compiles them into a database for retrieval when somebody does a search. Their system utilizes TextRunner to extract facts from the web pages. Their assumption that there exists a single correct answer to put into the database is similar to our goal of identifying the best answer.

Production Systems

When doing a Google search, sometimes Google will produce a quick answer. Although not published, it appears to be extracting the more frequently occurring answer found in snippets from selected websites. Systems like ask.com and Wolfram Alpha are designed to produce answers to questions, not just links to potentially relevant web sites. Systems like Yahoo! Answers only get answers from other people.

ARCHITECTURE

The foundation for this research is a system called GROK, which stands for Global Repository of Ordinary Knowledge. GROK was developed by the authors to provide a robust question-answering platform between Askers and Answerers.

In the simplest case, the GROK Client starts with a question, and each of GROK Experts attempts to provide one or more candidate answers. The Experts are typically wrappers for websites such as NASA, Wikipedia or Google.

Figure 1 is simplified, as it omits the shared ontology. It also doesn't really show that there are many Clients, and that the Experts can be agents, software, or humans contacted via email.

GROK Experts

GROK Experts are registered with the GROK Server for each domain that they have expertise in. Questions will come in from users. Sources like Google and Wikipedia will have broad knowledge covering all domains. Some questions might be answerable through software run on the expert's computer, while others might be answered by an email sent to a human expert.

GROK Google Expert

The GROK experts that we used for this research are tuned to extract information in an expected form, from a specific website. GROK can also ask human experts and consult the output of running software, but that is not used for our results in this paper. For example, the NASA website has tables full of answers for astronomy questions. In some cases, such as Wikipedia, they have Resource Description Framework descriptors to access the information directly, but in most cases, a custom wrapper has to be created to extract the information from the web page directly.

The GROK Google expert is different. It generates a series of queries, as if the user typed them, and examines the two or three line snippets returned for each match. All questions are processed by this expert.

GROK Expert Confidence Levels

This analysis considers four different levels of reliability, or confidence (Table 1).

Figure 1. Simplified GROK sequence diagram

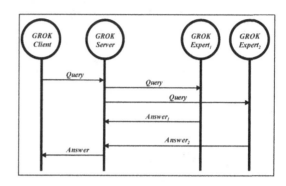

The scale factor only has meaning relative to the other scale factors. For example, a single candidate answer with High level of confidence (300) is equivalent to 10 candidate answers with Low confidence (30 each). These ratios are arbitrary; additional research is needed to tune these ratios. Clearly, websites are not equally likely to have correct answers. There is no a priori way to exclude websites, nor are there any websites that are guaranteed to be correct.

Google responses can only have two confidence values. When a match is made for the full pattern, such as "The diameter of Pluto is …" the confidence is considered to be Low. If less than 10 candidate answers are found this way, an additional query is attempted with just the object and attribute, such as "diameter Pluto". Any candidate answers returned for this query are considered to be Very Low confidence, because it looks through the entire snippet for any numbers followed by a valid unit. A candidate answer might not be referring to Pluto or its diameter, but the answer will still have a distance unit in it.

A research project has been initiated by the authors to quantify website confidence. The idea is to create a large collection of Questions across different domains. Send all questions through the GROK system collect all candidate answers. Reduce the web site sources to their DNS name (www.nasa.gov for example) instead of the full URL. Now, collect all the candidate responses for each DNS name and assess an average correctness for them based on the methodology

Table 1. Expert confidence levels

Level	Scale Factor	Example
High	300	NASA
Medium	100	Wikipedia
Low	30	Google – full pattern
Very Low	0.5	Google – no pattern

from this research paper. This measure becomes an indicator for website confidence. Preliminary results are showing that websites like www.nasa. gov are showing very high confidence, confirming expectations.

GROK Server

The GROK server knows what information is available, but doesn't actually know anything. The best way to think of this is that the server knows the column names and types of all the tables in the database, but none of the actual data in the tables. It knows about domains, and which experts can answer questions in each domain. It is really just a broker that distributes questions and collects candidate answers. These candidate answers are then consolidated into a single consensus answer that is delivered back to the GROK Client.

GROK Clients

Users may wish to find answers to domain-specific questions. Perhaps computer programs need information as well, such as weather forecasts. The GROK system can be used to distribute the question to multiple Experts. GROK will consolidate and normalize answers from multiple experts, into a single consensus answer.

In this research, the GROK Client is a program that reads a prepared list of questions spanning several different domains.

Shared Ontology

When questions are posed to the GROK system, they are set in the context of a shared ontology. The idea is similar to Cyc (Matuszek, et al., 2005), but this ontology is much less detailed. When a user wishes to know the diameter of Pluto, for example, the ontology snippet in Figure 2 is shared between the GROK components.

Topics are very high level concepts, and follow the object-oriented pattern of inheritance. Objects and attributes have to be from the types and attributes in the ontology that is shared between all users and experts. Note that there are no instances of objects in the ontology, e.g., Pluto is not a known concept.

Questions and Answers

Questions are represented using plain text XML. Figure 3 contains a sample question.

Each expert receives questions like that in Figure 3, and replies with a list of XML answers (Figure 4).

A variety of methods are available to communicate these XML messages between the GROK components. For this research, simple TCP/IP sockets are used.

Figure 2. Ontology for Planet

```
<type name="CelestialObject">
  <attribute name="Name"
       type="String" />
  <attribute name="Radius"
       type="Distance" />
  <attribute name="Diameter"
       type="Distance" />
  <attribute name="Mass"
       type="Mass" />
</type>
<type name="Planet"
       parent="CelestialObject">
  <attribute name="WhichStar"
       type="Star" />
  <attribute name="HasRings"
       type="Boolean" />
```

Figure 3. Sample XML question

```
<question qtopic="Astronomy"
    qclass="Planet"
    qobject="Pluto"
    qattribute="Diameter" />
```

Figure 4. Sample XML answer

```
<answer avalue="2337.5"
    adelta="37.5"
    aunits="km"
    aurl="http://www.pd.astro.it/
        E-MOSTRA/NEW/A2024PLU.HTM" />
```

Units Conversion

Another part of GROK is the automatic conversion of units, e.g., from miles to kilometers, which is processed inside the GROK server. Figure 5 shows how the Distance type is represented.

In the future, this unit conversion processing could be handled through some form of internet web service.

STATISTICAL FOUNDATION

Suppose one had two numbers in hand, like 210 and 211. We assume that the first value has an implied range of 205 to 215, while the second has an implied range of 210.5 to 211.5. In order to

Figure 5. Sample unit conversions

```
<measures>
  <type name="Distance" base="foot">
    <unit name="mile" abbrev="mi"
        factor="5280"/>
    <unit name="meter" abbrev="m"
        factor="3.280839895"/>
    <unit name="kilometer" abbrev="km"
        factor="3280.839895"/>
    <unit name="kilometre"
        factor="3280.839895"/>
    <unit name="foot" plural="feet"
        factor="1"/>
    <unit name="inch" plural="inches"
        factor="0.08333333333"/>
```

determine what answer to use as the consensus answer, it is necessary to compare them in some fashion. We describe our technique and show that it is identical to a probability model.

Interval Supports

In our system, comparing two numbers is based on converting them into intervals and computing the support (overlap) between them. Given any two intervals along a continuous line, there are several different ways one can support the other. Call these intervals A and B. A ranges from A_{LO} to A_{HI}, and B from B_{LO} to B_{HI}. All intervals are non-trivial, i.e., $A_{HI} > A_{LO}$ and $B_{HI} > B_{LO}$. There are four possibilities:

1. A is inside B. ($B_{LO} \leq A_{LO} < A_{HI} \leq B_{HI}$).
2. B is inside A. ($A_{LO} \leq B_{LO} < B_{HI} \leq A_{HI}$).
3. A is disjoint from B. ($A_{HI} < B_{LO}$ or $A_{LO} > B_{HI}$).
4. A partially overlaps B. ($A_{LO} \leq B_{LO} \leq A_{HI} \leq B_{HI}$ or $B_{LO} \leq A_{LO} \leq B_{HI} \leq A_{HI}$).

If A is totally inside B, then it supports B 100%, which is equivalent to asserting that A implies B. If A and B are disjoint, then the support is zero. If there is partial overlap between A and B, then there is partial support. Here is a definition of the 'supports' relationship:

A supports B = 0 if $A_{HI} < B_{LO}$ or $A_{LO} > B_{HI}$.

Otherwise, A supports B =
$$\frac{\min\left(A_{HI}, B_{HI}\right) - \max\left(A_{LO}, B_{LO}\right)}{A_{HI} - A_{LO}}$$

Consider Figure 6, looking at the diameter of Pluto, in miles. The horizontal axis represents the candidate answers given in response to a Google query, one answer per hash mark.

Figure 7 contains the same chart as Figure 6, but zoomed in on the vertical axis to 1350 to 1500 miles.

Figure 6. Diameter of Pluto responses

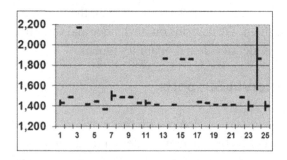

Figure 7. Diameter of Pluto, zoomed view

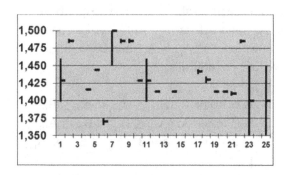

Each small horizontal bar shows a candidate answer, and the vertical bar shows the implied interval for that answer. For example, the first candidate answer was given as 2300 km, which implies 2250 to 2350 km, which is the same as 1429 ± 31 miles, which is 1398 to 1460 miles, as labeled "1" in Figure 7. Table 2 contains the 25 candidate answers for these charts.

When two answers, including their implied ranges, have a partial overlap, the amount of support is computed to a value between zero and one. For example, consider the first candidate answer (call it A) and the amount of support given by the fifth candidate answer (call it B), which is 1500 miles, with an implied range of 50. So

$$A_{LO} = 1398$$

$$B_{LO} = 1450$$

$$A_{HI} = 1460$$

Table 2. Pluto diameter candidate responses

#	Value	Units	Miles	Delta
1	2300	KM	1,429	31.1
2	2390	KM	1,485	3.1
3	2170	MILES	2,170	5.0
4	1416	MILES	1,416	0.5
5	1444	MILES	1,444	0.5
6	1370	MILES	1,370	5.0
7	1500	MILES	1,500	50.0
8	2390	KM	1,485	3.1
9	2390	KM	1,485	3.1
10	1429	MILES	1,429	0.5
11	2300	KM	1,429	31.1
12	2274	KM	1,413	0.3
13	1865	MILES	1,865	2.5
#	Value	Units	Miles	Delta
14	2274	KILOME-TERS	1,413	0.3
15	1860	MILES	1,860	5.0
16	1860	MILES	1,860	5.0
17	2320	KM	1,442	3.1
18	1430	MILES	1,430	5.0
19	2274	KILOME-TERS	1,413	0.3
20	2274	KILOME-TERS	1,413	0.3
21	2270	KM	1,411	3.1
22	1485	MILES	1,485	2.5
23	1400	MILES	1,400	50.0
24	3000000	METERS	1,864	310.7
25	1400	MILES	1,400	50.0

$$B_{HI} = 1550$$

$$\text{Support} = (A_{HI} - B_{LO}) / (A_{HI} - A_{LO}) = (1460 - 1450) / (1460 - 1398) = 0.16129$$

So the 2300 km answer supports the 1500 mile answer about 16%.

Conditional Bayes Probabilities

The above 'supports' relation is equivalent to a traditional Bayes conditional probability, Prob (A | B) = Prob (A and B) / Prob (B), if some simplifying assumptions are made. The first assumption is that an interval is equivalent to a uniform distribution. The second is that the range of possible values is continuous. That is, the assertion "the value is in the interval A" is equivalent to asserting a uniform distribution, "the value is equally likely to be any value in the interval A".

To show the equivalence between the Bayes calculations and the Support calculations, we will make one further assumption, namely that the values come from a finite range of possible values. Let us call that range U, with values ranging from U_{LO} to U_{HI}. All values must lie within U.

$$Prob(B) = (B_{HI} - B_{LO}) / (U_{HI} - U_{LO})$$

$$Prob(A \text{ and } B) = Overlap / (U_{HI} - U_{LO})$$

The amount of overlap is the smaller of the high values minus the larger of the low values. So,

$$Overlap = min(A_{HI}, B_{HI}) - max(A_{LO}, B_{LO})$$

Hence, $Prob(A | B) = [min(A_{HI}, B_{HI}) - max(A_{LO}, B_{LO})] / (A_{HI} - A_{LO})$

which is exactly as shown in the Interval Supports section previously.

Ranking Answers

A more general answer, e.g., 3.14 for π, will tend to be supported by more specific answers, e.g., 3.14159. Our assumption is that many answers tend to be approximations of the correct/accepted answer. In order to prefer more specific answers over more general answers, we rank candidate answers by the amount of support they *receive* from the other candidate answers, rather than the amount of support they *give*.

The ranking of the candidate answers is based on computing the support between all pairs of answers, and adding them up for each answer. The candidate answer that gives the most support to the other answers is chosen as the "best" or consensus answer. Note that the opposite approach is valid as well, choosing the candidate answer that receives the most support. The difference is that the former approach tends to find a more precise answer while the latter tends to find very broad answers.

EXAMPLE ANALYSIS

To illustrate the analysis, the two questions in Table 3 will be studied in some detail. The Q column is just a reference question number.

Tables 4 and 5 contain the candidate answers, all from Google. Note that, in the ontology, atomic radius of an element is defined to have an absolute possible upper limit of 1,000 picometers. This applies to all elements and is just a mechanism to reduce bizarre candidate answers. For question 26, seven candidate answers were eliminated because they far exceeded this limit.

Table 4 contains the 23 candidate answers for question 1 (What is the Total Area of the Aland Islands?).

Based on the preceding analysis, the consensus answer of 1512 sq. km was chosen because it has the most support from other candidate answers. In addition to the ten answers (marked with *) of 1512 sq. km., the 583 and 584 sq. miles answers (marked with +) are all partially supported by the answer of 1512 sq. km.

Table 3. Sample questions

Q	Object	Attribute	Target Answer (*)
1	Aland Islands	Total Area	13,517 sq km
2	Amazon River	Length	6,992 km

(*) These target answers were extracted from the 2008/9 Wikipedia Selection for Schools.

Table 4. Responses for question 1

1512 square kilometers (*)	1512 square kilometers (*)
584 sq mi (+)	583 sq. mi (+)
970 square miles	1512 square kilometres (*)
1512 square kilometres (*)	583 sq. mi (+)
583 sq. mi (+)	1512 square kilometres (*)
1512 square kilometers (*)	583 sq. mi (+)
583 sq. mi (+)	1512 square kilometres (*)
1512 square kilometers (*)	583 sq. mi (+)
584 sq mi (+)	1512 square kilometres (*)
1426 sq. km.	583 sq. mi (+)
1426 sq. km.	1512 square kilometers (*)
1426 sq. km.	

Table 5. Responses for question 2

3 m	0 in	3969 mi (+)
1600 km	4050 mi	5597 m
1000 mi	1609 m	0 m
4380 km	6387 km (*)	2300 miles
2720 mi	3969 mi (+)	6450 km
110 feet	5597 m	4000 mi (+)
4380 km	4380 km	6387 km (*)
2720 mi	2720 mi	3969 mi (+)
4170 miles	6516 kilometers	5597 m
6296 km	6400 km (+)	6762 km
8 feet	3977 mi	4202 mi
3 m	7050000 km	5597 m
3 m	2722020 mi	
3 m	6387 km (*)	

Question 2 (What is the Length of the Amazon River?) got 40 candidate answers (Table 5).

The candidate answer (marked with *) of 6387 km supports the most answers. It is only given in three of the answers, but it supports five other answers (marked with +).

Comparing Answers

The consensus answer is first converted to the same units as the target answer. To compare a consensus answer to the target answer in our evaluation, we define a distance measure. Let the consensus answer be A_{LO} to A_{HI}, with A_{MID} halfway between. Similarly, let the target answer be B_{LO} to B_{HI}, with B_{MID} halfway. Then, ansDistance is defined as:

$$\frac{|A_{LO} - B_{LO}| + |A_{MID} - B_{MID}| + |A_{HI} - B_{HI}|}{3\,|B_{MID}|}$$

ansDistance is a simplified version of the average distance between corresponding points on the intervals. Consider an example, where the consensus answer (A) is 80 ± 40 and the target answer (B) is 50 ± 30.

$$\text{ansDistance} = \text{average}(|40\text{-}20|, |80\text{-}50|, |120\text{-}80|) / 150 = 0.20$$

BASELINE AND THREE EXPERIMENTAL CONDITIONS

The baseline experimental condition includes unit conversion, implicit precision, and different confidence levels for different sources. The baseline is expected to have the best performance.

Condition 1: (no Unit Conversions, "No Conv.") Does not allow candidate answers in different units to support each other. For example, answers in miles and kilometers are valid, but are prevented from supporting each other.

Condition 2: (no Implied Precision, "No Impl."), All values are considered to be totally precise. For example, 4001 miles does not support 4000 miles under this condition.

Condition 3: (no Confidence Levels, "No Conf.") Does not consider the confidence of the source, e.g., an answer from Google is given the same weight as an answer from NASA. For the Wikipedia Development Phase, the only source activated was Google, so the only confidence levels were Low and Very Low. (Low corresponds to a Google search for a particular way of phrasing the answer, while Very Low corresponds to a keyword search).

The core of the research starts with a baseline configuration consisting of all available logic. Our hypothesis is that the baseline should have the best overall performance. Then three experimental conditions are tried, where each hypothesis is disabled one at a time (Table 6).

There were three phases to this research. The first phase was used to get the functionality operational and computations validated. The second phase was a detailed study into the three conditions described below. The third phase was the testing phase and was used to validate the results of the second phase.

Phase 1: Initial Development

A total of 115 questions were used for the initial development phase. Here are some representative questions:

- What is the diameter of Pluto?
- What is the radius of Pluto?
- How many grams are in a ton?
- How far is it to Miami from Chicago?
- What is the atomic mass of Copper?
- What is the length of the Nile?
- What is the area of Vietnam?
- What is the area of Alabama?

Table 6. Baseline and experimental conditions

Experimental Conditions:	Unit Conversions	Implied Precision	Confidence Levels
Baseline	✓	✓	✓
1. No Conv.	✗	✓	✓
2. No Impl.	✓	✗	✓
3. No Conf.	✓	✓	✗

During the initial development phase, considerable emphasis was placed on the approach, i.e., making sure all the statistics were calculated correctly, all the answers were consolidating correctly into a single consensus answer, etc. Also, the wrappers for sources like Google, Wikipedia, the CIA World Fact Book (www.cia.gov/library/publications/the-world-factbook), etc. were all implemented and tested.

Phase 2: Wikipedia Development

Wikipedia has developed a secondary school online encyclopedia. It can be downloaded and used for research purposes. This website was used to create a list of 1,418 numeric questions and target answers. Of the 1,418 questions, 278 did not return enough answers for analysis, leaving a total of 1,140 questions.

Figure 8 indicates the performance of each condition. The y axis is the count of the questions in that accuracy range. The accuracy values are based on the ansDistance distance measure, so values closer to zero imply greater accuracy. A value of zero means the experimental condition got precisely the target Wikipedia answer. Values in the range 0 to 1/4 are within 25% of the target answer, and a value of One or more means it was off by 100% or more.

For example, Condition 3 (no confidence) got 448 of the 1,140 questions slightly wrong, but still within 25% of the target answer. Overall, the baseline and each of the conditions got a large fraction of the answers within 25% of the target answer. The rightmost two groups of bars (3/4 to 1 and One or more) respectively represent cases where the consensus answer is far from the target. Usually, an answer in the 3/4 to 1 group corresponds to where the consensus answer is very small relative to the target answer (can't be off by more than 100%). The One or more group corresponds to where the consensus answer is very large relative to the target answers (more than twice as much).

Figure 8. Wikipedia Development Phase accuracy

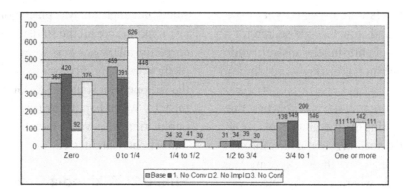

It is interesting to note that Condition 1 (No Conv, no conversion of units) actually got more answers exactly right (420 to 367). Possibly this is because it introduces no errors from unit conversion. The total of the exact plus close (0 to 1/4 including Zero) is 826 for baseline and 811 for condition 1, which indicates that the baseline condition was comparable to condition 1.

It is also interesting to note that condition 2 (No Impl, no implied precision) did not get very many answers exactly the same as the target answer (92), but got quite a few answers close to it (626).

In order to compare each condition to the baseline result, a Paired Difference test is performed. The difference between the Baseline ansDistance and the experimental condition ansDistance is computed. Roughly ansDistance corresponds to (consensus-target)/target, which means that a negative difference between the baseline ansDistance and a condition ansDistance means that the baseline predicted a better answer. However, since values can be wildly different, even off by orders of magnitude in some cases, the difference is limited to the range -1 to 1.

Based on all 1,140 questions, the Paired Difference computation is seen in Table 7.

These T test values are very significant and show that the average difference was negative with very high confidence (p << .001). That is, the Baseline outperformed the three conditions on this measure.

Likewise, a Signed Z test is performed. It is similar to the Paired Difference Test, but only the sign of the difference is considered (possible values -1, 0 or 1). A value of -1 means the baseline got a better answer than the experimental condition. A value of 0 means both were equally accurate and 1 means the baseline got a worse answer than the experimental condition.

Based on all 1,140 questions, the signed Z test computation is seen in Table 8.

The Z value for the first condition shows a fairly high certainty that the Condition 1 had better performance than the Baseline (p < .05). The second condition is shown to have worse performance than the Baseline (p << .001). But the third condition has nearly the same performance as the baseline.

Phase 3: Testing

Two major sources were used for the testing phase. No code changes were made for this phase; all pro-

Table 7. Paired difference results, Wikipedia Phase

Computation	Cond 1. No Conv.	Cond 2. No Impl.	Cond 3. No Conf.
Avg. Diff	-0.0109	-0.0854	-0.0042
Sample Var.	0.0549	0.1722	0.0104
T Statistic	-6.70	-16.74	-13.71

Table 8. Signed Z test results, Wikipedia phase

Computation	Cond 1. No Conv.	Cond 2. No Impl.	Cond 3. No Conf.
Baseline worse	192	257	49
Baseline better	152	691	51
Z = signed test	2.16	-14.10	-0.20

Table 9. Test phase question counts

Topic	Class	Attribute	Total
Chemistry	Molecule	Temperature	310
		Weight	647
Geography	County	Area	3,143
	State	Area	52
Total			4,152

cessing was done using the techniques developed during the previous phase. The questions were taken from very different domains to validate the results (Table 9).

The target answer source for the chemistry (molecular) data was www.reciprocalnet.org while the source for the geographic information was quickfacts.census.gov. It is difficult to judge the true accuracy of these sources. Of the 4,152 questions, 159 did not return any candidate answers at all in the baseline or one or more of the three conditions, so they were excluded from the analysis. Leaving a total of 3,993 questions. The average number of candidate answers was about 5.8 and the maximum was 101 (for the Area of Texas).

Figure 9 indicates the performance of each condition. As before, a value of zero means the experimental condition got precisely the target answer. Values in the range 0 to 1/4 are within 25% of the target answer. A value of One or more means it was off by 100% or more.

The rightmost two groups of bars in Figure 9 (3/4 to 1 and One or more) respectively represent cases where the consensus answer is likely very small relative to the target answer (can't be off by more than 100%) or is very large relative to the target answers (more than twice as much).

In this case, the number of answers that approximately match the target answer (0 to 1/4 group) is roughly double the number of answers that exactly match (Zero group). There is also an apparent tendency to get very small answers relative to the target answer (3/4 to 1) compared to answers that are too large (One or more). Both

of these observations are a direct consequence of the chosen question set, which is dominated by questions about the areas of counties. Areas of counties are difficult to define precisely due to factors like bordering waters, which helps justify the first observation.

Also, when a county area answer is incorrect, we observed that it is much more likely to be a smaller area than a larger area.

In order to compare each condition to the baseline result, a Paired Difference test is performed. The difference between the Baseline ansDistance and the conditional ansDistance is computed. However, since values can be wildly different, even off by many orders of magnitude in some cases, the difference is limited to the range -1 to 1. A negative difference indicates that the baseline had a more accurate answer.

Based on all 3,993 questions, the Paired Difference computation is seen in Table 10.

The Baseline outperformed all the other conditions on the paired difference test (p << .001).

Likewise, a Signed Z test is performed. It is similar to the Paired Difference Test, but only the sign of the difference is considered (possible values -1, 0 or 1).

Based on all 3,993 questions, the Signed Z test computation is seen in Table 11.

The Z value for all three conditions shows a fairly high certainty that each condition had a significant impact on performance. Again, the baseline outperformed each of the experimental conditions (p << 0.001).

Figure 9. Test phase accuracy

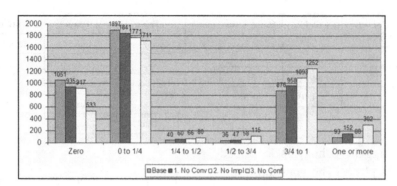

Experimental Conclusions

There were mixed results from the Signed Z test from our Wikipedia Development phase; however, the other three statistical tests validate our hypotheses, in particular, the Paired Difference Test and Signed Z Test from our Test phase. It is clear that numeric answers should be treated with implied precision. In addition, unit conversion and the reliability of sources are important to take into account.

KNOWN ISSUES AND FUTURE RESEARCH

Multiple Values

When talking about real world values, especially those with units attached to them, it is very often the case that the value depends on what is being measured. Consider, for example, the length of a year. One might say 365 days, or 365.25 or 365.2425, or some variation on that. But, in fact, there are many different ways of measuring a year. Wikipedia, for example, lists 11 different kinds of astronomical years (see en.wikipedia.org/wiki/Year#Astronomical_years). A Julian year has exactly 365.25 days, while a Sidereal year is just slightly longer. Note also, that the length of year varies ever so slightly due to many small factors like solar winds and lunar gravity.

Consider also the diameter of Jupiter. Does that refer to the equatorial diameter? One of the many polar diameters? An average or median diameter? Jupiter may not even have a well-defined surface. Jupiter is a giant ball of gas and liquid with little, if any, solid surface. Instead, the planet's surface is composed of dense [...] clouds, according to NASA (see www.nasa.gov/worldbook/jupiter_worldbook.html).

Judging Source Reliability

In this experiment, it was necessary to quantify relative source reliabilities. The ratios between

Table 10. Paired difference results, Test phase

Computation	Cond 1. No Conv.	Cond 2. No Impl.	Cond 3. No Conf.
Avg. Diff	-0.0385	-0.0586	-0.1240
Sample Var.	0.0738	0.1160	0.1296
T Statistic	-33.00	-31.89	-60.45

Table 11. Signed Z test results, Test phase

Computation	Cond 1. No Conv.	Cond 2. No Impl.	Cond 3. No Conf.
Baseline worse	324	1224	76
Baseline better	673	2022	691
Z = signed test	-11.05	-14.01	-22.21

High, Medium, Low, and Very Low are derived empirically, but are arbitrary. Different ratios will influence the results. It is especially difficult to assign reliability to human sources, without some form of feedback system. We intend to incorporate ideas from TextRunner (Yin, Han, & Yu, 2007) into future versions of our system.

Duplicate Websites

In the process of analyzing multiple sources to see how well they support each other, the results can be easily contaminated by duplicate websites. It seems that many websites copy-and-paste values from other more reputable websites. The act of copying from a source probably indicates that the source is somewhat reliable, but this is not a principled analysis. In this experiment, no attempt was made to reconcile sources to see if they were clones.

Considerable research is already being done is this area (e.g., Galland, Marian, Abiteboul, & Senellart, 2010). Dong, Berti-Equille, and Srivastava (2009) are especially interesting in tracking the dependency history of redundant website information over time.

Dates, Non-Numeric Values and Missing Units

Strings and dates can have similar analysis. One might consider Brisbane and Brisbaine to support each other for the capital of Australia. Also, days clearly support months, for example July 4, 2009 clearly supports July 2009. But the quantification of the support is slightly different. Consider also the population of Spain, which usually does not have any explicit units. The analysis in this experiment is applicable, other than Units Analysis.

Second Place, Third Place, and So Forth

This experiment assumes that a single, best answer is expected. It should be possible to return a ranked list of answers, each with a relative confidence to the others.

Adding More Knowledge Sources

Sites such as Yahoo! (www.yahoo.com) and Google both have instant answer sources. They have a higher reliability than just a Google search and should be considered as sources. There are also many domain specific sites that can be used for specialized queries. At the moment, adding a new source means adding a new wrapper with custom code. It is possible that patterns will emerge to facilitate the simpler extraction of values from websites. At the moment, writing a new wrapper involves a considerable amount of custom code and testing.

Systems like FACTO (Yin, Tan, & Liu, 2011) scan through web sites looking for attribute-value tables. It is possible that this approach can be used to help extract useful information from websites, reducing the need for manual wrapper creation.

CONCLUSION

The GROK architecture provides a good framework for experimenting with numeric question answering on the web. It allows candidate answers to come from different sources, including Google, Wikipedia, NASA, CIA World Fact Book, and many others. Furthermore, it is able to collect and consolidate multiple answers into a single consensus answer, and then to compare that against a target answer.

The three main hypotheses suggested in the research were all validated. Each of the following was demonstrated to improve performance:

- Doing unit conversions.
- Using an implied precision for numbers.
- Considering the confidence of the source.

These results were achieved during the Wikipedia Development phase, and validated during the Test phase.

REFERENCES

Cafarela, M. J., Downey, D., Soderland, S., & Etzioni, O. (2005). KnowItAll: Fast, scalable information extraction from the Web. In *Proceedings of the Human Language Technology Conference and Conference on Empirical Methods in Natural Language Processing* (pp. 563-570).

Clarke, C., Cormack, G. V., & Lynam, T. R. (2001). Exploiting Redundancy in Question Answering. In *Proceedings of the 24th Annual International ACM Conference on Research and Devel-opment in Information Retrieval (SIGIR)* (pp. 358-365).

Dong, X. L., Berti-Equille, L., & Srivastava, D. (2009). Integrating Conflicting Data: The Role of Source Dependence. In *Proceedings of the Very Large Databases (VLDB) Conference* (pp. 550-561).

Ferret, O., Grau, B., Hurault-Plantet, M., Illouz, G., & Jacquemin, C. (2001). Terminological Variants for Document Selection and Question/Answer Matching. In *Proceedings of the Workshop on Open-Domain Question Answering (ODQA)* (Vol. 12). Stroudsburg, PA: Association for Computational Linguistics.

Galland, A., Marian, A., Abiteboul, S., & Senellart, P. (2010). Corroborating Information from Disagreeing Views. In *Proceedings of the 3rd ACM International Conference on Web Search and Data Mining (WSDM)* (pp. 131-140).

Katz, B. (1997). Annotating the World Wide Web Using Natural Language. In *Proceedings of the 5th RIAO Conference on Computer Assisted Information Searching on the Internet.*

Katz, B., Felshin, S., Yuret, D., Ibrahim, A., Lin, J., Marton, G., et al. (2002). Omnibase: Uniform Access to Heterogeneous Data for Question Answering. In *Proceedings of the 7th International Workshop on Applications of Natural Language to Information Systems,* Stockholm, Sweden (pp. 230-234).

Kwok, C., Etzioni, O., & Weld, D. S. (2001). Scaling question answering to the web. *ACM Transactions on Information Systems*, *19*(3), 242–262. doi:10.1145/502115.502117.

Lin, J., & Katz, B. (2003). Question Answering from the Web Using Knowledge Annotation and Knowledge Mining Techniques. In *Proceedings of 12th International Conference on Information and Knowledge Management,* New Orleans, LA (pp. 116-123).

Matuszek, C., Witbrock, M., Kahlert, R. C., Cabral, J., Schneider, D., Shah, P., et al. (2005). Searching for Common Sense: Populating Cyc™ from the Web. In *Proceedings of the 20th National Conference on Artificial Intelligence,* Pittsburgh, PA.

Roussinov, D., Fan, W., & Robles-Flores, J. (2008). Beyond keywords: Automated question answering on the web. *Communications of the ACM*, *51*(9), 60–65. doi:10.1145/1378727.1378743.

Singh, M., & Huhns, M. (2005). *Service-Oriented Computing: Semantics, Processes, Agents.* Chichester, UK: John Wiley & Sons.

White, M., Cardie, C., & Ng, V. (2002). Detecting Discrepancies in Numeric Estimates Using Multidoc-ument Hypertext Summaries. In *Proceedings of the 2nd International Conference on Human Language Technology Research (HLT).*

Yates, A., Banko, M., Broadhead, M., Cafarella, M., Etzioni, O., & Soderland, S. (2007). TextRunner: Open Information Extraction on the Web. In *Proceedings of Human Language Technologies: The Annual Conference of the North American Chapter of the Association for Computational Linguistics: Demonstrations* (pp. 25-26). Stroudsburg, PA: Association for Computational Linguistics.

Yin, X., Han, J., & Yu, P. S. (2007). Truth Discovery with Multiple Conflicting Information Providers on the Web. In *Proceedings of the Knowledge Discovery and Data Mining (KDD) Conference*.

Yin, X., Tan, W., & Liu, C. (2011). FACTO: A Fact Lookup Engine Based on Web Tables. In *Proceedings of the World Wide Web Conference (WWW)*, Hyderabad, India (pp. 507-516).

This work was previously published in the International Journal on Semantic Web and Information Systems, Volume 7, Issue 1, edited by Amit P. Sheth,, pp. 1-17, copyright 2011 by IGI Publishing (an imprint of IGI Global).

Chapter 12
Semantics Discovery via Human Computation Games

Jakub Šimko
Slovak University of Technology, Slovak Republic

Michal Tvarožek
Slovak University of Technology, Slovak Republic

Mária Bieliková
Slovak University of Technology, Slovak Republic

ABSTRACT

The effective acquisition of (semantic) metadata is crucial for many present day applications. Games with a purpose address this issue by transforming computational problems into computer games. The authors present a novel approach to metadata acquisition via Little Search Game (LSG) – a competitive web search game, whose purpose is the creation of a term relationship network. From a player perspective, the goal is to reduce the number of search results returned for a given search term by adding negative search terms to a query. The authors describe specific aspects of the game's design, including player motivation and anti-cheating issues. The authors have performed a series of experiments with Little Search Game, acquired real-world player input, gathered qualitative feedback from the players, constructed and evaluated term relationship network from the game logs and examined the types of created relationships.

INTRODUCTION

Knowledge and semantics are needed both in quality and quantity. Many contemporary applications rely on (semantic) metadata in order to provide their intended functionality (Siorpaes & Simperl, 2010). Consequently, the creation or acquisition of such metadata is crucial to their effective operation and ultimately user satisfaction. Knowledge representations, from formal ontologies to lightweight taxonomies and flat folksonomy-like term networks, are especially vital to advanced

DOI: 10.4018/978-1-4666-3610-1.ch012

information processing tasks that need to process semantic relationships between entities. Typical examples of applications are metadata-based search engines or faceted browsers (Tvarožek & Bieliková, 2010), which require either document annotations or faceted classifications, (personalized) e-learning systems (Barla et al., 2010), which require complex course metadata, information repositories that need resource interlinks and annotations (e.g., Wikipedia), or Semantic Web applications that require formal ontologies. The use of concept relationships is also widely used in exploratory search tasks (Marchionini, 2006) like search query expansion (Ungrangsi, Anutariya, & Wuwongse, 2010) or visualization and navigation in information spaces (Stewart, Scott, & Zelevinsky, 2008).

Rather than use of semantics, more problematic is their acquisition. While automated approaches are able to provide quantity, in comparison with human oriented approaches (expert work, crowdsourcing) they vary in the quality of semantics they provide. The concept of *games with a purpose* (GWAP) emerged within the human computing initiative in recent years and stresses the use of human problem-solving capabilities via specially engineered games to address so called *human intelligence problems* (HITs) that are currently too difficult to solve by machine approaches (e.g., image annotation) (Siorpaes & Hepp, 2008a). By transforming computational problems into engaging computer games, GWAPs enable us to take advantage of human computing power without having to pay for expensive human resources while also providing the scalability to web-scale tasks. Several successful games like the image annotation ESP Game (von Ahn & Dabbish, 2008) have already shown the potential of this approach, especially for creation of web semantics (Siorpaes & Hepp, 2008a).

However, the creation of GWAPs is not a straightforward process, because it is specific to each human intelligence problem that it tries to solve. Although some effort has been spent on developing generic methodologies for GWAP creation (von Ahn & Dabbish, 2008; Siorpaes & Hepp, 2008a; Vickrey et al., 2008), they remain applicable only to narrow problem domains. In this paper, we examine design aspects of existing GWAPs (e.g., player input validation, anti-cheating, scoring system) – their shared characteristics and specifics to support the effort of devising a broader methodology, at least for the Semantic Web domain.

Our own contribution to the field of GWAPs for the Semantic Web includes *Little Search Game* – a novel game for the discovery of semantic links between terms and the successive construction of a term network. *Little Search Game* is a web search game, where players compete in reducing the number of search results by entering queries in a special format. The query consists of one normal search term, given to players before the game starts, and several negative terms entered by players, like "star –movie –wars –death". This query format forces players (in order to be successful in the game) to use negative terms with frequent common co-occurrences with the initial term (i.e., related to it). We collect this information via game logs and aggregate it into a lightweight term network of term relationships. The game has also the unique ability to discover term relationships as perceived by humans, some of which are hard to detect using statistical corpora analysis. Therefore the resulting lightweight term network is suitable for applications like learning support frameworks (Barla et al., 2010), exploratory search tools (Šimko, Tvarožek, & Bieliková, 2010) or as a subject for further semantic enrichment.

We present the details of the *Little Search Game*'s mechanics and term network construction. We further discuss the system of ladders and anti-cheating techniques employed. Next, based on our previous experiments, we briefly present quantitative results of the game deployment and validation of the acquired term network. Next, we discuss the attractiveness of the game with results of a player feedback survey. Lastly, we discuss the extension of the produced term network into a more ontology-like structure through naming of its relationships, and present experimental results examining the relationship types of the term network.

SEMANTIC ACQUISITION TECHNIQUES

Many approaches for knowledge and semantics acquisition have been developed. Automatic approaches to metadata creation address the requirements of web-scale information processing: they extract term relationships by mining text corpora using latent semantic analysis (Park & Ramamohanarao, 2009) or by exploiting existing taxonomies (El Sayed, Hacid, & Zighed, 2007) or folksonomies (Barla & Bieliková, 2009), sometimes within specialized domains (Nenadić & Ananiadou, 2006; Šimko, 2011; Šimko & Bieliková, 2009). Products of such approaches (and also of our game) are term networks, similar to human-created folksonomies: graphs with terms or concepts as nodes, connected to others by relationships of a single type. More formally the network can be represented by a set of RDF triplets with only one possible predicate (which also raises the issue of posterior acquisition of true relationship types).

Other semantics acquisition approaches focus on the discovery of ontology triplets via harvesting of statements (sentences) within a text corpus. Approaches described by Pantel and Pennacchiotti (2008) or Sanchez (2010) extract triplets by searching for occurrences of predicates manually picked beforehand (general, e.g., "part of" or domain specific) and identifying subjects and objects they are bound with. An interesting "inversion" of this approach was developed by Weichselbraun et al. (2010) which labels already existing relationships. The method mines a text corpus looking for co-occurrences of terms coupled in unlabeled relationships and looks up for candidate predicates (Weichselbraun, Wohlgenannt, & Scharl, 2010).

While automatic methods are capable of delivering quantity (e.g., number of terms or concepts and relationships), they vary in quality (e.g., relevance of relationships) (Wang, Maynard, Peters, Bontcheva, & Cunningham, 2005) and often cannot cover nuances and unusual situations in corpora thus producing metadata that need additional validation by human experts. Human resources however are usually scarce and too expensive to be practically viable for web-scale tasks. Perhaps the most comprehensive manually created knowledge base and inference system today is CYC, which despite more than 30 years of concentrated human effort (more than a person-century) still has to achieve widespread practical acceptance and impact on the Web (Lenat, 1995). Consequently, the limited availability of metadata impedes the deployment of advanced applications and seriously hinders Semantic Web adoption.

GAMES WITH A PURPOSE

The basic premise of games with a purpose is that players willingly play a game and are rewarded by non-monetary values (e.g., fun), while they solve a corresponding problem as a side effect of the game (Krause, Takhtamysheva, Wittstock, & Malaka, 2010). To illustrate the potential of GWAPs for web-scale problem solving, we cite statistics provided by the Entertainment Software Association (2011). These indicate that about 273.5 million games were sold in 2009, corresponding to more than 550 million human-hours, if each game was played at least for two hours, still not considering games freely available on the Web (e.g., *Farmville* on Facebook). We believe that this sheer volume of untapped and potentially available human computing power could be partially harnessed to provide the resources necessary to create the semantic metadata required to bring the Semantic Web vision yet one step closer.

Despite the fact that games with a purpose present a recent development enabled by the Web and the number of online users as potential players, they have already been used to perform various tasks, mostly related to semantics and metadata acquisition. GWAPs take advantage of common features such as player consensus and their designers also have to address several common issues (game attractiveness, motivation, cheating prevention) in order to create a successful GWAP.

Aspects of GWAP Design

The basic principle lies in *solving a computational problem via a carefully engineered game providing enjoyable experience to players*, who are usually unaware of its true purpose. Players engage in the game because it provides some non-monetary incentive, such as fun and entertainment. When playing, players' actions are logged and subsequently processed to generate useful artifacts, e.g., metadata. The practicality of GWAPs for web-scale problems comes from their properties:

- Massive parallelization due to the large number of potential players and their willingness to play.
- Human intelligence can effectively solve many problems presently unsolvable by machine approaches.
- Ability to achieve correct results even on noisy inputs via collaboration and agreement of multiple players.

Based on their properties, GWAPs present a unique opportunity to exploit human computation for the solving of complex, large scale problems virtually for free (relative to the size of the solved task). This is especially important in the Semantic Web scenario, which deals with huge amounts of information that needs to be processed by humans. From a design point of view, GWAPs share several issues and aspects that need to be considered during game design:

How Player Output is Validated: The game concept has to overcome this paradox: the purpose of the game is to create new useful artifacts by tracking player actions, which only humans are able to do (otherwise the game is not needed), yet needs to validate the correctness of such artifacts automatically. Furthermore, this must be done immediately after the game ends to provide players with scoring feedback and motivate them to play more and create more useful artifacts. The winning conditions and useful artifact production must correlate, which GWAPs address in these ways:

- Ideally, a single-player approach implements techniques of automatic evaluation of the created artifacts (Terry et al., 2009). This is often strongly problem-specific and not applicable to most problems.
- Some games solve the issue using an online multiplayer scheme, where players validate each others' inputs (von Ahn & Dabbish, 2008; Ho, Chang, Lee, Hsu, & Chen, 2009; Hladká et al., 2009; Siorpaes & Hepp, 2008a). However, this often results in the cold start problem due to the lack of players upon initial game deployment who would be willing to play at the same time. Many games solve this issue by introducing bot-players (von Ahn & Dabbish, 2008; Siorpaes & Hepp, 2008a).
- In case of other single-player games, some GWAPs use bootstrapping techniques for result evaluation: they first test player reliability using problem (game) instances that have a known solution. They further mix the instances with known and unknown solutions to keep the player from creating invalid artifacts (Seneviratne & Izquierdo, 2010).

How Entertainment is Provided: According to Hunicke et al. (2004) players of computer games may be entertained by several game aesthetic factors (Hunicke, LeBlanc, & Zubek, 2004). In games with a purpose these usually include: (1) social experience – interaction with other players (von Ahn & Dabbish, 2008; Tuulos, Scheible, &

Nyholm, 2007), (2) self-challenge – overcoming a player's own previous achievement, joy of reaching the goal (Seneviratne & Izquierdo, 2010; Terry et al., 2009) and (3) competition among players – either in duels or via a ladder system (Hladká et al., 2009; Chamberlain & Poesio, 2009; Ho et al., 2009 ; von Ahn & Dabbish, 2008).

How Does the Game Prevent Cheating Attempts: Computer games, especially multiplayer and competitive, suffer from cheating attempts and dishonest player behavior (bypassing rules, exploiting bugs). In games with a purpose, cheating may not only destroy the fairness of the game but also cause invalid problem solutions to be generated. Solutions are often problem specific, i.e., the state space of the game can be analyzed and rule gaps identified. The common practice is also cross-validation among opponents (Ho et al., 2009). In the worst cases, beta testing of a game with live deployment quickly discloses problems with cheating.

The majority of the GWAPs rely on online multiplayer mode of gameplay to validate correctness of the players' actions and artifacts that are inferred based on their actions. The number of these games indicates the relative ease of implementing this principle, which also comes with the opportunity of implicit cheating prevention and potential social experience for players that seems to be a very strong incentive and motivation to play (Kuo et al., 2009).

GWAPs for Semantic Web

In the Semantic Web domain, GWAPs are being employed for various tasks ranging from resource annotation (multimedia or texts) to ontology building. A comprehensive summary of existing semantics acquisition GWAPs was created by Thaler, Siorpaes, Simperl, and Hofer (2011) and is maintained in the *Insemtives* web page (http://www.insemtives.eu/games.php). We distinguish two major groups of GWAPs based on their purpose: *resource annotation* – metadata

acquisition games for multimedia (von Ahn & Dabbish, 2008; Seneviratne & Izquierdo, 2010; Barrington, O'Malley, Turnbull, & Lanckriet, 2009; Ho et al., 2009; Dasdan et al., 2009), textual resources (Chamberlain & Poesio, 2009; Hladká et al., 2009) or web pages (Law, Mityagin, & Chickering, 2009), and domain modeling games, involving tasks like common sense facts collecting (von Ahn & Dabbish, 2008; Kuo et al., 2009) and validation (Herdağdelen & Baroni, 2010), term associations acquisition (Vickrey et al., 2008) or ontology alignment (Siorpaes & Hepp, 2008a).

In the field of multimedia annotation, von Ahn's *ESP game* corresponds to an output-agreement game where two players must enter the same tag within a given time limit, given a common image as input and a set of taboo tags. Based on practical experience, as of 2008, 200,000 players have entered more than 50 million tags effectively solving the problem of image tagging via collaborative player agreement on image tags (von Ahn & Dabbish, 2008).

Similarly to the *ESP game*, *KissKissBan* is an image labeling game that extends the original *ESP game* with additional anti-cheating aspects (Ho et al., 2009), since the original concept was prone to abuse if players agreed beforehand on the keywords they would input. While *ESP game* addressed this problem by selecting random players who ideally did not know each other or by using system level measures, *KissKissBan* extends the gameplay model with a "blocker" player whose task is to prevent the other two players from forming a unified strategy by monitoring the progress of the game and selecting taboo words on the fly.

Peekaboom is an inversion-problem game, which is designed to support the annotation of objects in images (von Ahn & Dabbish, 2008). Again, two random players aim to find agreement – one plays the describer who is given an input, another one plays the guesser who must produce the input based on the description from the describer thus finishing the game.

As a non-multiplayer GWAP example working on the bootstrapping principle, the image annotation framework of Seneviratne and Izquierdo (2010) can be used. Here, a single player is annotating a pack of images with tags and receives his score only afterward. Some of the images in the set are already annotated and the scores is computed based on player's performance on those, plus the game uses some other heuristics for assumption whether the player is honest or not. Players are aware of the scoring methods, so their best option to gain the highest possible score is to be honest all the time (Seneviratne & Izquierdo, 2010).

The bootstrapping approach for image annotation was also used in the *FishEye* game devised by Thaler et al. (2011) although with a different technique of assigning annotations: instead of writing tags, players decide by putting images (fishes) into graphically stylized baskets, thus saying which of the given images belong to a specific concept assigned for each game round. This makes the task more comfortable for players (Thaler, Siorpaes, Mear, Simperl, & Goodman, 2011) and adds to effective "purpose encapsulation" exercised by the game's design (e.g., graphically stylized metaphor of fish catching).

Multimedia annotation GWAPs comprise mostly image annotation games. However, similar principles can also be used for annotation of video or audio streams. In the *Tagatune* game (Law, von Ahn, Dannenberg, & Crawford, 2007), players need to agree whether they are listening to the same track or not by exchanging text messages (from which tag descriptions are extracted automatically). In *HeardIt* (Barrington et al., 2009), two players have to agree on the same values of certain attributes that describe an audio stream, which produces a (rather "supervised") track categorization. Similarly to that, Siorpaes and Hepp (2008b) devised the *OntoTube* game for categorizing video streams.

In case of textual resource annotation, the task of providing characteristic terms to a resource is successfully performed by automated natural language processing approaches. A more complex problem, suitable for human solving, is identification of co-references (matching nouns and pronouns in texts, referencing the same object). Two GWAPs were designed to fulfill this task: *PlayCoref* (Hladká et al., 2009) and *PhraseDetectives* (Chamberlain & Poesio, 2009). In *PlayCoref*, two players compete in marking co-references by matching nouns with pronouns. The score is afterward computed by validating player guesses against the opponent and also by comparison with the results of an automated co-reference detection approach (Hladká et al., 2009). *PhraseDetectives* is slightly different as it works in two rounds: annotation and validation (in which the opponents validate each others' guesses) (Chamberlain & Poesio, 2009).

In this paper, we describe a GWAP involving search query formulation by players. Some resource annotation GWAPs also utilize this feature. In *Thumbs-up,* the player, given two images and one query that retrieved them, has to decide which image suits the query better (Dasdan et al., 2009). In the game *Intentions*, two players have to agree, whether they see the same web page or not (each player retrieves one and cannot see the opponent's one). They reversely construct search queries to retrieve the original. They cannot see each other's queries, but may review other results from opponent's queries. The purpose here is to decorate initial web pages with relevant terms (Law et al., 2009).

Games with a purpose have also been employed in the field of domain modeling. Siorpaes and Hepp (2008a) devised a set of interactive games for the Semantic Web whose purpose was the creation of annotations (*OntoTube, OntoBay*) but also ontology linking (*OntoPronto*) and ontology alignment (*SpotTheLink*) (Siorpaes & Hepp, 2008a; Thaler, Simperl, & Siorpaes, 2011). Several other GWAPs have been devised particularly in the field of ontology creation. *Verbosity* by Luis von Ahn, also an inversion-problem game, is played by two anonymous players where player B guesses a word (noun) given to player A. Player A describes the given word using other nouns inserted into preset sentence stubs either as subjects or objects. As players play, they discover common-sense facts about the words they play with – they connect them with relationships, typical for ontologies ("consists of", "is a", "is opposite of"), transformed to natural language sentence stubs. The correctness of the described relationships stems from the fact that in the end, player B guesses the correct original word and also by cross-validation among game instances (von Ahn & Dabbish, 2008). The game *Verbosity* is the main source of facts for the *ConceptNet* ontology.

Another ontology-population game is *OntoGalaxy* by Krause et al. (2010). In this single player game, designed graphically as an action game in space, players have to collect word-labeled freighters owing toward their ship, but only those labeled with a word satisfying certain conditions, given at the start of the game (e.g., "it must be touchable by hand"). The strengths of *OntoGalaxy* are its sophisticated graphics and good encapsulation of its purpose into its gameplay thus hiding it from players (Krause et al., 2010).

Concept game (Herdağdelen & Baroni, 2010) is an example of a GWAP oriented on the validation of common-sense facts obtained by automated means. Prior to gameplay, candidate triplet statements are acquired by an automated corpus-based method using seeds from the *ConceptNet* ontology. During the game, players encounter triplets being displayed by a slot machine (each feature on one of three cylinders). If a player thinks that a meaningful statement was rolled, he may "claim" money for it (effectively telling that he considers it valid). Based on other player choices, the player gets awarded or punished (Herdağdelen & Baroni, 2010). The game uses the bootstrapping approach

of artifact validation, supported by heuristics indicating player's trustworthiness, similarly to Seneviratne's image annotation framework (Seneviratne & Izquierdo, 2010).

To summarize, games with a purpose have already shown significant potential to harness human computational capabilities for web-scale problems with respect to the cost of man-hours required. Although some authors formulated several best design practices (Siorpaes & Hepp, 2008a; von Ahn & Dabbish, 2008), there still is no universal methodology for GWAP creation, which is often performed in an ad hoc way. Consequently, the transformation of arbitrary problems into a GWAPs, abuse detection and prevention, and on-demand metadata creation (e.g., how to focus GWAP to create/extend metadata in a desired way) are still challenging open problems.

LITTLE SEARCH GAME PRINCIPLES

In order to acquire a term relationship network (i.e., a light-weight semantic structure) we improve upon the state-of-the-art in games with a purpose by devising *Little Search Game*. It is a web search query formulation game, in which players reduce the number of results returned by a search engine to a minimum, using specially formatted queries (e.g., "star −movie −wars −death"), which force them to reveal their perception of term relationships. It is a single player, casual browser game that motivates players to play via ranked competition and mental challenges (game attractiveness factors defined by Hunicke et al., 2004).

The game utilizes the principle of negative search, in which the original set of web search results is stripped of a subset of results containing specific negative terms, to construct a term relationship network by mining the game query logs. At the start of the game, the player is given a task in the form of a positive query term that yields a certain number of search results. The player's task is to reduce the number of results by adding proper negative terms to the given initial query term. The lower the final number of results, the better rank the player gets. In order to achieve the best results, players must enter negative terms that have high co-occurrences with the task term on the Web. This principle is also the key for term relationship networks acquisition since players interpret the co-occurrence of terms as a semantic relationship between them and vice versa (Šimko, Tvarožek, & Bieliková, 2011).

The winning condition of *Little Search Game* is evaluated automatically unlike in multiplayer-based games (von Ahn & Dabbish, 2008; Ho et al., 2009; Law et al., 2007; Barrington et al., 2009) or bootstrap-based games (Seneviratne & Izquierdo, 2010; Thaler et al., 2011). Though the scoring only approximates the value of relationships created (best terms for the game are not necessarily best for the game's purpose and vice versa), it is sufficient to keep players motivated. This allowed us to design the game as a single player game. Consequently, the game does not suffer from the cold start problem caused by lack of players and neither requires a previously created set of data for score computation and result verification. Feedback to players is given immediately after the game ends. Since it cannot rely on mutual player

control to prevent cheating, we use preventive rules to reduce dishonest player behavior and also impose a posterior cheating detection heuristics.

Game Scenario

The following scenario illustrates a typical use of *Little Search Game* (the interface of the game is shown in Figure 1; the current implementation utilizes the Google search engine):

1. The player selects a task term or lets the game select one for him (we prefer to select tasks not yet played by the player), for example "star". The game queries a search engine with this term and displays the number of results, in this case nearly 500 million.

2. The player enters negative terms (fields on the left in Figure 1). He first uses the term "movie" (thus creating the query "star –movie"), because he feels that the words "star" and "movie" are commonly used within the same phrase in many web sites. After submitting this attempt, the search engine now returns only 400 million results. The change can be seen in Figure 1 in the middle of the game interface where the relative numbers of results per attempt (query) is shown.

Figure 1. Example of the Little Search Game interface with negative terms (left), attempt history (center) and ranking ladder (right)

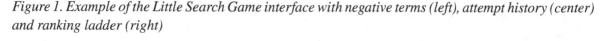

3. The player may continue to refine the query by entering or overwriting the negative terms. He is limited to use up to *N* negative terms at once (we chose *N = 6* to provide sufficient possibilities for players while not overloading them with too many options and to challenge the player to come up with the best terms). There is no penalty for performing more attempts; the players are free to refine their queries (and to enter new words) as much as they want. They usually do, until they are satisfied with their rank in the ranking ladder displayed on the right side of the interface (Figure 1).

4. When the player is satisfied with the results, he confirms the results and may review the rankings or play the same or another term in the next round. The ladder system is further discussed in section "Effectiveness of the game".

Term Network Inference

The format of the game queries forces players to reveal their perception of term relatedness with a given task term. If several players agree on the relatedness of the same term pair, we can arguably promote this relationship into the collaboratively created term relationship network (a subset of the *Little Search Game* term network is shown in Figure 2).

We represent log entries for term network creation as triplets (p_i, t_j, N_{ij}) where

- $p_i; p_i \in P$ is a player identifier where P is the set of all players.
- $t_j; t_j \in T$ is a task term where T is the set of all task terms.
- $N_{ij} = \{n_{ij1}, ..., n_{ijn}\}$ is a set of negative terms that player p_i used at least once when solving task t_j. Also let $\forall n; n \in N$ where N is the set of all negative words.

Figure 2. Subset of the created term network

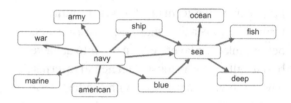

Note that there is no information about time, order, number of results for a particular attempt or the number of uses of a specific negative word. Though we also log this additional information, it is not needed for basic network creation. The only important fact is that the user used a negative term, which he at some point thought to be related to the task term (which it should occur often with). We call the first occurrence of the player, task term and negative term triplet a *vote* $l = (p_i, t_j, n_k)$ of vote set $L : P \times T \times N$.

If the number of votes with the same combination of task and negative term is greater than 5 (a constant we chose based on previous experience with such scenarios, i.e., we assume that the agreement of five players is satisfactory), the oriented relationship in the term network is created with the task word as the source node and the negative word as the target node. The relationship has two other attributes: the total number of votes that contain the source term as task word ω_t and the total number of votes for the particular relationship ω_p.

The *Little Search Game* term network is defined as a graph G consisting of the set of nodes V (containing task terms T and negative terms N) and set of edges E:

$$G(V, E)$$

$$V : T \cup N$$

$$E : V \times V \times \mathbb{N} \times \mathbb{N}$$

A term network edge $e; e \in E$ is a quartet $e = (t, n, \omega_t, \omega_p)$ where $t \in T$ and $n \in N$. Using values ω_t and ω_p we define the weight w of the edge relative to other edges outgoing from the same node:

$$w = \frac{\omega_p}{\omega_t}$$

The value w enables us to sort edges outgoing from a node by their relative strength.

Effectiveness of the Game

To evaluate the problem solving potential of games with a purpose, Luis von Ahn suggested the use of *throughput* (the number of problem instances solved in one man-hour) multiplied by the *average lifetime play* (ALP) – the total number of hours dedicated to the game by one player. The ALP factor corresponds to the attractiveness of the game, which is crucial to maintaining player interest (von Ahn & Dabbish, 2008). The game system influences both factors, which are usually contradictory.

In *Little Search Game* some of the attractiveness is motivated by the element of challenge (i.e., by the opportunity to outdo oneself), which is represented by a mental challenge for players to come up with negative terms which really help them (Hunicke et al., 2004). The second part of attractiveness is competition (Hunicke et al., 2004). The challenge aspect is always present in the game, even if the player plays it alone. On the other hand, the competition depends on the overall fairness of the game (i.e., cheating detection and prevention handled primarily by word banning policy) and the ladder system.

The ladder is in fact the critical point in which the attractiveness and throughput contradict. From the attractiveness standpoint, all players should play the same set of task words, as that would be the only fair way to compare players (i.e., to compare their result counts for the same game tasks). But from the throughput standpoint, only a limited number of players is required for playing the same task, since we only need to collect enough votes to acquire the most relevant relationships in the term network (we opted for 10 relationships per term, this depends on the purpose of the network, for instance, for exploring the term network visually within exploratory search applications, 10 was sufficient). Allowing players to continue playing one task over and over again for the sake of competition would be inefficient, since new relationships would appear at a decreasing rate and be less relevant. Since we aimed to discover at least some relationships for many terms (and not many relationships for few terms), we devised a strategy for assigning task words effectively, without breaking the competition system.

As a compromise, we organize gameplay into rounds lasting from several days to weeks starting with an empty ladder. In each round, a set of task words is played and every task has a separate ladder, created as an ascending list of the achieved result counts (the best player has the lowest count). There is no penalty for playing the same task several times and all players can play all tasks, since we want to motivate players to play as much as possible to obtain more data. However, only the single best task result is recorded in the ladder.

We also devised an overall ladder (empty at round start), to which a player receives points depending on his ranks in individual task ladders. The first player in the task ladder receives 100 points to the overall ladder, the second 99 points etc. Consequently, players receive points even for low ranks (in terms of hundreds of players) and are motivated to play multiple tasks which significantly increases throughput.

Based on the traffic in the last game round, the length of the next round and number of tasks in the next task set is determined to optimize throughput and to generate the desired 10 relationships for each task term. However, the length of a round should not be shorter than about 3 days (to give more casual players enough time to compete) and the number of task words higher than about 20 (to make all tasks playable in a reasonable amount of time).

Purposeful Task Word Selection

The strategy of selecting task words for LSG influences its outcome in several ways. Firstly, it enables us to control the "growth" of the term network: by introducing or ceasing the usage of certain terms, one can control the number of relationships created for that term. This can be exploited to complement similar existing term networks by "expanding" their nodes.

Secondly, task selection has impact on the attractiveness of the game. Players must be somewhat familiar with the task words they are given. If they do, they are going to be more effective in the game and therefore more satisfied. For general players, general terms should be used which yields general relationships. However, domain-specific scenarios are also possible. If the search query is made over a domain-specific corpus, indexed prior to gameplay (e.g., via tools such as *Lucene,* http://lucene.apache.org/) and the game is played by a group of users with some degree of expertise within this field, then it yields relationships specific for that domain. We observed this effect in our experiments, where a significant number of players were students of IT: when they were given the task word "cellular" one of their negative term responses was "automaton" – a purely domain specific relationship.

A further extension of the game's concept can lie in the task selection strategy as the means of setting the difficulty of the tasks given to players to keep them challenged. The difficulty of the task correlates with the specificity of the task term (more specific = more difficult). Also, it can be modified by automated evaluation of past

successes of other players with the task term (for example the relative decrease of the number of results).

Another possibility to acquire domain specific networks is to allow players to choose in which domain they want to play the game or assign tasks according to existing models of user interests (if available, for example in conjunction with a proxy server) (Kramár, Barla, & Bieliková, 2010). One of our aims is to use the game with groups of students during their courses (which act also as domains) and utilize the resulting relationships within the learning support system ALEF (Adaptive Learning Framework) (Barla et al., 2010) that uses lightweight semantics to model the syllabus of a course, helps students navigate through the course domain and is used for learning object recommendation.

GAME DEPLOYMENT

We devised *Little Search Game* as a web browser game (using the Silverlight platform) backed with .NET web services and the MS SQL database. Its current implementation is called *Little Google Game* (http://mirai.fiit.stuba.sk/LittleGoogleGame) as we used Google (via AJAX API) as the game's web search engine. However, any search engine supporting negative term search is applicable. To access WordNet (for filtering only meaningful negative terms), we used the WordNet.Net library.

During the first deployment, the game was played by 30 players with an initial set of 20 arbitrary chosen task words (*Path, Bomb, Water, Castle, Cellular, Brain, Culture, Masquerade, Jaguar, Future, Star, Navy, President, Rontgen, Einstein, Easter, Worm, Beer, Forest, Sea*). Players played up to 300 games and submitted about 2000 queries. Even after such a small number of games, we were able to construct the base of a term network comprising more than 100 nodes of negative terms. To expand the term network, further task terms in later phases of deployment were picked from target terms of the strongest relationships in the graph.

Besides the casual game mode, we devised the tournament mode, which is suitable for organizing a game competition during various events (e.g., conferences). In the tournament mode, players solve different sets of tasks, but can also participate as regular players. We used the tournament mode during the Student Research Conference IIT. SRC 2010 at our university. Participants, mostly students, were motivated to participate via a tournament prize, but many of them played also the regular game tasks (off the prized competition).

Another release of the game was during a showcase, where a minor number of games was played. So far, the game was played by about 300 players with 3,800 played games and 27,200 submitted queries. The total number of task terms used in the game so far is 40 and players guessed over 3,200 negative terms.

The resulting network contains 400 nodes and 560 edges. However, the distribution of relationships per task term differs between game type in which it was used (tournament tasks were played much more than tasks used during the showcase). After imposing an additional log analysis restriction, that only the 10 strongest relationships per task term are considered, the resulting network shrunk to 183 nodes and 220 edges.

TERM NETWORK VALIDATION

We validated the acquired term network for semantic soundness. We conducted an experiment with a group of 18 judges (from various professions, aged 18-35) to evaluate the soundness of 20 term relationship (Šimko et al., 2011). Twelve of those relationships were from the network acquired using the game, 8 were created randomly (i.e., not sound). The relationships were shuffled so the

judges were not able to figure out what they were expected to select. Judges were asked to assign each relationship a value between 1 ("definitely irrelevant") and 4 ("definitely relevant") to describe their opinion on the term pair's semantic soundness. They were also asked to evaluate pairs in an oriented manner, i.e., whether the term B is within the top ten most relevant terms for term A, but not necessarily vice versa.

After the judges submitted their votes, we computed their group opinion on soundness of each judged term pair. The outcome for each pair could be "sound", "not sound" and "controversial" in case that none of previous two options received more than two thirds of votes. To compute the number of votes, options 1 and 4 were counted with double weight (since the judges were more confident about them).

The experiment has shown that 10 out of 11 term pairs from the created term network were semantically sound, and one pair was not sound, which corresponds to almost 91% correctness. The twelfth relationship could not be evaluated, since it was marked as controversial – it was the pair "cellular – automaton" which makes sense for informatics (who were the prevailing group among players), but not in general.

HIDDEN RELATIONSHIPS

When considering methods for automatic term relationship extraction, term co-occurrence in documents comes to mind. However, the semantic soundness of term pairs does not necessarily correspond to the co-occurrence frequency of terms in large text corpora, such as the Web. For instance, the term pair "brain – tumor" is arguably a relevant connection, but those words, in fact, occur only sporadically together in web documents. On the other hand a pair "substance – argument" is a nonsense connection, despite that those terms occur ten times more frequently (according to their sole frequency of occurrence). This brings unwanted *noise* to co-occurrence based term network extraction, since the relevant pairs are "hidden" among irrelevant pairs with higher co-occurrence rates. The situation is best illustrated by the scheme on Figure 3.

Little Search Game is able to identify these "hidden" term relationships. Although the players' winning goal is to identify term pairs with high co-occurrence rates, they interpret this as finding of terms relevant to the task term (which in their opinion also has the best chances for significant co-occurrence). Players thus sometimes enter negative terms that they *believe* will help them in reducing the number of search results but in fact do not significantly reduce the result set. If such terms are "hidden", they are quickly abandoned by players as useless, but remain in the game logs where they provide valuable information upon network extraction.

To validate, how many "hidden" term relationships our term network contains, we conducted an experiment, which examined the co-occurrence of term relationships present in the *Little Search Game* (LSG) network (Šimko et al., 2011). Also, co-occurrences in a nonsense term pair set (created by random term pairing) were acquired to determine the "noise" level. We used the whole Web as a text corpus, accessed via the *Bing* search engine.

To determine the co-occurrence ratio of two terms, the search engine is queried for each term separately and then by conjunctive clause of both terms (e.g., "sea AND blue"). These three queries yield three result counts – p_s, p_t and i – which represent the cardinalities of result sets of the two terms and the intersection of those sets. The co-occurrence ratio of the search term to the target term is defined as $r_s = i / p_s$ (or $r_s = i / p_t$ for the reverse relationship).

We acquired the source-target co-occurrence ratios for the relationships in the LSG network and also for nonsense relationships in three reference sets. We used three sets composed of three dif-

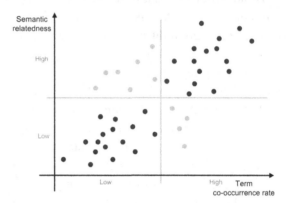

Figure 3. Hidden term relationships – expectations (black) and reality (black and grey). Some semantically sound term relationships have their text corpus co-occurrence rates below the rates of nonsense term pairs and vice versa

ferent sized corpora of the most frequent words in the English language (800, 5,000 and 50,000 words), excluding stopwords. This was due to the fact, that more frequent terms, event semantically unrelated, produce higher level of noise. For our experiment, the relevant set was the medium sized (5,000 words) since it covered the terms used in the LSG network.

The measured values are plotted in Figures 4 and 5. If we look at the reference sets, we see that for the medium sized corpus, the noise starts to be significant at the ratio of 35%. Around 40% of the LSG term network relationships have co-occurrence rates below that value, which means they can be considered "hidden". The game is therefore able to discover a significant amount of relationships that cannot be retrieved by statistical corpora analysis.

Relationship Types

The LSG term network is a lightweight structure of untyped term associations. It is therefore relevant to discover, whether those relationships can be upgraded to more ontology-like triplets, for instance by assigning them appropriate types as predicates. Although the method of doing so

Figure 4. Distribution of term network relationships by the real co-occurrence of the paired terms

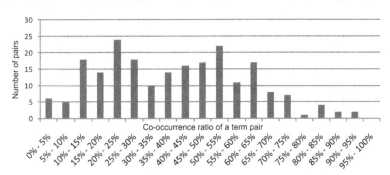

Figure 5. Distribution of the nonsense (reference) relationships by the real co-occurrence of the paired terms. Three differently sized corpora are used

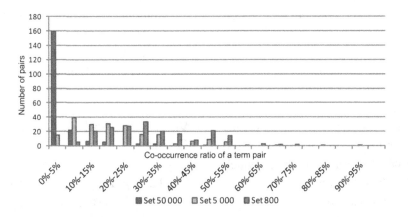

is also the subject of our future work, we conducted experiments to examine the feasibility of such efforts. In the experiments, we again tested the soundness of the LSG term network relationships and examined which types of relationships are mostly present in the LSG network. We also examined the degree of possible enrichment of an existing knowledge base that we can achieve by adding relationships from our network. At the end of this section, we outline two possible scenarios how to perform relationship labeling over the LSG term network as our future work.

We have queried the existing general knowledge base of common facts – the *ConceptNet* ontology (MIT Media Lab, n. d.) – for types of LSG network relationships. We were interested in

(1) how many of them are actually represented in such a knowledge base and (2) of what types they were. Additionally, we also conducted a manual (two judges agreement) evaluation of all the relationships in the LSG network and assigned each of them the overall semantic soundness and one of the relationship types (defined by *ConceptNet*).

We picked the *ConceptNet* for several reasons. It contains common sense facts (incidentally, co-created by another GWAP, Verbosity) (von Ahn & Dabbish, 2008) what makes it suitable to use as a reference dataset. Second, it has a defined set of 23 possible general predicates, which allowed us to type the LSG network relationships with some precision, but has not dispersed them into too small categories.

Hypotheses were defined as follows: Relationships of the LSG are semantically sound and are of various types. In the existing knowledge base, most of the terms used in LSG network were also present in the form of concepts, but the knowledge base comprises only a limited number of (mostly rigid) LSG network relationships.

Data

We worked with 400 relationships created by *Little Search Game*, the relationships were sorted according to their strength based on how many votes they received during gameplay. As knowledge base, we used *ConceptNet 3.0* accessible via an online REST API.

Process

Two independent judges manually evaluated each relationship in the LSG network. Both judges evaluated the soundness with one of the three values (sound, maybe sound and not sound), which after merging of both evaluation yielded five possible combinations. Judges also assigned one of the 23 relationship types (e.g., *IsA*, *HasA*, *UsedFor*, *CapableOf*) to each LSG relationship with an option to assign a default unknown type, which was also assumed if the judges had not reached an agreement. The automatic retrieval of relationship types from *ConceptNet* was straightforward.

Evaluation

We analyzed the collected data with these findings:

- The manual evaluation has shown that from 400 examined relationships 80% were semantically sound, 8% rather controversial and 12% not sound (which is less than in the previous experiment, however, the "strongest" 100 relationships still had 93% soundness with only one 1% marked as not sound).

- The *ConceptNet* comprises only 164 (41%) out of 400 relationships we worked with. We consider this to be a strong argument for putting effort into enriching such knowledge bases with relationships acquired by *Little Search Game*.

- The distribution of relationship types in the manually annotated set and *ConceptNet* set differs (as shown in Figure 6). First, many of the *ConceptNet* evaluated relationships were taxonomic (IsA) while various dependencies (Desires, Causes...) were virtually absent in *ConceptNet*. Generally, *ConceptNet* relies roughly on 6 types of relationships, while the manually annotated set appears to be much richer in types what further stresses the usefulness of naming LSG created relationships.

Verb Retrieval via Little Search Game

The basic game principle of *Little Search Game* can be modified to serve the relationship labeling purpose: (1) The task query can comprise two nouns (of the unnamed relationship) instead of single one. (2) The possible negative terms could be restricted to verbs.

The rest of the game rules remain untouched. The advantage of this modification is that players do not have to learn a new game principle; they just switch the game to different mode. Since the players (as demonstrated earlier) think about game tasks on a conceptual level, we argue that they will (as a first choice) use verbs effectively describing some of the valid predicates between the given terms. A minor drawback of this approach is the bypassing of the sentence syntax the player has in mind and the introduction of ambiguity in deciding what is the left or right feature in the triplet, however, even the assignment of a predicate is valuable.

Figure 6. Relative distribution of relationship types in the manually evaluated set and ConceptNet

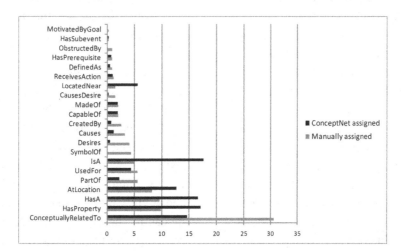

Mining Sentences on the Web

The second method that we propose for labeling the relationships of the LSG network relies on mining text for triplet-like statements comprising terms of the unnamed relationship. The main idea is to retrieve relevant web (or domain corpora) documents for each unnamed relationship using a web search engine, then parsing sentences containing relationship terms and finally analyzing those sentences for triplet statements. A similar approach was already implemented by McDowell and Carafella for unsupervised instance population for ontology classes and exploring relationships (Mcdowell & Cafarella, 2008).

In this method, the system of result ranking implemented by search engines is exploited. Since it takes into account the co-location of terms within the documents, it can retrieve relevant web documents to mine for relatively small cost: the most relevant documents will rank high in the result list. We propose sentence mining in several ways:

- **Three-Term Sentences:** A huge corpus of potentially relevant documents allows us to look only for three-term sentences, containing always two of our relationship terms and a third term which will be con-

sidered as a third part of a triplet. With the use of part-of-speech identification (e.g., using WordNet) we could identify predicates for noun-noun bigrams (common case of unnamed relationships), but also nouns complementing the "noun-predicate" which are sometimes also present in the LSG network.

- Using the option prior, we could search for any label (type) for a relationship. We could however, focus only on a limited set of general types of relationships as they are in many cases sufficient (e.g., *IsA, HasA, LocatedNear* as seen in *ConceptNet*). The lookup can then be performed using the predefined set of manually created sentence stubs characteristic for expressing the relationship (e.g., "A such as B" for "IsA" relationships).

Banned Terms

Game rules must be defined to preserve fairness and eliminate opportunity for abuse (besides "hard line" hacks, such as attacking network communication or the software itself). Abuse is usually done by a small group of (somehow curious) players, but especially in case of games with ladders, these players can ruin the whole system of fairness and cause regular players to abandon a game. With respect to games with a purpose, rules also have to eliminate possibilities for player behavior that does not support the game's purpose (e.g., not solving the problem correctly).

In *Little Search Game* the only player action that affects the game outcome are the negative term entries. After a few games, curious players realized that entering stopwords either from a language standpoint (e.g., "star –is –the –over") or Web standpoint (e.g., "star –download –page –table –menu") yields very few search results for all search terms and thus promotes them to top ranks in ladders with scores impossible to achieve by "proper" means. Some of the "web stopwords" like "menu" or "download" originate from their widespread use on websites, others like "page" or "table" occurs widely within HTML source code. As search engines include them into indexes, they bring an unwanted bias into the game.

We addressed this issue of "killer words" by defining a set of terms allowed to be used in the game, before the game was released:

- The terms must be contained within a dictionary (we used *WordNet,* http://wordnet. princeton.edu) within one of its parts of speech: nouns, adjectives, verbs or adverbs (i.e., we exclude most semantic-less terms). Before a game attempt is sent to the search engine, the negative terms are checked against the dictionary, which also helps us detect misspelled terms.
- Using the same term as the task term is forbidden; we also use *WordNet* to check for morphs of the task term.
- Most frequent words in the English language (the language of the game) are excluded. We used the set of the 200 most frequent words in the texts of Wikipedia.
- HTML tags and some other words common on the Web are excluded. This manually prepared set of terms was extended with additional words that were banned from use during the first days of game deployment.

Though we proactively devised these rules, some of the non-suitable words were only discovered after having been abusively used by players after the game was released. Thus we devised a term abuse detection heuristic that suggests suspicious words to game administrators (who may eventually decide to ban additional terms). The premise is that possibly abusive words would appear in the attempts of leading players and eventually be used multiple times for different tasks and their result yield would be significantly lower than the nearest ranking attempts.

Our heuristic works in these steps:

1. Collect (three) highest ranking players for each task.
2. Exclude players that rank in just one task ladder.
3. Collect negative terms for each of the remaining players' best attempts in tasks where they ranked high.
4. Exclude terms appearing in only one task.
5. Mark terms that appear in more than two tasks or that are contained in attempts yielding significantly fewer results (more than 10% than the next ranking attempt) as suspicious and pass them to an administrator.

We compute the "universal effectiveness" for suspicious terms as a guideline to administrators (to determine if they are truly stopwords) by querying for their co-occurrence within a set of 10 manually selected reference terms (with a small mutual co-occurrence on Web). If the intersection with them is high, the terms should probably be banned.

Formally: let $S = \{s_1, ..., s_n\}$ be a set of suspicious terms. For each s_i we construct a set $P_i = \{p_{i1}, ..., p_{im}\}$ of ordered pairs $p_{ij} = (r_j, q_{ji})$ where $r_j \in R$ is a reference term belonging to the set of reference terms $R = \{r_1, ..., r_m\}$ and q_{ji} is a search query of reference term r_j and the suspicious term s_i formatted as "r_j AND s_i". The search engine when queried by elements of each ordered pair p_{ij} yields elements of another ordered pair (σ_j, ψ_{ij}) where $\sigma_j; \sigma_j \in \mathbb{N}$ is the number of results yielded for the reference term r_j only and $\psi_{ij}; \psi_{ij} \in \mathbb{N}$ is the number of results yielded for query q_{ji}. Relatively high values of ψ_{ij} against σ_j (more than 30%) in the majority of reference terms, argued strongly for the banning of terms, though the final decision was made by game administrators.

After the game was released, the list of banned terms has increased from around 230 terms to 430. Using our heuristic we discovered about 30 non-suitable terms; the rest was manually inferred. Sometimes, one abused term indicated potential use of other similar terms. One example of discovered abusable terms was numbers and digits as some are present in WordNet. Since players received no penalty for trying to find "killer words", we have observed repeated attempts to do so. In fact, we welcomed their efforts as they helped us make the game fairer.

Attempts rejected due to use of banned words were returned to players with an explaining message – players were aware of all the aforementioned criteria. Unfortunately, some terms had to be excluded from the game (and thus the resulting term network) even though they arguably had semantic meaning and legitimacy to be used as negative terms in certain tasks (e.g., "restaurant –menu" or "school –table", where "menu" and "table" are banned due to being common in web content and HTML code). Such terms had to be sacrificed in order to keep the game fair; though they could still be used as task words.

Game Attractiveness and Explicit User Feedback

Game attractiveness plays an important role in evaluating the game's problem solving potential. Luis von Ahn mentions the average lifetime play factor (von Ahn & Dabbish, 2008), which depends mostly on a game's ability to maintain player interest in the game by providing fun. However, the overall game potential is also dependent on the game's ability to spread and attract new players. Thus to evaluate our game from the attractiveness point of view, we conducted the following player survey.

Environment

The survey was conducted during a showcase venue called Researchers' Night, which took place in a shopping mall where visitors had the opportunity to observe or try out various scientific experiments in a joyful and popular way. This included the *Little Search Game*, located in one of the showcase kiosks. The game principles as well as its purpose were explained with the help of a poster.

Participants

Visitors of the showcase were aged 14 years or older but comprised mostly adults. From about 70 players, 34 voluntarily completed the questionnaire after they had played several games. All of the participants had previous experience with web search, but approximately half of them were not aware of the negative search feature.

Data

We integrated a built-in questionnaire into the *Little Search Game* interface to pair player answers with their gaming sessions.

Task

Players were asked to choose one of the given answers to questions shown in Table 1. All participants answered all questions. The questions focused on whether and how players understood the game and its purpose, their general attitude to games and particularly the *Little Search Game*, the game's potential for viral spreading and their attitude towards the game's purpose. Participants could also fill in an optional free-text field to explain their answers. We also collected some feedback during informal interviews with the participants.

The result summary of the survey is shown in Table 1. From the attention attraction standpoint, the game was not self-explanatory: less than half of the players understood it only after reading the manual. Informally, some players mentioned that even with the manual, they would not be interested in the game if they came across it, because they prefer a self explaining interface. Not surprisingly, the non-awareness of the concept of negative search was also a drawback for players. However, once it was clear, players were more willing to play the game repeatedly.

On the other hand, once players understood the game principles, they considered the game interesting (question number 4 was indirectly aimed at the attention-keeping aspect of the game). Around 82% of participants expressed their interest and nearly one third of them would recommend the game further, which shows the game's viral spreading potential.

In the survey, we also asked about the perception of the game's purpose. First, we asked whether the players understood the purpose at all, which came out in correlation to understanding the game (since the explanation of the purpose was an integral part of the explanation of the game). Then we asked whether the purpose was the only motivation to play the game. A small, though significant number of players responded yes, which means that altruism may help overcome the initial barrier of lacking game attractiveness and argues

for disclosing the purpose of the game to potential players. Note, that this does not mean that the players must feel the purpose in game (through rule deformations), which may lead to disturbance of players as shown by Krause et al. (2010).

CONCLUSION AND FUTURE WORK

The creation and maintenance of web-scale semantic metadata (e.g., ontologies or lightweight semantic networks) has so far been an open problem. Games with a purpose (GWAP), a paradigm to human computing pioneered by Luis von Ahn and Dabbish (2008), emerged as an alternative way to provide solutions to complex computational problems. They employ the power of human minds, superior to machine computation in many tasks (such as knowledge delivery, extraction and reasoning), while retaining the quantitative capabilities of web-scale computation through mass parallelization.

We devised and evaluated a novel approach to term network acquisition – *Little Search Game*, which effectively combines a GWAP with a web search engine to address collaborative semantic metadata acquisition. We described the basic premise behind *Little Search Game* in which players extend the initial query with negative terms in order to reduce the total number of results as much as possible thus supplying us with their perception of term relatedness. The game is single player and thus does not suffer from the cold start problem. Our evaluation has conclusively shown that:

- *Little Search Game* can be used to create very precise term networks with relatively little human effort.
- *Little Search Game* can be used to identify term relationships which are normally not discoverable by statistical analysis of web corpora due to low co-occurrence of the respective terms. This can be achieved by exploiting player perception of term relatedness instead of statistical text analysis

Table 1. Results of the attractiveness survey from the Little Search Game showcase experiment

Question/Answer	Answer count
1. Have you understood the game?	
No.	2
Yes, after reading the manual.	16
Yes, after spoken explanation by the game's author.	16
2. Have you understood the purpose of this game (acquisition of term relationships)?	
No.	4
Yes.	30
3. Do you play computer games?	
Not at all.	7
Casually.	18
Regularly.	9
4. Would you play Little Search Game again?	
One time was enough.	6
Yes, I would like to play again.	18
Yes, I would like to play again and would recommend it to my friends	10
5. If you did not know that the game had an useful purpose, would you play it?	
I would play it anyway.	29
If the game was not useful, I would not play it.	5

which cannot identify these relationships due to noise.

- The game-created term relationships are of various types and are good candidates for extension into ontology triplets and incorporation into existing knowledge bases.
- The proposed heuristic can be effectively used to identify potentially abusive terms used by players thus lowering administrative workload of game administrators.
- 82% of players were interested in the game and played it despite some drawbacks in the intuitiveness of its user interface. Almost 30% of players were inclined to recommend the game to others supporting its viral spreading to new players.

Future work will focus on the enhancement of several game aspects. We plan to increase the game's attractiveness by improving its interface to be more intuitive and by employing it in a more social way to engage players in the competition. We plan to integrate a messaging mechanism that will notify players about ranking changes and motivate them to respond to them.

Labeling of the relationships of the LSG term network is also one of our future goals. Our aim is to employ textual corpora mining techniques seeking for sentences containing bigrams of the term network and extracting third elements of the contained statements to form triplets. We also plan to introduce a modification of the LSG, where two nouns (already connected within LSG network) act as a task query. Allowed only to enter verbs as negative search terms, players would effectively label unnamed relationships with predicates.

We also aim to develop strategies for term network expansion, where the goal is to cover as many terms as possible with focused expansion of the most "relevant" terms for a particular task, where the term network is employed. We plan to create relationships "on demand", also considering relationship strengths that can be derived from additional logged data (e.g., order of negative terms). For example, we want to support search query expansion of the most common queries and use the game in conjunction with our adaptive proxy-server for web search and browsing, where we collect bags of words via collecting and mining user search logs (Kramár et al., 2010). Here, term relationships help with grouping of user profiles or content-based recommendations.

ACKNOWLEDGMENT

This work was supported by grants No. VG1/0675/11, APVV 0208-10 and it is a partial result of the Research and Development Operational Program for the projects Support of Center of Excellence for Smart Technologies, Systems and Services, ITMS 26240120005 and Research and Development Operational Program for the projects Support of Center of Excellence for Smart Technologies, Systems and Services II, ITMS 26240120029, co-funded by ERDF. The authors wish to thank all members of the Personalized Web research group (pewe.fiit.stuba.sk) for their help with experiments.

REFERENCES

Barla, M., & Bieliková, M. (2009). On deriving tagsonomies: keyword relations coming from crowd. In N. T. Nguyen, R. Kowalczyk, & S.-M. Chen (Eds.), *Proceedings of the First International Conference on Computational Collective Intelligence: Semantic Web, Social Networks and Multiagent Systems* (LNCS 5796, pp. 309-320).

Barla, M., Bieliková, M., Ezzeddinne, A. B., Kramár, T., Šimko, M., & Vozár, O. (2010). On the impact of adaptive test question selection for learning efficiency. *Computers & Education, 55*(2), 846–857. doi:10.1016/j.compedu.2010.03.016.

Barrington, L., O'Malley, D., Turnbull, D., & Lanckriet, G. (2009). User-centered design of a social game to tag music. In *Proceedings of the ACM SIGKDD Workshop on Human Computation* (pp. 7-10). New York, NY: ACM.

Chamberlain, J., Poesio, M., & Kruschwitz, U. (2009). A demonstration of human computation using the phrase detectives annotation game. In *Proceedings of the ACM SIGKDD Workshop on Human Computation* (pp. 23-24). New York, NY: ACM.

Dasdan, A., Chris, D., Kolay, S., Alpern, M., Han, A., Chi, T., et al. (2009). Thumbs-up: a game for playing to rank search results. In *Proceedings of the ACM SIGKDD Workshop on Human Computation* (pp. 36-37). New York, NY: ACM.

El Sayed, A., Hacid, H., & Zighed, D. (2007). Mining semantic distance between corpus terms. In *Proceedings of the ACM First PhD Workshop in CIKM* (pp. 49-54). New York, NY: ACM.

Entertainment Software Association. (2011). *Industry facts.* Retrieved from http://www.theesa.com/facts/index.asp

Herdağdelen, A., & Baroni, M. (2010). The concept game: Better commonsense knowledge extraction by combining text mining and a game with a purpose. In *Proceedings of the AAAI Fall Symposium on Commonsense Knowledge* (pp. 52-57). Palo Alto, CA: AAAI Press.

Hladká, B., Mírovský, J., & Schlesinger, P. (2009). Designing a language game for collecting coreference annotation. In *Proceedings of the 3rd Linguistic Annotation Workshop* (pp. 52-55). Stroudsburg, PA: Association for Computational Linguistics.

Ho, C.-J., Chang, T.-H., Lee, J.-C., Hsu, J. Y.-j., & Chen, K.-T. (2009). KissKissBan: a competitive human computation game for image annotation. In *Proceedings of the ACM SIGKDD Workshop on Human Computation* (pp. 11-14). New York, NY: ACM.

Hunicke, R., Leblanc, M., & Zubek, R. (2004). MDA: A formal approach to game design and game research. In *Proceedings of the 19th National Artificial Intelligence Conference on Challenges in Games* (pp. 1-5). Palo Alto, CA: AAAI Press.

Kramár, T., Barla, M., & Bieliková, M. (2010). Disambiguating search by leveraging the social network context based on the stream of user's activity. In P. De Bra, A. Kobsa, & D. Chin (Eds.), *Proceedings of the 18th International Conference on User Modeling, Adaptation, and Personalization* (LNCS 6075, pp. 387-392).

Krause, M., Takhtamysheva, A., Wittstock, M., & Malaka, R. (2010). Frontiers of a paradigm: exploring human computation with digital games. In *Proceedings of the ACM SIGKDD Workshop on Human Computation* (pp. 22-25). New York, NY: ACM.

Kuo, Y.-l., Lee, J.-C., Chiang, K.-y., Wang, R., Shen, E., Chan, C.-w., & Hsu, J. Y.-j. (2009). Community-based game design: experiments on social games for commonsense data collection. In *Proceedings of the ACM SIGKDD Workshop on Human Computation* (pp. 15-22). New York, NY: ACM.

Law, E. L., Mityagin, A., & Chickering, M. (2009). Intentions: a game for classifying search query intent. In *Proceedings of the 27th International Conference Extended Abstracts on Human Factors in Computing Systems* (pp. 3805-3810). New York, NY: ACM.

Law, E. L., von Ahn, L., Dannenberg, R. B., & Crawford, M. (2007). Tagatune: A game for music and sound annotation. In *Proceedings of the 8th International Conference on Music Information Retrieval* (pp. 361-364). Vienna, Austria: Austrian Computer Society.

Lenat, D. B. (1995). Cyc: a large-scale investment in knowledge infrastructure. *Communications of the ACM*, *38*(11), 33–38. doi:10.1145/219717.219745.

Marchionini, G. (2006). From finding to understanding. *Communications of the ACM*, *49*(4), 41–46. doi:10.1145/1121949.1121979.

McDowell, L. K., & Cafarella, M. (2008). Ontology-driven, unsupervised instance population. *Web Semantics*, *6*, 218–236. doi:10.1016/j. websem.2008.04.002.

Media Lab, M. I. T. (n. d.). *Common sense computing initiative*. Retrieved from http://csc.media. mit.edu/conceptnet

Nenadić, G., & Ananiadou, S. (2006). Mining semantically related terms from biomedical literature. *ACM Transactions on Asian Language Information Processing*, *5*(1), 22–43. doi:10.1145/1131348.1131351.

Pantel, P., & Pennacchiotti, M. (2008). Automatically harvesting and ontologizing semantic relations. In *Proceeding of the Conference on Ontology Learning and Population: Bridging the Gap between Text and Knowledge* (pp. 171-195). Amsterdam, The Netherlands: IOS Press.

Park, L. F., & Ramamohanarao, K. (2009). An analysis of latent semantic term self-correlation. *ACM Transactions on Information Systems*, *27*(2), 1–35. doi:10.1145/1462198.1462200.

Sanchez, D. (2010). A methodology to learn ontological attributes from the web. *Data & Knowledge Engineering*, *69*(6), 573–597. doi:10.1016/j. datak.2010.01.006.

Seneviratne, L., & Izquierdo, E. (2010). An interactive framework for image annotation through gaming. In *Proceedings of the International Conference on Multimedia Information Retrieval* (pp. 517-526). New York, NY: ACM.

Šimko, J., Tvarožek, M., & Bieliková, M. (2010). Semantic history map: Graphs aiding web revisitation support. In *Proceedings of the International Workshop on Database and Expert Systems Applications* (pp. 206-210). Washington, DC: IEEE Computer Society.

Šimko, J., Tvarožek, M., & Bieliková, M. (2011). Little search game: term network acquisition via a human computation game. In *Proceedings of the 22nd ACM Conference on Hypertext and Hypermedia* (pp. 57-62). New York, NY: ACM.

Šimko, M. (2011). Automated domain model creation for adaptive social educational environments. *Information Sciences and Technologies Bulletin of the ACM Slovakia*, *3*(2), 119–121.

Šimko, M., & Bieliková, M. (2009). Automatic concept relationships discovery for an adaptive e-course. In *Proceedings of the 2ⁿᵈ International Conference on Educational Data Mining* (pp. 171-179). Cordoba, Spain: EDM.

Siorpaes, K., & Hepp, M. (2008a). Ontogame: weaving the semantic web by online games. In *Proceedings of the 5th European Semantic Web Conference on the Semantic Web: Research and Applications* (pp. 751-766). Berlin, Germany: Springer-Verlag.

Siorpaes, K., & Hepp, M. (2008b). Games with a purpose for the Semantic Web. *IEEE Intelligent Systems*, *23*(3), 50–60. doi:10.1109/MIS.2008.45.

Stewart, R., Scott, G., & Zelevinsky, V. (2008). Idea navigation: structured browsing for unstructured text. In *Proceedings of the 26th SIGCHI Conference on Human Factors in Computing Systems* (pp. 1789-1792). New York, NY: ACM.

Terry, L., Roitch, V., Tufail, S., Singh, K., Taraq, O., Luk, W., & Jamieson, P. (2009). Harnessing human computation cycles for the FPGA placement problem. In *Proceedings of the International Conference on Engineering of Reconfigurable Systems and Algorithms* (pp. 188-194). Las Vegas, NV: CSREA Press.

Thaler, S., Siorpaes, K., Mear, D., Simperl, E., & Goodman, C. (2011). SeaFish: A game for collaborative and visual image annotation and interlinking. In G. Antoniou, M. Grobelnik, E. Simperl, B. Parsia, D. Plexousakis, P. De Leenheer, & J. Pan (Eds.), *Proceedings of the International Conference on the Semantic Web: Research and Applications* (LNCS 6644, pp. 466-470).

Thaler, S., Siorpaes, K., Simperl, E., & Hofer, C. (2011). *A survey on games for knowledge acquisition* (Tech. Rep. No. 2011-05-01). Innsbruck, Austria: University of Innsbruck.

Tvarožek, M., & Bieliková, M. (2010). Generating exploratory search interfaces for the semantic web. In *Proceedings of the Second IFIP TC Symposium on Human-computer Interaction* (Vol. 332, pp. 175-186). New York, NY: Springer.

Ungrangsi, R., Anutariya, C., & Wuwongse, V. (2010). Enhancing folksonomy-based content retrieval with semantic web technology. *International Journal on Semantic Web and Information Systems*, *6*(1), 19–38. doi:10.4018/jswis.2010010102.

Vickrey, D., Bronzan, A., Choi, W., Kumar, A., Turner-Maier, J., Wang, A., & Koller, D. (2008). Online word games for semantic data collection. In *Proceedings of the Conference on Empirical Methods in Natural Language Processing* (pp. 533-542). Morristown, NJ: Association for Computational Linguistics.

von Ahn, L., & Dabbish, L. (2008). Designing games with a purpose. *Communications of the ACM*, *51*, 58–67. doi:10.1145/1378704.1378719.

Wang, T., Maynard, D., Peters, W., Bontcheva, K., & Cunningham, H. (2005). Extracting a domain ontology from linguistic resource based on relatedness measurements. In *Proceedings of the IEEE/WIC/ACM International Conference on Web Intelligence* (pp. 345-351). Washington, DC: IEEE Computer Society.

Weichselbraun, A., Wohlgenannt, G., & Scharl, A. (2010). Refining non-taxonomic relation labels with external structured data to support ontology learning. *Data & Knowledge Engineering*, *69*(8), 763–778. doi:10.1016/j.datak.2010.02.010.

This work was previously published in the International Journal on Semantic Web and Information Systems, Volume 7, Issue 3, edited by Amit P. Sheth,, pp. 23-45, copyright 2011 by IGI Publishing (an imprint of IGI Global).

Compilation of References

Adida, B., Birbeck, M., McCarron, S., & Pemberton, S. (2008). *RDFa in XHTML: Syntax and processing*. Retrieved from http://www.w3.org/TR/rdfa-syntax/

Adobe Developer Technologies. (2005). *Extensible Metadata Platform (XMP) specification*. San Jose, CA: Adobe Systems Incorporated. Retrieved from http://partners.adobe.com/public/developer/en/xmp/sdk/XMP-specification.pdf

Adomavicius, G., & Tuzhilin, A. (2005). Toward the Next Generation of Recommender Systems: A Survey of the State-of-the-Art and Possible Extensions. *IEEE Transactions on Knowledge and Data Engineering, 17*(6), 734–749. doi:10.1109/TKDE.2005.99.

Adomavicius, G., & Tuzhilin, A. (2011). Context-Aware Recommender Systems. In Ricci, F., Rokach, L., Shapira, B., & Kantor, P. B. (Eds.), *Recommender Systems Handbook* (pp. 217–253). doi:10.1007/978-0-387-85820-3_7.

Agrawal, R., & Srikant, R. (1994). Fast algorithms for mining association rules in large data-bases. In J. B. Bocca, M. Jarke, & C. Zaniolo (Eds.), *Proceedings of the International Conference on Very Large Data Bases* (pp. 487-499). San Francisco, CA: Morgan Kaufmann.

Agrawal, R., & Srikant, R. (1994). Fast algorithms for mining association rules in large databases. In *Proceedings of the 20th International Conference on Very Large Data Bases* (pp. 487-499). San Francisco, CA: Morgan Kaufmann.

Agrawal, R., Imielinski, T., & Swami, A. (1993). Mining association rules between sets of items in large databases. In *Proceedings of the ACM SIGMOD International Conference on Management of Data* (pp. 207-216). New York, NY: ACM Press.

Ahern, S., King, S., Naaman, M., Nair, R., & Yang, J. H.-I. (2007). ZoneTag: Rich, community-supported context-aware media capture and annotation. In *Proceedings of the Mobile Spatial Interaction Workshop at the SIGCHI Conference on Human Factors in Computing Systems*, San Jose, CA. New York, NY: ACM.

Ahn, J., Brusilovsky, P., Grady, J., He, D., & Syn, S. Y. (2007). Open User Profiles for Adaptive News Systems: Help or Harm? In *Proceedings of the 16th International World Wide Web Conference* (pp. 11-20).

Alexander, K., Cyganiak, R., Hausenblas, M., & Zhao, J. (2009). Describing linked datasets - on the design and usage of void, the "vocabulary of interlinked datasets". In *Proceedings of the Linked Data on the Web Workshop and the 18th International World Wide Web Conference*, Madrid, Spain.

Alfonseca, E., & Manandhar, S. (2002). Extending a lexical ontology by a combination of distributional semantics signatures. In *Proceedings of the 13th International Conference on Knowledge Engineering and Knowledge Management, Ontologies and the Semantic Web* (pp. 1-7). Berlin, Germany: Springer-Verlag.

Alfonseca, E., Moreno-Sandoval, A., Guirao, J. M., & Ruiz-Casado, M. (2006). The Wraetlic NLP Suite. In *Proceedings of the 5th International Conference on Language Resources and Evaluation*.

Anand, S. S., & Mobasher, B. (2007). Contextual Recommendation. In Berendt, B., Hotho, A., Mladenic, D., & Semeraro, G. (Eds.), *From Web to Social Web: Discovering and Deploying User and Content Profiles* (pp. 142–160). doi:10.1007/978-3-540-74951-6_8.

Anguelov, D., Lee, K.-C., Gokturk, S. B., & Sumengen, B. (2007). Contextual identity recognition in personal photo albums. In *Proceedings of the International Conference on Computer Vision and Pattern Recognition*, Minneapolis, MN (pp. 1-7). Washington, DC: IEEE Computer Society. Retrieved from http://robotics.stanford.edu/~drago/ Papers/ cvpr2007.pdf

Antoniou, G., & Bikakis, A. (2007). DR-Prolog: A System for Defeasible Reasoning with Rules and Ontologies on the Semantic Web. *IEEE Transactions on Knowledge and Data Engineering*, *19*(2), 233–245. doi:10.1109/ TKDE.2007.29.

Antoniou, G., Billington, D., Governatori, G., & Maher, M. J. (2006). Embedding Defeasible Logic into Logic Programming. *Theory and Practice of Logic Programming*, *6*(6), 703–735. doi:10.1017/S1471068406002778.

Antoniou, G., Dimaresis, N., & Governatori, G. (2009). A Modal and Deontic Defeasible Reasoning System for Modelling Policies and Multi-Agent Systems. *Expert Systems with Applications*, *36*(2), 4125–4134. doi:10.1016/j. eswa.2008.03.009.

Antoniou, G., Skylogiannis, T., Bikakis, A., & Bassiliades, N. (2007). DR-BROKERING: A Semantic Brokering System. *Knowledge-Based Systems*, *20*(1), 61–72. doi:10.1016/j.knosys.2006.07.006.

Antoniou, G., & van Harmelen, F. (2004). *A Semantic Web Primer*. Cambridge, MA: MIT Press.

Araujo, S., de Vries, A., & Schwabe, D. (2011). *Serimi results for OAEI 2011*. Paper presented at the Ontology Matching Workshop on Ontology Alignments Evaluation Initiative.

Artosi, A., Governatori, G., & Sartor, G. (1996). Towards a computational treatment of deontic defeasibility. In M. Brown & J. Carmo (Eds.), *Deontic Logic Agency and Normative Systems: Workshop on Computing* (pp. 27-46). Berlin, Germany: Springer-Verlag.

Ashri, R., Payne, T., Marvin, D., Surridge, M., & Taylor, S. (2004). Towards a Semantic Web Security Infrastructure. In *Proceedings of the AAAI Spring Symposium on Semantic Web Services* (pp. 84-91). Menlo Park, CA: AAAI Press.

Assmann, U., Henriksson, J., & Maluszynski, J. (2006). Combining safe rules and ontologies by interfacing of reasoners. In J. Alferes, J. Bailey, W. May, & U. Schwertel (Eds.), *Proceedings of the 4th International Conference on Principles and Practice of Semantic Web Reasoning* (LNCS 4187, p. 33-47).

Augurusa, E., Braga, D., Campi, A., & Ceri, S. (2003). Design and implementation of a graphical interface to XQuery. In G. B. Lamont, H. Haddad, G. A. Papadopoulos, & B. Panda (Eds.), *Proceedings of the ACM Symposium on Applied Computing* (pp. 1163-1167). New York, NY: ACM Press.

Baader, F., Ganter, B., Sertkaya, B., & Sattler, U. (2007). Completing description logic knowledge bases using formal concept analysis. In M. Veloso (Ed.), *Proceedings of the 20th International Joint Conference on Artificial Intelligence*, Hyderabad, India (pp. 230-235).

Baader, F., Calvanese, D., McGuinness, D. L., Nardi, D., & Patel-Schneider, P. F. (Eds.). (2003). *The description logic handbook: Theory, implementation, and applications*. Cambridge, UK: Cambridge University Press.

Baader, F., Calvanese, D., McGuinness, D., Nardi, D., & Patel-Schneider, P. (Eds.). (2007). *The Description Logic Handbook* (2nd ed.). Cambridge, UK: Cambridge University Press. doi:10.1017/CBO9780511711787.

Baader, F., Calvanese, D., McGuinness, D., Nardi, D., & Patel-Schneider, P. (Eds.). (2007). *The description logic handbook: Theory, implementation, and applications* (2nd ed.). Cambridge, UK: Cambridge University Press. doi:10.1017/CBO9780511711787.

Badea, L., & Nienhuys-Cheng, S.-H. (2000). A refinement operator for description logics. In J. Cussens & A. Frisch (Eds.), *Proceedings of the 10th International Conference on Inductive Logic Programming* (LNAI 1866, pp. 40-59).

Baeza-Yates, R., & Ribeiro-Neto, B. (1999). *Modern Information Retrieval*. Reading, MA: Addison-Wesley.

Balby Marinho, L., Buza, K., & Schmidt-Thieme, L. (2008). Folksonomy-based collabulary learning. In *ISWC '08: Proceedings of the 7th International Conference on the Semantic Web* (pp. 261-276). Berlin, Germany: Springer-Verlag.

Baldi, M., Baralis, E., & Risso, F. (2005). Data mining techniques for effective and scalable traffic analysis. In A. Clemm, O. Festor, & A. Pras (Eds.), *Proceedings of the IEEE International Symposium on Integrated Network Management* (pp. 105-118). Washington, DC: IEEE Computer Society.

Baralis, E., Cagliero, L., Cerquitelli, T., D'Elia, V., & Garza, P. (2010). Support driven opportunistic aggregation for generalized itemset extraction. In *Proceedings of the IEEE Conference on Intelligent Systems* (pp. 102-107). Washington, DC: IEEE Computer Society.

Baralis, E., Cagliero, L., Cerquitelli, T., Garza, P., & Marchetti, M. (2009). Context-aware user and service profiling by means of generalized association rules. In J. D. Velasquez, S. A. Rios, R. J. Howlett, & L. C. Jain (Eds.), *Proceedings of the International Conference on Knowledge-Based and Intelligent Information & Engineering Systems* (pp. 50-57). Berlin, Germany: Springer.

Baralis, E., Garza, P., Quintarelli, E., & Tanca, L. (2007). Answering XML queries by means of data summaries. *ACM Transactions on Information Systems*, 25(3), 1–33. doi:10.1145/1247715.1247716.

Barla, M., & Bieliková, M. (2009). On deriving tagsonomies: keyword relations coming from crowd. In N. T. Nguyen, R. Kowalczyk, & S.-M. Chen (Eds.), *Proceedings of the First International Conference on Computational Collective Intelligence: Semantic Web, Social Networks and Multiagent Systems* (LNCS 5796, pp. 309-320).

Barla, M., Bieliková, M., Ezzeddinne, A. B., Kramár, T., Šimko, M., & Vozár, O. (2010). On the impact of adaptive test question selection for learning efficiency. *Computers & Education*, 55(2), 846–857. doi:10.1016/j.compedu.2010.03.016.

Barrington, L., O'Malley, D., Turnbull, D., & Lanckriet, G. (2009). User-centered design of a social game to tag music. In *Proceedings of the ACM SIGKDD Workshop on Human Computation* (pp. 7-10). New York, NY: ACM.

Barthelmess, P., Kaiser, E., & McGee, D. R. (2007). Toward content-aware multimodal tagging of personal photo collections. In *Proceedings of the 9th International Conference on Multimodal Interfaces*, Nagoya, Aichi, Japan (pp.122-125). New York, NY: ACM. Retrieved from http://home.comcast.net/~pbarthelmess/ Publications/Photos/icmi259-barthelmess.pdf

Bassiliades, N., Antoniou, G., & Vlahavas, I. (2006). A Defeasible Logic Reasoner for the Semantic Web. *International Journal on Semantic Web and Information Systems*, 2(1), 1–41. doi:10.4018/jswis.2006010101.

Bassiliades, N., & Vlahavas, I. (2006). R-DEVICE: An Object-Oriented Knowledge Base System for RDF Metadata. *International Journal on Semantic Web and Information Systems*, 2(2), 24–90. doi:10.4018/jswis.2006040102.

Batini, C., & Scannapieco, M. (2006). *Data quality: Concepts, methodologies and techniques (data-centric systems and applications)*. New York, NY: Springer.

Berners-Lee, T. (2006). *Linked data* (Tech. Rep.). Retrieved from http://www.w3.org/DesignIssues/Linked-Data.html

Berners-Lee, T., Hollenbach, J., Lu, K., Presbrey, J., Prud'hommeaux, E., & Schraefel, M. (2008). Tabulator Redux: Browsing and Writing Linked Data. In *Proceedings of the WWW International Workshop on Linked Data on the Web*, Beijing, China.

Berners-Lee, T., Hendler, J., & Lassila, O. (2001). The Semantic Web. *Scientific American*, 284(5), 34–43. doi:10.1038/scientificamerican0501-34.

Berners-Lee, T., Hendler, J., & Lassila, O. (2001). The Semantic Web. *Scientific American*, 284, 34–43. doi:10.1038/scientificamerican0501-34 PMID:11396337.

Bickhard, M. H. (2008). The social ontology of persons. In Carpendale, J., & Müller, U. (Eds.), *Social interaction and the development of knowledge* (pp. 111–132). Mahwah, NJ: Lawrence Erlbaum.

Bieber, P., & Cuppens, F. (1993). Expression of Confidentiality Policies with Deontic Logic. In Meyer, J. C., & Wieringa, R. J. (Eds.), *Deontic Logic in Computer Science: Normative System Specification* (pp. 103–123). Chichester, UK: John Wiley & Sons.

Biemann, C. (2005). Ontology learning from text: A survey of methods. *LDV Forum*, 20(2), 75–93.

Billsus, D., & Pazzani, M. J. (1999). A Personal News Agent that Talks Learns and Explains. In *Proceedings of the 3rd International Conference on Autonomous Agents* (pp. 268-275).

Billsus, D., & Pazzani, M. J. (2000). User Modeling for Adaptive News Access. *User Modeling and User-Adapted Interaction*, *10*(2), 147–180. doi:10.1023/A:1026501525781.

Bizer, C., & Schultz, A. (2010). The r2r framework: Publishing and discovering mappings on the web. In *Proceedings of the 1st International Workshop on Consuming Linked Data*, Shanghai, China.

Bizer, C., Cyganiak, R., & Heath, T. (2007). *How to publish linked data on the web* (Tech. Rep.). Berlin, Germany: Freie Universität Berlin. Retrieved from http://www4.wiwiss. fu-berlin.de/bizer/pub/LinkedDataTutorial/20070727/

Blackburn, P., de Rijke, M., & Venema, Y. (2001). *Modal Logic*. Cambridge, UK: Cambridge University Press.

Blake, C., & Merz, C. (2010). *UCI repository of machine learning databases*. Retrieved July 25, 2011, from http://archive.ics.uci.edu/ml

Bleiholder, J., & Naumann, F. (2009). Data fusion. *ACM Computing Surveys*, *41*(1), 1–41. doi:10.1145/1456650.1456651.

Bloehdorn, S., Haase, P., Sure, Y., & Voelker, J. (2006). Ontology evolution. In Davies, J., Studer, R., & Warren, P. (Eds.), *Semantic Web Technologies: Trends and Research in Ontology-based Systems*. New York, NY: Wiley. doi:10.1002/047003033X.ch4.

Boella, G., & van der Torre, L. (2004). An agent oriented ontology of social reality. In *Proceedings of the International Conference on Formal Ontology in Information Systems*, Torino, Italy.

Bojārs, U., Heitmann, B., & Oren, E. (2007). A prototype to explore content and context on social community sites. In *Proceedings of the International Conference on Social Semantic Web* (pp. 47-58). Retrieved from http://www.eyaloren.org/pubs/cssw2007.pdf

Boley, H. (2004). *An Integrated Positional-Slotted Language for Semantic Web Knowledge*. Retrieved from http://www.ruleml.org/submission/ruleml-shortation.html

Boley, H. (2006). The RuleML Family of Web Rule Languages: Invited talk. In *Proceedings of 4th Workshop on Principles and Practice of Semantic Web Reasoning*, Budva, Montenegro (LNCS 4187, pp.1-15).

Bonatti, P. A., Duma, C., Fuchs, N., Nejdl, W., Olmedilla, D., Peer, J., & Shahmehri, N. (2006). Semantic Web Policies - a Discussion of Requirements and Research Issues. In *Proceedings of the 3rd European Semantic Web Conference,* Budva, Montenegro (LNCS 4011, pp. 712-724).

Borgida, A. (1996). On the relative expressiveness of description logics and predicate logics. *Artificial Intelligence*, *82*(1-2), 353–367. doi:10.1016/0004-3702(96)00004-5.

Borgida, A. (1996). On the relative expressiveness of description logics and predicate logics. *Artificial Intelligence*, *82*(1-2), 353–367. doi:10.1016/0004-3702(96)00004-5.

Boström, H., & Asker, L. (1999). Combining divide-and-conquer and separate-and-conquer for efficient and effective rule induction. In S. Dzeroski & P. Flach (Eds.), *Proceedings of the 9th International Workshop on Inductive Logic Programming (ILP-99)* (LNCS 1634, pp. 33-43).

Bottazzi, E., Catenacci, C., Gangemi, A., & Lehmann, J. (2006). From collective intentionality to intentional collectives: An ontological perspective. *Cognitive Systems Research*, *7*, 192–208. doi:10.1016/j.cogsys.2005.11.009.

Bottazzi, E., & Ferrario, R. (2009). Preliminaries to a DOLCE ontology of organisations. *International Journal of Business Process Integration and Management*, *4*(4), 225–238. doi:10.1504/IJBPIM.2009.032280.

Bouquet, P., Stoermer, H., & Bazzanella, B. (2008). An entity name system (ens) for the semantic web. In *Proceedings of the 5th European Semantic Web Conference on the Semantic Web: Research and Applications*, Tenerife, Spain (pp. 258-272).

Brandt, S., Küsters, R., & Turhan, A.-Y. (2002). Approximation and difference in description logics. In D. Fensel et al. (Eds.), *Proceedings of the International Conference on Knowledge Representation* (pp. 203-214). San Francisco, CA: Morgan Kaufmann.

Braun, S., Schmidt, A., & Walter, A. (2007). Ontology maturing: a collaborative web 2.0 approach to ontology engineering. In *Proceedings of the Workshop on Social and Collaborative Construction of Structured Knowledge (CKC) at the 16th International World Wide Web Conference*.

Braun, S., Kunzmann, C., & Schmidt, A. (2010). People tagging & ontology maturing: Towards collaborative competence management. In Randall, D., & Salembier, P. (Eds.), *From CSCW to Web2.0: European Developments in Collaborative Design Selected Papers from COOP08*. Berlin, Germany: Springer-Verlag. doi:10.1007/978-1-84882-965-7_7.

Breslin, J. G., Harth, A., Bojars, U., & Decker, S. (2005). Towards semantically interlinked online communities. In A. Gómez-Pérez & J. Euzenat (Eds.), *Proceedings of the 2nd European Semantic Web Conference: Research and Applications*, Heraklion, Greece (LNCS 3532, pp. 71-83). Retrieved from http://sw.deri.org/2004/12/sioc/index.pdf

Briendel, J. T., Grosee, I. R., Krishnamurty, S., Altidor, J., Wildeden, J., Trachtenberg, S., & Witherell, P. (2011). Towards industrial implementation of emerging semantic technologies. In *Proceedings of the ASME International Design Engineering Technical Conferences & Computers and Information in Engineering Conference*.

Broder, A. Z. (1997). On the resemblance and containment of documents. In *Proceedings of the International Conference on Compression and Complexity of Sequences*, Salerno, Italy (pp. 21-29). Washington, DC: IEEE Computer Society. Retrieved from http://www.cs.princeton.edu/courses/archive/spr05/cos598E/bib/broder97resemblance.pdf

Broersen, J., Dastani, M., Hulstijn, J., Huang, Z., & van der Torre, L. (2001). The BOID Architecture: Conflicts between Beliefs, Obligations, Intentions and Desires. In *Proceedings of the 5th International Conference on Autonomous Agents,* Montreal, QC, Canada (pp. 9-16). New York, NY: ACM.

Bryl, V., Giuliano, C., Serafini, L., & Tymoshenko, K. (2010). Supporting natural language processing with background knowledge: Coreference resolution case. In *Proceedings of the 9th International Semantic Web Conference*, Shanghai, China (pp. 80-95).

Buitelaar, P., & Cimiano, P. (Eds.). (2008). *Ontology Learning and Population: Bridging the Gap between Text and Knowledge*. Amsterdam, The Netherlands: IOS Press.

Buneman, P., Davidson, S., Hillebrand, G., & Suciu, D. (1996). A Query Language and Optimization Techniques for Unstructured Data. In H. V. Jagadish & I. S. Mumick (Eds.), *Proceedings of the ACM SIGMOD International Conference on Management of Data* (pp. 505-516). New York, NY: ACM Press.

Buntine, W. (1988). Generalized subsumption and its application to induction and redundancy. *Artificial Intelligence*, *36*(2), 149–176. doi:10.1016/0004-3702(88)90001-X.

Burke, R. (2002). Hybrid recommender systems: Survey and experiments. *User Modeling and User-Adapted Interaction*, *12*(4), 331–370. doi:10.1023/A:1021240730564.

Cafarela, M. J., Downey, D., Soderland, S., & Etzioni, O. (2005). KnowItAll: Fast, scalable information extraction from the Web. In *Proceedings of the Human Language Technology Conference and Conference on Empirical Methods in Natural Language Processing* (pp. 563-570).

Canny, J. (2002). Collaborative filtering with privacy via factor analysis. In *Proceedings of the 25th Annual International ACM SIGIR Conference on Research and Development in Information Retrieval*, Tampere, Finland (pp. 238-245). New York, NY: ACM. Retrieved from http://www.cs.berkeley.edu/~jfc/'mender/sigir.pdf

Cantador, I., Bellogín, A., & Castells, P. (2008b). Ontology-based Personalised and Context-aware Recommendations of News Items. In *Proceedings of the 2008 IEEE/WIC/ACM International Conference on Web Intelligence and Intelligent Agent Technology* (pp. 562-565).

Cantador, I., Bellogín, A., Fernández-Tobías, I., & López-Hernández, S. (in press). Semantic Contextualization of Social Tag-based Item Recommendations. In *Proceedings of the 12th International Conference on E-Commerce and Web Technologies*.

Cantador, I., Szomszor, M., Alani, H., Fernández, M., & Castells, P. (2008). Enriching Ontological User Profiles with Tagging History for Multi-Domain Recommendations. In *Proceedings of the 1st International Workshop on Collective Semantics: Collective Intelligence and the Semantic Web* (pp. 5-19).

Cantador, I., Bellogín, A., & Castells, P. (2008a). A Multilayer Ontology-based Hybrid Recommendation Model. *AI Communications*, *21*(2-3), 203–210.

Cantador, I., Fernández, M., Vallet, D., Castells, P., Picault, J., & Ribière, M. (2008). A Multi-Purpose Ontology-Based Approach for Personalised Content Filtering and Retrieval. In Wallace, M., Angelides, M., & Mylonas, P. (Eds.), *Advances in Semantic Media Adaptation and Personalization* (pp. 25–51). doi:10.1007/978-3-540-76361_2.

Cao, D. X., Ramani, K., Li, Z., Raskin, V., Liu, Y., & Li, Z. (2010). Developing customer preferences for concept generation by using engineering ontologies. In *Proceedings of the ASME International Design Engineering Technical Conferences & Computers and Information in Engineering Conference*.

Castano, S., Ferrara, A., Lorusso, D., Näth, T. H., & Möller, R. (2008). Mapping validation by probabilistic reasoning. In *Proceedings of the 5th European Semantic Web Conference on the Semantic Web: Research and Applications*, Tenerife, Spain (pp. 170-184).

Castano, S., Ferrara, A., & Montanelli, S. (2006). Matching ontologies in open networked systems: Techniques and applications. *Journal on Data Semantics*, *5*, 25–63.

Ceri, S., Gottlob, G., & Tanca, L. (1990). *Logic programming and databases*. New York, NY: Springer.

Cetina, K. K. (1997). Sociality with objects: Social relations in postsocial knowledge societies. *Theory, Culture & Society*, *14*(4), 1–30. doi:10.1177/026327697014004001.

Chamberlain, J., Poesio, M., & Kruschwitz, U. (2009). A demonstration of human computation using the phrase detectives annotation game. In *Proceedings of the ACM SIGKDD Workshop on Human Computation* (pp. 23-24). New York, NY: ACM.

Choi, J.-Y., Yang, S., Ro, Y. M., & Plataniotis, K. N. (2008). Face annotation for personal photos using context-assisted face recognition. In *Proceedings of the 1st ACM International Conference on Multimedia Information Retrieval*, Vancouver, BC, Canada (p. 44). New York, NY: ACM.

Chu, W., & Park, S. T. (2009). Personalized Recommendation on Dynamic Content Using Predictive Bilinear Models. In *Proceedings of the 18th International World Wide Web Conference* (pp. 691-700).

Cilibrasi, R., & Vitanyi, P. (2007). The Google similarity distance. *IEEE Transactions on Knowledge and Data Engineering*, *19*(3), 370–383. doi:10.1109/TKDE.2007.48.

Cimiano, P., Mädche, A., Staab, S., & Voelker, J. (2009). Ontology learning. In Staab, S., & Studer, R. (Eds.), *Handbook on Ontologies* (2nd ed.). Berlin, Germany: Springer. doi:10.1007/978-3-540-92673-3_11.

Cimiano, P., Mädche, A., Staab, S., & Völker, J. (2009). Ontology learning. In Staab, S., & Studer, R. (Eds.), *Handbook on Ontologies* (pp. 245–267). Berlin, Germany: Springer. doi:10.1007/978-3-540-92673-3_11.

Clark & Parsia. (2011). *Pellet: OWL 2 reasoner for Java*. Retrieved from http://clarkparsia.com/pellet/

Clarke, C., Cormack, G. V., & Lynam, T. R. (2001). Exploiting Redundancy in Question Answering. In *Proceedings of the 24th Annual International ACM Conference on Research and Devel-opment in Information Retrieval (SIGIR)* (pp. 358-365).

Claypool, M., Gokhale, A., Miranda, T., Murnikov, P., Netes, D., & Sartin, M. (1999). Combining Content-Based and Collaborative Filters in an Online Newspaper. In *Proceedings of the SIGIR 1999 Workshop on Recommender Systems: Algorithms and Evaluation*.

Clifton, C., Cooley, R., & Rennie, J. (2004). TopCat: Data mining for topic identification in a text corpus. *IEEE Transactions on Knowledge and Data Engineering*, *16*(8), 949–964. doi:10.1109/TKDE.2004.32.

Cohen, W. W., Ravikumar, P., & Fienberg, S. E. (2003). A Comparison of String Distance Metrics for Name-Matching Tasks. In *Proceedings of the IJCAI'03 Workshop on Information Integration on the Web* (pp. 73-78).

Cohen, W. W., Ravikumar, P., & Fienberg, S. E. (2003). A comparison of string metrics for matching names and records. In *Proceedings of the KDD Workshop on Data Cleaning and Object Consolidation*.

Cohen, W. W., Ravikumar, P., Fienberg, S. E., & Rivard, K. (2003). *Second string project*. Retrieved from http://secondstring.sourceforge.net

Cohen, W., & Hirsh, H. (1992). Learnability of description logics. In *Proceedings of the 4th Annual Workshop on Computational Learning Theory*. New York, NY: ACM Press.

Cohen, W., & Hirsh, H. (1994). Learning the CLASSIC description logic. In P. Torasso, J. Doyle, & E. Sandewall (Eds.), *Proceedings of the 4th International Conference on the Principles of Knowledge Representation and Reasoning* (pp. 121-133). San Francisco, CA: Morgan Kaufmann.

Cohen, P. R., & Kjeldsen, R. (1987). Information Retrieval by Constrained Spreading Activation in Semantic Networks. *Information Processing & Management, 23*(4), 255–268. doi:10.1016/0306-4573(87)90017-3.

Cohen, P. R., & Levesque, H. J. (1990). Intention is Choice with Commitment. *Artificial Intelligence, 42*(2-3), 213–261. doi:10.1016/0004-3702(90)90055-5.

Collins, A. M., & Quillian, M. R. (1969). Retrieval time from semantic memory. *Journal of Verbal Learning and Verbal Behavior, 8,* 240–248. doi:10.1016/S0022-5371(69)80069-1.

Consens, M. P., & Mendelzon, A. O. (1990). Graphlog: a Visual Formalism for Real Life Recursion. In D. J. Rosenkrantz & Y. Sagiv (Eds.), *Proceedings of the ACM SIGACT-SIGMOD-SIGART Symposium on Principles of Database Systems* (pp. 404-416). New York, NY: ACM Press.

Cour, T., Srinivasan, P., & Shi, J. (2006). Balanced graph matching. *Advances in Neural Information Processing Systems, 19,* 313–320.

Crestani, F. (1997). Application of Spreading Activation Techniques in Information Retrieval. *Artificial Intelligence Review, 11*(6), 453–482. doi:10.1023/A:1006569829653.

Cudré-Mauroux, P., Haghani, P., Jost, M., Aberer, K., & de Meer, H. (2009). idMesh: Graph-based disambiguation of linked data. In *Proceedings of the 18th International World Wide Web Conference,* Madrid, Spain (pp. 591-600).

d'Amato, C., Fanizzi, N., & Esposito, F. (2008). Query answering and ontology population: An inductive approach. In S. Bechhofer et al. (Eds.), *Proceedings of the 5th European Semantic Web Conference (ESWC2008)* (LNCS 5021, pp. 288-302).

Damiani, E., Oliboni, B., Quintarelli, E., & Tanca, L. (2003). *Modeling Semistructured Data by using graph-based constraints* (Tech. Rep. No. 27/03). Milano, Italy: Politecnico di Milano, Dipartimento di Elettronica e Informazione.

Das, A., Datar, M., Garg, A., & Rajaram, S. (2007). Google News Personalisation: Scalable Online Collaborative Filtering. In *Proceedings of the 16th International World Wide Web Conference* (pp. 271-280).

Dasdan, A., Chris, D., Kolay, S., Alpern, M., Han, A., Chi, T., et al. (2009). Thumbs-up: a game for playing to rank search results. In *Proceedings of the ACM SIGKDD Workshop on Human Computation* (pp. 36-37). New York, NY: ACM.

Davies, J. F., Grobelnik, M., & Mladenic, D. (2008). *Semantic knowledge management: Integrating ontology management, knowledge discovery, and human language technologies.* New York, NY: Springer.

Davis, M., Smith, M., Canny, J., Good, N., King, S., & Janakiraman, R. (2005). Towards context-aware face recognition. In *Proceedings of the 13th Annual ACM International Conference on Multimedia,* Singapore (pp. 483-486). Retrieved from http://fusion.sims.berkeley.edu/GarageCinema/pubs/pdf/pdf_89FB89A7-2534-412F-A815230DFDB32CDC.pdf

De Raedt, L. (2008). *Logical and Relational Learning.* Berlin, Germany: Springer. doi:10.1007/978-3-540-68856-3.

De Raedt, L. (2008). *Logical and relational learning.* New York, NY: Springer. doi:10.1007/978-3-540-68856-3.

De Raedt, L., & Ramon, J. (2004). Condensed representations for inductive logic programming. In Dubois, D., Welty, C. A., & Williams, M. A. (Eds.), *Principles of knowledge representation and reasoning* (pp. 438–446). Menlo Park, CA: AAAI Press.

Dehaspe, L., & Toivonen, H. (1999). Discovery of frequent DATALOG patterns. *Data Mining and Knowledge Discovery, 3,* 7–36. doi:10.1023/A:1009863704807.

Dey, A. K., & Abowd, G. D. (2000). Towards a better understanding of context and context-awareness. In *Proceedings of the Workshop on The What, Who, Where, When, and How of Context-Awareness at the Conference on Human Factors in Computing Systems,* The Hague, The Netherlands.

Dey, A. K. (2001). Understanding and using context. *Personal and Ubiquitous Computing, 5*(1), 4–7. doi:10.1007/s007790170019.

Dey, A. K. (2001). Understanding and Using Context. *Personal and Ubiquitous Computing*, *5*(1), 4–7. doi:10.1007/s007790170019.

Dhillon, I. S., & Modha, D. S. (2001). Concept decompositions for large sparse text data using clustering. *Machine Learning*, *42*(1-2), 143–175. doi:10.1023/A:1007612920971.

Dong, X. L., Berti-Equille, L., & Srivastava, D. (2009). Integrating Conflicting Data: The Role of Source Dependence. In *Proceedings of the Very Large Databases (VLDB) Conference* (pp. 550-561).

Dong, X., Berti-Equille, L., & Srivastava, D. (2009). Integrating conflicting data: The role of source dependence. In *Proceedings of the 35th International Conference on Very Large Databases*, Lyon, France (pp. 550-561).

Dong, X., Halevy, A., & Madhavan, J. (2005). Reference reconciliation in complex information spaces. In *Proceedings of the ACM SIGMOD International Conference on Management of Data* (pp. 85-96).

Donini, F., Lenzerini, M., Nardi, D., & Schaerf, A. (1998). -log: Integrating datalog and description logics. *Journal of Intelligent Information Systems*, *10*(3), 227–252. doi:10.1023/A:1008687430626.

Dorai, C., & Ventakesh, S. (2003). Bridging the semantic gap with computational media aesthetics. *IEEE MultiMedia*, *10*(2), 15–17. doi:10.1109/MMUL.2003.1195157.

Džeroski, S., & Lavrač, N. (Eds.). (2001). *Relational data mining*. New York, NY: Springer.

El Sayed, A., Hacid, H., & Zighed, D. (2007). Mining semantic distance between corpus terms. In *Proceedings of the ACM First PhD Workshop in CIKM* (pp. 49-54). New York, NY: ACM.

Elmagarmid, A., Ipeirotis, P., & Verykios, V. (2007). Duplicate record detection: A survey. *IEEE Transactions on Knowledge and Data Engineering*, *19*(1), 1–16. doi:10.1109/TKDE.2007.250581.

Entertainment Software Association. (2011). *Industry facts*. Retrieved from http://www.theesa.com/facts/index.asp

Eris, O. (2002). *Perceiving, comprehending, and measuring design activity through the questions asked while designing* (Unpublished doctoral dissertation). Stanford University, Stanford, CA.

Esposito, F., Fanizzi, N., Iannone, L., Palmisano, I., & Semeraro, G. (2004). Knowledge-intensive induction of terminologies from metadata. In F. van Harmelen et al. (Eds.), *Proceedings of the 3rd International Semantic Web Conference (ISWC2004)* (LNCS 3298, pp. 441-455).

Euromonitor International. (2010). *Global Market Information Database (GMID)*. Retrieved January 19, 2010, from http://www.portal.euromonitor.com

Euzenat, J., & Shvaiko, P. (2007). *Ontology matching*. Heidelberg, Germany: Springer-Verlag.

Fanizzi, N., d'Amato, C., & Esposito, F. (2008). Conceptual clustering and its application to concept drift and novelty detection. In *Proceedings of the 5th European Semantic Web Conference on the Semantic Web: Research and Applications* (pp. 318-332). Berlin, Germany: Springer-Verlag.

Fanizzi, N., d'Amato, C., & Esposito, F. (2008a). DL-FOIL: Concept learning in description logics. In F. Zelezný & N. Lavrač (Eds.), *Proceedings of the 18th International Conference on Inductive Logic Programming (ILP2008)* (LNAI 5194, pp. 107-121).

Fanizzi, N., d'Amato, C., & Esposito, F. (2008b). Statistical learning for inductive query answering on OWL ontologies. In A. Sheth (Eds.), *Proceedings of the 7th International Semantic Web Conference (ISWC2008)* (LNCS 5318, pp. 195-212).

Fanizzi, N., d'Amato, C., & Esposito, F. (2010). Induction of concepts in web ontologies through terminological decision trees. In J. L. Balcázar et al. (Eds.), *Proceedings of the ECML PKDD 2010 Conference: Part I* (LNAI 6321, pp. 442-457).

Fanizzi, N., Esposito, F., Ferilli, S., & Semeraro, G. (2003). A methodology for the induction of ontological knowledge from semantic annotations. In F. Turini & A. Cappelli (Eds.), *Proceedings of the 8th Conference of the Italian Association for Artificial Intelligence (AI*IA2003)* (LNAI 2829, pp. 65-77).

Fanizzi, N., Ferilli, S., Iannone, L., Palmisano, I., & Semeraro, G. (2005). Downward refinement in the $\mathcal{ALN}$ description logic. In *Proceedings of the 4th International Conference on Hybrid Intelligent Systems (HIS2004)* (pp. 68-73). Washington, DC: IEEE Computer Society.

Fanizzi, N., Iannone, L., Palmisano, I., & Semeraro, G. (2004). Concept formation in expressive description logics. In Boulicaut, J.-F. et al., (Eds.), *Proceedings of the 15th European Conference on Machine Learning (ECML2004)* (LNAI 3201, pp. 99-113).

Fanizzi, N., d'Amato, C., & Esposito, F. (2009a). Inductive classification of semantically annotated resources through reduced coulomb energy networks. *International Journal on Semantic Web and Information Systems*, *5*(4), 19–38. doi:10.4018/jswis.2009100102.

Fanizzi, N., d'Amato, C., & Esposito, F. (2009b). Metric-based stochastic conceptual clustering for ontologies. *Information Systems*, *34*(8), 792–806. doi:10.1016/j.is.2009.03.008.

Fellegi, I. P., & Sunter, A. B. (1969). A theory for record linkage. *Journal of the American Statistical Association*, *64*(328), 1183–1210. doi:10.2307/2286061.

Ferret, O., Grau, B., Hurault-Plantet, M., Illouz, G., & Jacquemin, C. (2001). Terminological Variants for Document Selection and Question/Answer Matching. In *Proceedings of the Workshop on Open-Domain Question Answering (ODQA)* (Vol. 12). Stroudsburg, PA: Association for Computational Linguistics.

Fitzpatrick, D. (2003). Searle and collective intentionality: The self-defeating nature of internalism with respect to social facts. *American Journal of Economics and Sociology*, *62*(1), 45–66. doi:10.1111/1536-7150.t01-1-00002.

Fleischman, M., & Hovy, E. (2002). Fine grained classification of named entities. In *Proceedings of the 19th International Conference on Computational Linguistics* (pp. 1-7).

Fowler, D., Crowder, R. M., Guan, T., Shadbolt, N., & Wills, G. (2010). Requirements for semantic Web applications in engineering. In *Proceedings of the ASME International Design Engineering Technical Conferences & Computers and Information in Engineering Conference*.

Fox, E. A., & Shaw, J. A. (1994). Combination of multiple searches. In *Proceedings of the 2nd Text Retrieval Conference TREC2 NIST SP 500215* (pp. 243-252). Gaithersburg, MD: NIST.

Franklin, M. J., Halevy, A. Y., & Maier, D. (2005). From databases to dataspaces: A new abstraction for information management. *SIGMOD Record*, *34*(4), 27–33. doi:10.1145/1107499.1107502.

Frawley, W. (1992). *Linguistic semantics*. Mahwah, NJ: Lawrence Erlbaum.

Fürber, C., & Hepp, M. (2010). Using SPARQL and SPIN for data quality management on the semantic web. *Business Information Systems*, *47*(2), 35–46. doi:10.1007/978-3-642-12814-1_4.

Galland, A., Marian, A., Abiteboul, S., & Senellart, P. (2010). Corroborating Information from Disagreeing Views. In *Proceedings of the 3rd ACM International Conference on Web Search and Data Mining (WSDM)* (pp. 131-140).

Gates, S. C., Teiken, W., & Cheng, K.-S. F. (2005). Taxonomies by the numbers: building high-performance taxonomies. In O. Herzog, H.-J. Schek, N. Fuhr, A. Chowdhury, & W. Teiken (Eds.), *Proceedings of the ACM International Conference on Information and Knowledge Management* (pp. 568-577). New York, NY: ACM Press.

Gero, J. S., & Maher, M. L. (1993). *Modeling creativity and knowledge-based creative design*. Mahwah, NJ: Lawrence Erlbaum.

Gil, Y. (2011). Interactive knowledge capture in the new millennium: How the semantic web changed everything. *The Knowledge Engineering Review*, *26*, 45–51. doi:10.1017/S0269888910000408.

Girgensohn, A., Adcock, J., Cooper, M., Foote, J., & Wilcox, L. (2003). Simplifying the management of large photo collections. In *Proceedings of the Ninth IFIP TC13 International Conference on Human-Computer Interaction*. Amsterdam, The Netherlands: IOS Press.

Glaser, H., Millard, I., & Jaffri, A. (2008). Rkbexplorer. com: a knowledge driven infrastructure for linked data providers. In *Proceedings of the 5th European Semantic Web Conference on the Semantic Web: Research and Applications*, Tenerife, Spain (pp. 797-801).

Gligorov, R., Aleksovski, Z., ten Kate, W., & van Harmelen, F. (2007). Using Google distance to weight approximate ontology matches. In *Proceedings of the 16th International World Wide Web Conference*, Banff, AB, Canada (pp. 767-775).

Goldman, S. A., Kwek, S., & Scott, S. D. (2003). Learning from examples with unspecified attribute values. *Information and Computation, 180*(2), 82–100. doi:10.1016/S0890-5401(02)00030-5.

Gómez-Pérez, A., Fernández-López, M., & Corcho, O. (2004). *Ontological engineering.* New York, NY: Springer.

Gottlob, G. (1992). Complexity Results for Nonmonotonic Logics. *Journal of Logic and Computation, 2*, 397–425. doi:10.1093/logcom/2.3.397.

Governatori, G., & Rotolo, A. (2004). Defeasible Logic: Agency, Intention and Obligation. In *Proceedings of the 7th International Workshop on Deontic Logic in Computer Science,* Madeira, Portugal (pp. 114-128).

Governatori, G., Hulstijn, J., Riveret, R., & Rotolo, A. (2007). Characterising Deadlines in Temporal Modal Defeasible Logic. In *Proceedings of the 20th Australian Joint Conference on Artificial Intelligence (AI 2007)* (pp. 486-496).

Governatori, G. (2005). Representing Business Contracts in RuleML. *International Journal of Cooperative Information Systems, 14*(2-3), 181–216. doi:10.1142/S0218843005001092.

Governatori, G., Padmanabhan, V., Rotolo, A., & Sattar, A. (2009). A Defeasible Logic for Modelling Policy-based Intentions and Motivational Attitudes. *Logic Journal of the IGPL, 17*(3), 227–265. doi:10.1093/jigpal/jzp006.

Governatori, G., & Rotolo, A. (2008a). BIO Logical Agents: Norms, Beliefs, Intentions in Defeasible Logic. *Journal of Autonomous Agents and Multi Agent Systems, 17*(1), 36–69. doi:10.1007/s10458-008-9030-4.

Governatori, G., & Rotolo, A. (2008b). A Computational Framework for Institutional Agency. *Artificial Intelligence and Law, 16*(1), 25–52. doi:10.1007/s10506-007-9056-y.

Gracia, J., & Mena, E. (2008). Matching with CIDER: Evaluation report for the OAEI 2008. In *Proceedings of the 3rd Ontology Matching Workshop and the 7th International Semantic Web Conference*, Karlsruhe, Germany.

Gracia, J., d'Aquin, M., & Mena, E. (2009). Large scale integration of senses for the Semantic Web. In *Proceedings of the 18th International World Wide Web Conference*, Madrid, Spain.

Grosof, B., Horrocks, I., Volz, R., & Decker, S. (2003). Description logic programs: combining logic programs with description logic. In *Proceedings of the 12th International Conference on World Wide Web (WWW03)* (pp. 48-57). New York, NY: ACM.

Gruber, T. R. (1993). Toward principles for the design of ontologies used for knowledge sharing. *International Journal of Human-Computer Studies, 43*(5), 907–928. doi:10.1006/ijhc.1995.1081.

Guarino, N., & Welty, C. (2002). Identity and subsumption. In Green, R., Bean, C. A., & Myaeng, S. H. (Eds.), *The semantics of relationships: An interdisciplinary perspective* (pp. 111–125). Dordrecht, The Netherlands: Kluwer Academic.

Guo, S., Dong, X., Srivastava, D., & Zajac, R. (2010). Record linkage with uniqueness constraints and erroneous values. In *Proceedings of the 36th International Conference on Very Large Databases*, Singapore (pp. 417-428).

Haake, J. M., Hussein, T., Joop, B., Lukosch, S., Veiel, D., & Ziegler, J. (2010). Modeling and Exploiting Context for Adaptive Collaboration. *International Journal of Cooperative Information Systems, 19*(1-2), 71–120. doi:10.1142/S0218843010002115.

Halpin, H., Hayes, P. J., McCusker, J. P., McGuinness, D. L., & Thompson, H. S. (2010). When owl:sameas isn't the same: An analysis of identity in linked data. In *Proceedings of the 9th International Semantic Web Conference*, Shanghai, China (pp. 305-320).

Han, J., & Fu, Y. (1995). Discovery of multiple-level association rules from large databases. In *Proceedings of the 21st International Conference on Very Large Data Bases* (pp. 420-431). San Francisco, CA: Morgan Kaufmann.

Han, J., & Fu, Y. (1999). Mining multiple-level association rules in large databases. *IEEE Transactions on Knowledge and Data Engineering, 11*(5).

Hasan, T., & Jameson, A. (2008). Bridging the motivation gap for individual annotators: What can we learn from photo annotation systems? In *Proceedings of the 1st Workshop on Incentives for the Semantic Web at the 7th International Semantic Web Conference*, Karlsruhe, Germany. Retrieved from http://km.aifb.uni-karlsruhe.de/ws/ insemtive2008/hasan2008insemtive.pdf

Hassanzadeh, O., Lim, L., Kementsietsidis, A., & Wang, M. (2009). A declarative framework for semantic link discovery over relational data. In *Proceedings of the 18th International Conference on World Wide Web* (pp. 1101-1102).

Hatzivassiloglou, V., Gravano, L., & Maganti, A. (2000). An investigation of linguistic features and clustering algorithms for topical document clustering. In N. J. Belkin, P. Ingwersen, & M.-K. Leong (Eds.), *Proceedings of the ACM SIGIR Conference on Research and Development in Information Retrieval* (pp. 224-231). New York, NY: ACM Press.

Heisig, P., Caldwell, N. H. M., Grebici, K., & Clarkson, P. J. (2010). Exploring knowledge and information needs in engineering from the past and for the future – results from a survey. *Design Studies, 31*(5), 499–532. doi:10.1016/j.destud.2010.05.001.

Hellmann, S., Lehmann, J., & Auer, S. (2011). Learning of OWL class expressions on very large knowledge bases and its applications. In Sheth, A. (Ed.), *Semantic Services, Interoperability and Web Applications: Emerging Concepts* (pp. 104–130). Hershey, PA: IGI Global.

Hepp, M. (2008). GoodRelations: An ontology for describing products and services offers on the Web. In A. Gangemi & J. Euzenat (Eds.), *Proceedings of the 16th International Conference on Knowledge Engineer: Practice and Patterns* (LNCS 5268, pp. 329-346).

Hepp, M. (2011). *The product types ontology: Good identifiers for product types based on Wikipedia.* Retrieved April 20, 2011, from http://www.productontology.org/

Hepp, M., & Radinger, A. (2010). *eClassOWL- The Web ontology for products and services.* Retrieved April 18, 2011, from http://www.heppnetz.de/projects/eclassowl/

Hepp, M. (2006). Products and services ontologies: A methodology for deriving OWL ontologies from industrial categorization standards. *International Journal on Semantic Web and Information, 2*(1), 72–99. doi:10.4018/jswis.2006010103.

Hepp, M. (2007). Possible ontologies: How reality constrains the development of relevant ontologies. *IEEE Internet Computing, 11*, 90–96. doi:10.1109/MIC.2007.20.

Hepp, M., Siorpaes, K., & Bachlechner, D. (2007). Harvesting wiki consensus: Using Wikipedia entries as vocabulary for knowledge management. *IEEE Internet Computing, 11*, 54–65. doi:10.1109/MIC.2007.110.

Herdağdelen, A., & Baroni, M. (2010). The concept game: Better commonsense knowledge extraction by combining text mining and a game with a purpose. In *Proceedings of the AAAI Fall Symposium on Commonsense Knowledge* (pp. 52-57). Palo Alto, CA: AAAI Press.

Herlocker, J. L., Konstan, J. A., Terveen, L. G., & Riedl, J. T. (2004). Evaluating collaborative filtering recommender systems. *ACM Transactions on Information Systems, 22*(1), 5–53. doi:10.1145/963770.963772.

Herman, I. (2009). *W3C Semantic Web Frequently Asked Questions.* Retrieved February 20, 2011, from http://www.w3.org/RDF/FAQ

Heymann, P., & Garcia-Molina, H. (2006, April). *Collaborative creation of communal hierarchical taxonomies in social tagging systems* (Tech. Rep. No. 2006-10). Palo Alto, CA: Stanford University.

Hilpinen, R. (2001). Deontic Logic. In Goble, L. (Ed.), *The Blackwell Guide to Philosophical Logic* (pp. 159–182). Oxford, UK: Blackwell.

Hippisley, A., Cheng, D., & Ahmad, K. (2005). The head-modifier principle and multilingual term extraction. *Natural Language Engineering, 11*(2), 129–157. doi:10.1017/S1351324904003535.

Hladká, B., Mírovský, J., & Schlesinger, P. (2009). Designing a language game for collecting coreference annotation. In *Proceedings of the 3rd Linguistic Annotation Workshop* (pp. 52-55). Stroudsburg, PA: Association for Computational Linguistics.

Ho, C.-J., Chang, T.-H., Lee, J.-C., Hsu, J. Y.-j., & Chen, K.-T. (2009). KissKissBan: a competitive human computation game for image annotation. In *Proceedings of the ACM SIGKDD Workshop on Human Computation* (pp. 11-14). New York, NY: ACM.

Hofmann, T. (1999). The cluster-abstraction model: Unsupervised learning of topic hierarchies from text data. In T. Dean (Ed.), *Proceedings of the International Joint Conference on Artificial Intelligence* (pp. 682-687). San Francisco, CA: Morgan Kaufmann.

Hofstadter, D. R. (1983). Metamagical Themas: Computer Tournaments of the Prisoner's Dilemma Suggest How Cooperation Evolves. *Scientific American*, *248*(5), 16–26. doi:10.1038/scientificamerican0583-16.

Hogan, A., Harth, A., Passant, A., Decker, S., & Polleres, A. (2010). Weaving the pedantic web. In *Proceedings of the Linked Data on the Web World Wide Web Workshop*, Raleigh, NC. Retrieved from http://sw.deri.org/~aidanh/docs/pedantic_ldow10.pdf

Hornsby, J. (1997). Collectives and Intentionality. *Philosophy and Phenomenological Research*, *57*(2), 429–434. doi:10.2307/2953732.

Horrocks, I., Patel-Schneider, P., Boley, H., Tabet, S., Grosof, B., & Dean, M. (2004). *SWRL: A semantic web rule language combining OWL and RuleML*. Retrieved from http://www.w3.org/Submission/SWRL/

Horrocks, I., Patel-Schneider, P., & van Harmelen, F. (2003). From $\mathcal{SHIQ}$ and RDF to OWL: The Making of a Web Ontology Language. *Journal of Web Semantics*, *1*(1), 7–26. doi:10.1016/j.websem.2003.07.001.

Hotho, A., Jäschke, R., Schmitz, C., & Stumme, G. (2006). Emergent Semantics in BibSonomy. In *Proceedings of the Workshop on Applications of Semantic Technologies*.

Hu, W., Chen, J., & Qu, Y. (2011). A self-training approach for re- solving object coreference on the semantic web. In *Proceedings of the 20th International World Wide Web Conference*, Hyderabad, India (pp. 87-96).

Huhtala, Y., Karkkainen, J., Porkka, P., & Toivonen, H. (1999). TANE: An efficient algorithm for discovering functional and approximate dependencies. *The Computer Journal*, *42*(2), 100–111. doi:10.1093/comjnl/42.2.100.

Hunicke, R., Leblanc, M., & Zubek, R. (2004). MDA: A formal approach to game design and game research. In *Proceedings of the 19th National Artificial Intelligence Conference on Challenges in Games* (pp. 1-5). Palo Alto, CA: AAAI Press.

Hustadt, U., Motik, B., & Sattler, U. (2004). Reducing -Description Logic to Disjunctive Datalog Programs. In D. Dubois, C. Welty, & M. A. Williams (Eds.), Principles of knowledge representation and reasoning (pp. 152–162). Menlo Park, CA: AAAI Press.

Huynh, D. F., Karger, D. R., & Miller, R. C. (2007). Exhibit: Lightweight structured data publishing. In *Proceedings of the 16th International World Wide Web Conference*.

Iannone, L., Palmisano, I., & Fanizzi, N. (2007). An algorithm based on counterfactuals for concept learning in the semantic web. *Applied Intelligence*, *26*(2), 139–159. doi:10.1007/s10489-006-0011-5.

Iannone, L., Palmisano, I., & Fanizzi, N. (2007). An algorithm based on counterfactuals for concept learning in the semantic web. *Applied Intelligence*, *26*, 139–159. doi:10.1007/s10489-006-0011-5.

Ienco, D., & Meo, R. (2008). Towards the automatic construction of conceptual taxonomies. In I.-Y. Song, J. Eder, & T. M. Nguyen (Eds.), *Proceedings of the International Conference on Data Warehousing and Knowledge Discovery* (pp. 327-336). Berlin, Germany: Springer.

InfoTrends/CAP Ventures. (2004). *Mobile imaging: Technology trends, consumer behavior, and business strategies* (Tech. Rep.). Retrieved from http://www.capv.com/home/Multiclient/ MobileImaging.html

Inuzuka, N., Kamo, M., Ishii, N., Seki, H., & Itoh, H. (1997). Tow-down induction of logic programs from incomplete samples. In S. Muggleton (Ed.), *Selected Papers from the 6th International Workshop on Inductive Logic Programming (ILP96)* (LNAI 1314, pp. 265-282).

Ioannou, E., Nejdl, W., Niederée, C., & Velegrakis, Y. (2010). On-the-fly entity-aware query processing in the presence of linkage. In *Proceedings of the 36th International Conference on Very Large Databases*, Singapore (pp. 429-438).

Ioannou, E., Niederée, C., & Nejdl, W. (2008). Probabilistic entity linkage for heterogeneous information spaces. In *Proceedings of the 20th International Conference on Advanced Information Systems Engineering*, Montpellier, France (pp. 556-570).

Ioannou, E., Niederée, C., Velegrakis, Y., Bonvin, N., Mocan, A., Papadakis, G., et al. (2010). *Intelligent entity matching and ranking* (Tech. Rep. No. D3.1). Brussels, Belgium: OKKAM.

Isele, R. (2011). *Link specification language*. Retrieved from http://www4.wiwiss.fu-berlin.de/bizer/silk/spec

Jaffri, A., Glaser, H., & Millard, I. (2008). URI disambiguation in the context of Linked Data. In *Proceedings of the WWW International Workshop on Linked Data on the Web*, Beijing, China.

Jain, P., Hitzler, P., Yeh, P. Z., Verma, K., & Sheth, A. P. (2009). Linked data is merely more data. In *Proceedings of the AAAI International Conference on Linked Data Meets Artificial Intelligence* (pp. 82-86). Retrieved April 18, 2011, from http://www.aaai.org/ocs/index.php/SSS/SSS10/paper/download/1130/1454

Jean-Mary, Y., Shironoshita, E., & Kabuka, M. (2009). Ontology matching with semantic verification. *Web Semantics: Science. Services and Agents on the World Wide Web, 7*(3), 235–251. doi:10.1016/j.websem.2009.04.001.

Johansson, I. (2004). *Ontological investigations: An inquiry into the categories of nature, man and society* (2nd ed.). Frankfurt, Germany: Verlag.

Jones, G. J., Quested, D. J., & Thomson, K. E. (2000). Personalised Delivery of News Articles from Multiple Sources. In *Proceedings of the 4th European Conference on Research and Advanced Technology for Digital Libraries* (pp. 340-343).

Józefowska, J., Lawrynowicz, A., & Lukaszewski, T. (2010). The role of semantics in mining frequent patterns from knowledge bases in description logics with rules. *Theory and Practice of Logic Programming, 10*(3), 251–289. doi:10.1017/S1471068410000098.

Kagal, L., Berners-Lee, T., Connolly, D., & Weitzner, D. (2006, July 16-20). Using Semantic Web Technologies for Open Policy Management on the Web. In *Proceedings of the 21st National Conference on Artificial Intelligence (AAAI 2006)*. Menlo Park, CA: AAAI Press.

Katz, B. (1997). Annotating the World Wide Web Using Natural Language. In *Proceedings of the 5th RIAO Conference on Computer Assisted Information Searching on the Internet.*

Katz, B., Felshin, S., Yuret, D., Ibrahim, A., Lin, J., Marton, G., et al. (2002). Omnibase: Uniform Access to Heterogeneous Data for Question Answering. In *Proceedings of the 7th International Workshop on Applications of Natural Language to Information Systems,* Stockholm, Sweden (pp. 230-234).

Kautz, H. A., & Selman, B. (1991). Hard Problems for Simple Default Theories. *Artificial Intelligence, 28*, 243–279. doi:10.1016/0004-3702(91)90011-8.

KEGG. (2010). *Genes database*. Retrieved from http://www.genome.jp/kegg/genes.html

Kemke, C. (2001). *About the ontology of actions* (Tech. Rep. No. MCC-01-328). University Park, NM: Computing Research Laboratory, New Mexico State University.

Kietz, J. (2003). Learnability of description logic programs. In S. Matwin & C. Sammut (Eds.), *Proceedings of the International Conference on Inductive Logic Programming* (LNCS 2583, pp. 117-132).

Kietz, J.-U. (2002). Learnability of description logic programs. In S. Matwin & C. Sammut (Eds.), *Proceedings of the 12th International Conference on Inductive Logic Programming* (LNAI 2583 pp. 117-132).

Kietz, J.-U., & Morik, K. (1994). A polynomial approach to the constructive induction of structural knowledge. *Machine Learning, 14*(2), 193–218. doi:10.1023/A:1022626200450.

Kim, O., Jayaram, U., Jayaram, S., & Zhu, L. J. (2009). An ontology mapping application using shared ontology approach and a bridge ontology. In *Proceedings of the ASME International Design Engineering Technical Conferences & Computers and Information in Engineering Conference.*

Kim, O., Jayaram, U., Jayaram, S., & Zhu, L. J. (2010). ITrain: Ontology-based integration of information and methods in computer-based training (CBT) and immersive training (IMT) for assembly simulation. In *Proceedings of the ASME International Design Engineering Technical Conferences & Computers and Information in Engineering Conference.*

Kim, J.-O., & Mueller, C. W. (1978). *Introduction to factor analysis: what it is and how to do it* (10th ed.). Thousand Oaks, CA: Sage.

Kirk, D., Sellen, A., Rother, C., & Wood, K. (2006). Understanding photowork. In *Proceedings of the SIGCHI Conference on Human Factors in Computing Systems* (pp. 761-770). New York, NY: ACM.

Kivinen, J., & Mannila, H. (1995). Approximate inference of functional dependencies from relations. *Theoretical Computer Science, 149*(1), 129–149. doi:10.1016/0304-3975(95)00028-U.

Klyne, G., & Carroll, J. J. (2004). *Resource Description Framework (RDF): Concepts and abstract syntax*. Retrieved from http://www.w3.org/TR/2004/REC-rdf-concepts-20040210/

Knublauch, H., Fergerson, R. W., Noy, N. F., & Musen, M. A. (2004). The Protégé OWL Plugin: An open development environment for semantic web applications. In S. A. McIlraith, D. Plexousakis, & F. van Harmelen (Eds.), In *Proceedings of the Semantic Web Conference* (LNCS 3298, p. 229-243).

Kolaczek, G. (2002). Application of Deontic Logic in Role-based Access Control. *International Journal of Applied Mathematics and Computer Science, 12*(2), 269–275.

Konstan, J. A., Miller, B. N., Maltz, D., Herlocker, J. L., Gordon, L. R., & Riedl, J. (1997). GroupLens: Applying Collaborative Filtering to Usenet News. *Communications of the ACM, 40*(3), 77–87. doi:10.1145/245108.245126.

Kontopoulos, E., Bassiliades, N., Governatori, G., & Antoniou, G. (2008). Extending a Defeasible Reasoner with Modal and Deontic Logic Operators. In *Proceedings of the Workshop on Logics for Intelligent Agents and Multi-Agent Systems (WLIAMAS 2008), IEEE/WIC/ACM International Conference on Web Intelligence and Intelligent Agent Technology,* Sydney, NSW, Australia (pp. 626-629). Washington, DC: IEEE Computer Society.

Kontopoulos, E., Bassiliades, N., Governatori, G., & Antoniou, G. (2011). Visualizing Semantic Web Proofs of Defeasible Logic in the DR-DEVICE System. *Knowledge-Based Systems, 24*(3), 406–419. doi:10.1016/j.knosys.2010.12.001.

Koparanova, M. G., & Risch, T. (2002). Completing CAD data queries for visualization. In *Proceedings of the International Database Engineering and Applications Symposium* (p. 130).

Köpcke, H., & Rahm, E. (2010). Frameworks for entity matching: A comparison. *Data & Knowledge Engineering, 69*, 197–210. doi:10.1016/j.datak.2009.10.003.

Köpcke, H., Thor, A., & Rahm, E. (2010). Evaluation of entity resolution approaches on real-world match problems. *Proceedings of the Very Large Data Base Endowment, 3*(1-2), 484–493.

Koren, Y., & Bell, R. B. (2011). Advances in Collaborative Filtering. In Ricci, F., Rokach, L., Shapira, B., & Kantor, P. B. (Eds.), *Recommender Systems Handbook* (pp. 145–186). doi:10.1007/978-0-387-85820-3_5.

Koudas, N., Sarawagi, S., & Srivastava, D. (2006). Record linkage: similarity measures and algorithms. In *Proceedings of the ACM SIGMOD International Conference on Management of Data*, Chicago, IL (pp. 802-803).

Kramár, T., Barla, M., & Bieliková, M. (2010). Disambiguating search by leveraging the social network context based on the stream of user's activity. In P. De Bra, A. Kobsa, & D. Chin (Eds.), *Proceedings of the 18th International Conference on User Modeling, Adaptation, and Personalization* (LNCS 6075, pp. 387-392).

Krause, M., Takhtamysheva, A., Wittstock, M., & Malaka, R. (2010). Frontiers of a paradigm: exploring human computation with digital games. In *Proceedings of the ACM SIGKDD Workshop on Human Computation* (pp. 22-25). New York, NY: ACM.

Kravari, K., Kontopoulos, E., & Bassiliades, N. (2010a, May 4-7). EMERALD: A Multi-Agent System for Knowledge-based Reasoning Interoperability in the Semantic Web. In *Proceedings of the 6th Hellenic Conference on Artificial Intelligence (SETN 2010)*, Athens, Greece (pp. 173-182).

Kravari, K., Kontopoulos, E., & Bassiliades, N. (2010b). Trusted Reasoning Services for Semantic Web Agents. *Informatica: International Journal of Computing and Informatics, 34*(4), 429–440.

Krótzsch, M., Vrandecic, D., Vólkel, M., Haller, H., & Studer, R. (2007). Semantic Wikipedia. *Journal of Web Semantics*, *5*, 251–261. doi:10.1016/j.websem.2007.09.001.

Kuffner, T. A., & Ullman, D. G. (1990). The information requests of mechanical design engineers. *Design Studies*, *12*(1), 42–50. doi:10.1016/0142-694X(91)90007-J.

Kuo, Y.-l., Lee, J.-C., Chiang, K.-y., Wang, R., Shen, E., Chan, C.-w., & Hsu, J. Y.-j. (2009). Community-based game design: experiments on social games for commonsense data collection. In *Proceedings of the ACM SIGKDD Workshop on Human Computation* (pp. 15-22). New York, NY: ACM.

Kwok, C., Etzioni, O., & Weld, D. S. (2001). Scaling question answering to the web. *ACM Transactions on Information Systems*, *19*(3), 242–262. doi:10.1145/502115.502117.

Lam, H., & Governatori, G. (2009). The Making of SPINdle. In G. Governatori, J. Hall, & A. Paschke (Eds.), *Proceedings of the 2009 International Symposium on Rule Interchange and Applications* (LNCS 5858, pp. 315-322).

Lavelle, B., Byrne, D., Gurrin, C., Smeaton, A. F., & Jones, G. J. F. (2007). Bluetooth familiarity: Methods of calculation, applications and limitations. In *Proceedings of the 9th International Conference on Human Computer Interaction with Mobile Devices and Services Mobile Interaction with the Real World*, Singapore. Retrieved from http://www.medien.ifi.lmu.de/mirw2007/ papers/ MIRW2007_Lavelle.pdf

Law, E. L., Mityagin, A., & Chickering, M. (2009). Intentions: a game for classifying search query intent. In *Proceedings of the 27th International Conference Extended Abstracts on Human Factors in Computing Systems* (pp. 3805-3810). New York, NY: ACM.

Law, E. L., von Ahn, L., Dannenberg, R. B., & Crawford, M. (2007). Tagatune: A game for music and sound annotation. In *Proceedings of the 8th International Conference on Music Information Retrieval* (pp. 361-364). Vienna, Austria: Austrian Computer Society.

Lee, A. S. (2004). Thinking about social theory and philosophy for information systems. In Mingers, J., & Willcocks, L. (Eds.), *Social theory and philosophy for information systems*. Chichester, UK: John Wiley & Sons.

Lehmann, J. (2007). Hybrid learning of ontology classes. In P. Perner (Ed.), *Proceedings of the 5th International Conference on Machine Learning and Data Mining in Pattern Recognition (MLDM2007)* (LNCS 4571, pp. 883-898).

Lehmann, J. (2009). DL-Learner: Learning concepts in description logics. *Journal of Machine Learning Research*, *10*, 2639–2642.

Lehmann, J. (2010). *Learning OWL Class Expressions*. Heidelberg, Germany: AKA Heidelberg.

Lehmann, J., Auer, S., Bühmann, L., & Tramp, S. (2011). Class expression learning for ontology engineering. *Journal of Web Semantics*, *9*(1), 71–81. doi:10.1016/j.websem.2011.01.001.

Lehmann, J., & Hitzler, P. (2010). Concept learning in description logics using refinement operators. *Machine Learning*, *78*(1-2), 203–250. doi:10.1007/s10994-009-5146-2.

Lehmann, J., & Hitzler, P. (2010). Concept learning in description logics using refinement operators. *Machine Learning*, *78*, 203–250. doi:10.1007/s10994-009-5146-2.

Lenat, D. B. (1995). Cyc: a large-scale investment in knowledge infrastructure. *Communications of the ACM*, *38*(11), 33–38. doi:10.1145/219717.219745.

Levy, A., & Rousset, M. C. (1998). Combining Horn rules and description logics in CARIN. *Artificial Intelligence*, *104*, 165–209. doi:10.1016/S0004-3702(98)00048-4.

Ley, M. (2005). *DBLP bibliography server*. Retrieved July 25, 2011, from http://dblp.uni-trier.de/xml

Lieberman, H., Rosenzweig, E., & Singh, P. (2001). Aria: An agent for annotating and retrieving images. *IEEE Computer*, *34*(7), 5762. doi:10.1109/2.933504.

Li, J., Tang, J., Li, Y., & Luo, Q. (2009). RiMOM: A dynamic multistrategy ontology alignment framework. *IEEE Transactions on Knowledge and Data Engineering*, *21*(8), 1218–1232. doi:10.1109/TKDE.2008.202.

Lin, J., & Katz, B. (2003). Question Answering from the Web Using Knowledge Annotation and Knowledge Mining Techniques. In *Proceedings of 12th International Conference on Information and Knowledge Management*, New Orleans, LA (pp. 116-123).

Lindley, S. E., Durrant, A., Kirk, D., & Taylor, A. (2009). Collocated social practices surrounding photos. *International Journal of Human-Computer Studies, 67*(12), 995–1004. Retrieved from http://research.microsoft.com/pubs/115365/ IJHCS_Editorial.pdf doi:10.1016/j.ijhcs.2009.08.004.

Lisi, F. A., & Esposito, F. (2008). Learning $\mathcal{SHIQ}$ +log rules for ontology evolution. In A. Gangemi et al. (Eds.), *Proceedings of the 5th Workshop on Semantic Web Applications and Perspectives (SWAP2008)* (Vol. 426). CEUR-WS.org.

Lisi, F., & Esposito, F. (2004). Efficient evaluation of candidate hypotheses in $\mathcal{AL}$ -log. In R. Camacho, R. King, & A. Srinivasan (Eds.), *Proceedings of the 14th International Conference on Inductive Logic Programming* (LNCS 3194, pp. 216-233).

Lisi, F., & Malerba, D. (2003a). Bridging the gap between horn clausal logic and description logics in inductive learning. In A. Cappelli & F. Turini (Eds.), *Proceedings of the 8th Congress of the Italian Association for Artificial Intelligence on Advances in Artificial Intelligence* (LNCS 2829, pp. 49-60).

Lisi, F., & Malerba, D. (2003b). Ideal refinement of descriptions in $\mathcal{AL}$ -log. In T. Horvath & A. Yamamoto (Eds.), *Proceedings of the 13th International Conference on Inductive Logic Programming* (LNCS 2835, pp. 215-232).

Lisi, F. (2008). Building rules on top of ontologies for the semantic web with inductive logic programming. *Theory and Practice of Logic Programming, 8*(03), 271–300. doi:10.1017/S1471068407003195.

Lisi, F. (2010). Inductive logic programming in databases: From Datalog to $\mathcal{DL}$ +log. *Theory and Practice of Logic Programming, 10*(3), 331–359. doi:10.1017/S1471068410000116.

Lisi, F., & Esposito, F. (2009). On ontologies as prior conceptual knowledge in inductive logic programming. In Berendt, B., Mladenic, D., de Gemmis, M., Semeraro, G., Spiliopoulou, M., & Stumme, G., et al. (Eds.), *Knowledge discovery enhanced with semantic and social information* (Vol. 220, pp. 3–18). New York, NY: Springer. doi:10.1007/978-3-642-01891-6_1.

Lisi, F., & Malerba, D. (2004). Inducing multi-level association rules from multiple relations. *Machine Learning, 55*, 175–210. doi:10.1023/B:MACH.0000023151.65011.a3.

Liu, H., Maes, P., & Davenport, G. (2006). Unravelling the Taste Fabric of Social Networks. *International Journal on Semantic Web and Information Systems, 2*(1), 42–71. doi:10.4018/jswis.2006010102.

Li, Z., Raskin, V., & Ramani, K. (2008). Developing engineering ontology for information retrieval. *Journal of Computing and Information Science in Engineering, 8*(1), 011003. doi:10.1115/1.2830851.

Li, Z., Yang, M. C., & Ramani, K. (2009). A methodology for engineering ontology acquisition and validation. *Artificial Intelligence for Engineering Design, Analysis and Manufacturing, 23*(1), 37. doi:10.1017/S0890060409000092.

Lokhorst, G.-J. C. (1996). Reasoning about actions and obligations in first-order logic. *Studia Logica, 57*(1), 221–237. doi:10.1007/BF00370676.

Lopez, V., Nikolov, A., Fernandez, M., Sabou, M., Uren, V., & Motta, E. (2009). Merging and ranking answers in the Semantic Web: The wisdom of crowds. In *Proceedings of the 4th Asian Se- mantic Web Conference*, Shanghai, China (pp. 135-152).

Maedche, A., & Staab, S. (2000). Discovering conceptual relations from text. In *Proceedings of the 14th European Conference on Artificial Intelligence* (pp. 321-325). Amsterdam, The Netherlands: IOS Press.

Maedche, A., & Staab, S. (2001). Ontology learning for the semantic web. *IEEE Intelligent Systems, 16*(2), 72–79. doi:10.1109/5254.920602.

Maedche, A., & Staab, S. (2004). Ontology learning. In Staab, S., & Studer, R. (Eds.), *Handbook on ontologies*. New York, NY: Springer.

Maher, M. J., & Governatori, G. (1999). A Semantic Decomposition of Defeasible Logics. In *Proceedings of the 16th National Conference on Artificial Intelligence*, Orlando, FL (pp. 299-305). Menlo Park, CA: AAAI Press.

Mannila, H., & Toivonen, H. (1997). Levelwise search and borders of theories in knowledge discovery. *Data Mining and Knowledge Discovery, 1*(3), 241–258. doi:10.1023/A:1009796218281.

Manning, C. D., Raghavan, P., & Schütze, H. (2008). *Introduction to information retrieval.* Cambridge, UK: Cambridge University Press. Retrieved from http://nlp.stanford.edu/IR-book/pdf/irbookonlinereading.pdf

Marchionini, G. (2006). From finding to understanding. *Communications of the ACM, 49*(4), 41–46. doi:10.1145/1121949.1121979.

Masolo, C., Guizzardi, G., Vieu, L., Bottazzi, E., & Ferrario, R. (2005). *Relational roles and qua-individuals.* Paper presented at the AAAI Fall Symposium on Roles, an Interdisciplinary Perspective.

Masolo, C., Vieu, L., Bottazzi, E., Catenacci, C., Ferrario, F., Gangemi, A., et al. (2004, June 2-5). *Social roles and their descriptions.* Paper presented at the Ninth International Conference on the Principles of Knowledge Representation and Reasoning, Whistler, BC, Canada.

Masolo, C., Borgo, S., Gangemi, A., Guarino, N., & Oltramari, A. (2003). *WonderWeb Deliverable D18: Ontology Library.* Trento, Italy: Laboratory for Applied Ontology – ISTC-CNR.

Matuszek, C., Witbrock, M., Kahlert, R. C., Cabral, J., Schneider, D., Shah, P., et al. (2005). Searching for Common Sense: Populating Cyc™ from the Web. In *Proceedings of the 20th National Conference on Artificial Intelligence,* Pittsburgh, PA.

McCusker, J., & McGuinness, D. (2010). Towards identity in linked data. In *Proceedings of the OWL Experiences and Directions Seventh Annual Workshop,* Karlsruhe, Germany.

McDowell, L. K., & Cafarella, M. (2008). Ontology-driven, unsupervised instance population. *Web Semantics, 6,* 218–236. doi:10.1016/j.websem.2008.04.002.

Media Lab, M. I. T. (n. d.). *Common sense computing initiative.* Retrieved from http://csc.media.mit.edu/conceptnet

Meilicke, C., Völker, J., & Stuckenschmidt, H. (2008). Learning disjointness for debugging mappings between lightweight ontologies. In *Proceedings of the 16th International Conference on Knowledge Engineering: Practice and Patterns* (pp. 93-108).

Melnik, S. (2002). Similarity flooding: a versatile graph matching algorithm. In *Proceedings of the 18th International Conference on Data Engineering,* San Jose, CA (pp. 117-128).

Meyer, J.-J. C. (2001). Epistemic Logic. In Goble, L. (Ed.), *The Blackwell Guide to Philosophical Logic.* Oxford, UK: Blackwell.

Meyer, J.-J. C. (2003). Modal Epistemic and Doxastic Logic. In Gabbay, D., & Guenthner, F. (Eds.), *Handbook of Philosophical Logic* (2nd ed., *Vol. 10,* pp. 1–38). Dordrecht, The Netherlands: Kluwer.

Middleton, S. E., Roure, D. D., & Shadbolt, N. R. (2004). Ontology-based Recommender Systems. In Staab, S., & Studer, R. (Eds.), *Handbook on Ontologies* (pp. 477–498). Berlin, Germany: Springer-Verlag.

Mika, P. (2005). Flink: Semantic Web Technology for the Extraction and Analysis of Social Networks. *Journal of Web Semantics, 3*(2-3), 211–223. doi:10.1016/j.websem.2005.05.006.

Miller, G. (1995). WordNet: A Lexical Database for English George. *Communications of the ACM, 38*(11), 39–41. doi:10.1145/219717.219748.

Miller, G. (1995). WordNet: a lexical database for English. *Communications of the ACM, 38*(11), 39–41. doi:10.1145/219717.219748.

Miller, G. A., Beckwith, R., Fellbaum, C., Gross, D., & Miller, K. (1990). Wordnet: An on-line lexical database. *International Journal of Lexicography, 3,* 235–244. doi:10.1093/ijl/3.4.235.

Mitchell, J. (2011). *How many photos are uploaded to Facebook each day?* Retrieved June 26, 2011, from http://www.quora.com/ How-many-photos-are-uploaded-to-Facebook-each-day

Mitchell, T. (1982). Generalization as search. *Artificial Intelligence, 18*(2), 203–226. doi:10.1016/0004-3702(82)90040-6.

Mitchell, T. (1982). Generalization as search. *Artificial Intelligence, 18,* 203–226. doi:10.1016/0004-3702(82)90040-6.

Mobasher, B., Jin, X., & Zhou, Y. (2004). Semantically Enhanced Content-based Collaborative Filtering on the Web. In Berendt, B., Hotho, A., Mladenic, D., Van Someren, M., & Spiliopoulou, M. (Eds.), *Web Mining: From Web to Semantic Web* (pp. 57–76). doi:10.1007/978-3-540-30123-3_4.

Moghaddam, B., Jebara, T., & Pentland, A. (2000). Bayesian face recognition. *Pattern Recognition*, *33*(11), 1771–1782. doi:10.1016/S0031-3203(99)00179-X.

Monaghan, F. (2008). *Context-aware photograph annotation on the social Semantic Web* (Doctoral dissertation, National University of Ireland). Retrieved from http://sw.deri.org/~ferg/publications/thesis.pdf

Monaghan, F., & O'Sullivan, D. (2007). Leveraging ontologies, context and social networks to automate photo annotation. In B. Falcidieno, M. Spagnuolo, Y. S. Avrithis, I. Kompatsiaris, & P. Buitelaar (Eds.), *Proceedings of the 2nd International Conference on Semantics and Digital Media Technologies*, Genoa, Italy (LNCS 4816, pp. 252-255).

Moreau, E., Yvon, F., & Cappé, O. (2008). Robust similarity measures for named entities matching. In *COLING '08: Proceedings of the 22nd International Conference on Computational Linguistics* (pp. 593-600). Morristown, NJ: Association for Computational Linguistics.

Morris, J. (2008). *The role of ontology in modern expert systems development*. Retrieved March 20, 2011, from http://www.slideshare.net/jcmorris/the-role-of-ontology-in-modern-expert-systems-dallas-2008-presentation

Motik, B., Sattler, U., & Studer, R. (2005). Query Answering for OWL-DL with Rules. *Journal of Web Semantics*, *3*(1), 41–60. doi:10.1016/j.websem.2005.05.001.

Murshed, S. M. M., Dixon, A., & Shah, J. J. (2009). Neutral definition and recognition of assembly features for legacy system reverse engineering. In *Proceedings of the ASME International Design Engineering Technical Conferences & Computers and Information in Engineering Conference*.

Naaman, M. (2005). *Leveraging geo-referenced digital photographs* (Doctoral dissertation, Stanford University). Retrieved from http://infolab.stanford.edu/~mor/research/naamanthesis.pdf

Naaman, M., Harada, S., Wangy, Q., Garcia-Molina, H., & Paepcke, A. (2004). Context data in georeferenced digital photo collections. In *Proceedings of the 12th International Conference on Multimedia* (pp. 196-203). New York, NY: ACM.

Naaman, M., Yeh, R. B., Garcia-Molina, H., & Paepcke, A. (2005). Leveraging context to resolve identity in photo albums. In *Proceedings of the 5th ACM/IEEE-CS Joint Conference on Digital Libraries*. (pp. 178-187). New York, NY: ACM.

Naaman, M., & Nair, R. (2008). Zonetag's collaborative tag suggestions: What is this person doing in my phone? *IEEE MultiMedia*, *15*(3), 34–40. doi:10.1109/MMUL.2008.69.

Nadjarbashi-Noghani, M., Zhang, J., Sadat, H., & Ghorbani, A. A. (2005). PENS: A Personalised Electronic News System. In *Proceedings of the 3rd Annual Communication Networks and Services Research Conference* (pp. 31-38).

Nenadić, G., & Ananiadou, S. (2006). Mining semantically related terms from biomedical literature. *ACM Transactions on Asian Language Information Processing*, *5*(1), 22–43. doi:10.1145/1131348.1131351.

Ngomo, A.-C. N., & Auer, S. (2011). LIMES - a time-efficient approach for large-scale link discovery on the web of data. In *Proceedings of the International Joint Conference on Artificial Intelligence*, Barcelona, Spain.

Nicklas, D., Ranganathan, A., & Riboni, D. (2010). A survey of context modeling and reasoning techniques. *Pervasive and Mobile Computing*, *6*(2), 161–180. doi:10.1016/j.pmcj.2009.06.002.

Nienhuys-Cheng, S., & de Wolf, R. (1997). *Foundations of inductive logic programming* (*Vol. 1228*). New York, NY: Springer.

Nijssen, S., & Kok, J. (2001). Faster association rules for multiple relations. In *Proceedings of the 17th International Joint Conference on Artificial Intelligence* (pp. 891-896). San Francisco, CA: Morgan Kaufmann.

Nijssen, S., & Kok, J. N. (2003). Efficient frequent query discovery in FARMER. In N. Lavrac, D. Gamberger, H. Blockeel, & L. Todorovski (Eds.), *Proceedings of the 7th European Conference on Knowledge Discovery in Databases* (LNCS 2838, pp. 350-362).

Nikolov, A., Uren, V., & Motta, E. (2010). Data linking: Capturing and utilising implicit schema-level relations. In *Proceedings of the 3rd Workshop on Linked Data on the Web*, Raleigh, NC.

Nikolov, A., Uren, V., Motta, E., & de Roeck, A. (2008a). Integration of semantically annotated data by the KnoFuss architecture. In *Proceedings of the 16th International Conference on Knowledge Engineering and Knowledge Management*, Acitrezza, Italy (pp. 265-274).

Nikolov, A., Uren, V., Motta, E., & de Roeck, A. (2008b). Refining instance coreferencing results using belief propagation. In *Proceedings of the 3rd Asian Semantic Web Conference*, Bangkok, Thailand (pp. 405-419).

Nikolov, A., d'Aquin, M., & Motta, E. (2011). *Unsupervised instance coreference resolution using a genetic algorithm (Tech. Rep. No. kmi-11-02)*. Milton Keynes, UK: Knowledge Media Institute.

NIST. (2002). *STEP/EXPRESS and XML*. Retrieved February 25, 2011, from http://xml.coverpages.org/stepExpressXML.html#step-part28

Niu, X., Rong, S., Zhang, Y., & Wang, H. (2011). Zhishi. links results for oaei 2011. In *Proceedings of the 10th International Semantic Web Conference*, Bonn, Germany.

Noessner, J., Niepert, M., Meilicke, C., & Stuckenschmidt, H. (2010). Leveraging terminological structure for object reconciliation. In *Proceedings of the 7th Extended Semantic Web Conference*, Crete, Greece (pp. 334-348).

Nute, D. (1994). Defeasible logic. In Gabbay, D. (Ed.), *Handbook of Logic and Artificial Intelligence (Vol. 3*, pp. 353–395). Oxford, UK: Oxford University Press.

Nute, D. (1998). Norms, Priorities, and Defeasible Logic. In McNamara, P., & Prakken, H. (Eds.), *Norms, Logics and Information Systems* (pp. 201–218). Amsterdam, The Netherlands: IOS Press.

O'Hare, N., & Smeaton, A. F. (2009). Context-aware person identification in personal photo collections. *IEEE Transactions on Multimedia, 11*(2).

O'Toole, A. J., Phillips, P. J., Jiang, F., Ayyad, J., Penard, N., & Abdi, H. (2007). Face recognition algorithms surpass humans matching faces over changes in illumination. *IEEE Transactions on Pattern Analysis and Machine Intelligence, 29*(9), 1642–1646. doi:10.1109/TPAMI.2007.1107 PMID:17627050.

Pantel, P., & Pennacchiotti, M. (2008). Automatically harvesting and ontologizing semantic relations. In *Proceeding of the Conference on Ontology Learning and Population: Bridging the Gap between Text and Knowledge* (pp. 171-195). Amsterdam, The Netherlands: IOS Press.

Papakonstantinou, Y., Garcia-Molina, H., & Widom, J. (1995). Object Exchange across Heterogeneous Information Sources. In P. S. Yu & A. L. P. Chen (Eds.), *Proceedings of the International Conference on Data Engineering* (pp. 251-260). Los Alamitos, CA: IEEE Computer Society Press.

Paredaens, J., Peelman, P., & Tanca, L. (1995). G–Log: A Declarative Graphical Query Language. *IEEE Transactions on Knowledge and Data Engineering, 7*(3), 436–453. doi:10.1109/69.390249.

Park, L. F., & Ramamohanarao, K. (2009). An analysis of latent semantic term self-correlation. *ACM Transactions on Information Systems, 27*(2), 1–35. doi:10.1145/1462198.1462200.

Pearl, J. (1988). *Probabilistic reasoning in intelligent systems: networks of plausible inference*. San Francisco, CA: Morgan Kaufmann.

Pham, D. H., Governatori, G., Raboczi, S., Newman, A., & Thakur, S. (2008). On Extending RuleML for Modal Defeasible Logic. In N. Bassiliades, G. Governatori, & A. Paschke (Eds.), *Proceedings of the International Symposium on Rule Representation, Interchange and Reasoning on the Web (RuleML 2008)*, Orlando, FL (LNCS 5321, pp. 89-103).

Picault, J., Ribière, M., Bonnefoy, D., & Mercer, K. (2011). How to Get the Recommender Out of the Lab? In Ricci, F., Rokach, L., Shapira, B., & Kantor, P. B. (Eds.), *Recommender Systems Handbook* (pp. 333–365). doi:10.1007/978-0-387-85820-3_10.

Pingdom. (2011). *Internet 2010 in numbers* [Web log post]. Retrieved June 26, 2011, from http://royal.pingdom.com/2011/01/12/ internet-2010-in-numbers/

Popper, K. (1945). *The open society and its enemies.* London, UK: Routledge.

Porter, M. F. (1980). An algorithm for suffix stripping. *Program, 14*(3), 130–137. doi:10.1108/eb046814.

Porter, M. F. (1997). An algorithm for suffix stripping. In Sparck Jones, K., & Willett, P. (Eds.), *Readings in information retrieval* (pp. 313–316). San Francisco, CA: Morgan Kaufmann.

Prud'hommeaux, E., & Seaborne, A. (2007). *W3C: SPARQL query language for RDF.* Retrieved February 25, 2011, from http://www.w3.org/TR/rdf-sparql-query/

Quinlan, J. (1990). Learning logical definitions from relations. *Machine Learning, 5,* 239–266. doi:10.1007/BF00117105.

Quinlan, R. (1990). Learning logical definitions from relations. *Machine Learning, 5,* 239–266. doi:10.1007/BF00117105.

Räck, C., Arbanowski, S., & Steglich, S. (2006). Context-aware, Ontology-based Recommendations. In *Proceedings of the 2006 International Symposium on Applications and the Internet Workshops* (pp. 98-104).

Rahm, E., & Bernstein, P. A. (2001). A survey of approaches to automatic schema matching. *The Very Large Data Base Journal, 10*(4), 334–350. doi:10.1007/s007780100057.

Raimond, Y., Sutton, C., & Sandler, M. (2008). Automatic interlinking of music datasets on the semantic web. In *Proceedings of the Linking Data on the Web Workshop,* Beijing, China.

Ramezani, M. FriedrichWitschel, H., Braun, S., & Zacharias, V. (2010). Using machine learning to support continuous ontology development. In *EKAW 2010: 17th International Conference on Knowledge Engineering and Knowledge Management.*

Rastogi, V., Dalvi, N., & Garofalakis, M. (2011). Large-scale collective entity matching. *Proceedings of the Very Large Data Base Endowment, 4*(4), 208–218.

Rettinger, A., Nickles, M., & Tresp, V. (2009). Statistical relational learning with formal ontologies. In W. L. Buntine, M. Grobelnik, D. Mladenic, & J. Shawe-Taylor (Eds.), *Proceedings of the European Conference on Machine Learning and Knowledge Discovery in Databases, Part II* (LNCS 5782, pp. 286-301).

Reverend Sam. (2010). *SimMetrics.* Retrieved from http://sourceforge.net/projects/simmetrics

Rissland, E. L., & Skalak, D. B. (1991). CABARET: Rule Interpretation in a Hybrid Architecture. *International Journal of Man-Machine Studies, 34*(6), 839–887. doi:10.1016/0020-7373(91)90013-W.

Riveret, R., Rotolo, A., & Governatori, G. (2007). Interaction between Normative Systems and Cognitive Agents in Temporal Modal Defeasible Logic. In G. Boella, L. van der Torre, & H. Verhagen (Eds.), *Proceedings of the Normative Multi-Agent Systems (NorMAS) Conference,* Dagstuhl, Germany.

Robinson, E. H. (2010). An ontological analysis of states: Organizations vs. legal persons. *Applied Ontology, 5*(2), 109–125.

Rodden, K., & Wood, K. R. (2003). How do people manage their digital photographs? In *Proceedings of the ACM Conference on Human Factors in Computing Systems,* Fort Lauderdale, FL (pp. 409-416). New York, NY: ACM. http://www.rodden.org/kerry/chi2003.pdf

Rodrнguez, M. A., Rodrguez, M. A., Egenhofer, M. J., & Egenhofer, M. J. (2003). Determining semantic similarity among entity classes from different ontologies. *IEEE Transactions on Knowledge and Data Engineering, 15,* 442–456. doi:10.1109/TKDE.2003.1185844.

Rosati, R. (2005). Semantic and computational advantages of the safe integration of ontologies and rules. In F. Fages & S. Soliman (Eds.), *Proceedings of the Third International Workshop on Principles and Practice of Semantic Web Reasoning* (LNCS 3703, pp. 50-64).

Rosati, R. (2006). $\mathcal{DL}$ +log: Tight integration of description logics and disjunctive datalog. In *Proceedings of the 10th International Conference on Principles of Knowledge Representation and Reasoning* (pp. 68-78). Menlo Park, CA: AAAI Press.

Roussinov, D., Fan, W., & Robles-Flores, J. (2008). Beyond keywords: Automated question answering on the web. *Communications of the ACM, 51*(9), 60–65. doi:10.1145/1378727.1378743.

Rouveirol, C., & Ventos, V. (2000). Towards learning in CARIN- $\mathcal{ALN}$. In J. Cussens & A. Frisch (Eds.), *Proceedings of the 10th International Conference on Inductive Logic Programming* (LNAI 1866, pp. 191-208).

Rouveirol, C., & Ventos, V. (2000). Towards Learning in CARIN- $\mathcal{ALN}$. In J. Cussens & A. Frisch (Eds.), *Proceedings of the 10th International Conference on Inductive Logic Programming* (LNCS 1866, pp. 191-208).

Rowe, W. (1999). Agent causation. In Audi, R. (Ed.), *The Cambridge dictionary of philosophy* (2nd ed., pp. 14–15). Cambridge, UK: Cambridge University Press.

Ruckhaus, E., Kolovski, V., Parsia, B., & Cuenca Grau, B. (2006). Integrating Datalog with OWL: Exploring the $\mathcal{AL}$ -log Approach. In S. Etalle & M. Truszczynski (Eds.), *Proceedings of the 22nd International Conference on Logic programming* (LNCS 4079, p. 455-456).

Ryan, M. (2005). Social action. In Ritzer, G. (Ed.), *Encyclopedia of social theory* (Vol. 2, pp. 714–715). Thousand Oaks, CA: Sage.

Säis, F., Pernelle, N., & Rousset, M.-C. (2007). L2R: A logical method for reference reconciliation. In *Proceedings of the Twenty-Second Conference on Artificial Intelligence*, Vancouver, BC, Canada (pp. 329-334).

Säis, F., Pernelle, N., & Rousset, M.-C. (2008). Combining a logical and a numerical method for data reconciliation. *Journal of Data Semantics, 12*, 66–94.

Sanchez, D. (2010). A methodology to learn ontological attributes from the web. *Data & Knowledge Engineering, 69*(6), 573–597. doi:10.1016/j.datak.2010.01.006.

Sarwar, B., Karypis, G., Konstan, J., & Reidl, J. (2001). Item-based collaborative filtering recommendation algorithms. In *WWW '01: Proceedings of the 10th International Conference on World Wide Web* (pp. 285-295). New York, NY: ACM.

Schalley, A. C. (2004). Representing verbal semantics with diagrams an adaptation of the UML for lexical semantics. In *Proceedings of the 20th International Conference on Computational Linguistics*, Geneva, Switzerland.

Scharffe, F., Liu, Y., & Zhou, C. (2009). RDF-AI: an architecture for RDF datasets matching, fusion and interlink. In *Proceedings of the Workshop on Identity and Reference in Knowledge Representation*, Pasadena, CA

Schild, U. J., & Herzog, S. (1993). The Use of Meta-rules in Rule Based Legal Computer Systems. In *Proceedings of the 4th International Conference on Artificial Intelligence and Law (ICAIL'93)* (pp. 100-109). New York, NY: ACM Press.

Schrijver, A. (1998). *Theory of linear and integer programming*. New York, NY: John Wiley & Sons.

Searle, J. R. (1983). *Intentionality: An essay in the philosophy of mind*. Cambridge, UK: Cambridge University Press.

Searle, J. R. (1995). *The construction of social reality*. New York, NY: Free Press.

Searle, J. R. (2008). Social ontology and political power. In Smith, B., Mark, D. M., & Ehrlich, I. (Eds.), *The mystery of capital and the construction of social reality* (pp. 19–34). Chicago, IL: Open Court.

Searle, J. R. (2010). *Making the social world: The structure of human civilization*. New York, NY: Oxford University Press.

Segaran, T., Evans, C., & Taylor, J. (2009). *Programming the semantic Web*. Sebastopol, CA: O'Reilly Media.

Semeraro, G., Esposito, F., Malerba, D., Fanizzi, N., & Ferilli, S. (1998). A logic framework for the incremental inductive synthesis of Datalog theories. In N. Fuchs (Ed.), *Proceedings of 7th International Workshop on Logic Program Synthesis and Transformation* (LNCS 1463, pp. 300-321).

Seneviratne, L., & Izquierdo, E. (2010). An interactive framework for image annotation through gaming. In *Proceedings of the International Conference on Multimedia Information Retrieval* (pp. 517-526). New York, NY: ACM.

Sevilmis, N., Stork, A., Smithers, T., Posada, J., Pianciamore, M., Castro, R., et al. (2005). Knowledge sharing by information retrieval in the semantic Web. In A. Gómez-Pérez & J. Euzenat (Eds.), *Proceedings of the Second European Semantic Web Conference: Research and Applications* (LNCS 3532, pp. 251-287).

Shafer, G. (1976). *A mathematical theory of evidence.* Princeton, NJ: Princeton University Press.

Shenoy, P. P. (1992). Valuation-based systems: a framework for managing uncertainty in expert systems. In Zadeh, L., & Kacprzyk, J. (Eds.), *Fuzzy logic for the management of uncertainty* (pp. 83–104). New York, NY: John Wiley & Sons.

Sheth, A. (2010). Computing for human experience: Semantics-empowered sensors, services, and social computing on the ubiquitous Web. *IEEE Internet Computing, 14*(1), 88–91. doi:10.1109/MIC.2010.4.

Shoval, P., Maidel, V., & Shapira, B. (2008). An Ontology-Content-based Filtering Method. *International Journal of Information Theories and Applications, 15*, 303–318.

Sieg, A., Mobasher, B., & Burke, R. (2007). Ontological User Profiles for Personalized Web Search. In *Proceedings of the AAAI 2007 Workshop on Intelligent Techniques for Web Personalization* (pp. 84-91).

Šimko, J., Tvarožek, M., & Bieliková, M. (2010). Semantic history map: Graphs aiding web revisitation support. In *Proceedings of the International Workshop on Database and Expert Systems Applications* (pp. 206-210). Washington, DC: IEEE Computer Society.

Šimko, J., Tvarožek, M., & Bieliková, M. (2011). Little search game: term network acquisition via a human computation game. In *Proceedings of the 22nd ACM Conference on Hypertext and Hypermedia* (pp. 57-62). New York, NY: ACM.

Šimko, M., & Bieliková, M. (2009). Automatic concept relationships discovery for an adaptive e-course. In *Proceedings of the 2ⁿᵈ International Conference on Educational Data Mining* (pp. 171-179). Cordoba, Spain: EDM.

Šimko, M. (2011). Automated domain model creation for adaptive social educational environments. *Information Sciences and Technologies Bulletin of the ACM Slovakia, 3*(2), 119–121.

Singh, M., & Huhns, M. (2005). *Service-Oriented Computing: Semantics, Processes, Agents.* Chichester, UK: John Wiley & Sons.

Siorpaes, K., & Hepp, M. (2008a). Ontogame: weaving the semantic web by online games. In *Proceedings of the 5th European Semantic Web Conference on the Semantic Web: Research and Applications* (pp. 751-766). Berlin, Germany: Springer-Verlag.

Siorpaes, K., & Hepp, M. (2008b). Games with a purpose for the Semantic Web. *IEEE Intelligent Systems, 23*(3), 50–60. doi:10.1109/MIS.2008.45.

Skylogiannis, T., Antoniou, G., Bassiliades, N., Governatori, G., & Bikakis, A. (2007). DR-NEGOTIATE – A System for Automated Agent Negotiation with Defeasible Logic-Based Strategies. *Data & Knowledge Engineering, 63*(2), 362–380. doi:10.1016/j.datak.2007.03.004.

Smeulders, A. W. M., Worring, M., Santini, S., Gupta, A., & Jain, R. (2000). Content-based image retrieval at the end of the early years. *IEEE Transactions on Pattern Analysis and Machine Intelligence, 22*(12), 1349–1380. doi:10.1109/34.895972.

Smith, B. (2003). Ontology. In Floridi, L. (Ed.), *The Blackwell guide to the philosophy of computing and information* (pp. 155–166). Malden, MA: Blackwell.

Smith, B. (2008). Searle and de Soto: The new ontology of the social world. In Smith, B., Mark, D. M., & Ehrlich, I. (Eds.), *The mystery of capital and the construction of social reality* (pp. 35–51). Chicago, IL: Open Court.

Smith, B., & Grenon, P. (2004). The cornucopia of formal ontological relations. *Dialectica, 58*(3), 279–296. doi:10.1111/j.1746-8361.2004.tb00305.x.

Smith, B., & Searle, J. (2003). The construction of social reality: An exchange. *American Journal of Economics and Sociology, 62*(1), 285–309. doi:10.1111/1536-7150.t01-1-00012.

Soininen, T., & Niemela, I. (1998). Developing a Declarative Rule Language for Applications in Product Configuration. In G. Gupta (Ed.), *Proceedings of International Symposium on Practical Aspects of Declarative Languages (PADL)* (pp. 305-319). Berlin, Germany: Springer-Verlag.

Sowa, J. F. (2009). *Building, Sharing, and Merging Ontologies*. Retrieved from http://www.jfsowa.com/ontology/ontoshar.htm

Srikant, R., & Agrawal, R. (1995). Mining generalized association rules. In *Proceedings of the 21st International Conference on Very Large Data Bases* (pp. 407-419). San Francisco, CA: Morgan Kaufmann.

Srikant, R., & Agrawal, R. (1995). Mining generalized association rules. In U. Dayal, P. M. D. Gray, & S. Nishio (Eds.), *Proceedings of the International Conference on Very Large Data Bases* (pp. 407-419). San Francisco, CA: Morgan Kaufmann.

Staab, S., & Studer, R. (Eds.). (2009). *Handbook on Ontologies* (2nd ed.). Berlin, Germany: Springer. doi:10.1007/978-3-540-92673-3.

Stanford University. (2011). *What is protégé-OWL?* Retrieved from http://protege.stanford.edu/overview/protege-owl.html

Stewart, R., Scott, G., & Zelevinsky, V. (2008). Idea navigation: structured browsing for unstructured text. In *Proceedings of the 26th SIGCHI Conference on Human Factors in Computing Systems* (pp. 1789-1792). New York, NY: ACM.

Stoilos, G., Stamou, G., & Kollias, S. (2005). A string metric for ontology alignment. In *Proceedings of the 4th International Semantic Web Conference*, Galway, Ireland (pp. 624-637).

Stoutland, F. (2008). The ontology of social agency. *Analyse & Kritik, 30*, 533–551.

Stumme, G., Hotho, A., & Berendt, B. (2006). Semantic Web Mining: State of the art and future directions. *Journal of Web Semantics, 4*(2), 124–143. doi:10.1016/j.websem.2006.02.001.

Suh, B., & Bederson, B. B. (2007). Semi-automatic photo annotation strategies using event based clustering and clothing based person recognition. *Interacting with Computers, 19*(4), 524–544. doi:10.1016/j.intcom.2007.02.002.

Sujiyama, K., Hatano, K., & Yoshikawa, M. (2004). Adaptive Web Search Based On User Profile Constructed Without Any Effort From Users. In *Proceedings of the 13th International World Wide Web Conference* (pp. 675-684).

Swiss Institute of Bioinformatics. (2011). *UniProt knowledgebase: SwissProt protein knowledge knowledgebase: TrEMBL protein database (user manual)*. Retrieved from http://web.expasy.org/docs/userman.html

Szomszor, M., Alani, H., & Cantador, I. OHara, K., & Shadbolt, N. R. (2008). Semantic Modelling of User Interests based on Cross-Folksonomy Analysis. In *Proceedings of the 7th International Semantic Web Conference* (pp. 632-648).

Szykman, S., Sriram, R. D., Bochenek, C., Racz, J. W., & Senfaute, J. (2000). Design repositories: Engineering design's new knowledge base. *IEEE Intelligent Systems, 15*(3), 48–55. doi:10.1109/5254.846285.

Tan, P.-N., Steinbach, M., & Kumar, V. (2006). *Introduction to Data Mining*. Boston, MA: Addison-Wesley.

Teege, G. (1994). A subtraction operation for description logics. In P. Torasso et al. (Eds.), *Proceedings of the 4th International Conference on Principles of Knowledge Representation and Reasoning* (pp. 540-550). San Francisco, CA: Morgan Kaufmann.

Terry, L., Roitch, V., Tufail, S., Singh, K., Taraq, O., Luk, W., & Jamieson, P. (2009). Harnessing human computation cycles for the FPGA placement problem. In *Proceedings of the International Conference on Engineering of Reconfigurable Systems and Algorithms* (pp. 188-194). Las Vegas, NV: CSREA Press.

Tessier, S., & Wang, Y. (2011). Ontology-based representation and verification to enable feature interoperability between CAD systems. In *Proceedings of the ASME International Design Engineering Technical Conferences & Computers and Information in Engineering Conference*.

Thaler, S., Siorpaes, K., Mear, D., Simperl, E., & Goodman, C. (2011). SeaFish: A game for collaborative and visual image annotation and interlinking. In G. Antoniou, M. Grobelnik, E. Simperl, B. Parsia, D. Plexousakis, P. De Leenheer, & J. Pan (Eds.), *Proceedings of the International Conference on the Semantic Web: Research and Applications* (LNCS 6644, pp. 466-470).

Thaler, S., Siorpaes, K., Simperl, E., & Hofer, C. (2011). *A survey on games for knowledge acquisition* (Tech. Rep. No. 2011-05-01). Innsbruck, Austria: University of Innsbruck.

Tomasello, M., & Rakoczy, H. (2003). What makes human cognition unique? From individual to shared to collective intentionality. *Mind & Language*, *18*(2), 121–147. doi:10.1111/1468-0017.00217.

TPC. (2005). *The TPC benchmark H. Transaction Processing Performance Council.* Retrieved July 25, 2011, from http://www.tpc.org/tpch/default.asp

Trypuz, R. (2008). *Formal ontology of action: A unifying approach.* Poland: Wydawnictwo KUL.

Tuffield, M. M., Harris, S., Dupplaw, D. P., Chakravarthy, A., Brewster, C., & Gibbins, N. ... Wilks, Y. (2006). Image annotation with photocopain. In *Proceedings of the First International Workshop on Semantic Web Annotations for Multimedia*, Edinburgh, UK. Retrieved from http://www.image.ntua.gr/swamm2006/resources/paper09.pdf

Tummarello, G., Delbru, R., & Oren, E. (2007). Sindice.com: Weaving the open linked data. In *Proceedings of the 6th International Semantic Web Conference*, Busan, Korea (pp. 552-565).

Turk, M. A., & Pentland, A. P. (1991). Eigenfaces for recognition. *Journal of Cognitive Neuroscience*, *3*(1), 71–86. doi:10.1162/jocn.1991.3.1.71.

Tvarožek, M., & Bieliková, M. (2010). Generating exploratory search interfaces for the semantic web. In *Proceedings of the Second IFIP TC Symposium on Human-computer Interaction* (Vol. 332, pp. 175-186). New York, NY: Springer.

Udrea, O., Getoor, L., & Miller, R. J. (2007). Leveraging data and structure in ontology integration. In *Proceedings of the ACM SIGMOD International Conference on Management of Data*, Beijing, China (pp. 449-460).

Ungrangsi, R., Anutariya, C., & Wuwongse, V. (2010). Enhancing folksonomy-based content retrieval with semantic web technology. *International Journal on Semantic Web and Information Systems*, *6*(1), 19–38. doi:10.4018/jswis.2010010102.

US Census Bureau. (2010). *International Data Base (IDB).* Retrieved January 19, 2010, from http://www.census.gov/ipc/www/idb/

Vallet, D., Castells, P., Fernández, M., Mylonas, P., & Avrithis, Y. (2007). Personalized Content Retrieval in Context Using Ontological Knowledge. *IEEE Transactions on Circuits and Systems for Video Technology*, *17*(3), 336–346. doi:10.1109/TCSVT.2007.890633.

Van Rijsbergen, C. (1979). *Information Retrieval.* Newton, MA: Butterworth-Heinemann.

Veltkamp, R. C., & Tanase, M. (2002). *Content-based image retrieval systems: A survey* (Tech. Rep. No. TR UUCS-2000-34). Utrecht, The Netherlands: Utrecht University. Retrieved from http://www.aa-lab.cs.uu.nl/cbirsurvey/cbir-survey/

Venema, Y. (2001). Temporal Logic. In Goble, L. (Ed.), *The Blackwell Guide to Philosophical Logic* (pp. 203–223). Oxford, UK: Blackwell.

Vickrey, D., Bronzan, A., Choi, W., Kumar, A., Turner-Maier, J., Wang, A., & Koller, D. (2008). Online word games for semantic data collection. In *Proceedings of the Conference on Empirical Methods in Natural Language Processing* (pp. 533-542). Morristown, NJ: Association for Computational Linguistics.

Vincenty, T. (1975). Direct and inverse solutions of geodesics on the ellipsoid with application of nested equations. *Survey Review*, *23*(176), 88–93.

Viola, P., & Jones, M. (2001). Robust real time object detection. In *Proceedings of the IEEE ICCV Workshop on Statistical and Computational Theories of Vision*, Vancouver, BC, Canada. Washington, DC: IEEE Computer Society. Retrieved from http://research.microsoft.com/en-us/um/people/viola/Pubs/Detect/violaJones_IJCV.pdf

Völker, J., Vrandecic, D., Sure, Y., & Hotho, A. (2007). Learning disjointness. In E. Franconi et al. (Eds.), *Proceedings of the 4th European Semantic Web Conference (ESWC 2007)* (LNCS 4519, pp. 175-189).

Volz, J., Bizer, C., Gaedke, M., & Kobilarov, G. (2009). Discovering and maintaining links on the web of data. In *Proceedings of the 8th International Semantic Web Conference* (pp. 650-665).

Volz, J., Bizer, C., & Gaedke, M. (2009). *Web of data link maintenance protocol (Technical Report)*. Berlin, Germany: Frei Universität Berlin.

von Ahn, L., & Dabbish, L. (2008). Designing games with a purpose. *Communications of the ACM, 51*, 58–67. doi:10.1145/1378704.1378719.

W3C. (2004). *SKOS: Simple knowledge organization system*. Retrieved from http://www.w3.org/2004/02/skos

Wagenaar, W. A. (1986). My memory: A study of autobiographical memory over six years. *Cognitive Psychology, 18*, 225–252. doi:10.1016/0010-0285(86)90013-7.

Wang, T., Maynard, D., Peters, W., Bontcheva, K., & Cunningham, H. (2005). Extracting a domain ontology from linguistic resource based on relatedness measurements. In *Proceedings of the IEEE/WIC/ACM International Conference on Web Intelligence* (pp. 345-351). Washington, DC: IEEE Computer Society.

Ware, R. (1988). Group action and social ontology. *Analyse & Kritik, 10*, 48–70.

Watson, M. (2010). *Practical semantic Web and linked data application*. Retrieved February 20, 2011, from http://www.markwatson.com/

Weber, M. (1978). *Economy and society*. Berkeley, CA: University of California Press. (Original work published 1968).

Weichselbraun, A., Wohlgenannt, G., & Scharl, A. (2010). Refining non-taxonomic relation labels with external structured data to support ontology learning. *Data & Knowledge Engineering, 69*(8), 763–778. doi:10.1016/j.datak.2010.02.010.

Welty, C. (1999). Ontologies: Expert systems all over again? In *Proceedings of the American Association for Artificial Intelligence National Conference*.

White, M., Cardie, C., & Ng, V. (2002). Detecting Discrepancies in Numeric Estimates Using Multidoc-ument Hypertext Summaries. In *Proceedings of the 2nd International Conference on Human Language Technology Research (HLT)*.

Widdows, D. (2003). Unsupervised methods for developing taxonomies by combining syntactic and statistical information. In *Proceedings of the 2003 Conference of the North American Chapter of the Association for Computational Linguistics on Human Language Technology* (Vol. 1, pp. 197-204). Morristown, NJ: Association for Computational Linguistics.

Wight, C. (2004). State agency: Social action without human activity? *Review of International Studies, 30*, 269–280. doi:10.1017/S0260210504006060.

Wikipedia. (2010). *Semantic web stack*. Retrieved March 25, 2011, from http://en.wikipedia.org/wiki/Semantic_Web_Stack

Wikipedia. (2011a). *Linked data*. Retrieved March 25, 2011, from http://en.wikipedia.org/wiki/Linked_Data

Wikipedia. (2011b). *Semantic web*. Retrieved March 25, 2011, from http://en.wikipedia.org/wiki/Semantic_Web

Winkler, W. (2006). *Overview of record linkage and current research directions* (Tech. Rep. No. 2006-2). Washington, DC: Statistical Research Division, U.S. Census Bureau.

Winkler, W. E. (1999). The state of record linkage and current research problems (Tech. Rep.). Suitland, MD: Statistical Research Division, U.S. Census Bureau.

Witherell, P., Krishnamurty, S., Grosse, I., & Wileden, J. (2009). Semantic relatedness measures for identifying relationships in product development processes. In *Proceedings of the ASME International Design Engineering Technical Conferences & Computers and Information in Engineering Conference*.

Witschel, H. F. (2005). Using decision trees and text mining techniques for extending taxonomies. In *Proceedings of the Workshop on Learning and Extending Lexical Ontologies by Using Machine Learning (ONTOML)*, Bonn, Germany.

Wood, Z., & Galton, A. (2009). A taxonomy of collective phenomena. *Applied Ontology, 4*, 267–292.

World Wide Web Consortium. (W3C). (2009). *OWL 2 Web Ontology Language*. Retrieved July 25, 2011, from http://www.w3.org/TR/owl-overview/

Wu, X., Zhang, L., & Yu, Y. (2006). Exploring social annotations for the semantic web. In *WWW '06: Proceedings of the 15th International Conference on World Wide Web* (pp. 417-426). New York, NY: ACM.

Wunsch-Vincent, S., & Vickery, G. (2006). *Participative web: User-created content* (Report No. DSTI/ICCP/IE(2006)7/FINAL). Paris, France: OECD. Retrieved from http://www.oecd.org/dataoecd/57/14/38393115.pdf

Xu, X., Huang, J., Wan, J., & Jiang, C. (2008). A method for measuring semantic similarity of concepts in the same ontology. In *IMSCCS '08: Proceedings of the 2008 International Multi-symposiums on Computer and Computational Sciences* (pp. 207-213). Washington, DC: IEEE Computer Society.

Yang, D., & Powers, D. M. W. (2005). Measuring semantic similarity in the taxonomy of wordnet. In *ACSC '05: Proceedings of the 28th Australasian Conference on Computer Science* (pp. 315-322). Australian Computer Society, Inc.

Yates, A., Banko, M., Broadhead, M., Cafarella, M., Etzioni, O., & Soderland, S. (2007). TextRunner: Open Information Extraction on the Web. In *Proceedings of Human Language Technologies: The Annual Conference of the North American Chapter of the Association for Computational Linguistics: Demonstrations* (pp. 25-26). Stroudsburg, PA: Association for Computational Linguistics.

Yin, X., Han, J., & Yu, P. S. (2007). Truth Discovery with Multiple Conflicting Information Providers on the Web. In *Proceedings of the Knowledge Discovery and Data Mining (KDD) Conference.*

Yin, X., Tan, W., & Liu, C. (2011). FACTO: A Fact Lookup Engine Based on Web Tables. In *Proceedings of the World Wide Web Conference (WWW),* Hyderabad, India (pp. 507-516).

Zacharias, V., & Braun, S. (2007). Soboleo- social bookmarking and lightweight ontology engineering. In *Proceedings of the WWW'07 Workshop on Construction of Structured Knowledge.*

Zhang, L., Wu, X., & Yu, Y. (2006). Emergent Semantics from Folksonomies: A Quantitative Study. *Journal of Data Semantics on Emergent Semantics,* 168-186.

Zhan, P., Jayaram, U., Kim, O., & Zhu, L. J. (2010). Knowledge representation and ontology mapping methods for product data in engineering applications. *Journal of Computing and Information Science in Engineering,* 10(2). doi:10.1115/1.3330432.

Zhao, M., Teo, Y. W., Liu, S., Chua, T.-S., & Jain, R. (2006). Automatic person annotation of family photo album. In H. Sundaram, M. Naphade, J. R. Smith, & Y. Rui (Eds.), *Proceedings of the 5th International Conference on Image and Video Retrieval* (LNCS 4071, pp. 163-172).

Zhou, M., Bao, S., Wu, X., & Yu, Y. (2007). An unsupervised model for exploring hierarchical semantics from social annotations. In *Proceedings of the 6th International Semantic Web Conference and 2nd Asian Semantic Web Conference (ISWC/ASWC 2007), Busan, South Korea* (LNCS 4825, pp. 673-686).

Zhu, L.J., Jayaram, U., Jayaram, S. & Kim, O. (2010). Querying and Reasoning with Product Engineering Ontologies-Moving Past Modeling. Proceeding of 2010 ASME IDETC/CIE Conference.

Zhu, L.J., Jayaram,U., Jayaram, S. & Kim, O. (2009). Ontology-Driven Integration of CAD/CAE Applications: Strategies and Comparisons. Proceeding of 2009 ASME IDETC/CIE Conference

Zhu, L. J., Jayaram, U., & Kim, O. (2012). Semantic applications enabling reasoning in product assembly ontologies: Moving past modeling. *Journal of Computing and Information Science in Engineering,* 12(1). doi:10.1115/1.3647878.

About the Contributors

Amit Sheth is an educator, researcher, and entrepreneur. He is a LexisNexis Eminent Scholar (an endowed faculty position, funded by LexisNexis and the Ohio Board of Regents), an IEEE Fellow, and the director of theOhio Center of Excellence in Knowledge-enabled Computing (Kno.e.sis) at Wright State University. which conducts research in Semantic Web, services computing, and scientific worklfows. His current work encompasses WWW subareas of Semantic Web, Social Web, Semantic Sensor Web/WoT and semantics enabled services and cloud computing, and their innovative applications to health, fitness and well being, and several other industries.

Earlier, Dr. Sheth was a professor at the University of Georgia, where he started the LSDIS lab in 1994, and he served in R&D groups at Bellcore, Unisys, and Honeywell. His h-index of 75 and the 23K+ citations to his publications places him among the top 100 in Computer Science and top few in WWW. His research has led to several commercial products, many deployed applications and two successful companies. He serves as technology and business advisor to startups and additional commercialization of his research continues. He is on several journal editorial boards, is the Editor-in-Chief of the *International Journal on Semantic Web and Information Systems* (IJSWIS), joint Editor-in-Chief of *Distributed and Parallel Databases* (DAPD), and a co-editor of two Springer book series (*Semantic Web and Beyond: Computing for Human Experience,* and*Advanced Database Systems*) (http://knoesis.org/amit).

* * *

Maria Bieliková received her Master degree (with summa cum laude) in 1989 and her PhD. degree in 1995, both from the Slovak University of Technology in Bratislava. Since 2005, she has been a full professor, presently at the Institute of Informatics and Software Engineering, Slovak University of Technology in Bratislava. Her research interests are in the areas of software web-based information systems, especially personalized context-aware web-based systems including domain and user modeling and social networks. She co-authored over 60 papers in international scientific journals and she is editor of more than 30 proceedings, six of them published in Lecture Notes in Computer Science series of Springer. She is a senior member of IEEE and ACM, a member of the IEEE Computer Society and the International Society for Web Engineering.

Tom Bylander is an Associate Professor in the Department of Computer Science at the University of Texas at San Antonio. He received his B.S. from the University of South Dakota in 1979 and his Ph.D. from the Ohio State University in 1986. His research interests are in machine learning and abductive reasoning.

Alfio Ferrara is assistant professor of Computer Science at the University of Milano, where he received his PhD in Computer Science in 2005. His research interests include database and semi-structured data integration, Web-based information systems, ontology engineering, and knowledge representation and evolution. On these topics, he works in national and international research projects, including the recent EU projects BOEMIE (Bootstrapping Ontology Evolution with Multimedia Information Extraction) and INTEROP (Interoperability Research for Networked Enterprises Applications and Software). He is also author of several articles and papers in international journals and conferences about ontology management and matching.

Siegfried Handschuh is a Senior Lecturer at the National University of Ireland, Galway (NUIG) and leader of the Semantic Collaboration research stream, as well as of the Semantic Information System and Language Engineering Group (SmILE), at the Digital Enterprise Research Institute (DERI). Siegfried holds Honours Degrees in both Computer Science and Information Science and a PhD from the University of Karlsruhe. He published over 100 papers as books and journal, book chapters, conference, and workshop contributions, mainly in the areas of Annotation and Authoring for the Semantic Web, Knowledge Acquisition, Information Visualization and Social Semantic Collaboration.

Uma Jayaram is an Associate Professor at Washington State University. With Dr. Sankar Jayaram she established the VRCIM lab at WSU. Through a successful industry/university/Government consortium, practical applications of their research have provided US manufacturing companies with technologies to compete successfully in a global economy. She has worked closely with many industry and government agencies in her area of expertise, such as, CAD/CAM, PLM, Virtual Reality for design evaluations and training, and ontologies for collaboration and communication between engineering applications. She is also a co-founder of three companies in the areas of CAD and virtual reality.

Okjoon Kim received his MS and PhD degrees from Washington State University (Pullman, WA) in Mechanical Engineering in 2007 and 2011 respectively under the guidance of Dr. Uma Jayaram and Sankar Jayaram in the VRCIM (Virtual Reality Computer Integrated Manufacturing) laboratory. He has worked on fundamental research in the areas of virtual reality and knowledge representation in CAD/CAE. He has made contributions in the use of ontology-based semantic knowledge approaches to solve engineering problems, such as knowledge transfer between different CAD/CAE tools, knowledge sharing between different types of training tools, and knowledge retention through semantic online communities. He is now a Senior Software Engineer at Integrated Engineering Solutions.

Francesca A. Lisi, PhD in Computer Science, is currently an Assistant Professor at the University of Bari (Italy). Active in the field of Inductive Logic Programming (ILP) for about 15 years, she investigates the intersection between Machine Learning and Knowledge Representation aiming at Semantic Web applications. She has given several seminars and tutorials on this topic and been awarded with 2006 Cyc Prize for her research idea of refining ontologies with ILP. She is (co)-author of more than 50 peer-reviewed papers.

Fergal Monaghan is a Research Team Lead at SAP Research within the Business Intelligence (BI) Practice. He holds an Honours Degree in Electronic & Computer Engineering and a Ph.D. from the National University of Ireland, Galway (NUIG) received while a researcher at the Digital Enterprise Research Institute (DERI). His research interests include context-aware systems at the intersection of society, the Internet of Things and Web of Data. Most recently his work focuses on decision rationale capture, tracking and change management via argumentation mining and reasoning. He has patented his work and published several times.

Andriy Nikolov is a research associate at the Knowledge Media Institute, The Open University, UK. He defended his PhD degree in Computer Science in 2010 on the topic of semantic data fusion and published several scientific papers on the topic. His research focuses on the problems of semantic data integration, in particular, discovering and connecting linked data sources. He is also involved in research on semantic data management on small-scale devices and semantic sensor networks. He participated in several national and international research initiatives, in particular, EU projects X-Media and SmartProducts.

Steven O'Hara is a PhD student in the Computer Science Department at the University of Texas at San Antonio. He received his B.S. and M.S. degrees from UTSA in 1981 and 1985. His research interests are in artificial intelligence and legacy programming language modernization.

David O'Sullivan (Ph.D.) is a Director of Research at the School of Engineering and Informatics, National University of Ireland, Galway. His research interests are in innovation management where he directs a number of industry sponsored research projects. His most recent projects include innovation management within SMEs and distributed innovation management across extended enterprises. David has a number of publications including books – *Applying Innovation* (Sage); *Manufacturing Systems Redesign* (Prentice-Hall); *Reengineering the Enterprise* (Chapman & Hall); and *The Handbook of IS Management* (Auerbach). David also works with leading organizations where innovation is a core value including IBM, Thermo King, Fujisawa, Hewlett-Packard and Boston Scientific.

Edward Heath Robinson (PhD) is an instructor of geographic information systems and human geography at the University of South Florida. He has recently completed his Ph.D. at the University at Buffalo as a fellow of the National Science Foundation's Integrative Graduate Education and Research Traineeship (IGERT) in Geographic Information Science. His current research area is the ontology of geopolitical entities, which he approaches from both the perspectives of philosophical ontology and ontology for information systems.

François Scharffe is associate professor at the University of Montpellier 2, France. He defended his PhD in computer science at the university of Innsbruck, Austria in 2009. His main focus is on reconciling data and ontologies on the semantic web. He published many international scientific publications on the topic, including two book chapters. François is also the scientific coordinator of the Datalift research project on publishing and interlinking semantic web data. He serves as program committee for the International Semantic Web Conference and for the Journal of Web Semantics.

Jakub Šimko received his Master degree (with cum laude) in 2010 from the Slovak University of Technology in Bratislava. Since then, he has been working as a PhD. student and researcher at the Institute of Informatics and Software Engineering at Faculty of Informatics and Information Technologies at the same university. His research interests are in the area of domain modeling, exploratory information retrieval, semantics acquisition, human computation and games with a purpose. He has co-authored over 10 papers published in scientific journals and proceedings and presented his work at several conferences including some supported by ACM and IEEE. He is a member of the ACM SIGWEB.

Michal Tvarožek received his Master degree with honors 'Magna cum laude' in 2007 and his PhD. degree, awarded with the Rector's award, in 2011, both from the Slovak University of Technology in Bratislava. Since then, he has been working as an assistant professor at the Faculty of Informatics and Information Technologies at the same university. His research interests are in the areas of exploratory information retrieval, adaptive user interfaces, and personalized web-based systems and user modeling. He has co-authored over 30 papers published in scientific journals and proceedings, and presented his work at several conferences including some supported by ACM, IEEE and IFIP. He ranked as the 2nd place winner in the ACM SRC Grand Finals 2010 with his work on "Personalized Semantic Web exploration based on adaptive faceted browsing". He is a member of the Slovak Society for Computer Science and ACM.

Lijuan Zhu obtained her PhD in Mechanical Engineering at Washington State University, advised by Dr. Uma Jayaram and Sankar Jayaram. The significance of her work relates to advancing the engineering product design process through the use of the Semantic Web for engineering domains. Lijuan's research interests include virtual reality applications for engineering design and manufacturing, integrated frameworks for engineering tools, and use of ontologies for collaboration between engineering applications. She is now employed as a Senior Software Engineer at Autodesk.

Index